Mastering™
Network Security
Second Edition

Chris Brenton
Cameron Hunt

SYBEX® San Francisco London

Associate Publisher: Neil Edde

Acquisitions and Developmental Editor: Chris Denny

Editor: Pat Coleman

Production Editor: Elizabeth Campbell

Technical Editor: Andy Leaning

Graphic Illustrator: Tony Jonick

Electronic Publishing Specialist: Maureen Forys, Happenstance Type-O-Rama

Book Designer: Maureen Forys, Happenstance Type-O-Rama

Proofreaders: Dave Nash, Nancy Riddiough

Indexer: Ted Laux

Cover Design: Design Site

Cover Illustrator: Tania Kac, Design Site

This book is dedicated to bleary-eyed, sleep-deprived, socially-inept, autistically savantic misfit technophiliacs...

—Cameron Hunt

Acknowledgments

I HAVE TO THANK Princess Knikki for keeping my creditors silenced, Mistress Elizabeth for providing a carrot along with a stick, Patsie (Pat Coleman) for being the ultimate professional, Chris Denny for enthusiasms, and all manufacturers of caffeine products.

—Cameron Hunt

Contents at a Glance

Contents

Introduction

SOME OF US CAN REMEMBER a time when securing a network environment was a far easier task than it seems to be today. As long as every user had a password and the correct levels of file permissions had been set, we could go to sleep at night confident that our network environment was relatively secure. This confidence may or may not have been justified, but at least we *felt* secure.

Then along came the Internet and everything changed. The Internet has accelerated at an amazing rate the pace at which information is disseminated. In the early 1990s, most of us would not hear about a security vulnerability unless it was reported by a major magazine or newspaper. Even then, the news release typically applied to an old version of software that most of us no longer used anyway. These days, hundreds of thousands of people can be made privy to the details of a specific vulnerability in less than an hour.

This is not to say that all this discussion of product vulnerabilities is a bad thing. Actually, quite the opposite is true. Individuals with malicious intent have always had places to exchange ideas. Pirate bulletin boards have been around since the 1980s. Typically, it was the rest of us who were left out in the cold with no means of dispersing this information to the people who needed it most: the network administrators attempting to maintain a secure environment. The Internet has become an excellent means by which to get vulnerability information into the hands of the people responsible for securing their environments.

Increased awareness also brings increased responsibility. This is not only true for the software company that is expected to fix the vulnerability; it is also true for the network administrator or security specialist who is expected to deploy the fix. Any end user with a subscription to a mailing list can find out about vulnerabilities as quickly as the networking staff. This greatly increases the urgency of deploying security-related fixes as soon as they are developed. (As if we didn't have enough on our plates already!)

So, along with all our other responsibilities, we need to maintain a good security posture. The first problem is where to begin. Should you purchase a book on firewalls or on securing your network servers? Maybe you need to learn more about network communications to be able to understand how these vulnerabilities can even exist. Should you be worried about running backups or redundant servers?

One lesson that has been driven home since the publication of the first edition of this book is the need to view security not as a static package, but rather as a constant process incorporating all facets of networking and information technology. You cannot focus on one single aspect of your network and expect your environment to remain secure. Nor can this process be done in isolation from other networking activities. This book provides system and network administrators with the information they need to run a network with multiple layers of security protection, while considering issues of usability, privacy, and manageability.

What This Book Covers

Chapter 1 starts with the idea that our technology, as well as the context in which that technology is used, should be thought of as a series of embedded systems. Using traditional system analysis vocabulary and techniques to understand and describe all the components in our security landscape ensures that we have a good understanding of the relationship and impact that our various components have on one another.

Chapter 2 extends the idea of systems to discuss security systems and security itself in a context of a continual (and recursive) process of discovery, analysis, planning, and implementation.

In Chapter 3, you'll get an overview of how systems communicate across a network. The chapter looks at how the information is packaged and describes the use of protocols. You'll read about vulnerabilities in routing protocols and which protocols help to create the most secure environment. Finally, the chapter covers services such as FTP, HTTP, and SMTP, with tips on how to use them securely.

Chapter 4 gets into topology security. In this chapter, you'll learn about the security strengths and weaknesses of different types of wiring, as well as different types of logical topologies, such as Ethernet and frame relay. Finally, you'll look at different types of networking hardware, such as switches, routers, and Layer-3 switching, to see how these devices can be used to maintain a more secure environment.

Chapter 5 discusses perimeter security devices such as packet filters and firewalls. You will create an access control policy (based on the security policy created in Chapter 2) and examine the strengths and weaknesses of different firewalling methods. Also included are some helpful tables for developing your access control policy, such as a description of all of the TCP flags as well as descriptions of ICMP type code.

In Chapter 6, we'll walk you through installing and configuring the Cisco PIX firewall, one of the most popular firewall devices in recent times. You'll be able to see not just the packet-filtering options of the firewall, but also how to set up stateful analysis, URL filtering, and even logging with syslog.

Chapter 7 discusses intrusion detection systems (IDSs). You'll look at the traffic patterns an IDS can monitor, as well as some of the technology's limitations. As a specific IDS example, you will take a look at Snort. This open-source tool is one of the most popular IDS products, and we'll talk about operating system preparation, installation, and how to configure an IDS to detect common network attacks.

Chapter 8 looks at authentication and encryption. You will learn why strong authentication is important and what kinds of attacks exploit weak authentication methods. You'll also read about different kinds of encryption and how to select the right algorithm and key size for your encryption needs.

Read Chapter 9 to learn about virtual private networking (VPN), including when the deployment of a VPN makes sense and what options are available for deployment. As a specific example, you will see how to use Microsoft Windows 2000 to create a VPN.

Chapter 10 discusses viruses, Trojan horses, and worms. This chapter illustrates the differences between these applications and shows exactly what they can and cannot do to your systems. You will see different methods of protection and some design examples for deploying prevention software.

Chapter 11 is all about disaster prevention and recovery, peeling away the layers of your network to see where disasters can occur. The discussion starts with network cabling and works its way inside your network servers. You'll even look at creating redundant links for your WAN. The chapter ends by discussing the setup and use of the VERITAS Storage Replicator.

Chapter 12 discusses Microsoft Windows networking technologies, specifically NT server, Windows 2000, and .NET. You'll look at designing a domain structure that will enhance your security posture, as well as how to use policies. We'll discuss working with user accounts' logging and file permissions, as well as some of the password insecurities with Windows NT/2000. Finally, you'll read about the security features of the new .NET line of servers from Microsoft.

Chapter 13 is all about Unix (and the Unix clones, Linux and FreeBSD). Specifically, you'll see how to lock down a system running the Linux operating system. You'll look at user accounts, file permissions, and IP services. This chapter includes a detailed description of how to rebuild the operating system kernel to enhance security even further.

Ever wonder how an evil villain might go about attacking your network resources? Read Chapter 14, which discusses how attackers collect information, how they might go about probing for vulnerabilities, and what types of exploits are available. You'll also look at some of the canned software tools that are available to attackers.

Chapter 15 shows you how you can stay informed about security vulnerabilities. This chapter describes the information available from both product vendors and a number of third-party resources. Vulnerability databases, websites, and mailing lists are discussed.

Who Should Read This Book

The book is specifically geared toward the individual who does not have ten years of experience in the security field—but is still expected to run a tight ship. If you are a security guru who is looking to fill in that last five percent of your knowledge base, this may not be the book for you.

If, however, you are looking for a practical guide that will help you to identify your areas of greatest weakness, you have come to the right place. This book was written with the typical network or system administrator in mind, those administrators who have a good handle on networking and the servers they are expected to manage, but who need to find out what they can do to avoid being victimized by a security breach.

Network security would be a far easier task if we could all afford to bring in a $350-per-hour security wizard to audit and fix our computer environment. For most of us, however, this is well beyond our budget constraints. A strong security posture does not have to be expensive—but it does take time and attention to detail. The more holes you can patch within your networking environment, the harder it will be for someone to ruin your day by launching a network-based attack.

If you have any questions or comments regarding any of the material in this book, feel free to e-mail us at cbrenton@sover.net or cam@cameronhunt.com.

Chapter 1

A Systems Analysis Approach to Information Technology

WE ALL PROBABLY HAVE an idea about what the word *system* means. For those of us who work in information technology, the term has become a catch-all that covers everything from an operating system on a single computer to the Internet itself. Now, we know you're probably thinking that we're going to spend a whole chapter convincing you that because your network is complex, securing it will also be complex. You would be right!

But we're going to do more than that. We're actually going to give you a small tour through the idea of complexity and how it relates to anything that gets labeled a "system." The goal is to give you several principles that you can apply to any complex system—whether that system is a network, a data recovery procedure, or a security decision tree—in order to build one or more models. These models not only provide a common reference for author and reader, but are valuable tools in their own right in understanding, planning, implementing, and managing any complex group of interrelating, dynamically operating parts. And if anything fits that description, it's a computer network (the thing we're trying to secure, remember?)

Featured in this chapter:

◆ An introduction to systems analysis

◆ Applying systems analysis to information technology

An Introduction to Systems Analysis

Systems analysis is the formal term for the *process* (which we cover in Chapter 2) that uses systems principles to identify, reconstruct, optimize, and control a system. Now, the trick is you have to be able to walk through that process while taking into account multiple objectives, constraints, and resources. Simple, but what's the point? Well, ultimately we want to create possible courses of action, together with their risks, costs, and benefits. And that, in a nutshell, is what network security is all about—choosing among multiple security alternatives to find the best one for our system, given our constraints (technical or financial, typically).

The principles that make up systems analysis come from several theories of information and systems. Let's look at Information Theory first. In its broadest sense, the term *information* is interpreted to include any and all messages occurring in any medium, such as telegraphy, radio, or television, and the signals involved in electronic computers and other data-processing devices. Information Theory (as initially devised in 1948 by Claude E. Shannon, an American mathematician and computer scientist) regards information as *only* those symbols that are unknown (or uncertain) to the receiver.

What's the difference between symbols that are known vs. symbols that are unknown? First, think of long distance communication a little more than a century ago, in the days of Morse Code and the telegraph. Messages were sent leaving out nonessential (predictable or known) words such as *a* and *the*, while retaining words such as *baby* and *boy* (defined as unknown information in Information Theory). We see the same kind of behavior in today's text messaging—minimal words and abbreviations come to stand for entire phrases.

Shannon argued that unknown information was the only true information and that everything else was redundant and could be removed. As a result, the number of bits necessary to encode information was called the *entropy* of a system. This discovery was incredibly important because it gave scientists a framework they could use to add more and more bandwidth (using compression, or the removal of redundant information) to the same medium. For example, modems increased their speed to the point they were transmitting 56,000 bits of information a second, even though the physical medium of the phone line could represent only 2400 changes (known as bauds) a second.

The reason I point out Information Theory and Shannon's definition of information is to illustrate a central concept of understanding systems: you don't have to know *everything* about a system to model it; you only need to know the unknown or nonredundant parts of a system (the information) that can affect the operation of a system as a whole. You can ignore everything else; for all practical purposes, it doesn't exist.

System analysis also draws heavily from another discipline, Systems Theory. Traditional Systems Theory tends to focus on complex (from the Latin *complexus*, which means "entwined" or "twisted together") items such as biological organisms, ecologies, cultures, and machines. The more items that exist and are intertwined in a system, the more complex. Newer studies of systems tend to look not only at items that are complex, but at items that are also *adaptive*. The assumption is that underlying principles and laws are general to any type of complex adaptive system, principles that then can be used to create models of these systems. The following are some of these principles:

Complexity Systems are complex structures, with many different types of elements that influence one another. For example, a computer network encompasses software, different layers of protocols, multiple hardware types, and, of course, human users—all interacting and influencing one another.

Mutuality The elements of a system operate at the same time (in real time) and cooperate (or not). This principle creates many simultaneous exchanges among the components. A negative example of this is a positive feedback loop! Imagine a computer that creates a log entry every time the CPU utilization is greater than 50 percent. Now, imagine the consequences that would occur if every time the system writes an error log, it forces the CPU to be used greater than—— you guessed it—50 percent.

Complementarity Simultaneous exchanges among the elements create subsystems that interact within multiple processes and structures. The result is that multiple (hierarchical) models are needed to describe a single system.

Evolvability Complex adaptive systems tend to evolve and grow as the opportunity arises, as opposed to being designed and implemented in an ideal manner. Now, this definitely sounds like most computer networks we've been privy too—patchworks of various brands, capabilities, and complexities, implemented in pieces as time and resources allow.

Constructivity Systems tend to grow (or scale), and as they do so, they become bound (in the sense of heritage) to their previous configurations (or models) while gaining new features. Anyone who has worked at an organization over an extended period of time has seen this happen. No matter how large the network grows (unless there was a major overhaul somewhere), it still seems to fundamentally reflect the small, original network it originated from, even with additional capabilities and features added over the life of the system.

Reflexivity Both positive and negative feedback are at work. Because this feedback affects both static entities and dynamic processes, the system as a whole begins to reflect internal patterns. You'll notice that the physical network begins to reflect the way you use that network.

The original Systems Theory was developed in the 1940s by Ludwig von Bertalanffy (1901–72), a biologist, who realized that there were no effective models to describe how biological organisms worked in their environment. Physicists at the time could make a small model of the solar system (through a process of both analysis and reductionism, breaking the components and functions down to their smallest, simplest parts) that would accurately predict planetary orbits while ignoring the universe at large. Biologists, however, could not completely separate an organism from its environment and still study it; it would die of starvation, cold, or boredom. As a result, the systems approach tries to combine the analytic and the synthetic methods, using both a holistic and reductionist view.

Again, think of how this applies to a computer network. Systems inside and outside the network make up the environment of the network itself. Although we can break down the parts and functions of a network, we can truly understand it only by looking at the dynamic interaction of the network with other components, whether those components are other networks or human beings.

To identify a system means to identify a boundary. The reality, especially in our connected world, is that boundaries are often arbitrarily dictated and defined, not necessarily created through physical reality. Placing a firewall between your business LAN and the Internet may or may not establish a boundary between two systems. It all depends on the model—the way in which you view your network.

Assuming that we *have* defined a boundary between the system and its environment, we can add some concepts that define how a system interacts with said environment. In the following illustration, *input* is defined as any information added into the system from the environment. *Throughput* is defined as those changes made to the input by the system. *Output*, of course, is what leaves the system and crosses the boundary back into the environment.

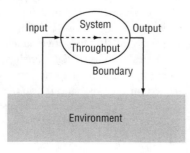

Of course, the environment itself is made up of one or more systems, and we rapidly reach the conclusion that defining a system (which really means defining a boundary between one system and its environment) is really a matter of scale and perspective—a concept that lets us begin to see systems in a hierarchical order (more on this later). Whereas we might view the Internet and our internal LAN as two separate systems, that model no longer functions as effectively when we consider remote workers accessing our network through a VPN (virtual private network) or even a web mail session secured through SSL (Secure Sockets Layer).

If we look at a system as a whole, we don't necessarily need to be aware of all its parts. This perspective is called the *black box view*, seeing a system as something that takes in input and produces output, with us being ignorant of the throughput. (Seeing the innards would then be called a *white box view.*) Although the black box view doesn't necessarily satisfy our inner control freak, it's not always necessary to see the innards of a process in order to implement and maintain it. (Remember the definition of *information* according to Information Theory?) This approach is common in the complex world of information technology, where we often work with black box abstractions of data operations.

In the realm of object-oriented programming languages such as C# and Java, reducing a code object to a black box is considered a primary strength. We are able to use the functionality of a code object (written by another programmer) in programs of our own without knowing *how* the object does the work. As long as the methods used to access the capabilities of the object or its accessible properties don't change, the authors can change, update, or rework their object in any way they desire. Our code can stay the same!

The challenge in dealing with information technology, as well as in dealing with *any* complex adaptive system, is to identify when we should use black or white approaches. And the capability of using both black and white approaches illustrates another principle that we mentioned earlier: systems are hierarchical. At the higher (or unified) level, you get an abstraction of the system as a whole. At the lower (reduced) level, you see many interrelating components, but you don't necessarily know how they fit together.

According to the traditional analytic approach (the one that existed before von Bertalanffy came along), that low level view is all that is necessary to understand a system. In other words, if you know the precise state of every component in the system, you should be able to understand how the system functions. Anyone who has ever tried to optimize an operating system for a given task (such as a web server or a database server) knows how limiting this model can be, simply because performance rarely scales in a linear fashion. In other words, increasing the number of users by a specific amount doesn't always guarantee the same rate (proportional or not) of resource utilization.

In the same fashion, doubling the amount of RAM doesn't automatically increase RAM-based performance by the same percentage. Computer components don't (often) exist in simple, linear cause-and-effect relationships; rather they live in complex networks of interdependencies that can only be understood by their common purpose: creating the functionality of the system as a whole. Looking at RAM or disk I/O or a CPU as individual elements isn't sufficient to understand resource utilization until you understand the relationship each of these elements has to the others— something not readily apparent by simply dissecting their design.

All this might seem like common sense, and if you've spent any time dealing with computer networks, you've probably come to the belief that these ideas are true, even if you haven't known *why* they are true. Most IT workers have an emotional reaction (and not necessarily a positive one) to the overwhelming complexity and unpredictability normally experienced by trying to understand, let alone manage, a complex system. Add in the feedback (in the *systems* sense of the word) of human users (each with their own method of interacting and altering that system), and we now have to struggle with a complex *adaptive* system.

But we're not done yet. Remember that we said that systems have hierarchies? Understanding that systems can affect the structure and functionality of subsystems and, likewise, that subsystems can influence the behavior of a parent system or systems (both directions of influence occurring simultaneously and repeatedly over a period of time) is crucial in Systems Theory, which also states that systems tend to mimic (in a general sense) the structures and the functions of their parent systems.

Let's look at a biological example. (Later on in the book, we'll look at some technical examples.) The cells in your body have boundaries (the cell wall), inputs (the structures on the cell wall that bind to proteins and usher them into the body of the cell), and outputs (internal cell structures that eject waste through the cell wall to the outside). Your body as a whole has inputs (your mouth and nose), outputs, and a boundary (the skin). Both your body, as a parent system, and your cells, as subsystems, have to take in nourishment. Both transform that input into an output. Although the specifics are different, the functions are the same: to allow sustenance, growth, and repair.

Similar structures also exist in the hierarchy of systems. The inputs on your body serve not only to transport nourishment, but also to analyze and prepare it for the body. Likewise, the inputs on the cell (located on the cellular wall itself) identify and "format" the proteins for the use of the cell. Systems Theory, ultimately, asserts that there are universal principles of organization that hold for all systems (biological, social, or informational) and that we can use these principles to understand, build, and manipulate those systems.

Now that we have a better understanding of the theory of information and systems, we need a practical way not just to understand a complex system, but to predict how the system will respond to changes. Such a method allows us not only to understand the security risks a computer network might face, but the consequences (especially the unforeseen ones) of trying to mitigate that risk. The name given to this practical method of managing systems is *systems analysis, decision analysis*, or even *policy analysis*. We'll use the traditional term *systems analysis*.

The systems analysis model is a multidisciplinary field that includes programming, probability and statistics, mathematics, software engineering, and operations research. Although you don't need a background in any of these areas to use the model, understanding the background will help you use the tools. The typical systems analysis process goes something like this:

1. Define the scope of a problem.

2. Determine the objectives, constraints, risks, and costs.

3. Identify alternative courses of action.

4. Evaluate the alternatives according to the constraints (feasibility), the fixed costs (cost-effectiveness), the ratio of benefits to cost (cost-benefit), or the ratio of benefits to risk (risk-benefit)

5. Recommend an alternative that will meet the needs of a decision maker (without violating the constraints of the system).

Sounds easy enough, right? What we're doing is creating a model of the system. This model allows us to apply metrics (measurable behaviors of the components, their behaviors, and relationships) in order to make decisions on what courses of actions will allow us to meet our objectives.

Two major challenges are associated with systems analysis of network security. The first is to assign realistic values to the frequency of threats. As we'll illustrate later, the frequency of a threat is one of the primary ways we determine the actual risk to a system. The second challenge is to decide which evaluation criteria to use (the items from step 4). Traditional computer network security has attempted to use all the criteria in the decision making process, while giving the greatest weight to cost-benefit. We'll follow that same plan throughout the book, but we'll also mention some exceptions to the rule.

Now that we have a list of the steps in the systems analysis process, let's walk through each of them in more detail.

Define the Scope of the Problem

In systems analysis, a problem is something in the system or its environment that requires the system to change. As we'll illustrate in greater detail later in this book, the *scope* of network security includes protecting the system from data corruption and ensuring the availability of data, no matter where the threat originates. The result of this definition of scope is that even if we have no external environmental threat from hackers, we still need to determine if the design of a network itself could put our data at risk, for example, by not providing sufficient levels of data redundancy.

In a practical sense for any individual involved in network security, defining the scope of the problem comes down to two questions: what and why? The first question is essentially about responsibility: what assets (or systems) are you in charge of protecting? This quickly moves beyond a technical arena into the specifics of your business, job, or role within a security effort. Once you clarify the *what* of your work, you can start to define the *why.* In other words, you can evaluate the current state of the system (*state* being formally defined as the current value of any variable element in a system) and decide what needs to be changed.

We'll introduce the formal security process in Chapter 2, but you can probably guess that in an ideal, formal setting, you receive a document that clarifies the areas (or systems) of your responsibility. You then attempt to determine the current state of the system, followed by an analysis of the problem. In network security specifically, this means identifying and quantifying the risks to your data, including the systems that process, store, and retrieve that data.

Determine Objectives, Constraints, Risks, and Cost

In systems analysis, an *objective* is simply the outcome desired after a course of action is followed. Because objectives (like systems) usually exist in a hierarchy (descending from general to specific, nonquantified to highly quantified), we usually refer to higher-level, abstract objectives as *goals.* Specific quantifiable objectives are referred to as *targets.*

An example of a goal/target combination is a corporate website. The *goal* is to maintain the functionality and integrity of the website as a whole. A *sub-goal* is to protect against web page defacement. Two specific *targets* that support that sub-goal (which, in turn, supports the overall goal) are to apply vendor security patches to the web server within five hours of release and to create a secure, mirrored content server that overwrites the master website with correct content every five minutes.

Nice and easy, right? The problem comes when we have multiple objectives that are contradictory or competitive (also known as conflicting objectives). We usually see conflicting objectives when more than one party is responsible for the state (remember the definition of state?) of a system. You probably already know how rampant conflicting objectives are in the security world, because implementing security almost always comes down to restricting behavior or capability (or increasing cost). Unfortunately, restricting system capability tends to conflict with the central purpose of information systems, which is to enable and ease behavior or capability. For example, think of how quickly you find notes hidden under keyboards when password complexity and length requirements are enforced in an organization!

Fortunately, systems analysis gives us a method for resolving conflicts by providing hierarchical decision makers. Because the means of achieving your goal of system security might conflict with the accountant's goal of maintaining a low cost of the system, a decision maker at a higher level is usually required to determine either which goal takes precedence or (more commonly in the real world) how to change the constraints of each goal so that they are no longer in opposition. In other words, executive-level decisions are often required to reach a compromise between two competing goals.

A byproduct of conflict resolution is the creation of *proxy* objectives—replacing generalized objectives with those that can be measured in some quantifiable way. An example of proxy objectives is illustrated by multiple security plans, each with a quantified cost/benefit ratio, that are presented to senior management, who make the final decision on how much risk they are willing to accept (the greater the risk, the less *initial* cost).

So what are constraints? According to systems analysis, a *constraint* is a limit in the environment or the system that prevents certain actions, alternatives, consequences, and objectives from being applied to a system. A simple, but limited way to understand this idea is to think of the difference between what is *possible* to do in a system and what is *practical*. Thinking of a constraint this way makes it easier to identify the consequences of any given course of action on a system.

A good example is a requirement mandating that biometric security devices (such as a fingerprint scanner) be used on every desktop computer in an organization. Although using a fingerprint scanner would achieve a major goal of network security (and is technically possible in most cases), you could easily run into constraints—initial equipment cost, client enrollment (storing authenticated copies of every employee's fingerprints), and non-biometric capable access devices (such as a Palm Pilot or other PDA) that make the solution unworkable according to other goals (such as maintaining your security within a certain budget).

We know this sounds complicated, and it is. Using systems analysis to guide you in your security process has great rewards, but it also requires you to have a thorough knowledge of your network inventory (hardware, software, and configuration), business procedures and policies, and even some accounting. Using formal worksheets and checklists to guide you through the process is highly recommended, as is hiring a consultant who specializes in systems analysis in a security context.

Once you identify your objectives and initial constraints (additional constraints usually show up when you are defining various courses of action), you need to identify risk. Risk, in systems analysis, can actually mean several things. For our purpose, we'll choose *risk assessment*, which is a two part process. The first part is identifying the impact (measured, from a security perspective, in cost) of a threat (defined as a successful attack, penetration, corruption, or loss of service), and the second part is quantifying the probability of a threat.

We can use the web page defacement example to illustrate risk assessment. We begin by identifying the threat (a successful web page defacement) in terms of the cost to the organization. Now things become difficult to quantify. How much money does an organization lose when investor and customer confidence is lowered (or lost) when a page is defaced? What if the particular page was interactive and the defacement breaks or inhibits commercial interactions?

We could even break the threat down to finer details, assigning cost to each individual defaced page, varied by the amount of time the page was defaced; the time of day, month, and year the defacement took place; the amount of publicity received; and the functionality that was broken.

You must also consider another type of impact: does the system state change after a threat? In other words, the process needed to deface your web page most likely results in the attacker having some level of control over your system. This, according to strictly defined systems analysis, has changed the state of your system, especially if you extend your concept of your system to include those individuals who are authorized to use your system. Once your system state has changed (for better or worse), new threats are possible, requiring a repeat of the entire risk assessment process. This recursive, hierarchical analysis helps us to establish a multilayered defense, something we'll refer to as *defense in depth*.

Once impact is quantified, you have to asses the probability of a threat (remembering our definition of a threat as an *actual occurrence* of a specific negative event, not just a possible one). How do you assess the probability of a threat against a system? One of the places you can start is through simple comparison: identify all the known characteristics of systems that have succumbed to that threat in the past. In our web page defacement example, you compare your system (including operating system, web server configuration, level of dynamic code, public exposure and opinion of the website, and so on) to those that have been defaced before.

This sounds relatively straightforward, but you can't stop here. You also need to attempt to weigh those system characteristics in susceptibility to the threat. Using an example from history: Which contributed more to the Department of Justice website defacement (the one that left then-Attorney General Janet Reno with a Hitler-like mustache!)—the operating system or the type of web server running on the operating system? This is a little bit more difficult to determine and takes experience along with knowing *how* the threat was carried out. We quickly come to the conclusion that we need another hierarchy, a hierarchy of threats. Although the end threat is still web page defacement, an attacker could use multiple methods to deface a page. The threat probability is then a combination of which methods of attack are the most popular, along with which system configurations are most susceptible to those popular attacks.

Remember that we're speaking of system configuration in the systems analysis sense of the term. Part of your website system is the *environment* in which it operates, including the popularity and publicity associated with that site. If you are, say, a U.S. military organization, the state of your system guarantees a higher level of interest. That raised interest can translate into a higher frequency and sophistication of attack. In this example, not only has the *frequency* of the threat possibly changed, but also the nature of the threat *itself*.

Once you identify your objectives, constraints, and risks, you're ready to decide on *courses of action*— nothing more than the ways in which an objective will be met. Multiple courses of action are defined as *alternatives*, and then only if they are mutually exclusive. For example, an objective requires a standard biometric authentication device across an organization. If the decision makers in the organization are trying to decide between fingerprint scanners and iris scanners, they are said to be selecting from two alternatives. If the organization decides that it could use both alternatives together in a standardized fashion—fingerprint scanners for desktops, iris scanners for server rooms (or combine elements from two mutually exclusive alternatives)—a new, distinct alternative has been created (and possibly a new objective, depending on how strictly that objective was originally defined).

Defining an alternative means to establish the feasibility, costs, benefits, and risks associated with a course of action—a process that usually occurs repeatedly, starting with a multitude of alternatives that are gradually integrated and combined until at last you reach a small collection of alternatives. At this point, the process usually stops for a couple of reasons:

◆ You don't have sufficient information to continue an evaluation. Perhaps no one has yet conducted a TCO (Total Cost of Ownership) study comparing biometric authentication with centrally stored user profiles against a system using smart dongles that store an encrypted copy of the user's profile in an embedded chip.

◆ All the alternatives that could meet the objective are greater than the budget constraint (an objective/constraint conflict), which (as we mentioned earlier) usually requires the intervention of a higher-level decision maker.

And, after all your hard work, all that is left to do is present your proposal to the decision makers. Although it can be bad enough if someone questions your results, it's worse when your decision makers don't understand your methodology. Might we recommend a remedy for that situation? We have it on good authority that a copy of *Mastering Network Security* goes well with *any* color of gift wrap. Oh, and remember to bookmark this chapter!

Applying Systems Analysis to Information Technology

Now that we've covered the general theory of systems analysis, let's apply it to IT systems specifically. This approach might seem like unnecessary repetition, but it's actually an attempt to reinforce important concepts while adding details that are specific to issues you'll face in dealing with security.

When you begin to analyze your network (in preparation to secure it), you'll actually break it down into four general areas:

Data   The nature of the information stored and processed on the system

Technology   The different types of technology used in the system

Organization   How the organization as a whole uses the system

Individuals   Key decision makers and personalities that use the system

The Nature of the Data

Understanding your organization and the type of work it does goes a long way toward understanding the type of data stored and processed on your system. Translating this into specifics follows a task orientation: what is your system used for? Some smaller organizations are primarily processing and storing groupware—common address books, shared or centrally stored files, and simple databases, along with e-mail and a website or two. Larger organizations tend to break down their network segments, and the network technical divisions begin to mirror the network logical divisions. For example, a company places its Internet-accessible resources (web servers, mail servers, and so on) on a network that is separate from its internal network (for security and performance reasons, among others). In this case, a parent system (the functionality) is driving a change in a subsystem (the technology).

The Types of Technology

Technology itself helps define the structure of the system, but primarily as background. In other words, understanding the technological topology of your system will help you formulate your constraints, identify and quantify your threats, and ultimately play a big part in formulating your risk assessment.

How the Organization Uses the System

Understanding how your organization uses the system can be easier in larger organizations, in which the network tends to follow organizational lines along centers of power or divisions of labor. However, even in smaller organizations, understanding how the network is used and *perceived* by the organization becomes critical to projecting the consequences of your various courses of action. Those consequences play a primary role in determining which alternatives you choose to solve a problem.

How Individuals Use the System

This task is not just about evaluating the technical ability of individuals in an organization or simply identifying those with the most influence. It also concerns determining the relationship those individuals have with the system and determining their knowledge of how the system as a whole works, even to the point of the organization's relationship with the system.

Models and Terminology

Once you look at your network through these types of filters, you're actually ready to start defining the subsystems. Selecting where to draw the border of a subsystem is always difficult, but, again, systems analysis gives us some direction. Object-Oriented Systems Analysis (OSA) takes the concept of the black box discussed earlier and uses it to create object-based models using the components of the network, using three model types:

ORM (Object-Relationship Model)   Defines objects (and classes of objects), how objects relate to classes, and how objects map to real-world components

OBM (Object-Behavior Model)   Defines the actions of objects (used to define how and why an object changes state)

OIM (Object-Interaction Model)   Defines how objects influence one another

OBJECT-RELATIONSHIP MODEL

So what's an object, and how is it different from a black box? An object is a label we apply to a single thing that has a unique identity either physically or conceptually. Here are a few IT objects:

◆   Router #13

◆   www.go-sos.com

◆   An inventory database

◆   The first primary partition of the second hard drive of the web server

In OSA, objects are represented with a lowercase labeled dot:

●

router #13

Objects can be grouped into one or more *object classes*, such as the following:

◆ Router

◆ URL

◆ Database

◆ Partition

Object classes are represented with a cylinder and an uppercase label:

For an object to be a member of an object class, it has to meet the constraints. That might seem obvious, but think about the Routers class in the previous example. It's easy to think of a dedicated router as belonging to the Router class, but what about a Windows 2000 server that shares files, hosts e-mail, and provides a VPN connection between a small office and corporate headquarters? Although we don't necessarily think of this machine as a router, it acts in that capacity (by routing traffic over the VPN). Including it in the Router class would depend on the constraints of our Router class; in other words, how we define the class determines what objects qualify for membership.

NOTE *Objects can migrate from class to class as class constraints change or as the state of the object changes.*

Objects can have a relationship, which is represented by a simple line between them and labeled with a sentence that describes the relationship. Usually, however, this relationship reflects a relationship *set* between object classes. Relationships are grouped into sets when they connect to the same object classes and represent the same *logical* connection among objects. To illustrate a relationship set, we draw the two object classes as boxes and connect them:

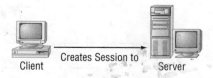

When a relationship set has multiple connections, these connections are referred to as the *arity* of the set. Two connections make a set binary, three connections make a set ternary, and four connections make a set quaternary. Relationships with five or more connections are referred to as *x-ary*, with x reflecting the number of connections. When illustrating a relationship set with more than one connection, a diamond is used to interconnect the lines:

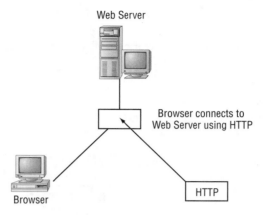

To give us an even better level of detail, we can treat the relationship set as an object, which in this case is called Session:

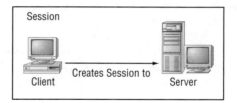

Treating the relationship set as an object allows us to link the Session object to other objects or object classes (in this cases, byproducts or characteristics of the session):

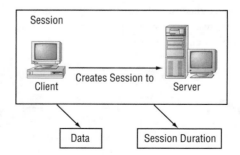

The figure above illustrates that a Session object (really a relationship set) has a relationship between a Data object class and a Session Duration class, much as any network session in the real world has data associated with it, along with an amount of time the session existed.

But something is still missing. When working with relationship sets, you need to clarify the constraints. There are three types:

Participation   Defines (for every connection) how many times an object class or object can participate in the relationship set.

Co-occurrence   Similar to participation, co-occurrence specifies how many times an object can participate in a relationship set with another object. This can also apply to object collections.

General   Defines what is allowed or not allowed in a relationship. This can be expressed as a formal math/logic statement or as a simple statement.

Let's look at an illustrated example of a Participation constraint:

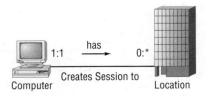

This illustration tells us that a Computer object (belonging to the Computer object class) has to have one (but only one) Location object (again, of the Location object class). A Location object, however, doesn't even have to have a single corresponding Computer object, but *can* have an infinite number of Computer objects. For example, if you define a Location object to have a value of Corporate, it is tied to all the Computer objects that are mapped to physical machines at the corporate office (a one-to-many relationship for all you database programmers out there).

This makes sense, but you could quickly run into a problem. What happens if you decide to map a laptop (a *map* in OSA is the term used to denote an association between a physical item and a logical object) to the Computer class? Because a Computer object can only have one location (as defined by the Participatory constraint), you could have difficulty if you are analyzing objects over time with an expectation that the Location value won't change! You can solve that problem by simply mapping laptops to a Laptop class that doesn't have the same constraint.

The following illustration shows how Co-occurrence constraints can limit the number of objects that can be associated with an object (or a group of objects) in a relationship set:

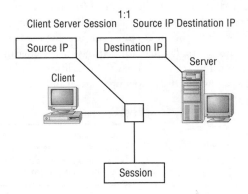

This example is also fairly straightforward. When Client, Server, and Session objects are in a relationship set, there can be only one Source IP and Destination IP object in that set. This arrangement is similar to real-life network communications, in which the source and destination IP addresses don't change for the duration of a session between a client and a server.

Whereas both of the previous examples illustrate constraints that arise from the workings of the objects themselves (or, in other words, the interaction of the objects *determined* the constraint), General constraints often represent constraints imposed on the objects. An example of general constraints is often seen in IT systems in which policies exist about how the system *should* be used, as shown in the following illustration:

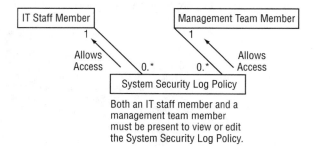

The previous illustration shows how a simple text sentence is used to create the General constraint. Because IT security policies are all about limiting the use of a system, General constraints are used frequently.

Once you model the objects and their relationships in the system, you're ready to examine their state, defined in OSA through the Object-Behavior Model as the activity or status of an object. We illustrate state by using an oval and writing the name of the state inside that oval:

How do you determine all the states an object can have? That's really up to you; you use your experience and understanding of the object you are representing. States are binary—either on or off—and they are activated and deactivated when control (or flow) transitions to another state. Exceptions to this rule are threads (you can turn on multiple threads), prior conjunction (turning off multiple states when one is turned on), and subsequent conjunction (turning multiple states on when one is turned off).

A transition is also formally diagrammed in OSA, sometimes with an identifier, but always with a trigger and an action. The trigger defines the conditions under which a transition fires, along with the resulting action, as shown in the following illustration:

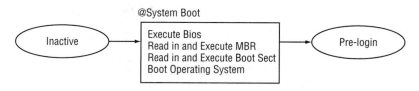

In the previous illustration, we used an event-based trigger (hence the *@* sign). Event-triggered transitions execute their action the moment the event becomes true. Conditional triggers (informal statements not preceded with *@*) cause the transition the *entire time* they are true.

Now that you can illustrate objects and relationships using ORM and use multiple state transitions (known as state nets) to show how objects behave, you can use the Object-Interaction Model to show how objects and states are changed through interaction. Here is a basic example of an interaction:

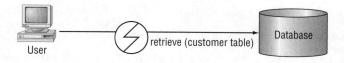

Both User and Database are object classes, with the interaction defined by a circle with a zigzag; *retrieve* is the action, and *customer table* is the object transferred in the transaction. We can use a more complete illustration to show how object class, state changes, and interactions would work together:

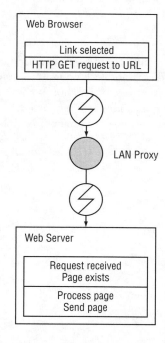

This is a complete (although simplified) example of putting all the pieces of the OSA together to represent your network as a system. Remember also that this is just an introduction to familiarize you with the concepts and symbols. Many specialized security consultants will use these diagrams to document your network, analyze courses of action, and present you with alternatives that meet your criteria and solve your problems. Knowing how to read their documentation will aid you in making better decisions. Although you might not go to the same lengths in analyzing or illustrating your own network, the principles remain the same.

Formal systems analysis makes understanding the environment of a system as important as understanding the system itself. This can be more difficult, especially determining which elements of an environment actually influence the system, especially those items that remain unknown. Once you start making a list of items that *might* influence or affect your system, you identify the techniques to determine if they do. Here are some items to look for:

Data   The flow of information streaming into a system

Technology   The limitations and capabilities of other systems that interact with our own

Competition   The capabilities of other organizations

Individuals   People whose activities could influence our system, such as crackers

Capital   The quantity of resources held by systems outside our own

Regulations   The legal limitations faced by all systems

Opportunities   The innovations and capabilities not yet integrated into our own system

Summary

By formally documenting your system, you can better understand the vulnerabilities and the threats it faces. By using the same theory and techniques to document your security alternatives (including their consequences), you can make better choices about *how* to secure your system. In the next chapter, we'll take these techniques and place them in a dynamic context of the security process—an important reminder that security is a constant effort, not just a project to complete!

Chapter 2

Security as a Process

IN THE FIRST CHAPTER, we talked about understanding information technology as a system that includes the individuals that interact with the technology, as well as the organization that invests in and controls the system. We provided you with some concepts that you can use to define and document your system as a whole. In this chapter, we'll take the static snapshot of a system and move it into a dynamic environment that is constantly changing. Because of constant change, securing your IT resources is no longer a single straightforward action, but a series of continual steps that make up a never-ending process.

Featured in this chapter:

◆ The myth of total security

◆ Risk mitigation

◆ The system development lifetime cycle

◆ Constant vigilance

Survival of the Fittest: The Myth of Total Security

Total and complete network security is a myth. Our belief in that statement comes from experience, but *why* total security is a myth really comes from the system model as explained in Chapter 1. If you think of your network as a pseudo-organism that lives in a constantly changing environment, it's not hard to see how your systems are constantly evolving to respond to the demands and threats placed upon them and how those threats (again, seen as co-existing organisms in a media and Internet-connected environment) change themselves to be more and more effective.

Let's take a step back for a moment so that we can suggest an idea that might seem like something out of a science fiction movie, but is in reality just another model, another way of looking at your relationship with computer systems: you and your network are one being, one entity, a cyborg. In this model, your network doesn't end at the keyboard, the firewall, or the modem. It ultimately ends in the decision makers who control the funds and direction of your network. In this view, then, your organization's IT budget is as much a part of your computer network as a router or cabling infrastructure, and so are those individuals (or policies) that determine how that budget is employed.

This cyborg entity—your organization (and its information technology)—lives in an environment made up of employees, floods, crackers, and software and hardware vendors, not to mention the business in which your organization is involved. In fact, if we were to borrow a metaphor from a certain visionary of a rather well-known company headquartered in Redmond, Washington, your information technology makes up a digital nervous system for your organization.

Although we like that metaphor (let's say we're embracing it), we see a need to alter it to better fit the topic of this book (let's say we're extending it). You see, the problem with viewing security as just dealing with a *digital* nervous system is to ignore the human beings who also make up that nervous system, whether we're looking at those people as users of the system or as decision makers of the system. In the context of security, both types of individuals can be equally detrimental. For example, an end user unknowingly opens an infected e-mail attachment, and a business executive won't fund an intrusion detection system for a critical web server. Both individuals have quite different levels of interaction and control of the system, but their (negative) impact is real.

Seeing these two types of users in a biological example can explain how our view of security must be scaled out large enough to see the entire picture. We like to think of the end user as our nose—one that isn't discriminating enough to realize that the milk in the jug is just a little too old to be safely put on our cereal in the morning. The safeguards might be in place, but they are ignored because of some other motivation. For example, an employee ignores virus warnings in order to see the attached dancing reindeer animation, or we occasionally ignore the fact that our expired soy milk can make us just as sick as expired dairy milk.

Sometimes our bodies just don't produce enough white cells. Or, if our white cells don't have experience in fighting a newly introduced disease, we might suffer until they learn how to handle the new invader. Our executive who chooses not to fund a key piece of security technology can be seen in this light. And, just like our immune system, all it usually takes is one (nonfatal) failure of our security to convince a key decision maker to invest in the appropriate level of protection.

Continuing in this biological model, think of security education as a vaccine, a way of shocking the system into preparing for a potential onslaught. Like a vaccine, the experience can be unpleasant, especially if we are rehearsing (like the body does) for what would happen in a real attack. Although we might suffer an uncomfortable fever while the body adjusts to the dead or deformed bugs used in a vaccine, our company might suffer anything from loss of productive time (for education, meetings, and system reconfiguration) to embarrassment (from the discovery that data recovery procedures don't work) from simulating a cracker attack or computer worm infection.

We can take this model even further. We've all received virus hoaxes in e-mail. The most damaging are those that tell a user to look for a specific virus file (which is actually a critical system component!) in order to delete it. When people take these warnings seriously, they can cause unwarranted damage or reduce their functionality. This is exactly what happens to someone who suffers from diabetes, arthritis, or allergies. Their body is overzealous, sees innocent system components (such as knee joints or a pancreas) or elements of the environment (food allergies) as the enemy, and attacks. Likewise, rashly placing extreme security measures (which usually have the dual impact of increasing cost and lowering ease of use and functionality of a system) can limit the system in varying degrees—some of them ultimately crippling—just like diabetes.

Well, everything seems nice and pat in this biological model. Your system gets an infection; but because you've been inoculated (your antivirus program has a database consisting of virus signatures allowing it to recognize known hostile code in your system), your white blood cells recognize the virus and can kill it. Your users open attachments on a whim, so you start with a company attachment policy and an education program. This could extend to more extreme measures, such as creating a quarantine directory for all e-mail attachments or even prohibiting all files transferred on e-mail! You might be tempted to think that apart from keeping your virus packages updated you're pretty much done. But again, the biological model works against you. Remember that your network (along with your organization) is going to experience some level of change, whether through growth, reduction, or just simple age. These changes alter the system state, which means that new threats are possible, and new internal weaknesses could put your information at danger.

At the same time your system is changing, the environment is changing also. Viruses become more sophisticated, denial of service (DoS) attacks are on the rise. Even new legislation mandating penalties for privacy or data disclosure (not to mention civil lawsuits involving past e-mail) are being enacted with greater frequency. As information technology becomes ubiquitous in the operation of any business—in fact, in any type of social discourse—it becomes more valuable. And things that are valued are stolen, exploited, or fought over in the courts.

Survival of the fittest works right into this model of your network in a big, bad world of hostile threats. If a lawsuit succeeds because incriminating evidence is found in a stored e-mail, future lawsuits will pursue the same avenue of attack. If a highly successful virus is publicized as using an innovative vector (*vector* being the medical term for how a disease is transmitted), other virus writers will embrace and extend that method to make increasingly virulent strains. If there is a trend in the past ten years of computer security, it is that the number and intensity of attacks have increased even in proportion to the growth of information systems themselves.

Before you start cursing Darwin, realize that many positive benefits are associated with the concept of survival of the fittest, which is known in the IT world as *best of breed*. By allowing products, processes, and concepts to duke it out in an ever-connected world, the overall quality, robustness, capability, and efficiency of our networks are improved. Think of how e-mail and instant messaging have become both a boon and a bane to organizations and have contributed to fundamental changes in how they are organized. Even the U.S. military is suffering from an identity crisis brought about by the decentralization offered (or compelled) by quick and inexpensive peer-to-peer communication methods.

So how can you, the security expert, keep your network healthy in the face of internal weaknesses and external threats? The same way that biological organisms stay healthy: you evolve in the most efficient manner possible. This evolution touches not just the technology used to process and store information, but the people, leadership, and procedures themselves. In other words, you have to evolve your entire organization. Don't panic; security professionals face this challenge constantly. The key is to learn how the successful ones do it.

Risk Mitigation: Case Studies of Success and Failure

"Hey, I think we've been hacked!" The phone call, from a network administrator for a local insurance company, came on a Saturday afternoon. We were surprised. We had reviewed this company's production network environment extensively, and the thought that an attack had been successful provided a significant amount of personal discomfort! Like police officers, however, our first thought was to preserve the crime scene.

"Did you unplug the computer from the network?" we asked.

"Yup," he replied.

"Good!" we exclaimed. "Don't turn it off! We'll be there in a half hour."

As we drove, we started reviewing our procedures for isolating a system, identifying its current state, imaging the drive, and conducting a forensic analysis of the contents. We were concerned. This company was a major player in the insurance industry, and Congress was up in arms about financial and medical data and its protection. We knew there could be possible legal ramifications if data had been exposed, not to mention embarrassment.

The company was fortunate: the server was a Windows 2000 server that was deployed on an isolated network with its own Internet access. The server was being used as a test for an upcoming Microsoft Exchange deployment. Its only network service was the web server, which was used to provide Outlook web access functionality. It held no actual sensitive data; even the passwords were specific to that machine.

We took a case history of the machine, which helped explain why it had become victim in a company that was fairly sophisticated in their security—both technically and procedurally. This particular computer had been a backup server, unplugged and stored in a corner for several months, missing the rounds of continual server updates and checks that occurred as a matter of policy in this company. Active (and unpatched) for only three days, it had fallen victim to hostile code known as Solaris/sadmind.worm. Sadmind (also known as Sadmin) is a parasitic worm that uses Solaris machines to find unpatched Microsoft web servers and deface them, replacing the default home page with a black background and red words expressing a vulgar and hostile sentiment toward the United States. The company also benefited from timing and obscurity. The web page defacement had been discovered within three hours of the penetration itself, which had occurred on a weekend, and to a system known to and used by only a few select IT staff members.

Even knowing the attack was from a worm, and therefore the result of an automated (and most likely unattended) attack, we still had a concern that the compromised system had been used as a beachhead to explore and attack the network at large. Although the attack signatures of sadmind were in plain view in the log of the web server, no other logging capabilities had been activated on the server. Even the router connecting the network to the Internet lacked intrusion-detection or packet-capturing services.

Fortunately, there were only two other servers on this little mini test network, and not only were both patched and updated, they had extensive logging enabled. Through the web logs, we could see the unsuccessful infection attempts by a sadmind worm from an external machine—the same machine that had infected the first test server. We could also see that there had been no communication from the infected server to either of the other test servers. Although we couldn't completely rule out an attack had been attempted (or was successful!) without further time-consuming testing, we were confident that adding a monitoring capability to the test network router (along with setting intrusion-detection alarms) would most likely uncover all but the most sophisticated infection. Along with a complete rebuild (and repatching) of the infected test server, we were almost done. When queried by the network administrator, we told him that the most important correction was not one of a technical nature, but procedural.

"You need to update your checklist and intrusion-detection procedures," we said. "Make sure that before any machine is activated it has the latest patches and is in line with your company policy about logging, monitoring, and intrusion detection, including setting intrusion alerts and regular review of logs for all machines, not just those in production."

As we said earlier, they were lucky. The assault was automated, not further exploited, and located on an isolated test system without real data, but they also had a good foundation to work with. It was only through an oversight, a procedural quirk if you will, that they fell victim to the worm. This kind of incident—an attack happening despite sound principles and consistent analysis—is a security professional's worst nightmare and unfortunately happens all too often. Understanding why oversights happen can help us catch them, and no example better illustrates this than the tragedy of *Apollo 1*.

On January 27, 1967, Apollo astronauts Mission Commander Edward White, Command Module Pilot Virgil "Gus" Grissom, and Lunar Module Pilot Roger Chaffee sat in the Apollo Command Module at the Kennedy Space Center, in Cape Canaveral, Florida. While the three space-suited men lay in the conical spacecraft, they participated in a Plugs Out Test, evaluating the capsule as if it were independently operating in the depth of space. As a result, the cabin was filled with pure oxygen at a higher pressure than the air outside the cabin, simulating what it would be like for the astronauts to be traveling in the vacuum of space.

At 6:31 PM a cry was heard over the radio, "Fire, I smell fire!" Because the inner door to the capsule only opened inward, the astronauts were trapped, unable to fight against the now-massive internal pressures created by the fire. Within seconds the module ruptured, spitting flame and toxic gases into two levels of the complex. Finally, after five minutes had passed, the workers were able to move through the dense and poisonous smoke to the capsule and begin the process of opening the hatch and removing the dead.

In the investigation that followed, much attention was focused on the pure oxygen environment of the cabin. NASA, however, patiently explained that pure oxygen made the most sense given all the other risk factors (including the decompression sickness that could occur during space walks). Instead, they insisted, they had attempted to *mitigate the risk of fire* by reducing the amount of flammable material in the cockpit. But notice in the following quote how they went about *determining* that fire risk:

> "...it can be seen in retrospect that attention was principally directed to individual testing of the material. What was not fully understood by...NASA was the importance of considering the fire potential of combustibles in a system of all materials taken together in the position which they would occupy in the spacecraft and in the environment of the spacecraft." (House Committee on Science and Astronautics, Subcommittee on NASA Oversight, Investigation into Apollo 204 Accident Hearings, 3 vols., 90th Cong., 1st session, 10 April to 10 May 1967, pp. 175-76. Emphasis added)

In addition, NASA had not adequately planned for how to handle a fire if it did occur, especially on the ground during a testing phase. As one of the NASA astronauts reportedly said, it was "a failure of imagination." This disaster, along with the near-disaster of Apollo 13, began a tradition of multiple layers of redundancy—something that we emulate in network security through the concept of *defense in depth*. It also shows us the importance of multilayered contingency plans. What happens when our contingency plan fails or has a problem?

In short, we are arguing that *repetition with recursion* is one of the singular principles of information security. Review a system again and again, looking closer and expanding outward in a never-ending cycle, always seeking more. Of course, the pragmatist will immediately note that this principle runs in direct opposition to that of *resource conservation.* In other words, don't spend money (in the form of time, effort, or capital) unless it would cost more not to—the cost-benefit ratio. Although a balance has to be achieved, there is still a lack of awareness of the dynamic nature of systems—a dynamic nature that requires us to continually walk through the security process. Many variations of the security process are possible, but we can get a general model of the process from—where else?—systems analysis!

The Systems Development Life Cycle (SDLC): Security as a Process from Beginning to End

The SDLC is a method used by system developers and programmers to formalize the implementation of any system-based process—from the initial project definition to the phasing out or replacement of the system. The exact number of steps in the process can vary, but for our purposes we'll use five major phases broken into sublayers:

1. Initiation
    - Conceptual Definition
    - Functional Requirement Determination
    - Protection Specifications Development
    - Design Review
2. Development and Acquisition
    - Component and Code Review
    - System Test Review
    - Certification
3. Implementation
4. Operation and Maintenance
5. Disposal

Initiation is defined as the beginning of the security process. Ideally, of course, security is implemented and integrated along with the full IT system itself. In reality, many times the security process is begun long after a system has been installed and operating. Most security professionals consider this phase the most important and, usually, the most rushed.

Conceptual Definition

Before any work can proceed, you must understand the scope of the security process. You can think of *scope* as defining the boundary of responsibility of the security system or, in other words, the boundary of the system you are charged with protecting. The conceptual definition is also important for another reason: it helps define the responsibility and scope of the individuals involved in the security process. This becomes critical if multiple individuals are involved in the security process, especially if those individuals are from multiple departments (or even from outside companies). You can think of the conceptual definition as the *spirit* of the security system—the guiding ideas and principles that will be made real through the formal and detail-specific implementation plans that will follow in subsequent steps and phases.

Functional Requirement Determination

Although your beginning objectives are initially (and generally) defined in the Conceptual Definition, in this phase you begins to specify the details of your objectives—from high-level goals to specific targets. In practical terms, this breaks down into several activities:

Interviews   Interviews serve to clarify and identify what specifically needs to be protected—both data and data processing. Your primary goal is to discover and categorize the data by criticality. As a natural result of this process, you also identify the business processes that are used to store, retrieve, and manipulate that data. The result is that you break your entire network into a series of subsystems whose performance and compliance with your security goals (and targets) can be measured. Measurement is critical, because it provides you with the central indicator of the effectiveness of the security process as a whole—in other words, justifying the expense (in effort and equipment) of performing the security process.

External Reviews   You use a current and historical review of the security environment, along with industry best practices, to establish a benchmark of environmental threats and supports. Visiting sites of organizations that have similar objectives and constraints, along with understanding technology trends and capabilities, are excellent ways to augment this step.

Gap Analysis   This step consists of taking the combined information gathered from the internal and external reviews and matching it with the objectives defined originally in the Conceptual Definition. What remains is the difference between what is and what should be, including identifying which areas of technology, business process, organizational culture, end-user knowledge, and budgeting are necessary to close the gap.

Another term for gap is *risk*, as we defined the term in the Chapter 1. The final product created from this phase is a Requirements Definition, a detailed analysis of what is needed to mitigate those risks identified by comparing your *actual* system state with your *objective* state.

Protection Specifications Development

Once your system is modeled and compared to your objectives, and your risks are defined, you're ready to roll up our sleeves and go to work. At this stage of the process, you create a detailed design of your new system security, starting with a general system model that matches your goals and then burrowing down into matching specific technologies, configurations, procedures, and changes to your various targets.

Because this design is the blueprint for the system, this phase usually produces the most formal documentation, even for the simplest implementations. Oversights or incorrect judgments made at this phase can cripple the success of the project. Some of the typical issues covered in the design (and translated to specific sections of the documentation) are as follows:

Executive Summary   This section usually contains a condensed overview of the objectives and constraints used to arrive at the plan. These items are usually referred to as the *selection criteria*, along with the decisions leading to the particular design. Because the repetitive and recursive process of analyzing and combining alternatives might not be apparent to key decisions makers, decision rationale is also included.

Selection Methodology   This section spells out your specific criteria, along with how you ranked them based on your initial objectives and constraints. It's also helpful to demonstrate how you evaluated the different combinations of criteria.

Alternatives   Although not every alternative at every level needs to be included, the most contested or competing alternatives should be listed with their respective pros and cons.

Recommendation   The meat of the document, this section contains the specific design details, along with the final rationale criteria.

Design Review

Any good plan needs a final reality check. We find that after being immersed in the discovery, definition, and design steps, we can sometimes miss simple things. Another pair of trusted eyes can help us avoid embarrassment. But more important, the Design Review phase is an opportunity to present your design and its implications to your decision makers. It also serves to clarify job responsibility among all individuals, teams, and organizations involved with the project. The review should reiterate how all the logical pieces are expected to flow together and interoperate.

Development and Acquisition

Get out the credit card. We're going shopping! Once your design is finished and reviewed and the final go-ahead given, you need to assemble or create your tools, including prototypes and test systems to verify that your configurations function correctly and in the manner that you expect. If your security effort is part of a larger system rollout, you'll have additional tasks, such as reviewing the code or applications that will be installed and testing your security system in the context of the network as a whole.

Component and Code Review

Once you purchase of develop a specific security tool, program, or component, you have to evaluate it in a lab or prototype environment. Although it seems obvious that you want to make sure the components work as advertised, you're also using this time to look for any unknown or unexpected behavior and consequences. Breaking this review into steps helps focus on specific areas of concern:

Component functionality   This step verifies that a particular security technology actually works according to your expectations and the requirements of the security system as a whole.

Component configuration   You also have to test the various configurations of a component to make sure they work as planned. Sometimes you discover additional configurations that might help or harm the system, and naturally you have to determine the implications for the component functionality and the system as a whole if those configurations are activated.

Component maintenance   This step often provides an opportunity for the groups or individuals responsible for maintaining the component to establish workable procedures and methods for maintaining, updating, and troubleshooting it.

Code review   A final (and separate) step from the rest, the code review is your last opportunity to explore sensitive or mission-critical areas of program code to look for bugs or fundamental design problems. Because the most common exploits of Internet-exposed network services are due to buffer overflows (explained later), finding code that could allow such an attack is the highest priority of this step.

System Test Review

Once you individually prototype and review your tools and technologies, you need to prototype them as a whole system—the lesson that was learned from the *Apollo 1* disaster. Although you look at similar issues of functionality, configuration, and maintenance in the Configuration and Code Review phase, you also use this step as an opportunity to determine the training and implementation efforts necessary to put the system into production. Specifically, prototyping the entire system helps with the following areas:

System functionality   Assuming that each component functions individually as planned, you must still verify that they will work in concert. This step in the prototype process can reveal negative, unpredicted side-effects of mixing a range of technologies and their various configurations with the established policies, procedures, and business processes of an organization.

System configuration   Altering the configuration of your components while they are interacting as a system can also highlight hidden problems and weaknesses.

System maintenance   Understanding the implications of component interactions can also help you develop a detailed plan for maintenance, upgrades, and troubleshooting, including the establishment of a baseline for behavior and performance and an estimated support budget. Again, the emphasis is on issues that present themselves only when the components are interacting.

System training   What education requirements are necessary for those individuals interacting with the system? Do support staff need to upgrade their technical skills? Do end users need basic training on how to use the system?

System implementation   One of the most significant benefits of prototyping a security system is learning which obstacles you might encounter in the actual implementation. Being able to document solutions to those implementation problems, along with simple exposure experience to the system itself, is an invaluable investment.

Certification

Similar to having an outside party review your design, certifying your prototype means that you verify a *working* design—a working system that meets your criteria. Once your prototype is verified (your mix of technologies and configurations has been simulated to the most practical degree possible), you can gain the permission to progress to the most dangerous step of all—the implementation.

Implementation

One of the most common IT statistics invoked today (usually used to scare project managers and bean counters everywhere) is that only 70 percent of all IT projects succeed. And when they fail, it's usually in the implementation process. Somehow, somewhere along the path, we inevitably miss things, or worse, the environment or the system changes enough from the beginning of the security process that our solution no longer meets the objectives, or the objectives themselves change!

Assuming that your design and prototype were sound, there are still great challenges. From our experience, those obstacles usually come in the form of the users of the system. So how might we mitigate the risk of acceptance among our users? The usual answer is to provide simple system education. When you teach users how to interact with the new rules and technologies that have been put in place, they will become comfortable with them and accepting of them. Once they understand the system, the users will embrace it and become proactive in carrying the mission of information security into all facets of their work.

Although we believe that education can provide understanding and acceptance, we also believe that there is more to successful internalization and acceptance than simple exposure to the methods and technologies of the new system. Like any of us, users of a system have a need to understand why the system has changed. In other words, psychologically, they perform their own cost-benefit analysis. Are the changes they have to make in their own established, functional habits worth it?

This is a valid question. And although ideally you could have gained the support of users back in the design stage and augmented it by providing user access and input in the prototype stage, the question inevitability gets asked again (even if so silently) by every user the moment that they have to give up their old way of doing things. You can answer the question in several ways. One way, of course, is to have a high degree of user involvement from the beginning of the security process, as we've mentioned. Additionally, if feasible, you can provide a phased transition (if practical) from the old system to the new one. And finally, you can resort to tactics used by every successful parent on the planet—bribery and delay!

Start by assuring your users that while their favorite feature might not have made it into this cycle of implementation, you will personally make every effort to include it in the next cycle of system evaluation. By the way, it's helpful to actually present the users with a schedule of cycles you will be using to reevaluate and reimplement fixes in the security system. By issuing new schedules that list their desired features matched to the expected implementation date, you not only convince users to start the acceptance process, but you provide leverage to management to provide you with the resources necessary to implement that feature. (Bribery works both up and down!)

Although it may seem that we're taking a tongue-in-cheek approach to the problem of user adoption, we're only slightly teasing. Getting end users to accept the system is the only way to reduce your chances that they will misuse it! Consider the Love Bug worm, a viral attachment to an e-mail message that used the address book of the victim to propagate. The worm had a devastating rate of infection, even in organizations that had strict policies about not activating attachments. The reason? The psychological need by humans to be validated (or the curiosity that led them wonder why their boss suddenly expressed an amorous interest in them).

Our final thought is this: the only way to increase the chances that your system will be used as designed is to understand and accept the changes in usability demanded by the most important stakeholders. If you don't, you'll spend the rest of the time convincing your users that they don't want the changes they believe they do. Neither is easy, and only you can decide which is better for the system as a whole.

Accreditation

There has been a growing trend in the security community to recommend insurance for critical business technology and systems, especially for e-commerce sites. That these sites are often the most visible victims of cracker attacks is certainly a factor, but not the only factor. History has shown that as any specific resource gains value in proportion to the overall value of a product, that resource has been insured, whether it is a building, an actor, or a web server. Although it is easy to put a price on equipment failure, it is an entirely different matter to put a price on an organization's reputation—let alone determine the extent of the damage. In the end, most organizations focus their coverage on immediate and short-term damage to stock prices following such a dramatic incident.

Some feel that insuring a system expresses doubt about the ability of the organization to properly defend it. What they are missing is that this type of insurance isn't usually designed specifically for an external, directed, hostile cracker attack against a computer system; rather, it is an attempt to cover the loss of a critical system against anything that might threaten it, whether that is a web-page defacement, a natural physical disaster, or hardware failure. Seen in this light, insuring a system makes much more sense.

Insurance companies often want to verify that a system meets a reasonable minimum level of security before they will cover it in a policy. As a result, the last step of your implementation should be an accreditation review. Often performed by an outside organization (but not necessarily the insurance company itself), this review verifies that the system meets the design objectives, which means that ideally you have included an insurance company's criteria in your Conceptual Definition at the beginning of the security process.

Accreditation also helps key stakeholders in the project (think senior management, investors, clients, employees, and so on) have confidence in your efforts. That confidence leads to the most important resource a security professional can maintain—credibility. Having credibility is more important than trust, although credibility encompasses trust. Credibility translates into support. Support translates into providing requested resources, and nothing can hamper a security effort like not dedicating enough to the security budget.

Operation and Maintenance

Like war itself, this phase can be filled with long stretches of tedium and boredom, followed by brief interludes of sheer terror. Days after days of updates to operating systems, web servers, and virus scan software can be interrupted by a 2 AM page from the firewall that it is about to go under from a massive DDoS (Distributed Denial of Service) attack. Operating a system is more than day-to-day maintenance; you also have to defend and recover the system in the face of threats. Although the sexy battles are with script-kiddy cyberpunks or dissatisfied, disgruntled IT ex-employees, your data is just as endangered by the high temperature levels in the server room, the misconfigured backup tape software, and the executive that insists on deleting key system files to make space for the latest Shakira mp3.

Maintenance is where the security battle is usually lost. Technology and business are both moving fast. Some say that businesses (and even whole economies) are changing in the same duration as dictated by Moore's Law—18 months. While you are scrambling to update your web server with the latest security fixes, you also have to be on the lookout for wireless access points that give someone in the next building local access to your network, and you have to be on call when your CEO loses her PDA (holding the companies not-yet-released earnings report) at the beach.

Ultimately, you will need to take a step back from the day-to-day chaos of your system and evaluate it again from top to bottom. There might even come a time when instead of small fixes, you have to reinvent the security from the ground up. This is happening more and more frequently as companies grow, merge, acquire, and implement whole new infrastructures. When that day comes, you might have to think not just about what to add, but what to get rid of.

Disposal

Making the choice about which business procedures and technologies to use is difficult. Sometimes you're presented with a simple choice—the old way or a new way, but not both, at least, not at the same time in the same place. But occasionally you decide that it's just not worth doing what you're doing now. Yes, your old way still functions and still meets the primary objectives, but it starts to conflict with your constraints, especially as they concern cost. This usually occurs when the price of maintaining a system is equal to or greater than the cost to implement and support a new system. You can also be presented with weaknesses that have been discovered in the old way that create or increase a threat against your system. Of course, getting rid of components (or your system as a whole) should never increase the danger level, but, again, that's an ideal.

Steady As It Goes: Putting the "Constant" Back into Vigilance

So, you have a security system. You're pretty darned satisfied. You've had a successful implementation, your maintenance is going well, and you've even scheduled a review of the system process. But you have a little whisper of doubt. What have you missed? Documents, policies, and procedures can only provide some comfort. After all, they are only tools to help the willing.

You know you need to be vigilant; you know you need to be constant. How you accomplish those goals will depend on the uniqueness of you, your system, and its environment. However, may we suggest something we've learned from many long nights of patrol and guard duty observation both in the military and in civilian life? For the watcher, routine is the enemy. Not only does repetition blind you, it also allows a hostile enemy to better plan for your vulnerability. Now, we understand that checklists and standards allow us to work efficiently. And, of course, we've preached against complexity; both of those principles are correct. However, if you are concerned about what you don't know, you need to be prepared to change how and when you look.

This can actually be a rewarding experience, and on levels not just psychological. By evaluating the performance of your system at unusual times, you can learn about issues affecting the system that don't present themselves at other times. Remember that crackers try to disguise their efforts and make inroads in the dead of night or during the busiest times, for example, on a Monday morning when not-yet-caffeinated workers are more likely to fudge a password. But you can also learn that system performance as a whole decreases in unexpected ways during that logon time—something your network administrator might likely be interested in knowing.

One of the ways we like to test our systems is to set up some formal evaluations by external experts, otherwise known as Tiger teams. We provide a strict, agreed-upon set of parameters of what they are allowed or not allowed to do. We establish joint monitoring procedures and set a start and a stop time. Then, as we look over their shoulders, they put our defenses through their paces. Not only do we learn some of the latest cracker techniques, we also get a good idea of what we've done well and what we've been missing. And while we usually leave a little more humble, we also have a lot of fun!

Our final note for this chapter, before we move on to the more technical concepts that make up the meat of this book, is that the sequential process we've outline is becoming more and more compressed and less sequential as the rate of system evolution advances. In reality, we either conduct, or prepare to conduct, each phase at the same time because we rarely implement a network system (let alone a security system) all at once. Although this can be frustrating, and potentially dangerous, it also means we can more quickly incorporate the best security tools as they become available and proven. By focusing on providing redundant levels of security for your data and the systems that retrieve, store, and process that data, you increase your tolerance for mistakes, mistakes that are inevitable in our rapidly changing environment, system, and organization.

Summary

Building on the work of the first chapter, the material we've just covered illustrates how perfect (and effortless) security is a myth. As with any endeavor, we focus on reducing our risk in the most cost-effective way through a continual cycle of analysis, planning, implementation, and maintenance. Finally, we talked about the need to constantly maintain our alertness. In the next chapter, we'll start looking at the technical nuts and bolts of how networks function.

## Chapter 3

Understanding How Network Systems Communicate

IN THIS CHAPTER, WE'LL review how networked systems move data from point A to point B. We're assuming that you already understand the basics of networking, such as how to assign a valid network address to a device. This chapter will focus on exactly what is going on behind the scenes and along your network cabling. This knowledge is critical in order to give context to the security concepts covered in subsequent chapters.

Featured in this chapter:

◆ The anatomy of a frame of data

◆ A protocol's job

◆ The OSI model

◆ Routers

◆ Connectionless and connection-oriented communications

◆ Network services

◆ Upper-layer communications

The Anatomy of a Frame of Data

When data is moved along a network, it is packaged inside a delivery envelope called a *frame*. Frames are topology-specific. An Ethernet frame needs to convey different information than a Token Ring or an ATM (asynchronous transfer mode) frame (also sometimes called a cell). Since Ethernet is by far the most popular topology, we'll cover it in detail here.

Ethernet Frames

An Ethernet frame is a set of digital pulses transmitted onto the transmission medium in order to convey information. An Ethernet frame normally can be anywhere from 64 to 1518 bytes (a byte being 8 digital pulses or bits) in size. In 1998, the maximum frame length was extended to 1522 bytes in order to support VLAN (virtual local area network) tags, but this is rarely implemented. Regardless of the exact size, Ethernet frames are organized into four sections:

◆ Preamble

◆ Header

◆ Data

◆ Frame-check sequence

Preamble   A *preamble* is a defined series of communication pulses that tells all receiving stations, "Get ready—I've got something to say." The standard preamble is seven bytes, followed by a single start-of-frame byte signifying that the real data starts now.

NOTE   *Because the preamble is considered part of the communication process and not part of the actual information being transferred, it is not usually included when measuring a frame's size.*

Header   A *header* always contains information about who sent the frame and where it is going. It may also contain other information, such as how many bytes the frame contains; this information is referred to as the *length field* and is used for error checking. If the receiving station measures the frame differently than the size indicated in the length field, it asks the transmitting system to send a new frame. If the length field is not used, the header may instead contain a *type field* that describes what type of Ethernet frame it is.

NOTE   *The header size is always 14 bytes.*

Data   The *data* section of the frame contains the actual data the station needs to transmit, as well as any protocol information, such as source and destination IP address. The data field can be anywhere from 46 to 1500 bytes in size. If a station has more than 1500 bytes of information to transfer, it breaks up the information over multiple frames and identifies the proper order by using *sequence numbers*. Sequence numbers identify the order in which the destination system should reassemble the data. This sequence information is also stored in the data portion of the frame.

If the frame does not have 46 bytes' worth of information to convey, the station pads the end of this section by filling it with 1 (remember that digital connections use binary numbers). Depending on the frame type, this section may also contain additional information that describes the protocol or method of communication the systems are using.

Frame-Check Sequence (FCS)   The *frame-check sequence* ensures that the data received is actually the data sent. The transmitting system processes the FCS portion of the frame through an algorithm called a *cyclic redundancy check* (CRC). This CRC takes the values of the above fields and creates a 4-byte number. When the destination system receives the frame, it runs the same CRC and compares it with the value within this field. If the destination system finds a match, it assumes the frame is free of errors and processes the information. If the comparison fails, the destination station assumes that something happened to the frame in its travels and requests that another copy of the frame be sent by the transmitting system.

NOTE   *The FCS size is always 4 bytes.*

The Frame Header Section

Now that you have a better understanding of what an Ethernet frame is, let's take a closer look at the header section. The header information is ultimately responsible for identifying who sent the data and where the sender wanted it to go.

The header contains two fields to identify the source and destination of the transmission. These are the *node addresses* of both the source and destination systems. This number is also referred to as the *media access control* (MAC) address. The node address is a unique number that is used to serialize network devices (such as network cards or networking hardware) and is a unique identifier that distinguishes it from any other networking device in the world. No two networking devices should ever be assigned the same number. Think of this number as equivalent to a telephone number. Every home with a telephone has a unique phone number so that the phone company knows where to direct the call. In this same fashion, a system uses the destination system's MAC address to send the frame to the proper system.

NOTE *The MAC address has nothing specifically to do with Apple's computers and is always represented in all capital letters. It is the number used by all the systems attached to the network (PCs and Macs included) to uniquely identify themselves.*

This 6-byte, 12-digit hexadecimal number is broken into two parts. The first half of the address is the manufacturer's identifier. A manufacturer is assigned a range of MAC addresses to use when serializing its devices. Some of the more prominent MAC addresses appear in Table 3.1.

TABLE 3.1: COMMON MAC ADDRESSES

FIRST THREE BYTES OF MAC ADDRESS	MANUFACTURER
00000C	Cisco
0000A2	Bay Networks
0080D3	Shiva
00AA00	Intel
02608C	3Com
080009	Hewlett-Packard
080020	Sun
08005A	IBM

TIP *The first three bytes of the MAC address can be a good troubleshooting aid. If you are investigating a problem, try to determine the source MAC address. Knowing who made the device might put you a little closer to determining which system is giving you trouble. For example, if the first three bytes are 0000A2, you know you need to focus your attention on any Bay Networks device on your network. The IEEE (Institute of Electrical and Electronics Engineers) stores a list of the MAC codes assigned to manufacturers at* http://standards.ieee.org/regauth/oui.

The second half of the MAC address is the serial number the manufacturer has assigned to the device.

One address worthy of note is FF-FF-FF-FF-FF-FF. This address is referred to as a *broadcast address*. A broadcast address is special: it means that all systems receiving this packet should read the included data. If a system sees a frame that has been sent to the broadcast address, it reads the frame and processes the data if it can.

NOTE *You should never encounter a frame that has a broadcast address in the source node field. The Ethernet specifications do not include any conditions under which the broadcast address should be placed in the source node field.*

How do you find out what the destination node address is so that you can send data to a system? After all, network cards do not ship with phone books. Finding a node address is done with a special frame referred to as an *address resolution protocol* (ARP) frame. The function of ARP depends on which protocol you're using (such as IPX [Internetwork Packet Exchange], IP [Internet Protocol], NetBEUI [NetBIOS Enhanced User Interface], and so on).

For an example, see Figure 3.1. This is a decode of the initial packet from a system that wants to send information to another system on the same network. Notice the information included within the decode. The transmitting system knows the IP address of the destination system, but it does not know the destination node address. Without this address, local delivery of data is not possible. ARP is used when a system needs to discover the destination system's node address.

NOTE *A frame* decode *is the process of converting a binary frame transmission to a format that can be understood by a human being. Typically, this is done using a network analyzer.*

FIGURE 3.1

A transmitting system attempting to discover the destination system's node address

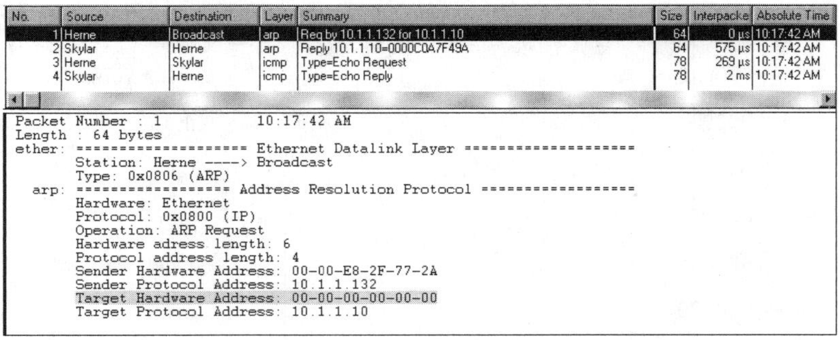

Keep in mind that ARP is only for local communications. When a packet of data crosses a router, the Ethernet header is rewritten so that the source node address is that of the router, not the transmitting system. This means that a new ARP request may need to be generated.

Figure 3.2 shows how this works. Our transmitting system (Fritz) needs to deliver some information to the destination system (Wren). Since Wren is not on the same subnet as Fritz, it transmits an ARP in order to discover the node address of Port A on the local router. Once Fritz knows this address, Fritz transmits its data to the router.

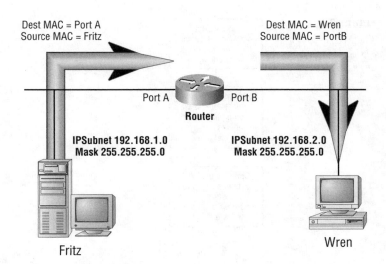

FIGURE 3.2

Node addresses are used for local communications only.

Our router then needs to send an ARP out of Port B in order to discover the node address of Wren. Once Wren replies to this ARP request, the router strips off the Ethernet frame from the data and creates a new one. The router replaces the source node address (originally Fritz's node address) with the node address of Port B. It also replaces the destination node address (originally Port A) with the node address of Wren.

NOTE   In order for the router to communicate on both subnets, it needs two unique node addresses, one for each port. If Fritz were launching an attack against Wren, you could not use the source node address within the frame on Wren's subnet in order to identify the transmitting system. Although the source node address will tell you where the data entered this subnet, it will not identify the original transmitting system.

When Fritz realized that Wren was not on the same subnet, he went looking for a router. A system will run through a process similar to that shown in Figure 3.3 when determining how best to deliver data. Once a system knows where it needs to send the information, it transmits the appropriate ARP request.

All systems are capable of caching information learned through ARP requests. For example, if Fritz wanted a few seconds later to send another packet of data to Wren, he would not have to transmit a new ARP request for the router's node address since this value is saved in memory. This memory area is referred to as the *ARP cache.*

ARP cache entries are retained for a period defined by each manufacturer; 60 seconds, 2 minutes, and 4 hours are common retention periods. After that, they are typically flushed out and must be learned again through a new ARP request. It is also possible to create static ARP entries, which creates a permanent entry in the ARP cache table. This way, a system is no longer required to transmit ARP requests for nodes with a static entry.

For example, you could create a static ARP entry for the router on Fritz's machine so that it would no longer have to transmit an ARP request when looking for this device. The only problem would occur if the router's node address changed. If the router were to fail and you had to replace it with a new one, you would also have to go back to Fritz's system and modify the static ARP entry because the new router would have a different node address.

FIGURE 3.3

The ARP decision process

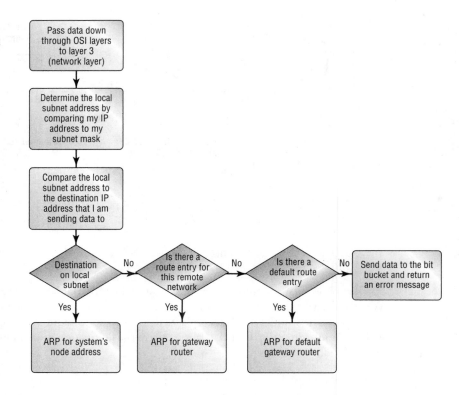

A Protocol's Job

You have seen that when a system wants to transfer information to another system, it does so by creating a frame with the target system's node address in the destination field of the frame header. This method of communication is part of your topology's communication rules. This transmission raises the following questions:

- Should the transmitting system simply assume the frame was received in one piece?

- Should the destination system reply, saying, "I received your frame, thanks!"?

- If a reply should be sent, does each frame require its own acknowledgment, or is it OK to send just one for a group of frames?

- If the destination system is not on the same local network, how do you figure out where to send your data?

- If the destination system is running e-mail, transferring a file, and browsing web pages on the source system, how does it know which application this data is for?

This is where a protocol comes in. A protocol's job is to answer these questions—as well as any others that might pop up in the course of the communication. When we talk about IP, IPX, AppleTalk, or NetBEUI, we are talking about protocols. So why are the specifications that characterize a protocol not simply defined by the topology?

The answer is: diversity. If the communication properties of IP were tied into the Ethernet topology, everyone would be required to use Ethernet for all network segments; this includes wide-area network links. You could not choose to use Token Ring or ATM, because these services would only be available on Ethernet. By defining a separate set of communication rules (protocols), these rules can now be applied over any OSI-compliant topology. This was not the case with legacy systems, which is why the OSI model was developed.

The OSI Model

In 1977, the International Organization for Standardization (ISO) developed the *Open Systems Interconnect Reference Model* (OSI model) to help improve communications between different vendors' systems. The ISO was a committee representing many organizations, whose goal was not to favor a specific method of communication but to develop a set of guidelines that would allow vendors to ensure that their products would interoperate.

The ISO was setting out to simplify communications between systems. Many events must take place in order to ensure that data first reaches the correct system and is then passed along to the correct application in a useable format. A set of rules was required to break down the communication process into a simple set of building blocks.

SIMPLIFYING A COMPLEX PROCESS

The OSI model is analogous to the process of building a house. Although the final product may seem a complex piece of work, it is much simpler when broken down into manageable sections.

A good house starts with a foundation. Rules define how wide the foundation wall must be, as well as how far below the frost line it needs to sit. After that, the house is framed off, or *packaged*. Again, rules define how thick the lumber must be and how far each piece of framing can span without support.

Once the house is framed, there is a defined process for putting on a roof, adding walls, and even connecting the electrical system and plumbing. By breaking down this complicated process into small, manageable sections, building a house becomes easier. This breakdown also makes it easier to define who is responsible for which section. For example, the electrical contractor's responsibilities include running wires and adding electrical outlets, but not shingling the roof.

The entire structure becomes an interwoven tapestry with each piece relying on the others. For example, the frame of our house requires a solid foundation. Without it, the frame will eventually buckle and fall. The frame may also require that load-bearing walls be placed in certain areas of the house in order to ensure that the frame does not fall in on itself.

The OSI model strives to set up these same kinds of definitions and dependencies. Each portion of the communication process becomes a separate building block. This makes it easier to determine what each portion of the communication process is required to do. It also helps to define how each piece will be connected to the others.

The OSI model consists of seven layers. Each layer describes how its portion of the communication process should function, as well as how it will interface with the layers directly above it, below it, and adjacent to it on other systems. This allows a vendor to create a product that operates on a certain level and to be sure it will operate in the widest range of applications. If the vendor's product follows a specific layer's guidelines, it should be able to communicate with products created by other vendors that operate at adjacent layers.

To use the analogy of a house for just a moment, think of the lumber yard that supplies main support beams used in house construction. As long as the yard follows the guidelines for thickness and material, builders can expect beams to function correctly in any house that has a proper foundation structure.

Figure 3.4 is a representation of the OSI model in all its glory. Let's take the layers one at a time to determine the functionality expected of each.

Physical Layer   Describes the specifications of our transmission media, connectors, and signal pulses. A repeater or a hub is a physical layer device because it is frame-stupid and simply amplifies the electrical signal on the wire and passes it along.

Data-Link Layer   Describes the specifications for topology and communication between local systems. Ethernet is a good example of a data-link layer specification because it works with multiple physical layer specifications (twisted-pair cable, fiber) and multiple network layer specifications (IPX, IP). The data-link layer is the "door between worlds," connecting the physical aspects of the network (cables and digital pulses) with the abstract world of software and data streams. Bridges and switches are considered data-link devices because they are frame aware. Both use information specific to the frame header to regulate traffic.

Network Layer   Describes how systems on different network segments find one another; it also defines network addresses. A network address is a name or a number assigned to a group of physically connected systems.

NOTE   *The network address is assigned by the network administrator and should not be confused with the MAC address assigned to each network card. The purpose of a network address is to facilitate data delivery over long distances. Its functionality is similar to the zip code used when mailing a regular letter.*

IP, IPX, and AppleTalk's Datagram Delivery Protocol (DDP) are all examples of network-layer functionality. Service and application availability are based on functionality prescribed at this level.

NOTE   *For more detail about network layer functionality, see the section "More on the Network Layer" later in this chapter.*

Transport Layer   Deals with the actual manipulation of your data and prepares it for delivery through the network. If your data is too large for a single frame, the transport layer breaks it into smaller pieces and assigns sequence numbers. Sequence numbers allow the transport layer on the other receiving system to reassemble the data into its original content. While the data link layer performs a CRC check on all frames, the transport layer can act as a backup check to ensure that all the data was received and is usable. Examples of transport layer functionality are IP's Transmission Control Protocol (TCP), User Datagram Protocol (UDP), IPX's Sequence Packet Exchange (SPX), and AppleTalk's AppleTalk Transaction Protocol (ATP).

FIGURE 3.4

The OSI model

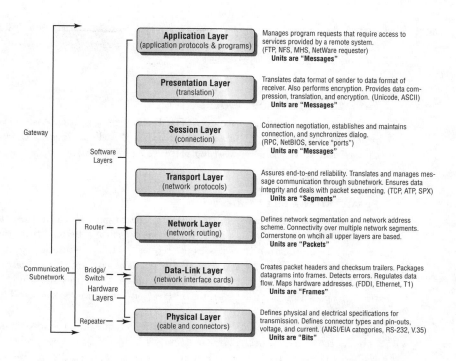

Session Layer   Deals with establishing and maintaining a connection between two or more systems. It ensures that a query for a specific type of service is made correctly. For example, if you try to access a system with your web browser, the session layers on both systems work together to ensure that you receive HTML pages and not e-mail. If a system is running multiple network applications, it is up to the session layer to keep these communications orderly and to ensure that incoming data is directed to the correct application. In fact, the session layer maintains unique conversations within a single service. For example, imagine downloading two distinct web pages from the same website at the same time (from the same computer). The session layer maintains the integrity of each file transfer—making sure that the two data streams aren't mixed up or otherwise confused by the receiving system.

Presentation Layer   Ensures that data is received in a format that is usable to applications running on the system. For example, if you are communicating over the Internet using encrypted communications, the presentation layer is responsible for encrypting and decrypting this information. Most web browsers support this kind of functionality for performing financial transactions over the Internet. Data and language translations are also done at this level.

Application Layer   Responsible for determining when access to network resources is required. The label *application layer* is a bit misleading, because this term does not describe the actual program that a user may be running on a system. For example, Microsoft Word does not function at the application layer of the OSI model. If a user tries to retrieve a document from their home directory on a server, however, the application layer networking software is responsible for delivering the request to the remote system.

NOTE   *In geek lingo, the layers are numbered in the order we've described them. If we were to state that switches function at Layer 2 of the OSI model, you would interpret this to mean that switches work within the guidelines provided by the data-link layer of the OSI model.*

How the OSI Model Works

Let's look at an example to see how these layers work together. Assume you're using your word-processing program, and you want to retrieve a file called `resume.txt` from your home directory on a remote server. The networking software running on your system would react similarly to the description that follows.

FORMULATING A FILE REQUEST

The application layer detects that you are requesting information from a remote file system. It formulates a request to that system that `resume.txt` should be read from disk. Once it has created this request, the application layer passes the request to the presentation layer for further processing.

The presentation layer determines if it needs to encrypt this request or perform any type of data translation. Once this is determined and completed, the presentation layer adds any information it needs to pass along to the presentation layer on the remote system and forwards the packet down to the session layer.

The session layer checks which application is requesting the information and verifies which service is being requested from the remote system (file access). The session layer adds information to the request to ensure that the remote system knows how to handle this request. It then passes all this information along to the transport layer.

The transport layer ensures that it has a reliable connection to the remote system and begins the process of breaking down all the information so that it can be packaged into frames. If more than one frame is required, the information is split, and each block of information is assigned a sequence number. These sequenced chunks of information are passed one at a time down to the network layer.

The network layer receives the blocks of information from the transport layer and adds the network address for both this and the remote system. This is done to each block before it is passed down to the data-link layer.

At the data-link layer, the blocks are packaged into individual frames. As shown in Figure 3.5, all the information added by each of the previous layers (as well as the actual file request) must fit into the 46- to 1500-byte data field of the Ethernet frame. The data-link layer then adds a frame header, which consists of the source and destination MAC addresses, and uses this information (along with the contents of the data field) to create a CRC trailer. The data-link layer is then responsible for transmitting the frame according to the topology rules in use on the network. Depending on the topology, this could mean listening for a quiet moment on the network, waiting for a token, or waiting for a specific time division before transmitting the frame.

NOTE   *The physical layer does not add any information to the frame.*

The physical layer is responsible for carrying the information from the source system to its destination. Because the physical layer has no knowledge of frames, it is simply passing along the digital signal pulses transmitted by the data-link layer. The physical layer is the medium by which a connection is made between the two systems; it is responsible for carrying the signal to the data-link layer on the remote system.

Your workstation has successfully formulated your data request ("Send me a copy of `resume.txt`.") and transmitted it to the remote system. At this point, the remote system follows a similar process, but in reverse.

RECEIVING DATA ON THE REMOTE SYSTEM

The data-link layer on the remote system reads in the transmitted frame. It notes that the MAC address in the destination field of the header is its own and recognizes that it needs to process this request. It performs a CRC check on the frame and compares the results with the value stored in the frame trailer. If these values match, the data-link layer strips off the header and trailer and passes the data field up to the networking layer. If the values do not match, the data-link layer sends a request to the source system asking that another frame be sent.

The network layer on the remote system analyzes the information recorded by the network layer on the source system. It notes that the destination software address is its own. Once this analysis is complete, the network layer removes information related to this level and passes the remainder up to the transport layer.

The transport layer receives the information and analyzes the information recorded by the transport layer on the source system. If it finds that packet sequencing was used, it queues any information it receives until all the data has been received. If any of the data is missing, the transport layer uses the sequence information to formulate a reply to the source system, requesting that this piece of data be resent. Once all the data has been received, the transport layer strips out any transport information and passes the full request up to the session layer.

FIGURE 3.5

The location of each layer's information within our frame

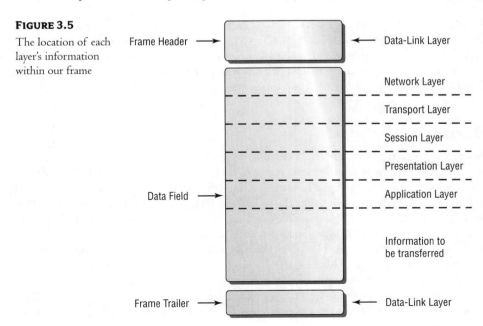

The session layer receives the information and verifies that it is from a valid connection. If the check is positive, the session layer strips out any session information and passes the request up to the presentation layer.

The presentation layer receives the frame and analyzes the information recorded by the presentation layer on the source system. It then performs any translation or decryption required. Once translation or decryption is complete, it strips out the presentation layer information and passes the request up to the application layer.

The application layer ensures that the correct process running on the system receives the request for data. Because this is a file request, it is passed to whichever process is responsible for access to the file system.

This process then reads the requested file and passes the information back to the application layer. At this point, the entire process of passing the information through each of the layers repeats. If you're amazed that the requested file is retrievable in anything less than a standard coffee break, you have a good idea of the magnitude of what happens when you request a simple file.

More on the Network Layer

As we mentioned earlier, the network layer is used to deliver information between *logical networks*.

NOTE   *A logical network is simply a group of systems assigned a common network address by the network administrator. These systems might be grouped together because they share a common geographical area or a central point of wiring.*

The terminology used for network addresses depends on the protocol in use. If the protocol in use is IPX, the logical network is simply referred to as a network address. With IP, it is a *subnet*, and with AppleTalk, it is called a *zone*.

NOTE   *NetBEUI is a nonroutable protocol, although NetBEUI can be thought of as overlapping the transport, network, and (the LLC portion of the) data-link layer. NetBEUI does not use network numbers and does not have the ability to propagate information between logical network segments. A nonroutable protocol is a set of communication rules that expects all systems to be connected locally. A nonroutable protocol has no direct method of traveling between logical networks. A NetBEUI frame is incapable of crossing a router without some form of help.*

Routers

Routers are used to connect logical networks, which is why they are sometimes referred to in the IP world as *gateways*. Figure 3.6 shows the effect of adding a router to a network. Notice that protocols on either side of the device must now use a unique logical network address. Information destined for a nonlocal system must be routed to the logical network on which the system resides. The act of traversing a router from one logical network to another is referred to as a *hop*. When a protocol hops a router, it must use a unique logical network address on both sides.

So how do systems on one logical network segment find out what other logical segments exist on the network? Routers can either be statically programmed with information describing the path to follow in order to find remote networks, or they can use a special type of maintenance frame such as the routing information protocol (RIP) to relay information about known networks. Routers use these frames and static entries to create a blueprint of the network known as a *routing table*.

FIGURE 3.6

The effects of adding a router to the network

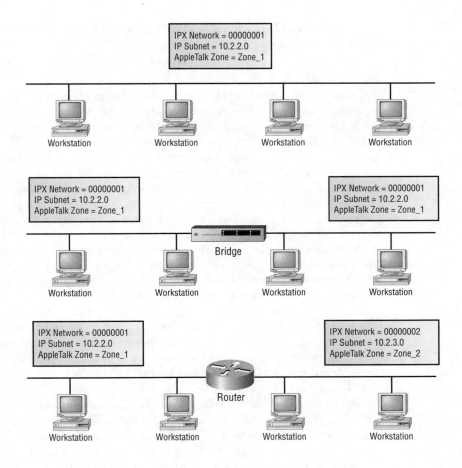

NOTE *Routing tables tell the router which logical networks are available to deliver information to and which routers are capable of forwarding information to that network.*

Routing Tables

You can think of a routing table as being like a road map. A road map shows all the streets in a local city or town in much the same way a routing table keeps track of all the local networks.

Without having some method for each of these routers to communicate and let one another know who is connected where, communication between logical network segments would be impossible.

There are four methods for populating routing tables:

◆ Static

◆ Distance vector

◆ Link state

◆ Label switching

Although each method has its own ways of providing routing functionality, each implementation can be classified into one of these four categories.

Static Routing

Static routing is the simplest way to get information from one system to another. Used mostly in IP networks, a static route defines a specific router as the point leading to a specific network. Static routing does not require routers to exchange route information: it relies on a configuration file that directs all traffic bound for a specific network to a particular router. This, of course, assumes that you can predefine all the logical networks with which you want to communicate. When this is not feasible (for example, when you are communicating on the Internet), you can designate a single router as a default to receive all traffic destined for networks that have not been predefined. When static routing is used, most workstations receive an entry for the default router only.

For example, let's assume we configure a system to have a default route that points to the router Galifrey. As the system passes information through the network layer, it analyzes the logical network of the destination system. If the system is on the same logical network, the data-link layer adds the MAC address of that system and transmits the frame onto the wire. If the system is on some other logical network, the data-link layer uses the MAC address for Galifrey and transmits the frame to it. Galifrey is then responsible for ensuring that the frame gets to its final destination.

The benefits of this type of routing are simplicity and low overhead. A workstation is not required to know or care about what other logical networks might be available and how to get to them. It has only two possibilities to worry about—deliver locally or deliver to Galifrey. This can be useful when there is only one possible route to a final destination. For example, most organizations have only one Internet connection. Setting up a static route that points all IP traffic to the router that borders this connection might be the easiest way to ensure that all frames are delivered properly. Because all routing information is configured at startup, routers do not need to share route information with other routers. Each system is only concerned with forwarding information to its next default route. There is no need to have any dynamic routing frames propagated through the network, because each router has been preset as to where it should forward information.

Although static routing is easy to use, it does suffer from some major drawbacks that severely limit its application. When redundant paths are provided, or even when multiple routers are used on the same logical network, you may find it more effective to use a routing method that can exchange dynamic routing information. Dynamic routing allows routing tables to be developed on the fly, which can compensate for hardware failures. Both distance vector and link state routing use dynamic routing information to ensure that routing tables stay up-to-date.

Although static routing is high maintenance, it is also the most secure way to build your routing tables. Dynamic routing allows routing tables to be updated dynamically by devices on the network. An attacker can exploit this feature to feed your routers incorrect routing information, thus preventing your network from functioning properly. In fact, depending on the dynamic routing protocol you use, an attacker might only need to feed this bogus information to a single router. The compromised router would then take care of propagating this bogus information throughout the rest of the network.

Each static router is responsible for maintaining its own routing table. Thus, if one router is compromised, the effects of the attack are not automatically spread to every other router. A router using static routing can still be vulnerable to ICMP (Internet Control Message Protocol) redirect attacks, but its routing tables cannot be corrupted through the propagation of bad route information.

NOTE *For more information on ICMP, see Chapter 5.*

Distance Vector Routing

Distance vector is the oldest and most popular way to create routing tables. This is primarily due to the routing information protocol (RIP), which is based on distance vector. For many years, distance vector routing was the only dynamic routing option available, so it has found its way onto many networks.

Distance vector routers build their tables on secondhand information. A router will look at the tables being advertised by other routers and simply add 1 to the advertised hop values to create its own table. With distance vector, every router broadcasts its routing table once per minute.

PROPAGATING NETWORK INFORMATION WITH DISTANCE VECTOR

Figure 3.7 shows how propagation of network information works with distance vector.

FIGURE 3.7

A routed network about to build its routing tables dynamically

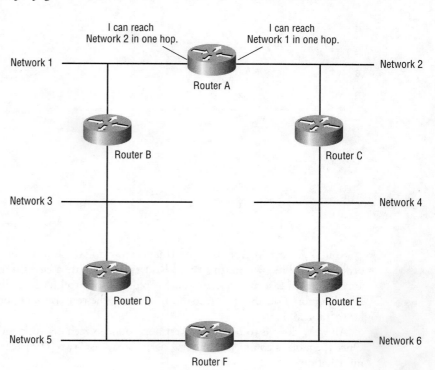

Router A has just come online. Because the two attached networks (1 and 2) have been programmed into it, Router A immediately adds these to its routing table, assigning a hop value of 1 to each. The hop value is 1 instead of 0 because this information is relative to other attached networks, not the router. For example, if the router is advertising the route to Network 1 on Network 2, one hop is appropriate because any system sending information to Network 1 from Network 2 would have to travel one hop (the router itself) to get there. A router usually does not advertise routing information about a directly attached network on that network itself. Thus, the router should not transmit a RIP frame stating, "I can reach Network 1 in one hop," on Network 1 itself.

So Router A sends out two RIP packets, one on each network, to let any other devices know about the connectivity it can provide. When Routers B and C receive these packets, they reply with RIP packets of their own. Remember that the network was already up and running. All the other routers have already had an opportunity to build their tables. From these other RIP packets, Router A collects the information shown in Table 3.2.

TABLE 3.2: ROUTING INFORMATION RECEIVED BY ROUTER A

ROUTER	NETWORK	HOPS TO GET THERE
B	3	1
B	5	2
B	6	3
B	4	4
B	2	5
C	4	1
C	6	2
C	5	3
C	3	4
C	1	5

Router A then analyzes this information, picking the lowest hop count to each network in order to build its own routing table. Routes that require a larger hop count are not discarded but are retained in case an alternate route is required due to link failure. These higher hop values are simply ignored during the normal operation of the router. Once complete, the table appears similar to Table 3.3.

All we've done is to pick the lowest hop count to each network and add 1 to the advertised value. Once the table is complete, Router A again broadcasts two RIP packets, incorporating this new information.

TABLE 3.3: ROUTER A'S ROUTING TABLE

NETWORK	HOPS TO GET THERE	NEXT ROUTER
1	1	Direct connection
2	1	Direct connection
3	2	B
4	2	C
5	3	B
6	3	C

Now that Routers B and C have noted that there is a new router on the network, they must reevaluate their routing tables, as well. Before Router A came online, the table for Router B would have looked like Table 3.4.

TABLE 3.4: ROUTER B'S ROUTING TABLE BEFORE ROUTER A INITIALIZES

NETWORK	HOPS TO GET THERE	NEXT ROUTER
1	1	Direct connection
2	5	D
3	1	Direct connection
4	4	D
5	2	D
6	3	D

Now that Router A is online, Router B will modify its table to reflect the information shown in Table 3.5.

TABLE 3.5: ROUTER B'S ROUTING TABLE AFTER ROUTER A INITIALIZES

NETWORK	HOPS TO GET THERE	NEXT ROUTER
1	1	Direct connection
2	2	A
3	1	Direct connection
4	3	A
5	2	D
6	3	D

It takes two RIP updates on the same logical network to get to this point. The first time Router A sent a RIP to Router B, it only knew about Network 2, as you can see in Figure 3.7. It was not until Router C sent a reply RIP that Router A had to send a second RIP frame to Router B, incorporating this new information. Table 3.5 is broadcast with only the direct common network information being removed (Network 1). This means that while Router A was updating Router B with the information it had learned from Router C, it was also relaying back the route information originally sent to it by that router (Router B). The only difference is that Router A has increased by 1 each hop count reported by Router B.

Because the hop value is larger than what Router B currently has in its tables, Router B simply ignores this information.

Router C goes through a similar process, adjusting its table according to the information it receives from Router A. Again, it requires two RIP frames on the same logical network to yield a complete view of the entire network so that Router C can complete the changes to its tables.

These changes then begin to propagate down through the network. Router B updates Router D when A first comes online and then again when it completes its tables. This activity continues until all the routers have an accurate view of the new network layout. The amount of time that is required for all routers to complete their table changes is known as the time to *convergence*. The convergence time is important, because a routing table is in a state of flux until all routers become stabilized with their new tables.

TIP Keep in mind that in a large network, convergence time can be quite long, as RIP updates are only sent once or twice a minute.

DISTANCE VECTOR ROUTING PROBLEMS

Our distance vector routing table has been almost completely built on secondhand information. Any route that a router reports with a hop count greater than 1 is based on what it has learned from another router. When Router B tells Router A that it can reach Network 5 in two hops or Network 6 in three, it is fully trusting the accuracy of the information it has received from Router D. If, as a child, you ever played the telephone game (in which each person in a line receives a whispered message and tries to convey it exactly to the next), you quickly realize that secondhand information is not always accurate.

Figure 3.8 shows a simple network layout. It consists of four logical networks separated by three routers. Once the point of convergence is reached, each router will have created a routing table, as shown in the diagram.

Now, let's assume that Router C dies a fiery death and drops offline. This makes Network 4 unreachable by all other network segments. Once Router B realizes that Router C is offline, it reviews the RIP information it has received in the past, looking for an alternate route. At this point, distance vector routing starts to break down. Because Router A has been advertising that it can get to Network 4 in three hops, Router B simply adds 1 to this value and assumes it can now reach Network 4 through Router A. Relying on secondhand information clearly causes problems: Router B cannot reach Network 4 through Router A, now that Router C is offline.

As you can see in Figure 3.9, Router B now begins to advertise that it can reach Network 4 in four hops. Remember that RIP frames do not identify *how* a router will get to a remote network, only that it *can* and how many hops it will take to get there. Without knowing how Router A plans to reach Network 4, Router B has no idea that Router A is basing its route information on the tables it originally received from Router B.

FIGURE 3.8

Given the diagrammed network, each router would construct its routing table.

Network 1

Router A

Network 2

Network	Hops	Next Router
1	1	Direct
2	1	Direct
3	2	B
4	3	B

Router B

Network 3

Network	Hops	Next Router
1	2	A
2	1	Direct
3	1	Direct
4	2	C

Router C

Network 4

Network	Hops	Next Router
1	3	B
2	2	B
3	1	Direct
4	1	Direct

FIGURE 3.9

Router B incorrectly believes that it can now reach Network 4 through Router A and updates its tables accordingly.

Network 1

Router A

Network 2

Network	Hops	Next Router
1	1	Direct
2	1	Direct
3	2	B
4	3	B

Router B

Network 3

Router C

Network 4

Network	Hops	Next Router
1	2	A
2	1	Direct
3	1	Direct
4	4	A

So Router A receives a RIP update from Router B and realizes that it has increased the hop count to Network 4 from 2 to 4. Router A then adjusts its table accordingly and begins to advertise that it now takes 5 hops to reach Network 4. It would again RIP, and Router B would again increase the hop count to Network 4 by 1.

NOTE *This phenomenon is called* count to infinity *because both routers continue to increase their hop counts forever. Because of this problem, RIP routing limits the maximum hop count to 15; other distance vector protocols have higher maximum hop counts. Any route that is 16 or more hops away is considered unreachable and is subsequently removed from the routing table. This allows our two routers to figure out in a reasonable amount of time that Network 4 can no longer be reached.*

Reasonable is a subjective term, however. Remember that RIP updates are sent out only once or twice a minute. Thus, it may be a minute or more before our routers buy a clue and realize that Network 4 is gone. With a technology that measures frame transmissions in the microsecond range, a minute or more is plenty of time to wreak havoc with communications. For example, let's look at what is taking place on Network 2 while the routers are trying to converge.

Once Router C drops offline, Router B assumes that it has an alternative route to Network 4 through Router A. Any packets it receives are checked for errors and passed along to Router A. When Router A receives the frame, it performs an error check again. It then references its tables and realizes it needs to forward the frame to Router B in order to reach Network 4. Router B again receives the frame and sends it back to Router A.

This process is called a *routing loop*. Each router plays hot potato with the frame, assuming the other is responsible for its delivery and passing it back and forth. Although our example describes only one frame, imagine the amount of bandwidth lost if a considerable amount of traffic is destined for Network 4. With all these frames looping between the two routers, very little bandwidth is available on Network 2 for any other systems that need to transmit information.

Fortunately, the network layer has a method for eliminating this problem, as well. As each router handles the frame, it is required to decrease a hop counter within the frame by 1. The hop counter is responsible for recording how many routers the information has crossed. As with RIP frames, this counter has a maximum value of 15. As the information is handled for the 16th time (the counter drops to 0), the router realizes that the information is undeliverable and simply drops the information.

Although this 16-hop limitation is not a problem for the average corporate network, it can be a severe limitation in larger networks. For example, consider the vast size of the Internet. If RIP were used throughout the Internet, certain areas of the Internet could not reach many resources.

SECURITY CONCERNS WITH RIP

Besides our RIP routing tables being built on secondhand information, this information is never actually verified. For example, if Router B claims to have the best route to a given network, none of the other routers verify this information. In fact, they do not even verify that this information was sent from Router B or that Router B even exists!

Needless to say, this lack of verification can be a gaping security hole. It is not all that difficult to propagate bogus routing information and bring an entire network to its knees. This is a clear example of how one savvy but malicious user can interrupt communications for an entire network. This weakness was partially overcome in RIP version 2, which included simple authentication for RIP packets but still left a lot to be desired.

Because of this security concern and the other problems we've noted, many organizations use static routing or deploy a more advanced distance vector such as Cisco's IGRP (Interior Gateway Routing Protocol) or link state routing protocols such as OSPF (Open Shortest Path First). Besides eliminating many of the convergence problems found in RIP, OSPF also brings authentication to the table, requiring routers to supply a password in order to participate in routing updates. Although not infallible, this method dramatically increases the security in a dynamic routing environment.

Link State Routing

Link state routers function in a similar fashion to distance vector, but with a few notable exceptions. Most important, link state routers use only firsthand information when developing their routing tables. Not only does this help to eliminate routing errors, it drops the time to convergence to nearly zero. Imagine that our network in Figure 3.7 has been upgraded to use a link state routing protocol. Now let's bring Router A online and watch what happens.

PROPAGATING NETWORK INFORMATION WITH LINK STATE

As Router A powers up, it sends out a type of packet referred to as a *hello*. The hello packet is simply an introduction that states, "Greetings! I am a new router on this network; is there anybody out there?" This packet is transmitted on both of its ports and will be responded to by Routers B and C.

Once Router A receives a reply from Routers B and C, it creates a *link state protocol* (LSP) frame and transmits it to Routers B and C. An LSP frame is a routing maintenance frame that contains the following information:

- ◆ The router's name or identification
- ◆ The networks to which it is attached
- ◆ The hop count or cost of getting to each network
- ◆ Any other routers on each network that responded to its hello frame

Routers B and C then make a copy of Router A's LSP frame and forward the frame in its entirety along through the network. Each router receiving Router A's LSP frame then copies the information and passes it along. With link state routing, each router maintains a copy of every other router's LSP frame. The router can use this information to diagram the network and thus build routing tables. Because each LSP frame contains only the route information that is local to each router that sent it, this network map is created strictly from firsthand information. A router simply fits the LSP puzzle pieces together until its network picture is complete.

Router A then makes an LSP frame request from either Router B or C. An LSP frame request is a query requesting that the router forward a copy of all known LSP frames. Because each router has a copy of all LSP frames, either router is capable of supplying a copy from every router on the network. This arrangement avoids making Router A request this information from each router individually, thus saving bandwidth. Once an LSP network is up and running, updates are transmitted every two hours or whenever a change takes place (such as a router going offline).

CONVERGENCE TIME WITH LINK STATE

Our link state network is up and running. Note that Routers B and C were not required to recompute their routing tables. They simply added the new piece from Router A and continued to pass traffic. Thus, convergence time is nearly zero. The only change required of each router is to add the new piece to its tables. Unlike distance vector, updates were not required in order to normalize the routing table. Router B did not need a second packet from Router A, telling it which networks were available through Router C. Router B simply added Router A's LSP information to its existing table and was already aware of the links.

RECOVERING FROM A ROUTER FAILURE IN A LINK STATE ENVIRONMENT

Let's revisit Figure 3.9 to look at how link state routing reacts when a router goes offline. Again, for the purpose of this example, let's assume that our routing protocol has been upgraded from distance vector to link state. Let's also assume that our routing tables have been created and that traffic is passing normally.

If Router C is shut down normally, it transmits a maintenance frame (known as a *dying gasp*) to Router B, informing Router B that it is about to go offline. Router B then deletes the copy of Router C's LSP frame that it has been maintaining and forwards this information to Router A. Both routers now have a valid copy of the new network layout and realize that Network 4 is no longer reachable. If Router C is not brought down gracefully but again dies a fiery death, there would be a short delay before Router B realizes that Router C is no longer acknowledging packets sent to it. At this point, Router B realizes that Router C is offline. It deletes Router C's LSP frame from its table and forwards the change to Router A. Again, both systems have a valid copy of the new network layout. Because we are dealing with strictly firsthand information, there are none of the pesky count-to-infinity problems that we experienced with distance vector. Our router tables are accurate, and our network is functioning with a minimal amount of updating. This allows link state to traverse a larger number of network segments. The maximum is 127 hops, but this number can be fewer, depending on the implementation.

SECURITY WITH LINK STATE ROUTING

Most link state routing protocols support some level of authenticating the source of dynamic route updates. Although it is not impossible to incorporate this functionality into distance vector routing, most distance vector routing protocols predate the need to authenticate routing table updates. Authentication is an excellent way to ensure that each router accepts routing table updates only from a trusted host. Although authentication is not 100 percent secure, it is a far cry from trusting every host on the wire.

For example, OSPF supports two levels of authentication: password and message digest. *Password authentication* requires each router that will be exchanging route table information to be preprogrammed with a password. When a router attempts to send OSPF routing information to another router, it includes the password string as verification. Routers using OSPF will not accept route table updates unless the password string is included in the transmission. This helps to ensure that table updates are accepted only from trusted hosts. The drawback to this authentication method is that the password is transmitted as clear text. Thus, an attacker who is monitoring the network with a packet analyzer can capture the OSPF table updates and discover the password. An attacker who knows the password can use it to pose as a trusted OSPF router and transmit bogus routing table information.

Message digest is far more secure in that it does not exchange password information over the wire. Each OSPF router is programmed with a password and a key-ID. Before transmitting an OSPF table update, a router processes the OSPF table information, password, and key-ID through an algorithm in order to generate a unique message digest, which is attached to the end of the packet. The message digest provides an encrypted way to verify that the router transmitting the table can be considered a trusted host. When the destination router receives the transmission, the destination router uses the password and key-ID it has been programmed with to validate the message digest. If the message is authentic, the routing table update is accepted.

TIP   *Although it is possible to crack the encryption used by OSPF, doing so takes time and lots of processing power. Thus, OSPF with message digest authentication is an excellent choice for updating dynamic routing information over insecure networks.*

Label Switching and MPLS

In an effort to integrate packet traffic direction capabilities present in both Layer 2 (referring to the second level of the OSI model) switches and in Layer 3 routers, while at the same time removing some of the speed constraints inherent in traditional routing tables, vendors have pushed the concept of tagging packets with labels representing predetermined, optimized routes. The foremost protocol representing this effort is called MPLS (Multiprotocol Label Switching) and is defined in RFC 3031, Multiprotocol Label Switching Architecture. Although there is no single MPLS standard, many of the technologies that fall under the heading of MPLS have already received standard status from the IETF (Internet Engineering Task Force).

Because the MPLS process avoids the time-intensive process of routing table lookup, router performance can better emulate the speed of switches—Layer 2 devices that merely examine the MAC address of a packet and make a simple forwarding decision. Initially, this speed increase was enough to justify the development and deployment of the protocol. As router speeds increased with the advances of their ASIC (application-specific integrated circuit) chips, so called Layer 3 switches came to market promising switchlike speeds while retaining the traditional table-based routing protocols.

MPLS, however, provides benefits beyond speed increases:

Path definition   MPLS provides a mechanism by which routes can be predetermined throughout the network.

Class performance   Packet types can be assigned classes. Classes can then be given various levels of priority, and priority is the primary method for augmenting the network performance of a given class of traffic..

VWAN (Virtual Wide Area Network)   MPLS can create unencrypted IP tunnels throughout their network, removing the need for specialized VPN (virtual private network) applications on network hosts.

ATM emulation   Many WAN carriers (your T1 provider, for example) use SONET (Switched Optical Network) for Layer 1, use ATM for Layer 2, and force IP onto Layer 3. MPLS provides the same ability to segment and optimize traffic—all in Layer 3. This allows a greater flexibility and simplifies network management.

In MPLS, all packets are assigned one or more *labels*. These labels are used to associate the packet with an FEC (Forwarding Equivalence Class). FECs are used by MPLS to create LSPs (Label Switch Paths), specific routes through an MPLS-enabled network. By associating packets with the FEC label assigned to an LSP, administrators can force packets to follow predetermined network routes, give priority to some FECs over others, and provide services typically associated with ATM such as class billing (charging a client for the amount of traffic sent using a specific type of data such as multimedia).

LABELS

The MPLS label is placed in between the IP header and the Layer 2 information (including the MAC address) and is made up of 32 bits. These bits are broken down into four fields:

Label   A 20-bit area that carries the actual FEC information.

CoS   A 3-bit area that stores Cost of Service information, which is used to determine how long a packet can be delayed in a router before it is discarded.

Stack   A single-bit area that designates the position of the label in a multilabel hierarchy, required when multiple labels are applied to a single packet.

TTL   An 8-bit area that designates the Time To Live of a packet.

FEC (FORWARDING EQUIVALENCY CLASS)

FECs are used to define a collection of packet evaluation criteria. Thus, all packets associated with an FEC can be treated and routed in the same manner. Packets are usually assigned an FEC when they arrive at the border of an MPLS network (also called an MPLS *domain*) by an LSR (Label Switch Router), an MPLS-capable router. The LSR looks at the interface on which the packet arrived, at the IP header, and possibly at the application layer (Layer 7) data itself in order to determine which FEC to assign to the packet.

LSP (LABEL SWITCH PATH)

An LSP is actually an abstracted object that is associated with MPLS labels. Because multiple traffic flows can be combined in a hierarchy, you can think of an LSP as a container that is capable of holding various labels in a *label stack*, with each label defining a particular path inside the network.

Let's look at an example that will help you understand how the LSP works as an object. An MPLS domain consists of five routers—R1 through R5. Routers R1 and R5 function at the border of the domain, and routers R2, R3, and R4 operate inside the domain. A packet entering the domain at R1 can be given an LSP containing two labels. One label defines a virtual path directly connecting R1 to R5. The other label, considered subordinate in the label hierarchy, actually maps the path of the packet *inside* the domain, from R2 to R4.

The packet is first processed by R1, which determines that the ultimate destination of the packet is to leave the domain through R5 and, as a result, assigns a label to the packet that represents that fact. Additionally, R1 assigns a second label to the packet that will be used only by internal LSRs to route the packet *until* it reaches R5. After classifying and labeling the packet, R1 forwards it to R2. Because the top-level label reflects a FEC in which R2 doesn't participate, R2 continues down the label hierarchy to the second label, which does apply. R2 determines that the next router that should receive the packet is R3 and forwards it accordingly. This process continues until the packet arrives at R5, at which point the router reads the top-level packet and then forwards that packet out of the MPLS domain accordingly. Functionally, the various labels in an LSP are used to associate Layer 3 routes with Layer 2 switched paths—mappings that are used by the LSRs in an MPLS network to actually perform the MPLS functions.

LDP (LABEL DISTRIBUTION PROTOCOL)

Because all LSRs in an MPLS network need a common understanding of label-to-FEC associations, a protocol is needed to transfer that information to all LSRs that make up the LSP. The LDP is simply the standard by which label definitions are propagated through the network. The following requirements are common to any specific protocol used to implement LDP:

Discovery   LSRs have to know where other LSRs are located in order to maintain communication.

Message classes   All messages are defined as being Discovery, Adjacency, Label Advertisement, or Notification.

TCP (Transmission Control Protocol)   With the exception of Discovery messages, all LDP traffic relies on the connection-oriented nature of TCP.

LDP defines several label distribution modes:

Demand or Unsolicited   Labels are either requested from participating LSRs or received without warning.

Order or Independent   LSPs are maintained externally by an administrator (ordered) or generated from the LSRs themselves (independent).

Liberal or Conservative   This mode determines how labels will hold their FEC associations in the midst of network reconfiguration.

Two competing implementations of LDP are used to actually chart and create the paths through an MPLS network, creating the LSP:

RSVP-TE   An extension of the RSVP QoS (Quality of Service) protocol that allows for route determination and label transfer.

CR-LDP   An extension of the original LDP that also allows for route determination and adds QoS capabilities. Most of today's MPLS routers support RSVP-TE, including those from Nortel, the vendor of CR-LDP.

TRAFFIC ENGINEERING

In addition to predefined (or *explicit*) routing, MPLS allows for additional capabilities referred to as Traffic Engineering (TE). TE allows for additional restraints and conditions to be taken into account by the various LSRs when determining the route a packet will take through the MPLS domain. Specifically, MPLS uses the following components to provide this functionality:

CSPF (Constraint Shortest Path First)   This component modifies the OSPF protocol to allow classes and other constraints to figure into path determination.

Reservations   Both RSVP and CR-LDP can reserve bandwidth throughout an LSP for specific packet classes.

Link state   Extending IGP allows for network changes to be communicated throughout the network to the various LSRs.

TRAFFIC ISOLATION

Similar to ATM or frame relay, MPLS can create virtual network segments. Although doing so does not provide the encrypting or authentication functions of a complete VPN, it is an additional layer of security to already-encrypted VPN traffic. Various alterations have been suggested that would allow the integration of IPsec (IP Security) into the MPLS standard, but these are still in their infancy.

QoS (QUALITY OF SERVICE)

MPLS allows traditional IP QoS features to be applied to Layer 2 connections, providing a significantly increased level of detail in controlling network data. Although you can add custom QoS features, interoperability becomes problematic. Typical MPLS deployments use a three-tiered level of service:

Premium   This tier was designed primarily for multimedia data. Packets in this tier must have the highest priority and least possible latency in order to avoid time delay.

Critical   Although reducing latency is the primary goal of the Premium class, Critical requires only that the delivery of a packet is guaranteed, applying connection-oriented principles to all data regardless of the transport protocol.

Basic   This entry-level tier makes minimal or no promises as to latency or delivery, relying instead on the higher-layer protocols and applications of the hosts themselves to resolve packet loss.

Connectionless and Connection-Oriented Communications

We can now get our information from Point A to Point B, regardless of whether the systems are on the same logical network. This raises the question, Once we get there, how do we carry on a proper conversation? This is where the transport layer comes in.

The transport layer is where we begin to set down the rules of communication etiquette. It's not enough that we can get this information from one system to another; we also have to ensure that both systems are operating at the same level of decorum.

As an analogy, let's say you pull up to the finest restaurant in the city in your GMC Pacer and proceed to the front door sporting your best set of leather chaps, Harley jacket, and bandanna. Once inside, you greet the maitre d' with "Yo wimp, gimme a table and some grub, NOW!" Surprisingly, you're escorted out of the restaurant at gunpoint. What went wrong? Why, you employed improper etiquette, of course—everyone knows the correct term is not "grub" but "escargot."

You can avoid such verbal breakdown, as well as those in network communications, by ensuring that all parties involved are communicating at the same level of etiquette. There are two forms of network communication etiquette:

◆ Connection-oriented

◆ Connectionless

Connection-Oriented Communications

A *connection-oriented* communication exchanges control information referred to as a *handshake* prior to transmitting data. The transport layer uses the handshake to ensure that the destination system is ready to receive information. A connection-oriented exchange will also ensure that data is transmitted and received in its original order.

Modems are heavy users of connection-oriented communications because they need to negotiate a connection speed prior to sending any information. In networking, this functionality is accomplished through the use of a transport layer field referred to as a *flag* in the IP and AppleTalk world or as a *connection control field* under IPX. Only connection-oriented communications use these fields. When IP is the underlying routing protocol, TCP is used to create connection-oriented communications. IPX uses SPX (Sequenced Packet Exchange), and AppleTalk uses ATCP (AppleTalk Control Protocol) to provide this functionality. As a communication session is started, the application layer (not necessarily the program you are using) specifies if it needs to use a connection-oriented protocol. Telnet is just such an application. When a Telnet session is started, the application layer requests TCP as its transport service in order to better ensure reliability of the connection. Let's look at how this session is established to see how a handshake works.

At your workstation, you type **telnet thor.foobar.com** to establish a remote connection to that system. As the request is passed down through the transport layer, TCP is selected to connect the two systems so that a connection-oriented communication can be established. The transport layer sets the synchronization (SYN) flag to 1 and leaves all other flags at 0. IP uses multiple flag fields and uses the binary system to set values. Thus, the only possible values of an IP flag are 1 and 0. IPX and ATCP use a hexadecimal value because their frames contain only one flag field. The one field, therefore, can contain more than two values.

By setting SYN to 1 and all other fields to 0, we let the system on the other end (`thor.foobar.com`) know that we want to establish a new communication session with the system. This request is then passed down the remaining layers, across the wire to the remote system, and then up through its OSI layers.

If the service is available on the remote system (more on services in a moment), the request is acknowledged and sent back down the stack until it reaches the transport layer. The transport layer then sets the SYN flag to 1, as did the originating system, but it also sets the acknowledgment (ACK) flag to 1. This lets the originating system know that its transmission was received and that it's OK to send data. The request is then passed down the stack and over the wire back to the original system.

The original system then sets the SYN flag to 0 and the ACK flag to 1 and transfers this frame back to Thor. This lets Thor know, "I'm acknowledging your acknowledgment, and I'm about to send data." At this point, data is transferred, with each system being required to transmit an acknowledgment for each packet it receives.

Figure 3.10 shows a Telnet session from the system Loki to the system Thor. Each line represents a different frame that has been transmitted from one system to the other. Source and destination systems are identified, and some summary information about the frame is displayed. Notice that the first three frames are identified as TCP frames, not Telnet, and that they perform the handshaking just described. Once TCP establishes the connection-oriented connection, Telnet can step in to transfer the data required. The TCP frames that appear later in the conversation are for acknowledgment purposes. As stated, with a connection-oriented protocol every frame must be acknowledged. If the frame was a request for information, the reply can be in the form of delivering the requested information. If a frame is sent that does not require a reply, however, the destination system is still required to acknowledge that the frame was received.

If you're still a bit fuzzy on handshaking and connection-oriented communications, let's look at an analogy. Let's say you call a friend to inform him you'll be having a network Quake party on Saturday night and that he should come by with his laptop. You follow these steps:

◆ You dial your friend's phone number (SYN=1, ACK=0).

◆ Your friend answers the phone and says, "Hello" (SYN=1, ACK=1).

◆ You reply by saying, "Hi, Fred, this is Dave" (SYN=0, ACK=1).

You then proceed to transfer the data about your upcoming party. Every time you pause, Fred either transfers back information ("Yes, I'm free Saturday night.") or sends some form of acknowledgment (ACK) to let you know he has not yet hung up.

When the conversation is complete, you both tear down the connection by saying goodbye, which is a handshake to let each other know that the conversation is complete and that it's OK to hang up the phone. Once you hang up, your connection-oriented communication session is complete.

The purpose of connection-oriented communications is simple. They provide a reliable communication session when the underlying layers might be considered less than stable. Ensuring reliable connectivity at the transport layer helps to speed up communication when data becomes lost. This is because the data does not have to be passed all the way up to the application layer before a retransmission frame is created and sent. Although this is important in modem communications, in which a small amount of noise or a crossed line can kill a communication session, it is not as useful with network-based communication. TCP and SPX originate from the days when the physical and data-link layers could not always be relied on to successfully transmit information. These days, this is less a concern because reliability has increased dramatically.

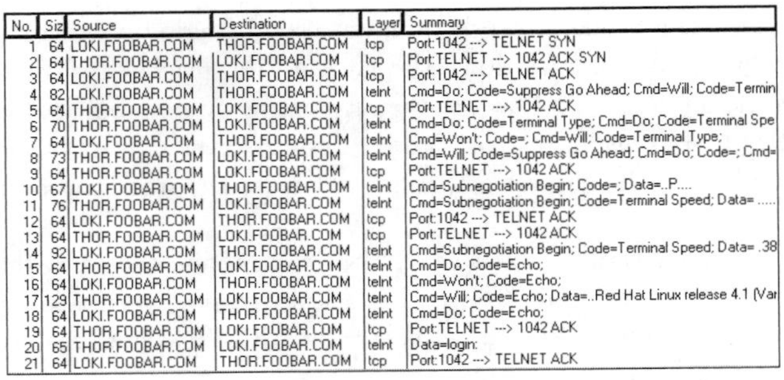

FIGURE 3.10

An example of a connection-oriented communication

No.	Siz	Source	Destination	Layer	Summary
1	64	LOKI.FOOBAR.COM	THOR.FOOBAR.COM	tcp	Port:1042 ---> TELNET SYN
2	64	THOR.FOOBAR.COM	LOKI.FOOBAR.COM	tcp	Port:TELNET ---> 1042 ACK SYN
3	64	LOKI.FOOBAR.COM	THOR.FOOBAR.COM	tcp	Port:1042 ---> TELNET ACK
4	82	LOKI.FOOBAR.COM	THOR.FOOBAR.COM	telnt	Cmd=Do; Code=Suppress Go Ahead; Cmd=Will; Code=Termin
5	64	THOR.FOOBAR.COM	LOKI.FOOBAR.COM	tcp	Port:TELNET ---> 1042 ACK
6	70	THOR.FOOBAR.COM	LOKI.FOOBAR.COM	telnt	Cmd=Do; Code=Terminal Type; Cmd=Do; Code=Terminal Spe
7	64	LOKI.FOOBAR.COM	THOR.FOOBAR.COM	telnt	Cmd=Won't; Code=; Cmd=Will; Code=Terminal Type;
8	73	THOR.FOOBAR.COM	LOKI.FOOBAR.COM	telnt	Cmd=Will; Code=Suppress Go Ahead; Cmd=Do; Code=; Cmd=
9	64	THOR.FOOBAR.COM	LOKI.FOOBAR.COM	tcp	Port:TELNET ---> 1042 ACK
10	67	LOKI.FOOBAR.COM	THOR.FOOBAR.COM	telnt	Cmd=Subnegotiation Begin; Code=; Data=..P....
11	76	THOR.FOOBAR.COM	LOKI.FOOBAR.COM	telnt	Cmd=Subnegotiation Begin; Code=Terminal Speed; Data= .....
12	64	THOR.FOOBAR.COM	LOKI.FOOBAR.COM	tcp	Port:1042 ---> TELNET ACK
13	64	THOR.FOOBAR.COM	LOKI.FOOBAR.COM	tcp	Port:TELNET ---> 1042 ACK
14	92	LOKI.FOOBAR.COM	THOR.FOOBAR.COM	telnt	Cmd=Subnegotiation Begin; Code=Terminal Speed; Data= .38
15	64	THOR.FOOBAR.COM	LOKI.FOOBAR.COM	telnt	Cmd=Do; Code=Echo;
16	64	LOKI.FOOBAR.COM	THOR.FOOBAR.COM	telnt	Cmd=Won't; Code=Echo;
17	129	THOR.FOOBAR.COM	LOKI.FOOBAR.COM	telnt	Cmd=Will; Code=Echo; Data= .Red Hat Linux release 4.1 (Var
18	64	LOKI.FOOBAR.COM	THOR.FOOBAR.COM	telnt	Cmd=Do; Code=Echo;
19	64	THOR.FOOBAR.COM	LOKI.FOOBAR.COM	tcp	Port:TELNET ---> 1042 ACK
20	65	THOR.FOOBAR.COM	LOKI.FOOBAR.COM	telnt	Data=login:
21	64	LOKI.FOOBAR.COM	THOR.FOOBAR.COM	tcp	Port:1042 ---> TELNET ACK

Connectionless Communications

A *connectionless* protocol does not require an initial handshake or acknowledgments to be sent for every packet. When you use a connectionless transport, it makes its best effort to deliver the data but relies on the stability of the underlying layers, as well as application layer acknowledgments, to ensure that the data is delivered reliably. IP's User Datagram Protocol (UDP) and IPX's NetWare Core Protocol (NCP) are examples of connectionless transports. Both protocols rely on connectionless communications to transfer routing and server information, as well. Although AppleTalk does not use connectionless communication for creating data sessions, AppleTalk does use it when advertising servers with its Name-Binding Protocol (NBP). Broadcasts are always transmitted using a connectionless transport.

As an example of connectionless communications, check out the Network File System (NFS) session in Figure 3.11. NFS is a service that allows file sharing over IP. It uses UDP as its underlying transport protocol. Notice that all data acknowledgments are in the form of a request for additional information. The destination system (Thor) assumes that the last packet was received if the source system (Loki) requests additional information. Conversely, if Loki does not receive a reply from Thor, NFS takes care of requesting the information again. As long as we have a stable connection that does not require a large number of retransmissions, allowing NFS to provide error correction is an efficient method of communicating because it does not generate unnecessary acknowledgments.

FIGURE 3.11

NFS uses UDP to create a connectionless session.

No.	Size	Source	Destination	Layer	Summary
1	198	LOKI.FOOBAR.COM	THOR.FOOBAR.COM	nfs	Call Lookup ???/games.tar.gz
2	174	THOR.FOOBAR.COM	LOKI.FOOBAR.COM	nfs	Reply Lookup for games.tar.gz
3	182	LOKI.FOOBAR.COM	THOR.FOOBAR.COM	nfs	Call Get File Attributes for games.tar.gz
4	142	THOR.FOOBAR.COM	LOKI.FOOBAR.COM	nfs	Reply Get File Attributes
5	194	LOKI.FOOBAR.COM	THOR.FOOBAR.COM	nfs	Call Read From File games.tar.gz; Offset 0; 1024 bytes
6	1,170	THOR.FOOBAR.COM	LOKI.FOOBAR.COM	nfs	Reply Read From File; 1024 bytes
7	194	LOKI.FOOBAR.COM	THOR.FOOBAR.COM	nfs	Call Read From File games.tar.gz; Offset 1024; 1024 bytes
8	1,170	THOR.FOOBAR.COM	LOKI.FOOBAR.COM	nfs	Reply Read From File; 1024 bytes
9	194	LOKI.FOOBAR.COM	THOR.FOOBAR.COM	nfs	Call Read From File games.tar.gz; Offset 2048; 1024 bytes
10	1,170	THOR.FOOBAR.COM	LOKI.FOOBAR.COM	nfs	Reply Read From File; 1024 bytes
11	194	LOKI.FOOBAR.COM	THOR.FOOBAR.COM	nfs	Call Read From File games.tar.gz; Offset 3072; 1024 bytes
12	1,170	THOR.FOOBAR.COM	LOKI.FOOBAR.COM	nfs	Reply Read From File; 1024 bytes
13	194	LOKI.FOOBAR.COM	THOR.FOOBAR.COM	nfs	Call Read From File games.tar.gz; Offset 4096; 1024 bytes
14	1,170	THOR.FOOBAR.COM	LOKI.FOOBAR.COM	nfs	Reply Read From File; 1024 bytes
15	194	LOKI.FOOBAR.COM	THOR.FOOBAR.COM	nfs	Call Read From File games.tar.gz; Offset 5120; 1024 bytes
16	1,170	THOR.FOOBAR.COM	LOKI.FOOBAR.COM	nfs	Reply Read From File; 1024 bytes
17	194	LOKI.FOOBAR.COM	THOR.FOOBAR.COM	nfs	Call Read From File games.tar.gz; Offset 6144; 1024 bytes
18	1,170	THOR.FOOBAR.COM	LOKI.FOOBAR.COM	nfs	Reply Read From File; 1024 bytes
19	194	LOKI.FOOBAR.COM	THOR.FOOBAR.COM	nfs	Call Read From File games.tar.gz; Offset 7168; 1024 bytes
20	1,170	THOR.FOOBAR.COM	LOKI.FOOBAR.COM	nfs	Reply Read From File; 1024 bytes
21	194	LOKI.FOOBAR.COM	THOR.FOOBAR.COM	nfs	Call Read From File games.tar.gz; Offset 8192; 1024 bytes
22	1,170	THOR.FOOBAR.COM	LOKI.FOOBAR.COM	nfs	Reply Read From File; 1024 bytes
23	194	LOKI.FOOBAR.COM	THOR.FOOBAR.COM	nfs	Call Read From File games.tar.gz; Offset 9216; 1024 bytes

Let's look at another analogy to see how this type of communication differs from the connection-oriented communication described earlier. Again, let's say you call Fred to invite him and his laptop to your network Quake party on Saturday night. You call Fred's number but this time get his answering machine. You leave a detailed message indicating when the party will take place and what he should bring. Unlike the first call, which Fred answered, you are now relying on the following:

◆ Your ability to dial the correct phone number, as you did not reach your friend to confirm that this number was in fact his

◆ The fact that the phone company did not drop your phone connection in the middle of your message (answering machines do not ACK—unless, of course, you talk until the beep cuts you off)

◆ The answering machine's proper recording of the message—without eating the tape

◆ The ability of Fred's cat to discern between the tape and a ball of yarn

◆ The absence of a power failure (which would cause the machine to lose the message)

◆ Fred's retrieval of this message between now and the date of the party

As you can see, you have no real confirmation that your friend will actually receive the message. You are counting on the power company, the answering machine, and so on to enable Fred to get your message in a timely manner. If you wanted to ensure the reliability of this data transmission, you could send an application layer acknowledgment request in the form of "Please RSVP by Thursday." If you did not get a response by then, you could try transmitting the data again.

So, which is a better transport to use: connectionless or connection-oriented? Unfortunately, the answer is whichever your application layer specifies. If Telnet wants TCP, you cannot force it to use UDP.

Security Implications

One technology that has made good use of the flag field of connection-oriented communications is firewalls. A firewall uses the information in the flag field to determine if a connection is inbound or outbound and, based on its rule table, either accept or deny the connection.

For example, let's say our firewall rules allow internal users access to the Internet but block external users from accessing internal systems. This is a common security policy. How do we accomplish this?

We cannot simply block all inbound traffic, because this would prohibit internal users from ever receiving a reply to their data requests. We need some way to allow replies back in while denying external systems the ability to establish connections with internal systems. The secret to this is TCP flags.

Remember that a TCP-based session needs to handshake prior to sending data. If we block all inbound frames that have the SYN field set to 1 and all other fields set to 0, we can prevent any external user from establishing a connection with our internal system. Because these settings are only used during the initial handshake and do not appear in any other part of the transmission, this is an effective way of blocking external users. If external users cannot connect to an internal system, they cannot transmit data to or pull data from that system.

NOTE *Many firewalls deny all UDP connections—UDP does not have a flag field, and most firewalls have no effective way of determining if the data is a connection request or a reply. This is what has made* dynamic packet filtering *firewalls so popular: they monitor and remember all connection sessions. With dynamic packet filtering you can create a filter rule that accepts UDP packets from an external host only when that host has been previously queried for information using UDP. This ensures that only UDP replies are allowed back in past the firewall. Although a packet filter or some proxy firewalls can only effectively work with TCP connections, a dynamic packet filtering firewall can safely pass UDP as well.*

Network Services

We can now find our remote system and ensure that both systems are using the same level of communications. Now, how do we tell the server what we want? Although computers are powerful tools—capable of processing many requests per second—they still have a problem with the phrase, "You know what I mean?" This is why we need a way to let a system know exactly what we want from it. It would be a real bummer to connect to a slick new website only to have the server start spewing e-mail or routing information at you because it had no idea which of its data you're looking for.

To make sure the computer knows what you want from it, you need to look to the session layer.

NOTE *You may remember from our discussion of the session layer that it is the layer responsible for ensuring that requests for service are formulated properly.*

A *service* is a process or application that runs on a server and provides some benefit to a network user. E-mail is a good example of a value-added service. A system may queue your mail messages until you connect to the system with a mail client in order to read them. File and print sharing are two other common examples of network services.

Services are accessed by connecting to a specific port or socket. Think of ports as virtual mail slots on the system, and you'll get the idea. A separate mail slot (port number) is designated for each service or application running on the system. When a user wants to access a service, the session layer is responsible for ensuring that the request reaches the correct mail slot or port number.

On a Unix or NT-based Microsoft systems (NT/2000/XP/.NET) system, IP port numbers are mapped to services in a file called (oddly enough) `services`. An abbreviated output of a `services` file is shown in Table 3.6. The first column identifies the service by name, and the second column identifies the port and transport to be used. The third column is a brief description of the functionality provided by the service. Table 3.6 is only a brief listing of IP services with focus on ports frequently used in firewall configuration. More information can be found in request for comment (RFC) 1700.

TABLE 3.6: AN ABBREVIATED SERVICES FILE

NAME OF SERVICE	PORT AND TRANSPORT	FUNCTIONALITY
ftp-data	20/tcp	Used to transfer actual file information
ftp	21/tcp	Used to transfer session commands
ssh, pcAnywhere	22/tcp	Secure connection to local shell, remote control
telnet	23/tcp	Creates a remote session
smtp	25/tcp	E-mail delivery
whois	43/tcp	Internic domain name lookup
domain	53/tcp	Domain name queries
domain	53/udp	DNS zone transfers
bootps	67/udp	bootp server
bootpc	68/udp	bootp client
pop3	110/tcp	PostOffice V.3
Identd/auth	113/tcp	Required for IRC chat connections
nntp	119/tcp	Network News Transfer
ntp	123/tcp	Network Time Protocol

Continued on next page

TABLE 3.6: AN ABBREVIATED SERVICES FILE *(continued)*

NAME OF SERVICE	PORT AND TRANSPORT	FUNCTIONALITY
ntp	123/udp	Network Time Protocol
netbios-ns	137/tcp	nbns
netbios-ns	137/udp	nbns
netbios-dgm	138/tcp	nbdgm
netbios-dgm	138/udp	nbdgm
netbios-ssn	139/tcp	nbssn
IMAP	143/tcp	Internet Message Access Protocol
snmp	161/udp	Simple Network Management Protocol
snmp-trap	162/udp	Simple Network Management Protocol
ssl	443/tcp	Secure Sockets Layer
SMB	445/tcp	Server Message Block
MS-RPC	593/tcp	Microsoft Remote Procedure Call
MS SQL	1433/tcp	Microsoft SQL Server
ICA	1494/tcp	Independent Computer Architecture used by Citrix for remote computer control
Oracle	1521	Oracle SQL protocol
MSTS	1604/tcp	Microsoft Terminal Server
RADIUS	1645/tcp	RADIUS authentication
RADIUS	1646/tcp	RADIUS accounting
rdp	3399/tcp	Microsoft Terminal Server

NOTE   *These port numbers are not Unix-specific. For example, any operating system using SMTP (Simple Mail Transfer Protocol) should use port 25.*

According to the file summarized in Table 3.6, any TCP request received on port 23 is assumed to be a Telnet session and is passed up to the application that handles remote access. If the requested port is 25, it is assumed that mail services are required, and the session is passed up to the mail program.

The file in Table 3.6 is used on Unix systems by a process called the *Internet daemon* (inetd). Inetd monitors each of the listed ports on a Unix system and is responsible for *waking up* the application that provides services to that port. This is an efficient means of managing the system for infrequently accessed ports. The process is only active and using system resources (memory, CPU time, and so on) when the service is actually needed. When the service is shut down, the process returns to a sleep mode, waiting for inetd to call on it again.

Applications that receive heavy use should be left running in a constant listening mode. For example, web server access usually uses port 80. Web server is not listed in the `services` file in Table 3.6 as a process to be handled by inetd. This is because a web server can be called upon to service many requests in the course of a day. It is more efficient to leave the process running all the time than to bother inetd every time you receive a page request.

All these port numbers are referred to as *well-known ports*. Well-known ports are de facto standards used to ensure that everyone can access services on other machines without needing to guess which port number is used by the service. For example, there is nothing stopping you from setting up a web server on port 573, provided that the port is not in use by some other service. The problem is that most users will expect the service to be available on port 80 and may be unable to find it. Sometimes, however, you switch ports on purpose—we will look at that shortly.

NOTE   A de facto standard *is a standard by popularity; it is not a rule or law.*

Ports 0–1023 are defined by the Internet Assigned Numbers Authority (IANA) for most well-known services. Although ports have been assigned beyond 7200, the ports below 1024 traditionally made up the bulk of Internet communications. As more and more types and brands of Internet communication become popular, the number of ports in use has dramatically escalated. This can make controlling, or even monitoring, these communications difficult. Typically, an organization will limit file-sharing protocols (such as Napster, Kazaa, and Gnutella) or instant messaging clients (such as AOL's Instant Messenger and Microsoft's MSN Messenger) in order to simplify their network security. Because of the dynamic nature of the internet, these assignments are not hard-and-fast rules; rather, they are guides to ensure that everyone offers public services on the same port. For example, if you want to access Microsoft's web page, you can assume it offers the service on port 80, because this is the well-known port for that service.

When a system requests information, it not only specifies the port it wants to access but also which port should be used when returning the requested information. Port numbers for this task are selected from 1024 to 65535 and are referred to as *upper port numbers*.

To illustrate how this works, let's revisit our Telnet session in Figure 3.10. When Loki attempts to set up a Telnet session with Thor, it does so by accessing port 23 on Thor (port 23 is the well-known service port for Telnet). If we look at frame number 2, we see that Thor is sending the acknowledgment (ACK) back on port 1042. This is because the session information in the original frame that Loki sent Thor specified a source port of 1042 and a destination port of 23. The destination port identified where the frame was going (port 23 on Thor), and the source port identified which port should be used when sending replies (port 1042 on Loki). Port 23 is our well-known service port, and port 1042 is our upper port number used for the reply.

Upper reply ports are assigned on the fly. It is nearly impossible to predict which upper port a system will request information to be received on because the ports are assigned based on availability. For this reason, packet filters used for firewalling purposes are sometimes incorrectly set up to leave ports above 1023 open all the time in order to accept replies.

This leads to one of the reasons that a port other than a well-known port may be used to offer a service. A savvy end user who realizes that a packet filter will block access to the web server on port 80 running on her system might assign the service to some upper port number such as 8001. Because the connection will be made above port 1023, it may not be blocked. The result is that despite your corporate policy banning internal websites and a packet filter to help enforce it, this user can successfully advertise her website provided she supplies the port number (8001) along with the universal resource locator (URL). The URL would look similar to this:

```
http://thor.foobar.com:8001
```

The :8001 tells your web browser to access the server using port 8001 instead of 80. Because most packet filters have poor logging facilities, the network administrator responsible for enforcing the policy of "no internal websites" would probably never realize it exists unless they stumble across it.

TIP *The next time your boss accuses you of wasting time by cruising cracker sites on the Web, correct them by replying, "I am performing a security audit by looking at references to our internal network infrastructure as documented by the cracking underground. Because you denied my request for an intrusion detection system, this is the only way to effectively determine if we have been cracked." If you're not fired on the spot, quickly submit a PO for a new IDS (intrusion detection system) while the event is fresh in the boss's mind.*

Speaking of switching port numbers, try to identify the session in Figure 3.12. Although the session is identified as SMTP, it is actually a Telnet session redirected to port 25 (the well-known port for SMTP). We've fooled the analyzer recording this session into thinking that we simply have one e-mail system transferring e-mail to another. Most firewalls will be duped in the same fashion because they use the destination port to identify the session in progress—they do not look at the actual applications involved. This type of activity is usually analogous to someone *spoofing* or faking an e-mail message. Once you've connected to the remote e-mail system, you're free to pretend the message came from anywhere. Unless the routing information in the mail header is checked (most user-friendly e-mail programs simply discard this information), the actual origin of this information cannot be traced.

FIGURE 3.12

Although this looks like a normal transfer of mail, it is actually someone spoofing a mail message to the destination system.

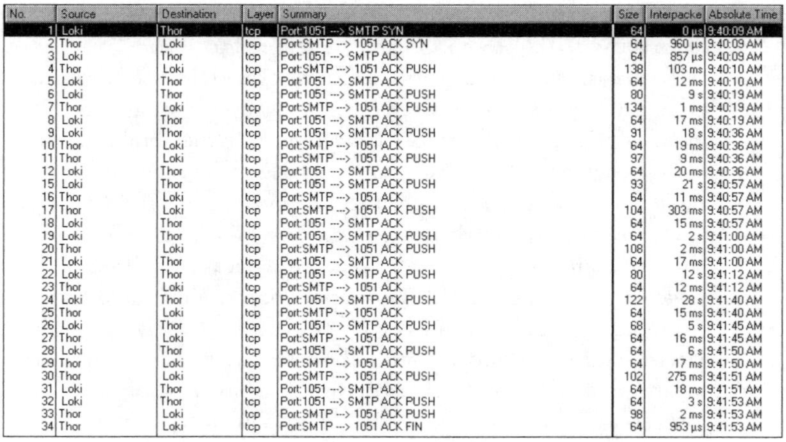

No.	Source	Destination	Layer	Summary	Size	Interpacke	Absolute Time
1	Loki	Thor	tcp	Port:1051 ---> SMTP SYN	64	0 µs	9:40:09 AM
2	Thor	Loki	tcp	Port:SMTP ---> 1051 ACK SYN	64	960 µs	9:40:09 AM
3	Loki	Thor	tcp	Port:1051 ---> SMTP ACK	64	857 µs	9:40:09 AM
4	Thor	Loki	tcp	Port:SMTP ---> 1051 ACK PUSH	138	103 ms	9:40:10 AM
5	Loki	Thor	tcp	Port:1051 ---> SMTP ACK	64	12 ms	9:40:10 AM
6	Loki	Thor	tcp	Port:1051 ---> SMTP ACK PUSH	80	9 s	9:40:19 AM
7	Thor	Loki	tcp	Port:SMTP ---> 1051 ACK PUSH	134	1 ms	9:40:19 AM
8	Loki	Thor	tcp	Port:1051 ---> SMTP ACK	64	17 ms	9:40:19 AM
9	Loki	Thor	tcp	Port:1051 ---> SMTP ACK PUSH	91	18 s	9:40:36 AM
10	Thor	Loki	tcp	Port:SMTP ---> 1051 ACK	64	19 ms	9:40:36 AM
11	Thor	Loki	tcp	Port:SMTP ---> 1051 ACK PUSH	97	9 ms	9:40:36 AM
12	Loki	Thor	tcp	Port:1051 ---> SMTP ACK	64	20 ms	9:40:36 AM
15	Loki	Thor	tcp	Port:1051 ---> SMTP ACK PUSH	93	21 s	9:40:57 AM
16	Thor	Loki	tcp	Port:SMTP ---> 1051 ACK	64	11 ms	9:40:57 AM
17	Thor	Loki	tcp	Port:SMTP ---> 1051 ACK PUSH	104	303 ms	9:40:57 AM
18	Loki	Thor	tcp	Port:1051 ---> SMTP ACK	64	15 ms	9:40:57 AM
19	Loki	Thor	tcp	Port:1051 ---> SMTP ACK PUSH	64	2 s	9:41:00 AM
20	Thor	Loki	tcp	Port:SMTP ---> 1051 ACK PUSH	108	2 ms	9:41:00 AM
21	Loki	Thor	tcp	Port:1051 ---> SMTP ACK	64	17 ms	9:41:00 AM
22	Loki	Thor	tcp	Port:1051 ---> SMTP ACK PUSH	80	12 s	9:41:12 AM
23	Thor	Loki	tcp	Port:SMTP ---> 1051 ACK	64	12 ms	9:41:12 AM
24	Loki	Thor	tcp	Port:1051 ---> SMTP ACK PUSH	122	28 s	9:41:40 AM
25	Thor	Loki	tcp	Port:SMTP ---> 1051 ACK	64	15 ms	9:41:40 AM
26	Loki	Thor	tcp	Port:SMTP ---> 1051 ACK PUSH	68	5 s	9:41:45 AM
27	Thor	Loki	tcp	Port:SMTP ---> 1051 ACK	64	16 ms	9:41:45 AM
28	Loki	Thor	tcp	Port:1051 ---> SMTP ACK PUSH	64	6 s	9:41:50 AM
29	Thor	Loki	tcp	Port:SMTP ---> 1051 ACK	64	17 ms	9:41:50 AM
30	Thor	Loki	tcp	Port:SMTP ---> 1051 ACK PUSH	102	275 ms	9:41:51 AM
31	Loki	Thor	tcp	Port:1051 ---> SMTP ACK	64	18 ms	9:41:51 AM
32	Loki	Thor	tcp	Port:1051 ---> SMTP ACK PUSH	64	3 s	9:41:53 AM
33	Thor	Loki	tcp	Port:SMTP ---> 1051 ACK PUSH	98	2 ms	9:41:53 AM
34	Thor	Loki	tcp	Port:SMTP ---> 1051 ACK FIN	64	953 µs	9:41:53 AM

Such spoofing is what has made *intrusion detection systems* (IDS) so popular—they can be programmed to catch this type of activity. Look at Figure 3.12 again, but this time check out the frame size used by the transmitting system. Notice that the largest frame sent is 122 bytes. This indicates a Telnet session, as Telnet requires that each character typed be acknowledged. Had this been an actual e-mail system transferring data, we would have seen packet sizes closer to 1500 bytes, because SMTP does not require that only a single character be sent in every frame. A good IDS can be tuned to identify such inconsistencies.

Figure 3.13 shows the final output of this spoofing session. Without the header information, you might actually believe this message came from bgates@microsoft.com. The fact that the message was never touched by an e-mail system within the Microsoft domain indicates that it is a phony. We've used this example in the past when teaching Internet and security classes. Do not believe everything you read, especially if it comes from the Internet!

FIGURE 3.13

The output from our spoofed mail message

```
From bgates@microsoft.com  Wed Feb  5 16:42:21 1997
Return-Path: <bgates@microsoft.com>
Received: from loki.foobar.com (loki.foobar.com [10.2.2.20])
          by thor.foobar.com (8.8.4/8.8.4) with SMTP
          id QAA00887 for cbrenton@thor.foobar.com; Wed, 5 Feb 1997 16:41:04 -0500
Date: Wed, 5 Feb 1997 16:41:04 -0500
From: bgates@microsoft.com (Bill Gates)
Message-Id: <199702052141.QAA00887@thor.foobar.com>
Subject: Quake Party
Status: R

The party sounds cool! I'll bring the P5's and the cheeze wiz!

Later...
```

Port numbers are also used to distinctly identify similar sessions between systems. For example, let's build on Figure 3.10. We already have one Telnet session running from Loki to Thor. What happens if four or five more sessions are created? All sessions have the following information in common:

Source IP address: 10.2.2.20 (loki.foobar.com)

Destination IP address: 10.2.2.10 (thor.foobar.com)

Destination port: 23 (well-known port for Telnet)

The source ports will be the only distinctive information that can be used to identify each individual session. Our first connection has already specified a source port of 1042 for its connection. Each sequential Telnet session that is established after that would be assigned some other upper port number to uniquely identify it. The actual numbers assigned would be based on what was not currently being used by the source system. For example, ports 1118, 1398, 4023, and 6025 may be used as source ports for the next four sessions. The actual reply port number does not really matter; what matters is that it can uniquely identify that specific session between the two systems. If we were to monitor a number of concurrent sessions, the transaction would look similar to Figure 3.14. Now we see multiple reply ports in use to identify each session.

IP is not the only protocol to use ports. AppleTalk and IPX also use ports, which are referred to as *sockets*. Unlike IP and AT, which use decimal numbers to identify different ports, IPX uses hexadecimal numbers. Well-known and upper ports function the same with AppleTalk and IPX as they do with IP. AppleTalk and IPX simply do not have as many services defined.

FIGURE 3.14

Multiple Telnet sessions in progress between Loki and Thor

No.	Source	Destination	Layer	Summary	Size
1	LOKI.FOOBAR.COM	THOR.FOOBAR.COM	telnt	Data=l	64
2	THOR.FOOBAR.COM	LOKI.FOOBAR.COM	telnt	Data=l	64
3	LOKI.FOOBAR.COM	THOR.FOOBAR.COM	tcp	Port:1036 ---> TELNET ACK	64
4	LOKI.FOOBAR.COM	THOR.FOOBAR.COM	telnt	Data=s	64
5	THOR.FOOBAR.COM	LOKI.FOOBAR.COM	telnt	Data=s	64
6	LOKI.FOOBAR.COM	THOR.FOOBAR.COM	tcp	Port:1036 ---> TELNET ACK	64
7	LOKI.FOOBAR.COM	THOR.FOOBAR.COM	telnt	Data=.	64
8	THOR.FOOBAR.COM	LOKI.FOOBAR.COM	telnt	Data=.	64
9	LOKI.FOOBAR.COM	THOR.FOOBAR.COM	tcp	Port:1036 ---> TELNET ACK	64
10	THOR.FOOBAR.COM	LOKI.FOOBAR.COM	telnt	Data=install.log.	64
11	LOKI.FOOBAR.COM	THOR.FOOBAR.COM	tcp	Port:1036 ---> TELNET ACK	64
12	THOR.FOOBAR.COM	LOKI.FOOBAR.COM	telnt	Data=[cbrenton@thor /tmp]$	80
13	LOKI.FOOBAR.COM	THOR.FOOBAR.COM	tcp	Port:1036 ---> TELNET ACK	64
14	LOKI.FOOBAR.COM	THOR.FOOBAR.COM	telnt	Data=l	64
15	THOR.FOOBAR.COM	LOKI.FOOBAR.COM	telnt	Data=l	64
16	LOKI.FOOBAR.COM	THOR.FOOBAR.COM	tcp	Port:1038 ---> TELNET ACK	64
17	LOKI.FOOBAR.COM	THOR.FOOBAR.COM	telnt	Data=s	64
18	THOR.FOOBAR.COM	LOKI.FOOBAR.COM	telnt	Data=s	64
19	LOKI.FOOBAR.COM	THOR.FOOBAR.COM	tcp	Port:1038 ---> TELNET ACK	64
20	LOKI.FOOBAR.COM	THOR.FOOBAR.COM	telnt	Data=.	64
21	THOR.FOOBAR.COM	LOKI.FOOBAR.COM	telnt	Data=.	64
22	LOKI.FOOBAR.COM	THOR.FOOBAR.COM	tcp	Port:1038 ---> TELNET ACK	64
23	THOR.FOOBAR.COM	LOKI.FOOBAR.COM	telnt	Data=install.log.	71
24	LOKI.FOOBAR.COM	THOR.FOOBAR.COM	tcp	Port:1038 ---> TELNET ACK	64
25	THOR.FOOBAR.COM	LOKI.FOOBAR.COM	telnt	Data=[cbrenton@thor /tmp]$	80
26	LOKI.FOOBAR.COM	THOR.FOOBAR.COM	tcp	Port:1038 ---> TELNET ACK	64
27	LOKI.FOOBAR.COM	THOR.FOOBAR.COM	telnt	Data=l	64
28	THOR.FOOBAR.COM	LOKI.FOOBAR.COM	telnt	Data=l	64
29	LOKI.FOOBAR.COM	THOR.FOOBAR.COM	tcp	Port:1039 ---> TELNET ACK	64
30	LOKI.FOOBAR.COM	THOR.FOOBAR.COM	telnt	Data=s	64
31	THOR.FOOBAR.COM	LOKI.FOOBAR.COM	telnt	Data=s	64
32	LOKI.FOOBAR.COM	THOR.FOOBAR.COM	tcp	Port:1039 ---> TELNET ACK	64

File Transfer Protocol (FTP): The Special Case

In all our examples so far, the source system would create a single service connection to the destination system when accessing a specific service. Unless multiple users requested this service, only a single connection session was required.

FTP is used to transfer file information from one system to another. FTP uses TCP as its transport and ports 20 and 21 for communication. Port 21 is used to transfer session information (username, password, commands), and port 20 is referred to as the *data port* and is used to transfer the actual file.

Figure 3.15 shows an FTP command session between two systems (Loki is connecting to Thor). Notice the three-packet TCP handshake at the beginning of the session, which was described in the discussion on connection-oriented communications earlier in this chapter. All communications are using a destination port of 21, which is simply referred to as the FTP port. Port 1038 is the random upper port used by Loki when receiving replies. This connection was initiated by Loki at port 1038 to Thor at port 21.

Figure 3.16 shows Loki initiating a file transfer from Thor. Lines 7, 8, and 9 show the TCP three-packet handshake. Lines 10 through 24 show the actual data transfer.

FIGURE 3.15

An FTP command session between two systems

No.	Size	Source	Destination	Layer	Summary
1	64	LOKI.FOOBAR.COM	THOR.FOOBAR.COM	tcp	Port:1038 ---> FTP SYN
2	64	THOR.FOOBAR.COM	LOKI.FOOBAR.COM	tcp	Port:FTP ---> 1038 ACK SYN
3	64	LOKI.FOOBAR.COM	THOR.FOOBAR.COM	tcp	Port:1038 ---> FTP ACK
4	164	THOR.FOOBAR.COM	LOKI.FOOBAR.COM	ftp	Reply:(Service ready for new user.)
5	64	LOKI.FOOBAR.COM	THOR.FOOBAR.COM	tcp	Port:1038 ---> FTP ACK
6	73	LOKI.FOOBAR.COM	THOR.FOOBAR.COM	ftp	Command=USER(User Name)
7	64	THOR.FOOBAR.COM	LOKI.FOOBAR.COM	tcp	Port:FTP ---> 1038 ACK
8	95	THOR.FOOBAR.COM	LOKI.FOOBAR.COM	ftp	Reply:(User name okay, need password.)
9	64	LOKI.FOOBAR.COM	THOR.FOOBAR.COM	tcp	Port:1038 ---> FTP ACK
10	71	LOKI.FOOBAR.COM	THOR.FOOBAR.COM	ftp	Command=PASS(Password)
11	64	THOR.FOOBAR.COM	LOKI.FOOBAR.COM	tcp	Port:FTP ---> 1038 ACK
12	88	THOR.FOOBAR.COM	LOKI.FOOBAR.COM	ftp	Reply:(User logged in, proceed.)
13	64	LOKI.FOOBAR.COM	THOR.FOOBAR.COM	ftp	Command=SYST(System Operating System Type)
14	77	THOR.FOOBAR.COM	LOKI.FOOBAR.COM	ftp	Reply:(Name system type.)
15	64	LOKI.FOOBAR.COM	THOR.FOOBAR.COM	tcp	Port:1038 ---> FTP ACK
16	66	LOKI.FOOBAR.COM	THOR.FOOBAR.COM	ftp	Command=TYPE(Representation Type)
17	64	THOR.FOOBAR.COM	LOKI.FOOBAR.COM	tcp	Port:FTP ---> 1038 ACK
18	78	THOR.FOOBAR.COM	LOKI.FOOBAR.COM	ftp	Reply:(Command okay.)
19	64	LOKI.FOOBAR.COM	THOR.FOOBAR.COM	tcp	Port:1038 ---> FTP ACK

This is where things get a bit weird. Loki and Thor still have an active session on ports 1038 and 21, as indicated in Figure 3.15. Figure 3.16 is a second, separate session running parallel to the one shown in Figure 3.15. This second session is initiated in order to transfer the actual file or data.

FIGURE 3.16

An FTP data session

No.	Size	Source	Destination	Layer	Summary
2	66	LOKI.FOOBAR.COM	THOR.FOOBAR.COM	ftp	Command=TYPE(Representation Type)
3	78	THOR.FOOBAR.COM	LOKI.FOOBAR.COM	ftp	Reply:(Command okay.)
4	79	LOKI.FOOBAR.COM	THOR.FOOBAR.COM	ftp	Command=PORT(Data Port)
5	88	THOR.FOOBAR.COM	LOKI.FOOBAR.COM	ftp	Reply:(Command okay.)
6	77	LOKI.FOOBAR.COM	THOR.FOOBAR.COM	ftp	Command=RETR(Retrieve File)
7	64	THOR.FOOBAR.COM	LOKI.FOOBAR.COM	tcp	Port:FTP-DATA ---> 1037 SYN
8	64	LOKI.FOOBAR.COM	THOR.FOOBAR.COM	tcp	Port:1037 ---> FTP-DATA ACK SYN
9	64	THOR.FOOBAR.COM	LOKI.FOOBAR.COM	tcp	Port:FTP-DATA ---> 1037 ACK
10	132	THOR.FOOBAR.COM	LOKI.FOOBAR.COM	ftp	Reply:(File status okay; about to open data connection.)
11	1,518	THOR.FOOBAR.COM	LOKI.FOOBAR.COM	tcp	Port:FTP-DATA ---> 1037 ACK
12	1,518	THOR.FOOBAR.COM	LOKI.FOOBAR.COM	tcp	Port:FTP-DATA ---> 1037 ACK
13	64	LOKI.FOOBAR.COM	THOR.FOOBAR.COM	tcp	Port:1037 ---> FTP-DATA ACK
14	1,518	THOR.FOOBAR.COM	LOKI.FOOBAR.COM	tcp	Port:FTP-DATA ---> 1037 ACK
15	1,518	THOR.FOOBAR.COM	LOKI.FOOBAR.COM	tcp	Port:FTP-DATA ---> 1037 ACK
16	1,518	THOR.FOOBAR.COM	LOKI.FOOBAR.COM	tcp	Port:FTP-DATA ---> 1037 ACK
17	64	LOKI.FOOBAR.COM	THOR.FOOBAR.COM	tcp	Port:1037 ---> FTP-DATA ACK
18	64	LOKI.FOOBAR.COM	THOR.FOOBAR.COM	tcp	Port:1034 ---> FTP ACK
19	1,518	THOR.FOOBAR.COM	LOKI.FOOBAR.COM	tcp	Port:FTP-DATA ---> 1037 ACK PUSH
20	1,518	THOR.FOOBAR.COM	LOKI.FOOBAR.COM	tcp	Port:FTP-DATA ---> 1037 ACK
21	1,518	THOR.FOOBAR.COM	LOKI.FOOBAR.COM	tcp	Port:FTP-DATA ---> 1037 ACK
22	1,518	THOR.FOOBAR.COM	LOKI.FOOBAR.COM	tcp	Port:FTP-DATA ---> 1037 ACK
23	64	LOKI.FOOBAR.COM	THOR.FOOBAR.COM	tcp	Port:1037 ---> FTP-DATA ACK
24	1,518	THOR.FOOBAR.COM	LOKI.FOOBAR.COM	tcp	Port:FTP-DATA ---> 1037 ACK

There is something else a bit odd about this connection: look closely at line number 7. Thor—not Loki—is actually initiating the TCP three-packet handshake in order to transfer the file information. Although Loki was responsible for initiating the original FTP command session to port 21, Thor is actually initiating the FTP data session.

In order to support FTP sessions to the Internet, you must allow connections to be established from Internet hosts on port 20 to your internal network. If your firewall device does not allow you to define a source port for inbound traffic (which some do not), you must leave all ports above 1023 completely open! Not exactly the most secure security stance.

A second type of FTP transfer is known as *passive FTP* (PASV FTP). Passive FTP is identical to standard FTP in terms of sending commands over port 21. The difference between PASV FTP and standard FTP lies in how the data session is initiated. PASV FTP is the mode supported by most web browsers.

Before transferring data, a client can request PASV mode transmission. If the FTP server acknowledges this request, the client is allowed to initiate the TCP three-packet handshake, instead of the server. Figure 3.17 shows a capture of two systems using PASV FTP. Packet 21 shows "This workstation" (or FTP client) requesting that PASV FTP be used. In packet 22, the FTP server responds, stating that PASV mode is supported.

Notice what occurs in packet 23. Our FTP client initiates the TCP three-packet handshake in order to transfer data. This fixes one problem but causes another. Since the client initiates the session, we can now close inbound access from port 20. This lets us tighten up our inbound security policy a bit. To initiate this passive session, however, the client is using a random upper port number for the source and destination. Thus, the port the client will use to transfer data can and will change from session to session. In order to support PASV FTP, you must allow outbound sessions to be established on all ports above 1023. Not a very good security stance if you are looking to control outbound Internet access (such as a policy forbidding Internet Quake games).

As if all this were not enough to deal with, administrators can run into another problem with FTP when they use a firewall or Network Address Translation (NAT) device. The problem arises because FTP uses two separate sessions.

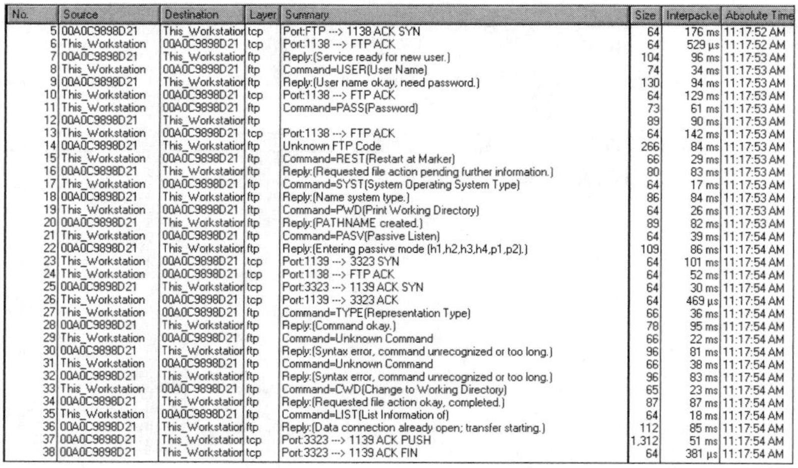

FIGURE 3.17

A passive mode
FTP session

No.	Source	Destination	Layer	Summary	Size	Interpacket	Absolute Time
5	00A0C9898D21	This_Workstation	tcp	Port:FTP ---> 1138 ACK SYN	64	176 ms	11:17:52 AM
6	This_Workstation	00A0C9898D21	tcp	Port:1138 ---> FTP ACK	64	529 μs	11:17:52 AM
7	00A0C9898D21	This_Workstation	ftp	Reply:(Service ready for new user.)	104	96 ms	11:17:53 AM
8	This_Workstation	00A0C9898D21	ftp	Command=USER(User Name)	74	34 ms	11:17:53 AM
9	00A0C9898D21	This_Workstation	ftp	Reply:(User name okay, need password.)	130	94 ms	11:17:53 AM
10	This_Workstation	00A0C9898D21	tcp	Port:1138 ---> FTP ACK	64	129 ms	11:17:53 AM
11	This_Workstation	00A0C9898D21	ftp	Command=PASS(Password)	73	61 ms	11:17:53 AM
12	00A0C9898D21	This_Workstation	ftp		89	90 ms	11:17:53 AM
13	This_Workstation	00A0C9898D21	tcp	Port:1138 ---> FTP ACK	64	142 ms	11:17:53 AM
14	00A0C9898D21	This_Workstation	ftp	Unknown FTP Code	266	84 ms	11:17:53 AM
15	This_Workstation	00A0C9898D21	ftp	Command=REST(Restart at Marker)	66	29 ms	11:17:53 AM
16	00A0C9898D21	This_Workstation	ftp	Reply:(Requested file action pending further information.)	80	83 ms	11:17:53 AM
17	This_Workstation	00A0C9898D21	ftp	Command=SYST(System Operating System Type)	64	17 ms	11:17:53 AM
18	00A0C9898D21	This_Workstation	ftp	Reply:(Name system type.)	86	84 ms	11:17:53 AM
19	This_Workstation	00A0C9898D21	ftp	Command=PWD(Print Working Directory)	64	26 ms	11:17:53 AM
20	00A0C9898D21	This_Workstation	ftp	Reply:(PATHNAME created.)	89	82 ms	11:17:53 AM
21	This_Workstation	00A0C9898D21	ftp	Command=PASV(Passive Listen)	64	39 ms	11:17:54 AM
22	00A0C9898D21	This_Workstation	ftp	Reply:(Entering passive mode (h1,h2,h3,h4,p1,p2).)	109	86 ms	11:17:54 AM
23	This_Workstation	00A0C9898D21	tcp	Port:1139 ---> 3323 SYN	64	101 ms	11:17:54 AM
24	This_Workstation	00A0C9898D21	tcp	Port:1138 ---> FTP ACK	64	52 ms	11:17:54 AM
25	00A0C9898D21	This_Workstation	tcp	Port:3323 ---> 1139 ACK SYN	64	30 ms	11:17:54 AM
26	This_Workstation	00A0C9898D21	tcp	Port:1139 ---> 3323 ACK	64	469 μs	11:17:54 AM
27	This_Workstation	00A0C9898D21	ftp	Command=TYPE(Representation Type)	66	36 ms	11:17:54 AM
28	00A0C9898D21	This_Workstation	ftp	Reply:(Command okay.)	78	95 ms	11:17:54 AM
29	This_Workstation	00A0C9898D21	ftp	Command=Unknown Command	66	22 ms	11:17:54 AM
30	00A0C9898D21	This_Workstation	ftp	Reply:(Syntax error, command unrecognized or too long.)	96	81 ms	11:17:54 AM
31	This_Workstation	00A0C9898D21	ftp	Command=Unknown Command	66	38 ms	11:17:54 AM
32	00A0C9898D21	This_Workstation	ftp	Reply:(Syntax error, command unrecognized or too long.)	96	83 ms	11:17:54 AM
33	This_Workstation	00A0C9898D21	ftp	Command=CWD(Change to Working Directory)	65	23 ms	11:17:54 AM
34	00A0C9898D21	This_Workstation	ftp	Reply:(Requested file action okay, completed.)	87	87 ms	11:17:54 AM
35	This_Workstation	00A0C9898D21	ftp	Command=LIST(List Information of)	64	18 ms	11:17:54 AM
36	00A0C9898D21	This_Workstation	ftp	Reply:(Data connection already open; transfer starting.)	112	85 ms	11:17:54 AM
37	00A0C9898D21	This_Workstation	tcp	Port:3323 ---> 1139 ACK PUSH	1,312	51 ms	11:17:54 AM
38	00A0C9898D21	This_Workstation	tcp	Port:3323 ---> 1139 ACK FIN	64	381 μs	11:17:54 AM

NOTE   *NAT allows you to translate IP addresses from private numbers to legal numbers. This is useful when the IP addresses you are using on your network were not assigned to you by your ISP. We will talk more about NAT when we discuss firewalls in Chapter 5.*

While you are transferring a large file over the Internet (let's say the latest 60MB patch file from Microsoft), your control session to port 21 stays quiet. This session is not required to transmit any information during a file transfer until the transfer is complete. Once it is complete, the systems acknowledge over the control session that the file was in fact received in its entirety.

If it has taken a long time to transfer the file (say, more than an hour), the firewall or NAT device may assume that the control session is no longer valid. Since it has seen no data pass between the two systems for a long period of time, the device assumes that the connection is gone and purges the session entry from its tables. This is a bad thing—once the file transfer is complete, the systems have no means to handshake to ensure that the file was received. The typical symptom of this problem is that the client transferring or receiving the file hangs at 99 percent complete.

Luckily, most vendors make this timeout setting adjustable. If you are experiencing such symptoms, check your firewall or NAT device to see if it has a TCP timeout setting. If so, simply increase the listed value. Most systems default to a timeout value of one hour.

Other IP Services

Many application services are designed to use IP as a transport. Some are designed to aid the end user in transferring information, and others have been created to support the functionality of IP itself. In this section, we'll describe some of the most common services, including the transport used for data delivery and the well-known port number assigned to the service.

BOOT PROTOCOL (*BOOTP*) AND DYNAMIC HOST CONFIGURATION PROTOCOL (DHCP)

IP addresses can be assigned to host systems in three ways:

Manually   The user manually configures an IP host to use a specific address.

Automatically A server automatically assigns a specific address to a host during startup.

Dynamically A server dynamically assigns free addresses from a pool to hosts during startup.

Assigning addresses manually is the most time-consuming method but the most fault tolerant — and, many would argue, the most secure. It requires that each IP host be configured with all the information the system requires to communicate using IP. Manual assignment is most appropriate for systems that must maintain the same IP address or systems that must be accessible even when the IP address server is down. Web servers, mail servers, and any other servers providing IP services are usually manually configured for IP communications.

`Bootp` supports automatic address assignment. A table is maintained on the `bootp` server that lists each host's MAC number. Each entry also contains the IP address to be used by the system. When the `bootp` server receives a request for an IP address, it references its table and looks for the sending system's MAC number, returning the appropriate IP address for that system. Although this simplifies management, because all administration can be performed from a central system, the process is still time-consuming, because each MAC address must be recorded. It also does nothing to free IP address space that is not in use.

DHCP supports both automatic and dynamic IP address assignments. When addresses are dynamically assigned, the server issues IP addresses to host systems from a pool of available numbers. The benefit of a dynamic assignment over automatic assignment is that only the hosts that require an IP address have one assigned. Once complete, the IP addresses can be returned to the pool to be issued to another host.

NOTE *The amount of time a host retains a specific IP address is referred to as the* lease period. *A short lease period ensures that only systems requiring an IP address have one assigned. When IP is only used occasionally, a small pool of addresses can support a large number of hosts.*

The other benefit of DHCP is that the server can send more than just address information. The remote host can also be configured with its host name, default router, domain name, local DNS (domain name server) server, and so on. This allows an administrator to remotely configure IP services to a large number of hosts with a minimal amount of work. A single DHCP server can service multiple subnets.

The only drawbacks with DHCP are the following:

◆ Broadcast traffic increases. (Clients send an all-networks broadcast when they need an address.)

◆ Address space stability is compromised if the DHCP server is shut down.

◆ Any DHCP-enabled computer that gets access to the network receives an IP address—even if that system is unauthorized.

On many systems, the tables that track who has been assigned which addresses are saved in memory only. When the system goes down, this table is lost. When you restart the system, IP addresses may be assigned to systems that were already leased to another system before the shutdown. If this occurs, you may need to renew the lease on all systems or wait until the lease time expires. This also means that unauthorized leases are not recorded or logged—something that might hinder your over-all intrusion detection plan.

NOTE *Both* bootp *and DHCP use UDP as their communication transport. Clients transmit address requests from a source port of* 68 *to a destination port of* 67.

DOMAIN NAME SERVICE (DNS)

DNS is responsible for mapping host names to IP addresses and vice versa. It is the service that allows you to connect to Novell's web server by entering www.novell.com, instead of having to remember the system's IP address. All IP routing is done with addresses, not names. Although IP systems do not use names when transferring information, names are easier for people to remember; DNS was developed to make reaching remote systems easier. DNS allows a person to enter an easy-to-remember name while allowing the computer to translate this into the address information it needs to route the requested data.

DNS follows a hierarchical, distributed structure. No single DNS server is responsible for keeping track of every host name on the Internet. Each system is responsible for only a portion of the framework.

Figure 3.18 shows an example of how DNS is structured. Visually it resembles a number of trees strapped to a pole and hanging upside down. The *pole* is not meant to represent the backbone of the Internet; it simply indicates DNS connectivity between the domains. The systems just below the pole are referred to as the root name servers. Each root name server is responsible for one or more top-level domains. Examples of top-level domains are the .com, .edu, .org, .mil, or .gov found at the end of a domain name. Every domain that ends in .com is said to be part of the same top-level domain.

FIGURE 3.18

A visual representation of the hierarchical structure of DNS

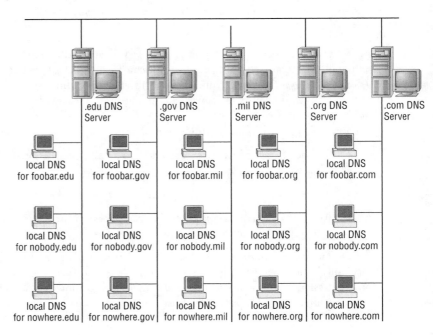

The root name servers are responsible for keeping track of the DNS servers for each subdomain within a top-level domain. They do not know about individual systems within each subdomain; they only know about the DNS servers that are responsible for them. Each subdomain DNS server is responsible for tracking the IP addresses for all the hosts within its domain.

Let's walk through an example to see how it works. Let's say you're part of the `foobar.com` domain. You are running a web browser and enter the following URL:

`http://www.sun.com`

Your system first checks its DNS cache (if it has one) to see if it knows the IP address for `www.sun.com`. If it does not, it forms a DNS query and asks one of the DNS servers within the `foobar.com` domain for the address. (A DNS query is simply a request for IP information.) Let's assume the system it queries is `ns.foobar.com`.

If `ns.foobar.com` does not have this information cached, it also forms a DNS query and forwards the request to the root name server responsible for the top-level domain `.com`, because this is where the Sun domain is located.

The root name server consults its tables and forms a reply similar to this: "I do not know the IP address for `www.sun.com`. I do, however, know that `ns.sun.com` is responsible for all the hosts within the `sun.com` domain. Its IP address is `10.5.5.1`. Please forward your query to that system." This reply is then sent to `ns.foobar.com`.

`ns.foobar.com` now knows that if it needs to find a system with the `sun.com` domain, it needs to ask `ns.sun.com`. `ns.foobar.com` caches this name server information and forwards the request to `ns.sun.com`.

`ns.sun.com` in turn consults its tables and looks up the IP address for `www.sun.com`. `Ns.sun.com` then forwards the IP address to `ns.foobar.com`. `Ns.foobar.com` caches this address and forwards the answer to your system. Your system can now use this IP address information to reach the remote web server.

If you think that there is a whole lot of querying going on, you have a good understanding of the process. The additional traffic is highly preferable, however, to the amount of overhead that would be required to allow a single system to maintain the DNS information for every system on the Internet.

As you may have noticed, DNS makes effective use of caching information during queries. This helps to reduce traffic when looking up popular sites. For example, if someone else within `foobar.com` now attempted to reach `www.sun.com`, the IP address for this system has been cached by `ns.foobar.com`. It can now answer this query directly.

The amount of time that `ns.foobar.com` remembers this information is determined by the *time to live* (TTL) set for this address. The TTL is set by the administrator responsible for managing the remote name server (in this case `ns.sun.com`). If `www.sun.com` is a stable system, this value may be set at a high value, such as 30 days. If it is expected that the IP address for `www.sun.com` is likely to change frequently, the TTL may be set to a lower value, such as a few hours.

NOTE *DNS uses TCP and UDP transports when communicating. Both use a destination port of 53.*

CAVEATS ABOUT THE TTL SETTINGS

Let's look at an example to see why it is important to properly manage your TTL settings. Let's say the e-mail relay for foobar.com is run from the system mail.foobar.com. Let's also assume that a high TTL value of 30 days has been set in order to reduce the number of DNS queries entering the network from the Internet. Finally, let's assume that your network has changed ISPs, and you have been assigned a new set of IP numbers to use when communicating with the Internet.

The network is readdressed, and the changeover takes place. Immediately users begin to receive phone calls from people saying that e-mail sent to their address is being returned with a delivery failure notice. The failure is intermittent—some e-mail gets through, while other messages fail.

What went wrong? Since the TTL value has been set for 30 days, remote DNS servers will remember the old IP address until the TTL expires. If someone sent mail to the foobar.com domain the day before the changeover, it may be 30 days before their DNS server creates another query and realizes that the IP address has changed! Unfortunately, the domains most likely affected by this change are the ones you exchange e-mail with the most.

You can resolve this failure in a couple of ways:

1. Ignore it and hide under your desk. Once the TTL expires, e-mail delivery will return to normal.

2. Contact the DNS administrator for each domain you exchange e-mail with and ask them to reset their DNS cache. This will force the remote system to look up the address the next time an e-mail message must be sent. This option is not only embarrassing—it may be impossible when dealing with large domains such as AOL or CompuServe.

Avoiding this type of failure takes some fundamental planning. Simply turn down the TTL value to an extremely short period of time (such as one hour) at least 30 days prior to the changeover. This forces remote systems to cache the information for only a brief amount of time. Once the changeover is complete, you can adjust the TTL back up to 30 days to help reduce traffic. Thirty days is a good TTL value for systems that are not expected to change their host name or address.

With the introduction of Active Directory, Microsoft has adopted DNS as the primary method of locating all resources that are shared on the network, not just web or FTP servers. As a result, companies are often forced to choose between maintaining two separate DNS structures—one for use by resources on the internal network, and another for resources exposed to the external network—or populating a single DNS server with information about their internal network, something that heightens the security risk for the entire network.

Recent DNS advances also allow DHCP clients to dynamically populate a DNS server with their host name and newly acquired IP address when they receive a new lease from a DHCP server. Fortunately, you can configure newer DNS implementations to allow this update only when a client has authenticated with the DNS server.

HYPERTEXT TRANSFER PROTOCOL (HTTP)

HTTP is used in communications between web browsers and web servers. It differs from most services in that it does not create and maintain a single session while a user is retrieving information from a server. Every request for information—text, graphics, or sound—creates a separate session, which is terminated once that request is completed. A web page with lots of graphics needs multiple simultaneous connections in order to be loaded onto a browser. It is not uncommon for a web browser to create 10, 20, or even 50 sessions with a web server just to read a single page.

Since version 1.0, HTTP has included Multipurpose Internet Mail Extension (MIME) to support the negotiation of data types. This has helped HTTP to become a truly cross-platform service, since MIME allows the web browser to inform the server about what type of file formats it can support. MIME also allows the server to alert the web browser as to what type of data it is about to receive. This allows the browser to select the correct, platform-specific viewing or playing software for the data it is about to receive.

NOTE   *HTTP uses the TCP transport and a destination port of 80 when communicating. When used as part of a secure web session (through SSL), HTTP uses port 443.*

POST OFFICE PROTOCOL (POP)

Post Office Protocol is typically used when retrieving e-mail from a Unix shell account. It allows a user to read their e-mail without creating a Telnet connection to the system. When you dial in to your ISP to retrieve your e-mail, you are typically using POP to retrieve e-mail from a Unix system.

When a Unix user receives an e-mail message, it is typically stored in the `/var/spool/mail` directory. Normally this message can be retrieved remotely by telnetting to the system and running the `mail` command. Although it is a useful utility, `mail` does not have much of a user interface. To the inexperienced user, the commands can seem cryptic and hard to remember.

POP allows a user to connect to the system and retrieve their mail using their username and password. POP does not provide shell access; it simply retrieves any e-mail messages the user may have pending on the system.

A variety of e-mail clients are available that support POP (POP3 is the latest version), so the user has a good amount of freedom to choose the e-mail client they like best.

When using POP3, the user can either leave their messages up on the POP server and view them remotely (*online mail*) or download the messages to the local system and read them offline (*offline mail*). Leaving the messages on the server allows the system administrator to centrally back up everyone's e-mail when backing up the server. The drawback, however, is that if the user never deletes their messages (we've seen mailboxes with more than 12,000 messages), the load time for the client can be excruciatingly long. Because a copy of each message is left on the server, all messages must be downloaded every time the client connects.

The benefit of using the POP client in offline mode is that users can create local folders to organize old messages. Because messages are stored locally, the load time for new messages is relatively short. This can provide a dramatic improvement in speed when the POP server is accessed over a dial-up connection. Only local folders can be used. POP3 does not support the use of global or shared folders. The downside to offline mode is that each local system must be backed up to ensure recovery in the event of a drive failure. Most POP clients operate in offline mode.

One of POP3's biggest drawbacks is that it does not support the automatic creation of global address books. Only personal address books can be used. For example, if your organization is using a

POP3 e-mail system, you have no way of automatically viewing the addresses of other users on the system. This leaves you with two options:

◆ You can manually discover the other addresses through some other means and add them to your personal address book.

◆ You can require that the system administrator generate a list of e-mail addresses on the system and e-mail this list to all users. Each user can then use the file to update their personal address book.

Neither option is particularly appealing, so POP is best suited for the home Internet user who does not need sharable address books or folders. For business use, the IMAP4 protocol (discussed in the next section) is more appropriate.

When a message is delivered by a POP3 client, the client forwards the message either back to the POP server or on to a central e-mail relay. Which of these is performed depends on how the POP client is configured. In either case, the POP client uses SMTP (discussed in an upcoming section) when delivering new messages or replies. This forwarding system, not the POP client, is ultimately responsible for the delivery of the message.

By using a forwarding e-mail relay, the POP client can disconnect from the network before the message is delivered to its final destination. Although most SMTP messages are delivered quickly (in less than one second), a busy e-mail system can take 10 minutes or more to accept a message. Using a forwarding system helps to reduce the amount of time a remote POP client is required to remain dialed in.

If the e-mail relay encounters a problem (such as a typo in the recipient's e-mail address) and the message cannot be delivered, the POP client will receive a delivery failure notice the next time it connects to the POP server.

NOTE   *POP3 uses TCP as a transport and communicates using a destination port of 110.*

INTERNET MESSAGE ACCESS PROTOCOL, VERSION 4 (IMAP4)

IMAP was designed to be the next evolutionary step from the Post Office Protocol. Although it has the same features as POP, it includes many more, which allow it to scale more easily in a workgroup environment.

As with POP3, the user can either leave messages on the server and view them remotely (*online mail*) or download the messages to the local system and read them offline (*offline mail*). IMAP, however, supports a third connection mode referred to as disconnected (more about that a bit later).

In online mode, all messages are stored on the IMAP server. Although it can be time-consuming to start up a POP e-mail client in online mode if many messages are involved, IMAP avoids this problem through the use of *flags*.

As you've seen, when a POP client connects to a POP server, the client simply authenticates and begins to download messages. All messages on the server are considered new and unread, which means that the user's entire inbox must be transferred before messages can be viewed or read. When an IMAP client connects to an IMAP server, however, it authenticates and checks the flag status on existing messages. Flagging allows a message to be marked as "seen," "deleted," or "answered." This means that an IMAP client can be configured to collect only messages that have not been seen, avoiding the transfer of the entire mailbox.

In offline mode, connection time can be reduced through the use of *previewing*. Previewing allows the user to scan the header information of all new messages without actually transferring them to their local system. If the user is looking to remotely retrieve only a specific message, they can choose which messages to receive and which messages to leave on the server as unread. The user can also delete messages based on the header information or file size without having to transfer them to the local system first. This can be a real time-saver if you usually retrieve your e-mail remotely and you receive a lot of unsolicited advertisements.

IMAP includes a third connection mode not supported by POP, referred to as *disconnected*. (Someone certainly had a twisted sense of humor when they called it that. you can just see the poor support people pulling their hair out over this one: "I disconnected my computer just like the instructions said, so how come I can't see my e-mail?") When a remote IMAP client is operating in disconnected mode, it retrieves only a copy of all new messages. The originals are left on the IMAP server. The next time the client connects to the system, the server is synchronized with any changes made to the cached information. This mode has a few major benefits:

◆ Connection time is minimized, reducing network traffic and/or dial-in time.

◆ Because messages are centrally located, they can be backed up easily.

◆ Because all messages are server-based, e-mail can be retrieved from multiple clients and/or multiple computers.

The last benefit is extremely useful in an environment where people do not always work from the same computer. For example, an engineer who works from home a few days a week can easily keep their e-mail synchronized between home and work computers. When working in offline mode, as most POP clients do, e-mail retrieved by the engineer's work system would not be viewable on their home system. An IMAP client does not have this limitation.

Another improvement over POP is that IMAP supports the writing of messages to the server. This allows a user to have server-based folders instead of just local folders. These folders can be synchronized in disconnect mode, as well.

IMAP also supports group folders. This allows e-mail users to have *bulletin board* areas where messages can be posted and viewed by multiple people. This functionality is similar to news under NNTP (Network News Transfer Protocol). (A description of NNTP and news follows.) Using group folders is an excellent way to share information. For example, the Human Resources department could set up a group folder for corporate policy information, reducing the need to create printed manuals.

TIP *If you are using IMAP or if your current e-mail system supports group folders, create a folder titled* `computer sup-`*`port`* *or something similar. In it you can post messages providing support for some of your most common support calls. This can help reduce the number of support calls received and provide the user with written directions about how to work through a problem. You can even add screen captures, which can make resolving the problem much easier than walking through it over the phone would.*

IMAP has been designed to integrate with the Application Configuration Access Protocol (ACAP). ACAP is an independent service that allows a client to access configuration information and preferences from a central location. Support for ACAP enhances the portability of IMAP even further.

For example, our engineer who works from home a few days a week could also store their personal address book and configuration information on the server. If they are at work and add a new name and e-mail address to their address book, that name would be available on their home system. This would not be true with POP because each client has a separate address book saved on each local system. ACAP also ensures that any configuration changes take effect on both systems.

ACAP provides e-mail administrators some control when setting up corporate standards for users when accessing e-mail. For example, the administrator can set up a global address book that everyone can access.

NOTE *IMAP uses TCP as a transport with a destination port of 143.*

NETWORK FILE SYSTEM (NFS)

NFS provides access to remote file systems. The user can access the remote file system as if the files were located on the local system. NFS provides file access only. This means that other functionality such as processor time or printing must be provided by the local system.

NFS requires configuration changes on both the server and the client. On the server, the file system to be shared must first be *exported*. This is done by defining which files are to be made sharable. This can be a single directory or an entire disk. You must also define who has access to this file system.

On the client side, the system must be configured to *mount* the remote file system. On a Unix machine this is done by creating an entry in the system's /etc/fstab file, indicating the name of the remote system, the file system to be mounted, and where it should be placed on the local system. In the Unix world, this is typically a directory structure located under a directory. In the DOS world, the remote file system may be assigned a unique drive letter. DOS and Windows require third-party software in order to use NFS.

While it offers a convenient way to share files, NFS suffers from a number of functional deficiencies. File transfer times are slow when compared to FTP or NetWare's NCP protocol. NFS has no file-locking capability to ensure that only one user can write to a file. As if this were not bad enough, NFS makes no assurances that the information has been received intact. I've seen situations where entire directories have been copied to a remote system using NFS and have become corrupted in transit. Because NFS does not check data integrity, the errors were not found until the files were processed.

NOTE *NFS uses the UDP transport and communicates using port 2049; some newer versions also use TCP. You may also need to open TCP/UDP on port 111 for NFS to operate. Port 111 is for Portmapper, a mechanism through which the server tells the client which high port to use*

NETWORK NEWS TRANSFER PROTOCOL (NNTP)

NNTP is used in the delivery of *news*. News is very similar in functionality to e-mail, except messages are delivered to *newsgroups*, not end users. Each newsgroup is a storage area for messages that follow a common thread or subject. Instead of an e-mail client, a news client is used to read messages that have been posted to different subject areas.

For example, let's say you are having trouble configuring networking on your NetWare server. You could check out the messages that have been posted to the newsgroup `comp.os.netware.connectivity` to see if anyone else has found a solution to the same problem. There are literally tens of thousands of newsgroups on a wide range of subjects. My own personal favorites are

```
comp.protocols

alt.clueless

alt.barney.dinosaur.die.die.die
```

In order to read news postings, you must have access to a *news server*. News servers exchange messages by relaying any new messages they receive to other servers. The process is a bit slow: it can take three to five days for a new message to be circulated to every news server.

News is very resource intensive. It's not uncommon for a news server to receive several gigabits of information per week. The processes required to send, receive, and clean up old messages can eat up a lot of CPU time, as well.

News has dwindled in appeal over the last few years due to an activity known as *spamming*. Spamming is the activity of posting unsolicited or off-subject messages. For example, at the time of this writing `comp.os.netware.connectivity` contains 383 messages. Of these, 11 percent are advertisements for get-rich-quick schemes, 8 percent are ads for computer-related hardware or services, 6 percent are postings describing the sender's opinion on someone or something using many superlatives, and another 23 percent are NetWare-related but have nothing to do with connectivity. This means that only slightly more than half the postings are actually on-topic. For some groups the percentages are even worse.

NOTE   *NNTP uses TCP as a transport and port 119 for all communications.*

NetBIOS over IP

NetBIOS over IP is not a service *per se*, but it does add session layer support to enable the encapsulation of NetBIOS traffic within an IP packet. This is required when using Windows NT or Samba, which use NetBIOS for file and printer sharing. If IP is the only protocol bound to an NT server, it is still using NetBIOS for file sharing via encapsulation.

Samba is a suite of programs that allows Unix file systems and printers to be accessed as shares. In effect, this makes the Unix system appear to be an NT server. Clients can be other Unix systems (running the Samba client) or Windows 95/98/NT/2000 systems. The Windows clients do not require any additional software, because they use the same configuration as when they are communicating with an NT/2000 server.

The source code for Samba is available as freeware on the Internet. More than 15 different flavors of Unix are supported.

NOTE   *When NetBIOS is encapsulated within IP, both TCP and UDP are used as a transport. All communications are conducted on ports 137–139.*

Simple Mail Transfer Protocol (SMTP)

SMTP is used to transfer e-mail messages between systems. SMTP uses a message-switched type of connection: each e-mail message is processed in its entirety before the session between two systems is terminated. If more than one message must be transferred, a separate session must be established for each e-mail message.

SMTP is capable of transferring ASCII text only. It does not have the ability to support rich text or transfer binary files and attachments. When these types of transfers are required, an external program is needed to first translate the attachment into an ASCII format.

The original programs used to provide this functionality were uuencode and uudecode. A binary file would first be processed by uuencode to translate it into an ASCII format. The file could then be attached to a e-mail message and sent. Once received, the file would be processed through uudecode to return it to its original binary format.

Uuencode/uudecode has been replaced by the use of MIME. While MIME performs the same translating duties, it also compresses the resulting ASCII information. The result is smaller attachments, which produce faster message transfers with reduced overhead. Apple computers use an application called Binhex, which has the same functionality as MIME. MIME is now supported by most Unix and PC e-mail systems.

Uuencode/uudecode, Binhex, and MIME are not compatible. If you can exchange text messages with a remote e-mail system but attachments end up unusable, you are probably using different translation formats. Many modern e-mail gateways provide support for both uuencode/uudecode and MIME to eliminate such communication problems. Some even include support for Binhex.

NOTE   *SMTP uses the TCP transport and destination port 25 when creating a communication session.*

SIMPLE NETWORK MANAGEMENT PROTOCOL (SNMP)

SNMP is used to monitor and control network devices. The monitoring or controlling station is referred to as the *SNMP management station*. The network devices to be controlled are required to run SNMP *agents*. The agents and the management station work together to give the network administrator a central point of control over the network.

NOTE   *The SNMP agent provides the link into the networking device. The device can be a manageable hub, a router, or even a server. The agent uses both static and dynamic information when reporting to the management station.*

The *static information* is data stored within the device in order to identify it uniquely. For example, the administrator may choose to store the device's physical location and serial number as part of the SNMP static information. This makes it easier to identify which device you're working with from the SNMP management station.

The *dynamic information* is data that pertains to the current state of the device. For example, port status on a hub would be considered dynamic information, as the port may be enabled or disabled depending on whether it is functioning properly.

The SNMP management station is the central console used to control all network devices that have SNMP agents. The management station first learns about a network device through the use of a *management information base* (MIB). The MIB is a piece of software supplied by the network device vendor, usually on floppy disk. When the MIB is added to the management station, it teaches the management station about the network device. This helps to ensure that SNMP management stations created by one vendor will operate properly with network devices produced by another.

Information is usually collected by the SNMP management station through *polling*. The SNMP management station will issue queries at predetermined intervals in order to check the status of each network device. SNMP only supports two commands for collecting information: `get` and `getnext`. The `get` command allows the management station to retrieve information on a specific operating parameter. For example, the management station may query a router to report on the current status of one of its ports. The `getnext` command is used when a complete status will be collected from a device. Instead of forcing the SNMP management station to issue a series of specific `get` commands, `getnext` can be used to sequentially retrieve each piece of information a device can report on.

SNMP also allows for the controlling of network devices through the command `set`. The `set` command can be used to alter some of the operational parameters on a network device. For example, if your `get` command reported that port 2 on the router was disabled, you could issue a `set` command to the router to enable the port.

SNMP typically does not offer the same range of control as a network device's management utility. For example, while you may be able to turn ports on and off on your router, you would probably be unable to initialize IP networking and assign an IP address to the port. The amount of control available through SNMP is limited by which commands are included in the vendor's MIB, as well as the command structure of SNMP itself. The operative word in SNMP is "simple." SNMP provides only a minimal amount of control over network devices.

While most reporting is done by having the SNMP management station poll network devices, SNMP does allow network devices to report critical events immediately back to the management station. These messages are called *traps*. Traps are sent when an event occurs that is important enough to not wait until the device is again polled. For example, your router may send a trap to the SNMP management console if it has just been power cycled. Because this event will have a grave impact on network connectivity, it is reported to the SNMP management station immediately instead of waiting until the device is again polled.

NOTE *SNMP uses the UDP transport and destination ports 161 and 162 when communicating.*

SSH

SSH is used when a remote communication session is required with some other system on the network. Its functionality is similar to a mainframe terminal, remote control session, or Telnet. Unlike Telnet, however, SSH provides for advanced security features required in today's hostile networking environment. One of these features can require that the client initiating the session provide proof of identity through an electronic signature known as a key (see Chapter 9). Once authenticated, the same key is used to generate an encrypted session that hides everything transmitted between the client and server.

Additionally, SSH provides other functionality missing in Telnet. It is possible to "wrap" other services inside the authenticated, encrypted session, such as an ftp session, or even a completely separate IP session.

NOTE *SSH uses the TCP transport and destination port 22 by default when creating a communication session.*

IRC

IRC (Internet Relay Chat) protocol allows clients to communicate in real time. It is made up of various separate networks (known as *nets*) of IRC servers. Users run a client that connects them to a server on one of the nets. The server relays information to and from other servers on the same net. Once connected to an IRC server, a user will be presented with a list of one or more topical *channels*. Channel names usually begin with a #, such as #irchelp, and since all servers on a given net share the same list of channels, users connected to any server on that net can communicate with one another.

NOTE   *Channels that begin with an & instead of a # are local to a given server only, and are not shared with other servers on the net.*

Each IRC client is distinguished from other clients by a unique nickname (or *nick*). Servers store additional information about each client, including the real name of the host that the client is running on, the username of the client on that host, and the server to which the client is connected.

Operators are those clients that have been given the ability to perform maintenance on the IRC nets, such as disconnecting and reconnecting servers as needed to correct for any network routing problems. Operators can also forcibly remove other clients from the network by terminating their connection. Operators can be assigned to a server, or just to a channel, and they are identified by an @ symbol next to their nick.

IRC has actually gotten a bad security rap in recent years. Hackers have used the unregulated and distributed nature of the servers and channels to provide an infrastructure to control *zombies*—everyday computers that been taken over by hackers through back doors. Zombies are used to generate millions of packets simultaneously, creating a *DDoS* (Distributed Denial of Service Attacks).

IRC, like active ftp, relies on the server to make a connection back to the client, but unlike ftp, this connection is for the purpose of identifying the server. Previous security flaws in the authentication component (called an ident service) allowed hackers to gain control of a computer through that component.

NOTE   *IRC can use both TCP and UDP as transports, and most modern IRC servers listen on ports 6667–7000.*

Upper Layer Communications

Once we get above the session layer, our communications become pretty specific to the program we're using. The responsibilities of the presentation and application layers are more a function of the type of service requested than the underlying protocol in use. Data translation and encryption are considered *portable features*.

NOTE   *Portable means that these features can be applied easily to different services without regard for the underlying protocol. It does not matter if I'm using IP or IPX to transfer my data, the ability to leverage these features will depend on the application in use.*

For example, Lotus has the ability to encrypt e-mail messages prior to transmission. This activity is performed at the presentation layer of the program. It does not matter if I'm connecting to my e-mail system via TCP, SPX, or a modem. The encryption functionality is available with all three protocols, because the functionality is made available by the program itself. Lotus Notes is not dependent on the underlying protocol.

Summary

In this chapter, we began by discussing the anatomy of an Ethernet frame and how systems on a local Ethernet segment communicate. We also covered how routing is used to assist communication in large networking environments. From there we looked at the different methods of connection establishment and finished off the chapter by discussing IP services.

In the next chapter, we will begin to look at some of the insecurities involved in everyday communications. We will look at how building security into your core network design can not only improve performance (always a good thing)—it can make your data less susceptible to attack, as well.

Chapter 4

Topology Security

In this chapter, we will look at the communication properties of network transmissions. You will also see what insecurities exist in everyday network communications and how you can develop a network infrastructure that alleviates some of these problems.

Featured in this chapter:

- ◆ Understanding network transmissions
- ◆ Topology security
- ◆ Basic networking hardware

Understanding Network Transmissions

It is no accident that the National Security Agency, which is responsible for setting the encryption standards for the U.S. government, is also responsible for monitoring and cracking encrypted transmissions that are of interest to the government. In order to know how to make something more secure, you must understand what vulnerabilities exist and how these can be exploited.

This same idea applies to network communications. In order to be able to design security into your network infrastructure, you must understand how networked systems communicate with one another. Many exploits leverage basic communication properties. If you are aware of these communication properties, you can take steps to ensure that they are not exploited.

Digital Communication

Digital communication is analogous to Morse code or the early telegraph system: certain patterns of pulses represent different characters during transmission. Figure 4.1 shows an example of a digital transmission. A voltage placed on the transmission medium is considered a binary 1. The absence of a signal is interpreted as a binary 0.

Because this waveform is so predictable and the variation between acceptable values is so great, it is easy to determine the state of the transmission. This is important if the signal is electrical, because the introduction of noise to a circuit can skew voltage values slightly. As shown in Figure 4.2, even when there is noise in the circuit, you can still see what part of the signal is a binary 1 and which is a 0.

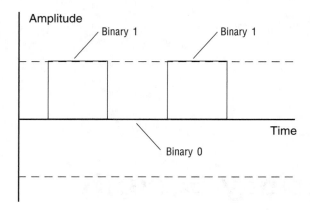

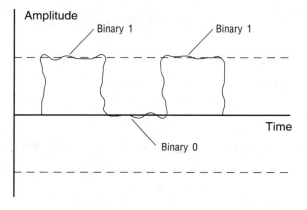

This simple format, which allows digital communication to be so noise-resistant, can also be its biggest drawback. The information for the ASCII character *A* can be transmitted with a single analog wave or vibration, but transmitting the binary or digital equivalent requires eight separate waves or vibrations (to transmit 01000001). Despite this inherent drawback, digital communication is usually much more efficient than analog circuits, which require a larger amount of overhead in order to detect and correct noisy transmissions.

NOTE Overhead *is the amount of additional information that must be transmitted on a circuit to ensure that the receiving system gets the correct data and that the data is free of errors. Typically, when a circuit requires more overhead, less bandwidth is available to transmit the actual data. This is like the packaging used for shipping. You didn't want hundreds of little Styrofoam acorns, but they're there in the box taking up space to ensure that your item is delivered safely.*

When you have an electric circuit (such as an Ethernet network that uses twisted-pair wiring), you need to pulsate your voltage in order to transmit information. This means your voltage state is constantly changing, which introduces your first insecurity: electromagnetic interference.

Electromagnetic Interference (EMI)

EMI is produced by circuits that use an alternating signal, like analog or digital communications (referred to as an *alternating current* or an *AC circuit*). EMI is not produced by circuits that contain a consistent power level (referred to as a *direct current* or a *DC circuit*).

For example, if you could slice one of the wires coming from a car battery and watch the electrons moving down the wire (kids: don't try this at home), you would see a steady stream of power moving evenly and uniformly down the cable. The power level would never change: it would stay at a constant 12 volts. A car battery is an example of a DC circuit, because the power level remains stable.

Now, let's say you could slice the wire to a household lamp and try the same experiment (kids: *definitely* do not try this at home!). You would now see that, depending on the point in time when you measured the voltage on the wire, the measurement would read anywhere between −120 volts and +120 volts. The voltage level of the circuit is constantly changing. Plotted over time, the voltage level resembles an analog signal.

As you watched the flow of electrons in the AC wire, you would notice something interesting. As the voltage changes and the current flows down the wire, the electrons tend to ride predominantly on the surface of the wire. The center point of the wire shows almost no electron movement at all. If you increase the frequency of the power cycle, more and more of the electrons travel on the surface of the wire, instead of at the core. This effect is somewhat similar to what happens to a water skier—the faster the boat travels, the closer to the top of the water the skier rides.

As the frequency of the power cycle increases, energy begins to radiate at a 90° angle to the flow of current. In the same way that water ripples out when a rock breaks its surface, energy moves out from the center core of the wire. This radiation is in a direct relationship with the signal on the wire; if the voltage level or the frequency is increased, the amount of energy radiated also increases (see Figure 4.3).

This energy has magnetic properties and is the basis of how electromagnets and transformers operate. The downside to all of this is that the electromagnetic radiation can be measured in order to "sniff" the signal traveling down the wire. Electricians have had tools for this purpose for many years. Most electricians carry a device that they can simply connect around a wire in order to measure the signal traveling through the center conductor.

FIGURE 4.3

A conductor carrying an AC signal radiating EMI

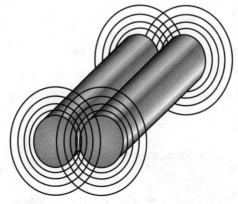

Copper wire conducting AC signal

More sophisticated devices can measure the EMI radiation coming off an electrical network cable and actually record the digital pulses traveling down the wire. Once a record of these pulses is made, it is a simple matter to convert them from a binary format to a format that humans can read. (Although a serious geek is just as happy reading the information in binary format, we did specifically say "humans.")

NOTE *Although twisted-pair cabling has become popular because of its low cost, it is also extremely insecure. Most of today's networks are wired using unshielded twisted pair. Since twisted pair is used for the transmission of electrical signals, EMI is produced. Because the cable does not use any shielding, it is extremely easy to detect the EMI radiating from each of the conductors. Although twisted pair is an excellent choice for general network use, it is not a good selection if the information traveling along the wire needs to remain 100 percent secure.*

Your first point of vulnerability, therefore, is your actual network cables. People typically overlook these when evaluating the security of a network. Although an organization may go to great lengths to secure its computer room, a web of cabling may be running through the ceilings. This can be even more of a problem if an organization is located in shared office space and cabling runs through common areas.

A would-be attacker would never have to go near a computer room or wiring closet to collect sensitive information. A stepladder and a popped ceiling tile are all that's needed to create an access point to your network. A savvy attacker might even use a radio transmitter to relay the captured information to another location. This means that the attacker can safely continue to collect information for an extended period of time.

Fiber-Optic Cable

Fiber-optic cable consists of a cylindrical glass thread center core 62.5 microns in diameter wrapped in cladding that protects the central core and reflects the light back into the glass conductor. This is then encapsulated in a jacket of tough KEVLAR fiber.

The whole thing is then sheathed in PVC (polyvinyl chloride) or Plenum. The diameter of this outer sheath is 125 microns. Because of the diameter measurements, this cabling is sometimes referred to as 62.5/125 cable. Although the glass core is breakable, the KEVLAR fiber jacket helps fiber-optic cable stand up to a fair amount of abuse. Figure 4.4 shows a fiber-optic cable.

Unlike twisted-pair cable, fiber-optic cable uses a light source for data transmission. This light source is typically a light-emitting diode (LED) that produces a signal in the visible infrared range. On the other end of the cable is another diode that receives the LED signals. The type of light transmission can take one of two forms: single mode or multimode.

TIP *Never look into the beam of an active fiber-optic cable! The light intensity is strong enough to cause permanent blindness. If you must visually inspect a cable, first make sure that it is completely disconnected from the network. Just because a cable is dark for a moment does not mean it is inactive. The chance of blindness or visual "dead spots" is too high to take risks—unless you know the cable is completely disconnected.*

FIGURE 4.4

A stripped-back fiber-optic cable

LIGHT DISPERSION

You'll see light dispersion if you shine a flashlight against a nearby wall: the light pattern on the wall will have a larger diameter than the flashlight lens. If you hold two flashlights together and shine them both against the wall, you'll get a fuzzy area in the middle where it's difficult to determine which light source is responsible for which portion of the illumination. The farther from the wall you move, the larger this fuzzy area becomes. This is, in effect, what limits the distance on multimode fiber-optic cable (that is, if you can call 1.2 miles a distance limitation for a single cable run). As the length of the cable increases, it becomes more difficult for the diode on the receiving end to distinguish between the different light frequencies.

Single-mode fiber-optic cable consists of an LED that produces a single frequency of light. This single frequency is pulsed in a digital format to transmit data from one end of the cable to another. The benefit of single-mode fiber-optic cable over multimode is that it is faster and will travel longer distances (in the tens-of-miles range). The drawbacks are that the hardware is extremely expensive and installation can be tedious at best. Unless your company name ends with the word *Telephone* or *Utility*, single-mode fiber-optic cable would be overkill.

Multimode transmissions consist of multiple light frequencies. Because the light range does not need to be quite so precise as single-mode, the hardware costs for multimode are dramatically less than for single-mode. The drawback of multimode fiber-optic cable is *light dispersion*, the tendency of light rays to spread out as they travel.

Because multimode transmissions are light-based instead of electrical, fiber-optic cable benefits from being completely immune to all types of EMI monitoring. There is no radiation to monitor as a signal passes down the conductor. Although it might be possible to cut away part of the sheath in order to get at the glass conductor, this might cause the system to fail, thus foiling the attacker. However, newer fiber-optic systems are more resilient and, ironically, more susceptible to monitoring from this kind of attack.

Fiber-optic cable has one other major benefit: it can support large bandwidth connections—10MB, 100MB, and even gigabit Ethernet. So along with security improvements, there are performance improvements. This is extremely helpful in justifying the use of fiber-optic cable within your network; you can satisfy both bandwidth and security concerns. If Woolly Attacker is going to attempt to tap into your network in order to monitor transmissions, he will to want to choose a network segment with a lot of traffic so that he can collect the largest amount of data. Coincidentally, these are also the segments where you would want to use fiber-optic cable in order to support the large amount of data flowing though this point in the network. By using fiber-optic cable on these segments, you can help to protect the integrity of your cabling infrastructure.

Bound and Unbound Transmissions

The atmosphere is referred to as an *unbound medium*—a circuit with no formal boundaries. It has no constraints to force a signal to flow within a certain path. Twisted-pair cable and fiber-optic cable are examples of bound media, because they restrain the signal to within the wire. An unbound transmission is free to travel anywhere.

Unbound transmissions bring a host of security problems. Since a signal has no constraints that confine it within a specific area, it becomes that much more susceptible to interception and monitoring. The atmosphere is capable of transmitting a variety of signal types. The most commonly used are light and radio waves.

LIGHT TRANSMISSIONS

Light transmissions through the atmosphere use lasers to transmit and receive network signals. These devices operate similarly to a fiber-optic cable circuit, except without the glass medium.

Because laser transmissions use a focused beam of light, they require a clear line of sight and precise alignment between the devices. This helps to enhance system security, because it severely limits the physical area from which a signal can be monitored. The atmosphere limits the light transmission's effective distance, however, as well as the number of situations in which it can be used.

Unbound light transmissions are also sensitive to environmental conditions; a heavy mist or snowfall can interfere with their transmission properties. This means that it is easy to interrupt a light-based circuit—thus denying users service. Still, light transmissions through the atmosphere make for a relatively secure transmission medium when physical cabling cannot be used.

RADIO WAVES

Radio waves used for networking purposes are typically transmitted in the 1–20GHz range and are referred to as *microwave* signals. These signals can be fixed frequency or spread spectrum in nature.

Fixed Frequency Signals

A *fixed frequency signal* is a single frequency used as a carrier wave for the information you want to transmit. A radio station is a good example of a single frequency transmission. When you tune in to a station's carrier wave frequency on your FM dial, you can hear the signal that is riding on it.

A *carrier wave* is a signal that is used to carry other information. This information is superimposed onto the signal (in much the same way as noise), and the resultant wave is transmitted into the atmosphere. This signal is then received by a device called a *demodulator* (in effect, your car radio is a demodulator that can be set for different frequencies), which removes the carrier signal and passes along the remaining information. A carrier wave is used to boost a signal's power and to extend the receiving range of the signal.

Fixed frequency signals are easy to monitor. Once an attacker knows the carrier frequency, they have all the information they need to start receiving your transmitted signals. They also have all the information they need to jam your signal, thus blocking all transmissions.

Spread Spectrum Signals

A *spread spectrum signal* is identical to a fixed frequency signal, except multiple frequencies are transmitted. The reason multiple frequencies are transmitted is the reduction of interference through noise. Spread spectrum technology arose during wartime, when an enemy would jam a fixed frequency signal by transmitting on an identical frequency. Because spread spectrum uses multiple frequencies, it is much more difficult to disrupt.

Notice the operative words "more difficult." It is still possible to jam or monitor spread spectrum signals. Although the signal varies through a range of frequencies, this range is typically a repeated pattern. Once an attacker determines the timing and pattern of the frequency changes, they are in a position to jam or monitor transmissions.

NOTE *Because it is so easy to monitor or jam radio signals, most transmissions rely on encryption to scramble the signal so that it cannot be monitored by outside parties. We cover encryption in Chapter 9.*

Terrestrial vs. Space-Based Transmissions

Two methods can be used to transmit both fixed frequency and spread spectrum signals. These are referred to as *terrestrial* and *space-based* transmissions.

Terrestrial Transmissions   *Terrestrial transmissions* are completely land-based radio signals. The sending stations are typically transmission towers located on top of mountains or tall buildings. The range of these systems is usually line of sight, although an unobstructed view is not required. Depending on the signal strength, 50 miles is about the maximum range achievable with a terrestrial transmission system. Local TV and radio stations are good examples of industries that rely on terrestrial-based broadcasts. Their signals can only be received locally.

Space-Based Transmissions   *Space-based transmissions* are signals that originate from a land-based system but are then bounced off one or more satellites that orbit the earth in the upper atmosphere. The greatest benefit of space-based communications is range. Signals can be received from almost every corner of the world. The space-based satellites can be tuned to increase or decrease the effective broadcast area.

Of course, the larger the broadcast range of a signal, the more susceptible it is to being monitored. As the signal range increases, so does the possibility that someone knowledgeable enough to monitor your signals will be within your broadcast area.

Choosing a Transmission Medium

You should consider a number of security issues when choosing a medium for transferring data across your network. Keep in mind that any security concerns (read: objectives) will have to be balanced by other system objectives such as flexibility and cost. Although it is currently the most maligned network technology, the 802.11b protocol has also enabled rapid and flexible network access for thousands of businesses and individuals. Creative solutions that meet your security requirements while still allowing for the deployment of these popular communications media can be considered a best practice.

HOW VALUABLE IS MY DATA?

As you saw in earlier chapters, the typical attacker must feel like they have something to gain by assaulting your network. Do you maintain databases that contain financial information? If so, someone might find the payoff high enough to make it worth the risk of staging a physical attack.

Of course, there is another consideration. Because of the growth in laws (and law suits) concerning data privacy and integrity, especially as applied to specific industries (health care) and types of data (financial), you must also consider the compliance levels your network has to meet in order to avoid legal liability or retain insurance coverage.

WHICH NETWORK SEGMENTS CARRY SENSITIVE DATA?

Your networks carry sensitive information on a daily basis. To protect this information, you need to understand the workflow of how it is used. For example, if you identify your organization's accounting information as sensitive, you should know where the information is stored and who has access to it. A small workgroup with its own local server will be far more secure than an accounting database that is accessed from a remote facility using an unbound transmission medium.

TIP *Be careful when analyzing the types of services that will be passing between your facilities. For example, e-mail is typically given little consideration, yet it usually contains more information about your organization than any other business service. Considering that most e-mail systems pass messages in the clear (if an attacker captures this traffic, it appears as plain text), e-mail should be one of your best-guarded network services.*

TIP *Care should also be given to the applications that pass sensitive data. Even the most highly encrypted traffic can be rendered ineffective if the program passing the data is vulnerable to hostile attack—attacks that would lead to the compromise of the system holding the data!*

WILL AN INTRUDER BE NOTICED?

It's easy to spot an intruder when an organization consists of three of four people. Scale this to three or four thousand, and the task becomes proportionately difficult. If you are the network administrator, you may have no say in the physical security practices of your organization. You can, however, strive to make eavesdropping on your network a bit more difficult.

When you select a physical medium, keep in mind that you may need to make your network more resilient to attacks if other security precautions are lacking—especially as our definition of a "local" network logically extends to an Internet-connected laptop half a world away.

ARE BACKBONE SEGMENTS ACCESSIBLE?

If a would-be attacker is going to monitor your network, they are going to look for central nodes where they can collect the most information. Wiring closets and server rooms are prime targets because these areas tend to be junction points for many communication sessions. When laying out your network, pay special attention to these areas and consider using a more secure medium (such as fiber-optic cable) when possible.

Consider these issues carefully when choosing a method of data transmission. Use the risk analysis information you collected in Chapter 2 to cost-justify your choices. Although increasing the level of topology security might appear to be an expensive proposition, the cost may be more than justified when compared with the cost of recovering from an intrusion.

Topology Security

Now that you have a good understanding of the transmission media available for carrying your data, let's look at how these media are configured to function as a network. *Topology* is defined as the rules for physically connecting and communicating on given network media. Each topology has its own set of rules for connecting your network systems and even specifies how these systems must "speak" to one another on the wire. By far the most popular local area network (LAN) topology is Ethernet.

LAN Topologies

The past decade has seen a major change in LAN infrastructure, with Ethernet emerging victorious from its battle with Token Ring as the topology of choice. Beginning with the new century, however, wireless technologies are rapidly encroaching and crossing LAN/WAN boundaries, even as speed and security concerns persist.

ETHERNET

In Chapter 3, you saw what type of information is included within an Ethernet frame. Now we will examine how Ethernet moves this information from one system to another across a network. The better you understand network communication properties, the easier it will be to secure your network.

NOTE   *Ethernet was developed in the late 1970s by Xerox; it later evolved into the IEEE specification 802.3 (pronounced "eight-oh-two-dot-three"). Its flexibility, high transmission rate (at the time, anyway), and nonproprietary nature quickly made it the networking topology of choice for many network administrators.*

Ethernet's ability to support a wide range of cable types, low-cost hardware, and plug-and-play connectivity has caused it to find its way into more corporate (as well as home) networks than any other topology.

Ethernet's communication rules are called *Carrier Sense Multiple Access with Collision Detection* (CSMA/CD). This is a mouthful, but it's simple enough to understand when you break it down:

◆   *Carrier sense* means that all Ethernet stations are required to listen to the wire at all times (even when transmitting). By "listen," we mean that the station should be constantly monitoring the network to see if any other stations are currently sending data. By monitoring the transmissions of other stations, a station can tell if the network is open or in use. This way, the station does not just blindly transfer information and interfere with other stations. Being in a constant listening mode also means that the station is ready when another station wants to send it data.

◆   *Multiple access* simply means that more than two stations can be connected to the same network, and that all stations are allowed to transmit whenever the network is free. It is far more efficient to allow stations to transmit only when they need to than it is to assign each system a time block in which it is allowed to transmit. Multiple access also scales much more easily as you add more stations to the network.

◆   *Collision detection* answers the question: "What happens if two systems think the circuit is free and try to transmit data at the same time?" When two stations transmit simultaneously, a *collision* takes place. A collision is similar to interference, and the resulting transmission becomes mangled and useless for carrying data. As a station transmits data, it watches for this condition; if it detects such a condition, the workstation assumes that a collision has taken place. The station will back off, wait for a random period of time, and then retransmit.

NOTE   *Each station is responsible for determining its own random waiting period before retransmission. This helps to ensure that each station is waiting for a different period of time, avoiding another collision. In the unlikely event that a second collision does occur (the station backs off but is again involved in a collision), each station is required to double its waiting period before trying again. Two or more consecutive collisions are referred to as a multiple collision.*

If you were to chart CSMA/CD, it would look something like Figure 4.5. This process takes place after the ARP (Address Resolution Protocol) decision process discussed in Chapter 3.

An integral part of Ethernet communications is that each system is constantly monitoring the transmissions of all the other stations on the wire. Unfortunately, this is also Ethernet's biggest security flaw. It is possible to configure a system to read all this information it receives. This is commonly referred to as a *promiscuous mode* system.

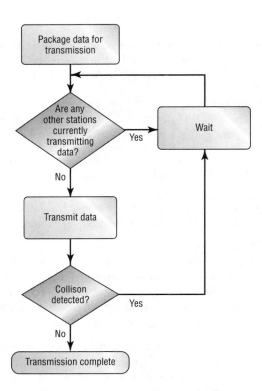

A network administrator can leverage promiscuous mode to monitor a network from one central station so that errors and network statistics can be gathered. A network analyzer is effectively a computer operating in promiscuous mode. Since a station is listening to all network traffic anyway, a simple software change allows a system to actually record all the information it sees.

Unfortunately, the existence of promiscuous mode also means that a not-so-honest person might be able to eavesdrop on network communications or steal sensitive information. This is particularly a problem because most information passed along a computer network is transmitted as clear text. See Figure 4.6 for an example of this output.

FIGURE 4.6

A packet capture of
a network file

```
Packet Number : 13          3:52:02 PM
Length : 66 bytes
ether: ==================== Ethernet Datalink Layer ====================
       Station: Skylar ----> This_Workstation
       Type: 0x0800 (IP)
  ip:  ==================== Internet Protocol ====================
       Station:10.1.1.100 ---->10.1.1.25
       Protocol: TCP
       Version: 4
       Header Length (32 bit words): 5
       Precedence: Routine
            Normal Delay, Normal Throughput, Normal Reliability
       Total length: 48
       Identification: 21249
       Fragmentation not allowed, Last fragment
       Fragment Offset: 0
       Time to Live: 128 seconds
       Checksum: 0x9148(Valid)
  tcp: ================== Transmission Control Protocol ==================
       Source Port: 258
       Destination Port: 1027
       Sequence Number: 417610
       Acknowledgement Number: 898472
       Data Offset (32-bit words): 5
       Window: 8510
       Control Bits: Acknowledgement Field is Valid (ACK)
            Push Function Requested (PSH)
       Checksum: 0x5DB5(Valid)
       Urgent Pointer: 0
```

To minimize the amount of information that can be collected with a network monitor or analyzer, you can segment network traffic to isolate network communications by using a switch or a router—although many sophisticated techniques exist that can bypass the filtering capability of a switch. These devices (and their limitations) are discussed in the "Basic Networking Hardware" section of this chapter.

WIRELESS

Both 802.11b and, increasingly, Bluetooth wireless standards can be implemented as LAN technologies, with upcoming upgrades to both promising faster data throughput and increased security. (Bluetooth was originally conceived as more of a "personal" network connecting a PDA to a laptop or a laptop to a printer.) As vendors increasingly integrate wireless capability into network devices ranging from printers to PDAs, the security threats to unsecured wireless access points have reached mythic proportions.

WiFi

Advertised as an 11Mbps half-duplex (meaning that a wireless station can't transmit and receive at the same time) protocol, WiFi (formally known as 802.11b) operates in the 2.4GHz range, which means that some newer cordless phones can interfere with optimal operation. Also, the reality is that most communication occurs from between 2.5Mbps and 4.5Mbps, with speeds decreasing as space between the access point and wireless station increase or as barriers (such as walls) are placed between them.

A WiFi topology operates in one of two modes—Ad-Hoc or Infrastructure. In Ad-Hoc mode, all wireless-capable devices talk directly to one another. In Infrastructure mode, all wireless traffic passes through one or more *access points*. Access points are used primarily to provide nonwireless networks (and devices) access to the wireless LAN and vice versa.

Access points also operate in modes:

NAT   In this mode, the access point acts like a Network Address Translation router, in that traffic can originate from the wireless network and travel to the wired network. Traffic originating from the wired network, however, is not allowed to flow back. This configuration is common when an office or a home network has multiple computers that need to share a single, public IP address on the Internet.

Bridge   Access points acting as bridges transparently connect wireless and wired networks, while still providing the traffic segmentation features found in bridges and switches.

NAT + Bridge   Access points can bridge wired and wireless networks and then use a WAN port to NAT that traffic onto a distinct network. This configuration is common in offices that have a mix of wired and wireless computers that need NAT services.

Security for wireless networks is provided by WEP (Wired Equivalent Privacy). Although WEP includes both a low (64-bit) and high (128-bit) encryption mode, several flaws in the WEP infrastructure itself have rendered it unreliable and vulnerable to attack. Vendors are responding to this problem by providing proven industry-strength encryption on the wireless cards themselves, although not all these devices will interoperate.

802.11a

The 802.11a standard is a sister technology to WiFi (they both use the same Media Access Control standard). Although still grouped under the WiFi banner, there are some significant differences—primarily in how they use the radio spectrum. The 802.11a standard uses a technology called OFDM (Orthogonal Frequency-Division Multiplexing), a signal modulation technique that uses frequencies in the range of 5GHz. OFDM provides for a greater use of available bandwidth than earlier technologies, which allows the theoretical top speed of 802.11a to approach 54Mbps.

Although the 802.11a components are more expensive and use more power than WLAN devices, the newer technologies (and operating frequencies) mean that they are less susceptible to the interference from cordless phones, microwave ovens, Bluetooth networks, and even WiFi networks themselves! Although this is helpful in the United States, 802.11a is not a worldwide standard (WiFi is), 802.11a devices can't communicate with WiFis, and they use the same vulnerable WEP encryption as WiFi. And finally, because higher frequencies are more easily absorbed, the 5GHz signals don't penetrate walls and windows as easily, significantly limiting their range indoors to 50 meters, as opposed to the 100 meters for WiFi.

With all these concerns, will 802.11a find a place in today's home and office networks? The most likely scenario is that high-bandwidth multimedia devices will take the most advantage of the higher data rates offered by the protocol. In fact, some vendors see it as the super-fast alternative for Bluetooth—limited range, high resistance against interference—all perfect qualities for a transfer mechanism from a digital camera to a laptop.

Bluetooth

Originally designed as a cable replacement technology, Bluetooth technology is being integrated directly into laptops, PDAs, cell phones, and printers, as opposed to 802.11b, which is usually implemented as a distinct network device. With a much more limited range and data throughput (10 meters and 1Mbps as opposed to the 11Mbps and 300+ of 802.11b), Bluetooth is still eight times faster than the average parallel port.

Although the abilities of 802.11b seem dramatic in comparison, Bluetooth still embodies fundamental infrastructure improvements, including support for full-duplex communications and a more sophisticated interference immunity provided by a spread spectrum made up of more than 79 (as opposed to the 11 of 802.11b) frequencies.

Bluetooth devices are separated into three classes based on the amount of power they use, as shown in Table 4.1.

When two Bluetooth-enabled devices attempt to communicate, they use LMP (Link Manager Protocol) to initiate, authenticate, and manage sessions, along with device power management. When more than two devices communicate in a session, they are said to join a *piconet*. A piconet is a network that operates like 802.11b in Ad-Hoc mode, with the difference that one of the devices will become a master (with the rest remaining slaves) for the purpose of maintaining the frequency hopping in sync. Multiple piconets (as many as 10) can be connected to form *scatternets*, although this is seen as impractical.

TABLE 4.1: CLASSES OF BLUETOOTH DEVICES

CLASS	POWER (IN MILLIWATTS)	RANGE (IN METERS)
1	100	100
2	1–2.5	10
3	1	0.1–10

Bluetooth security is broken into three modes for devices:

SM1   Also called promiscuous mode. A device operating in SM1 will allow any other device to initiate a session.

SM2   Security is enforced after a session is initiated. Although still leaving devices vulnerable to an intermediate (man-in-the-middle) attack, SM2 enables flexible security policies to be applied to sessions.

SM3   All sessions, regardless of connection status, are wrapped in an encryption and authentication wrapper

Additionally, service *levels* are applied to both devices and services. Devices can either be *trusted* or *untrusted*, with trusted devices gaining access to a full range of services. Although untrusted devices can be limited from all services, they can also be granted access to a controlled subset of services. Services have three security levels:

Authentication/Authorization   To access a service at this level, devices must first authenticate themselves (prove their identity) and then receive authorization (their identity must be on an approved list for access). If a device is trusted, access is granted automatically. Untrusted devices can gain access, but only through user intervention.

Authentication   Services with the authentication service level require only that the identity of the device be assured.

Open   Services at this level are said to be *promiscuous*—open to all devices without restriction.

Most wireless security experts are in agreement that although future weaknesses might be found, Bluetooth is generally secure and provides a level of sophistication lacking in WLAN, as long as vendors continue to implement the security capabilities by default.

Wide Area Network Topologies

Wide area network (WAN) topologies are network configurations that are designed to carry data over a great distance. Unlike LANs, which are designed to deliver data between many systems, WAN topologies are usually point to point. *Point to point* means that the technology was developed to support only two nodes sending and receiving data. If multiple nodes need access to the WAN, a LAN is placed behind it to accommodate this functionality. Here are some of the more common private circuit topologies.

Leased lines are dedicated analog or digital circuits that are paid for on a flat-rate basis. Whether you use the circuit or not, you pay a fixed monthly fee. Leased lines are point-to-point connections that connect one geographical location to another. The maximum throughput on a leased line is 56Kbps.

A *T1* is a full-duplex signal (each end of the connection can transmit and receive simultaneously) over two-pair wire cabling. This wire pair terminates in a receptacle that resembles the square phone jacks used in older homes. T1s are used for dedicated point-to-point connections in the same way that leased lines are. Bandwidth on a T1 is available in increments from 64Kb up to 1.544Mb. T1s use time division to break the two wire pairs into 24 separate channels. *Time division* is the allotment of available bandwidth based on time increments. This arrangement is extremely useful because a T1 can carry both voice and data at the same time.

Typically, you can deploy leased lines or T1s in two ways:

◆ The circuit constitutes the entire length of the connection between the two organizational facilities (such as a branch office and a main office).

◆ The leased line is used for the connection from each location to its local exchange carrier. Connectivity between the two exchange carriers is then provided by some other technology, such as frame relay (discussed in the next section).

The first of these two options creates the more secure connection, but at a much higher cost. Using a private circuit for end-to-end connectivity between two geographically separated sites is the best way to ensure that your data is not monitored. Although it is still possible to sniff one of these circuits, an attacker would need to gain physical access to some point along its path. The attacker would also need to be able to identify the specific circuit to monitor. Telephone carriers are not known for using attacker-friendly labels such as "Bank XYZ's financial data: monitor here."

The second option is simply used to get your signal to the local exchange carrier. From there, data travels over a public network, such as frame relay.

Frame Relay

Frame relay is a *packet-switched* technology. Because data on a packet-switched network can follow any available circuit path, such networks are represented by clouds in graphical presentations such as Figure 4.7.

Frame relay must be configured as a *permanent virtual circuit* (PVCs), meaning that all data entering the cloud at point A is automatically forwarded to point B. These end points are defined at the time the service is leased. For large WAN environments, frame relay can be far more cost effective than dedicated circuits because you can run multiple PVCs through a single WAN connection.

For example, let's say you have four remote sites that require a 56Kb connection to the home office. To construct this network out of dedicated circuits, you would need a 56Kb leased line connection at each of the remote sites, as well as four 56Kb leased line connections running into the main office.

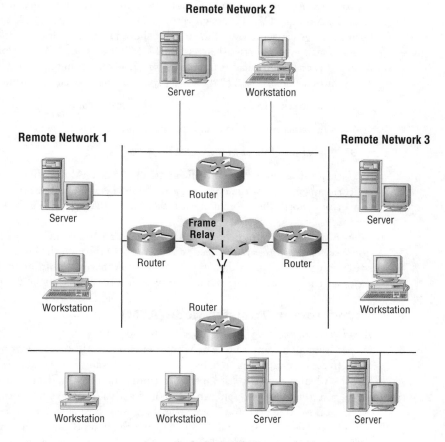

FIGURE 4.7

A WAN frame relay cloud connecting three remote networks to a corporate office

With frame relay, however, you could replace the four dedicated connections at the main office with one fractional T1 connection and simply activate four channels of the T1 circuit to accept the data. By requiring only a single circuit at the main site, you can reduce your WAN costs.

In fact, there is nothing that says the CIR (Committed Information Rate—the rate per second, under normal conditions, that the frame connection can deliver data) at the main office must equal the CIR value of all your remote sites. For example, let's assume that the connections to your remote site are used strictly for transferring e-mail. If bandwidth requirements are low, you might be able to drop the CIR at the main office from 256Kb to 128Kb. As long as the combined traffic to your four remote sites never exceeds 128Kb, you would not even notice a drop in performance. This would reduce your WAN costs even further.

NOTE *The packet-switched network is a shared medium. Your exchange carrier uses the same network for all PVCs it leases out. In effect, you are sharing available bandwidth with every other client.*

Your connection point into the cloud is defined through the use of a *Data Link Connection Identifier* (DLCI). A unique DLCI is assigned to each router that connects to the cloud. The DLCI lets the local exchange carrier know which PVC it should map to your connection.

As long as everyone uses their assigned DLCI, life is good. The problem occurs when someone incorrectly, or with malicious intent, assigns their router the same DLCI as your circuit. This can cause traffic to be diverted to their network. For this to occur, the following conditions must be met:

1. The attacker must be connected to the same local exchange carrier.

2. The attacker must be connected to the same physical switch.

3. The attacker must know your DLCI.

Clearly, this is not the most difficult attack to stage. Although it would be expensive (unless the attacker can gain access to another organization's network and "borrow" that connection), this attack may be well worth the effort if the attacker knows that sensitive information will be passing across the link.

Also, a would-be attacker can actually redirect a PVC to another geographical location. Although doing so would eliminate the need to be connected through the same local carrier and the same switch in order to capture data, the attacker would have to infiltrate the exchange carrier's management system. Although this is not an easy task, it has been done in the past.

Asynchronous Transfer Mode (ATM)

Asynchronous Transfer Mode (ATM) is a point-to-point WAN technology most commonly implemented at speeds ranging from 25 to 622Mbps and beyond. Although ATM was initially very popular as a cost-effective, scalable, and reliable alternative to traditional leased lines, it also has significant vulnerabilities when it comes to user authentication, data integrity, data availability, and data privacy, and it has begun to lose some popularity compared with advancements in other less-expensive technologies. ATM works differently from frame relay because it breaks up data into fixed-size packets known as *cells*. These cells are quite small (53 bytes), which allows them to transmit video, audio, and computer data over the same network, all the while making sure that no single type of data monopolizes the bandwidth.

The cell-based packets of ATM aren't compatible with packet-filtering firewalls, because these firewalls would have to be considered the endpoint of a point-to-point ATM connection. The over-head of *segmentation and reassembly* (SAR) of ATM packets simply wouldn't be efficient. Also, because ATM services can transfer non-IP traffic, there are vulnerabilities not associated with IP traffic (and therefore not covered by traditional IP-based network security mechanisms).

So how would a cracker get access to your ATM data? The first method depends on your transport media. Although most ATM is run on fiber-optic cables, this is not necessarily the cracker-showstopper you would think. Crackers have eavesdropped on fiber-optic by pulling away the insulation and then bending the fiber-optic enough to force some of the light out of the transmission path (but not enough to completely terminate the session and thus alert someone to their actions).

The second method takes advantage of the virtual circuit running on a network: switched (SVC) or permanent (PVC). Most SVC management systems have an Add to Call feature that allows any system to join a session currently in progress. If the SVC administrator has not predefined and closed a session, any person can join in and eavesdrop. PVCs are also vulnerable through their management systems, especially if their interfaces are Telnet- or web-based. On these interfaces, a cracker can take advantage of sniffing passwords (in the case of Telnet) or in exploiting weaknesses in implementation (web-based utilities).

Once a cracker has access to your network (and can create their own PVC or SVC), they can use the Interim Local Management Interface (ILMI) or Private Network-to-Network Interface (PNNI) to change the routing of your ATM network and send the data directly to a system on the Internet they control.

Wireless

Known as *broadband fixed wireless*, WAN solutions are gaining in popularity as speed increases, hardware prices decrease, and reliability concerns prove to be unfounded. Most commercial providers of wireless WAN services include comprehensive data encryption as part of their service, although the level of encryption can vary among providers.

Although designed to be only a LAN wireless solution, the 802.11b standard has become so popular as an inter- and intraoffice solution that many stories abound in the popular media about *whacking*, or wireless hacking. The process involves sensitive but inexpensive directional antennae that are used to locate and exploit wireless hubs physically located inside office buildings, but without encryption or authentication requirements that would keep a cracker from gaining access to the LAN as if they were sitting at a desk inside the building. Adding to the embarrassment was the revelation that the encryption level built into the standard was easily cracked. Vendors are responding to this threat by upgrading their equipment to add strong levels of encryption by default for all wireless communications.

Basic Networking Hardware

These days there is a plethora of networking products to consider when planning your network infrastructure. There are devices for everything from connecting computer systems to the network to extending a topology's specifications to controlling network traffic. Sometimes your choices are limited. For example, to connect an office computer to the network, you must have a network card.

Many of these devices, when used correctly, can also help to improve your network security. In this section, we'll take a look at some common networking hardware and discuss which can be used to reinforce your security posture.

Hubs

Hubs are probably the most common piece of network hardware next to network interface cards. Physically, they are boxes of varying sizes that have multiple female RJ45 connectors. Each connector is designed to accept one twisted-pair cable outfitted with a male RJ45 connector. This twisted-pair cable is then used to connect a single server or workstation to the hub.

Hubs are essentially multiport repeaters that support twisted-pair cables in a star typology. Each node communicates with the hub, which in turn amplifies the signal and transmits it out each of the ports (including back out to the transmitting system). Hubs work at the electrical level.

Almost as popular as wire-only hubs and switches, wireless hubs/switches combine hub and switching functions with a wireless Access Point. Most current popular models also include a dedicated WAN port (for DSL or cable modem connection) and basic firewall, logging, and NAT functions. Several wireless standards exist, from the highly popular 11MB 802.11b standard to its faster, newer cousin, the 54MB 802.11a.

Bridges

Although bridges as distinct pieces of hardware are a relic of the past, their functionality is still retained in today's *switches*. To better understand that functionality, however, it will help to review what bridges *were*. Essentially a bridge was a small box with two network connectors that attached to two separate portions of the network, a bridge incorporated the functionality of a hub (signal amplification), but it actually looked at the frames of data, which was a great benefit.

In our discussion of Ethernet in Chapter 3, we introduced the concept of a data frame and described the information contained within the frame header. Bridges put this header information to use by monitoring the source and destination MAC address in each frame of data. By monitoring the source address, the bridge learns where all the network systems are located. It constructs a table, listing which MAC addresses are directly accessible by each of its ports. It then uses that information to play traffic cop and regulate the flow of data on the network. Let's look at an example.

In the network in Figure 4.8, Betty needs to send data to the server Thoth. Because everyone on the network is required to monitor the network, Betty first listens for the transmissions of other stations. If the wire is free, Betty transmits a frame of data. The bridge is also watching for traffic and will look at the destination address in the header of Betty's frame. Because the bridge is unsure of which port the system with MAC address 00C08BBE0052 (Thoth) is connected to, it amplifies the signal and retransmits it out Port B.

FIGURE 4.8

Betty transmits data to the server Thoth by putting Thoth's MAC address into the destination field of the frame.

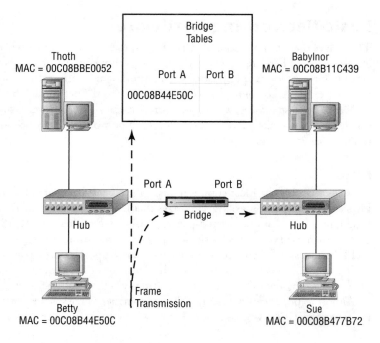

When Thoth replies to Betty's request, as shown in Figure 4.9, the bridge looks at the destination address in the frame of data again. This time, however, it finds a match in its table, noting that Betty is also attached to Port A. Because it knows Betty can receive this information directly, it drops the frame and blocks it from being transmitted from Port B. The bridge also makes a new table entry for Thoth, recording the MAC address as being off Port A.

FIGURE 4.9

Thoth's reply to Betty's message

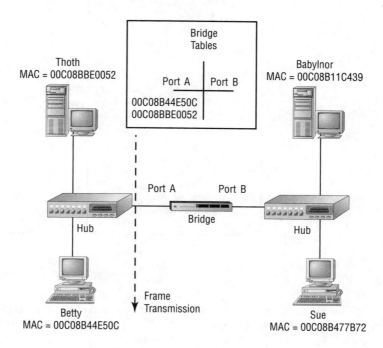

For as long as the bridge remembers each station's MAC address, all communications between Betty and Thoth are isolated from Sue and Babylnor. *Traffic isolation* is a powerful feature; systems on both sides of the bridge can carry on conversations at the same time, effectively doubling the available bandwidth. The bridge ensures that communications on both sides stay isolated, as if they were not even connected. Because stations cannot see transmissions on the other side of the bridge, they assume the network is free and send their data.

Each system needs to contend for bandwidth only with systems on its own segment. There is no way for a station to have a collision outside its segment. Thus, these segments are referred to as *collision domains*, as shown in Figure 4.10. Notice that one port on each side of the bridge is part of each collision domain. This is because each of its ports will contend for bandwidth with the systems to which it is directly connected. Because the bridge isolates traffic within each collision domain, there is no way for separated systems to collide their signals. The effect is a doubling of potential bandwidth.

Also notice that splitting the network into two collision domains has increased the security of the network. For example, let's say that the system named Babylnor becomes compromised. An attacker has gained high-level access to this system and begins capturing network activity in order to look for sensitive information.

FIGURE 4.10

Two separate colli-
sion domains

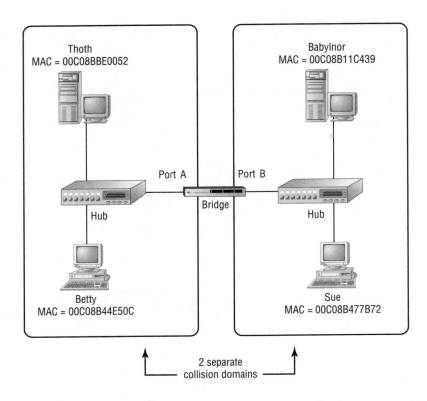

Given the network design, Thoth and Betty can carry on a conversation with relative security. The only traffic that will find its way onto Babylnor's collision domain is broadcast traffic. You may remember from Chapter 3 that a broadcast frame needs to be delivered to all local systems. For this reason, a bridge will also forward broadcast traffic. By using a bridge in this situation, you get a double bonus light. You have not only increased performance, but security as well.

So what happens when traffic needs to traverse the bridge? As mentioned, when a bridge is unsure of the location of a system, it always passes the packet along just in case. Once the bridge learns that the system is in fact located off its other port, it continues to pass the frame along as required.

If Betty begins communicating with Sue, for example, this data crosses the bridge and is transmitted onto the same collision domain as Babylnor. This means that Babylnor can capture this data stream. Although the bridge helped to secure Betty's communications with Thoth, it provides no additional security when Betty begins communicating with Sue.

To secure both of these sessions, you would need a bridge capable of dedicating a single port to each system. This type of functionality is provided in a device referred to as a *switch*.

Switches

Switches embody the marriage of hub and bridge technology. They resemble hubs in appearance, having multiple RJ45 connectors for connecting network systems. Instead of being a dumb amplifier like a hub, however, a switch functions as though it has a little miniature bridge built into each port.

A switch keeps track of the MAC addresses attached to each of its ports and routes traffic destined for a certain address only to the port to which it is attached.

Figure 4.11 shows a switched environment in which each device is connected to a dedicated port. The switch learns the MAC identification of each station once a single frame transmission occurs (identical to a bridge). Assuming that this has already happened, you now find that at exactly the same instant Station 1 needs to send data to Server 1, Station 2 needs to send data to Server 2, and Station 3 needs to send data to Server 3.

FIGURE 4.11

A switch installation showing three work-stations and three servers that need to communicate

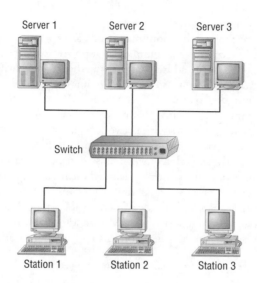

There are some interesting things about this situation. The first is that each wire run involves only the switch and the station attached to it. Each collision domain is limited to only these two devices, because each port of the switch is acting like a bridge. The only traffic seen by the workstations and servers is any frame specifically sent to them or to the broadcast address. As a result, all three stations see little network traffic and can transmit immediately. This is a powerful feature that goes a long way toward increasing potential bandwidth. Given our example, if this is a 10Mbps topology, the effective throughput has just increased by a factor of 3. All three sets of systems can carry on their conversations simultaneously, because the switch isolates them from one another. Although the network is still technically 10Mbps Ethernet, potential throughput has increased to 30Mbps.

Besides increasing performance dramatically, you have also increased security. If any one of these systems becomes compromised, the only sessions that can be monitored are sessions with the compromised system. For example, if an attacker gains access to Server 2, they will not be able to monitor communication sessions with Servers 1 or 3, only Server 2.

Monitoring devices can only collect traffic that is transmitting within their collision domain. Since Server 2's collision domain consists of itself and the switch port it is connected to, the switch does an effective job of isolating System 2 from the communication sessions being held with the other servers. Although this is a wonderful security feature, it does make legitimate monitoring of your network somewhat cumbersome, which is why many switches include a *monitoring port*.

A monitoring port is simply a port on the switch that can be configured to receive a copy of all data transmitted to one or more ports. For example, you can plug your analyzer into port 10 of the switch and configure the device to listen to all traffic on port 3. If port 3 is one of your servers, you can now analyze all traffic flowing to and from this system.

This situation can also be a potential security hole. If an attacker is able to gain administrative access to the switch (through Telnet, HTTP, SNMP, or the console port), they would have free rein to monitor any system connected to, or communicating through, the switch. To return to our example, if the attacker could access Server 2 and the switch itself, they are now in a perfect position to monitor all network communications.

Even without access to the switch's monitoring port, a cracker can still get access to network traffic, if only temporarily. In recent years, a number of sophisticated attacks have been created that force the switch to dump the MAC address table (something that a switch will do on its own if there are a large quantity of network changes in a short amount of time—such as unplugging all the cables and putting them back into different ports). Known as *MAC address poisoning*, the attack involves the cracker sending information to the switch that makes the switch think it has corrupted information in the table associating MAC addresses with network segments.

As a result, the switch *fails open*. It stops filtering network traffic in an attempt to remap which MAC addresses correspond to which network segments, thus allowing the hacker to eavesdrop on all network communication. Of course, once the switch has learned the network, it would normally reenable the switching function, but savvy attackers will continue to confuse the switch by sending false mapping information to the switch, keeping it in a state of perpetual learning. Newer switches include management functions that allow them to report when a MAC address table dump has occurred—an event that can trigger management alarms and alert you to an intruder on your network!

NOTE *Keep in mind that bridges, switches, and similar networking devices are designed primarily to improve network performance, not to improve security. Increased security is just a secondary benefit. These devices have not received the same type of abusive, real-world testing as, say, a firewall or a router product. A switch can augment your security policy, but it should not be the core device to implement it.*

Switching introduces a technology referred to as the *virtual local area network* (VLAN). Software running on the switch allows you to set up connectivity parameters for connected systems by workgroup (referred to as VLAN groups) instead of by geographical location. The switch's administrator is allowed to organize port transmissions logically so that connectivity is grouped according to each user's requirements. The "virtual" part is that these VLAN groups can span multiple physical network segments, as well as multiple switches. For example, by assigning all switch ports that connect to PCs used by accounting personnel to the same VLAN group, you can create a virtual accounting network.

Think of VLANs as being the virtual equivalent of taking an ax to a switch with many ports in order to create multiple switches. If you have a 24-port switch and you divide the ports equally into three separate VLANs, you essentially have three 8-port switches.

Essentially is the key word here, because you still have one physical device. Although this arrangement makes for simpler administration, from a security perspective it is not nearly as good as having three physical switches. If an attacker is able to compromise a switch using VLANs, they might be able to configure their connection to monitor any of the other VLANs on the device.

This situation can be extremely bad if you have one large switch providing connectivity on both sides of a traffic-control device such as a firewall. An attacker may not need to penetrate your firewall; they may find the switch to be a far easier target. At the very least, the attacker now has two potential ways into the network instead of just one.

Routers

A *router* is a multiport device that decides how to handle the contents of a frame, based on protocol and network information. To truly understand what this means, we must first look at what a protocol is and how it works. Until now, we've been happily communicating using the MAC address assigned to our networking devices. Our systems have used this number to contact other systems and transmit information as required.

The problem with this scheme is that it does not scale well. For example, what if you have 2000 systems that need to communicate with one another? You would now have 2000 systems fighting one another for bandwidth on a single Ethernet network. Even if you employ switching, the number of broadcast frames will eventually reach a point where network performance will degrade and you cannot add any more systems. This is where protocols such as IP and IPX come in.

NETWORK PROTOCOLS

At its lowest levels, a *network protocol* is a set of communication rules that provide the means for networking systems to be grouped by geographical area and common wiring. To indicate that it is part of a specific group, each of these systems is assigned an identical protocol network address.

Network addresses are kind of like zip codes. Let's assume someone mails a letter, and the front of the envelope simply reads Fritz & Wren, 7 Spring Road. If this happens in a very small town, the letter will probably get through (as if you'd used a MAC address on a LAN).

If the letter were mailed in a city such as Boston or New York, however, the Post Office would have no clue where to send it (although postal workers would probably get a good laugh). Without a zip code, they may not even attempt delivery. The zip code provides a way to specify the general area where this letter needs to be delivered. The postal worker processing the letter is not required to know exactly where Spring Road is located. They simply look at the zip code and forward the letter to the Post Office responsible for this code. It is up to the local Post Office to know the location of Spring Road and to use this knowledge to deliver the letter.

Protocol network addresses operate in a similar fashion. A protocol-aware device adds the network address of the destination device to the data field of a frame. It also records its own network address, in case the remote system needs to send a reply. This is where a router comes in. A router is a protocol-aware device that maintains a table of all known networks. It uses this table to help forward information to its final destination. Let's walk through an example to see how a routed network operates.

A ROUTED NETWORK EXAMPLE

Let's assume you have a network similar to that shown in Figure 4.12 and that System B needs to transmit information to System F.

FIGURE 4.12

An example of a
routed network

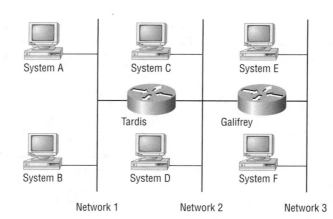

System B begins by comparing its network address to that of System F. If there is a match, System B assumes the system is local and attempts to deliver the information directly. If the network addresses are different (as they are in our example), System B refers to its routing table. If it does not have a specific entry for Network 3, it falls back on its default router, which in this case is Tardis. In order to deliver the information to Tardis, System B ARPs for Tardis's MAC address. System B then adds the network protocol delivery information for System F (the source and destination network numbers) to the data and creates a frame using Tardis's MAC address as the destination. It does this because System B assumes that Tardis will take care of forwarding the information to the destination network.

Once Tardis receives the frame, it performs a CRC check to ensure the integrity of the data. If the frame checks out, Tardis completely strips off the header and trailer. Tardis then analyzes the destination network address listed in the frame (in this case Network 3) to see if it is locally connected to this network. Since Tardis is not directly connected to Network 3, it consults its routing table to find the best route to get there. Tardis then discovers that Galifrey can reach Network 3.

Tardis now ARPs to discover the local MAC address being used by Galifrey. Tardis then creates a new frame around the data packet by creating a header consisting of its MAC address to the source address field and Galifrey's MAC address in the destination field. Finally, Tardis generates a new CRC value for the trailer.

Although all this stripping and re-creating seems like a lot of work, it is a necessary part of this type of communication. Remember that routers are placed at the borders of a network segment. The CRC check is performed to ensure that bad frames are not propagated throughout the network. The header information is stripped away because it is only applicable on Network 1. When Tardis goes to transmit the frame on Network 2, the original source and destination MAC addresses have no meaning. This is why Tardis must replace these values with values that are valid for Network 2.

Because the majority of the header (12 of the 14 bytes) needs to be replaced anyway, it is easier to simply strip the header completely away and create it from scratch. As for stripping off the trailer, once the source and destination MAC addresses change, the original CRC value is no longer valid. This is why the router must strip it off and create a new one.

NOTE   *A data field that contains protocol information is referred to as a* packet. *Although this term is sometimes used interchangeably with the term* frame, *a packet in fact describes only a portion of a frame.*

So Tardis has created a new frame around the packet and is ready to transmit it. Tardis transmits the frame out onto Network 2 so that the frame is received by Galifrey. Galifrey receives the frame and processes it in a similar fashion to Tardis. It checks the CRC and strips off the header and trailer.

Galifrey now repeats the earlier ARP process to find the address of System F. Once it has the MAC address, it builds a new frame around the packet and transmits it on the wire.

PROTOCOL SPECIFICITY

In order for a router to provide this type of functionality, it needs to understand the rules for the protocol being used. A router is *protocol specific*. Unlike a bridge, which will handle any valid topology traffic you throw at it, a router has to be specifically designed to support both the topology and the protocol being used. For example, if your network contains Banyan Vines systems, make sure that your router supports VinesIP.

Routers can be a powerful tool for controlling the flow of traffic on your network. If you have a network segment that is using IPX and IP but only IP is approved for use on the company backbone, simply enable IP support only on your router. The router will ignore any IPX traffic it receives.

A wonderful feature of routers is their ability to block broadcasts. (As we mentioned in Chapter 3, broadcasts are frames that contain all Fs for the destination MAC address.) Because any point on the other side of the router is a new network, these frames are blocked.

NOTE   *A counterpart to this is an* all-networks broadcast *that contains all Fs in both the network and MAC address fields. These frames are used to broadcast to local networks when the network address is not known. Most routers will still block these all-networks broadcasts by default.*

Most routers can also filter out certain traffic. For example, let's say your company enters a partnership with another organization. You need to access services on this new network but do not want to allow your partner to access your servers. To accomplish this, simply install a router between the two networks and configure it to filter out any communication sessions originating from the other organization's network.

Most routers use static packet filtering to control traffic flow. The specifics of how this works will be covered in Chapter 6. For now, just keep in mind that routers cannot provide the same level of traffic control that may be found in the average firewall. Still, if your security requirements are minimal, packet filtering may be a good choice. Chances are you will need a router to connect your networks, anyway.

A Comparison of Bridging/Switching and Routing

Table 4.2 presents a summary of the information discussed in the preceding sections. It provides a quick reference to the differences between controlling traffic at the data link layer (bridges and switches) and controlling traffic at the network layer (routers).

TABLE 4.2: BRIDGING/SWITCHING VERSUS ROUTING	
A BRIDGE (SWITCH):	**A ROUTER:**
Uses the same network address off all ports	Uses different network addresses off all ports
Builds tables based on MAC address	Builds tables based on network layer address
Filters traffic based on MAC information	Filters traffic based on network or host information
Forwards broadcast traffic	Blocks broadcast traffic
Forwards traffic to unknown addresses	Blocks traffic to unknown addresses
Does not modify frame	Creates a new header and trailer
Can forward traffic based on the frame header	Must always queue traffic before forwarding

Layer-3 Switching

Now that you have a clear understanding of the differences between a switch and a router, let's look at a technology that, on the surface, appears to mesh the two. (In fact, we've really talked a lot about this information already, but this is a good review.) The terms *Layer-3 switching*, *switch routing*, and *router switching* are used interchangeably to describe the same devices, and Layer-3 switching has become so popular that even more traditional Layer-2 devices perform the same function.

So what exactly is a switch router? The device is not quite as revolutionary as you might think. In fact, these devices are more an evolution of existing router technology. The association with the word *switch* is more for marketing appeal to emphasize the increase in raw throughput these devices can provide.

These devices typically (but not always) perform the same functions as a standard router. When a frame of data is received, it is buffered into memory, and a CRC check is performed. The topology frame is then stripped off the data packet. Just like a regular router, a switch router references its routing table to determine the best route of delivery, repackages the data packet into a frame, and sends it on its merry way.

How does a switch router differ from a standard router? The answer lies under the hood of the device. Processing is provided by application-specific integrated circuit (ASIC) hardware. With a standard router, all processing was typically performed by a single RISC (Reduced Instruction Set Computer) processor. In a switch router, components are dedicated to performing specific tasks within the routing process. The result is a dramatic increase in throughput.

Keep in mind that the real goal of these devices is to pass information along faster than the standard router. To accomplish this, a vendor may choose to do things slightly differently than the average router implementation in order to increase throughput (after all, raw throughput is everything, right?). For example, a specific vendor implementation might not buffer inbound traffic in order to perform a CRC check on the frame. Once enough of the frame has been read in order to make a routing decision, the device might immediately begin transmitting information out the other end.

From a security perspective, this may not always be a good thing. Certainly performance is a concern—but not at the cost of accidentally passing traffic that should have been blocked. Since the real goal of a switch router is performance, it may not be as nitpicky as the typical router about what it passes along.

Layer-3 switching has some growing up to do before it can be considered a viable replacement for the time-tested router. Most of today's routers can process more than one million packets per second. Typically, higher traffic rates are required only on a network backbone. To date, this is why switches have dominated this area of the network.

Switch routing may make good security sense as a replacement for regular switches, however. The ability to segregate traffic into true subnets instead of just collision domains brings a whole new level of control to this area of the network.

Like their router counterparts, some switch routers support access control lists (ACLs), which allow the network administrator to manipulate which systems can communicate between each of the subnets and what services they can access. This is a much higher level of granular control than is provided with a regular switch. Switch routing can help to fortify the security of your internal network without the typical degradation in performance. If your security requirements are light, a switch router might be just the thing to augment your security policy.

Summary

We've covered a lot of ground in this chapter. We discussed the basics of communication properties and looked at transmission media and hardware from a security perspective. We also discussed what traffic control options are available with typical network hardware.

In the next few chapters, we'll look at systems that are specifically designed to implement security policies. We will start by discussing firewalls and then work our way into intrusion detection systems.

Chapter 5

Firewalls

IN THIS CHAPTER, we'll discuss firewalls and their implementation—especially how they integrate with other network security devices such as an IDS (intrusion detection system) and network management products in general. Although most commercial firewalls provide the same basic services, not all of them implement their features in the same way. Therefore, you should select a firewall based on the security it provides, while ensuring that it is a proper fit for your business requirements.

For example, if the firewall you chose will not support AOL's Instant Messenger and IM is a critical business function, it might have been cheaper to simply buy a pair of wire cutters. Similarly, if your firewall meets your protection requirements, but doesn't integrate with your network management philosophy or tools, this might be enough to force the decision of another platform. Before we discuss firewalls, we'll review the information you need to collect in order to make an informed purchase decision.

Featured in this chapter:

- ◆ Defining an access control policy
- ◆ Understanding firewalls
- ◆ Firewall functions
- ◆ Firewall types
- ◆ Choosing a firewall type
- ◆ Additional firewall considerations
- ◆ Deploying a firewall

Defining an Access Control Policy

During the system analysis phase, you had to define what types of Internet traffic were required to fulfill business functions, as well as other, noncritical but acceptable traffic that is to be permitted. Once you define the type of traffic, you use how and when that traffic should be allowed (known as the *context*) to create your access control policy. An *access control policy* is simply a corporate policy that states which type of access is allowed across an organization's network perimeters. For example, your organization may have a policy that states, "Our internal users can access Internet websites and FTP sites or send SMTP mail, but we will only allow inbound SMTP mail from the Internet to our internal network."

An access control policy can also apply to different areas within an internal network. For example, your organization might have WAN links to supporting business partners or VPNs to allow home or remote workers and offices to connect. In this case, you might want to define a limited scope of access across this link to ensure that it is only used for its intended purpose.

An access control policy simply defines the directions of data flow to and from different parts of the network. It also specifies what type of traffic is acceptable, assuming that all other data types will be blocked. When defining an access control policy, you can use a number of parameters to describe traffic flow. Table 5.1 lists some common descriptors that can be implemented with a firewall.

TIP   *If you don't have an access control policy, you didn't finish your system analysis. An access control policy not only justifies your router, it specifies which resources are allowed to be accessed by which individuals, roles, or organizations. By not creating this policy you risk wasting resources or blocking legitimate network activity.*

TABLE 5.1: ACCESS CONTROL DESCRIPTORS

DESCRIPTOR	DEFINITION
Direction	A description of acceptable traffic flow based on direction. For example, traffic from the Internet to the internal network (inbound) or traffic from the internal network heading toward the Internet (outbound).
Service	The type of server application that will be accessed. For example, Web access (HTTP), File Transfer Protocol (FTP), Simple Mail Transfer Protocol (SMTP).
Specific Host	Sometimes more granularity is required than simply specifying direction. For example, an organization might want to allow inbound HTTP access, but to only a specific computer. Conversely, the organization might have only one business unit to which it wants to grant Internet web server access.
Individual Users	Many organizations have a business need to let certain individuals perform specific activities but do not want to open this type of access to everyone. For example, the company CFO may need to be able to access internal resources from the Internet because they do a lot of traveling. In this case, the device enforcing the access control policy attempts to authenticate anyone trying to gain access, to ensure that only the CFO can get through.
Time of Day	Sometimes an organization wants to restrict access during certain hours of the day. For example, an access control policy might state, "Internal users can access web servers on the Internet only between the hours of 5:00 P.M. and 7:00 A.M."

Continued on next page

TABLE 5.1: ACCESS CONTROL DESCRIPTORS *(continued)*

DESCRIPTOR	DEFINITION
Public or Private	At times it might be beneficial to use a public network (such as frame relay or the Internet) to transmit private data. An access control policy might define that one or more types of information should be encrypted as that information passes between two specific hosts or over entire network segments.
Quality of Service	An organization might want to restrict access based on the amount of available bandwidth. For example, let's assume that an organization has a web server that is accessible from the Internet and wants to ensure that access to this system is always responsive. The organization might have an access control policy that allows internal users to access the Internet at a restricted level of bandwidth when a potential client is currently accessing the web server. When the client is through accessing the server, the internal users would have 100 percent of the bandwidth available to access Internet resources.
Role	Administrators use roles to group individuals with similar access needs. This grouping simplifies the complexity of access control and eases administrative workloads.

Be creative and try to envision what type of access control your organization might require in the future. This will help to ensure that you will not quickly outgrow your firewall solution. A number of organizations have told us that they had zero interest in accessing their local network from the Internet. Many of these same clients came back within six months, looking for an Internet-based remote access solution. Always try to think in scale—not just according to today's requirements.

Definition of a Firewall

A *firewall* (unlike a simple router that merely directs network traffic) is a system or group of systems that enforces an access control policy on network traffic as it passes through access points. Once you determine the levels of connectivity you want to provide, it is the firewall's job to ensure that no additional access beyond this scope is allowed. It is up to your firewall to ensure that your access control policy is followed by all users on the network.

Firewalls are similar to other network devices in that their purpose is to control the flow of traffic. Unlike other network devices, however, a firewall must control this traffic while taking into account that not all the packets of data it sees are what they appear to be. For example, a bridge filters traffic based on the destination MAC (Media Access Control) address. If a host incorrectly labels the destination MAC address and the bridge inadvertently passes the packet to the wrong destination, the bridge is not seen as being faulty or inadequate. It is expected that the host will follow certain network rules, and if it fails to follow these rules, the host is at fault, not the bridge.

A firewall, however, must assume that hosts may try to fool it in order to sneak information past it. A firewall cannot use communication rules as a crutch; rather, it should expect that the rules will *not* be followed. This assumption places a lot of pressure on the firewall design, which must plan for every contingency.

When Is a Firewall Required?

Traditionally, firewalls have been used to control access between the internal network of an organization and the Internet, but as network boundaries have blurred (due to the additional of wireless networks, VPN for remote clients, and extranets) and as malicious code has proliferated, firewalls are increasingly becoming a basic function that is added to every network-capable host. At a minimum, however, there are situations in which firewalls are clearly necessary.

Dial-In Modem Pool and Client-Initiated VPN

A firewall can be used to control access from a dial-in modem pool or a client-initiated VPN (virtual private network). For example, an organization might have an access control policy that specifies that dial-in or VPN users can access only a single e-mail system. The organization does not want to allow access to other internal servers or to the Internet. A firewall can be used to implement this policy.

External Connections to Business Partners

Many organizations have permanent connections to remote business partners. This can create a difficult situation. The connection is required for business, but now someone has access to the internal network from an area where security is not controlled by the organization. A firewall can be used to regulate and document access from these links.

Between Departments

Some organizations (such as trading companies) are required to maintain internal firewalls between different areas of the network. This is to ensure that internal users only have access to the information they require. A firewall at the point of connection between these two networks enforces access control.

Hosts

Because good defense is implemented through a layered approach, software firewall functionality can be added to individual hosts—whether a server or a desktop—even if that host is on a network already protected from the Internet by a firewall. Because of the proliferation of inexpensive software firewall products such as ZoneAlarm, even hosts not necessarily running business-critical applications or hosting critical data can be protected through another line of defense.

NOTE *An explosion in personal software firewalls has mirrored the growth in home broadband (high-speed) Internet connections. Although you can choose from many such products, Zone Alarm has consistently garnered the best reviews for usability as well as comprehensive protection.*

Firewall Functions

Most of today's firewalls employ a combination of functions to protect networks from hostile traffic. The more common ones are the following:

- Static packet filtering

◆ Dynamic packet filtering

◆ Stateful filtering

◆ Proxy

Static Packet Filtering

Static packet filtering controls traffic by using information stored within the packet headers. As packets are received by the filtering device, the attributes of the data stored within the packet headers are compared against the access control policy (referred to as an *access control list* [ACL]). Depending on how this header information compares with the ACL, the traffic is either allowed to pass or dropped.

A static packet filter can use the following information when regulating traffic flow:

◆ Destination IP (Internet Protocol) address or subnet

◆ Source IP address or subnet

◆ Destination service port

◆ Source service port

◆ Flag (TCP only)

THE TCP FLAG FIELD

When the TCP (Transmission Control Protocol) transport is used, static packet filtering can use the flag field in the TCP header when making traffic control decisions. Figure 5.1 shows a packet decode of a TCP/IP (Transmission Control Protocol/Internet Protocol) packet. The Control Bits field identifies which flags have been set. Flags can be either turned on (binary value of 1) or turned off (binary value of 0).

FIGURE 5.1

A TCP/IP packet decode

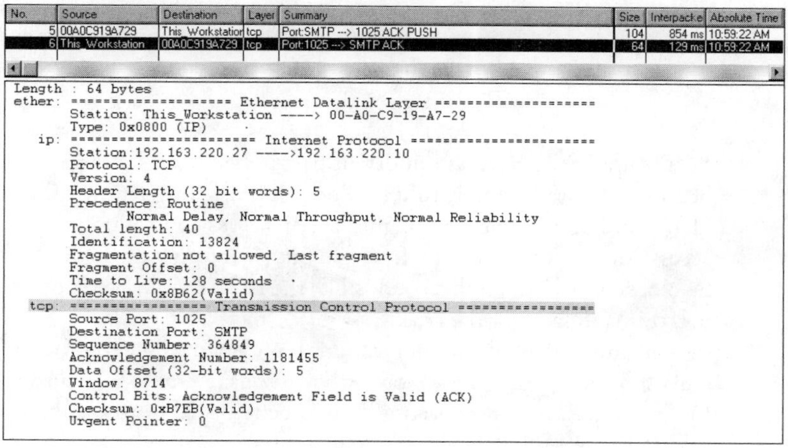

```
No.   Source          Destination      Layer  Summary                      Size  Interpacke  Absolute Time
  5 00A0C919A729    This_Workstation  tcp    Port:SMTP --> 1025 ACK PUSH   104   854 ms  10:59:22 AM
  6 This_Workstation 00A0C919A729    tcp    Port:1025 --> SMTP ACK        64    129 ms  10:59:22 AM

Length : 64 bytes
ether: ==================== Ethernet Datalink Layer ====================
       Station: This_Workstation ----> 00-A0-C9-19-A7-29
       Type: 0x0800 (IP)
   ip: ==================== Internet Protocol ====================
       Station:192.163.220.27 ---->192.163.220.10
       Protocol: TCP
       Version: 4
       Header Length (32 bit words): 5
       Precedence: Routine
             Normal Delay, Normal Throughput, Normal Reliability
       Total length: 40
       Identification: 13824
       Fragmentation not allowed, Last fragment
       Fragment Offset: 0
       Time to Live: 128 seconds
       Checksum: 0x8B62(Valid)
  tcp: ==================== Transmission Control Protocol ====================
       Source Port: 1025
       Destination Port: SMTP
       Sequence Number: 364849
       Acknowledgement Number: 1181455
       Data Offset (32-bit words): 5
       Window: 8714
       Control Bits: Acknowledgement Field is Valid (ACK)
       Checksum: 0xB7EB(Valid)
       Urgent Pointer: 0
```

So what does the flag field tell us? You might remember from our discussion of the TCP three-packet handshake in Chapter 3 that different flag values are used to identify different aspects of a communication session. The flag field gives the recipient hosts some additional information regarding the data the packet is carrying. Table 5.2 lists the valid flags and their uses.

TABLE 5.2: VALID TCP/IP FLAGS

TCP FLAG	DESCRIPTION
ACK (Acknowledgment)	Indicates that this data is a response to a data request and that there is useful information within the Acknowledgment Number field.
FIN (Final)	Indicates that the transmitting system wants to terminate the current session. Typically, each system in a communication session issues a FIN before the connection is actually closed.
PSH (Push)	Prevents the transmitting system from queuing data prior to transmission. In many cases, it is more efficient to let a transmitting system queue small chunks of data prior to transmission so that fewer packets are created. On the receiving side, Push tells the remote system not to queue the data, but to immediately push the information to the upper protocol levels.
RST (Reset)	Resets the state of a current communication session. Reset is used when a non-recoverable transmission failure occurs. It is a transmitting system's way of stating, "Were you listening to me? Do I have to say it again?" This is typically caused by a nonresponsive host or by a spouse enthralled by an afternoon sporting event.
SYN (Synchronize)	Used while initializing a communication session. This flag should not be set during any other portion of the communication process.
URG (Urgent)	Indicates that the transmitting system has some high-priority information to pass along and that there is useful information within the Urgent Pointer field. When a system receives a packet with the Urgent flag set, it processes the information before any other data that is waiting in the queue. This is referred to as processing the data *out-of-band*.

The flag field plays an important part in helping a static packet filter regulate traffic. This is because a firewall is rarely told to block all traffic originating off a specific port or going to a particular host. For example, you might have an access control policy that states, "Our internal users can access any service out on the Internet, but all Internet traffic headed to the internal network should be blocked." Although this sounds like the ACL should be blocking all traffic coming from the Internet, this is in fact not the case.

Remember that all communications represent a two-step process. When you access a website, you make a data request (step 1) to which the website replies by returning the data you requested (step 2). During step 2, you are expecting data to be returned from the Internet-based host to the internal system. If the second half of our statement were taken verbatim ("...all Internet traffic headed to the internal network should be blocked."), our replies would never make it back to the requesting host. We are back to the "wire cutters as an effective security device" model: our firewall would not allow a complete communication session.

FIN SCANNERS

Because a simple packet filter can block port scans, some people decided to become creative. The simple port scanner eventually evolved into the *FIN scanner*. A FIN scanner operates under a similar principle to the port scanner, except that the transmitted packets have FIN=1, ACK=1, and all other flags set to 0.

Now, since our packet filter is only looking to block packets that have SYN=1 and all other flags set to 0, these packets are happily passed along. The result is that an attacker can analyze the returning data stream to determine which hosts are offering what services. If the destination host returns an ACK=1, RST=1 (a generic system response for nonexistent services), the software knows that this is an unused port. If, however, the destination host returns an ACK=1, FIN=1 (the service is agreeing to close the connect), the FIN scanner knows that a service is monitoring that port. Our packet filter is unable to deter these scanning probes.

In addition, FIN scanning can be used to identify the operating system of the remote machine (which can then be used by a cracker to design a custom attack tuned toward the vulnerability of that machine). This is possible because most vendors implement TCP/IP a little differently, resulting in a unique "fingerprint."

This is where our flag field comes into play. Remember that during the TCP three-packet handshake, the originating system issues a packet with SYN=1 and all other flags equal to 0. The only time this sequence is true is when one system wants to establish a connection to another. A packet filter will use this unique flag setting to control TCP sessions. By blocking the initial connection request, a data session between the two systems cannot be established.

So to make our access control policy more technically correct, we would state, "All Internet traffic headed to the internal network with SYN=1 and all other flags equal to 0 should be blocked." Any other flag sequence is assumed to be part of a previously established connection and would be allowed to pass through.

This is clearly not the most secure way to lock down your network perimeter. By playing with the flag values, a would-be attacker can fool a static packet filter into allowing malicious traffic through. In this way, these predators stay one step ahead of these security devices.

For example, software programs called *port scanners* can probe a destination host to see if any service ports are open. The port scanner sends a connection request (SYN=1) to all the service ports within a specified range. If any of these connection requests causes the destination host to return a connection request acknowledgment (SYN=1, ACK=1), the software knows that a service is monitoring that port.

PACKET FILTERING UDP TRAFFIC

As if TCP traffic were not hard enough to control, UDP (User Datagram Protocol) traffic is actually worse. UDP provides even less information regarding a connection's state than TCP does. Figure 5.2 shows a packet decode of a UDP header.

Notice that our UDP header does not use flags to indicate a session's state. Thus, there is no way to determine if a packet is a data request or a reply to a previous request. The only information that can be used to regulate traffic is the source and destination port numbers. Even this information is of little use in many situations, because some services use the same source and destination port number.

FIGURE 5.2

A UDP header decode

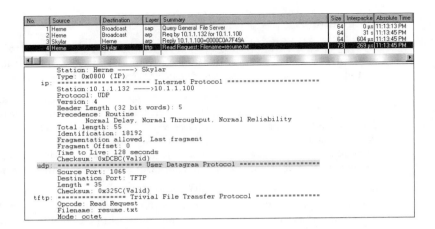

```
No.   Source      Destination  Layer  Summary                                    Size  Interpacke  Absolute Time
   1  Herne       Broadcast    sap    Query General File Server                   64   0 µs        11:13:13 PM
   2  Herne       Broadcast    arp    Req by 10.1.1.132 for 10.1.1.100            64   31 s        11:13:45 PM
   3  Skylar      Herne        arp    Reply 10.1.1.100=0000C0A7F49A               64   604 µs      11:13:45 PM
   4  Herne       Skylar       tftp   Read Request: Filename=resume.txt           73   269 µs      11:13:45 PM

         Station: Herne ----> Skylar
         Type: 0x0800 (IP)
    ip:  ====================== Internet Protocol ======================
         Station:10.1.1.132 ---->10.1.1.100
         Protocol: UDP
         Version: 4
         Header Length (32 bit words): 5
         Precedence: Routine
               Normal Delay, Normal Throughput, Normal Reliability
         Total length: 55
         Identification: 18192
         Fragmentation allowed, Last fragment
         Fragment Offset: 0
         Time to Live: 128 seconds
         Checksum: 0xDCBC(Valid)
   udp:  ====================== User Datagram Protocol ==================
         Source Port: 1065
         Destination Port: TFTP
         Length = 35
         Checksum: 0x325C(Valid)
  tftp:  ================= Trivial File Transfer Protocol ================
         Opcode: Read Request
         Filename: resume.txt
         Mode: octet
```

For example, when two Domain Name Servers (DNSs) are exchanging information, they use a source and destination port number of 53. Unlike many other services, they do not use a reply port of greater than 1023. Thus, a static packet filter has no effective means of limiting DNS traffic to only a single direction. You cannot block inbound traffic to port 53, because that would block data replies as well as data requests.

This is why, in many cases, the only effective way to control UDP traffic with a static packet filter is either to block the port or to let it through and hope for the best. Most people tend to stick with the former solution, unless they have an extremely pressing need to allow UDP traffic through (such as running networked Quake games, which use UDP port 26000).

PACKET FILTERING ICMP

The *Internet Control Message Protocol* (ICMP) provides background support for the IP protocol. It is not used to transmit user data, but is used for maintenance duty to ensure that all is running smoothly. For example, ping uses ICMP to ensure connectivity between two hosts. Figure 5.3 shows a packet decode of an ICMP header.

ICMP does not use service ports. A Type field identifies the ICMP packet type, and a Code field provides even more granular information about the current session. The Code field can be a bit confusing. For example, in Figure 5.3 the code states `Protocol Unreachable; Host Unreachable`. This could lead you to think that the destination system is not responding. If you compare the source IP address for this ICMP packet to the destination IP address in the section after `Original IP Packet Header`, you will notice that they are the same (`10.1.1.100`). So if the destination was in fact "unreachable," how could it have possibly sent this reply?

The combination of these two codes actually means that the requested service was not available. If you look at the top of Figure 5.3, you can see that the transmission that prompted this reply was a Trivial File Transfer Protocol (TFTP) request for `resume.txt`. Only a destination host will generate a protocol unreachable error. Table 5.3 identifies the Type field values for ICMP packets.

NOTE *Remember that UDP does not use a flag field. Thus, UDP is incapable of letting the transmitting system know that a service is not available. To rectify this problem, ICMP is used to notify the transmitting system.*

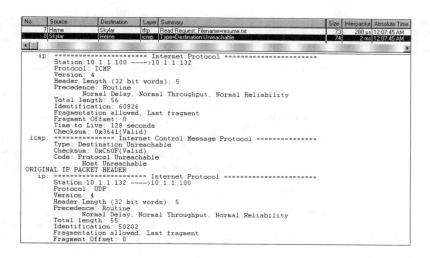

FIGURE 5.3

An ICMP header

TABLE 5.3: THE ICMP TYPE FIELD VALUES

TYPE	NAME	DESCRIPTION
0	Echo Reply	Responds to an echo request.
3	Destination Unreachable	Indicates that the destination subnet, host, or service cannot be reached.
4	Source Quench	Indicates that the receiving system or a routing device along the route is having trouble keeping up with the inbound data flow. Hosts that receive a Source Quench are required to reduce their transmission rate. This is to ensure that the receiving system will not begin to discard data due to an overload inbound queue.
5	Redirect	Informs a local host that another router or gateway device is better able to forward the data the host is transmitting. A Redirect is sent by local routers.
8	Echo	Requests that the target system return an echo reply. Echo is used to verify end-to-end connectivity as well as measure response time.
9	Router Advertisement	Used by routers to identify themselves on a subnet. This is not a true routing protocol, because no route information is conveyed. It is simply used to let hosts on the subnet know the IP addresses of their local routers.
10	Router Selection	Allows a host to query for router advertisements without having to wait for the next periodic update. Also referred to as a *router solicitation*.
11	Time Exceeded	Informs the transmitting systems that the time to live (TTL) value within the packet header has expired and the information never reached its intended host.
12	Parameter Problem	Is a catchall response returned to a transmitting system when a problem occurs that is not identified by one of the other ICMP types.

Continued on next page

TABLE 5.3: THE ICMP TYPE FIELD VALUES *(continued)*

TYPE	NAME	DESCRIPTION
13	Timestamp	Used when you are looking to quantify link speed more than system responsiveness. Timestamp is similar to an Echo request, except that a quick reply to a Timestamp request is considered more critical.
14	Timestamp Reply	Is a response to a Timestamp request.
15	Information Request	Has been superseded by the use of bootp and DHCP (Dynamic Host Configuration Protocol). This request was originally used by self-configuring systems in order to discover their IP address.
16	Information Reply	Is a response to an information request.
17	Address Mask Request	Allows a system to dynamically query the local subnet as to what is the proper subnet mask to be used. If no response is received, a host should assume a subnet mask appropriate to its address class.
18	Address Mask Reply	Is a response to an address mask request.
30	Traceroute	Provides a more efficient means of tracing a route from one IP host to another than using the legacy Traceroute command. This option can only be used when all intermediary routers have been programmed to recognize this ICMP type. Implementation is via a switch setting using the ping command.

Table 5.4 identifies valid codes that can be used when the ICMP type is Destination Unreachable (Type=3).

TABLE 5.4: THE ICMP TYPE 3 CODE FIELD VALUES

CODE	NAME	DESCRIPTION
0	Net Unreachable	The destination network cannot be reached due to a routing error (such as no route information) or an insufficient TTL value.
1	Host Unreachable	The destination host cannot be reached due to a routing error (such as no route information) or an insufficient TTL value.
2	Protocol Unreachable	The destination host you contacted does not offer the service you requested. This code is typically returned from a host; all others are returned from routers along the path.
3	Port Unreachable	The service that normally binds to this port is not active.
4	Fragmentation Needed and Don't Fragment Was Set	The data you are attempting to deliver needs to cross a network that uses a smaller packet size, but the Don't Fragment bit is set.
5	Source Route Failed	The transmitted packet specified the route that should be followed to the destination host, but the routing information was incorrect.

Table 5.5 identifies some of the valid codes that can be used when the ICMP type is redirect (Type=5).

TABLE 5.5: THE ICMP TYPE 5 CODE FIELD VALUES

CODE	NAME	DESCRIPTION
0	Redirect Datagram for the Network (or Subnet)	Indicates that another router on the local subnet has a better route to the destination subnet.
1	Redirect Datagram for the Host	Indicates that another router on the local subnet has a better route to the destination host.

Employing filtering on the values of the Type and the Code fields, we have a bit more granular control than simply looking at source and destination IP addresses. Not all packet filters can filter on all Types and Codes. For example, many will filter out Type=3, which is Destination Unreachable, without regard to the Code value. This limitation can cause some serious communication problems.

Let's assume you have a network configuration similar to the one shown in Figure 5.4. Your local network uses a Token Ring topology, and your remote business partner uses Ethernet. You want to give your business partner access to your local web server in order to receive the latest product updates and development information.

FIGURE 5.4

Problems blocking destination unreachable messages

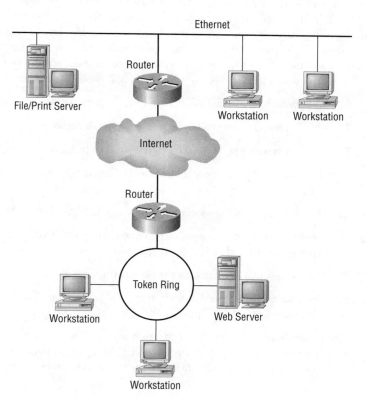

Now, let's also assume that your router is blocking inbound ICMP Destination Unreachable messages. You have done this in an effort to block Denial of Service (DoS) attacks by preventing external attackers from sending false Host Unreachable (Type=3, Code=1) messages. Since your router has limited packet-filtering ability, you must block all ICMP Type=3 traffic.

This situation can present you with some problems, however. When your business partner's employees try to access your local web server, they may not be able to view any HTML pages. This problem has the following symptoms and can be quite confusing:

◆ The browser on the workstation located on the Ethernet segment appears to resolve the destination host name to an IP address.

◆ The browser appears to connect to the destination web server.

◆ If either router provides session logging, traffic appears to flow between the two systems.

◆ The log on the local web server indicates that the workstation is connected to the web server and that a number of files were returned.

So what has gone wrong? Unfortunately, by blocking all Type=3 traffic you have blocked the Fragmentation Needed (Type=3, Code=4) error messages, as well. This prevents the router from adjusting the *maximum transmission unit* (MTU) of the traffic being delivered.

MTU describes the maximum payload size that can be delivered by a packet of data. In an Ethernet environment, the MTU is 1.5Kb. In a Token Ring environment, the MTU can be as large as 16Kb. When a router receives packets that are too large for a destination network, it sends a request to the transmitting system, asking it to break the data into smaller chunks (ICMP Type=3, Code=4). If the router tries to fragment this data itself, it might run into queuing problems if its buffers become full. For this reason, it is easier to have the remote system send smaller packets.

So if you watch the flow of data in Figure 5.4, you see the following:

1. An Ethernet workstation forms an HTML data request.

2. This request is delivered to the destination web server.

3. The two systems perform a TCP three-packet handshake using 64-byte packets.

4. Once the handshake is complete, the web server responds to the data request using a 16Kb MTU.

5. This reply reaches the router on the remote Ethernet network.

6. The Ethernet router issues a fragmentation request (IMCP Type=3, Code=4) back to the web server, asking that it use a 1.5Kb MTU.

7. The request makes it back to the border router at the Token Ring network.

8. This router checks its ACL, determines that it is supposed to drop all Destination Unreachable messages (ICMP Type=3), and drops the packet.

The fragmentation request never makes it back to your local network, and your remote business partner is unable to view your web pages. When using static packet filtering, always make sure that you fully understand the ramifications of the traffic you are blocking or allowing to pass through.

STATIC PACKET FILTERING SUMMARY

Static packet filters are nonintelligent filtering devices. They offer little protection against advanced types of attack. They look at a minimal amount of information in order to determine which traffic should be allowed to pass and which traffic should be blocked. Many routers can perform static packet filtering.

Dynamic Packet Filtering

Dynamic packet filtering takes static packet filtering one step further by maintaining a connection table in order to monitor the state of a communication session. It does not simply rely on the flag settings. This is a powerful feature that can be used to better control traffic flow.

For example, let's assume that an attacker sends your system a packet of data with a payload designed to crash your system. The attacker might perform some packet trickery in order to make this packet look like a reply to information requested by the internal system. A regular packet filter analyzes this packet, sees that the ACK bit is set, and is fooled into thinking that this is a reply to a data request. It then happily passes the information along to the internal system.

A dynamic packet filter would not be so easily fooled. When the information is received, the dynamic packet filter references its connection table (sometimes referred to as a *state table*). When reviewing the table entries, the dynamic packet filter realizes that the internal system never actually connected to this external system to place a data request. Since this information has not been explicitly requested, the dynamic packet filter throws the packet in the bit bucket.

DYNAMIC PACKET FILTERING IN ACTION

Let's take a look at how dynamic packet filtering works, in order to get a better idea of the increased security it can provide. In Figure 5.5, you can see two separate network configurations: in one the internal host is protected by a static packet filter, and in the other a dynamic packet filter is used.

FIGURE 5.5

The differences between static and dynamic packet filtering

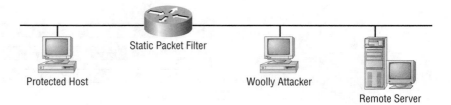

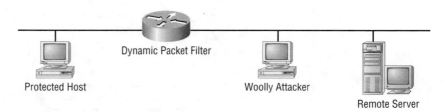

Now, let's look at some access rules to see how each of these two firewall devices handles traffic control. The ACL on both firewalls might look something like this:

- Allow the protected host to establish any service sessions with the remote server.

- Allow any session that has already been established to pass.

- Drop all other traffic.

The first rule allows the protected host to establish connections to the remote server. The only time a packet with the SYN bit set is allowed to pass is if the source address is from the protected host and the destination is the remote server. When this is true, any service on the remote server can be accessed.

The second rule is a catchall. Basically it says, "If the traffic appears to be part of a previously established connection, let it pass." In other words, all traffic is OK—provided that the SYN bit is not set and all other bits are off.

The third rule states that if any traffic does not fit neatly into one of the first two rules, drop it just to be safe.

Both of our firewall devices use the same ACL. The difference is in the amount of information each has available in order to control traffic. Let's transmit some traffic to see what happens.

In Figure 5.6, the internal system tries to set up a communication session with the remote server. Since all traffic passes the criteria set up in the access control lists, both firewalls allow this traffic to pass.

FIGURE 5.6

Connection establishment from the protected host

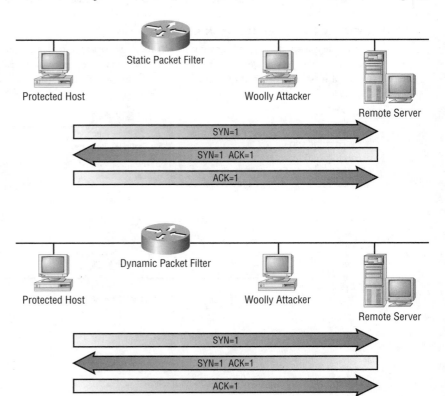

Once the handshake is complete, our protected host makes a data request. This packet has the ACK bit set, and possibly the PSH bit. When the remote server receives this request, it also responds with the ACK bit set and possibly the PSH bit, as well. Once the data transfer is complete, the session closes, each system transmitting a packet with the FIN bit set.

Figure 5.7 shows this established session passing data. Notice that we have no problems passing our firewall devices because of our second rule: "Allow any session that has already been established to pass." Each firewall is making this determination in a slightly different way, however.

Our static packet filter is simply looking at the flag field to see if the SYN bit is the only bit set. Since this is not true, the static packet filter assumes that this data is part of an established session and lets it pass through.

FIGURE 5.7

An established session between the two hosts

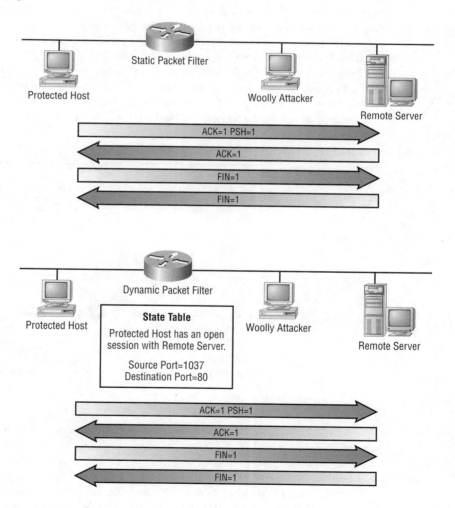

Our dynamic packet filter is doing the same check, but it also created a state table entry when the connection was first established. Every time the remote server tries to respond to the protected host, the state table is referenced to ensure the following:

◆ The protected host actually made a data request.

◆ The source port information matches the data request.

◆ The destination port information matches the data request.

In addition, the dynamic packet filter might even verify that the sequence and acknowledgment numbers match. If all this data is correct, the dynamic packet filter also allows the packets to pass. Once the FIN packets are sent by each system, the state table entry is removed. Additionally, if no reply is received for a period of time (anywhere from one minute to one hour, depending on the configuration), the firewall assumes that the remote server is no longer responding and again deletes the state table entry. This keeps the state table current.

Now let's say that Woolly Attacker notices this data stream and decides to attack the protected host. The first thing he tries is a port scan on the protected system to see if it has any listening services. As you can see in Figure 5.8, this scan is blocked by both firewall devices, because the initial scanning packets have the SYN bit set and all other bits turned off.

FIGURE 5.8

Both filtering methods can block a port scan.

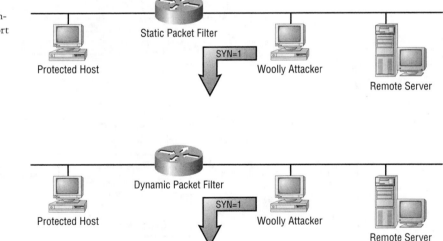

Not to be put off, Woolly Attacker attempts to perform a FIN scan by transmitting packets with the ACK and FIN bits set to 1. Now the results are a bit different. Since the packet filter is simply looking for the SYN bit being set to 1, it happily passes this traffic along, because this condition has not been met.

Our dynamic packet filter, however, is a bit more fussy. It recognizes that the SYN bit is not set and proceeds to compare this traffic with the state table. At this point, it realizes that our protected host has never set up a communication session with Woolly Attacker. There is no legitimate reason that Woolly Attacker should be trying to end a session if our protected host never created one in the first place. For this reason, the traffic is blocked, as shown in Figure 5.9.

FIGURE 5.9

The effects of performing a FIN scan

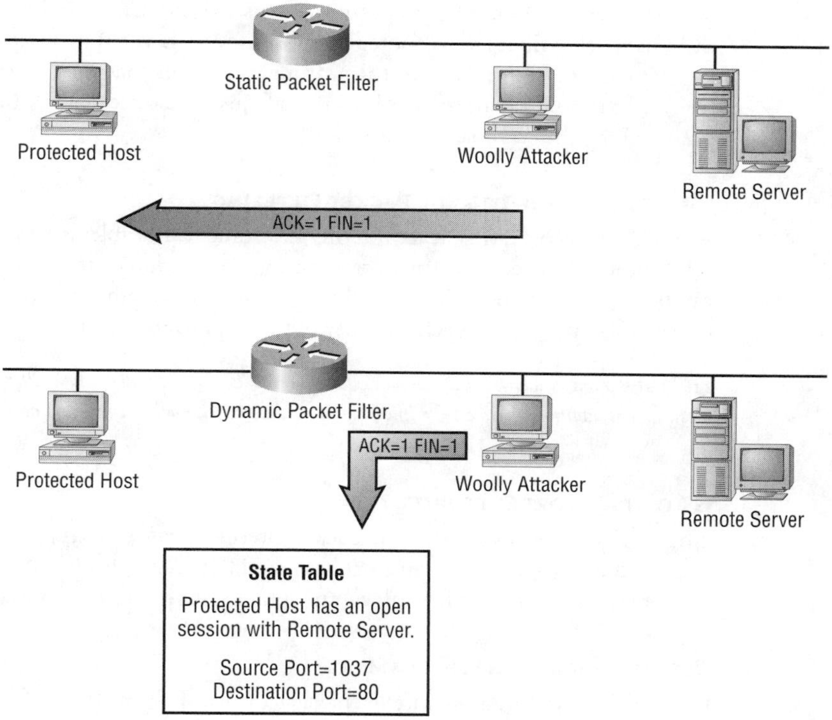

So what if Woolly Attacker tries to spoof the firewall by pretending to be the remote server? In order for him to perform this attack successfully, a number of conditions have to be met:

◆ Woolly Attacker has to spoof or assume the IP address of the remote server.

◆ If the address has been assumed, Woolly Attacker might have to take further measures to ensure that the remote server cannot respond to requests on its own.

◆ If the address has been spoofed, Woolly Attacker needs some way to read replies off the wire.

◆ Woolly Attacker needs to know the source and destination service ports being used so that his traffic will match the entries in the state table.

◆ Depending on the implementation, the acknowledgment and sequence numbers might have to match, as well.

◆ Woolly Attacker has to manipulate the communication session fast enough to avoid timeouts, both on the firewall and on the protected host.

So although it is possible to launch this type of attack, it is not easy to succeed. Clearly, Woolly Attacker would have to be very knowledgeable and feel that he has much to gain by going to all this effort.

Keep in mind that this discussion is theory only. Your actual mileage with a specific firewall product may vary. For example, at the time of this writing, Check Point's FireWall-1 product (which is a dynamic packet filter) has a touted feature that allows the state table to be maintained even after a rule set change. Unfortunately, this feature also means that state is not always maintained as effectively as it should be. In the FIN scan attack just described, Check Point's FireWall-1 would have passed along the scan packets, as well.

UDP Traffic and Dynamic Packet Filtering

As you have seen, static packet filtering has some real problems handling UDP traffic because the UDP header has zero information regarding connection state. This is where dynamic packet filtering can be extremely useful; the firewall itself is able to remember state information. It does not rely on information within the packet header but maintains its own tables regarding the state of all sessions.

TIP *It is strongly advised that dynamic packet filtering be used instead of static filtering when UDP traffic must be allowed through. The addition of state table information makes this firewall method far more secure with no loss in service.*

Is My Transport Supported?

The implementation of dynamic packet filtering is *transport specific*: it has to be specifically implemented for each protocol transport, such as TCP, UDP, and ICMP. When choosing a dynamic packet filter, make sure that the firewall can maintain state for all transports that you want to use.

Dynamic Packet Filter Summary

Dynamic packet filters are intelligent devices that make traffic-control decisions based on packet attributes and state tables. State tables enable the firewall device to "remember" previous communication packet exchanges and make judgments based on this additional information.

The biggest limitation of a dynamic packet filter is that it cannot make filtering decisions based on payload, which is the actual data contained within the packet. In order to filter on payload, you must use a proxy-based firewall.

Stateful Filtering

Stateful filtering improves on the power of dynamic packet filtering. First implemented by Check Point under the name Stateful Multilevel Inspection, stateful rules are protocol-specific, keeping track of the context of a session (not just its state). This allows filtering rules to differentiate between the various connectionless protocols (such as UDP, NFS [Network File System], and RPC [remote procedure call]), which—because of their connectionless nature—were previously immune to management by static filtering and were not uniquely identified by dynamic filtering.

The greatest addition that stateful filtering provides to dynamic filtering is the ability to maintain application state, not just connection state. Application state allows a previously authenticated user to create new connections without reauthorizing, whereas connection state just maintains that authorization for the duration of a single session.

An example of this is a firewall that allows internal access based on per-user authentication. If an authenticated user attempts to open another browser, a dynamic filtering router prompts the user for their password. Stateful filtering, however, recognizes that a preexisting (and concurrent) connection is being maintained with that same machine and automatically authorizes the additional session.

Proxy Servers

A *proxy server* (sometimes referred to as an *application gateway* or *forwarder*) is an application that mediates traffic between two network segments. Proxies are often used instead of filtering to prevent traffic from passing directly between networks. With the proxy acting as mediator, the source and destination systems never actually "connect." The proxy plays middleman in all connection attempts.

HOW A PROXY PASSES TRAFFIC

Unlike its packet-filtering counterparts, a proxy does not route any traffic. In fact, a properly configured proxy has all routing functionality disabled. As its name implies, the proxy stands in or speaks for each system on each side of the firewall.

For an analogy, think of two people speaking through a language interpreter. Although it is true that these two people are carrying on a conversation, they never actually speak to each other. All communication passes through the interpreter before being passed on to the other party. The interpreter might have to clean up some of the language used or filter out comments or statements that might seem hostile.

To see how this relates to network communications, see Figure 5.10. Our internal host wants to request a web page from the remote server. It formulates the request and transmits the information to the gateway leading to the remote network, which in this case is the proxy server.

Once the proxy receives the request, it identifies what type of service the internal host is trying to access. Since in this case the host has requested a web page, the proxy passes the request to a special application used only for processing HTTP sessions. This application is simply a program running in memory that has the sole function of dealing with HTTP communications.

FIGURE 5.10

A proxy mediating a communication session

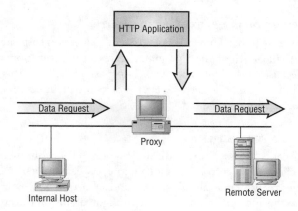

When the HTTP application receives the request, it verifies that the ACL allows this type of traffic. If the traffic is acceptable, the proxy formulates a new request to the remote server—only it uses itself as the source system. In other words, the proxy does not simply pass the request along; it generates a new request for the remote information.

This new request is then sent to the remote server. If the request were checked with a network analyzer, it would look like the proxy had made the HTTP request, not the internal host. For this reason, it responds to the proxy server when the remote server responds.

Once the proxy server receives the reply, it again passes the response up to the HTTP application. The HTTP application then scrutinizes the actual data sent by the remote server for abnormalities. If the data is acceptable, the HTTP application creates a new packet and forwards the information to the internal host.

As you can see, the two end systems never actually exchange information directly. The proxy constantly butts into the conversation to make sure that all goes securely.

NOTE   *Cisco has recently extended its packet filtering with NBAR (Network-Based Application Recognition), which can look at the first 400 bytes of a packet in an attempt to recognize the code fingerprints of known web server exploits (such as Code Red). Although similar in intent to application proxy filtering, NBAR doesn't actually proxy the session.*

Since proxies must "understand" the application protocol being utilized, they can also implement protocol-specific security. For example, you can configure an inbound FTP proxy to filter out all put and mput requests received by an external system. For example, you can create a read-only FTP server: people outside the firewall would be unable to send the FTP server the commands required to write a file. They could, however, perform a request for files, which would allow them to receive files from the FTP server.

TIP   *Proxy servers are application specific. In order to support a new protocol via a proxy, a proxy must be developed for that protocol. If you select a proxy firewall, be sure that it supports all the applications you want to use.*

There are stripped-down proxies know as *plug gateways*. These are not true proxies because they do not understand the application they are supporting. Plug gateways simply provide connectivity for a specific service port and offer little benefit beyond dynamic filtering.

CLIENT CONFIGURATION IN A PROXY ENVIRONMENT

Early proxy servers require all internal hosts to run connection software such as SOCKS or a modified winsock.dll file. Each of these programs serves a single function: to forward all nonlocal traffic to the proxy. Because of the high maintenance cost associated with this kind of proxy, not to mention the inflexibility for mobile clients, newer proxies usually function transparently. No special client configuration or software is required.

THE BENEFITS OF A PROXY CLIENT

A number of benefits are associated with running proxy client software. The first is ease of configuration. Since the client is designed to forward all nonlocal data requests to the proxy, the only required configuration information is a valid IP address and subnet mask. Router and DNS parameters can be ignored, because this information needs to be configured only on the proxy.

Proxy clients can also provide transparent authentication in order to validate outbound connection attempts based on logon name and password. For example, Novell's BorderManager integrates with eDirectory (similar to Microsoft's Active Directory) to transparently authenticate users as they access the Internet. As long as a user is authenticated to eDirectory, that user is not prompted for a password when accessing Internet resources.

NOTE *User authentication of outbound sessions is used for increased logging and management. If authentication is not used, a firewall must rely on the source IP address to identify who has accessed which Internet resources. This can be a problem; all a user has to do to change their identity is change their IP address. This can be a serious problem in a DHCP or bootp environment if you want to track all your users.*

THE LIABILITIES OF A PROXY CLIENT

Unfortunately, a number of liabilities are associated with using a proxy client. The first is deployment. If you have 1,000 machines that will need to use the proxy server, plan to load additional software on each of these machines. Software compatibility might also be a problem; some applications might not be compatible with the replacement winsock.dll file. For example, many Winsock replacements are still written to the 1.*x* specification, although there are now applications that require Winsock 2.*x*.

And what if many of your desktop machines do not run Windows? Many proxies do not provide client software for any operating system other than Windows. In this case, you have to be sure that all IP applications you want to use are SOCKS compliant. Although there are SOCKS versions of many IP applications such as Telnet and FTP, it's all too often the case that a favorite application is not SOCKS compliant.

Client software can also be a problem for mobile or laptop users. For example, let's say you are a laptop user who connects to the local network during the day and dials in to your Internet Service Provider (ISP) in the evening. In this case, you have to make sure that your proxy client is enabled during the day, but disabled at night. Not exactly the type of procedure you'd want to have your pointy-haired boss performing on a daily basis.

Finally, a proxy client can be a real problem if you have multiple network segments. The proxy client expects to forward all nonlocal traffic to the proxy server—not a good solution if you have a large network environment with many subnets. Although some configurations do allow you to exempt certain subnets from being forwarded to the proxy, this typically involves modifying a text file stored on the local workstation. Again, if you administer 1,000 desktop machines, plan on putting in quite a few long nights just to update all your desktop machines regarding a subnet address change.

TRANSPARENT PROXIES

Not all proxies require special client software. Some can operate as a *transparent proxy*, which means that all internal hosts are configured as though the proxy were a regular router leading to the Internet. As the proxy receives traffic, it processes the traffic in a fashion similar to our example in Figure 5.10.

If you decide that a proxy firewall is the best fit for your security requirements, make sure you also decide whether you want to use a transparent or a nontransparent proxy. The marketing material for many proxy packages can be a bit vague about whether the package requires special client software.

Typically, if a product claims to support SOCKS, it is not a transparent proxy. Make sure you know the requirements before investing in a firewall solution.

FILTERING HOSTILE CODE

As you have seen, proxies can analyze the payload of a packet of data and make decisions as to whether this packet should be passed or dropped. This is a powerful feature, one that gives the administrator far more ability to scrutinize what type of data should be allowed into the network. When it comes to content filtering, the first thing most security professionals think about isn't pornography; it's VBScript

VBScript is Microsoft's scripting language that is based on Visual Basic. Primarily used to create dynamic web pages and to create macros that add functionality to Microsoft's Office suite (Word, Excel, and so on), VBScript has been one of the primary vectors for hostile code in the past few years. The infamous "I Love You" worm sent copies of itself as an attachment to everyone listed in the infected system's address book. Those individuals promptly clicked the attachment in Outlook or Outlook Express (both VBScript-enabled programs), activating the script and repeating the cycle.

Other executable code is also considered dangerous, especially code that is attached to a file with an innocuous extension such as `.wav`. The Nimda virus, which comes as an attachment that is described in it's MIME (Multipurpose Internet Mail Extension) type as being a .WAV file (even though the actual extension is `.exe`). Because the default action for most Windows installations is to activate incoming `.wav` attachments, the `.exe` file is executed and infects the computer. Because of this vulnerability creators of hostile code routinely attempt to disguise the true nature of their attack. Deciding what types of files are truly benign can become quite difficult, but usually the attitude of "better safe than sorry" is the guiding principle behind firewall filtering.

NOTE   Multimedia infrastructure increasingly supports scripted capabilities in the files and the software players that display them. Microsoft's Windows Media Player (WMP), for instance, relies on scripting to maintain synchronization between certain types of video and audio tracks and also to update the appearance of the Player through the use of "skins." One reported problem occurs when a user receives an HTML-based e-mail message with an attachment that is defined by the MIME type as being a WMP skin, but in reality is an executable file. Because WMP is not affected by the security settings of Outlook, Outlook Express, and Internet Explorer, restricting how attachments are activated in any of those programs will not alter the behavior of WMP, which will execute any type of file with a multimedia MIME type

Considering the threat that hostile code can have on your network, what are the available solutions? Many proxy firewalls provide the ability to filter out some or all of various programming code. This allows users to continue accessing remote websites without fear of running a malicious application.

NOTE   Enabling these features blocks both good and bad code, without distinguishing between the two. In other words, your choices are all or nothing. There are, however, proxies that can selectively filter out only "known to be malicious" programming code. Although this allows some executable code to be passed through the proxy, it does so at a reduced level of security. These proxies can only filter out known problems; they cannot help with exploits that have yet to be discovered. Unless you stay on top of the latest exploits, you can still end up letting some malicious code past your firewall.

Firewall Types

Although most firewalls implement the functions described earlier, the actual implementation or firewall type is spread across four areas:

◆ Embedded

◆ Software

◆ Hardware

◆ Application

EMBEDDED FIREWALLS

When firewall functions are integrated into a router or a switch, the firewall is said to be *embedded*. Also known as choke-point firewalls, embedded firewalls usually perform only stateless inspection of packets at the IP level, resulting in faster performance but an increased vulnerability to hostile code.

SOFTWARE FIREWALLS

Software firewalls themselves come in two different types—enterprise class for performing routing functions for large networks, and a SOHO (Small Office, Home Office) class. Usually providing the full range of firewall features, software firewalls are installed on server-based hardware and operating systems (such as Linux, Unix, or Windows 2000).

HARDWARE FIREWALLS

Also known as *appliance* firewalls, hardware firewalls are intended to be *turnkey* systems. A turnkey system needs no extensive installation or configuration before it begins providing firewall services. Hardware firewalls, like software firewalls, can target either the enterprise or the SOHO markets.

APPLICATION FIREWALLS

Application firewalls are usually implemented as additional components to existing hardware or software firewalls. Their primary purpose is to provide a sophisticated level of content filtering for data traveling at the application level. As firewall functions increase in their capabilities, and filtering focuses increasingly on data at the application layer, application firewalls are becoming more and more specialized

Which Firewall Functions Should I Use?

There are no clear-cut absolutes for choosing a particular type of firewall solution, although advances in creating hybrid function routers mean that a reasonable investment can provide you with the full range of features without purchasing a firewall product separate from a router. Usually the distinguishing factor is the sophistication of the stateful inspection level performed by the router (or firewall), along with management, and VPN functions.. Additionally, you should consider cost, business need, and security requirements when you are looking for a proper solution.

Since static filtering is considered weak, it is the lowest level of perimeter security. It is also the most basic, however, because static filtering ability is built into most routers. If you have a permanent WAN connection, chances are you are using a router. If you have a router, you should be performing static packet filtering as a minimum.

Each of these firewalls has its strengths and weaknesses. Dynamic filtering is typically easier to work with than a proxy and has a better ability to meet most business needs, but it is not quite as competent at screening traffic as a proxy server might be. Although both a dynamic packet filter and a proxy will block traffic known to be bad, each can act a little differently in the face of dubious traffic.

For example, let's say you have two firewalls: a dynamic packet filter and a proxy. Each receives a packet of data that has the high-priority flag set for a certain application, and neither has been programmed as to how to handle this type of data. Typically (but not always), the dynamic packet filter passes questionable traffic, while the proxy drops it. In addition, since the proxy is application-aware, it further checks the contents of the actual data, while the dynamic packet filter does not. Again, this is a theoretical comparison between two forms of perimeter protection. Your actual mileage may vary, depending on the specific product you choose.

Proxies tend to be a bit more secure, but it can be more difficult to get them to fit a particular business need. For example, some proxies still have trouble supporting some of the instant messaging protocols or application-specific protocols such as Citrix MetaFrame.

Because some level of risk must be assumed, the challenge is to create cost-efficient multiple defensive layers protecting network assets while still maintaining usability of the system. A proper firewall selection meets all the business needs of connectivity while employing the highest level of security possible. Additionally, a good firewall product not only incorporates both dynamic packet filtering and proxy technology, but also VPN, monitoring, and intrusion detection services in order to provide the highest level of security and flexibility.

Which Type Should I Choose?

This topic has been the subject of many a religious war. Search the archives of any firewall mailing list, and you will find volumes on this topic. Just like a religious belief system, the selection of a proper firewall platform is a personal decision that you should make only after proper investigation.

This section is not going to tell you which platform to choose; it will simply point out some of the strengths and weaknesses of each platform and leave the final decision up to you. Just like choosing a proper firewall product, choosing the operating system to run it on is clearly not a one-size-fits-all prospect.

For the purposes of this discussion, we'll focus on the two most common firewall types—hardware and software. Because even hardware routers use software, we'll refer to them as *appliance* firewalls. Enterprise software firewalls usually run server hardware and operating systems, which we'll refer to as server-based. An example of a server-based firewall is Check Point's Firewall-1, which runs on various server operating systems (Windows, Solaris, and Linux). An *appliance-based firewall*, or *integrated solution*, is a firewall application that runs on proprietary hardware and software. For example, the Cisco PIX firewall is an example of an integrated device in which the entire system is not capable of being anything other than a firewall and does not include a hard drive or other traditional components of a server. Because of its integrated and proprietary nature, these boxes are traditionally faster and more robust and are considered more secure than server-based firewalls. Server-based firewalls, on the other hand, often provide additional configuration and support options and can be cheaper than integrated solutions.

Server-Based Firewalls

Server-based firewalls are applications that run on top of an operating system. Firewalls exist for the following platforms:

◆ Apple Mac OS X

◆ Unix (Solaris, HP-UX, IBM AIX)

◆ Linux

◆ Microsoft Windows NT, 2000, XP, and .NET

THE MAC OPERATING SYSTEM

The Mac operating system has undergone a radical change, starting in 2001 with the release of the consumer version of OS X (10). OS X is based on the NeXTStep operating system, which itself is based on the Mach kernel and BSD (Berkeley Software Distribution) Unix. Even though Apple has released the source code for the OS X kernel (called Darwin), it has made significant changes to it to adapt it to the Mac platform. Although no major security weaknesses have been discovered or exploited in OS X, the open-source nature of the operating system, along with the Unix heritage of OS X, allow many existing security products to be altered to run on the system—in addition to the firewall API (application programming interface) already built into the system.

Mac Strengths

So what distinguishes the Mac as an operating system from other notable server operating systems? As of OS X, less than most people would think. Because of it's Unix base and open-source nature, OS X provides the same feature-rich base as other Unix-like systems. Also, because the core operating system (Darwin) is open source, changes can be made to the core system to fix security bugs or add functionality.

In addition, most OS X server implementations rely on the same generic Unix components that other Unix-based systems do (such as the Apache Web Server, the MySQL database, and Sendmail mail server). There is still a widespread belief, however, that running a firewall on a Mac is inherently more secure simply because most crackers are unfamiliar with Mac technology. Although there are some reported vulnerabilities in applications that run on the Mac, few reports exist about weaknesses of the operating system itself—especially now that the core operating system is open sourced—meaning that more external eyes can review the code, discover errors, and release the code, all in a short period of time.

There is also the ease of configuration for basic firewall services. BrickHouse is a GUI front-end to the firewall API built into OS X. Although it only provides for static packet filtering, it also has fairly extensive logging capabilities. Fortunately for the more sophisticated user, the API is also accessible through the command line.

Finally, a firewall running on the new OS X will see benefits of performance (from a cutting-edge Unix-based operating system), configuration (each specific service can be turned on or off at will), and support tools (most Unix-based security support utilities will run on OS X).

Mac Weaknesses

Some significant weaknesses are actually the flip side of the Mac's strengths. Because the system is not well known, the possibility exists that many vulnerabilities are waiting to be discovered by any cracker who might make a serious attempt to penetrate it—especially in areas of the system that aren't open for public review (such as the graphical support areas).

Also, because a Mac server has only a limited number of configuration and application choices built into the firewall API, administrators may feel that they miss extras, such as the ability to highly customize the API to include additional security features such as sophisticated intrusion detection. Although some open-source solutions exist that provide these features, no vendor is yet producing an enterprise class version of an OS X software firewall.

THE UNIX OPERATING SYSTEM

Unix has been around far longer than other operating systems, including Microsoft Windows NT (and NT-based operating systems such as Windows2000, XP, and .NET), and the first firewalls were designed on Unix systems. Thus, the idiosyncrasies of the platform are well understood and documented, and the firewall products that run on it are stable. Although most versions of Unix are sold commercially (such as Sun's Solaris multiprocessor version, HP's HP-UX, and IBM's AIX), it is still considered a fairly open system because so much is known about its fundamental structure and services. When security weaknesses are discovered with Unix, they tend not to be with the core operating system, but with services and applications running on top of it.

Unix also has the benefit of outperforming other operating systems. This, combined with the many hardware platforms and configurations that support Unix, makes it a preferred operating system for intensive and large data operations. Good firewall practice dictates that all applications and components not essential to the operation of the firewall are disabled, and this is particularly easy to accomplish in Unix.

Unix Strengths

Specific strengths of Unix are many. It is highly configurable, is well understood by many in the security industry, and is the most prominent operating system in existence. Many resources are dedicated to understanding and fixing any security issues that might arise.

Unix is also considered a very stable, high-performing operating system. In addition, because of its ability to run on multiple hardware platforms (including advanced IBM and SGI servers) and on multiple-processor versions of these platforms, it can support high data rates required of any firewall supporting a large network. It is also relatively immune from the need to reboot the machine after configuration changes, something that has afflicted Windows NT systems.

There are more security and security support products for Unix than for any other platform (although Windows NT is a close second). This, coupled with its 30-year history, has made Unix the preferred choice for many large organizations.

Unix Weaknesses

So what are the negatives? Problems arise when inexperienced Unix administrators place firewalls on "out of the box" installations and don't disable the many vulnerable (but potentially valuable on a nonfirewall system) programs and services (*daemons*) that are enabled by default. And because many of these daemons are configured to run in the security context of the root (the all-powerful superuser account), they provide an attacker with complete access to the system once they have exploited vulnerable system components.

Deactivating daemons is relatively simple. Administrators simply remove or rename the scripts that activate the respective daemon at boot time or comment out the line in the `inetd.conf` configuration file, if the daemon is called by `inetd`. (See the following view of an `inetd.conf` configuration file.)

```
# These are standard services.
#
ftp     stream  tcp     nowait  root    /usr/sbin/tcpd  in.ftpd -l -a
telnet  stream  tcp     nowait  root    /usr/sbin/tcpd  in.telnetd
gopher  stream  tcp     nowait  root    /usr/sbin/tcpd  gn
#smtp   stream  tcp     nowait  root    /usr/bin/smtpd  smtpd
#nntp   stream  tcp     nowait  root    /usr/sbin/tcpd  in.nntpd
#
# Shell, login, exec and talk are BSD protocols.
#
shell   stream  tcp     nowait  root    /usr/sbin/tcpd  in.rshd
login   stream  tcp     nowait  root    /usr/sbin/tcpd  in.rlogind
#exec   stream  tcp     nowait  root    /usr/sbin/tcpd  in.rexecd
talk    dgram   udp     wait    root    /usr/sbin/tcpd  in.talkd
ntalk   dgram   udp     wait    root    /usr/sbin/tcpd  in.ntalkd
#dtalk  stream  tcp     waut    nobody  /usr/sbin/tcpd  in.dtalkd
#
# Pop and imap mail services et al
#
pop-2   stream  tcp     nowait  root    /usr/sbin/tcpd  ipop2d
pop-3   stream  tcp     nowait  root    /usr/sbin/tcpd  ipop3d
imap    stream  tcp     nowait  root    /usr/sbin/tcpd  imapd
#
# Tftp service is provided primarily for booting.  Most sites
# run this only on machines acting as "boot servers." Do not uncomment
# this unless you *need* it.
#
#tftp   dgram   udp     wait    root    /usr/sbin/tcpd  in.tftpd
#bootps dgram   udp     wait    root    /usr/sbin/tcpd  bootpd
#
# Finger, systat and netstat give out user information which may be
# valuable to potential "system crackers."  Many sites choose to disable
# some or all of these services to improve security.
#
# cfinger is for GNU finger, which is currently not in use in RHS Linux
#
finger  stream  tcp     nowait  root    /usr/sbin/tcpd  in.fingerd
```

```
#cfinger stream tcp      nowait root    /usr/sbin/tcpd  in.cfingerd
#systat stream  tcp      nowait guest   /usr/sbin/tcpd  /bin/ps -auwwx
#netstat stream tcp      nowait guest   /usr/sbin/tcpd  /bin/netstat -f inet
#
# Time service is used for clock synchronization.
#
time    stream  tcp      nowait nobody  /usr/sbin/tcpd  in.timed
time    dgram   udp      wait   nobody  /usr/sbin/tcpd  in.timed
#
# Authentication
#
auth    stream  tcp      nowait     nobody /usr/sbin/in.identd in.identd -l -e -o
#
# End of inetd.conf
```

More weaknesses are exploited in Unix on a weekly basis than on any other operating system. For example, CERT (the Computer Emergency Response Team at Carnegie Mellon) reported on September 15, 2000, that crackers were using two common vulnerabilities to conduct widespread attacks. The first vulnerability is with the `rpc.statd` daemon that is used to support NFS. The second is with `wu-ftpd`, an FTP server package provided by Washington University. Because these services are installed and activated on most Unix (and Linux) systems by default, administrators who install firewalls on default installations are leaving their entire network vulnerable.

Unix is considered a more difficult system to learn and administer than other operating systems, and the cost of a Unix system has traditionally been more expensive than other operating systems. And because there are so many documented weaknesses with Unix, an administrator has to invest more time in securing the system; otherwise an attacker with access to the same information on Unix vulnerabilities can take advantage of "so many holes."

OpenBSD: An Exception to the Unix rule

One Unix variation that minimizes the risk of preinstalled vulnerable daemons is OpenBSD. OpenBSD installs with no accessibility; the administrator is forced to manually choose which services and components will run.

Created and maintained by volunteers and distributed for free, OpenBSD is sometimes confused with Linux. In fact, it is a tightly controlled collaborative Unix project with specific goals. Although weaknesses can still be found, the response time to correct those weaknesses is considered the best in the industry, which, when coupled with a proactive attitude toward locating and correcting software errors, makes OpenBSD a compelling choice for many firewall administrators.

LINUX

What about Linux, the most significant challenger in the operating system wars in recent memory? Linux shares many of the strengths and weaknesses of Unix.

Linux Strengths

Like Unix, the Linux platform is highly configurable, stable, and well understood and has many available security-related products. The greatest attraction to Linux, however, is its open nature. In fact,

Linux is more open than OpenBSD, and many in the security industry favor this principle of expos-ing source code to as many eyes as possible in the search for errors and vulnerabilities. And the com-munal nature of the Linux community means a ready and willing support group for security specialists with concerns and questions.

Another advantage of Linux is a simple financial fact: the source code is freely distributed, some-thing that is becoming more appealing to organizations struggling to reign in IT costs. But it's not just the "free beer" appeal of Linux source code; it's the freedom to be able to modify the operating system in fundamental ways to suit an organization's particular needs. This can be contrasted with the increasingly restrictive (and expensive) nature of Microsoft licenses.

Within the past two years, all major hardware vendors (with the exception of Apple) have announced preloaded Linux systems, along with Linux technical support. Even major software ven-dors have announced that Linux is their operating system of choice, including Oracle, which moved all its internal Oracle databases to the platform.

Because of the free and open nature of the Linux system, many more firewall solutions exist for this platform than for any other. Although such a dizzying array of options can be overwhelming, it also means that Linux can be an ideal solution for customized security configurations.

Linux Weaknesses

Although Linux is considered very powerful, it is also considered more complex. The emphasis of the CLI (command-line interface) can be intimidating to a generation of computer users who have learned and relied on ease of a GUI. Because of the various distributions of Linux, each with dis-tinct locations of configuration files and kernel versions, maintaining consistency can become diffi-cult. Add to that the constant churn of bug fixes, service updates, and additional product functionality, and supporting Linux can increase the overall support cost for a network, especially without an overall system maintenance plan.

MICROSOFT WINDOWS NT

In contrast to Linux, Microsoft brings the power of familiarity. As Cervantes observed in *Don Quixote*, however, familiarity breeds contempt, and that's true of Microsoft Windows NT and Windows 2000.

NT Strengths

Since Windows NT is an extension of the Windows Desktop environment (by far the most popular operating system ever produced), NT is a far more familiar environment to the typical end user. The user is not forced to learn a completely new environment just to run firewall software. Even more important, a company is not required to hire additional resources just to manage its firewall.

In fact, NT systems have traditionally been less expensive than their Unix counterparts, and the fact that the investment in hardware and software (let alone expertise) is usually less for an NT-based system must be taken into account.

It is argued that familiarity augments security. Since people are familiar with NT, they are less likely to configure the platform incorrectly and cause a security problem. Although it may or may not be true that Unix can be configured to be a more secure environment, certainly a secure environ-ment can never be achieved if a user does not understand how to properly manage it.

Finally, the argument can be made for consistency. Since many organizations run NT for file, print, and application services, it makes sense to standardize on this one platform for all required services. This makes administration easier and more harmonious. It also helps to reduce or abolish compatibility problems.

NT Weaknesses

The greatest weakness attributed to NT is one of perception—that Microsoft is slow and reluctant to admit and correct security weaknesses. Although a third party discovered a weakness, privately notified Microsoft, and then notified the public because they waited for over a month for Microsoft to announce a patch, there is no evidence that this is a pattern. And although significant vulnerabilities have been discovered, they have, for the most part, been limited to services that are not preinstalled on NT and would not be placed on a firewall system, such as IIS (Internet Information Services), Microsoft's web server.

Because of the proprietary nature of NT, not much is known about the internal workings of the services, and they are not configurable to the same degree as Unix daemons. This might also provide some uncertainty for security specialists who are looking for the most secure platform with which to run their firewall.

Other negatives include the need to reboot NT servers after configuration changes (or even after several days or weeks of operation due to system instability) and the purchase and licensing fees associated with an NT server.

MICROSOFT WINDOWS 2000

How does Windows 2000 compare with Windows NT? Windows 2000 shares many common weaknesses with Windows NT, including its proprietary nature, the perceived reluctance on the part of Microsoft to admit (and remedy) vulnerabilities, and the significant costs associated with using a Windows product. Like NT, Windows 2000 has the strength of user familiarity and consistency throughout the network.

Windows 2000 does have some unique strengths that distinguish it from NT. First is the ability to make configuration changes without needing to restart the server. Second is the increased stability of the server, which lengthens its up time (and, therefore, increases reliability). And finally, the ability to centrally define and deploy comprehensive security settings (called Group Policies) gives a dramatic boost to security as a whole.

After several years of experience with Windows 2000, most security experts agree that the vulnerabilities of the system lie primarily in the additional services (such as the IIS web server) that run on top of the operating system. The core operating system, however, is seen to be primarily sound. In addition, Microsoft has released its own firewall for Windows 2000. Known as ISA Server (Internet Security and Acceleration), the software supports all major firewall functions and includes extras such as a web cache, intrusion detection, and integration with Microsoft's Active Directory.

MICROSOFT .NET

At the time of this writing, Microsoft's .NET Server family is still in beta. Microsoft plans to release four major versions of the .NET Server in the first or second quarter of 2003:

Windows .NET Web Server   Primarily used to host web services and applications, the web server includes partial VPN, AD (Active Directory), and PKI (Public Key Infrastructure) support, but doesn't include the Microsoft Internet Connection Firewall.

Windows .NET Standard Server   The entry-level server for small to mid-sized business, this server includes all security features except for clustering , MMS (Microsoft Metadirectory Services, which is used to integrate AD with third-party directories), and data.

Windows .NET Enterprise Server   The most full featured of all .NET servers, it includes all .NET security and redundancy services.

Windows .NET Datacenter Server   Focused on providing redundant data and load-balancing operations, this server lacks security features more suited for network-edge systems.

At the beginning of 2002, Microsoft began a major security initiative that included a stop in code production for a period of a month while all existing code was reviewed for bugs or other errors that could lead to security vulnerabilities. In addition, Foundstone, Inc., and CORE Security Technologies, two respected security auditing companies, performed a security analysis of the entire .NET framework (which includes the .NET servers) over the period of a year. They found that when properly implemented, the .NET technologies provide a highly detailed level of control over network resources, give administrators a complete set of tools to implement those controls, and move security decisions away from end users—all highly desirable results.

Appliance-Based Firewalls

Also called *integrated solutions*, appliance-based firewalls run on proprietary hardware and software and usually consist of a physically small box with network connections and a power source. Appliance-based firewalls include the following:

◆ Cisco PIX

◆ Check Point Firewall-1

◆ eSoft InstaGate

◆ SonicWALL PRO

◆ WatchGuard Firebox

Integrated firewalls provide an all-in-one solution, with the vendor supplying the hardware, software, and operating system. Integrated solutions are quite popular, especially for small businesses that do not have a full-time IT staff and require basic firewall functionality without the need for advanced customization. Larger businesses also rely on more expensive, higher-end integrated firewalls to handle the extreme traffic flow generated by having many computers that require protected access to the Internet or to handle e-commerce sites that have millions of visitors a day.

APPLIANCE STRENGTHS

The greatest benefit of integrated solutions is their short configuration time. Many firewalls are pre-configured to protect your network literally right out of the box. Simply by connecting the Internet into one port, and your internal network into another, the device begins to immediately filter network traffic. Small businesses benefit from this simplicity, especially when they do not have a full-time or experienced IT staff. If configuration is required, administration can be done from a simple web browser or from the installation of a proprietary administrative utility.

Performance is the other benefit most often cited by large corporations who purchase integrated firewalls. Because these firewalls use programmable hardware (also called *firmware*), they can operate at much higher speeds than those firewalls that have an extra layer of operating system and hardware (both of which are designed to do general computing tasks, and have not been optimized for firewall tasks).

This focus on dedicated design also has the potential of reducing firewall costs, since there is no requirement to purchase an operating system and licenses in addition to the firewall application; everything is included in a tightly integrated package by the vendor. This monolithic approach (where everything is controlled, designed, and supported by vendor) can actually increase security by minimizing the number of hands in the pie. And simplicity (having one vendor produce everything) is considered the Holy Grail of any security system.

APPLIANCE WEAKNESSES

On the other hand, such a monolithic approach to a firewall might limit the flexibility of a product or the ability to upgrade the underlying hardware (such as installing more RAM as desired in a server-based firewall). Appliances also limit an organization to one vendor for their entire security system, as opposed to using a modular system that could encourage "best of breed" for all components—the best operating system tied to the best firewall, which feeds into the best analysis system, with all three coming from different vendors.

Appliances have also been known to be more expensive than simple software solutions, and, at one time, depending on the level of complexity needed by your organization, you might be better served by going with a traditional software firewall. This has rapidly changed as prices have decreased (while capabilities increased) for appliances. Combined with the growth of appliances priced for the SOHO market, many businesses are finding appliances very appealing.

Additional Firewall Considerations

No matter what type of firewall you choose, you should analyze some potential features closely before selecting a specific firewall product. These features are common to all types of firewalls, so we'll review them here.

Address Translation

Address translation is considered a basic firewall function. Don't trust a firewall product that doesn't include this option. The conversion of an IP address from one value to another is called *address translation*. This feature has been implemented in most firewall products and is typically used when you do not want to let remote systems know the true IP address of your internal systems. Figure 5.11 shows the typical deployment of this configuration.

Our internal workstation wants to access an external website. It formulates a request and delivers the information to its default gateway, which in this case is the firewall. The desktop system has one minor problem, though: the subnet on which it is located is using private addressing.

FIGURE 5.11

Address translation

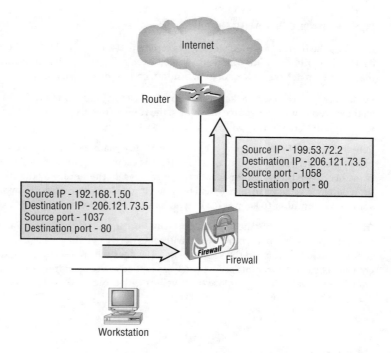

Private addressing is the use of IP subnet ranges. Any organization can use private addressing when addressing its internal hosts because these ranges are not permitted to be routed on the Internet. Although this means that we can use these addresses without fear of conflict, it also means that any request we send to a remote system will not know which route to take in order to reply. These ranges are as follows:

◆ 10.0.0.0–10.255.255.255

◆ 172.16.0.0–172.31.255.255

◆ 192.168.0.0–192.168.255.255

Although our workstation can reach the remote server, the remote server cannot reply. This is where address translation is useful: we can map the IP address of the workstation to some other legal IP address. In the case of Figure 5.11, we translated the desktop's IP address of 192.168.1.50 to the same legal address used by the external interface of the firewall, which is 199.53.72.2.

You can deploy address translation in three ways:

◆ By hiding NAT

◆ By using static NAT

◆ By using Port Address Translation (PAT)

IT'S ALL IN THE PORT NUMBERS

How does the firewall distinguish between replies that are coming back to this workstation and traffic that is destined for other systems or for the firewall itself? If the firewall is translating the address of all desktop machines to match the address of its own interface, how does it tell the difference between different sessions?

Look closely at the two packet headers in Figure 5.11, and you will see that one other value has been changed. Along with the source IP address, the firewall has also changed the source port number. This port number is used to identify which replies go to which system.

Remember that the source port is typically a value dynamically assigned by the transmitting system. This means that any value above 1023 is considered acceptable. There should be no problems with having the firewall change this value for accounting purposes. In the same way that the source port number can be used between systems to distinguish between multiple communication sessions, the firewall can use this source port number to keep track of which replies need to be returned to each of our internal systems.

Our firewall will modify the IP header information on the way out and transmit the packet to its final destination. On the way back, our firewall will again need to modify the IP header in order to forward the data to the internal system. In the reply packet, the destination IP address and service port will need to be changed because the remote server will have replied to the IP address and source port specified by the firewall. The firewall needs to replace these values with those used by the desktop workstation before passing along the information.

HIDING NAT

Hiding NAT functions exactly as shown in Figure 5.11. All internal IP hosts are hidden behind a single IP address. This can be the IP address of the firewall itself or some other legal number. Although hiding NAT can theoretically support thousands of concurrent sessions, multiple hiding addresses can be used if you require additional support.

The biggest limitation of hiding NAT is that it does not allow the creation of any inbound sessions. Since all systems are hidden behind a single address, the firewall has no way of determining which internal system the remote session request is destined for. Since there is no mapping to an internal host, all inbound session requests are dropped.

This limitation can actually be considered a feature, because it can help augment your security policy. If your policy states that internal users are not allowed to run their own servers from their internal desktop machines (web, FTP, and so on), hiding NAT for all desktop machines is a quick way to ensure that these services cannot be directly accessed from outside the firewall.

STATIC NAT

Static NAT functions similarly to hiding NAT, except that only a single private IP address is mapped to each public IP address used. This is useful if you have an internal system using private IP addresses, but you want to make this system accessible from the Internet. Since only one internal host is associated with each legal IP address, the firewall has no problem determining where to forward traffic.

For example, let's assume that you have an internal Exchange server and you want to enable SMTP functionality so that you can exchange mail over the Internet. The Exchange server has an

IP address of 172.25.23.13, which is considered private address space. For this reason, the host cannot communicate with hosts located on the Internet.

You now have two choices:

◆ You can change the address from a private number to a legal number for the entire subnet on which the Exchange server is located.

◆ You can perform static NAT at the firewall.

Clearly, the second option is far easier to deploy. It allows internal systems to continue communicating with the Exchange server using its assigned private address, while translating all Internet-based communications to a virtual legal IP address.

Static NAT is also useful for services that will break if hiding NAT is used. For example, some communications between DNS servers require that the source and destination port both be set to port 53. If you use hiding NAT, the firewall is required to change the source port to some random upper port number, thus breaking the communication session. By using static NAT, the port number does not need to be changed, and the communication sessions can be carried out normally.

TIP   *Most NAT devices allow you to use both static and hiding NAT simultaneously. This allows you to use static NAT on the systems that need it, while hiding the rest.*

PORT ADDRESS TRANSLATION (PAT)

Port address translation is utilized by most proxy firewall products. When PAT is used, all outbound traffic is translated to the external IP address used by the firewall, in a way similar to hiding NAT. Unlike hiding NAT, the external address of the firewall must be used. This cannot be set to some other legal value.

The method for dealing with inbound traffic varies from product to product. In some implementations, ports are mapped to specific systems. For example, all SMTP traffic directed at the firewall's external interface (which has a destination port number of 25) is automatically forwarded to a specific internal system. For a small environment, this limitation is rarely a problem. For large environments that operate multiple systems running the same type of server (such as multiple mail or FTP servers), this deficiency can be a major obstacle.

To get around this problem, some proxy servers can analyze data content in order to support multiple internal services. For example, a proxy might be able to forward all inbound SMTP e-mail addressed as user@eng.bofh.org to one internal e-mail system and forward e-mail addressed to user@hr.bofh.org to another.

If you have multiple internal servers running the same service, be sure that your firewall can distinguish between them. We've seen more than one organization that has been bitten by this limitation and has been forced to place servers outside the firewall. This is like walking to work in a blizzard because the shiny new Corvette you just purchased got stuck in a half-inch of snow.

Firewall Logging and Analysis

Although a firewall's primary function is to control traffic across a network perimeter, a close second is its ability to document and analyze all the traffic it encounters. Logging is important because it documents who has been crossing your network perimeter—and who has attempted to cross, but failed. Analysis is important because it might not be readily apparent from a casual view of the log which incidents are attempts to actually cross your perimeter and which are investigations for openings in the "fence" in preparation for a future attack.

What defines a good firewall log? Obviously, this comes down to personal preference. You should, however, consider a number of features:

◆ The log should present all entries in a clear, easy-to-read format.

◆ You should be able to view all entries in a single log so that you can better identify traffic patterns, although the ability to export the log data to an analysis tool is of even greater value.

◆ The log should clearly identify which traffic was blocked and which traffic was allowed to pass.

◆ Ideally, you should be able to manipulate the log, using filtering and sorting, to focus on specific types of traffic, although this feature is best suited to an analysis tool.

◆ The log should not overwrite itself or drop entries based on a specific size limitation.

◆ You should be able to securely view logs from a remote location.

◆ The logging software should have some method of exporting the log to at least one common format, such as ASCII text (preferably with some kind of delimiter). This allows you to manipulate the data further within a reporting tool, a spreadsheet, or a database program.

Kind of a tall order, but all are important features. It is rare that an attacker will gain access on the first try. If you schedule time to scrutinize the logs regularly, you may be able to thwart an attack before it even happens. A good logging tool will help.

For example, look at the log viewer shown in Figure 5.12. This is FireWall-1's log viewer, and it does a good job of fulfilling the criteria. The log is easy to read, is easy to follow, and can even be reviewed remotely from an alternate workstation through a secure session. You can even use the Select menu option to choose different filtering and sort options.

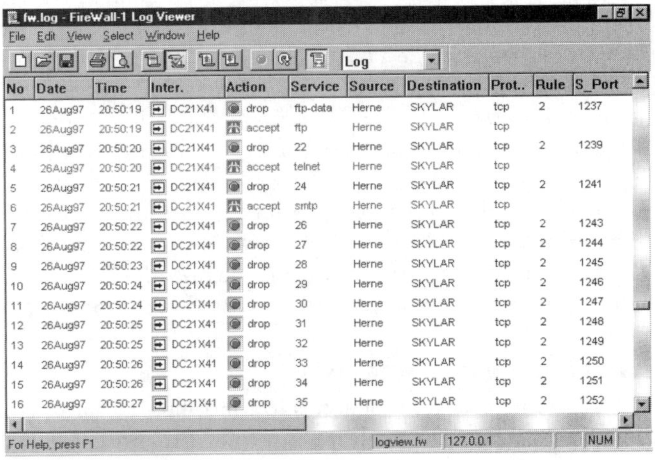

FIGURE 5.12

Firewall-1's log viewer

No	Date	Time	Inter.	Action	Service	Source	Destination	Prot..	Rule	S_Port
1	26Aug97	20:50:19	DC21X41	drop	ftp-data	Herne	SKYLAR	tcp	2	1237
2	26Aug97	20:50:19	DC21X41	accept	ftp	Herne	SKYLAR	tcp		
3	26Aug97	20:50:20	DC21X41	drop	22	Herne	SKYLAR	tcp	2	1239
4	26Aug97	20:50:20	DC21X41	accept	telnet	Herne	SKYLAR	tcp		
5	26Aug97	20:50:21	DC21X41	drop	24	Herne	SKYLAR	tcp	2	1241
6	26Aug97	20:50:21	DC21X41	accept	smtp	Herne	SKYLAR	tcp		
7	26Aug97	20:50:22	DC21X41	drop	26	Herne	SKYLAR	tcp	2	1243
8	26Aug97	20:50:22	DC21X41	drop	27	Herne	SKYLAR	tcp	2	1244
9	26Aug97	20:50:23	DC21X41	drop	28	Herne	SKYLAR	tcp	2	1245
10	26Aug97	20:50:24	DC21X41	drop	29	Herne	SKYLAR	tcp	2	1246
11	26Aug97	20:50:24	DC21X41	drop	30	Herne	SKYLAR	tcp	2	1247
12	26Aug97	20:50:25	DC21X41	drop	31	Herne	SKYLAR	tcp	2	1248
13	26Aug97	20:50:25	DC21X41	drop	32	Herne	SKYLAR	tcp	2	1249
14	26Aug97	20:50:26	DC21X41	drop	33	Herne	SKYLAR	tcp	2	1250
15	26Aug97	20:50:26	DC21X41	drop	34	Herne	SKYLAR	tcp	2	1251
16	26Aug97	20:50:27	DC21X41	drop	35	Herne	SKYLAR	tcp	2	1252

Look closely at the services reported in each of the packet entries in Figure 5.12. See anything strange? Our source system Herne appears to be attempting to connect to Skylar on every TCP service port sequentially. Our display starts at service port 20 (FTP-data) and continues one port at a time to port 35. This is an indication that Herne is running a port scanner against Skylar in order to see what services are offered.

In contrast to this is a log viewer such as the one used with Secure Computing's BorderWare firewall. This firewall maintains no less than six separate logs. Although this makes tracking a particular service a bit easier, it makes tracking a specific host far more difficult. You need to use a third-party program to combine the information and get a clear look at what is going on. Also, although the log in Figure 5.12 can be exported and saved using a simple menu option, BorderWare requires that you enable FTP administration and manually transfer the file to your local machine.

Keep the flexibility of the log interface in mind when you are selecting a firewall product. Although the firewall's ACL will typically be set and require few changes, plan to spend some time reviewing your firewall logs and analyzing traffic flow.

Virtual Private Networks (VPNs)

VPNs are considered a feature that sets a high-end firewall apart from the rest of the crowd. VPNs allow authenticated and encrypted access to an intranet through the public Internet. Instead of expensive point-to-point communication, LANs or mobile users can use inexpensive ISPs to communicate with their internal organization's resources.

However, simply providing basic VPN service is not enough. You'll need to determine what configuration, management, and encryption options your firewall provides for VPNs. In some cases a dedicated VPN solution that integrates into your firewall might provide the best results.

Intrusion Detection and Response

The ability of a firewall to notify an administrator while an attack is taking place should also enter the purchase and deployment decision. In the case of the high-profile DoS attacks that took place in February of 2000, the ability of the firewall systems to instantly notify the IT staff of unusual network activity allowed several sites to return to functionality within the hour.

Future firewall systems promise a degree of cooperation that would allow entire networks to respond to and reconfigure themselves in the event of an attack. Although experts feel that the technology for this level of proactive monitoring and response is feasible, challenges remain. To be truly effective, such a system requires the cooperation and communication of all affected parties, even if distinct (or even competitive) businesses and organizations are involved. Assuming such a level of communication and integration exists, the anonymity of an attacker becomes much more difficult to maintain, and the effects of an attack are neutralized much more quickly.

Formal and informal groups monitor and report intrusions, as well as virus, worms, and Trojan horse infections (such as the "I Love You" worm of May 2000). However, the reporting mechanisms are, more often than not, manual, requiring an "eyes on" approach. Ideally, reporting is automatic, standardized, and provide intelligent systems with enough information to allow for automatic or proactive defensive actions.

As a result of the need for automated response, many firewalls are providing IDS functions, and dedicated IDS systems are attempting, with mixed results, to automatically update firewall rule sets when attacks are detected. One of the challenges with this approach is the possibility that an attacker can take advantage of this dynamic interaction to close down valid ports. effectively producing an overreaction on the part of the IDS-firewall relationship.

Integration and Access Control

Firewalls are integrating more and more with other network systems and services. This trend promises to simplify administration, reduce complexity, and decrease TCO (Total Cost of Ownership), as firewalls no longer have to duplicate preexisting network infrastructure.

Examples of integration include directory and authentication services that eliminate redundant user account information and allow customizable authentication schemes. Two industry standards that provide these services are LDAP (Lightweight Directory Access Protocol) and RADIUS (Remote Authentication Dial-In User Service).

LIGHTWEIGHT DIRECTORY ACCESS PROTOCOL (LDAP)

LDAP creates a tunnel between two directory services or between a directory service and a client. For firewalls, this means that instead of creating user and group/role accounts redundantly, the system can use accounts and properties stored in a third-party directory service to determine access. This arrangement has a direct benefit of reducing the administrative burden of creating and managing duplicate user and group/role accounts, and it also reduces complexity—the greatest enemy to any security system. Examples of directory services include Microsoft's AD (Active Directory), Novell's NDS (NetWare Directory Services), iPlanet's Directory Server.

REMOTE AUTHENTICATION DIAL-IN USER SERVICE (RADIUS)

RADIUS offers an extensible and independent platform for authentication. Not only does this allow for customized authentication schemes (such as smart cards or biometric devices), RADIUS servers offload the actual authentication workload from the firewall (or LDAP-compliant directory services). By providing an infrastructure dedicated only to authentication, RADIUS simplifies and strengthens the authentication (and as a result, access) process.

TACACS+ (TERMINAL ACCESS CONTROLLER ACCESS CONTROL SYSTEM)

TACACS+ provides an alternative to RADIUS as a method for centralizing access. Like RADIUS, TACACS+ offloads the authentication from the firewall to another server. TACACS+, however, also provides accounting facilities and per-command authorization. On the down side, TACACS+ isn't nearly as well supported as RADIUS and as such is only available for some firewalls.

Third-Party Tools

Many of today's networks are a Frankenstein of multiple technologies from many vendors; although this may be an optimal collection of technology for your organization, it can be a nightmare to administer. Fortunately, new technologies are emerging that are designed to centrally monitor and manage all of your network devices and applications. An excellent example is HP's OpenView which provides management in the following areas:

- Applications
- Availability

- ◆ Networks

- ◆ Performance

- ◆ Services

- ◆ Systems

- ◆ Storage and Data

The ability for your firewall to work with third-party management tools could easily be a decisive factor in which product you choose.

But management is not the only area for which you can find third-party products. Many products, including Check Point's VPN-1, Cisco's PIX, and Microsoft's ISA allow other vendors to extend their features to include URL filtering, antivirus scanning, and e-mail spamming protection. These additional benefits might justify the (usually) increased cost of such a product.

You Decide

There are some strong arguments for each choice of firewall type. In order to make the proper selection for your environment, you will need to review all these arguments and decide which are more applicable to your particular environment.

Table 5.6 breaks down popular mid-range firewall products by features.

Firewall Deployment

You have selected a firewall product. Now the big question is how it should be placed within your network environment. Although opinions vary, the most common deployment is shown in Figure 5.13.

FIGURE 5.13

Where to place your firewall

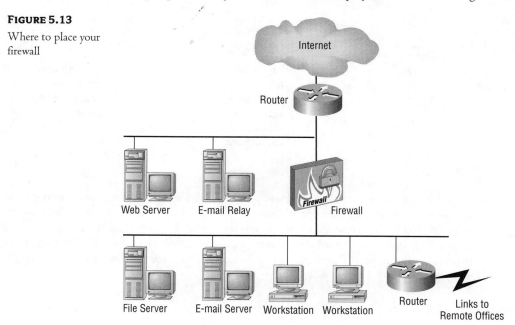

TABLE 5.6: POPULAR FIREWALL PRODUCTS COMPARED BY PRICE, FEATURE, AND PLATFORM

NAME	SERVICES (STATIC/DYNAMIC/ STATEFUL/PROXY)	OPERATING SYSTEMS (OR APPLIANCE)	ADDRESS TRANSLATION	FIREWALL LOGGING AND ANALYSIS	VPNs
Microsoft ISA	All (including application filters for H.323, streaming media, RPC, POP, and DNS)	Windows 2000, XP, .NET	Yes (dynamic and static)	Yes	Yes (IPSec, PPTP)
Check Point Firewall-1 NG	All (including more than 150 predefined application, service, and protocol filters)	NT/2000, Solaris, Linux	Yes (dynamic and static)	Monitoring current or past activity by port, service, protocol, and time of day	No (must purchase VPN-1 licenses) (including IPsec)
Cisco PIX 515E Firewall	All (includig application filters for VoIP, H.323 SIP, Skinny, and Microsoft NetMeeting)	Appliance	Yes (dynamic and static)	Add-on (Cisco Secure Policy Manager)	Yes; IPSec, PPTP (including option for dedicated VPN card)
eSoft InstaGate Pro	All	Appliance	Yes	SNMP	IPSec, PPTP
SonicWALL PRO 300	All	Appliance	Yes	Web page	IPSec, PPTP
WatchGuard Firebox 2500	All	Appliance (Linux OS), install and management done from Windows applications	Yes	Real time centralized logging, graphing, and analysis	IPSec

In this design, all internal systems are protected by the firewall from Internet-based attacks. Even remote sites connected to the organization via the WAN link are protected. All systems that are accessible from the Internet (such as the web server and the e-mail relay) are isolated on their own subnet. This subnet is referred to as a *demilitarized zone* (DMZ) because although it may be secure from attack, you cannot be 100 percent sure of its safety, as you are allowing inbound connections to these systems.

Intrusion Detection and Response	Integration and Access Control	Load Sharing and Fail Over	Other Services (including Integrated Third Party Tools)
Yes, ISS-based	Active Directory	Both through CARP (Cache Array Routing Protocol).	Web caching
Can be centrally coordinated (e-mail and SNMP reporting)	DES and 3DES, Secure ID, Axent Defender, IKE, IPSec, RADIUS, Secure ID, S/Key, TACACS, TACACS+, LDAP	Both (ClusterXL add-on module)	URL filtering, antivirus scanning (including Java and ActiveX), and e-mail spamming protection
Cisco Secure Policy Manager	RADIUS, TACACS+, PKI, PPPoE, DES, 3DES, and Web GUI	Failover (requires license and additional hardware)	URL blocking
Pager, e-mail, SNMP	CryptoCard, RADIUS, SecurID cards, S/Key	No	Additional services provided through SoftPak Applications: antiviurs, spam filter, modem communications, security check, VPN Manager
E-mail, SNMP	3DES, PPPoE, RADIUS, IKE	No	AutoUpdate, cookies, hacker prevention attacks, Java, NNTP, proxy blocking, antivirus
Email, pager	RCryptoCard, Internal ACL, Microsoft Windows NT, RADIUS, SecurID	Optional module	Optional services: anti-spam, high availability, McAfee anti-virus, VPN

Using a DMZ provides additional protection from attack. Since some inbound services are open to these hosts, an attacker might be able to gain high-level access to these systems. If this occurs, it is less likely that additional internal systems will be compromised, since these machines are isolated from the rest of the network.

You can add network cards to the firewall to control other types of remote access. For example, if the company has WAN links to business partners that are not officially part of the organization, you can create another subnet from an additional NIC card in the firewall. All routers connecting to these remote business partners are then located on this subnet. The firewall can control traffic between these sites and the internal network.

Additionally, you can use the static packet filtering capability of your router to increase security even further. This provides a multilayered wall of protection at your network perimeter. If an exploit is found in one of your security devices, the second device may be able to patch the leak.

There are many variations of this basic design. For example, you can install an additional type of firewall to the configuration you saw in Figure 5.13 to enhance security even more. For instance, if the firewall in the figure is a dynamic packet filter, you can place a proxy firewall behind it to better secure your Internet connection.

TIP It is always a good idea to place your firewall between any assets you want to protect so that all communication sessions must pass through the firewall. Although this may sound like an extremely basic idea, you might be surprised—if not shocked—at the way some organizations attempt to deploy a firewall.

Summary

This concludes our discussion of firewalls and how they work. Keep in mind the basic types and services that all firewalls offer, including:

- Static/dynamic/stateful/proxy filtering
- VPN capabilities
- Monitoring, logging, and analysis
- Extra services and third-party product integration

You should now be well equipped to select a firewall specifically for your organization's security and business needs.

In the next two chapters, we will look at some examples of how to set up and configure a few specific firewall products.

Chapter 6

Cisco's PIX Firewall

THERE ARE MANY FIREWALL products on the market, and selecting one to profile for this book was no easy task. In previous editions of this book, we demonstrated Check Point's Firewall-1, but in this edition we decided to profile one of the new generation of SOHO (small office, home office) firewall devices that have become ubiquitous with the widespread adoption of broadband (both DSL and cable) Internet access by business and individuals alike.

Featured in this chapter:

- ◆ An overview of PIX

- ◆ Installing PIX

- ◆ Configuring PIX

- ◆ Configuring PIX security

An Overview of PIX

The purpose of the Cisco PIX Firewall Series is to extend Cisco's famous presence to the emerging market of hardware-based firewalls—especially in smaller businesses. As a result, Cisco is attempting to provide enterprise service in a small box for networks that are connected to the Internet in an "always on" fashion.

Frankly, Cisco has done a good job of placing sophisticated capabilities in a relatively inexpensive, easy-to-administer, small package. Firewall features of PIX include the following:

Adaptive Security Algorithm (ASA)   The inspection process that looks at the state (or context) of each packet.

Access control   PIX predefines more than 85 protocols, services, and applications for rapid and flexible administration.

Virtual private network (VPN)   Using IPsec, PIX can interoperate with other VPN products.

Network Intrusion Detection System (NIDS)   Built-in intrusion detection can identify more than 55 types of Internet-based attacks.

URL filtering   When PIX is used with Cisco's Websense server, outgoing traffic can be filtered based on the URL.

Network Address Translation (NAT)   Multiple computers can share a single broadband connection.

In reality, PIX is a combination of hardware (the box) and an operating system (the PIX Firewall operating system). The box size depends on the PIX model, with the smaller models designed to fit on a desk and the larger models in a rack. In this chapter, we'll demonstrate the 501 model, which takes up slightly more space than the palm of your hand. The hardware has a few other features:

◆ 133MHz processor

◆ 16MB RAM

◆ WAN Ethernet connection

◆ Four LAN ports (switched, 10/100Mbps)

◆ Serial port (used to administer the firewall)

◆ Optional physical security lock

The operating system that is current as of this writing is version 6.1 and is dedicated to supporting the firewall hardware. Other operating system characteristics include the following:

◆ Default configuration for rapid installation

◆ Cisco PDM (PIX Device Manager), which provides web-based administration

◆ License-based user access (10 users by default, more based on a license that you can purchase)

◆ Integrated DHCP (Dynamic Host Configuration Protocol) server

◆ DES (Data Encryption Standard), 3DES (Triple DES), with optional license

Before you can take advantage of all these services, of course, you need to install the firewall. This in and of itself requires some planning and an understanding of your network.

Installing PIX

Before you actually plug everything in and boot up the firewall, you need to plan where it will be implemented in your network. You should also, at this point, have a good idea of what types of traffic you will allow through the firewall—in both directions. And, yes, we can get back up on our soap box to remind you of the first two chapters of this book and tell you that all these things should have been decided as part of your security policy, security plan, and implementation guide.

Typically, a manufacturer places last-minute additions and changes to a system in a file referred to as *release notes*. For example, the release notes for the PIX Firewall operating system version 6.1 specify that the DHCP capabilities can be upgraded to provide 256 IP addresses. This is a lot more than the original 128 limitation with previous versions.

After you review the release notes, you're ready to dive into the equipment. PIX comes with an accessory kit that includes CD-based documentation and software, a power cord, and rack-mounting hardware for PIX models greater than the 506—although all models can be placed on a desktop.

No matter where you place the firewall, consider the greatest threat to all electrical devices (except oceans and asteroids)—heat. Make sure that your firewall is vented and that there is enough air flow in the room where the firewall is located.

Let's take a look at the layout of the physical box of the firewall. Figure 6.1 shows the front panel, Figure 6.2 shows the rear panel, and Figure 6.3 is a close-up of the LEDs.

FIGURE 6.1

The PIX 501 front panel

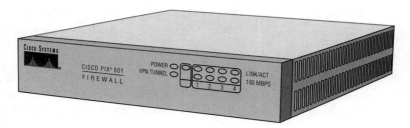

FIGURE 6.2

The PIX 501 rear panel

FIGURE 6.3

The PIX 501 front panel LEDs

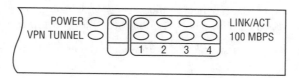

The LEDs provide a quick view of the current status of the firewall. Table 6.1 lists the LEDs, their various states, and descriptions.

TABLE 6.1: THE PIX 501 LEDs

LED	STATE	DESCRIPTION
Power	Green	Device is on
	Off	Device is off
Link/Activity	Flashing green	Represents network activity
	Green	Cable has power
	Off	No link
VPN Tunnel	Green	One or more IPsec VPN sessions have been created
	Off	No IPsec tunnels are active
100Mbps	Green	Port is operating at 100Mbps
	Off	Port is operating at 10Mbps

After you unpack the PIX, you can use the yellow Ethernet cable to connect the firewall to your hub or switch. The orange cable is included to connect your firewall to your WAN through a router, a DSL modem, or a cable modem. Connecting the power cable of the 501 activates it. (There is no power switch.)

Once power is running to the firewall, you should immediately see the power LEDs turn on. Also, if there are active links (LAN or WAN) into your firewall, you should see those corresponding lights glow and flicker in response to network activity. Finally, if any of your LAN links are 100Mbps, the 100Mbps light will also come on.

Installing PDM

The Cisco PIX Device Manager, or PDM, is the primary tool for configuring the PIX firewall. The PDM has a GUI interface and the following features:

◆ Task-based wizards that include many pre-filled menus.

◆ Visual monitoring of the firewall, all connections, the firewall NIDS, and interface traffic.

◆ The capability to create new configurations while maintaining backward compatibility with the Cisco Secure Policy Manager and other command-line options.

◆ Java-based interface stored on the firewall. (All that is required is a Java and JavaScript-capable web browser.)

◆ SSL (Secure Sockets Layer) communication between PDM and the firewall.

◆ Ability to administer (individually) multiple PIX firewalls from the same applet.

PDM is just the latest in a long trend toward graphical (as opposed to command-line) control of dedicated hardware devices such as firewalls, routers, and even switches. Keep in mind that although SSL capability is built into PIX, an additional license is required from Cisco to use 128-bit 3DES encryption. Because the weaker (and older) 56-bit DES can be broken relatively quickly, this investment is necessary.

The benefit of using a Java-based GUI is that your administration workstation isn't restricted to Windows machines; Solaris and Linux are also supported. Keep in mind, however, that if you have aggressive antivirus software, initializing PDM the first time can take a while. This shouldn't be a problem if you plan to customize the firewall or if you will keep the applet up and loaded continually.

PDM should already be installed on your PIX firewall (unless you are using a pre-6.0 version of the operating system). However, Cisco releases frequent updates to fix bugs and holes in the system; so you should download any updates. To do so, contact your Cisco reseller or partner to obtain the update file.

Now, you need to set up a TFTP (Trivial File Transfer Protocol) server, which you can download from the Cisco website (www.cisco.com). A TFTP server is typically included in most versions and distributions of Unix-based systems. You use the TFTP server to host PIX operating system updates, which are then downloaded and installed using a TFTP client integrated in the firewall itself.

Once you have the update file and configure a TFTP server to host it, you need to create a serial connection to your PIX. Follow these steps:

1. Connect the serial cable that came with your PIX from your administrative machine to the PIX.

2. If your administrative machine is Windows-based, launch the HyperTerminal program.

3. In the Connect To dialog box, select the next available COM port in the Connect Using field:

4. Click OK to open the Properties dialog box for your COM port:

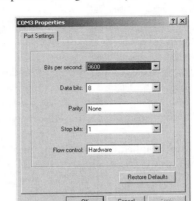

5. Increase the Bits Per Second option from 2400 to 9600, and click OK.

HyperTerminal attempts to connect to the PIX firewall. After approximately 30 seconds, you should see a series of messages scroll across the screen, ending with a prompt of `pixfirewall#`. At the prompt, enter the following command:

```
copy tftp://192.168.1.1/pdmnnn.bin flash:pdm
```

Replace `192.168.1.1` with the IP address of your actual TFTP server, and replace `pdmnnn.bin` with the actual filename of the operating system update. Once the update is copied, you need to actually activate it by entering configuration mode and setting up your administrative passwords. To do so, enter the `configure terminal` command, which results in a modified prompt:

```
pixfirewall (config)#
```

Now, enter the `setup` command and answer the next series of prompts, summarized in Table 6.2.

TABLE 6.2: PIX SETUP OPTIONS

PROMPT	WHAT TO ENTER
Enable Password	An alphanumeric password that can be a maximum of 16 characters
Clock, Year, Month, Day, Time	Time in UTC (Universal Coordinate Time)
Inside IP Address	The internal LAN address assigned to the PIX
Inside Network Mask	The subnet mask for the inside IP address
Host Name	A name for the firewall that can be a maximum of 16 characters
Domain Name	The domain name appended to the host name
PDM IP Address	The IP address of the administrative machine running the PDM

Next you'll see a summary of your selected options, and then you'll be prompted one final time to write the settings into the Flash memory of the firewall. Your firewall is now updated and configured with some initial settings.

Configuring PDM

Now that your firewall is activated, updated, and initialized, it's time to start PDM and perform a full configuration. Follow these steps:

1. Start your Java- and JavaScript-capable web browser.

2. Specify the HTTPS (HTTP Secure) protocol and then the IP address of the firewall, like this:

   `https://192.168.1.1`

   and then press Enter to open the Security Alert dialog box. (The `192.168.1.1` portion of this URL is the IP address of your firewall.)

3. Click Yes to accept the firewall's certificate and to open the Enter Network Password dialog box:

TIP   If you are using Internet Explorer, check the box in the lower-left corner so that you are not prompted every time to accept the certificate. If you are using Netscape Navigator (or Mozilla), you can check the Remember This Decision box for the same result.

4. If you chose to create a password during the PIX operating system update, enter it in the Password field. Otherwise, simply click OK.

Now that you are authenticated to the PIX, it will use your current browser window to launch another window that will actually host the PDM Java applet. When that applet is launched, you can close the original window.

At this point, PDM is active, and you can begin to configure the firewall. However, we'd like to cover a few PDM administrative concepts before you jump into the fray. The first is a comment on the size of your configuration parameters. PDM can't yet handle configurations of more than 2MB, and so keeping an eye on the size of your current configuration is an important task, especially as you become more confident with your system and begin designing your own sophisticated rules.

You can use Telnet (or the serial cable included with the firewall) to create a terminal session to the firewall. If you are using Windows 2000, simply open a command prompt, enter the following, and press Enter (192.168.1.1 is the IP address of your firewall):

```
telnet 192.168.1.1
```

You will be prompted for a password (the built-in password is `cisco`). Now, you need to enter `enable` mode. Follow these steps:

1. At the prompt, enter the enable password you set during your update of the PIX operating system. (The password is blank by default.)

2. At the enable prompt (`pixfirewall#`), type **show flashfs** and press Enter to display configuration size:

You can see that this part of the system is a little obtuse. Focus on the `file 1` line, specifically looking at the `length:` parameter. This is the number of bytes in your configuration file. Simply divide that number by 1024 to get the number of kilobytes in your configuration file. You can see that the size for this unit is a little over 1.8KB. Check from time to time to make sure you aren't approaching the 2MB limit.

Finally, keep in mind a couple of concepts about PDM. First, although you can run several PDM sessions concurrently, resource limitations on your computer (RAM, processor, and so on) can come into play. Second, if you have a slow link between your computer and the PIX, the PDM initialization time could be noticeable, with a minimum of 56Kbps required to effectively use PDM. If you notice that your computer is slow or is running low on resources, try closing and reopening your browser and then start PDM again.

Once PDM is configured and is working well on your system, it's time to actually configure the firewall itself.

Configuring PIX

You can use PIX in any of the three primary firewall configurations: bastion, three-way, or back-to-back. The basic models (like the one we're demonstrating) work with only two interfaces: inside and outside. Typically, however, you use PIX in a three-way firewall, acting as the central control point between the external network, the DMZ (De-Militarised Zone), and the internal network. In other words, all network traffic between the external network and your DMZ and internal networks flows through, and is subject to, the firewall.

PIX is preconfigured with two interfaces that are simply referred to as inside and outside. PIX uses security levels to determine how filtering rules are applied to the interfaces. (You can define a maximum of eight security levels.) Outside has a security level of 0, and inside has a security level of 100. The lower the number, the less protected an interface—relative to other interfaces. If you choose to set up a DMZ, define an additional interface and supply it with a security level greater than the outside interface, but lower than the inside interface. Keep in mind that there is no communication between security levels of the same number.

ADAPTIVE SECURITY ALGORITHM

Most current enterprise-level firewalls have some form of *context filtering*, more commonly referred to as *stateful filtering*. Cisco's implementation is known as ASA . ASA keeps track of all outgoing packets and records the pertinent session information. As incoming packets arrive at the firewall, they are compared with the stored state information to verify that they belong to a preexisting "conversation," or session, between a host on the inside of your network and a host on the outside.

ASA uses the following rules when it analyzes packets:

◆ Packets can't cross the firewall without matching a state.

◆ Outbound connections (connections originating from the inside) are always allowed, except when a specific access control list has been defined.

◆ All inbound connections (connections originating from the outside) are denied, unless an exception has been created. Multiple exceptions can be tied to a single translation (or *xlate*).

◆ Exceptions aside, no ICMP (Internet Control Message Protocol) packets are allowed through the firewall

◆ Attempts to bypass the rules are dropped (as opposed to rejected, which sends an ICMP status message back to the originator), and the attempts are logged.

We need to explain translations, or xlates. Cisco uses the term *xlates* to refer to packet forwarding, allowing external hosts to originate a connection to a host located on a DMZ or even on the internal network (although placing all Internet-accessible hosts on a DMZ is preferable). You define an xlate by associating a public IP address and port with a DMZ (or internal) host IP address and port. Once an xlate is defined, incoming exceptions can be tied to that xlate, allowing multiple types of traffic to be sent to DMZ hosts.

ASA is primarily designed to work with TCP (Transmission Control Protocol), because only TCP is stateful, and state is the basis of ASA analysis. So what about UDP (User Datagram Protocol) traffic? Remember that UDP is stateless and is common in streaming multimedia. When an outgoing UDP packet crosses PIX, it stores pseudo-state information about the packet (including time and destination IP address). When incoming UPD packets reach PIX, it attempts to match the "connection state" information to determine if the packets are valid. Even with this capability, PIX supports only DNS and a handful of multimedia protocols.

So how does ASA fit into the overall activity of the firewall? When the inside (or any interface with a security level higher than the outside interface) interface receives an outgoing packet, it uses ASA to verify the validity of the packet. PIX then checks to see if this packet is part of a preexisting session. If the packet is valid, but not part of a session, PIX creates a slot in the PIX state table, which stores the inside IP address and the global (or public) IP address used by NAT. The packet's source IP is then modified to store the global IP address, and the packet is sent.

Once an incoming packet reaches the outside interface, ASA compares it with the slot information stored in the state table, as well as with any other security restrictions that apply. If the packet is valid, PIX removes the destination IP address (the global address), replaces the actual IP address of the internal host, and then sends the packet to the interface where the original connection was made.

NETWORK ADDRESS TRANSLATION

As mentioned earlier, using NAT is a great way to protect the internal IP addresses from public exposure. Typically, you use NAT to encompass not only a one-to-one relationship between translated addresses (meaning that for every internal IP address there is an equally valid external IP address), but the more common one-to-many translation, in which a single public IP address is used for all internal private IP addresses. This one-to-many functionality is actually achieved through PAT (Port Address Translation), in which the various ports of the external IP address are used to distinguish the various connections created by internal hosts. By default, all these translations are dynamic; that is, they are performed at the moment the connection is created.

You can also configure NAT to create static translations. Static translations create a permanent association between an external IP address and a single internal IP address. This type of translation is the basis for the xlate and allows DMZ or internal-based servers to respond to connections originating on the external network.

ACCESS CONTROL

PIX can enforce user-based authorization and authentication in two ways:

Authentication, Accounting, and Authorization (AAA)   Allows PIX to use a TACACS+ (Terminal Access Controller Access Control System) or RADIUS (Remote Authentication Dial-In User Service) server to authenticate user accounts. Once the server verifies the identity of the user (and, optionally, any groups to which the account belongs), the PIX compares the user (or group) with an access control list

Access lists   Control connections and connection types. An access list restricts connections by three characteristics: source IP address, destination IP address, and/or port. The most restrictive access lists define all three characteristics.

As a result of AAA and access lists, PIX can support a type of proxy known as a *cut-through* proxy. Whereas most proxy servers analyze the entire protocol stack of each packet, a cut-through proxy simply authenticates the user requesting the connection and uses the stateful information of that connection to maintain a direct connection between the two communicating parties.

Cut-through proxies also let an administrator apply user-specific access control on outgoing (and incoming) sessions. The user enters the password as part of an HTTP, FTP, or even Telnet session. PIX then verifies the identity of the user, compares their authentication information with the appropriate access list, and creates the session.

ATTACK-SPECIFIC PROTECTION

Although you can (and should) apply many generic settings to a firewall (and we'll discuss those later in this chapter), PIX includes the following technologies that are designed to protect against certain specific types of network attacks:

Unicast RPF (Reverse Path Forwarding)   This simple feature compares incoming IP addresses to be sure they make sense in the context of your network. Outgoing packets are also analyzed and compared with the routing table to make sure that a route exists for the destination network. Although Unicast RPF is a good basic function, it isn't perfect. If an incoming packet doesn't match any known routes, it's impossible to determine its validity.

Flood Guard   Enabled by default, Flood Guard places limits on how many (and how often) login attempts are presented by AAA. If there were no limits, it would be possible to execute a DoS (Denial of Service) attack against the PIX by repeatedly attempting to create an authenticated session and then ignoring the subsequent login prompts, forcing the AAA to dedicate resources waiting for a login answer that never comes.

Flood Defender   This feature protects internal systems with a static NAT mapping (or xlate) from SYN floods. Remember that a SYN flood is made up of as many TCP connection requests as possible, in an effort to tie up the resources of the target in waiting to complete the TCP handshake. Flood Defender identifies SYN floods and in turn responds to TCP connection requests for the target server, until the SYN flood has passed.

FragGuard   Certain attacks (such as teardrop.c) create overlapping and offset packet fragments. These bad fragments can cause systems to crash or simply bypass normal packet security procedures. FragGuard fully reassembles ICMP error messages before sending them to internal systems, eliminating this weakness.

DNS Control   Enabled by default, DNS Control allows only a single DNS server response to a client DNS request, no matter how many servers have actually responded

ActiveX Blocking   When Microsoft implemented ActiveX capabilities in its operating systems, it placed no hard limits on the code itself (unlike Java, which had a "sandbox," or built-in limitations, on what it could do to the client system). PIX comments out all HTML `<object>` tags on web pages that it filters, effectively removing ActiveX controls from all browsed web pages.

Java Filtering   Although Java is protected from certain types of direct file manipulation, it is still possible for Java applets to originate attacks on an internal network. PIX disables the retrieval of Java applets by commenting out references to their location in the page. Although Java applets don't pose as critical a threat to systems as ActiveX components do, they can still be used as a form of network and system discovery.

URL Filtering   When PIX is used with the NetPartners Websense software, PIX can verify that URLs requested by an internal computer are allowed according to the policy defined on the Websense server.

Although these security features protect against specific attacks, the following additional supports are built into PIX for safely filtering specific applications and protocols:

RIPv2   PIX can support the MD5 authentication methods of RIPv2 (including a key per interface).

Configurable Proxy Pinging   You can protect PIX from exposure to ping attacks (or probing) by using this feature, which essentially defines how PIX responds to ICMP traffic (used by the `ping` command). However, if you will be passing VPN (IPsec or PPTP [Point-to-Point Tunneling Protocol]) traffic through PIX, you must enable ICMP type 3.

Mail Guard   Mail Guard allows only a minimal number of SMTP commands, and it logs all SMTP connections.

Multimedia and telephony protocols   PIX can seamlessly support the following protocols:

- ◆ RealAudio
- ◆ Streamworks
- ◆ CU-SeeMe
- ◆ Internet Phone
- ◆ IRC (Internet Relay Chat)
- ◆ Vxtreme
- ◆ VDO Live

◆ H.323

◆ SIP (Session Initiation Protocol)

NetBIOS over IP This capability is required if you have legacy Microsoft clients that require SMB (Server Message Block) access to servers on an external network.

All these features are excellent additions to a firewall, but we still haven't discussed the basic configuration of the firewall. In the next section, we'll walk through a complete, yet simple, configuration using the PDM.

Configuring PIX Security

So, you've completed your security plan, updated the PIX operating system, and configured your PDM. You feel ready to implement your plan. Let's start by looking at the main PDM screen, which is shown in Figure 6.4.

FIGURE 6.4

The default PDM screen, open at the Access Rules tab

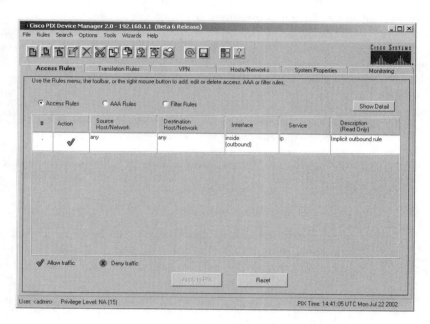

When you start PDM, the main screen opens at the Access Rules tab. The main screen contains an array of mostly colorful icons under the various menu options (the icons are gray if they can't be used) and six tabs. First, we'll walk through the tabs, and then we'll show you how to configure a basic firewall.

The Access Rules Tab

This tab displays all the restrictions and exceptions you implemented in PIX. Rules are categorized as follows:

Access   Essentially a simple packet filter, access rules use the source and destination IP addresses and ports of a packet to determine if it is allowed or denied access.

AAA   Packets are allowed if the AAA process is successful.

Filter   Requests from inside your network are filtered based on URLs (requires a URL filtering server such as Websense).

Remember that, by default, PIX allows internal computers to create sessions to external computers. (You can see this rule in Figure 6.4.) Also, by default, the firewall refuses packets from any less-secure network destined for a higher-level network. Thus, if you define an internal network with a security level of 100, a DMZ network with a security level of 50, and the external network with a security level of 0, connections originating from either the internal network or DMZ won't be allowed to cross into the external network.

The default access rule mode is ACL, although PIX is backward compatible with the Conduit and Outbound mode used with previous versions of the PIX firewall (and other Cisco routers). ACL rules are bundled together based on the interface to which they apply and are processed in order of their creation.

NOTE   *Before PIX will function as a firewall, it must be configured to perform NAT functions. These configurations are known as* implicit *rules and will actually allow basic network communications even though no ACL rules have been defined. We show you how to enable NAT functions in later in this chapter.*

Looking closer at Figure 6.4, you can see the following several fields in the Access Rules table:

A number indicating the order in which the rule is processed.

Action   The net effect of this rule, either allowing or prohibiting the affected packet.

Source Host/Network   Contains a list of the hosts (or networks) that are allowed to create connections to the addresses stored in the next field (Destination Host/Network). You can use the keyword **any**, which is a global acceptance for any host or network initiating traffic through the interface associated with the rule.

Destination Host/Network   The addresses that can receive traffic from the addresses listed in the Source Host/Network field.

Interface   The interface to which the rule applies. This field can hold several types of keywords:

◆   The name of your interface (such as "inside").

◆   The interface name with the **outbound** keyword in parentheses. This option applies the rule only to packets received on the interface that are destined for a *lower* security interface

◆   The **inbound** keyword (used only when you are using conduit-based rules from a previous PIX configuration).

Service A service name and (more important) a port number of the destination network service protected by the rule.

Description Specifies whether a rule is implicit (can't be edited) or has a source service (although this is rare).

Creating an access rule, then, is simply a matter of deciding what traffic should be allowed through the firewall. For the most part, the default access rules (along with a NAT rule allowing IP address translation for outgoing connections from your internal network) is sufficient for most networks that are not hosting any Internet-accessible services or using any particular multimedia services that PIX would normally block.. Of course, if you decide to add a server inside your network, you need to create special rules. If you create a DMZ network to host that server, you will have to create rules allowing access to those servers from the Internet.

Let's begin by creating a simple rule. The result is shown in Figure 6.5.

FIGURE 6.5

A simple access rule

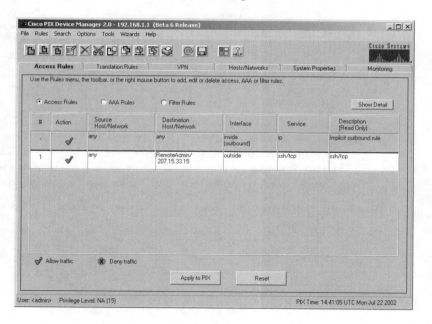

We'll summarize this rule first: any computer on the Internet can create an SSH (Secure Shell) connection to our RemoteAdmin server, which is on our private network. You can see this by reading the rule from left to right. Apart from the default rule allowing any outgoing traffic through, this rule is the first to be processed. Any computer on any network is allowed to initiate a connection to a computer named RemoteAdmin. PIX encourages you to use computer names to help you keep things straight—and so do we as long as the connection request arrives at the outside interface (defined as 207.15.33.15 as shown in the graphic) and the protocol of the connection is SSH.

Now, let's walk through the steps for creating this rule.

1. Click the Add A New Rule icon in the toolbar to open the Add Rule dialog box:

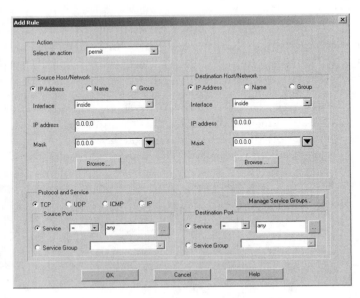

In the Add Rule dialog box, you can select all the details of the packet. To create the rule shown in Figure 6.5, you need to retain the permit action, and you need to alter the other three major sections (Source Host/Network, Destination Host/Network, and Protocol And Service).

2. In the Interface drop-down list, select Outside to open the Select Host/Network dialog box:

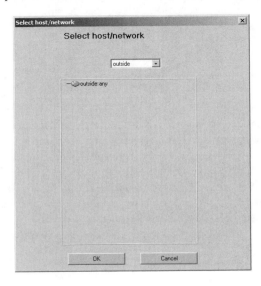

Because you haven't configured any networks or hosts, the only choice is to allow all hosts and networks sending packets through the outside interface. This is called the `outside:any` network.

3. Click OK to close the Select Host/Network dialog box.

4. Back in the Add Rule dialog box, enter the destination IP address and subnet mask of the server in the IP Address and Mask fields, as shown in Figure 6.6.

FIGURE 6.6

Source and destination configuration

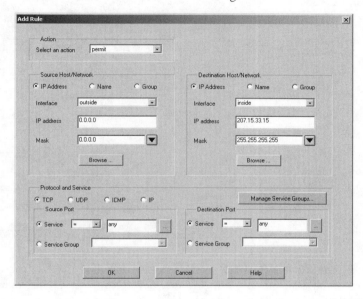

Now you need to specify the SSH protocol as the destination port. This filters out all traffic to the server that *isn't* SSH.

5. In the Destination Port section of the Protocol And Services section, click the Ellipsis button to the right of the Service radio button to open the Service dialog box:

6. Select the SSH service from the list, and then click OK.

Figure 6.7 shows the Add Rule dialog box after configuration.

FIGURE 6.7

The Add Rule
dialog box after
configuration

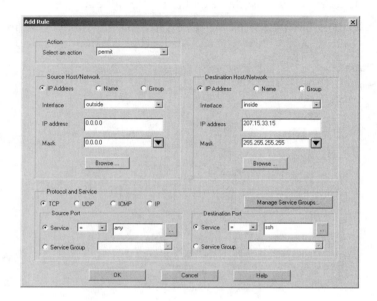

Notice that we left the Source Port to the default of any. This is because most client programs use a randomly available port as their source port. Defining a specific source port for a client program is usually a bad idea, unless you know for certain that it always binds to a specific port on the client machine. Also notice that there is a radio button under the Service option in both the Source Port and Destination port sections of the Protocol And Service section. Service Groups are simply named collections of protocols that need to be used together. This feature is commonly seen in applications that use multiple ports to support their functionality. For example, FTP uses two ports: port 21 for the actual data transfer, and port 20 for the logon information.

You're now ready to create the rule. Follow these steps:

1. In the Add Rules dialog box, click OK to open the Add Host/Network? dialog box:

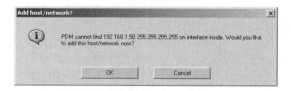

2. Click OK to open the Create Host/Network dialog box.

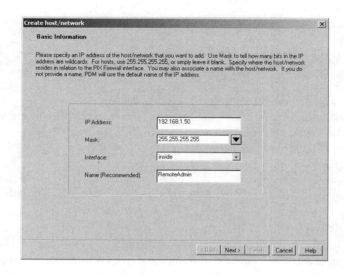

You use the Create Host/Network dialog box to verify (and change, if desired) the IP address, subnet mask, and related PIX interface of the server. You can also provide a common name to refer to the server.

3. Click Next to open the Edit Host/Network dialog box at the NAT tab, as shown in Figure 6.8.

FIGURE 6.8

The Edit Host/Network dialog box, open at the NAT tab

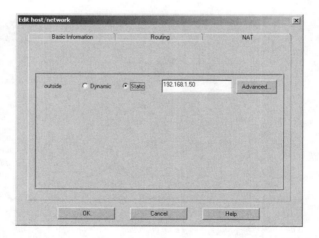

PIX has a limitation in that you can only define translation rules between an interface and another interface with a lower security level. NAT rules are either static or dynamic, and you can apply only one of each type to an interface. Static rules permanently map an IP address and port on a lower-security interface to an IP address on a higher-security interface, allowing an internal server to be accessible by hosts on the higher-security interface (that is, on the Internet).

Dynamic NAT, however, serves only to hide the internal IP addresses of hosts on higher-security networks. Essentially, Dynamic NAT is sufficient for simple networks that don't host any Internet-accessible servers. To expose services to the Internet, however, you define a static mapping, allowing incoming connections to the hosted services to pass through the firewall while blocking everything else.

In Figure 6.8, the Static option is selected, and we entered the (internal) IP address of the RemoteAdmin server. Clicking the Advanced button opens the Advanced NAT Options dialog box, in which you can specify additional options such as connection limits and SYN flood protection, and you can randomize TCP sequence numbers (activated by default). After you click OK, the NAT rule is created as appears as in Figure 6.5, earlier in this chapter. But you're not done yet. You still need to write the changes to PIX. To do so, click the Apply To PIX button at the bottom of the PDM window. This button is always displayed, no matter which tab you are working with.

AAA Rules

Access rules are firewall basics, but what about providing a higher level of user authentication? This requirement is common in organizations for which unauthorized Internet activity could have serious consequences. AAA rules allow you to specify what types of hosts, applications, or protocols require user authentication.

Before you can add an AAA rule, you need to add an AAA server to the PIX configuration. To do so, follow these steps:

1. In the main PDM screen, click the System Properties tab:

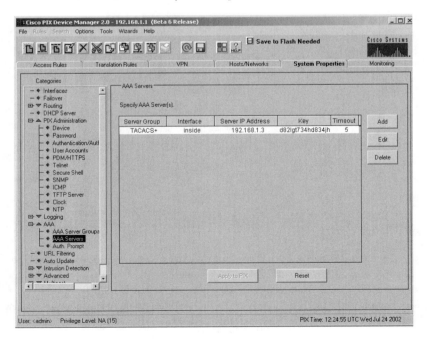

2. Select the AAA category in the left pane, and then select the AAA Servers subcategory.

3. Click the Add button to open the Add AAA Server dialog box:

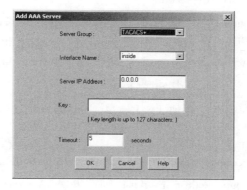

4. Select the desired server group (either TACACS+ or RADIUS).

5. Specify the appropriate PIX interface that will communicate with the AAA server.

6. Enter the AAA server IP address.

7. Insert the encryption key (which can be as many as 127 characters).

8. Alter the timeout interval, if necessary. (The default is 5 seconds.)

9. Click OK to close the Add AAA Server dialog box.

You can now create an AAA rule. To do so, follow these steps:

1. In the PDM main screen, click the Access Rules tab, and then click the AAA Rules radio button.

2. Click the Add A New Rule icon to open the Add Rule dialog box:

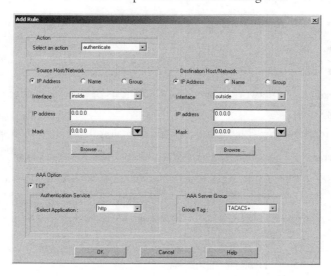

3. In the Select An Action drop-down list, select an action. Typically, this is Authenticate, but other options might be displayed (Do Not Authenticate, Authorize, Do Not Authorize, Account, Do Not Account).

4. In the Source Host/Network section, click an option button to indicate whether the Source and Destination Host/Network information will be an IP address, a host name, or a group.

5. In the Interface drop-down list, select the appropriate interface.

6. In the IP address field, enter the IP address.

7. In the Mask drop-down list, select the subnet mask, or click the Browse button to open the Browse dialog box and select from predefined host names and/or groups.

8. In the Select Application drop-down list in the AAA Option section, specify the authentication service to be used (options are any, http, telnet, and ftp).

9. In the Group Tag drop-down list, select the AAA Server Group that will handle this AAA rule.

10. Click OK to create the rule and return to the Access Rules tab of the PDM main screen.

The AAA Rules fields differ from those of the Access Rules in that they must integrate the PIX filtering capability with the authentication services of a TACACS+ or RADIUS server. The AAA Rules table contains the following:

The number in which the rule is evaluated. Each new Server Group or Action restarts the numbering.

Action The actions are as follows:

- Authenticate
- Do not authenticate
- Authorize
- Do not authorize
- Account
- Do not account

Source Host/Network Specifies which hosts or networks are required to authenticate using AAA.

Destination Host/Network Specifies the destination networks subject to this rule.

Interface The name of the interface where the AAA rule is applied.

Service The destination service that will force the AAA process to start. If this option is left at the default (any), all three service (http, ftp, and telnet) requests will require authentication.

Server Group Three possible entries are TACACS+, RADIUS, and a predefined Server Group

Once this rule is activated, users must enter a username and a password to browse the Internet. Some organizations combine this type of authentication with an extensive logging program to better support their security policy. Users must verify their identity before they surf the Web. The end result is that an organization can maintain detailed records on which individuals are visiting which sites. Organizations also use this type of authentication if unauthorized users might not be allowed to surf the Internet, but a restricted subset of authorized users are allowed access.

Filter Rules

Many organizations are (correctly) worried about hostile code and also want to ensure that their users are not looking at inappropriate web content. Filter rules allow you to define which ActiveX, Java, and JavaScript code will be allowed through the firewall. You can also use the services of a URL filtering server to define which websites are forbidden to your users. In this example, we'll configure a URL filter. Before you can add a URL filter, you need to define a URL filtering server. To do so, follow these steps:

1. In the main PDM screen, click the System Properties tab.

2. Select the URL filtering category in the left pane to display the URL Filtering box in the right pane:

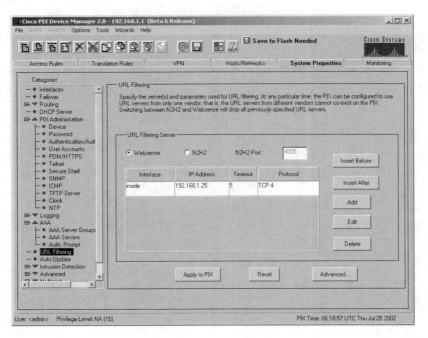

3. In the URL Filtering Server section, select the server type (either Websense or N2H2).

4. Click the Add button to open the Add Parameters for Websense URL Filtering dialog box.

5. In the Interface box, specify the appropriate PIX interface that will communicate with the URL filtering server.

6. In the IP Address box, enter the URL filtering server IP address.

7. Alter the timeout interval, if necessary, by entering a new number in the Timeout Interval box. (The default is 5 seconds.)

8. In the Protocol box, specify the protocol (choices are TCP 1, TCP 4, and UDP 4).

9. Click OK to close the Add Parameters for Websense URL Filtering dialog box.

If you are confident that you have sufficient response time and bandwidth in your network leave the default 5-second timeout interval. If you are using a newer version of Websense, you can select the TCP 4 option, which allows you to take advantage of some extra functionality, including the ability to perform a lookup on the name of the user requesting the URL. (The original TCP option is TCP 1, which provides only a limited subset of TCP filtering options.) UDP is also supported. Once your URL filtering server is configured, you can edit the Advanced URL Filtering settings.

Click the Advanced button in the URL Filtering category in the System Properties tab to open the Advanced URL Filtering dialog box:

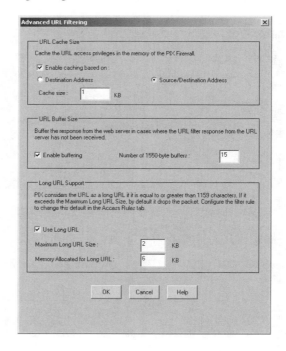

You use the settings in this dialog box to specify whether URL access privileges are cached in PIX memory, whether the PIX will buffer web server response if the URL filtering server is delayed, and how long URLs are handled.

These settings exist because Websense does more than just limit access based on prohibited URLs. It also relies on user-based access control lists to limit access based on user accounts. Because PIX always allows HTTP requests *out*, it might be necessary to buffer the response of the web server while the PIX waits for approval from the URL filtering server to allow the response *in* if the URL is allowed

Notice how the settings specify that PIX will retain access privileges based on the source and destination address. This specification reduces the number of calls to the URL Filtering server, while ensuring that only individuals allowed to that specific URL can retrieve it.

The option to enable URL buffering has been selected by creating 15 buffers of 1.5KB each, because there is the possibility that users will generate so many requests for web pages that the web server will respond before the URL filtering server tells PIX that the user is authorized. So that the web server response isn't lost (and an error returned to the user's browser), the PIX can cache the response until it receives the acceptance (or denial) from the URL filtering server. If PIX receives acceptance, it forwards the response to the client.

Finally, the option to enable long URL support has been configured. A URL is considered "long" if it exceeds 1159 characters. By default, a URL must be 2KB to be considered too "long"—a situation that might indicate hostile code appended to the URL. In this example, 6KB is set aside for long URLs.

NOTE   *This final setting can be a good idea if you have a lot of Hotmail users. (Hotmail is a web-based e-mail service from Microsoft.) In Hotmail, clicking a link in an e-mail message opens a new window. Instead of taking you directly to the new site, however, Hotmail actually embeds the new site under a Hotmail banner, reminding you of how you got to this particular page. The problem comes from the link itself: it points back to Hotmail, but appends the new link (and other control information) after it, something that can take up a lot of space.*

Now that you have configured a URL filtering server, you can create a Filter rule. Follow these steps:

1. Click the Add Filter icon to open the Add Rule dialog box:

2. In the Select An Action drop-down list, select Filter URL.

3. In the Source Host/Network and Destination Host/Network sections, specify either the IP information or the name of the host or network that will be subject to this rule. In this example, the filter will apply to connections originating inside the network.

4. In the URL Filtering Option section, check the CGI Truncate check box. This option removes any CGI script that is passed as part of a web request.

5. In the Long URL section, click the Deny radio button so that users will see a message saying that access is prohibited.

6. Click the No radio button to specify that if the URL server becomes unavailable, no outgoing connections will be allowed.

7. Click OK to close the Add Rule dialog box and return to the Access Rules tab on the main PDM screen:

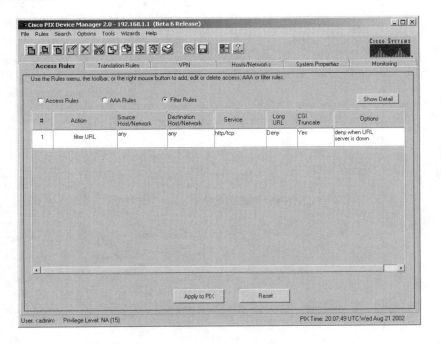

The Filter Rules fields are as follows:

The order in which the rule is evaluated.

Action   Keywords include the following:

◆ `filter ActiveX`

◆ `filter Java applet`

- ◆ `filter URL`

- ◆ `do not filter URL`

Source Host/Network   The addresses that are requesting the URL or code objects.

Destination Host/Network   The addresses that host the URL or code objects.

Service   The protocol that will be filtered.

Long URL   The action taken when a URL is longer than the maximum allowed value. The options are as follows:

- ◆ Drop

- ◆ Truncate

- ◆ Deny

CGI Truncate   Specifies whether CGI script can be embedded in a URL.

Options   Defines the action (allow or deny) to be taken by PIX when the URL filtering server cannot be reached.

Now that you've seen some of the options and an example of Access Rules, let's look in detail at the Translation Rules tab of the main PDM screen.

Translation Rules

Translation rules define how PIX performs NAT and PAT. Figure 6.9 shows the configuration based on the previous changes made in this chapter.

FIGURE 6.9

The Translation Rules tab

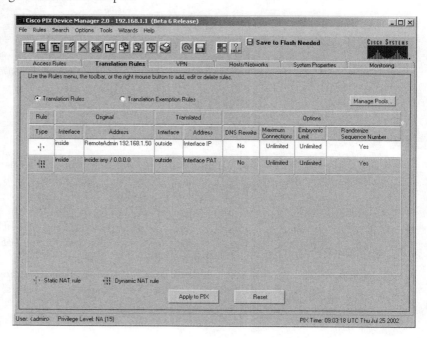

The first rule to be evaluated is the static rule that operates on the outside interface and allows external connections to be created to the internal server. (The Type icon indicates the one-to-one relationship of a static rule.) Essentially, remote users enter the IP address of the outside PIX interface in their SSH client software. When the SSH session request arrives at PIX, it is first evaluated for an access rule (which we created earlier). Once PIX authorizes the session, it checks for any translation rules on the outside interface, finds the first rule (which is currently the only rule applied to the external interface), uses this first translation rule to replace the original destination IP address (the IP address assigned to the outside PIX interface) with the IP address of the RemoteAdmin server (192.168.1.50), and then forwards the session data to the inside network, to be routed normally.

But what about the translation rule options? In the next example, you will delete the second (albeit original) rule that provided dynamic NAT/PAT services to the inside network and re-create it. In Figure 6.10, you can see a new translation rule (after deleting the dynamic rule).

FIGURE 6.10

The Add Address Translation Rule dialog box

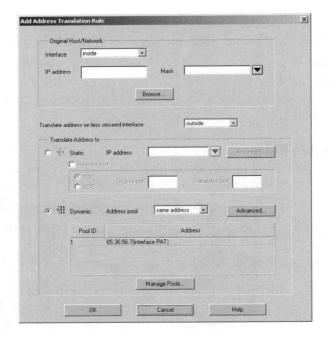

Figure 6.10 shows the default settings. Notice that when the Dynamic option is chosen, you are presented with (at least) one address pool, but this pool is made up of only one IP address! This actually makes sense, because, by default, you actually use only the single IP address bound to the outside interface (in this example, 65.36.56.7) to mask *all* your inside network hosts.

How is this possible? Because PAT actually creates a table inside PIX that forces each outgoing connection to use a distinct dynamic port (remember that there are 65,535 possible TCP *and* UDP ports), even though they are all sharing the same IP address. When PIX receives the external response, it consults the PAT table to replace the destination IP address with the appropriate inside IP address, based on the port used by the connection when it was first created.

It's actually possible to create multiple address pools by assigning multiple, valid external IP addresses to the outside interface. This is rarely done, however, simply because it is rare for more than 60,000 computers to send their traffic through a single firewall. However, it is possible that you want your outgoing sessions to use a different public IP address than the incoming sessions. In other words, hosts on the Internet connecting to your web server and using a static NAT translation point to one address (say, 65.36.56.7), but you want all your internal users to be seen as having a different address (say, 65.36.56.8) so that it is easier for you to distinguish traffic types in your firewall logs (and IDS alerts!).

In this case, you need to create a new pool. Follow these steps

1. In the Add Address Translation Rule dialog box, click the Manage Pools button, to open the Manage Global Address Pools dialog box:

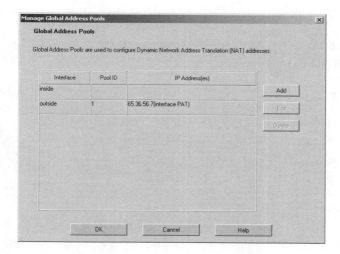

2. Click the Add button to open the Add Global Pool Item dialog box:

3. In the Interface drop-down list, select Outside.

We're choosing the outside interface because incoming response packets (returning packets from web servers and so on) need the correct (inside) address as the destination IP and port *before* they are evaluated inside PIX. PIX needs the correct internal (and typically private) IP address to send the packet on to that correct network.

4. Click the Port Address Translation (PAT) radio button.

5. In the IP Address field, enter the external IP address that will be used by this global pool.

6. Click OK to close the Add Global Pool Item dialog box and create the new global pool.

7. Click OK to close the Manage Global Address Pools dialog box.

8. In the Add Address Translation Rule dialog box, select the new address pool.

9. Click OK to create the new Address Translation Rule, as shown in Figure 6.11.

FIGURE 6.11

The Add Address Translation Rule dialog box

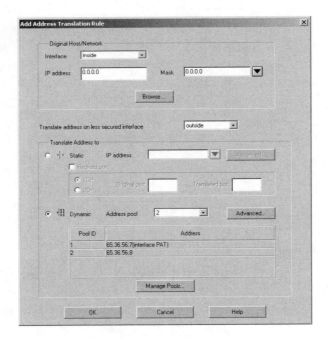

After you create the rule, review your results. Notice that the translated address now represents the new IP address that will be used only for dynamic translation (and not for the static translation of the server). This is a real benefit. When you review the firewall logs, you can rapidly distinguish between traffic originating from your internal network (most likely desktop web browsing and e-mail) and requests for your web server (which are more likely to contain hostile attacks or probes). Having a distinct IP address for your web server traffic also means you can more easily expose that data to database and script analysis.

To set the advanced NAT options, follow these steps:

1. In the Address Rules table, double-click the new rule you created to open the Edit Address Rule dialog box.

2. Click the Advanced button to open the Advanced NAT Options dialog box:

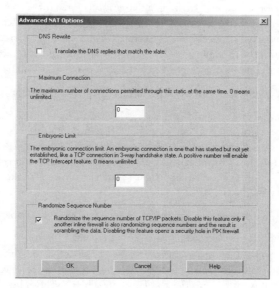

3. In the DNS Rewrite section, click the Translate The DNS Replies That Match The Date check box.

Selecting this option allows a DNS client on the outside network to resolve the name of a host on the internal network to a public IP address. In other words, let's say that your network is Active Directory–based, which means that all your internal hosts register themselves with your DNS server as they boot up. As a result, your DNS server that supports your Active Directory will list your server (assuming it is Windows 2000 based) as having an IP address of 192.168.1.50. This is correct for internal operations, but remember that external clients can't (and shouldn't) see that address— they use the external address (6.36.56.7) of PIX instead. Turning on the Translate The DNS Replies That Match The Date option tells PIX to rewrite DNS query results to reflect the public *outside* address, instead of the internal address that is actually stored (and returned) by the DNS server.

4. In the Maximum Connection section, accept the default.

This setting determines the maximum number of connections that can use this particular NAT rule, and zero means no restrictions. This option is rather obscure, and we can only imagine that you would implement it on static NAT rules with the intent to limit the number of connections allowed to a particular sensitive service, such as the static mapping to your server. Limiting the maximum connections to 1 means that only one remote administrator at a time can have access, a possibility that might work well for your security policy.

5. In the Embryonic Limit option, accept the default value of zero.

This section deals with a common DoS attack, in which an attacker creates multiple TCP connection requests but doesn't complete them, in an attempt to force the server to dedicate resources to "waiting" for the handshake process to complete. By specifying a number other than zero ,you can indicate how many of these partial connections are tolerated. Once the limit is exceeded, PIX itself answers any future connections until the number subsides below the limit, possibly indicating that an attack is over or, at the very least, that the performance pressure on a server (typically a web server) has subsided.

6. Click the check box in the Randomize Sequence Number section.

This setting works to avoid specific types of attacks that use the (normally) incremental nature of TCP sequence numbers. Remember that TCP sequence numbers are used by the hosts involved in a conversation to make sure that all packets are received. If attackers can predict the next sequence of packets expected by a firewall, they can attempt to hijack a valid session, passing hostile code or data through the firewall. Randomizing those sequence numbers makes it that much harder for a cracker to sneak data past the firewall.

7. Click OK to close the Advanced NAT Options dialog box.

Deciding which options to enable can be difficult. The more you know about your network, the better. This is where having a comprehensive (and detailed) baseline of your network will come into play. If you decide to keep a single DNS that resolves internal servers for both internal and external hosts, you might want to consider the Translate The DNS Replies That Match The Date option.

However, keep in mind that in the Active Directory default configuration, all computers, not just servers, have their IP address and domain names dynamically added to DNS servers. Thus, anyone on the Internet can send a series of requests to your DNS server and basically map your entire network (based on DNS names), and even if they can't see the actual (private) IP addresses, this information can still be valuable for a determined cracker.

You can apply the Maximum Connection option to this translation rule, and it might make sense as part of your defense-in-depth strategy. By limiting the number of remote administration connections to PIX, you can reduce the possibility that a cracker can be simultaneously accessing your server along with your administrators. By maintaining the connection limit at 1, you also have a rather cut-and-dried way to determine if a cracker *is* currently connected: no other (legitimate) administrator can remotely connect!

Although you can keep the default of randomizing sequence numbers, don't enable the embryonic limit unless (or until) your network becomes the target of a large number of DoS/DDoS attacks, and even then you want to coordinate with your ISP in an attempt to shut the problem down at the source, if at all possible.

Once you define access and translation rules, your basic firewall work is finished. You now have a configuration that will protect your internal network from common hostile attacks, filter out URLs based on a URL filtering server, and still allow incoming connections to your web server. Not too difficult, right? Before we show you a more complex example (that includes a DMZ), let's briefly walk through some of the other configurable options of PIX, starting with the VPN tab of the main PDM screen.

CONFIGURING VPN

The VPN tab (see Figure 6.12) contains several categories (and subcategories) of configurations. The PIX operating system actually embodies a fairly sophisticated set of VPN options, including acting as a VPN peer, server, and client. The first two categories (IPSec and IKE) deal with creating the VPN tunnel itself. The Remote Access category defines how PIX will act as a VPN server (either with Cisco's VPN protocol or Microsoft's L2TP/PPTP). The VPN System Options specify whether access checks apply to IPSec, L2TP, or PPTP traffic. The Easy VPN Remote category describes how PIX works with other Easy VPN products (as a client or server) and the options that are available.

FIGURE 6.12

The PDM VPN tab

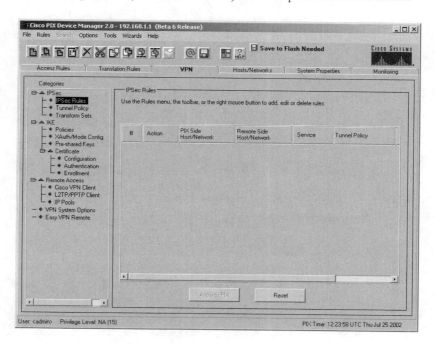

THE HOSTS/NETWORKS TAB

This tab (see Figure 6.13) is involved with the basic configuration of PIX itself. You use the options on this tab to create the hosts and, more important, the networks that PIX assigns to the various interfaces (also defined here). In essence, you use this tab to set up the network environments in which PIX exists. The Hosts part of this tab name refers to the fact that any rule that applies to a specific host (as opposed to a network in general) must also be defined. This might seem like overkill, but it really makes good management sense. Definitions of networks and hosts that you create on this tab are visible to *all* other functions provided by PIX, typically through a Browse button that lets you select to which host(s) or network(s) a rule will apply.

You can also define route and NAT settings on this tab. Keep in mind that PIX acts as a (sophisticated) router, not just a firewall. This capability becomes more involved when you introduce NAT/PAT functions into the mix, because NAT functions can cause routing functions to fail if the NAT process is not configured correctly.

FIGURE 6.13

The Hosts/Net-
works tab

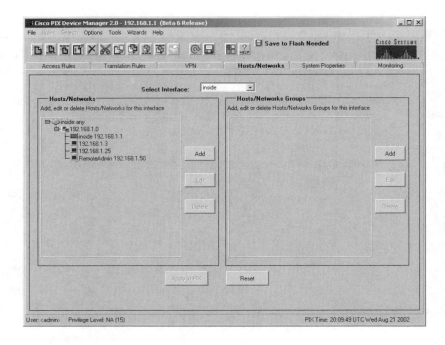

FIGURE 6.13

The Hosts/Net-
works tab

THE SYSTEM PROPERTIES TAB

The System Properties tab, which is shown in Figure 6.14, contains the categories listed and described in Table 6.3.

FIGURE 6.14

The System Proper-
ties tab

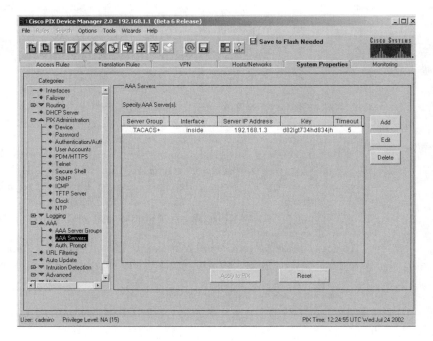

TABLE 6.3: THE SYSTEM PROPERTIES TAB CATEGORIES AND DESCRIPTIONS

CATEGORY	DESCRIPTION/SUBCATEGORY
Interfaces	Defines PIX interfaces, including route information.
Failover	Configures how PIX works with other PIX firewalls for fault tolerant operations.
Routing	Defines RIP, static routes, and proxy ARP settings.
DHCP Server	Allows PIX to act as a DHCP server.
PIX Administration	Defines how PIX is administered.
Logging	Controls how logging is configured, including logging failover services, PDM logging level, syslog capabilities, and logging debugging options.
AAA	Defines server groups and servers and specifies how authentication is prompted.
URL Filtering	Specifies which URL filter servers are configured, along with the various options for these servers.
Auto Update	Allows PIX to automatically update configuration and operating system parameters.
Intrusion Detection	Specifies IDS policies and which attack signatures to use.
Advanced	Enables sophisticated (and specific) attack recognition and response.
Multicast	Handles multicast operations (used for multimedia, primarily).
History Metrics	Allows you to review the performance of PIX in relation to your network traffic as whole. It includes information on access rules, translation rules, and URL filtering.

Most of the core configuration of PIX that supports rule creation takes place on this tab. Any option that doesn't warrant a separate tab is also located here.

Monitoring

Almost as detailed as the System Properties tab, the Monitoring tab, shown in Figure 6.15, contains a multitude of options that you can use to verify the operation of PIX as a whole, as well as the subcomponents used in PIX operation. Table 6.4 lists and describes these options.

TABLE 6.4: THE MONITORING TAB CATEGORIES AND DESCRIPTIONS

CATEGORY	DESCRIPTION
PDM Log	Defines the type of Unix syslog messages passed by the PIX
Secure Shell Sessions	Displays currently connected SSH sessions
Telnet Console Sessions	Displays currently connected Telnet sessions

Continued on next page

TABLE 6.4: THE MONITORING TAB CATEGORIES AND DESCRIPTIONS *(continued)*

CATEGORY	DESCRIPTION
User Licenses	Displays the number of licenses available, along with the total number of available licenses
PDM Users	Displays the current PDM sessions
DHCP Client	Shows the current DHCP client lease information
PPoE Client	Displays current PPoE configuration information, along with performance statistics
VPN Statistics	Subcategories include IKE, IPSec, L2TP, and PPTP session information
VPN Connection Graphs	Current IPSec and L2TP/PPTP connection information
System Graphs	Subcategories include data blocks, CPU utilization, failover status, and memory statistics
Connection Graphs	Subcategories include xlate status and a performance monitor
Miscellaneous Graphs	Displays IDS information
Interface Graphs	Displays dropped packets, total throughput, and other common interface statistics useful for troubleshooting and performance monitoring

FIGURE 6.15

The Monitoring tab

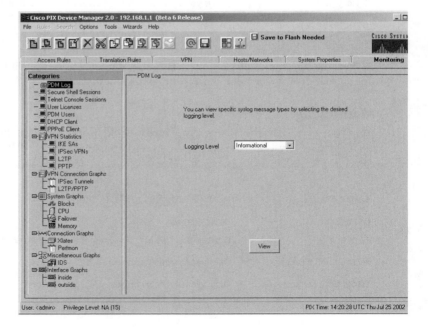

Although the Monitoring tab can provide you with a wealth of information (as well as being sheer eye candy for those inclined to statistics), it is no substitute for maintaining a history log. Log as extensively as your bandwidth will allow. This data will be invaluable later for analysis and forensic purposes (especially if you discover that you have, indeed, been attacked).

Handling the massive amount of information that comes from logging and monitoring is one of the greatest challenges with any security device that operates at the perimeter of a network. When you combine a firewall with an IDS (covered in Chapter 8), using automated tools to help filter and isolate important data becomes essential. Although many products can assist you in your analysis, they are useless unless you understand the fundamentals and recommended practices of logging. We highly recommend Counterpane's Log Analysis Resources website as a starting point and continual reference: `www.counterpane.com/log-analysis.html`.

TIP *Incorrectly configured firewalls are considered the root cause of many successful network-based attacks. Consider purchasing and implementing Cisco's Secure Policy Manager, which integrates the various policies and configurations of all Cisco devices on your network and can help you avoid configuration mistakes that would leave you network vulnerable.*

Summary

The PIX firewall is an excellent example of a typical enterprise-level firewall. Involving access lists, NAT rules, and URL filtering, PIX encompasses many of the common firewall functions required by today's networks. By using the PDM, you can easily (and graphically) configure your PIX firewall to provide sophisticated firewall functions, including NAT, URL filtering, and hostile code protection.

Chapter 7

Intrusion Detection Systems

INTRUSION DETECTION SYSTEMS (IDSs) represent a sophisticated concept that involves a variety of technologies. What is safe to say is that IDSs are becoming as essential to network security as the firewall, and, in fact, many of the distinctions between an IDS and a firewall are blurring.

We'll cover the following topics in this chapter:

- ◆ IDS types

- ◆ NIDS limitations

- ◆ Host-based NIDS

- ◆ NIDS fusion

- ◆ Snort: a popular NIDS

IDS Types

Traditionally, IDS has all been about analyzing network traffic to look for evidence of attack. Increasingly, however, IDS is also about scanning access logs and analyzing the characteristics of files to see if they have been compromised. And IDS has even been extended to the concept of honeypots—a fake network used to attract and distract crackers from the real network, all the while monitoring their actions.

The types of IDSs are categorized as follows:

Network Intrusion Detection System (NIDS)   Analyzes packets on a network and tries to determine if a cracker is trying to break into a system or cause a denial of service (DoS) attack. An NIDS typically runs on a hub or a router, analyzing all traffic flowing through that device. Snort, which we'll look at later in this chapter, is an example of an NIDS.

Host Intrusion Detection System (HIDS)   Similar to an NIDS, an HIDS analyzes network traffic sent to and from a single machine. Most of today's commercial NIDSs usually have some sort of HIDS element, and these systems are called hybrid IDSs.

System Integrity Verifier (SIV)   Keeps track of critical system files and notifies an administrator when they are altered (usually by a cracker attempting to replace a valid copy with a Trojan horse). Tripwire, which is discussed later in this chapter, is an example of an SIV.

Log File Monitor (LFM)   "Reads" the logs generated by network services looking for attack patterns. Swatch is an example of an LFM.

Honeypot   A deception system that has false services with well-known vulnerabilities to attract hacker attention or distract them from an actual system. The Deception Toolkit is an example of a honeypot.

In this chapter, we'll focus primarily on NIDS because, along with a firewall, it is the first line of defense. SIVs and LFMs are fairly straightforward. (LFMs actually look for many of the same attack signatures as NIDSs do.) Honeypots are still a black art and require a lot of additional resources.

Network Intrusion Detection System

To understand the traditional NIDS, think about having one or more network protocol experts (affectionately known as "bit weenies") armed with a network analyzer and watching passing traffic. These specialists know about all the latest exploits that an attacker might attempt to launch, and they diligently check every packet to see if any suspicious traffic is passing on the wire. If they find suspicious traffic, they immediately contact the network administrator and inform them of their findings.

Take the human element from this scenario, and you have a Network Intrusion Detection System. An NIDS captures all passing traffic on the network, just like a network analyzer. Once this information has been read into memory, the system compares the packets with a number of known attack patterns. For example, if the NIDS notices that a particular host is repeatedly sending SYN packets to another host without ever attempting to complete the connection, the NIDS identifies this as a SYN attack and takes appropriate action. A good NIDS may have well over 100 attack patterns saved in its database.

The action taken depends on the particular NIDS you are using and how you have it configured. All NIDSs can log suspicious events. Some will even save a raw packet capture of the traffic so that it can be analyzed later by the network administrator. Others can be configured to send out an alert, such as an e-mail message or a page. Many NIDSs can attempt to interfere with the suspicious transmission by resetting both ends of the connection. Finally, a few can interact with a firewall or a router to modify the filter rules and block the attacking host. (We'll discuss the benefits and drawbacks associated with each of these actions in detail later in this chapter.)

An NIDS traditionally consists of two parts:

◆ The *sensor*, which captures and analyzes the traffic

◆ The *console*, from which you can manage the sensor and run all reports

Network Intrusion Detection Systems are extreme resource hogs. Vendors typically recommend that you run the sensor on a dedicated system with 256MB of RAM and an Intel 300MHz Pentium III or Pro processor (or RISC equivalent if the sensor is running on Unix). Since an NIDS logs all traffic, copious amounts of disk space are required for its databases. Although about 100MB of disk space is usually recommended, plan to use a lot more unless you frequently purge the database or your network sees very little traffic. The requirements for the dedicated system running the console are about the same, except you must reserve enough disk space to store a copy of each sensor's database.

System Integrity Verifier

Consider the worst-case scenario: despite all your security precautions, a cracker penetrates your firewall, using an innovative attack that your NIDS can't detect. The end state is that your systems are compromised. What's worse, you have no idea. That's where a *filesystem IDS* comes into play. By creating a digital signature of all critical system files (the files most likely to be altered by Trojan horses or rootkits), your system can regularly re-compare these signatures with the actual files. If even a single bit is changed, your filesystem IDS will know about it and alert you.

NOTE *A rootkit is a collection of utilities, often masking as legitimate administrative programs, that allow an attacker to gain continued remote control of a system without being detected.*

The most popular filesystem IDS is Tripwire. Released as a commercial product for Windows and Unix, Tripwire has been made open source for Linux, once again confirming the advanced role Linux plays in the security world. Tripwire works by keeping track of a binary signature of a file, along with the size of the file over time. As is the case with any highly detailed security tool, optimizing the filters so they match your environment is the most difficult part of the process.

In fact, Tripwire is so sensitive that it is used for purposes other than IDS, such as ensuring that unauthorized software from users is not installed on a system or that critical system files haven't become corrupt through improper system shutdown. Tripwire can also play a significant part in the forensic analysis of your system if it actually is compromised.

Tripwire consists of the following:

◆ Configuration files control operation as a whole.

◆ Policy files dictate allowed activities.

◆ Report files generate e-mail message notifying an administrator when a file changes.

◆ A database contains the binary signatures of the files themselves.

Tripwire encrypts this database with a 1024-bit key based on the El Gamal algorithm. There are actually two sets of keys: a site key protects the policy and configuration files for Tripwire installations across a "site," and a local key protects the database (and report) files on individual systems.

Combining Tripwire with a traditional NIDS is a good foundation for securing and monitoring your system. We can take our integration efforts further, however, as you'll see in the next section.

Log File Monitor

Log files can be an incredible asset, but because they deal with so much information, only an automated approach will be successful. Even before you choose your monitoring software, you need to take the following three steps when you create a log file monitoring plan:

1. Determine what information you need out of your system.

2. Locate the logs that contain that information.

3. Define what types of entries will trigger alerts.

For example, you're worried about your e-mail system. You've had problems in the past with spammers relaying e-mail through your mail server (usually the result of misconfiguration on the part of the e-mail administrator). Although you believe you've corrected the problem, you'd like to be notified if someone misuses your system again. Once you determine *what* you want to know (has someone misused your system), you must determine which, of all your system logs, has that information. Depending on your e-mail system, that information could be in the Windows Application Event Log for Microsoft systems running the Microsoft Exchange e-mail server or in the `/var/log/maillog` file for a Linux system running the sendmail e-mail server.

Now, the difficult part: what will be the trigger(s)? A good starting place is to identify relay attempts and compare the IP address of the machine attempting the relay with a list of IP addresses that contain valid relay hosts. Additionally, you can look for the specific relay command in your log files (for example, the `expand` command in sendmail). One way to validate our LFM is to actually create an incident of the kind you're trying to find. This allows you to make sure that your LFM configuration will catch the actual incident.

Using LFMs with an NIDS and an SIV provides a robust approach to system security. For those looking for the highest level of sophistication, however, you need to get yourself a decoy—a honeypot.

Honeypot

One of the original honeypot stories comes from *The Cuckoo's Egg*, a book by Clifford Stoll (Pocket Books, 2000). In the 1980s, a cracker has been traced to Germany, but all attempts to pinpoint him further are frustrated by the German phone system, which is based on analog circuits. Tracing a connection takes time. To keep the cracker on the line, Cliff (along with the team helping him track this cracker) builds a series of fake computer files that purport to detail a new secret plane in development by the U.S. military. Their effort pays off: the cracker is so fascinated by the drawings and fake information that he stays connected long enough for his phone call to be traced.

From this example, you can see that a honeypot is nothing more than a series of resources that are meant to be probed, attacked, or compromised—all for the purpose of misleading a cracker (called a *production* honeypot) or understanding a cracker's methods (called a *research* honeypot). The value of a honeypot lies in simplicity. Any time a connection is sent to a honeypot, it is most likely a probe or an attack. Any connections from the honeypot indicate that it has been compromised.

A couple of advantages are associated with using honeypots:

◆ They collect data on how attackers penetrate and what they do once in the system.

◆ They help optimize resources. Crackers are hitting your honeypot, not your firewall or NIDS.

But there are some downsides.

◆ Honeypots are useless if the attacker doesn't take the bait.

◆ If the honeypot is not configured correctly, crackers can attack other resources on your network.

Because honeypot configuration is complicated and risky, don't implement a honeypot unless you are confident of your ability to install, monitor, and maintain it.

Typically, production honeypots are implemented as part of a larger security effort, with clearly defined parameters about what services will be offered and what actions will be taken once the system is compromised. All these decisions maximize the value of a honeypot while reducing the risk to your system or to others! For more information on honeypots, including how to set up, monitor, and maintain one, visit `http://project.honeynet.org`.

NIDS Limitations

So far, the various IDS types seem like wonderful security devices. Even though we'll focus the rest of the chapter on NIDS, keep in mind that the drawbacks and challenges of an NIDS can apply to the other IDS types as well. In fact, the authors of a popular column in the trade magazine *InfoWorld* declared NIDS dead at the end of the year 2000 because of switched network technologies, imperfect one-size-fits-all attack signatures, high-volume network traffic overloading NIDS systems, and encrypted network data hiding pertinent attack information from the NIDS system, while leaving web servers vulnerable. Many times NIDS systems simply cannot respond in time to prevent an attack. It is now apparent, however, that NIDS, while challenged, has only grown in popularity. Let's look at a common denial of service (DoS) attack to see why this has happened.

Teardrop Attacks

A teardrop attack occurs when an attacker sends fragments of data that a system is unable to reassemble. Some systems and services can freeze when overwhelmed by the sheer number of malformed packets.

To understand how a teardrop attack is used against a system, you must first understand the purpose of the fragmentation offset field and the length field within the IP header. A decode of an IP header is shown in Figure 7.1. The fragmentation offset field is typically used by routers. If a router receives a packet that is too large for the next segment, the router needs to fragment the data before passing it along. The fragmentation offset field is used along with the length field so that the receiving system can reassemble the datagram in the correct order. When a fragmentation offset value of 0 is received, the receiving system assumes either that this is the first packet of fragmented information or that fragmentation has not been used.

FIGURE 7.1

A decode of an IP header

```
Packet Number : 13              3:52:02 PM
Length : 66 bytes
ether: ==================== Ethernet Datalink Layer ====================
       Station: Skylar ----> This_Workstation
       Type: 0x0800 (IP)
   ip: ==================== Internet Protocol ====================
       Station:10.1.1.100 ---->10.1.1.25
       Protocol: TCP
       Version: 4
       Header Length (32 bit words): 5
       Precedence: Routine
           Normal Delay, Normal Throughput, Normal Reliability
       Total length: 48
       Identification: 21249
       Fragmentation not allowed, Last fragment
       Fragment Offset: 0
       Time to Live: 128 seconds
       Checksum: 0x9148(Valid)
  tcp: ================ Transmission Control Protocol =================
       Source Port: 258
       Destination Port: 1027
       Sequence Number: 417610
       Acknowledgement Number: 898472
       Data Offset (32-bit words): 5
       Window: 8510
       Control Bits: Acknowledgement Field is Valid (ACK)
           Push Function Requested (PSH)
       Checksum: 0x5DB5(Valid)
       Urgent Pointer: 0
```

If fragmentation has occurred, the receiving system uses the offset to determine where the data within each packet should be placed when rebuilding the datagram. For an analogy, think of a child's set of numbered building blocks. As long as the child follows the numbering plan and puts the blocks together in the right order, they can build a house, a car, or even a plane. In fact, they don't even need to know what they are trying to build. They simply have to assemble the blocks in the specified order.

The IP fragmentation offset works in much the same way. The offset tells the receiving system how far from the front of the datagram to place the included payload. If all goes well, this schema allows the datagram to be reassembled in the correct order. The length field is used as a verification check to ensure that there is no overlap and that data has not been corrupted in transit. For example, if you place fragments 1 and 3 within the datagram and then try to place fragment 2, but you find that fragment 2 is too large and will overwrite some of fragment 3, you know you have a problem.

At this point, the system tries to realign the datagrams to see if it can make them fit. If it cannot, the receiving system sends out a request that the data be resent. Most IP stacks can deal with overlaps or payloads that are too large for their segment.

LAUNCHING A TEARDROP ATTACK

A teardrop attack starts by sending a normal packet of data with a normal-sized payload and a fragmentation offset of 0. From the initial packet of data, a teardrop attack is indistinguishable from a normal data transfer. Subsequent packets, however, have modified fragmentation offset and length fields. This ensuing traffic is responsible for crashing the target system.

When the second packet of data is received, the fragmentation offset is consulted to see where within the datagram this information should be placed. In a teardrop attack, the offset on the second packet claims that this information should be placed somewhere within the first fragment. When the payload field is checked, the receiving system finds that this data is not even large enough to extend past the end of the first fragment. In other words, this second fragment does not overlap the first fragment; it is actually fully contained inside it. Since this is not an error condition that anyone expected, there is no routine to handle it, and this information causes a buffer overflow—crashing the receiving system. For some operating systems, only one malformed packet is required. Others will not crash unless multiple malformed packets are received.

NIDS VERSUS TEARDROP

How would a typical NIDS deal with this attack? When the teardrop attack is launched, the initial packet resembles a normal data transfer. From just looking at this first packet of information, an NIDS has no way of knowing that an attack is about to occur.

When the second packet is transmitted, the NIDS can put together the datagram fragments and identify that this is a classic example of a teardrop attack. The NIDS can then alert the networking staff and take preventive measures to stop the attack.

You only have one tiny little problem: if your attacker was lucky enough to identify an operating system that will crash with only one malformed packet, it is too late to prevent the attack from occurring. Although your networking staff will have the benefit of knowing that their server has just crashed, they probably already figured that out from the number of calls from irate users.

Although your intrusion detection system can tell you why the server crashed, it can't prevent the attack from occurring in the first place. To prevent future occurrences, you need to patch the system.

Why not simply block the attacking IP address? Your attacker is probably savvy enough to use IP spoofing, making it look as if the attack came from somewhere other than their real IP address. Unless your NIDS is on the same collision domain as the attacking system, it will be unable to detect that a spoofed address is being used. This means that your attacker can continue to randomly change the source IP address and launch successful attacks.

Other Known NIDS Limitations

In February 1998, Secure Networks, Inc. released a white paper about its testing of a number of intrusion detection systems. This testing discovered a number of vulnerabilities in NIDS that allow an attacker to launch a completely undetected attack.

Although some conclusions of the study are a bit melodramatic, the actual testing raises some valid points. In short, the study focused on two problem areas:

♦ NIDS detection of manipulated data

♦ Direct attacks on the NIDS itself

The conclusion of the study was that sniffer-based intrusion detection would never be capable of reliably detecting attacks.

DATA MANIPULATION

Virtually none of the intrusion detection systems in the study reassembled the IP packets in an identical manner to systems communicating via IP. This resulted in some inconsistencies between what the NIDS perceived was occurring within the packet stream and what the receiving system was able to process.

One problem was that some of the intrusion detection systems did not verify the checksum field with the IP header (refer to Figure 7.1). This would most certainly be done by the receiving system, and manipulating this field would cause the NIDS to record a different payload than the receiving system would process.

The example cited in the study was the PHF CGI attack. An NIDS attempts to detect this attack by looking for the character string phf within the payload portion of all HTTP requests. If this pattern is detected, the NIDS assumes that this attack is taking place. A savvy attacker could attempt to send a series of packets, each with one character that produced the string phoof. The attacker could then manipulate the checksum field so that each packet that contains the letter o has an invalid checksum. The result is that while the receiving system (which verifies the checksum) processes only the character string phf, the NIDS (which does not verify the checksum) reads this transmission as phoof.

Although this inconsistency in how traffic is processed is certainly a valid concern, it is not insurmountable. For example, ISS RealSecure, one of the packages that exhibited this problem, was fixed by the next product release. Such problems are typical in an infant technology. Firewall vendors have gone through a similar learning process and continue to make improvements even today. There is no reason to assume that network security will ever become a stagnant field.

ATTACKS AGAINST THE NIDS

Another issue raised by the Secure Networks study was the vulnerability of the NIDS to direct attacks. This concern is valid, because a direct attack against the NIDS might inhibit its ability to detect intrusions. By shutting down the NIDS, an attacker can launch an attack against the network without fear of detection.

NIDS VERSUS FIREWALL

A firewall acts as a perimeter guard. All traffic must pass through it to move from one section of a network to another. If the firewall is attacked and services are disrupted, it typically *fails close*, meaning that it is unable to pass traffic. Although this situation disrupts all transmissions, it prevents an attacker from disabling the firewall and launching an attack on an internal host.

An NIDS, on the other hand, does not sit between network segments. It is designed to run unobtrusively within a single collision domain. If the NIDS is disabled, it technically *fails open* because traffic flow is not disrupted. An attacker might be able to disable the NIDS while still gaining access to network resources. In this case, all attacks launched while the NIDS is offline are undocumented.

Again, this problem is not as insurmountable as the Secure Network study would make it seem. There is no legitimate reason for the intrusion detection system to be directly addressed by every network host. The act of sniffing network traffic does not require a valid IP address. Only the following systems require connectivity:

◆ The sensor

◆ The console

◆ A DNS system (if you want to resolve IP addresses to host names)

◆ The firewall or router (if you want to let the NIDS modify filtering rules)

You can easily segregate NIDS communications from the public network using a separate private network along with private IP address space. In fact, segregation can even be tunneled over the same network, as long as routing to this subnet is disabled. Although the sensor requires an IP protocol stack and thus an IP address on the main network, this IP address doesn't have to be valid. An example of this configuration is shown in Figure 7.2.

In Figure 7.2, the regular network systems are assigned address space from the 10.1.1.0 subnet. All systems within this subnet are allowed some level of Internet access, and the firewall is configured to use NAT (Network Address Translation) with these addresses. As far as the firewall is concerned, only the 10.1.1.0 network exists internally.

If you look closely at the figure, you will notice that the DNS system has two IP addresses: one for the 10.1.1.0 network and one for the 192.168.1.0 network. This device is specifically configured not to route any traffic between these two subnets. IP forwarding has been disabled: while the DNS system is able to communicate with systems on both subnets, it is unable to act as a router and forward traffic between them.

FIGURE 7.2

Managing NIDS through a separate subnet

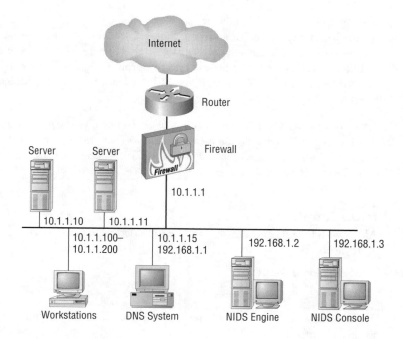

The NIDS sensor and monitor use address space from the `192.168.1.0` subnet. Although they can communicate with each other and the DNS system, they cannot communicate with any system using a `10.1.1.0` address because no devices are routing between the two network segments. The NIDS is also unable to send to or receive any data from systems outside the firewall.

What happens when the NIDS sensor tries to monitor traffic? As mentioned, the NIDS sensor captures all traffic on the network, not just traffic on its own subnet. It is perfectly capable of recording all traffic on the local network, including communications between systems on the `10.1.1.0` subnet and the Internet. It can then report these findings to the console via the `192.168.1.0` subnet.

What happens when either system needs to resolve an IP address to a host name? We did, after all, mention that the DNS system was incapable of routing information. Although this is true, it does not prohibit you from using the DNS system as a proxy to resolve address queries.

In Chapter 3, you saw that DNS is simply an Application layer service that translates host names to IP addresses and vice versa. When your sensor sends a DNS query to the DNS server, the server attempts to respond to the request with information stored locally (either through local domain files or via cached entries). If this is not possible, the DNS server attempts to contact one of the root name servers.

If the best route to the root name server is configured through the `10.1.1.15` IP address, such as by creating a default route that points to `10.1.1.1` on the firewall, the DNS server transmits the request using the source IP address `10.1.1.15`. The DNS server is not routing the query; it is acting as a proxy to resolve the query.

When it receives a reply to the query, the DNS server forwards the response to the sensor using the best route it knows. This requires the system to transmit using the `192.168.1.1` address. Again, the information is not being routed; it is being proxied by the DNS service. The NIDS can resolve DNS queries without using the same subnet address as the rest of the network.

The result is a hidden subnet that cannot be directly addressed from the Internet. An attacker would need to penetrate the firewall and compromise the DNS server to gain connectivity to either the NIDS sensor or the console. If the NIDS cannot be directly addressed, it obviously cannot be attacked.

TIP   As is the case with a firewall, an NIDS sensor that uses IP on the public network should be hardened before use. This hardening includes ensuring that the sensor has all the latest security patches installed and that the system is not running any unnecessary services. A hardened system is far more resistant to attack and is therefore a much better platform for running a security-monitoring process.

NIDS Countermeasures

Along with logging and alerting, an intrusion detection system has two other active countermeasures at its disposal:

◆   Session disruption

◆   Filter rule manipulation

These countermeasures depend on the specific product, but let's look at the general strengths and weaknesses of each method.

SESSION DISRUPTION

Session disruption is the easiest kind of countermeasure to implement. Although implementations vary, in its most basic form session disruption is produced by the NIDS resetting or closing each end of an attack session. This approach might not prevent the attacker from launching further attacks, but it does prevent the attacker from causing any further damage during the current session.

INTERNAL ATTACKS AGAINST THE NIDS

The NIDS sensor and console are vulnerable to internal attack, however. If someone on the 10.1.1.0 network discovers the IP address of the NIDS, it is a simple matter to change or spoof the local address in order to address these systems directly on the 192.168.1.0 subnet. This situation is referred to as "security through obscurity"—the systems remain secure only as long as no one knows where they are hidden. Still, by making these systems completely inaccessible from the Internet, you dramatically limit the scope of potential attack origination points and simplify the process of discovering the attacker.

When internal attacks are a concern, you can go with an NIDS that does not require an IP stack. For example, ISS RealSecure supports network monitoring from a system that does not have IP bound to the monitored network. With no IP address, the system is invulnerable to any form of IP-based attack. Of course, you have to make special considerations for the monitoring console. You will need to either run the NIDS console on the same system as the sensor or install a second network card in the sensor so that it can communicate with the console through a private subnet.

For example, your NIDS sensor detects a would-be attacker attempting to send the character string CWD ~root during an FTP session. If formulated correctly, this exploit provides the attacker with root-level FTP access on some older systems. This level of access is granted without any password authentication, and the attacker can read or write to any file on the system.

If session disruption is enabled, your NIDS sensor first identifies and logs this potential attack and then spoofs ACK-FIN packets to both ends of the session to tear down the connection. The NIDS sensor pretends to be the system on the other end of the connection. For example, it transmits an ACK-FIN to the attacker using the source IP address, port numbers, and sequence numbers of the FTP server. This effectively closes the communication session, preventing the attacker from accessing the file system. Depending on the NIDS sensor in use, it might then attempt to block all communications from the attacking host indefinitely or for a user-configurable period of time.

Although session disruption is a powerful feature, it is not without its limitations. The teardrop example given earlier in this chapter showed that the intrusion detection system was unable to block the attack. Although the NIDS has enough time to react to the FTP exploit, it can never react quickly enough to save a system from teardrop if only one malformed IP header can crash the system.

FILTER RULE MANIPULATION

Some NIDS sensors can modify the filter rules of a router or a firewall to prevent continued attacks. The sensor prevents the attacking system from transmitting additional traffic to the target host; the NIDS adds a new filter rule to the firewall that blocks all inbound traffic from the suspect IP address. Although filter rule manipulation is a powerful novelty, it is not without limitations. You should fully understand the implications of this feature before you enable it.

Filter rule manipulation can cause a problem if an attacker spoofs the address of an Internet server or site with which your organization needs to connect and then launches an attack. The NIDS will see the incoming attack, apply a filter rule to your router or firewall to block access from the attacker's source address (which is being spoofed), and in doing so prevent you from communicating with the site—a twist on the traditional DoS.

On the positive side, manipulating filter rules can prevent an attack with far less network traffic than session disruption. Once the NIDS modifies the filter rules, attack traffic ceases. With session disruption, the NIDS must continually attempt to close every attack session. If you have a persistent attacker, extra traffic could be added to the wire.

On the negative side, manipulating filter rules is not always 100 percent effective. For example, what if the source IP address of the attack is inside the firewall? In this case, modifying the filter rules has no effect. Since the attacking traffic never actually passes through the firewall, it is not subject to the filter rules. Thus, a filter change has no effect on the attack.

Also, a savvy attacker might use a spoofed IP address rather than a real one. Although the firewall might begin blocking the initial attack, all the attacker has to do is select another spoofed address to circumvent this new rule change. With session disruption, the NIDS reacts based on attack signature, not on source IP address. Session disruption can continually fend off the attack, but filter rule manipulation cannot. The NIDS can make successive rule changes, thus attempting to block all spoofed addresses as they are detected. If the attacker quickly varies the source IP address, however, the NIDS can never keep up. Remember that it takes a certain amount of time (typically 10–30 seconds) for the NIDS and the firewall to complete the filter change.

WARNING   *The ability to perform live filter rule changes can be exploited for a DoS attack. If the attacker purposely varies the source IP address to trigger multiple filter rule changes, the firewall can become so busy that it stops passing traffic. Any active sessions during the filter rule change might be terminated, as well.*

Clearly, you need to modify filter rules sparingly and only for attacks that are considered extremely detrimental. For example, just about every unpatched IP device or system produced before 1996 is vulnerable to the *ping of death*, an exploit that breaks the IP protocol stack on a target system by sending it an oversized ICMP (Internet Control Message Protocol) datagram. If you are running an environment that includes many older systems that have not been patched, modifying the filter rules to block these attacks makes a lot of sense. Although frequent rule changes can potentially cause a DoS, letting this traffic onto your network most certainly will interrupt all IP communications.

TIP   *The ping of death affects networking hardware as well as computer systems. Be sure that all your IP devices are patched against this form of attack.*

NOTE   *Not all intrusion detection systems are compatible with all firewalls and routers. For example, ISS RealSecure can modify only Check Point FireWall-1. At the time of this writing, RealSecure is not compatible with any other firewall product, although there are plans to add Cisco routers to a future release. So, while session disruption can be used by any NIDS that supports this feature, you can only use filter manipulation if you are using a compatible system that performs firewall functions.*

Host-Based IDS

Until now we have focused on intrusion detection systems that run on a dedicated server and monitor all passing network traffic. These devices control traffic within an entire collision domain. Host-based IDS products are designed to protect only a single system.

Host-based IDS functions similarly to a virus scanner. The software runs as a background process on the system you want to protect as it attempts to detect suspicious activity. Suspicious activity can include an attempt to pass unknown commands though an HTTP request or even modification to the file system. When suspicious activity is detected, the IDS can then attempt to terminate the attacking session and send an alert to the system administrator.

Some Drawbacks

A number of drawbacks are associated with host-based intrusion detection systems, which make them impractical for many environments. For starters, most can monitor only specific types of systems. For example, CyberCop Server by Network Associates can protect only web servers. If the server is running multiple services (such as DNS, file sharing, POP3, and so on), the host-based IDS system might not be able to detect an intrusion. Although most host-based intrusion detection systems do watch core server functions, such as modifications to a user's access rights, an attacker might find a way to disable the IDS before attempting any changes to the system. If the IDS becomes disabled, the attacker is free to wreak havoc on the system.

Another problem is that host-based intrusion detection systems simply run as a background process and do not have access to the core communication functionality of the system. The IDS is incapable of fending off attacks against the protocol stack itself. For example, it takes 10 or more teardrop packets to crash an unpatched NT server. Although this is more than ample time for an NIDS to react and take countermeasures, a host-based IDS is left helpless because it never even sees this traffic.

It can also be argued that there is a logistical flaw in running your intrusion detection software on the system you want to protect. If an attacker can infiltrate the system, the attacker might compromise the IDS, as well. This is an extremely bad thing: the attacker has just punched through your last line of security defense.

TIP   Only sloppy attackers fail to clean up after themselves by not purging logs and suspected processes. This is why many security experts suggest that system administrators forward all log entries to a remote system. If the system is compromised by an attacker, the logs cannot be altered. Extend this principle to your intrusion detection systems.

WHEN IS HOST-BASED IDS EFFECTIVE?

Despite all these drawbacks, host-based intrusion detection systems do have their place. For example, you have a web server you want to protect that is located on a DMZ (De-Militarized Zone) network segment. This DMZ is behind your firewall but in an isolated segment that contains only the web server. The firewall is configured to allow only HTTP traffic in to the web server.

In this situation, a host-based IDS product might be sufficient to protect the web server, because the firewall is providing most of your protection. The firewall should ensure that the only traffic allowed to reach the web server is HTTP requests. This means that you should not have to worry about any other services being compromised on the web server.

Your host-based intrusion detection system only has to ensure that no access requests, CGI/ Java exploits, and web-server specific exploits are included in these HTTP requests and passed along to the web server process running on the system. Although this is still no small feat, it does limit the scope of the kinds of exploits the NIDS will be expected to handle.

Host-based IDS can also be extremely useful in a fully switched environment. The reasoning behind this is shown in Figure 7.3. In this figure, all systems are directly connected to a backbone switch. This, in effect, gives every system its own collision domain: the switch isolates all unicast traffic so that only the two systems involved in the communication see the traffic.

Since the switch is isolating communication sessions, the network-based IDS is unable to see all the passing network traffic. If a workstation launches an attack against the intranet web server, the IDS is completely unaware that the attack is taking place and is thus unable to take countermeasures. The attack does not appear in the IDS logs, so no record is made of the event.

A host-based IDS would be in a much better position to protect the intranet web server. Since it runs on the system you want to protect, it is unaffected by the traffic isolation properties of the switch. It sees all the traffic that the web server sees, so it can protect the system from HTTP-based attacks.

TIP   Most switch vendors let you configure one of the switch's ports as a monitoring port. Doing so allows the switch to send a copy of all passing traffic to any system connected to this port. If you will be using a network-based IDS in a switched environment, connect it to this monitoring port to ensure that the IDS can verify all passing traffic.

FIGURE 7.3

A network-based IDS is incapable of seeing all traffic in a fully switched environment.

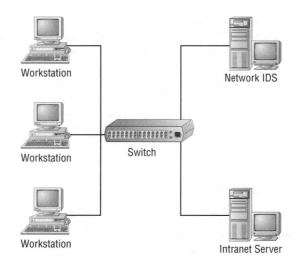

Workstation

Network IDS

Workstation   Switch

Workstation

Intranet Server

NIDS Fusion

In an attempt to not only overcome the limitations of traditional NIDS, but also allow for more proactive defense, NIDS research is pushing toward the integration—or to use the more common term of military origin, the *fusion*—of data. By combining the packet information (the actual information being communicated) from servers and hosts, along with information about other types and sources, NIDS systems can more accurately determine information about an attack. Additional data sources include the following:

Filesystem   Using Tripwire or some other type of software to create and compare file signatures can add a powerful last line of defense. Although using a filesystem IDS won't prevent a cracker from penetrating your system, it will at least notify you that system files have been altered, which can be the next best thing.

Simple Network Management Protocol (SNMP)   SNMP enables network devices to communicate with a centralized monitoring system and report *how* they are operating, not just what data is being transferred. An example is a router that updates a network monitoring system with the amount of traffic per second passing through a given interface (information that can be used by NIDS to determine if a cracker is attempting a DoS attack).

System logs   Most operating systems can be configured to record an extensive amount of detail concerning their overall state at any given moment, along with the specifics from each operating system component. Consider an e-mail server that logs not only the arrival time of e-mail messages, but also the IP address of the originating server. NIDS can use this information to trace the path of worm-carrying e-mails and to tell all e-mail servers in a system to filter out any e-mail originating from the offending server.

System messages   Although most pertinent system data is usually logged, this is not always the case—either through the fault of misconfiguration or simply because of an operating system weakness. NIDS uses system messages to create a greater overall picture of an entire network, which allows for combing the data (fusion) and retrieving meaning (pattern analysis) from the network's state.

Commands   Most operating systems are not designed or configured to record every single command issued by all users. NIDS fusion is designed to overcome just that limitation—illuminating patterns that might be missed by system logs themselves (which only report information of a direct system or security nature). An example is a command designed to delete proprietary company information—though extremely damaging to an organization, this deletion does not violate or affect system integrity.

User behavior   A corollary to monitoring user commands, monitoring normal user behavior over time creates patterns, and by constantly analyzing user account activity against that account's own profile, NIDS systems can determine if that account has been hijacked—before any greater violation or penetration of systems has yet occurred.

Although the concept of analyzing all user, system, and network data and behavior seems straightforward enough, in reality NIDS fusion is difficult; it relies on complicated mathematical formulas and requires some intense back-end resources to operate effectively—and even then it is still highly subjective and experimental. Nonetheless, NIDS fusion promises to revolutionize network defense through cooperative data-sharing and response by all networks affected by an attack.

Snort: A Popular NIDS

For the purpose of discussing how you set up an NIDS, we'll look at Snort, an open-source software project that has become one of the most popular of all NIDSs, even when compared with commercial products costing thousands of dollars. Snort isn't difficult to configure and use (in theory), but in reality avoiding false alarms is a constant challenge with any NIDS.

You can use Snort to sniff packets, log packets, and, of course, detect network intrusion. When sniffing packets, Snort simply displays those packets on the console. Logged packets are, of course, recorded on the hard drive. NIDS logging and alerting (matching and responding to suspect traffic) functions are based on configuring rules and responses.

By default, Snort logs the ruleset hits (a "hit" occurs when Snort detects a packet that matches the conditions defined in one or more rulesets) in ASCII and, when an alert is defined, displays the entire alert message along with the full packet header of the packet in question. The following six types of alerts are possible with Snort:

Full   The default; displays all information

Fast   Has a timestamp, the message, and source and destination IP address and port numbers

Socket   Sends alerts to a Unix socket (so that another program on the same machine can record the alerts)

Syslog   Sends alerts to the `syslog` daemon

Smb   Uses Samba to send a pop-up message to Windows machines

None   Generates no alerts

Be careful with your initial alert settings. The primary drawback to any NIDS system is the sheer number of false positives. In other words, your system will see attacks coming from all sides, when the reality is that a lot of ugly, poorly implemented networking protocols out there in the world give fits to any NIDS system you implement.

Snort Rules

Snort rules are nothing more than text entries that specify the characteristics of attack signatures and options on how the system can respond when it detects those characteristics. Most rules can be written in a single line. (Spanned lines require a backslash (\) at the end of each wrapped line.) A rule looks like this:

```
alert tcp any any -> 10.0.0.0/8 22 (msg: "ssh login";)
```

The first part of the rule (up to the opening parenthesis) is called the *rule header*. The rule header contains the action to be performed when this signature is recognized, the protocol involved, the source and destination IP addresses, and the source and destination port addresses. The second part of the rule is called the *rule option section*. Here is where you can specify which additional characteristics of suspect packets are reviewed by Snort before it takes action, as well as the specific alert message.

You can imagine that when you are writing multiple rules (possibly hundreds), entering the same IP address or protocol information in each rule can be tedious. Snort lets you define variables and values that can be reused throughout the entire ruleset. The format is as follows:

```
var <variable name> <variable value>
```

Let's look at an example. Let's say you have multiple internal private IP networks. You want Snort to notify you when it observes any TCP (Transmission Control Protocol) connection requests to any of your internal networks. Instead of having to define a rule for each network's IP address, you can simply define a variable that includes all the IP addresses on your internal network, like this:

```
var INT [10.0.0.0/8,192.168.1.0/24,192.168.2.0/24]
```

Once you define this variable, you can use it in a rule that notifies you when any network attempts to create a TCP connection to any of your internal networks:

```
alert tcp any any -> $INT any (flags: S, msg: "SYN packet";)
```

ACTIONS

Rule actions define what Snort does when it detects a packet that matches a rule pattern. There are five (default) actions in Snort:

Alert   Generates an alert (using the user-defined alert method) and logs the packet

Log   Logs only the packet

Pass   Allows the packet through without taking any action

Activate Generates an alert and then activates a dynamic (or log) rule

Dynamic A special type of log rule that is activated by another rule (known as an activate rule) as opposed to a packet

One of the great things about Snort is that you can customize it. You can create your own rule action (known as a rule type) and then use it in Snort as you would use any other action. The following example logs the information to a database:

```
ruletype dbalert
{
    type output
    output database: mysql, user=knikki dbname=snortie host=localhost
}
```

PROTOCOLS

Snort can analyze four protocols: TCP, UDP (User Datagram Protocol), ICMP, and IP (Internet Protocol). TCP looks at connection requests, something that is often abused by crackers in DdoS (distributed denial of service) attacks. UDP can also be used as part of a DdoS attack, but this is easily blocked. ICMP, the "messenger" of the TCP/IP protocol suite, can be used to sneak information in and out of firewalls. And IP information is always subject to tampering, unless something such as IPsec (IP Security) is used.

IP ADDRESSES

IP addresses follow the CIDR (Classless Inter-Domain Routing) nomenclature in which the IP address itself is followed by a forward slash and the number of bits in the subnet. For example, CIDR represents the network 192.168.1.0 with a subnet of 255.255.255.0 as:

192.168.1.0/24

Of course, variables can be used to represent IP addresses, lists of multiple comma-separated addresses, as well as the keyword any.

PORT NUMBERS

Like IP addresses, port numbers can use the any keyword, but they can also use ranges and negation. Ranges are specified using a colon (:) to separate the two numbers that mark the beginning and end of a range. For instance, 0:20 means all ports between 0 and 20. Port negation is expressed by using the bang (!) character, which can also be combined with a range to exclude a range of addresses.

DIRECTION

The direction of the flow of network traffic is indicated by the right arrow character ($\rightarrow$). Anything to the left of the arrow is the source; anything to the right is the destination. A more useful direction indicator is the greater-than less-than character (<>), which indicates that any source or destination combination will be tracked. In this case, Snort can follow a conversation between two hosts, increasing the chances of finding attacks, especially if you are performing more detailed and in-depth analysis of the log records produced by Snort.

RULE OPTIONS

Snort's reputation is really made through the many options that can be used, combined, and custom defined to operate on all the types of traffic defined by rule headers. Here is a list of some of Snort's predefined options:

KEYWORD	DESCRIPTION
msg	Defines alert message text
logto	Defines the location for an alternate log file
ttl	Evaluates the TTL (time to live) field of the IP packet
content	Defines a pattern to search for in the packet
session	Logs the Application layer information of a packet
uricontent	Specifies the URI (Universal Resource Identifier) pattern to be matched
stateless	Specifies that the rule match the packet regardless of state

One of our favorite option keywords is content. We can use content to search for any particular string. Typically, the most common worms and DdoS attacks have a well-publicized and static series of characters they use to overflow buffers or activate code on unsecured servers. By searching all packets for these well-known patterns, we can be alerted if we're being attacked by the most common tools. Although this won't (in and of itself) protect us from a targeted attack by a sophisticated cracker, the reality is that the most common threat (common in terms of quantity and type) that Internet-exposed servers face is from well-known or well-publicized exploits.

PREPROCESSORS

Preprocessors are the natural evolution from using custom-defined rule options. Essentially, pre-processors are plug-ins that allow third parties to code custom pattern machine and response actions. Regular users can then simply enable the plug-ins in the rules file to take advantage of their functionality. Many preprocessors exist (and you can write your own). The following are some popular preprocessors:

Stream4   Tracks large numbers of TCP streams, stateless attacks, and smaller-than-normal fragmentation that is commonly used to hide cracker activity

HHTP Decode   Converts Unicode URIs to ASCII

Portscan   Detects cracker-probing attempts

Spade (Statistical Packet Anomaly Detection Engine)   Detects nonspecific "weirdness" on a network that could indicate sophisticated cracker probing and attacks

One of our favorites among preprocessors is HTTP Decode. This powerful preprocessor takes any URI and reformats it into standard ASCII before passing it to the main Snort engine. The reason this is so important is that crackers use formatting tricks to hide their requests for powerful system commands (which are located outside the normal directory structure of a web server). Because most original Snort rules relied on ASCII to recognize these unusual and unauthorized requests, the same request encoded with Unicode was missed.

An example of HTTP Decode syntax (and of preprocessor syntax in general) is as follows:

```
preprocessor http_decode: 80
```

FORMATTING MODULES

Formatting modules (also called output modules) let you define the format and presentation of alerts and log entries. You can use multiple modules (a process called stacking) in a sequential fashion. Some of the modules are as follows:

alert_syslog   Specifies how the `syslog` daemon handles alerts

alert_fast   Displays a simple (and much faster) single-line alert

alert_full   Contains a full alert with full packet information

alert_smb   Sends a pop-up message with the alert text to the machine specified

alert_unixsock   Sends an alert to a program running on the same system

log_tcpdump   Formats the alert in the `tcpdump` fashion

xml   Formats SNML (Simple Network Markup Language), which is a reporting language based on XML (Extensible Markup Language)

database   Contains SQL-formatted alerts

csv   Sends alerts to a CSV (comma-separated value) file

The following example uses modules in a rule file:

```
output alert_syslog: LOG_AUTH LOG_ALERT
```

In this example, `output` is the keyword, `alert_syslog` is the module, and `LOG_AUTH` and `LOG_ALERT` are the facilities, or components, of the `syslog` daemon. In this fashion, you can specify that alerts not only are passed to the `syslog` daemon (which is the default, anyway), but even tell `syslog` how to handle those alerts once they are in its possession.

Now that you have an idea of how Snort works, let's look at how to install and configure it.

Before You Begin

For this walk-through, we will focus on the Linux version of Snort. Other popular platforms for Snort include OpenBSD and Solaris, although there is even a version for Windows NT/2000. Linux has the advantage of being very well known, documented, and supported in the open-source community. The disadvantage for some network administrators, of course, is that you need a good working knowledge of Unix command lines and configuration file syntax to feel comfortable working with Linux in general and with Snort in particular.

When we talk about NIDS resources, the general rule of thumb is this: if the system will be monitoring a low-bandwidth connection (T1 speeds or less), you will probably be better off running a single "killer" machine rather than two lower-quality computers. If you plan to monitor a network backbone or other high-traffic area, you might want to consider purchasing two appropriately outfitted systems.

Receiving and processing every packet on the wire takes a lot of CPU horsepower. Snort checks each packet for as many different suspect conditions as you define (another one its many strengths). Combine this with making log entries and launching countermeasures when required, and you have a very busy system.

WHERE TO PLACE YOUR NIDS

In deciding where to best place your NIDS, determine which systems you want to protect from which sources. It's good to clarify this point up front; you might find that you actually need more than one NIDS sensor. You should have a solid security objective in mind before you fill out a purchase request for hardware or software. Fortunately, because Linux can use lower-end hardware, you can use older systems that would normally be discarded and dedicate them to sniffing out the various network gateways.

One potential deployment is shown in Figure 7.4. In this configuration, both the DMZ and the internal connection of the firewall are monitored. This approach lets you verify all inbound traffic from the Internet. It also lets you reinforce the existing firewall. Both NIDS sensors are running without IP being bound to the public network segment. IP is running only on a network card that connects the sensors back to the console. With this arrangement, your NIDS sensors are completely invisible to all systems on the public network segment.

A few limitations are associated with this configuration, however. First, you will be unable to monitor attack traffic from the Internet that is targeted at the firewall. Although your firewall should be capable of logging such activity, you may not have the benefits of raw packet captures, dynamic filter rule manipulation, or any of the other features that an NIDS can offer. If your link to the Internet is a T1 or less, and you want to monitor Internet traffic only, you might be better off buying one really good server and running all NIDS functions outside the firewall. Since IP will not be needed on this system, it should be safe from attack.

Another limitation of the design in Figure 7.4 is that it does not allow you to monitor any of the unicast traffic generated between internal systems. If your goal is to monitor all network traffic, you might want to move your internal NIDS sensor to its own port on the switch and configure this switch port for monitoring. This approach allows you to see all traffic activity inside the firewall.

If your goal is to lock down the network as much as possible, you might want to combine these solutions: place one NIDS sensor outside the firewall and another NIDS sensor off a monitoring switch port, and configure both sensors to communicate with the console through a private subnet. This approach lets you monitor all passing traffic within your network while still maintaining control from a central console.

After you select the areas you want to monitor, you can select the number of NIDS sensors required, as well as the appropriate hardware.

HARDWARE REQUIREMENTS

Although requirements depend on your Linux distribution, we recommend the following minimum hardware requirements for running Snort:

- Pentium II 300MHz processor
- 128MB of RAM
- At least one PCI (Peripheral Component Interconnect) network card

FIGURE 7.4

A potential deploy-
ment of two NIDS
sensors

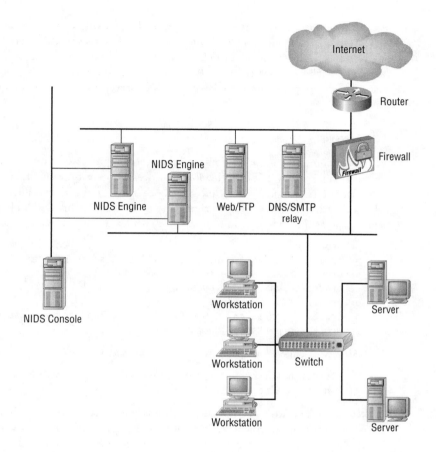

If you will be using Snort with a packet sniffer and will store copies of your network dumps on the hard drive, definitely dedicate hard drive space to that.

INSTALLING LINUX

Installing Linux is usually a straightforward process. However, optimizing a Linux installation to perform nothing but NIDS activities can be tricky primarily in determining what *not* to install. Fortunately, even if you install extra programs and services, you can easily disable them so that they don't automatically start and steal system resources. Consult the documentation that comes with your Linux distribution to determine how best to disable unnecessary services.

Configuring Snort

You can either compile Snort from scratch, or you can download an .rpm (Red Hat Package Manager) package that matches your Linux distribution from www.snort.org. After installing (or updating) Snort, you will begin by editing /etc/snort/snort.conf. The Snort distribution includes a sample snort.conf file to help you get on your way.

One of the first tasks is to configure variables that will represent your network and IP addresses that you might want to exclude from your scans. Examples of these variables include *INT*, *EXT*, and *DNS*. The values of these variables can be a list of networks or simply the keyword **any**. By placing the IP address of all DNS servers in the *DNS* variable, you can avoid a significant cause of false alarms. Look at the following example in which all the DNS servers used by hosts on the network are specified:

```
var INT any
var EXT_NET any
var DNS [4.2.2.1/8,4.2.2.2/8]
```

Next comes the preprocessors, and the more preprocessors you enable, the more triggers (and less performance) you get. The following preprocessors detect unusual fragmentation, allow for better connection tracking, convert Unicode to ASCII (the Unicode module is a newer version of HTTP Decode), detect Back Orifice (a common Trojan horse) scans, and look for port scans (we define a port scan as three requests in four seconds) while ignoring DNS servers:

```
preprocessor frag2
preprocessor stream4: detect_scans detect_state_problems
preprocessor stream4_reassemble: ports all
preprocessor unidecode: 80 8080
preprocessor bo: -nobrute
preprocessor portscan: 0.0.0.0/0 3 4 /var/log/snort/portscan.log
preprocessor portscan-ignorehosts: $DNS
```

After you define the preprocessors, you're ready to set up an output module to send alerts to a database:

```
output database: alert, mysql, user=lizbeth password=acrosstable dbname=snort
        host=localhost
```

Now you're ready to get down to business by specifying the rules. In reality, you simply specify a series of `include` statements that point to a directory that contains the various text files that make up each distinct rule. Fortunately, Snort comes with a rather serious collection of rules to detect the most common network exploits.

```
include /etc/snort/exploit.rules
include /etc/snort/scan.rules
include /etc/snort/finger.rules
include /etc/snort/ftp.rules
include /etc/snort/telnet.rules
```

After you configure the Snort rules, you need to tell the Snort daemon which interface(s) you want to scan for attacks. You do so by editing the `/etc/rc.d/init.d/snortd` file:

```
INTERFACE="eth0"
```

You can also edit `/etc/snort/recipients` to contain one or more e-mail addresses (one per line) that will receive Snort alerts. Once you finish with that, you're ready to start detecting. Simply restart Snort by issuing the following command (assuming you are using a Red Hat system):

```
service snort restart
```

and start checking your `/var/log/messages` file, your database, or your inbox for alerts!

Snort Alert Example

So, what do Snort alerts look like? One of the most common alerts you will get is from a port scan. A port scan is simply a rapid probing of your system(s) by some other entity on the Internet, typically an attempt to determine what services your computer is hosting. Although seeing frequent alerts could mean that you are the victim of hostile probing by a cracker, the reality could be benign. It is common for cable modem and DSL providers to probe the customers of their residential class services to verify that they are not running web and news servers—something typically prohibited because of bandwidth and security issues. Here are a few Snort alerts as they detect a port scan:

```
Jun 8 21:33:56 bubba snort[19226]: SCAN synscan portscan: 102.15.44.3:7543 ->
    14.16.1.101:21
Jun 8 21:33:56 bubba snort[19226]: SCAN synscan portscan: 102.15.44.3:24500 ->
    14.16.1.102:21
Jun 8 21:33:56 bubba snort[19226]: SCAN synscan portscan: 102.15.44.3:26344 ->
    14.16.1.103:21
Jun 8 21:33:56 bubba snort[19226]: SCAN synscan portscan: 102.15.44.3:2556 ->
    14.16.1.104:21
Jun 8 21:33:56 bubba snort[19226]: SCAN synscan portscan: 102.15.44.3:8745 ->
    14.16.1.105:21
Jun 8 21:33:56 bubba snort[19226]: SCAN synscan portscan: 102.15.44.3:33 ->
    14.16.1.106:21
Jun 8 21:33:56 bubba snort[19226]: SCAN synscan portscan: 102.15.44.3:5555 ->
    14.16.1.107:21
Jun 8 21:33:56 bubba snort[19226]: SCAN synscan portscan: 102.15.44.3:21 ->
    14.16.1.108:21
```

Now, what we find fascinating about this example is how Snort can detect a sophisticated attack of the type that would have gone unnoticed even three years ago. In this attack, the cracker is changing their port after every single probing packet. Notice also how they are actually only probing one port at a time across a broad range of IP addresses. This is an attempt to bypass a less-sophisticated NIDS that might not put it together that all these queries are part of a single probing effort (something that we can see quite readily with the information assembled this way).

Suggestions for Using Snort

Good rules are the key to not only detecting the Woolly Hacker, but also staying sane as you administer and maintain your Snort server. Here are some general suggestions:

- Be aware of case sensitivity. If you create a rule to determine if someone is attempting to log on with the username `administrator`, you will miss attempts that use `ADMINISTRATOR`. For content rules, you can overcome this problem using the `nocase` rule option, which tells Snort to ignore case sensitivity.

- Content rules are processed last. Thus, attempt to filter out packets (when possible) by means other than content *first*.

- Use a database. Log files are simpler and are certainly easier to configure, but they simply can't handle the massive amounts of information that Snort generates, especially in the beginning while you fine-tune your detection. Additionally, keep in mind that you'll recognize some attacks only by a thorough analysis of the logs produced by Snort. Keeping a detailed attack history will give you more credibility with your managers, and with a jury should your database be used as forensic evidence.

◆ Some users find that managing Snort via the command line is troublesome. Fortunately for them, a number of Snort management tools offer graphical utilities for front-end management and log analysis and even data conversion tools to convert Snort report data to other formats. Examples include the following:

  ◆ SnortSnarf, which produces HTML reports from Snort logs

  ◆ ACID (Analysis Console for Intrusion Detection), a PHP-based analysis engine

  ◆ SnortReport, a PHP-based front end for analyzing Snort logs stored in MySQL

  ◆ SnortWebMin, a plug-in module for the popular web-based administration tool Webadmin

You'll find a comprehensive list of Snort utilities at `http://snort.solution.de/files/downloads-other.html`.

Summary

In this chapter, you learned the basics of intrusion detection systems and how they can aid in securing a network environment. You saw some of the strengths and weaknesses of NIDS products in general. We even walked through the configuration of Snort and showed you an example of the alerts generated through a port scan.

The next chapter looks at authentication and encryption technology. Authentication and encryption have become extremely popular subjects as organizations race to provide connectivity over less-than-secure network channels.

Chapter 8

Authentication and Encryption

AUTHENTICATION AND ENCRYPTION ARE two intertwined technologies that help to ensure that your data remains secure. *Authentication* is the process of ensuring that both ends of the connection are in fact who they say they are. This applies not only to the entity trying to access a service (such as an end user) but to the entity providing the service (such as a file server or a website). *Encryption* helps to ensure that the information within a session is not compromised. This includes not only reading the information within a data stream, but altering it.

Although authentication and encryption each has its own responsibilities in securing a communication session, maximum protection can only be achieved when the two are combined. For this reason, many security protocols contain both authentication and encryption specifications.

Featured in this chapter:

- ◆ The need for improved security
- ◆ Requiring good authentication
- ◆ Encryption
- ◆ Requiring good encryption
- ◆ Encryption solutions

The Need for Improved Security

When IP (Internet Protocol) version 4, the version currently in use on the Internet, was created back in the '70s, network security was not a major concern. Although system security was important, little attention was paid to the transport used when exchanging information. When IP was first introduced, it contained no inherent security standards. The specifications for IP do not take into account that you might want to protect the data that IP is transporting. This approach will change with IP version 6, but it appears that wide acceptance of this new specification is still many years in the future.

IP currently transmits all data as clear text, which is commonly referred to as *transmitting in the clear.* Data and authentication information are not scrambled or rearranged; they are simply transmitted in raw form. To see how this appears, let's start by looking at Figure 8.1.

FIGURE 8.1

A packet decode of an authentication session initializing

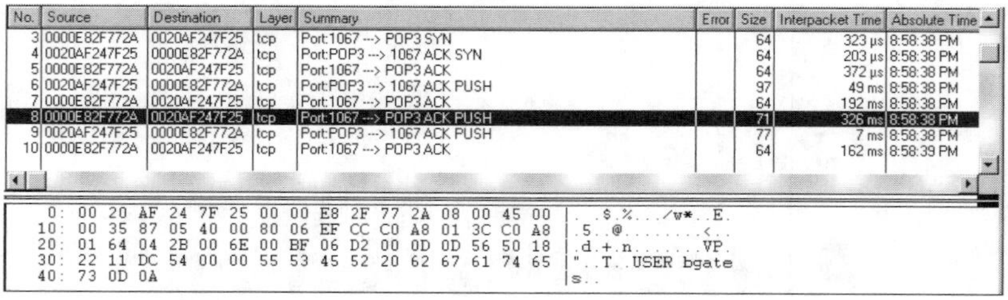

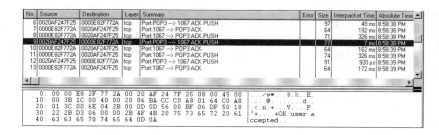

Figure 8.1 shows a network analyzer's view of a communication session. A user is in the process of retrieving e-mail with a POP3 (Post Office Protocol, version 3) e-mail client. Packets 3 through 5 are the TCP (Transmission Control Protocol) three-packet handshake used to initialize the connection. Packets 6 and 7 are the POP3 e-mail server informing the client that it is online and ready. In packet 8 we start finding some interesting information. If you look toward the bottom of Figure 8.1, you will see the decoded contents of the data field within packet 8. A POP3 client uses the USER command to pass the logon name to a POP3 server. Any text following the USER command is the name of the person who is attempting to authenticate with the system.

Figure 8.2 shows the POP3 server's response to this logon name. If you look at the decode for packet 9, you can see that the logon name was accepted. This tells us that the logon name captured in Figure 8.1 is in fact legitimate. If you can discover this user's password, you will have enough information to gain access to the system.

In Figure 8.3 you can see a decode of packet 11. This is the next set of commands sent by the POP3 e-mail client to the server. The client uses the PASS command to send the password string. Any text that follows this command is the password for the user attempting to authenticate with the system. As you can see, the password is plainly visible.

In Figure 8.4 we see a decode of packet 12. This is the server's response to the authentication attempt. Notice that the server has accepted the logon name and password combination. We now know that this was a valid authentication session and that we have a legitimate logon name and password combination in order to gain access to the system. In fact, if we decoded further packets, we would be able to view every e-mail message downloaded by this user.

FIGURE 8.2

The POP3 server accepting the logon name

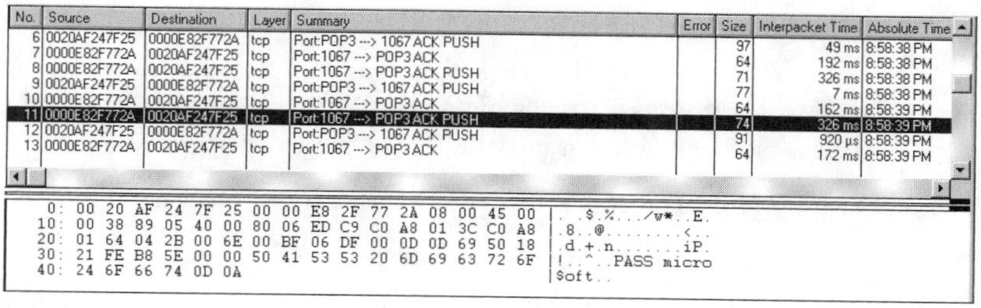

FIGURE 8.3

The POP3 client sending the user's password

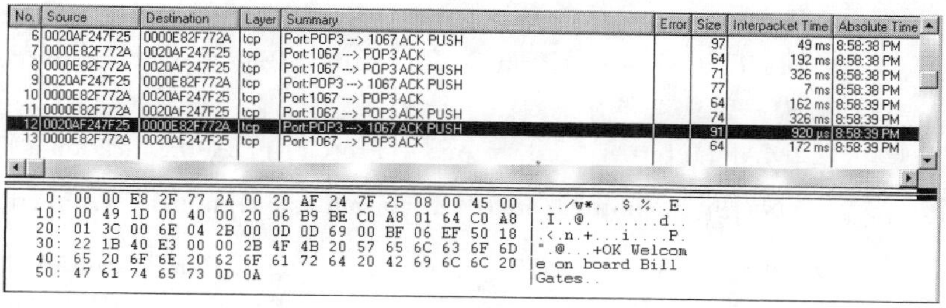

No.	Source	Destination	Layer	Summary	Error	Size	Interpacket Time	Absolute Time
6	0020AF247F25	0000E82F772A	tcp	Port:POP3 ---> 1067 ACK PUSH		97	49 ms	8:58:38 PM
7	0000E82F772A	0020AF247F25	tcp	Port:1067 ---> POP3 ACK		64	192 ms	8:58:38 PM
8	0000E82F772A	0020AF247F25	tcp	Port:1067 ---> POP3 ACK PUSH		71	326 ms	8:58:38 PM
9	0020AF247F25	0000E82F772A	tcp	Port:POP3 ---> 1067 ACK PUSH		77	7 ms	8:58:38 PM
10	0000E82F772A	0020AF247F25	tcp	Port:1067 ---> POP3 ACK		64	162 ms	8:58:39 PM
11	0000E82F772A	0020AF247F25	tcp	Port:1067 ---> POP3 ACK PUSH		74	326 ms	8:58:39 PM
12	0020AF247F25	0000E82F772A	tcp	Port:POP3 ---> 1067 ACK PUSH		91	920 μs	8:58:39 PM
13	0000E82F772A	0020AF247F25	tcp	Port:1067 ---> POP3 ACK		64	172 ms	8:58:39 PM

```
 0: 00 20 AF 24 7F 25 00 00 E8 2F 77 2A 08 00 45 00   . $.%.../w* . E.
10: 00 38 89 05 40 00 80 06 ED C9 C0 A8 01 3C C0 A8   .8..@........<..
20: 01 64 04 2B 00 6E 00 BF 06 DF 00 0D 0D 69 50 18   .d.+.n.......iP.
30: 21 FE B8 5E 00 00 50 41 53 53 20 6D 69 63 72 6F   !..^..PASS micro
40: 24 6F 66 74 0D 0A                                  $oft..
```

FIGURE 8.4

The POP3 server accepting the authentication attempt

No.	Source	Destination	Layer	Summary	Error	Size	Interpacket Time	Absolute Time
6	0020AF247F25	0000E82F772A	tcp	Port:POP3 ---> 1067 ACK PUSH		97	49 ms	8:58:38 PM
7	0000E82F772A	0020AF247F25	tcp	Port:1067 ---> POP3 ACK		64	192 ms	8:58:38 PM
8	0000E82F772A	0020AF247F25	tcp	Port:1067 ---> POP3 ACK PUSH		71	326 ms	8:58:38 PM
9	0020AF247F25	0000E82F772A	tcp	Port:POP3 ---> 1067 ACK PUSH		77	7 ms	8:58:38 PM
10	0000E82F772A	0020AF247F25	tcp	Port:1067 ---> POP3 ACK		64	162 ms	8:58:39 PM
11	0000E82F772A	0020AF247F25	tcp	Port:1067 ---> POP3 ACK PUSH		74	326 ms	8:58:39 PM
12	0020AF247F25	0000E82F772A	tcp	Port:POP3 ---> 1067 ACK PUSH		91	920 μs	8:58:39 PM
13	0000E82F772A	0020AF247F25	tcp	Port:1067 ---> POP3 ACK		64	172 ms	8:58:39 PM

```
 0: 00 00 E8 2F 77 2A 00 20 AF 24 7F 25 08 00 45 00   .../w*. .$.%.E.
10: 00 49 1D 00 00 40 00 20 06 B9 BE C0 A8 01 64 C0 A8   .I..@.. .....d..
20: 01 3C 00 6E 04 2B 00 0D 0D 69 00 BF 06 EF 50 18   .<.n.+...i....P.
30: 22 1B 40 E3 00 00 2B 4F 4B 20 57 65 6C 63 6F 6D   ".@...+OK Welcom
40: 65 20 6F 6E 20 62 6F 61 72 64 20 42 69 6C 6C 20   e on board Bill
50: 47 61 74 65 73 0D 0A                               Gates..
```

Passively Monitoring Clear Text

The POP3 authentication session in Figures 8.1 through 8.4 was captured using a network analyzer. A network analyzer can be either a dedicated hardware tool or a software program that runs on an existing system. You can purchase network analyzer software for less than $1000 for Windows or Mac platforms, and it is freely available for Windows and Unix.

Network analyzers operate as truly passive devices, meaning that they do not need to transmit any data to the network in order to monitor traffic. Although some analyzers do transmit traffic (usually in an effort to locate a management station), it is not a requirement. In fact, an analyzer does not even need a valid network address. Thus, a network analyzer can monitor your network without your knowledge. You have no way to detect its presence without tracing cables and counting hub and switch ports.

It is also possible for an attacker to load network analyzer software onto a compromised system. An attacker does not need physical access to your facility in order to monitor traffic. They can simply use one of your existing systems to capture the traffic. This is why it is so important to perform regular audits on your systems. You clearly do not want a passively monitoring attack to go unnoticed.

In order for a network analyzer to capture a communication session, it must be connected somewhere along the session's path. It could be connected on the network at some point between the system initializing the session and the destination system. It could also connect by compromising one of the systems at either end of the session. This means that an attacker cannot capture your network traffic over the Internet from a remote location. They must place some form of probe or analyzer within your network.

NOTE *As you saw in Chapter 4, you can reduce the traffic that an analyzer can capture using bridges, switches, and routers—although unencrypted wireless networks take you back to square one.*

Clear Text Protocols

POP3 is not the only IP service that communicates via clear text. Nearly every nonproprietary IP service that is not specifically designed to provide authentication and encryption services transmits data as clear text. Here is a partial list of clear text services:

FTP (File Transfer Protocol)   Authentication is clear text.

Telnet   Authentication is clear text.

SMTP (Simple Mail Transfer Protocol)   Contents of e-mail messages are delivered as clear text.

HTTP (Hypertext Transfer Protocol)   Page content and the contents of fields within forms are sent clear text.

IMAP (Internet Message Access Protocol)   Authentication is clear text.

SNMPv1 (Simple Network Management, version 1)   Authentication is clear text.

WARNING   *The fact that SNMPv1 uses clear text is particularly nasty. SNMP is used to manage and query network devices, including switches, routers, servers, and even firewalls. If the SMTP password is compromised, an attacker can wreak havoc on your network. SNMPv2 and SNMPv3 include a message algorithm similar to the one used with Open Shortest Path First (OSPF). This algorithm provides a much higher level of security and data integrity than the original SNMP specification. Unfortunately, not every networking device supports SNMPv2, let alone SNMPv3. Thus, SNMPv1 is still widely used today.*

Good Authentication Required

By now, the need for good authentication should be obvious. A service that passes logon information as clear text is far too easy to monitor. Easily snooped logons can be an even larger problem in environments that do not require frequent password changes, which gives our attacker plenty of time to launch an attack using the compromised account. Also of concern is that most users try to maintain the same logon name and password for all accounts. Thus, if an attacker can capture the authentication credentials from an insecure service (such as POP3),they might now have a valid logon name and passwords to other systems on the network, such as NT and NetWare servers.

Good authentication goes beyond validating the source attempting to access a service during initial logon. You should also validate that the source has not been replaced by an attacking host in the course of the communication session. This type of attack is commonly called *session hijacking*.

Session Hijacking

Consider the simple network drawing in Figure 8.5. A client is communicating with a server over an insecure network connection. The client has already authenticated with the server and has been granted access. Let's make this a fun example and assume that the client has administrator-level privileges. Woolly Attacker is sitting on a network segment between the client and the server and has been quietly monitoring the session, learning which port and sequence numbers being used to carry on the conversation.

FIGURE 8.5

An example of a man-in-the-middle attack

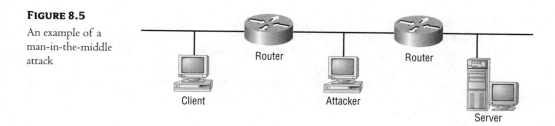

Now let's assume that Woolly Attacker wants to hijack the administrator's session in order to create a new account with administrator-level privileges. The first thing he does is force the client into a state where it can no longer communicate with the server. He can crash the client by sending it a Ping of death or using a utility such as WinNuke. He can also launch an attack such as an ICMP (Internet Control Message Protocol) flood. No matter which type of attack Woolly launches, his goal is to ensure that the client cannot respond to traffic sent by the server.

NOTE   *When an ICMP flood is launched against a target, the target spends so much time processing ICMP requests that it does not have enough time to respond to any other communications.*

Now that the client is out of the way, Woolly Attacker is free to communicate with the server as if he were the client. He can do this by capturing the server's replies as they head back to the client in order to formulate a proper response. If Woolly has an intimate knowledge of IP, he might even be able to completely ignore the server's replies and transmit port and sequence numbers based on the expected responses from the server. In either case, Woolly Attacker is now communicating with the server—except that the server thinks it is still communicating with the original client.

Therefore, good authentication should also verify that the source remains constant and has not been replaced by another system. This can be done by having the two systems exchange a secret during the course of the communication session. A secret can be exchanged with each packet transmitted or at random intervals during the course of the session. Obviously, verifying the source of every packet is far more secure than verifying the source at random intervals. The communication session would be even more secure if you could vary the secret with each packet exchange. This approach helps to ensure that your session is not vulnerable to session hijacking.

Verifying the Destination

The need to authenticate the source both before and during a communication session is apparent. What may not be apparent is the need to verify the server. Many people take for granted that they will either connect to the intended server or that they will receive some form of host unreachable message. It may not dawn on them that what they assume is the server may actually be an attacker attempting to compromise the network.

Later versions of Windows (post Windows95) used stronger types of authentication by default (discussed later in this chapter), culminating in the Kerberos protocol that makes both the client *and* the server authenticate to each other.

DNS POISONING

Another exploit that displays the need for authentication is *DNS poisoning*. DNS poisoning, also known as *cache poisoning*, is the process of handing out incorrect IP address information for a specific host with the intent to divert traffic from its true destination. Eugene Kashpureff proved this was possible in the summer of 1997 when he diverted requests for InterNIC hosts to his alternate domain name registry site called AlterNIC. He diverted these requests by exploiting a known vulnerability in DNS services.

When a name server receives a reply to a DNS query, it does not validate the source of the reply or ignore information not specifically requested. Kashpureff capitalized on these vulnerabilities by hiding bogus DNS information inside valid replies. The name server receiving the reply cached the valid information, as well as the bogus information. The result was that if a user tried to resolve a host within the InterNIC's domain (for example `rs.internic.net`, which is used for `whois` queries), they received an IP address within AlterNIC's domain and were diverted to a system on the AlterNIC network.

Although Kashpureff's attack can be considered little more than a prank, it does open the door to some far nastier possibilities. In an age when online banking is the norm, consider the ramifications if someone diverts traffic from a bank's website. An attacker, using cache poisoning to divert bank traffic to an alternate server, could configure the phony server to appear identical to the bank's legitimate server.

When a bank client attempts to authenticate to the bank's web server in order to manage their bank account, an attacker captures the authentication information and simply presents the user with a banner screen stating that the system is currently offline. Unless digital certificates are being used, the client has no way of knowing they are being diverted to another site unless they happen to notice the discrepancy in IP addresses.

NOTE   *Digital certificates are described in the "Digital Certificate Servers" section later in this chapter.*

It is just as important that you verify the server you are attempting to authenticate with as it is to verify the client's credentials or the integrity of the session. All three points in the communication process are vulnerable to attack.

Encryption 101

Cryptography is a set of techniques used to transform information into an alternate format that can later be reversed. This alternate format is referred to as the *ciphertext* and is typically created using a crypto algorithm and a crypto key. The *crypto algorithm* is simply a mathematical formula that is applied to the information you want to encrypt. The *crypto key* is an additional variable injected into the algorithm to ensure that the ciphertext is not derived using the same computational operation every time the algorithm processes information.

Let's say the number 42 is extremely important to you and you want to guard this value from peering eyes. You create the following crypto algorithm to encrypt this data:

```
data / crypto key + (2 x crypto key)
```

This process relies on two important pieces: the crypto algorithm itself and the crypto key. Both are used to create the ciphertext, a new numeric value. To reverse the ciphertext and produce an answer of 42, you need to know both the algorithm and the key. There are less secure crypto algorithms known as *Caesar ciphers* that do not use keys, but these are typically not used because they do not have the additional security of a crypto key. You only need to know the algorithm for a Caesar cipher in order to decrypt the ciphertext.

NOTE *Julius Caesar is credited as being one of the first people to use encryption. Using the substitution method, he shifted each letter of his message to the letter three places down in the alphabet. He replaced all his letter A's with D's, B's with E's, and so on. Because his generals were the only people aware of his algorithm, he considered his messages safe from untrusted messengers. This type of encryption is commonly referred to as the "Caesar cipher."*

Since encryption uses mathematical formulas, there is a symbiotic relationship between the following:

◆ The algorithm

◆ The key

◆ The original data

◆ The ciphertext

Knowing any three of these pieces allows you to derive the fourth. The exception to this is knowing the combination of the original data and the ciphertext. If you have multiple examples of both, you might be able to discover the algorithm and the key.

Methods of Encryption

The two methods of producing ciphertext are:

◆ The stream cipher

◆ The block cipher

The two methods are similar except for the amount of data each encrypts on each pass. Most of today's encryption schemes use some form of a block cipher.

STREAM CIPHER

Using the *stream cipher* is one of the simplest ways to encrypt data. When a stream cipher is employed, each bit of the data is sequentially encrypted using one bit of the key. A classic example of a stream cipher was the Vernam cipher used to encrypt Teletype traffic. The crypto key for the Vernam cipher was stored on a loop of paper. As the Teletype message was fed through the machine, one bit of the data was combined with one bit of the key in order to produce the ciphertext. The recipient of the ciphertext then reversed the process, using an identical loop of paper to decode the original message.

The Vernam cipher used a fixed-length key, which can actually be easy to deduce if you compare the ciphertext from multiple messages. To make a stream cipher more difficult to crack, you can use a crypto key that varies in length. A variable-length crypto key helps to mask any discernible patterns in the resulting ciphertext. In fact, by randomly changing the crypto key used on each bit of data, you can produce ciphertext that is mathematically impossible to crack. Using different random keys does not generate any repeating patterns that can give a cracker the clues required to break the crypto key. The process of continually varying the encryption key is known as a *one-time pad*.

Although virtually unbreakable, the one-time pad method is far less common than other methods of encryption because it produces overhead equivalent to the amount of plain text being protected. This, of course, creates additional traffic and decreases the efficiency of your network. However, a cryptographic system doesn't need to be unbreakable to be useful. It needs only to be strong enough to resists attacks by likely enemies for as long your information needs to be protected.

BLOCK CIPHER

Unlike stream ciphers, which encrypt every single bit, *block ciphers* encrypt data in chunks of a specific size. A block cipher specification identifies how much data should be encrypted on each pass (called a *block*) as well as what size key should be applied to each block. For example, the Data Encryption Standard (DES) specifies that DES-encrypted data should be processed in 64-bit blocks using a 56-bit key.

You can use a number of different algorithms when processing block cipher encryption. The most basic is to simply take the data and break it into blocks while applying the key to each. Although this method is efficient, it can produce repetitive ciphertext. If two blocks of data contain exactly the same information, the two resulting blocks of ciphertext will be identical, as well. As mentioned earlier, a cracker can use ciphertext that repeats in a nonrandom fashion to break the crypto key.

A better solution is to use earlier resultants from the algorithm and combine them with later keys. Figure 8.6 shows one possible variation. The data you want to encrypt is broken into blocks labeled DB1 through DB4. An *initialization vector* (IV) is added to the beginning of the data to ensure that all blocks can be properly ciphered. The IV is simply a random character string to ensure that two identical messages will not create the same ciphertext. To create your first block of ciphertext (CT1), you mathematically combine the crypto key, the first block of data (DB1), and the initialization vector (IV).

FIGURE 8.6

Block cipher
encryption

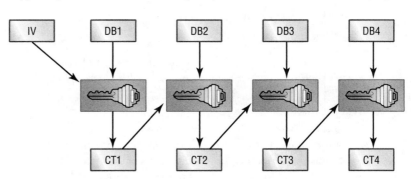

Key + IV + DB1 = CT1
Key + CT1 + DB2 = CT2
Key + CT2 + DB3 = CT3
Key + CT3 + DB4 = CT4

When you create the second block of ciphertext (CT2), you mathematically combine the crypto key, the first block of ciphertext (CT1), and the second block of data (DB2). Because the variables in your algorithm have changed, DB1 and DB2 could be identical, but the resulting ciphertext (CT1 and CT2) will contain different values. This helps to ensure that the resulting ciphertext is sufficiently scrambled so that it appears completely random. This process of using resulting ciphertext to encrypt additional blocks of data will continue until all the data blocks have been processed.

There are a number of variations on how to mathematically combine the crypto key, the initialization vector, and previously created ciphertext. All these methods share the same goal, which is to create a seemingly random character string of ciphertext.

PUBLIC/PRIVATE CRYPTO KEYS

So far, all the encryption techniques we have discussed use *secret key algorithms*. A secret key algorithm relies on the same key to encrypt and to decrypt the ciphertext. Thus, the crypto key must remain secret to ensure the confidentiality of the ciphertext. If an attacker learns your secret key, they can unlock all encrypted messages. This situation creates an interesting Catch-22, because you now need a secure method for exchanging the secret key in order to use the secret key to create a secure method of exchanging information!

In 1976, Whitfield Diffie and Martin Hellman introduced the concept of public cipher keys in their paper "New Directions in Cryptography." Not only did this paper revolutionize the cryptography industry; the process of generating public keys is now known as *Diffie-Hellman*.

In lay terms, a *public key* is a crypto key that has been mathematically derived from a private or secret crypto key. Information encrypted with the public key can only be decrypted with the private key; however, information encrypted with the private key cannot be decrypted with the public key. In other words, the keys are not symmetrical. They are specifically designed so that the public key is used to encrypt data, while the private key is used to decrypt ciphertext.

This eliminates the Catch-22 of the symmetrical secret key, because a secure channel is not required to exchange key information. Public keys can be exchanged over insecure channels while still maintaining the secrecy of the messages they encrypted. If your friend Fred Tuttle wants to send you a private message, all Fred has to do is encrypt it using your public key. The resulting ciphertext can then only be decrypted using your private key.

You can even use Diffie-Hellman to provide authentication. You authenticate by signing a message with your private key before encrypting it with the recipient's public key. *Signing* is simply a mathematical algorithm that processes your private key and the contents of the message. This creates a unique digital signature that is appended to the end of the message. Since the contents of the message are used to create the signature, your digital signature will be different on every message you send.

For example, let's say you want to send Fred a private message. First you create a digital signature using your private key, and then you encrypt the message using Fred's public key. When Fred receives the message, he first decrypts the ciphertext using his private key and then checks the digital signature using your public key. If the signature matches, Fred knows that the message is authentic and that it has not been altered in transit. If the signature does not match, Fred knows that either the message was not signed by your private key or that the ciphertext was altered in transit. In either event, the recipient knows that he should be suspicious of the contents of the message.

Encryption Weaknesses

Encryption weaknesses fall into three categories:

◆ Mishandling or human error

◆ Deficiencies in the cipher itself

◆ Brute force attacks

When deciding which encryption method best suits your needs, be sure you are aware of the weaknesses of your choice.

MISHANDLING OR HUMAN ERROR

Although the stupid user syndrome may be an odd topic to bring up when discussing encryption methods, it does play a critical role in ensuring that your data remains secure. Some methods of encryption lend themselves better to poor key management practices than others. When selecting a method of encryption, be sure you have the correct infrastructure required to administer the cipher keys in an appropriate manner.

Although a one-time pad may be the most secure cipher to use, you must be able to generate enough unique keys to keep up with your data encryption needs. Even if you use a regular secret key cipher, you must make sure that you have a secure method for exchanging key information between hosts. It does little good to encrypt your data if you are simply going to transmit your secret key over the same insecure channel.

Simple key management is one of the reasons that public/private cipher keys have become so popular. The ability to exchange key information over the same insecure channel that you want to use for your data has great appeal. This approach greatly simplifies management: you can keep your private key locked up and secure while transmitting your public key using any method you choose.

PROPER KEY MANAGEMENT IS KEY

Back in the 1940s, the Soviet Union was using a one-time pad to encrypt its most sensitive data. As you saw in the section on stream ciphers, it is mathematically impossible to break encryption using a one-time pad. This, of course, assumes that the user understands the definition of "one-time." Apparently, the Soviet Union did not.

Since cipher keys were in short supply, the Soviet Union began reusing some of its existing one-time pad keys by rotating them through different field offices. The assumption was that as long as the same office did not use the same key more than once, the resulting ciphertext would be sufficiently secure. (How many of you can see your pointy-haired boss making a similar management decision?)

Apparently, this assumption was off base: the United States was able to identify the duplicate key patterns and decrypt the actual messages within the ciphertext. For more than five years, the United States was able to track Soviet spying activity within the United States. This continued until information regarding the cracking activity was relayed to a double agent.

WARNING   *You must make sure that the public keys you use to encrypt data have been received from the legitimate source and not from an attacker who has swapped in a private key of their own. You can easily authenticate the validity of a public key through a phone call or some other means.*

CIPHER DEFICIENCIES

Determining whether there are any deficiencies in the cipher algorithm of a specific type of encryption is probably the hardest task a noncryptographer can attempt. You can, however, look for a few things to ensure that the encryption is secure:

◆ The mathematical formula that makes up the encryption algorithm should be public knowledge. Algorithms that rely on secrecy may very well have flaws that can be extorted to expedite cracking.

◆ The encryption algorithm should have undergone open public scrutiny. Anyone should be able to evaluate the algorithm and be free to discuss their findings. Analysis of the algorithm cannot be restricted by confidentiality agreements and cannot be contingent on the cryptographer's signing a nondisclosure agreement.

◆ The encryption algorithm should have been publicly available for a reasonable length of time to ensure that a proper analysis has been performed. An encryption algorithm with no known flaws that has only been publicly available for a few months has not stood the test of time. One of the reasons that many people trust DES encryption is that it has been around since 1976.

◆ Public analysis should have produced no useful weaknesses in the algorithm. This can be a gray area because nearly all encryption algorithms have some form of minor flaw. As a rule of thumb, the flaws within an algorithm should not dramatically reduce the amount of time needed to crack a key beyond what could be achieved by trying all possible key combinations.

By following these simple guidelines, you should be able to make an educated guess about the relative security of an encryption algorithm.

BRUTE FORCE ATTACKS

A brute force attack is simply an attempt to try all possible cipher key combinations in order to find the one that unlocks the ciphertext. This attack is also known as an *exhaustive key search*. The cracker makes no attempt to actually crack the key, but relies on the ability to try all possible key combinations in a reasonable amount of time. All encryption algorithms are vulnerable to brute force attacks.

The preceding paragraph contains a couple of key terms. The first is *reasonable*. An attacker must feel that launching a brute force attack is worth the time. If an exhaustive key search will produce your VISA platinum card number in a few hours, the attack might be worth the effort. If, however, four weeks of work are required to decrypt your father-in-law's chili recipe, a brute force attack might not be worth the attacker's effort.

The other operative word is *vulnerable*. Although all encryption algorithms are susceptible to a brute force attack, some may take so long to try all possible key combinations that the amount of time spent cannot be considered reasonable. For example, encryption using a one-time pad can be broken using a brute force attack, but the attacker had better plan on having many of their descendants carry on the work long after they are gone. To date, the earth has not existed long enough for an attacker to be able to break a proper one-time pad encryption scheme using existing computing power.

Therefore, the amount of time required to perform a brute force attack is contingent on two factors: how long it takes to try a specific key and how many possible key combinations there are. The amount of time required to try each key depends on the device providing the processing power. A typical desktop computer can test approximately five keys per second. A device specifically designed to break encryption keys might be able to process 200 keys or more per second. Of course, greater results can be achieved by combining multiple systems.

The number of possible key combinations is directly proportional to the size of the cipher key. Size does matter in cryptography: the larger the cipher key, the more possible key combinations exist. Table 8.1 shows some common encryption methods, along with their associated key size. Notice that as the size of the key increases, the number of possible key combinations increases exponentially.

TABLE 8.1: METHODS OF ENCRYPTION AND THEIR ASSOCIATED KEYS

ENCRYPTION	BITS IN KEY	NUMBER OF POSSIBLE KEYS
Netscape	40	1.1×10^6
DES	56	72.1×10^6
Triple DES (2 keys)	112	5.2×10^{33}
RC4/128	128	3.4×10^{38}
Triple DES (3 keys)	168	3.7×10^{50}
Future standard?	256	1.2×10^{77}

Of course, all this leads to the question: how long does it take to perform an exhaustive key search on a particular encryption algorithm? The answer should scare you. DES encryption (discussed in the DES section of this chapter) has become somewhat of an industry standard. Over the past few years, RSA Laboratories has staged a DES challenge to see how long it would take for a person or persons to crack a string of ciphertext and discover the message hidden inside.

In 1997, the challenge was completed in approximately five months. In January 1998, the challenge was completed in 39 days. By July 1998, the Electronic Frontier Foundation (EFF) was able to complete the challenge in less than three days.

The EFF accomplished this task through a device designed specifically for brute forcing DES encryption. The cost of the device was approximately $250,000—well within the price range of organized crime and big business. Just after the challenge, the EFF published a book entitled *Cracking DES* (O'Reilly and Associates, 1998), which completely documents the design of the device they used. Obviously, this has put a whole new spin on what key lengths are considered secure.

For more information on the RSA Challenge, which offers prizes ranging from $10,000 to $200,000 for successful decryption of highly secure keys, visit their website at www.rsasecurity.com.

Government Intervention

As you may know, the federal government regulates the export or use of encryption across U.S. borders. These regulations originated during World War II, when the use of encryption was thought to be limited to spies and terrorists. These regulations still exist today, in part because of the efforts of the National Security Agency (NSA). The NSA is responsible for monitoring and decrypting all communication that can be considered of interest to the security of the U.S. government.

Originally, the regulations controlled the cipher key size that could be exported or used across U.S. borders. For many rules, the limitation was a maximum key size of 40 bits, with few exceptions. Organizations that wanted to use a larger key size had to apply to the Department of Commerce and obtain a license to do so under the International Traffic in Arms Regulations (ITAR). This was typically sought by a financial institution or a U.S.-based company with foreign subsidiaries.

However, on October 19, 2000, the Bureau of Export Administration published a rule that embodied the changes made by the Clinton administration earlier that year which intended to liberalize export policy on not only the length, but also the type, of encryption products that could be exported. The major impetus for the change came from the administration's recognition that non-U.S. companies already provided encryption technologies that exceeded the export restrictions. Bowing to pressure not only from U.S. companies, but also countries in the European Union (EU), the change allows most encryption products to be exported without a governmental review to all 15 EU countries and 8 other trading parties.

So, what does this mean for you? Well, better encryption products domestically, for one. Because vendors don't have to produce two versions of their products (with distinct encryption strengths), there is more incentive to include greater encryption as opposed to keeping to the lowest common denominator.

Good Encryption Required

If you are properly verifying your authentication session, why do you even need encryption? Encryption serves two purposes:

- To protect the data from snooping
- To protect the data from being altered

In the section on clear text transmissions earlier in this chapter, you saw how most IP services transmit all information in the clear. This fact should be sufficient justification for using encryption to shield your data from peering eyes.

Encryption can also help to ensure that your data is not altered during transmission. Altering data during transmission is commonly referred to as a man-in-the-middle attack (as mentioned earlier), because it relies on the attacker's ability to disrupt the data transfer. Let's assume you have a web server configured to accept online catalog orders. Your customer fills out an online form, which is then saved on the web server in a plain text format. At regular intervals, these files are transferred to another system via FTP or SMTP.

If an attacker can gain access to the web server's file system, they can modify these text files prior to processing. A malicious attacker can then change quantities or product numbers to introduce inaccuracies. The result is a very unhappy client when the wrong order is received. Although this example assumes that the attacker has gained access to a file system, it is possible to launch a man-in-the-middle attack while information is in transit on the network, as well.

Although your attacker has not stolen anything, they have altered the data—and disrupted your business. Had this information been saved using a good encryption algorithm, this attack would have been far more difficult to stage because the attacker would not know which values within the encrypted file to change. Even if the attacker were a good guesser, the algorithm decrypting the cipher would detect the change in data.

Solutions

A number of solutions are available for providing authentication and encryption services. Some are products produced by a specific vendor, and others are open standards. Which option is right for you depends on your specific requirements. The following options are the most popular for providing authentication, encryption, or a combination. Most likely, one of these solutions can fill your needs.

Data Encryption Standard (DES)

DES was, for many years, the encryption standard used by the U.S. government for protecting sensitive, but not classified, data. The American National Standards Institute (ANSI) and the Internet Engineering Task Force (IETF) have also incorporated DES into security standards. DES is by far the most popular secret key algorithm in use today.

The original standard of DES uses a 40-bit (for export) or 56-bit key for encrypting data. The latest standard, referred to as *Triple DES*, encrypts the plain text three times using two or three different 56-bit keys. This approach produces ciphertext that is scrambled to the equivalent of a 112-bit or 168-bit key, while still maintaining backward compatibility.

DES is designed so that even if someone knows some of the plain text data and the corresponding ciphertext, there is no way to determine the key without trying all possible keys. The strength of DES encryption–based security rests on the size of the key and on properly protecting the key. Although the original DES standard has been broken in brute force attacks of only 56 hours, the new Triple DES standard should remain secure for many years to come.

Advanced Encryption Standard (AES)

As of May 26, 2002, the new standard used by the U.S government for protecting sensitive, but not classified, data is AES (Advanced Encryption Standard). This new standard was the result of a "best of breed" approach in which multiple encryption algorithms (MARS, RC6, Rijndael, Serpent, Twofish) were submitted and evaluated on the basis of not only brute protection, but also speed, maintenance, and administration. As a result of this process, the Rijndael algorithm was selected to be the official algorithm of the new standard.

Rijndael (as implemented in AES) is a symmetric block cipher that uses 128-, 192-, and 256-bit keys (in blocks of 128 bits). Although all the algorithms submitted to the government were considered strong enough for AES, Rinjdael excelled in areas of performance, efficiency, and flexibility. These areas take on additional importance when you understand that the protocol has to be implemented in hardware/software combinations with less power than traditional desktop computers (such as radios, key/card readers, and other devices).

And what about the IETF's opinion of AES and the AES algorithm? After performing a stuffy review of IETF protocols (including SSL [Secure Sockets Layer], S/MIME [Secure Multipurpose Internet Mail Extension], SSH [Secure Shell], and Kerberos, among others), they reached the conclusion that most protocols that already use encryption can be easily modified to accommodate it. As a result, by the end of 2003 all IETF protocols will be AES-capable, even though DES/3DES will still be supported a little beyond that date.

Digital Certificate Servers

As you saw in the section on public and private cipher keys, you can use a private key to create a unique digital signature. This signature can then be verified later with the public key to ensure that the signature is authentic. This process provides a strong method for authenticating a user's identity. A *digital certificate server* provides a central point of management for multiple public keys. This prevents every user from having to maintain and manage copies of every other user's public cipher key. For example, a Lotus Notes server can act as a digital certificate server, allowing users to sign messages using their private keys. The Notes server can then inform the recipient on delivery whether the Notes server could verify the digital signature.

Digital certificate servers, also known as *certificate authorities* (CAs), provide verification of digital signatures. For example, if Toby receives a digitally signed message from Lynn but does not have a copy of Lynn's public cipher key, Toby can obtain a copy of Lynn's public key from the CA to verify that the message is authentic. Also, let's assume that Toby wants to respond to Lynn's e-e-mail but wants to encrypt the message to protect it from prying eyes. Toby can again obtain a copy of Lynn's public key from the CA so that the message can be encrypted using Lynn's public key.

You can even use certificate servers to provide single sign-on and access control. You can map certificates to access control lists for files stored on a server in order to restrict access. When a user attempts to access a file, the server verifies that the user's certificate has been granted access. This approach allows a CA to manage nearly all document security for an organization.

NOTE *Netscape Certificate Server is a good example of a CA that supports file-level access control.*

The largest benefit comes from using a CA that supports X.509, an industry standard format for digital certificates. This approach allows certificates to be verified and information to be encrypted between organizations. If the predominant method of exchanging information between two domains is e-mail, a CA may be far more cost effective than investing in virtual private networking.

IP Security (IPSEC)

IPSEC (IP Security) is a set of protocols developed by the IETF to support the encryption and authentication of data at the IP layer of the OSI (Open Standards Interconnect) Reference Model and, as a result, has become a key technology in the deployment of VPNs (virtual private networks). The various protocols include the following:

AH (Authentication Header) This protocol is used to authenticate and validate packets—in other words, to digitally sign each packet. A receiving station can verify the identity of the sender of the message, but also the integrity of the data (that is, verify that the data hasn't been changed, either through corruption or malicious intent).

ESP (Encapsulating Security Protocol)   This protocol actually encrypts the data payload of a packet so that only the sender and receiver know the contents.

IPcomp (IP payload compression)   Because encryption can reduce the effectiveness of encryption, IPcomp works to compress the data and then hands it off to ESP for encryption.

IKE (Internet Key Exchange   Because AH and ESP use public/private keys to generate and exchange a symmetric session key, IKE is used to negotiate how that process takes place.

IPSEC can be used in two modes, transport and tunnel. *Transport mode* simply encrypts communication between two hosts. *Tunnel mode,* however, works to support VPNs by placing the entire encrypted IP packet into an additional IP packet so that the encrypted data is "tunneled" through to the destination. Both AH and ESP can operate in either transport or tunnel mode.

When you implement IPSEC, you need to give your system guidelines so that it knows which packets are to be processed by IPSEC. You do so by defining an IPSEC policy, which really comes down to deciding if IPSEC is applied to a specific type of packet or to a service as a whole.

For example, an IPSEC rule applies to all packets being sent to a specific destination network. This approach is most common when an IPSEC-aware router is used to establish a secure connection (possibly a VPN, but not necessarily) from one network to another. In this case, all packets, regardless of which service or client they originate from, are encrypted, as long as they are destined for the specific network.

If you want to set up an IPSEC-aware service (such as an e-mail server), you could also specify that all packets sent or received on a specific port—regardless of the origin or destination of the packets—is processed by IPSEC. In this case, IPSEC is said to be applied in a per-server fashion.

In addition to the flexibility of the functions performed by IPSEC, the standard also allows for a choice of encryption algorithms that can be used by AH and ESP, as well as by IKE. This feature is important when you are combining IPSEC with other security implementations from various vendors.

Kerberos

Kerberos is another authentication solution that is designed to provide a single sign-on to a heterogeneous environment. Kerberos allows mutual authentication and encrypted communication between users and services. Unlike security tokens, however, Kerberos relies on each user to remember and maintain a unique password.

When a user authenticates to the local operating system, a local agent sends an authentication request to the Kerberos server. The server responds by sending the encrypted credentials for the user attempting to authenticate to the system. The local agent then tries to decrypt the credentials using the user-supplied password. If the correct password has been supplied, the user is validated and given authentication tickets, which allow the user to access other Kerberos-authenticated services. The user is also given a set of cipher keys that can be used to encrypt all data sessions.

Once the user is validated, they are not required to authenticate with any Kerberos-aware servers or applications. The tickets issued by the Kerberos server provide the credentials required to access additional network resources. Although the user is still required to remember their password, they only need one password to access all systems on the network to which they have access.

One of the biggest benefits of Kerberos is that it is free. You can download and use the source code without cost. Many commercial applications, such as IBM's Global Sign-On (GSO) product, are also Kerberos-compatible but sport additional features and improved management. A number of security flaws have been discovered in Kerberos over the years, but most, if not all, have been fixed as of Kerberos V.

TIP *Chapter 12 contains more detailed information about Kerberos, in the context of Windows 2000.*

PPTP/L2TP

A discussion on encryption techniques would not be complete without at least mentioning *PPTP* (Point-to-Point Tunneling Protocol) and *L2TP* (Layer Two Tunneling Protocol). Developed by Microsoft, PPTP uses authentication based on the Point-to-Point Protocol (PPP) and encryption based on a Microsoft algorithm. Microsoft has integrated support for PPTP into all versions of Windows.

However, although this technology made for rapid and easy deployment of Microsoft VPNs, PPTP has never been considered secure. As a result, Microsoft took the best features of PPTP and merged them with Cisco's L2F (Layer Two Forwarding) to create L2TP. (This standard was later adopted by the IETF.) L2TP can use IPSEC for its authentication and encryption, and because IPSEC implementations can choose from among various algorithms, it is more flexible (and secure). There is an additional implementation and maintenance cost, however, because of IPSECs reliance on a public-key infrastructure.

L2TP can operate without IPSEC, however, and in this mode it uses the same authentication and access controls of PPP (Point to Point Protocol)—PAP (Password Authentication Protocol) and CHAP (Challenge Handshake Authentication Protocol), along with NCP (Network Control Protocol)—to handle the IP address assignment of the remote VPN client. (The VPN client can appear to the host network as having an IP address on the same, or complimentary, subnet.) Microsoft's implementation of L2TP can also use EAP (discussed next) for more flexible and stronger authentication.

EAP (Extensible Authentication Protocol)

EAP is an extension to PPP that allows for multiple authentication methods, including token cards, one-time passwords, public key authentication (using smart cards), and even Kerberos and RADIUS (see the next section). Microsoft provides for both CHAP and TLS (Transport Layer Security) with their implementation of EAP. TLS is a mutual authentication scheme (like Kerberos) that requires that both client and server prove their identity (through certificates) and is simply an extension (and improvement) of SSL.

Remote Access Dial-In User Service (RADIUS)

RADIUS allows multiple remote access devices to share the same authentication database. RADIUS provides a central point of management for all remote network access. When a user attempts to connect to a RADIUS client (such as a terminal access server), they are challenged for a logon name and password. The RADIUS client then forwards these credentials to the RADIUS server. If the credentials are valid, the server returns an affirmative reply, and the user is granted access to the network. If the credentials do not match, the RADIUS server replies with a rejection, causing the RADIUS client to drop the user's connection.

RADIUS has been used predominantly for remote modem access to a network. Over the years, it has enjoyed widespread support from such vendors as 3COM, Cisco, and Ascend. RADIUS is also starting to become accepted as a method for authenticating remote users who are attempting to access the local network through a firewall. Support for RADIUS has been added to Check Point's FireWall-1 and Cisco's PIX firewall.

The biggest drawback to using RADIUS for firewall connectivity is that the specification does not include encryption. Although RADIUS can perform strong authentication, it has no way to ensure the integrity of your data once the session is established. If you do use RADIUS authentication on the firewall, you will need an additional solution in order to provide encryption.

RSA Encryption

The *RSA encryption algorithm* was created by Ron Rivest, Adi Shamir, and Leonard Adleman in 1977. RSA is considered the de facto standard in public/private key encryption: it has found its way into products from Microsoft, Apple, Novell, Sun, and even Lotus. As a public/private key scheme, it can also perform authentication.

The fact that RSA is widely used is important when considering interoperability. You cannot authenticate or decrypt a message if you are using a different algorithm from the algorithm used to create it. Sticking with a product that supports RSA helps to ensure that you can exchange information with a large base of users. The large installation base also means that RSA has received its share of scrutiny over the years. This consideration is also important when you are selecting an algorithm to protect your data.

RSA Laboratories was the original owner of the algorithm, but in September 2000 they released it into the public domain. This release further confirms the position of the algorithm and will do nothing but increase its ubiquity in products and services.

Secure Shell (SSH)

SSH is a powerful method for performing client authentication and safeguarding multiple service sessions between two systems. Written by a Finnish student named Tatu Ylönen, SSH has received widespread acceptance within the Unix world. The protocol has even been ported to Windows and OS/2.

Systems running SSH listen on port 22 for incoming connection requests. When two systems running SSH establish a connection, they validate each other's credentials by performing a digital certificate exchange using RSA. Once the credentials for each system have been validated, Triple DES is used to encrypt all information that is exchanged between the two systems. The two hosts authenticate each other in the course of the communication session and periodically change encryption keys. This helps to ensure that brute force or playback attacks are not effective.

SSH is an excellent method for securing protocols that are known to be insecure. For example, Telnet and FTP sessions exchange all authentication information in the clear. SSH can encapsulate these sessions to ensure that no clear text information is visible.

Secure Sockets Layer (SSL)

Created by Netscape, *SSL* provides RSA encryption at the session layer of the OSI model. By encrypting at the session layer, SSL can be service independent. Although SSL works equally well with FTP, HTTP, and even Telnet, the main use of SSL is in secure Web commerce. Since the RSA encryption is a public/private key encryption, digital certificates are also supported. This allows SSL to authenticate the server and optionally authenticate the client.

Netscape includes SSL in its web browser and web server products. Netscape has even provided source code so that SSL can be adapted to other web server platforms. A webmaster developing a web page can flag the page as requiring an SSL connection from all web browsers. This allows online commerce to be conducted in a relatively secure manner.

SSL was the creation of Netscape, which then passed the standard to the Internet Engineering Task Force (IETF). The IETF built TLS (Transport Layer Security) from SSL, while still retaining backward compatibility. As a result, HTTPS (Hypertext Transfer Protocol Secure) supports both SSL and TLS.

Security Tokens

Security tokens, also called token cards, are password-generating devices that can be used to access local clients or network services. Physically, a token is a small device with an LCD display that shows the current password and the amount of time remaining before the password expires. Once the current password expires, a new one is generated. This approach provides a high level of authentication security, because a compromised password has a limited life span. Figure 8.7 shows a number of security tokens produced by Security Dynamics Technologies. These tokens are referred to as SecurID cards.

FIGURE 8.7

SecurID cards from Security Dynamics Technologies

Security tokens do not directly authenticate with an existing operating system or application. An agent is required to redirect the logon request to an authentication server. For example, FireWall-1 supports inbound client authentication via SecurID. When a user on the Internet wants to access internal services protected by FireWall-1, they use their SecurID token to authenticate at the firewall. FireWall-1 does not handle this authentication directly; rather, an agent on the firewall forwards the logon request to a SecurID authentication server, known as an *ACE/Server*. If the credentials are legitimate, validation is returned to the agent via an encrypted session, and the user is allowed access to the internal network.

Each security token is identified by a unit ID number. The unit ID number uniquely identifies each security token to the server. The unit ID is also used to modify the algorithm used to generate each password so that multiple tokens will not produce the same sequence of passwords. Since passwords expire at regular intervals (usually 60 seconds), the security token needs to be initially synchronized with the authentication server.

A number of benefits are associated with this type of authentication. First, users are no longer required to remember their passwords. They simply read the current password from the security token and use this value for authentication. This obviously removes the need for users to change their passwords at regular intervals, because this is done automatically by the security token. Also, it is far less likely that a user will give out their password to another individual because the token is a physical device that needs to be referenced during each authentication attempt. Even if a user does read off their password to another user, the consequences are minimized because the password is only valid for a short period of time.

Security tokens are an excellent way to provide authentication. Their only drawback is that they do not provide any type of session encryption. They rely on the underlying operating system or application to provide this functionality. For example, authentication information can still be read as clear text if an attacker snoops on a Telnet session. Still, the limited life span of any password makes this information difficult to capitalize on.

Simple Key Management for Internet Protocols (SKIP)

SKIP is similar to SSL in that it operates at the session level. Like SSL, SKIP can support IP services regardless of whether the services specifically support encryption. This feature is extremely useful when multiple IP services are running between two hosts.

What makes SKIP unique is that it requires no prior communication in order to establish or exchange keys on a session-by-session basis. The Diffie-Hellman public/private algorithm is used to generate a shared secret. This shared secret is used to provide IP packet–based encryption and authentication.

Although SKIP is extremely efficient at encrypting data, which improves VPN performance, it relies on the long-term protection of this shared secret to maintain the integrity of each session. SKIP does not continually generate new key values, as SSH does. Thus, SKIP encryption is vulnerable if the keys are not protected properly.

Summary

In this chapter, you saw why good authentication is important and what kinds of attacks can be launched if you do not use it. You also learned about encryption and the differences between secret and public/private algorithms. Finally, you looked at a number of authentication and encryption options that are currently available.

Now that you understand encryption, it is time to put it to use by creating a VPN. Extranets have become quite popular, and the ability to create a secure VPN has become a strong business need.

Chapter 9

Virtual Private Networking

NOT SINCE THE INTRODUCTION of the Internet has a single technology brought with it so much promise—or so much controversy. Virtual private networking (VPN) has been touted as the cure-all for escalating WAN expenses and has been feared for being the Achilles' heel in perimeter security. Obviously, the true classification of VPN technology lies somewhere in the middle.

Interestingly, it has been financial institutions, trading companies, and other organizations at high risk of attack that have spearheaded the deployment of VPN technology. Monetary and economic organizations have embraced VPNs to extend their network perimeter. But that isn't all—many small offices have also implemented VPNs to allow employees to work from home or to connect two offices together. Finally, some are finding that by using remote desktop viewing software instead of VPNs, they get many of the same benefits without the downsides.

In this chapter we'll cover:

◆ VPN basics

◆ Setting up a VPN

VPN Basics

A *virtual private network* session is an authenticated and encrypted communication channel across some form of public network, such as the Internet. Since the network is considered insecure, encryption and authentication are used to protect the data while it is in transit. Typically, a VPN is *service independent*, meaning that all information exchanged between the two hosts (Web, FTP [File Transfer Protocol], SMTP [Simple Mail Transfer Protocol], and so on) is transmitted along this encrypted channel.

Figure 9.1 shows a typical example of a VPN configuration. Two different networks are connected to the Internet. These two networks want to exchange information, but they want to do so in a secure manner, because some of the data they will be exchanging is private. To safeguard this information, a VPN is set up between the two sites.

FIGURE 9.1

An example of a
VPN between two
Internet sites

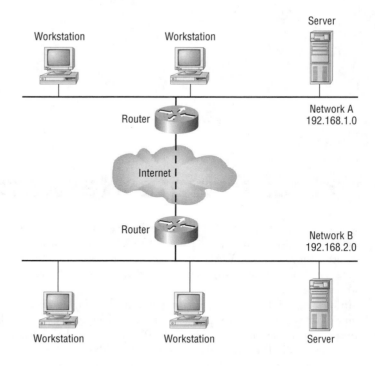

VPNs require some advance planning. *Before* establishing a VPN, the two networks must do the following:

◆ Set up a VPN-capable device on the network perimeter. This can be a router, a firewall, or a device dedicated to VPN activity.

◆ Know the IP subnet addresses used by the other site.

◆ Agree on a method of authentication and exchange digital certificates if required.

◆ Agree on a method of encryption and exchange encryption keys as required.

In Figure 9.1, the devices at each end of the VPN tunnel are the routers you are using to connect to the Internet. If these are recent Cisco routers, they can support IPsec (IP Security), which provides Diffie-Hellman authentication and 128-bit 3DES (Triple Data Encryption Standard) encryption.

You must configure the router on Network A so that all outbound traffic headed for the 192.168.2.0 subnet is encrypted using 3DES. This is known as the remote *encryption domain*. The router on Network A also must know that any data received from the router on Network B will require decryption. You configure the router on Network B in a similar fashion, encrypting all traffic headed for the subnet 192.168.1.0 while decrypting any replies received from the router on Network A. Data sent to all other hosts on the Internet is transmitted in the clear. Only communications between these two subnets are encrypted.

NOTE   *A VPN protects only communications sessions between the two encryption domains. Although it is possible to set up multiple VPNs, you must define multiple encryption domains.*

With some VPN configurations, a network analyzer placed between the two routers displays all packets using a source and destination IP address of the interfaces of the two routers. You do not get to see the IP address of the host that actually transmitted the data, nor do you see the IP address of the destination host. This information is encrypted along with the actual data within the original packet. Once the original packet is encrypted, the router encapsulates this ciphertext within a new IP packet using its own IP address as the source and a destination IP address of the remote router. This is called *tunneling*. Tunneling helps to ensure that a snooping attacker cannot guess which traffic crossing the VPN is worth trying to crack, since all packets use the two routers' IP addresses. Not all VPN methods support this feature, but it is nice to use when it is available.

Since you have a virtual tunnel running between the two routers, you have the added benefit of being able to use private address space across the Internet. For example, a host on Network A can transmit data to a host on the 192.168.2.0 network without requiring network address translation (NAT). The routers encapsulate this header information as the data is delivered along the tunnel. When the router on Network B receives the packet, it simply strips off the encapsulating packet, decrypts the original packet, and delivers the data to the destination host.

Your VPN also has the benefit of being platform and service independent. To communicate securely, your workstations do not have to use software that supports encryption. Secure communications are performed automatically as the traffic passes between the two routers. Thus, you can use services such as SMTP, which are transmitted in the clear, in a secure fashion—provided the destination host is on the remote encryption domain.

VPN Usage

Although VPNs are beginning to be widely deployed, they are being used for two primary applications:

- Replacement for dial-in modem pools
- Replacement for dedicated WAN links

VPNs aren't more widely deployed because of the extensive manual configuration effort typically required to implement them, especially if multiple hosts need to participate in secure communications. However, the need for secure communications is anything but unusual, and many types of inter-device communication could benefit from encryption. For example, two IPsec-compatible routers might dynamically handshake and exchange keys before passing SMTP traffic. When the delivery process is complete, the VPN can be torn down.

MODEM POOL REPLACEMENT

Modem pools have always been the scourge of the network administrator. Although stable solutions are available, they are usually priced beyond the budget of a small- to mid-sized organization. Some of the issues confronting administrators include the following:

- Modems that go off auto-answer
- Below-grade wiring

- Incorrectly configured hunt groups

- Remote workers using personal computers that might not be configured correctly or that are corrupted with a virus or other hostile code

A VPN solution for remote users can dramatically decrease support costs, as well as provide workers a way to work while not physically in the office. You don't have to maintain more phone lines or pay for 800 numbers. You are not required to upgrade your hardware every time a new modem standard is released or to upgrade your phone lines to support new technology, such as ISDN (Integrated Services Digital Network). All inbound access is managed through your Internet connection, a connection your company already maintains to do business on the Internet. And most important (considering this *is* a book on security), you force all access to your network to be scrutinized by your security system.

Access costs can be cheaper, as well. For example, many organizations maintain an 800 number so that employees have remote access to the network free of charge. Maintaining an 800 number can place a large cost burden on the organization, because the per-minute charge for using an 800 number can be double the cost of calling direct. Most ISPs charge $20 a month or less for unlimited access. Large ISPs, such as CompuServe, can even provide local dial-up numbers internationally. For heavy remote access users, it might be far more cost effective for an organization to reimburse the employee for an ISP account than it would be to pay 800-number charges.

Besides reducing infrastructure costs, you can reduce end-user support costs. The most frequent remote-access Helpdesk problem is helping the end user configure network settings and connect to the network. If the user first needs to dial in to an ISP, the ISP can provide this support. Your organization's Helpdesk needs to get involved only when the user can access resources out on the Internet but is having problems connecting to internal resources.

TIP *When selecting a firewall solution, consider whether you will provide end users with remote VPN access. Most firewall packages provide special client software so that an end user can create a VPN to the firewall.*

When deciding whether to provide end users with remote VPN access, you need to consider a few drawbacks. The first is the integrity of the remote workstation. With penetration tools such as L0pht's Netcat and the Cult of the Dead Cow's Back Orifice freely available on the Internet, it is entirely possible that the remote workstation can become compromised. Because most ISPs do not provide any type of firewall for dial-in users, dialed-in systems are wide open to attack. The remote client can be infiltrated by an attacker, who can then use the VPN tunnel to attack internal resources.

A second issue is incorrect configurations, especially if a user is utilizing a personal or home computer to create the VPN session. Because personal computers are typically not supported in an organization and therefore are not subject to corporate policies, there is no way to guarantee that a user will maintain correct settings over the lifecycle of the system.

DEDICATED WAN LINK REPLACEMENT

As you saw in Figure 9.1, you can use a VPN to connect two geographically separate networks over the Internet. A VPN is most advantageous when the two sites are separated by large distances, such as when your organization has one office in Germany and another in New York. Instead of having to pay for a dedicated circuit halfway around the world, each site can connect to a local ISP. The Internet is then used as a backbone to connect these two networks.

A VPN connection might even be advantageous when two sites are relatively close to each other. For example, if you have a business partner that you want to exchange information with but the expected bandwidth does not justify a dedicated connection, a VPN tunnel across an existing Internet connection might be just the ticket. In fact, it might even make life a bit easier.

In Figure 9.2, an internal network is protected by a firewall. A DMZ segment holds your web server and mail relay. Additionally, you have an extra network card in the firewall for managing security to a number of dedicated T1 lines. The T1 circuits connect you to multiple business partners and are used so that sensitive information does not cross the Internet. This sensitive information can be transmitted via e-mail or by FTP.

Although this setup appears straightforward on the surface, it can potentially create a number of problems. The first is routing. Your firewall needs to be programmed with the routing information for each of these remote networks. Otherwise, your firewall simply refers to its default route setting and sends this traffic out to the Internet. Although you can set these routing entries in advance, how will you update them if one of the remote networks makes a routing or subnet change? Although you could use RIP (Routing Information Protocol), you have already seen in Chapter 3 that this is an insecure routing protocol. Open Shortest Path First (OSPF) would be a better choice, but depending on the equipment at the other end of the link, you might not have the option of running OSPF.

You might also run into IP address issues. What if one of the remote networks is using NAT with private address space? If you perform a DNS (Domain Name System) lookup on one of these systems, you will receive the public IP address, not the private. You might have additional routing issues, or you might be required to run DNS entries for these systems locally. Also, what if two or more of the remote networks are using the same private address space? You might now be forced to run NAT on the router at your end of the connection just so your hosts can distinguish between the two networks.

SYSTEM CAPACITY CHECKLIST

If you will be providing client VPN access to your network, keep a sharp eye on system capacity. Here are some questions you should ask yourself:

◆ How many concurrent users will there be? More users means a need for more capacity.

◆ When will VPN clients connect remotely to your network? If most remote VPN access will take place during normal business hours, a faster Internet link and faster hardware might be required.

◆ What services will the clients access? If remote VPN access will be for bandwidth-intensive applications such as file sharing, a faster Internet link and faster hardware might be required, as well.

◆ What kind of encryption do you plan to use? If remote VPN access will be using a large key algorithm, such as 3DES, faster encryption hardware might be required.

FIGURE 9.2

A network using dedicated links to safeguard sensitive information

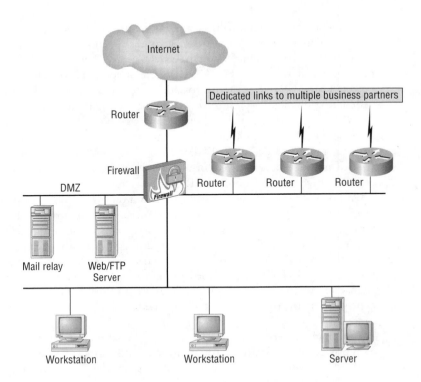

There is also a liability issue. What if an attacker at one of your remote business partners launches an attack against one of the other remote business partners? You have now provided the medium required for this attack to take place. Even if you can legally defend yourself, such a situation would certainly cause a lot of embarrassment and would strain your business relationships.

Replacing your dedicated business partner connections with VPNs resolves each of these problems. As long as you can ensure the integrity of the data stream, administering multiple VPNs is far simpler than managing multiple dedicated circuits.

As with remote client access, you must open a hole through your firewall to permit VPN traffic. Although strong authentication dramatically decreases the chances that an attacker can exploit this hole, it is a hole in your perimeter security just the same.

Selecting a VPN Product

When deciding which VPN product to use, look for the following features:

◆ Strong authentication

◆ Adequate encryption

◆ Adherence to standards

◆ Integration with other network services

Of course, this assumes that you have a choice when selecting a VPN product. If you are setting up a VPN to connect to a specific site, your options may be limited—simply because so many VPN solutions embody features that are proprietary. If you are setting up a VPN to communicate with a specific remote network, find out what VPN package that network is using. You can then determine your product options. A good example of this is key exchange. Although most VPNs use some form of IKE (Internet Key Exchange)—typically ISAKMP (Internet Security Association and Key Management Protocol)—not all these implementations are complementary. Fortunately, most VPN solutions let you specify a manual key—not an ideal solution for mixing VPN products, but at least workable in a transition.

STRONG AUTHENTICATION

Without strong authentication, you have no way to determine if the system at the other end of the VPN tunnel is what you think it is. The newer standard for authentication (replacing the aging and vulnerable Diffie-Hellman), IKE allows a shared secret to be created through the exchange of public keys. This exchange removes the need to exchange secret information through some alternative means.

TIP   *If you are not using a known and trusted certificate authority when exchanging public keys over the Internet, verify the key values through some other means, such as a phone call or fax.*

ADEQUATE ENCRYPTION

Notice that the word *adequate*—not *strong*—appears in the title of this section. You should determine what level of protection you actually require before selecting a method of encryption. The minimum standard of encryption is 3DES. Although VPN products still support 56-bit DES, computing power has advanced to the point that breaking this encryption is trivial.

The reason you want to choose the right level of encryption is performance. The stronger the encryption algorithm you use, the greater the delay the encryption and decryption processes introduce. Although it is always better to err on the side of caution by using a larger key, give some thought to what size key you actually need before assuming bigger is always better.

The type of key you use also affects performance. Secret key encryption, such as 3DES, is popular with VPNs because it is fast. Public/private encryption schemes, such as RSA (Rivest-Shamir-Adelman), can be 10 to 100 times slower than secret key algorithms that use the same size key. Key management with a public/private scheme requires more processor time. Many VPN products use a public/private key algorithm to initially exchange the secret key, but then use secret key encryption for all future communications.

ADHERENCE TO STANDARDS

You saw in Chapter 8 why it is important to stick with encryption schemes that have survived public scrutiny. The same holds true when selecting an encryption method for your VPN. Stick with an algorithm that has stood the test of time and has no significant vulnerabilities. For example, the only real deficiency found with DES is the small key size used in the original version. This can easily be rectified by using 3DES, which increases the number of keys.

Also make sure that the VPN product is compatible with other VPN solutions. Remember, you might achieve only partial compatibility, and that might be enough to satisfy your requirements. Having a good security plan (remember Chapter 2?) will prevent headaches when you get around to implementation.

INTEGRATION WITH OTHER NETWORK SERVICES

Newer VPN solutions can integrate with other services, including firewalls, user directories, and monitoring software. Check Point's VPN-1 is completely integrated into the entire Check Point management suite, allowing not only complete security integration, but also address translation and bandwidth allocation. The ability to centrally manage the authentication of VPN connections as well as control how much bandwidth each connection is allowed is a powerful feature.

Of course, the ideal VPN solution integrate products from different vendors. So far, success has been limited, although newer products are including industry standards such as LDAP (Lightweight Directory Access Protocol) and 3DES.

Microsoft is an example. Microsoft included a VPN solution in Windows 2000. The advantage, of course, is the integration of encryption and authentication technologies with Active Directory. Some vendors (such as Check Point) can mix their own VPN products with Microsoft VPN, allowing one centrally defined VPN policy to be applied equally to Microsoft and vendor-specific VPN access points. Also, because Active Directory is LDAP-compliant, third-party VPNs can base permissions on the user account information stored in Active Directory.

VPN Product Options

You have a number of options when selecting the kind of device to use for a VPN connection. These options fall into three categories:

◆ Firewall-based VPN

◆ Router-based VPN

◆ Dedicated software or hardware

The option you choose depends on your requirements, as well as on the equipment you already have.

FIREWALL-BASED VPN

The most popular VPN solution is *firewall integration*. Since you will probably want to place a firewall on your network perimeter anyway, it is a natural extension to let this device support your VPN connections. This arrangement provides a central point of management as well as direct cohesion between your firewall security policy and the traffic you want to let through your end of the tunnel.

The only drawback is performance. If you have a busy Internet circuit, and you want to use multiple VPNs with strong encryption on all of them, consolidating all these services on a single box might overload the system. Although overload will probably not be an issue for the average installation, keep scale and performance in mind while you are deciding where to terminate your VPN tunnel. Some firewalls, such as Check Point FireWall-1, do support encryption cards to reduce processor load. The encryption card fits in a standard PCI (Peripheral Component Interconnect) expansion slot and takes care of all traffic encryption and decryption. To use one of these cards, however, you must make sure that all your PCI slots are not currently being used by network cards.

ROUTER-BASED VPN

Another choice is your Internet border router. This is yet another device that you must install to connect to the Internet. Terminating the VPN at your border router lets you decrypt the traffic stream before it reaches the firewall. Although process load is still a concern, many routers now use application-specific integrated circuit (ASIC) hardware. This allows the router to dedicate certain processors for specific tasks, thus preventing any one activity from overloading the router.

The only real drawback to a router-based VPN solution is security. Typically (but not always), routers are extremely poor at providing perimeter security compared with the average firewall. An attacker might be able to spoof traffic past the router that the firewall will interpret as originating from the other side of the VPN tunnel. In such a case, the attacker might gain access to services that are typically not visible from other locations on the Internet.

DEDICATED HARDWARE OR SOFTWARE

If you have already purchased a firewall and router and neither supports VPN, all is not lost. You can still go with a hardware or software solution that is dedicated to creating VPN connections. For example, DEC's AltaVista Tunnel is an excellent product that supports tunnels to remote networks and remote-user VPNs. Since this in an independent product, it works with any existing firewall.

The biggest drawback to a dedicated solution is an additional point of administration and security management. If the device is outside the firewall, you have the same spoofing issues that you have with the router solution. If the device is inside the firewall, you might not be able to manage access using your firewall security policy. Most VPN solutions encrypt the original packet in its entirety. In this case, the IP header information is no longer available to the firewall to make traffic control decisions. Because all traffic passing from one end of the tunnel to the other uses the same encapsulating packet headers, the firewall cannot distinguish between an SMTP and a Telnet session encapsulated within the tunnel. You must rely on the dedicated VPN device to provide tools to control the type of traffic you want to let through your end of the tunnel.

VPN Alternatives

Not every remote-access solution requires a fully functional VPN. A number of products provide their own authentication and encryption. Some even allow access to additional network resources. For example, Citrix's WinFrame and MetaFrame products provide terminal server capability based on the Windows NT operating system. (Microsoft has its own version, called Terminal Services.) These Citric products also support decent authentication and encryption. Users on the Internet can use a Citrix client to access the Citrix server through an encrypted session. Once connected to the server, users can access any internal applications to which the system administrator has granted them access. A cheaper (albeit limited) alternative is VNC (Virtual Network Computer), an open-source remote desktop product that provides the ability to remotely view and control a desktop computer. Although security is not integrated (you need to use SSL [Secure Sockets Layer] or SSH [Secure Shell] to encapsulate the VNC traffic), and the Windows version allows only a single session, VNC does have the advantage of providing client and server software for Apple's OS X (there is a commercial product for OS 9), all versions of Windows, and Unix-based systems (such as Solaris, Linux, and BSD-based systems)—and they all interoperate.

The biggest drawback to these alternative solutions is that they require special software to be run on the client (and server, of course) to initiate the connection. You no longer have the service independence of a true VPN solution. This situation is changing, however, as vendors such as Citrix are working to make their products more universally accessible. For example, the latest versions of Win-Frame and MetaFrame (and Microsoft's Terminal Server) no longer require the use of a specialized client. You can now use an optional web browser plug-in that supports the latest versions of Netscape Navigator and Internet Explorer.

TIP   A browser plug-in is an excellent remote solution: a network administrator simply needs to make the plug-in software and configuration file available via a web server. Remote users can then download the required software (about 300KB) and connect to the Citrix server using their favorite web browser.

Setting Up a VPN

In the remainder of this chapter, we'll set up a VPN using Windows 2000. Many of these steps are conceptually similar or equal to what you would do to implement any VPN product.

Microsoft VPN supports both PPTP (Point-to-Point Tunneling Protocol) and L2TP (Layer 2 Tunneling Protocol). We'll show you how to set up a PPTP session because it's a straightforward process. L2TP VPNs are much more powerful, but they also involve establishing a PKI (Public Key Infrastructure) as well as additional work.

Preparing the System

This section assumes that you have a working Windows 2000 Server and a Windows 2000 Professional installation (although XP would also work, and 9x/Me with an additional client). We'll be using basic access rules to keep the demonstration simple—although simplicity is always a good idea when it comes to security.

Make sure that you have applied all Service Packs, hot fixes, and patches to your installations. Doing so will ensure that you don't have any known holes in your system and will also fix any known problems in the VPN software itself.

Our VPN Diagram

Figure 9.3 shows the VPN we'll create. A client machine uses an ISP to connect to a remote network site. This implementation is popular, as more and more workers are requesting (or demanding!) remote access to their networks so they can work at home or on the road.

We'll configure our VPN so that the client machine behaves as if it were physically connected to the remote network. The VPN server will assign a valid IP address for our internal LAN to the VPN client and then embed (or tunnel) this traffic through a session created by using valid Internet addresses.

FIGURE 9.3

An example of a VPN

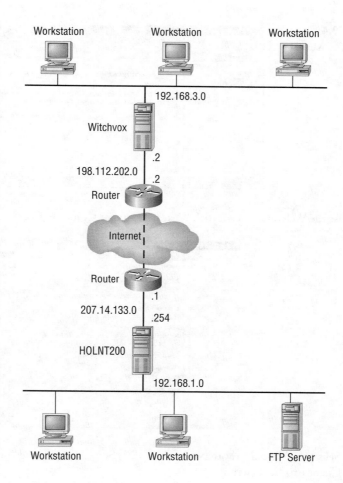

Configuring the VPN Server

We configure the VPN server through the RRAS (Routing and Remote Access) MMC (Microsoft Management Console) plug-in on a Windows 2000 Advanced Server. Follow these steps:

1. From the Desktop, choose Start ➢ Programs ➢ Administrative Tools ➢ Routing and Remote Access to open the Routing and Remote Access dialog box, which is shown in Figure 9.4.

NOTE   *In Figure 9.4, a down-pointing red arrow indicates that the VPN server is not yet configured.*

2. Choose Action ➢ Configure and Enable Routing and Remote Access to start the Routing and Remote Access Server Setup Wizard.

FIGURE 9.4

The RRAS MMC
dialog box

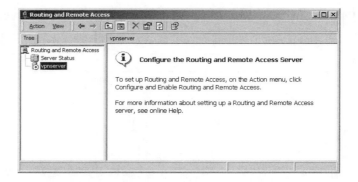

3. At the Welcome screen, click Next to open the Common Configurations screen:

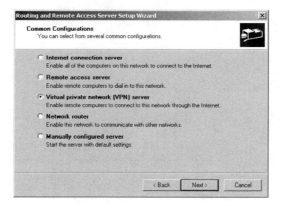

4. Select the Virtual Private Network (VPN) Server option, and click Next to open the Remote
Client Protocols screen:

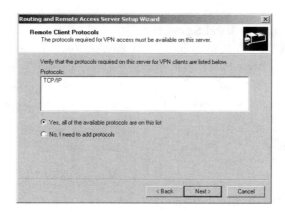

The Protocols box displays the protocols currently installed on the system. If you want client machines to pass a protocol that is not listed, click the No, I Need to Add Protocols option, click Next, and follow the on-screen instructions.

5. Select the protocol you want to use, and click Next to open the Internet Connection screen:

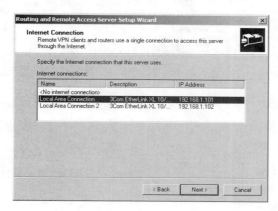

6. Select the connection that you want clients to use to access your server, and then click Next to open the IP Address Assignment screen, which is shown in Figure 9.5.

FIGURE 9.5

Select how IP addresses will be assigned

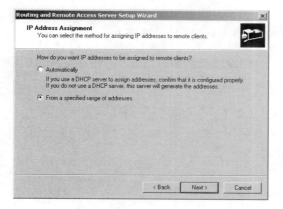

Now you must specify how your VPN clients will get the IP address that they will use for the VPN session. If you already have a DHCP server configured on your network, you can select the Automatically option. However, this requires that you enable the DHCP Proxy service on your VPN server. If you know that you'll have a limited (known) number of DHCP clients, you can choose to specify a range of IP addresses that the VPN server will directly assign to your VPN clients. In Figure 9.4, we chose this option.

7. Select how IP addresses will be assigned, and click Next. If you select the From a Specified Range of Addresses option, clicking next opens the Address Range Assignment screen, which is shown in Figure 9.6.

FIGURE 9.6

Assigning address ranges

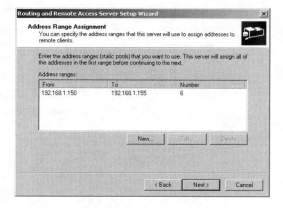

In this example, we created a simple range encompassing 6 addresses (from 192.168.1.150 to 192.168.1.155), as shown in Figure 9.6. Of course, you need to make sure that if you *do* have a DHCP server also operating on your network that you enter an exclusion so that the DHCP server won't assign duplicate addresses.

8. Assign an address range, and click Next to open the Managing Multiple Remote Access Servers screen, which is shown in Figure 9.7.

FIGURE 9.7

Managing remote access servers

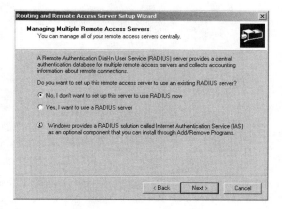

After you enable VPN clients to get an address on your LAN, you can choose to enable RADIUS (Remote Authentication Dial-In User Service) for VPN connections, as shown in Figure 9.x. ISPs commonly use RADIUS servers to authenticate dial-in users, but they're not required for a pure Windows environment, in which authentication is handled by Active Directory. You can use RADIUS to extend the normal capabilities of Active Directory, however, especially for smart cards or biometric devices that have not yet been integrated with Active Directory.

9. Click Next, and then click Finish to return to the RRAS MMC window.

Notice that the view of the RRAS MMC has changed dramatically, as shown in Figure 9.8. From this screen you can choose to do the following:

◆ Configure the server's interfaces

◆ Look at existing active VPN client connections

◆ Review the various VPN ports (each VPN client uses a single port)

◆ Review the IP routing table

◆ View or change your remote access policies

◆ Change remote access log settings

FIGURE 9.8

The RRAS MMC
after configuration

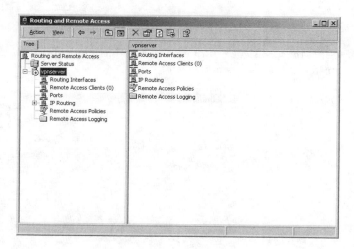

Now that your server is set up, you need to set up your VPN client and then test the VPN connection.

Configuring the VPN Client

Configuring the client consists of creating a VPN connection object on a Windows-based machine. (We'll use Windows 2000 Professional because the VPN client capability is built in.)

1. Choose Start ➢ Settings➢ Network and Dialup Connections ➢ Make New Connection to start the Make New Connection Wizard.

2. At the Welcome screen, click Next to open the Network Connection Type screen:

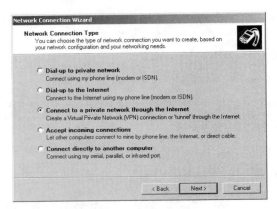

3. Select the Connect to a Private Network through the Internet option, and then click Next to open the Public Network screen:

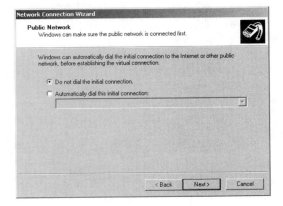

The wizard offers you the option to have the computer create the initial Internet connection before establishing the VPN session. This is useful if you're using an analog modem or an ISDN connection to connect to the Internet, but isn't required if we you using a cable, DSL, or other LAN connection that is always on. In these steps we assume a constant connection.

4. Select the Do Not Dial the Initial Connection option, and then click Next to open the Destination Address screen:

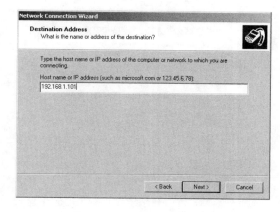

The Destination Address screen asks for the host name or IP address of the VPN server. Many organizations don't configure a DNS name for their VPN server out of security concerns, so you might have to contact your system administrator for the IP address. In this example, we enter the Internet-accessible IP address of our VPN server.

5. Enter a host name or an IP address, and then click Next to open the Connection Availability screen:

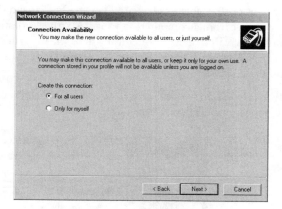

One of the features that makes Windows 2000 such a powerful choice for a desktop computer (this applies to XP also) is that it tightly segregates what different users of the same system can do. In the Connection Availability screen, you can specify whether all users of the client computer can use this connection or only the user account that is actually creating the connection itself. The For All Users is the default.

6. Specify that everyone can use the connection, and then click Next to open the Internet Connection Sharing screen. (If you select only your current user account, you won't be given the option to do Internet Connection Sharing).

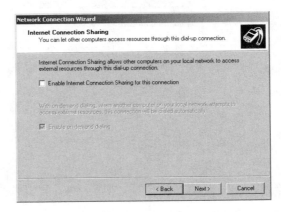

Many small businesses, especially those with two or more remote offices, can benefit from a VPN, but find it difficult to dedicate a whole computer at each office to act as a VPN server. By combining the capabilities of Microsoft's ICS (Internet Connection Sharing) with a standard VPN client, you can allow multiple computers at one location to use the VPN client capabilities of a Windows 2000 Professional (or XP) installation, while still using that computer to perform normal desktop functions.

The Internet Connection Sharing screen asks if you want to enable ICS for this VPN connection and, if so, if you want to enable on-demand dialing. On-demand dialing means that when your computer receives a packet from a computer on your LAN that is destined for a computer on your remote network, your VPN client automatically dials the modem or ISDN connection, creates the VPN session, and then passes the traffic. In this example, we chose to keep the default, which is to leave both options disabled.

7. Specify how you want to deal with ICS, and then click Next to open the Completing the Network Connections Wizard screen:

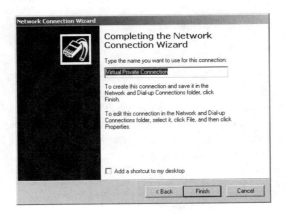

8. Enter a name for this VPN connection, and click the Add a Shortcut to My Desktop check box if you want to place a shortcut to the connection on your Desktop.

Giving a name to your connection might seem like a simple decision, but if you will be creating multiple VPN connections, this is a chance to avoid future confusion. To be even more helpful, you can include VPN connection naming standards in your security plan.

9. Click Finish to open the Connect Virtual Private Connection dialog box:

Testing the VPN

Although you can accept the defaults in the Connect Virtual Private Connection dialog box, you can also click the Properties button to open the Properties dialog box for your VPN connection. In this dialog box, you can configure various settings that apply to this specific connection. You can do the following:

- ◆ Alter the IP address or domain name of the DNS server
- ◆ Change dialing options, including retry parameters and authentication prompts
- ◆ Set advanced authentication and encryption options
- ◆ Install, configure, or remove protocols used in the VPN connection
- ◆ Enable or disable ICS and on-demand dialing

When you're ready to test the session, follow these steps:

1. Enter the user name and password required to connect to the VPN server, and click Connect to open the Connecting Virtual Private Connection dialog box:

2. When the system connects, it registers your machine on the remote network, displaying the following message:

3. When the connection is complete, the system display the Connection Complete dialog box:

4. Click OK to start the session.

For a final verification, you can browse your network to make sure that all remote network resources are available. Figure 9.9 shows the result of browsing to the internal IP address of our VPN server, 192.168.1.145. You can see the Program Files folder, which we shared on the VPN server.

FIGURE 9.9

Browsing the VPN server

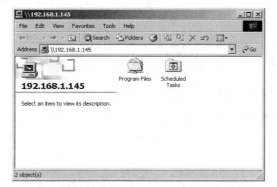

To close your VPN session, right-click the VPN connection object in your Network and Dial-up Connections folder, and choose Disconnect from the shortcut menu. (Or right-click the VPN connection icon in the status area and choose Disconnect from the shortcut menu.) And that's it—a simple and quick VPN session. Of course, your particular VPN session might be more complicated, especially if you have additional authentication, encryption, or administrative needs. Also, setting up multiple remote sites for VPN sessions involves some serious understanding and configuration of routing tables.

VERIFYING THE DATA STREAM

Although all this looks correct, the true test is to break out a network analyzer and decode the traffic being transmitted by the firewalls. Although the log entries claim that the traffic is being encrypted and decrypted, it never hurts to check. A network analyzer will show you the contents of the packets being transmitted. If you can read the financial information within the data stream, you know you have a problem.

Figure 9.10 shows a packet decode of an FTP session before it is encrypted by the firewall. Notice that you can clearly distinguish that this is an FTP session. You can also identify the IP addresses of the systems carrying on this conversation. If you review the information in the bottom pane, you can even see the data being transferred, which appears to be credit card information.

FIGURE 9.10

The data stream before it is encrypted

Figure 9.11 shows the same data stream, but from outside the firewall. This is what an attacker would see who was trying to capture data traveling along the VPN. Notice that the transport protocol for each packet is identified as 57. This identifies the transport as being a tunneling protocol and prevents you from seeing the real transport used in the encapsulated packet (in this case TCP) or the service that is riding on that transport (in this case FTP).

FIGURE 9.11

The data stream after it is encrypted

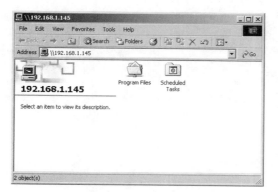

If you look at the middle pane, you will see that the source and destination IP addresses are that of the two computers used in this example. You do not see the true source and destination IP addresses of the data stream. This, combined with hiding the transport and service within the encrypted packet, helps to keep any one data transmission from looking more interesting to an attacker than any other. In fact, there is no certain method of verifying that all this captured traffic is from a single session. The packets listed in the top pane might be from different communication sessions that are taking place simultaneously. To find the FTP session, an attacker might be forced to decrypt hundreds or even thousands of packets.

The real test is the bottom pane. Notice that the data is now scrambled into ciphertext and is no longer readable. This scrambling prevents an attacker from being able to read the enclosed data, as you can in Figure 9.11. To get to this information, an attacker needs to identify which packets contain the financial information and decrypt them with a brute force attack.

Given these two packet traces, it is safe to say that your VPN is functioning properly and encrypting the data that flows between the two encryption domains.

Summary

In this chapter we defined the term *virtual private networking* and discussed when it is beneficial to use a VPN. We also covered what you should look for in a VPN product and what your options are for deployment. Finally, we walked through the steps for configuring a VPN between Microsoft Windows 2000 Professional, and Windows 2000 Server and looked at the effect this configuration has on the passing data stream.

In the next chapter, we'll look at viruses and how you keep these little pieces of destructive code off your network.

Chapter 10

Viruses, Trojans, and Worms

JUST ABOUT EVERY SYSTEM administrator has had to deal with a virus at one time or another. This fact is extremely disheartening, because these tiny pieces of code can cause an immense amount of damage. The loss in productivity and intellectual property can be expensive for any organization. Clearly, the cost of recovering from a virus attack more than justifies the cost of taking preventive measures.

Featured in this chapter:

- ◆ Viruses: the statistics
- ◆ What is a virus?
- ◆ Worms and Trojan horses
- ◆ Preventive measures
- ◆ Deploying virus protection

Viruses: The Statistics

Although virus statistics can be controversial, no one denies that they have a significant impact on personal and corporate productivity, as well as increasing the expense of information-processing systems as a whole.

NOTE   A Computer Economics study (one that is disputed by some in the industry) estimated a $13.2 billion dollar loss for 2001 when Love Bug ran rampant across IT systems world wide. This figure was actually a decrease of 23 percent from the year before.

Sophos, a maker of computer security products, noted some interesting facts about viruses in 2001:

- Although Code Red received an incredible amount of publicity in July, by the end of the year it didn't even place in the top 10 list of viruses seen "in the wild."

- Although experts predicted that PDA (Personal Digital Assistant) and mobile phone viruses would have an impact, none were observed.

- Two viruses (FunnyFile and Choke) attacked instant messaging programs.

- For the first time, truly effective cross-platform worms (Sadmind) and viruses (Lindose) were found.

- Prosecution of virus creators saw mixed results. Although the author of the Anna Kournikova worm was sentenced to only 150 hours of community service (only 50 U.S. companies would admit to infection by the worm), the creator of the Melissa virus struck a deal with prosecutors to lower his sentence from 5 years to 20 months in a federal prison. What is significant is that both the prosecution and the defense in the case admitted that the virus caused damage exceeding $80 million.

- In the context of security, viruses are also starting to be used as a mechanism to infiltrate firewalls. Crackers encode virus engines into attachments and then send them as e-mail to users behind a corporate firewall. The virus then deploys and distributes a Trojan horse around the corporate LAN. The Trojan payload itself does nothing destructive but simply establishes a link from the internal PCs back out to the cracker. Because this link is outbound, it is not blocked by the firewall, and the cracker now has a route into the corporate LAN.

What Is a Virus?

The precise definition of a virus has been hotly debated for many years. Experts have had difficulty describing the specific traits that characterize a true virus and separate it from other types of programs. To add to the confusion, people tend to lump viruses, worms, Trojan horses, and so on under the generic umbrella of "virus." This tendency is partly because no one industry-acceptable descriptor includes all these program types. Confusion continues over exactly what constitutes a virus.

The generally accepted definition of a virus is a program that can be broken into three functional parts:

- Replication
- Concealment
- Bomb

The combination of these three attributes makes the collective program a virus.

Replication

A virus must include some method of *replication*, that is, some way to reproduce or duplicate itself. When a virus reproduces itself in a file, the result is sometimes referred to as an *infection*. Since most people would never knowingly load a virus on their system, replication ensures that the virus has some method of spreading.

Replication occurs when the virus is loaded into memory and has access to CPU cycles. A virus cannot spread by simply existing on a hard disk. An infected file must be executed in order for a virus to become active. *Executed* is a generic term. For example, an infected executable file might be initiated from a command prompt, or an infected Microsoft Word document might be loaded into a text editor that can process embedded macros. In either event, some process is now using CPU cycles that help to spread the virus code.

FILE INFECTION

The method of replication can be the result of file infection or boot sector replication. *File infection* relies on the virus's ability to attach itself to a file. In theory, any type of file is vulnerable to attack. Attackers tend to focus, however, on files that provide some form of access to CPU cycles. This access can be through direct execution or through some secondary application processing the code.

For example, a Word document does not directly execute any type of command in memory. Word, however, can read macro commands embedded in a Word document and execute them in memory. So although it is the Word *document* that is actually infected, it is the Word *application* that provides the transport for replication. You can activate a macro-based virus simply by viewing a Word document or by viewing a document in any other application that relies on macros.

A similar type of virus that was popular many years ago leveraged vulnerabilities in DOS's ANSI.SYS driver. Any text document can contain embedded ANSI (American National Standards Institute) commands. If a user has the ANSI driver loaded, these commands can be parsed from a text file and executed, even if the user is simply viewing the text within the file. Some viruses have even embedded themselves in raw source-code files. When the code is eventually compiled, the virus becomes capable of accessing CPU cycles, thus replicating even further.

The most popular type of infection, however, affects direct executable files. In the PC world, these are files with a .COM, .EXE, .PIF, or .BAT file extension. A virus adds a small piece of code to the beginning of the file so that when the file is executed, the virus is loaded into memory before the actual application. The virus then places its remaining code within or at the end of the file.

Once a file becomes infected, the method of replication can take one of two forms: resident or nonresident. A *resident* replicating virus, once loaded into memory, waits for other programs to be executed and then infects them. Viruses such as Cabanas have shown that this is even possible on protected-memory systems such as Windows NT. A *nonresident* replicating virus selects one or more executable files on disk and directly infects them without waiting for them to be processed in memory. This infection occurs every time the infected executable is launched.

Sometimes a virus can take advantage of the extension search order of the operating system in order to facilitate the loading of the virus code without actually infecting the existing file. This type of virus is known as a *companion virus*. A companion virus works by ensuring that its executable file is launched before the legitimate file is launched.

Windows first tries to execute a file with a .COM extension, then a .EXE extension, and finally a .BAT extension (assuming they are in the same location in the file system; otherwise the files are executed in the order the system finds them as dictated by the path). Once a match is found, the operating system ends the search and executes the program. In our example, the operating system would find and execute the virus file (.COM extension) before the real program file (.EXE extension).

BOOT SECTOR REPLICATION

Boot sector replication viruses infect the system area of the disk that is read when the disk is initially accessed or booted. This area can include the master boot record, the operating system's boot sector, or both.

A virus infecting these areas typically takes the system instructions it finds and moves them to some other area on the disk. The virus is then free to place its own code in the boot record. When the system initializes, the virus loads into memory and simply points to the new location for the system instructions. The system then boots in a normal fashion—except the virus is now resident in memory.

NOTE   A boot sector virus can replicate without your executing any programs from an infected disk. Simply accessing the disk is sufficient. For example, most PCs do a systems check on boot-up that verifies the operation of the floppy drive. Even this verification process is sufficient to activate a boot sector virus if one exists on a floppy left in the machine, and the hard drive can also become infected.

Boot sector viruses rely on disk-to-disk contact to facilitate replication. Both disks must be attached to the same machine. For example, if you access a shared directory on a system with a boot sector virus, the virus cannot replicate itself to your local machine because the two machines do not share memory or processor cycles.

Programs known as *droppers,* however, can augment the distribution of boot sector viruses, even across a network. A dropper is effectively an installation utility for the virus. The dropper is typically coded to hide the virus contained within it and escape detection by antivirus software. It also poses as some form of useful utility in order to entice a user to execute the program. When the dropper program is executed, it installs the virus on the local system.

NOTE   By using a dropper, an attacker could theoretically infect a system with a boot sector virus even across a network. Once the virus is dropped, however, disk-to-disk access is required for further replication.

COMMON TRAITS OF FILE INFECTION AND BOOT SECTOR REPLICATION

What is common to file and to boot sector replication is that a virus must have some method of detecting itself to avoid potential corruption by performing a double infection. If a corruption does occur, the program can become unusable, or the user may suspect that something is wrong. In either event, the replication process may cease. If replication cannot continue, the virus is doomed to die out, just like any living organism.

AN INTERESTING CATCH-22

One of the methods used by virus programmers to ensure that duplication does not occur can also be used to detect the virus and prevent it from infecting files. Many virus programmers identify a code string that they know is unique to their particular virus. The virus is then programmed to look for this code string before it infects a file. If a match is found, the file is not infected.

Antivirus software can be programmed to look for this signature code string. This code string allows the software to quickly identify the existence of the virus. Also, by adding this code string to a file without the actual virus code, the file can be inoculated against infection by the actual virus.

Concealment

To facilitate replication, a virus must have one or more methods of masking its existence. If a running virus were to simply show up on your Windows Taskbar, you'd see a problem right away. Viruses employ a number of methods to camouflage their presence.

SMALL FOOTPRINT

Viruses tend to be small. Even a large virus can be less than 2KB in size. This small footprint makes it far easier for the virus to conceal itself on the local storage media and while it is running in memory. To ensure that a virus is as small as possible, most viruses are coded in assembly language.

If a virus is small enough, it can even attach itself to a file without noticeably affecting the overall file size. Viruses known as *cavity viruses* look for repetitive character sequences within a file (usually a null value) and overwrite this area for virus storage. In this way, the virus can store the bulk of its code in a file without affecting the reported file size.

ATTRIBUTE MANIPULATION

To protect files from virus infection, early DOS computer users set their executable file permissions to read-only. The thinking was that if the file could not be modified, a virus would be unable to infect it. Of course, virus programmers responded by adding code to the virus that allowed it to check the file's attributes before infection. If the attributes were set to read-only, the virus removed the read-only attribute, infected the file, and then reset the attributes to their original values. Needless to say, this method of protection is of little value against today's viruses.

This is not the case in a true multiuser environment, however, in which the permissions level can be set on a user-by-user basis. If administrator-level privileges are required to change a file's permissions, the virus cannot change these attributes when run from a regular user account.

Typically, regular users on Windows 2000 (or any other network operating system, for that matter) are given read-write access to a public directory. If a user's computer contracts a virus, the virus can spread to other machines by infecting files within the public directory, because the virus is able to modify these files. Also, if the administrator's computer becomes infected, all bets are off—this account does have write access to the public directory. Setting the minimum level of required permissions not only helps to enhance security, it can help prevent the spread of viruses, as well.

Along with permission attributes, viruses can also modify the date and time stamps associated with a file. This modification ensures that a user is not clued in to a problem by noticing that a file has been changed. Early virus scanners looked for date changes as part of their virus-detection routine. Since most of today's viruses restore the original date and time stamps after infection, this method of detection has become less than effective.

NOTE *Windows NT–based systems (Windows 2000, XP, and .NET) running NTFS (New Technology File System) are particularly vulnerable because they use data streams. A data stream is a hidden file that can be associated with a regular file. A data stream provides a hidden area in which an attacker can hide virus code. Data streams are not visible when you use Explorer or the* DIR *command. You must reference the stream directly (meaning you already know it exists) or use a tool specifically designed to find data streams, such as March Information System's StreamFind utility. You can find out more about StreamFind at* **www.march.co.uk***.*

STEALTH

Stealth allows a virus to hide the modifications made to a file or boot sector. When the virus is loaded into memory, it monitors system calls to files and disk sectors. When a call is trapped, the virus modifies the information returned to the process making the call so that it sees the original, uninfected information. This aids the virus in avoiding detection.

For example, many boot sector viruses contain stealth ability. If the infected disk is booted (thus loading the virus into memory), programs such as FDISK report a normal boot record. The virus is intercepting sector calls from FDISK and returning the original boot sector information. If you boot the system from a clean floppy disk, however, the drive is inaccessible. If you run FDISK again, the program reports a corrupted boot sector on the drive.

Concealment can also be accomplished by modifying the information reported by utilities such as DIR and MEM. Thus, a virus can hide its existence on the local storage medium and in physical memory. To use stealth, however, the virus must be actively running in memory, which means that the stealth portion of the virus is vulnerable to detection by antivirus software.

ANTIVIRUS COUNTERMEASURES

Some viruses include countermeasures to fight against detection. These viruses monitor the system for indications of an active virus scan and then take preventive measures to ensure that they go undetected. Think of countermeasures as stealth ability with an attitude.

For example, some viruses monitor system activity once they become active in memory. If the virus detects that a virus scan has been initiated, it attempt to fool the scanner into thinking that some other virus is present on the system. Typically, the reported virus requires some form of destructive cleaning that trashes the system if the virus is not actually present. The virus then attempts to seed itself within the file system so that if a recovery is attempted, the virus can infect the new configuration.

Like stealth, antivirus countermeasures rely on the virus's being active in memory so that the virus can monitor activity. Thus, it is important to boot a system from a boot disk you know to be clean before you attempt any repair. On DOS systems, it is also important to actually power cycle the system: many viruses can trap the Ctrl+Alt+Del key sequence and create a false warm boot. The virus can then remain active in memory, even though the system appears to have been restarted.

ENCRYPTION

Virus programmers have not overlooked the benefits of encryption. Encryption allows the virus programmer to hide telltale system calls and text strings within the program. By encrypting the virus code, virus programmers make the job of detecting the virus much more difficult.

Detection is not impossible, however, because many viruses use a simple form of encryption and the same key for all virus code. Although it might be difficult to retrieve the actual virus code, the decryption sequence is identical for all infected files. If you can break the decryption key, you can use it to detect all future instances of the virus. Even if the decryption key is not broken, the cipher string becomes a telltale signature that antivirus software can use to detect the virus.

The efficiency of this method of detecting encrypted viruses depends on the resulting cipher string. Remember that the antivirus software has no way of knowing whether it is looking at encrypted or plain text information. If the cipher string can be made to resemble some benign form of code, the antivirus software will have a difficult time differentiating between infected and noninfected files.

POLYMORPHIC MUTATION

A polymorphic virus can change its virus signature from infected file to infected file while still remaining operational. Many virus scanners detect a virus by searching for telltale signature code. Since a polymorphic virus can change its appearance between infections, it is far more difficult to detect.

One way to produce a polymorphic virus is to include a variety of encryption schemes that use different decryption routines. Only one of these routines is available in any instance of the virus. Thus, an antivirus scanner is unable to detect all occurrences of the virus unless all the decryption routines are known.

Knowing the decryption routines may be nearly impossible if the virus utilizes a random key or sequence when performing encryption. For example, many viruses include benign or dormant code that can be moved around within the virus before encryption without affecting the virus's operational ability. The cipher string created by the process varies with each instance of the virus, because the code sequence varies.

The most efficient way to create a polymorphic virus is to include hooks into an object module known as a *mutation engine*. Because this engine is modular, it can easily be added to any existing virus code. The mutation engine includes a random-number generator that helps to scramble the resulting ciphertext even further. Since a random-number generator is used, the resulting ciphertext becomes unpredictable and varies with every file infected. This can make the virus nearly impossible to detect, even for other instances of the virus itself.

Bomb

Our virus has successfully replicated itself and avoided detection. The question now becomes, What will the virus do next? Most viruses are programmed to wait for a specific event. This event can be almost anything—including the arrival of a specific date, the infection of a specific number of files, or even the detection of a predetermined activity.

Once this event occurs, the true purpose of the virus becomes evident. This purpose might be as benign as playing a tune through the computer's speakers or as destructive as completely wiping out all the information on the computer's hard drive.

Most bombs can perform a malicious task because the current Windows environments provide no clear containment between the operating system and the programs they run. A virus can have direct access to lower-level functions. This functionality is provided because the operating system expects programs to be trustworthy.

For example, Windows applications can directly address memory and the interrupt table. Although this functionality can help boost an application's performance by allowing it to circumvent the operating system, it also provides much of the functionality required for a virus to utilize stealth.

Although most bombs can't cause physical damage, they can still leave the computer unusable. Most of today's motherboards have a BIOS (Basic Input Output System) that holds the initial code used to boot the system. Because the operating system can update those BIOS commands, it's possible for a virus to completely erase the contents, leaving the motherboard dead and unrecoverable.

Social-Engineering Viruses

Although not a true virus in the strict sense of the term, a social-engineering virus can be just as troublesome as the real thing. Social-engineering viruses meet all the criteria of a normal virus, except they rely on people to spread the infection, not a computer. A good example of a social engineering virus is the Good Times virus hoax that has circulated on the Internet for many years. This e-mail message announces that a dangerous virus is being circulated via e-mail and has the ability to wipe out all the files on your computer. This message even claims that the virus's existence has been confirmed by AOL (who we all know is the world's authority on viruses). People concerned that their friends may be attacked by this virus then forward the hoax to every person in their address books.

How does a social-engineering virus meet the criteria that define a true virus?

REPLICATION

These viruses rely on two human traits in order to replicate themselves to other systems: good intentions and gullibility. Since it is human nature to help others, we are more than happy to circulate what appear to be virus warnings, e-mail requests from dying children, and the like to other computer users. Since it is also human nature to believe what we read—and perhaps to be a bit too lazy to verify information—we might forward the virus along without verification.

CONCEALMENT

To conceal the threat, the virus uses language that makes the message believable to the average user. For example, the message might claim that a company such as AOL, IBM, or Microsoft has verified the existence of the virus mentioned in the alert. Since these are computer-related companies familiar to the average user, the message appears authoritative.

BOMB

This is the part of social-engineering viruses that most people do not even think about. The "bomb" is wasted bandwidth, as well as unnecessary fear. Since the message is a hoax, bandwidth is wasted every time it is circulated. Since the sender assumes a sense of urgency with the message, the virus is typically sent out en masse. Unnecessary fear comes into play because the message usually includes a warning of disaster if it is ignored. (For example, the user's computer becomes infected by the hoax virus or the child with cancer dies because she did not receive enough e-mail to pay for her treatment.) This fear manifests itself as additional stress and worry. Thus the bomb is how these e-mails affect both computer resources and their human operators.

No virus scanner can detect social-engineering viruses. Only education and verifying information can keep these viruses from spreading.

NOTE *A wonderful resource for social engineering viruses is the Vmyths.com page at* `www.vmyths.com`.

Worms

Traditionally, a computer worm was considered an application that could replicate itself via a permanent or a dial-up network connection. Unlike a virus, which seeds itself within the computer's hard disk or file system, a worm is a self-supporting program. A typical worm maintains only a functional copy of itself in active memory; it does not even write itself to disk.

However, in the last few years, the boundary between worms and viruses has become increasingly blurry, starting with Melissa. Melissa was a worm/virus hybrid that could infect a system (like a virus) by modifying documents to include quotes from *The Simpsons* television show. But it could also use the Address Book in Microsoft Outlook and Outlook Express to resend itself (like a worm) to other clients, who were then subsequently infected by an attached document (which might be a confidential document!). In 2000, ILOVEYOU, another worm/virus hybrid, actually caused destruction by removing JPEG and MP3 files. (Some argue that ILOVEYOU was also a form of Trojan horse by presenting itself as a legitimate e-mail message.) Also, whereas Melissa limited itself to the first 50 addresses in a user's Address Book, ILOVEYOU used all addresses.

Code Red, the worm that received a significant amount of attention (along with a similarly acting but separately authored successor known as Code Red II), was also a "blended" threat that used DoS (Denial of Service) attacks, web page defacement, and a Trojan horse that executed after the main attack.

Nimda, however, was not only the most frequent example of hostile code to be seen in 2001, but was innovative in the way that it modified existing websites to offer infected code to web clients. Once infected, these clients searched for more vulnerable websites, and the cycle of infection continued.

At the end of 2001, a worm named Klez started making the rounds (and is still quite active as of this writing in the summer of 2002). Capable of disabling antivirus programs (along with other, legitimate programs), Klez can even present itself to a user as a patch to protect against itself!

NOTE *The name worm is derived from a 1975 story by John Brunner called "The Shockwave Rider." The story's hero uses a program called a "tapeworm" to destroy the totalitarian government's computer network. This destruction removes the government's power base, thus freeing the people under its control. Before the publication of this story, there was no universally agreed upon name to describe these programs (life imitating art, so to speak).*

THE VAMPIRE WORM

Worms have not always been considered a bad thing. In the 1980s, John Shock and Jon Hepps of Xerox were doing some wonderful worm research in order to show just how beneficial these programs could be. To this end, they created a number of worm programs and used them for administration on Xerox's network.

The most effective was the *vampire worm*. This worm sat idle during the day when system utilization was high. At night, however, the worm would wake up and use idle CPU time to complete complex and highly processor intensive tasks. The next morning, the vampire worm saved its work and went back to sleep.

The vampire worm was extremely effective until the day that Xerox employees came into work and found that all the computer systems had crashed from a malfunctioning process. When the systems were restarted, they were immediately crashed by the worm. This led to the worm's removal from all the network's systems and an end to further testing.

THE GREAT INTERNET WORM

Worms received little attention until November 3, 1988. This was the day after the great Internet worm had been released onto the Internet. In less than six hours, this 99-line program had effectively crippled all 6000 Sun and VAX systems connected to the Internet.

The program was written by Robert Morris, the son of one of the country's highest-ranking security experts at that time. It has been suggested that the writing of the worm was not a malicious act, but the effort of a son to break out from his father's shadow. This thinking is supported by the actual worm code, because the program does not perform any intentionally destructive functions.

What the worm did do was to start a small process running in the background of every machine it encountered. This experiment would have probably gone completely unnoticed—except for one minor programming flaw. Before infecting a host, the worm did not check to see if the system was already infected. This omission led to the multiple infection of systems. Although one instance of the worm created little processor load, dozens—or possibly hundreds—of instances would bring the system to its knees.

Administrators found themselves in a losing battle. As a system was cleaned and restarted, it again become quickly infected. When it was discovered that the worm was using Sendmail vulnerabilities to move from system to system, many administrators reacted by disconnecting from the Internet or by shutting down their e-mail systems. This reaction probably did more harm than good, because it effectively isolated the site from updated information on the worm including information on how to prevent infection.

From all the chaos that ensued from this incident, many good things did arise. It took an episode of this magnitude to change people's thinking regarding system vulnerabilities. At the time, such vulnerabilities were simply considered minor bugs. The Internet worm incident pushed these deficiencies into a class of their own. This incident spawned the creation of the Computer Emergency Response Team (CERT), an organization that is responsible for documenting, and helping to resolve, computer-related security problems.

THE WANK WORM

Although the Internet worm is probably the best known, it was certainly not the worst worm ever encountered. In October 1989, the WANK (Worms Against Nuclear Killers) worm was released on unsuspecting systems. Although highly destructive, this worm was unique in that it infected only DEC systems and used only the DECnet protocol. (It was not spread via IP.) This worm did the following:

- Sent e-mail (presumably to the worm's creator) identifying which systems it penetrated along with the logon names and passwords used

- Changed passwords on existing accounts

- Left additional trapdoor access into the system

- Found users on random nodes and rang them using the phone utility

- Infected local COM files so that the worm could reactivate later if it was cleaned from the system

- Changed the announcement banner to indicate that the system had been "WANKed"

- Modified the logon script to make it appear that all of a user's files were being deleted

- Hid the user's files after logon so that the user would be convinced that the files had been deleted

As you can imagine, this worm ruined more than one system administrator's day. It took quite some time to successfully purge this worm from all the infected systems.

Trojan Horses

A Trojan horse, as the name implies, is an application that hides a nasty surprise. This is a process or a function, specifically added by the Trojan horse's programmer, that performs an activity that the user is unaware of—and would probably not approve of. The visible application may or may not do anything that is actually useful. The hidden application is what makes the program a Trojan horse.

Because ILOVEYOU presented itself as a valid e-mail message (the virus code was actually stored in an attachment to the e-mail message), some consider it an example of a Trojan horse, even though an e-mail message isn't an application per se. Other hostile code examples blur the line, including an attack in which the MIME type of an attachment declared the virus to be a multimedia program, when in fact it was executable code (and kept the `.EXE` extension). Because Windows activates multimedia files by default, the executable slipped past the normal e-mail attachment security checks, and because the file ended in `.exe`, Windows executed it like any other program, leading to the infection of the system.

How Trojan Horses Are Different from Viruses

A pure Trojan horse (or "Trojan" for short) differs from a virus in that it does not replicate or attach itself to other files. A Trojan is a stand-alone application that had its bomb included from the original source code. It did not become malicious because of the effects of another application.

For example, a number of Unix Trojans are made to replace existing network applications. An attacker can replace the Telnet server process (`telnetd`) with one of their own creation. Although the program functions identically to the standard `telnetd` program, it quietly records all logon names and passwords that authenticate to the system. Conversely, the attacker can also replace the Telnet client application, giving them valid account information on remote systems. Thus, the attacker can systematically penetrate every server on a network.

Attackers have also created Trojans designed to be immediately destructive. For example, in April 1997, many people fell prey to the `AOL4FREE.COM` Trojan. Although users thought they had found a utility that would give them a free account on AOL, what they actually received was a wonderful tool for removing all those pesky files on a system's local hard drive. As soon as the program was launched, it permanently deleted all files on the rive C.

Did I Just Purchase a Trojan Horse?

Of course, not all Trojans were written by true attackers. For example, some users were extremely surprised to find out that when they joined the Microsoft Network, the software made a complete inventory of system hardware and software, including Microsoft software and competitors' products. When the user connected to the network, this information was automatically forwarded to Microsoft, which could collect marketing data and check for proper product licensing. Although Microsoft claimed that this information was being collected for technical support use only, many people considered it a clear invasion of privacy.

In many other situations, vendors add functionality at the expense of breaching a customer's security posture. For example, in May 1998 it was made public knowledge that 3COM, as well as a number of other network hardware vendors, were including "backdoor" accounts for access into their switch and router products. These undocumented accounts are typically invisible to the end user and cannot be deleted or disabled. Although vendors again claimed they had created these back doors for technical support reasons (in case an administrator forgets a password, for example), these back doors still leave the product horribly exposed and the administrator uninformed.

Such activities exist in a gray area between technical support and Trojans. Although these undocumented back doors are being added by reputable vendors, they compromise security and fail to make the customer aware of potential exposure. Clearly, backdoor access is a feature that many administrators would like to disable, but they have to learn of its existence first.

Preventive Measures

Now that you have seen the implications of these rogue programs, what can you do about them? The only foolproof way to identify a malicious program is to have a knowledgeable programmer review the source code. Since most applications are already in an executable format, this would require a step back to reverse engineer every file on the system. Obviously, doing so is too time-consuming and expensive to be a feasible option for the typical organization.

With this in mind, any other preventive measures will fall short of being 100 percent effective. You are faced with performing a risk analysis to determine just how much protection you actually require. You can employ many techniques to prevent infection. Each has its strengths and weaknesses, so a combination of three or more techniques is usually best.

Access Control

Establishing an access control policy is not only a good security measure; it can help to prevent the spread of rogue programs, as well. Access control should not be confused with file attributes (such as read-only or system), which an infecting program can easily change. True access needs to be managed through a multiuser operating system that allows the system administrator to set up file permission levels on a user-by-user basis.

Access control will not remove or even detect the existence of a rogue program. It is simply one method of helping your systems resist infection. For example, most viruses count on the infected machine having full access to all files (such as the default permissions under Windows NT). If a savvy system administrator modifies these default permissions so that users have only read access to their required executables, a virus is unable to infect these files.

NOTE   Access control does not work for all executables, however. Some actually require that they modify themselves during execution. Users need write access to these executables, and you can expect the time and date stamps to change regularly. How do you know which executables require write access? Usually you don't. It's a matter of trial and error to see which executables change their date and time stamps or break when write access is not provided. These self-writing executables are rare, however. You should not run into them often.

Checksum Verification

A *checksum*, or cyclic redundancy check (CRC), is a mathematical verification of the data within a file. A checksum allows the contents of the file to be expressed as a numeric quantity. If a single byte of data within the file changes, the checksum value changes, even if the file size remains constant. Typically, you first create a baseline of a noninfected system. The CRC is then performed at regular intervals to look for file changes.

A couple of drawbacks are associated with this method. First, a CRC cannot actually detect file infection; it can only look for changes. Thus, self-writing executables regularly fail the checksum verification. Also, even if the change is actually due to the result of a virus, a CRC has no way of cleaning the file. Finally, many viruses are specifically written to fool a CRC into thinking that the file information has not changed.

TIP *Although a CRC is a not the most effective check against viruses, it can be a big help in discovering Trojan horse replacements. A Trojan designed to replace an existing authentication service (such as Telnet or FTP client and server software) does not simply modify the existing files; it replaces them. This file replacement is flagged and reported by a checksum verification. A virus scanner, however, completely misses this problem, provided that the files don't include any viruslike code. Thus, the CRC is far more effective at identifying Trojans.*

Process Monitoring

Another method for preventing rogue programs from taking hold of a system is *process monitoring*. Process monitoring observes system activity and intercepts anything that looks suspicious. For example, the BIOS in most of today's desktop computers contains an antivirus setting. When enabled, this setting allows the computer to intercept all write attempts to the master boot record. If a boot sector virus attempts to save itself to this area, the BIOS interrupts the request and prompts the user for approval.

Again, there are a few problems. The first is that viruses and normal programs share a lot of similar attributes: it can be extremely difficult to distinguish between the two. For example, running the FDISK utility also triggers the BIOS virus warning just described. Even though FDISK is not a virus (unless you subscribe to the school of thought that all Microsoft programs are viruses), it still triggers the warning because its activity is considered suspicious. The result is referred to as a *false positive*—the BIOS thinks it has detected a virus when in fact it has not.

A second problem with process monitoring is the requirement of user intervention and proficiency. For example, a user who receives the false positive must be computer savvy enough to realize that a true virus was not actually detected, but that the normal operation of FDISK set off the alarm.

Then again, maybe there *is* in fact a boot sector virus on the floppy disk where FDISK is stored. If so, the user might assume that a false positive was reported when in fact there is an actual virus. Although this would trigger the BIOS virus alert at a different point in the process (when FDISK is loaded rather than when FDISK is closed), the end user needs a high level of skill and computer proficiency to identify virus problems accurately.

The problem of correctly distinguishing between a virus and a normal application becomes even more apparent when you start trying to monitor other types of activity. Should you consider file deletions suspicious? Certainly you will use a file maintenance utility to delete files from time to time, generating frequent false positives. The same is true for attempting to monitor file changes, memory swapping, and so on. A virus can perform all these activities, but a normal application can also perform them.

About the only useful process monitoring is the BIOS virus warning described earlier. Although the potential for false positive warnings exists, it is actually rather rare for a user to be running

FDISK or some other application that legitimately attempts to write to the boot sector. Typically, this occurs only if the user is installing a new operating system. Thus, the frequency of false positives is minimal.

Virus Scanners

The most popular way to detect viruses is through the use of virus-scanning software. Virus scanners use *signature files* to locate viruses in infected files. A signature file is simply a database that lists all known viruses, along with their specific attributes. These attributes include samples of each virus's code, the types of files it infects, and any other information that might be helpful in locating the virus. By using a separate file to store this information, you can update your software to detect the latest viruses by replacing this single file. You do not have to update the entire program. This practice is useful because many new viruses are detected each month.

When a scanner checks a file, it looks to see if any of the code in the file matches any of the entries in the signature file. When a match is found, the virus scanner notifies the user that a virus has been detected. Most scanners can then run a separate process that can clean the virus, as well.

The biggest limitation of virus scanners is that they can detect only known viruses. If your system happens to become infected by a newly created virus, a scanner may well miss it. This problem is particularly nasty when you are dealing with a polymorphic virus. As mentioned earlier in this chapter, polymorphic viruses can change their signature with each infection. In order for a virus scanner to be 100 percent effective against this type of virus, it must have a signature file that lists all possible polymorphic permutations. If even one permutation is missed, the virus scanner may fail to clean an infected file—and the virus can again infect the system.

TIP   *When selecting a virus scanner, look for one that not only has the capability of detecting many different viruses, but many different polymorphic strains, as well.*

Compressed or encrypted files can also cause problems for a virus scanner. Since both of these processes rearrange the way information is stored, a virus scanner might be unable to detect a virus hidden within the file.

For example, let's say you use PKZIP to compress a number of files in order to transport them on a floppy disk. You then use a virus scanner to check the disk in order to verify that none of the compressed files contains a virus. Unless the virus scanner you are using understands the ZIP file format (many do not), it can't detect a virus hidden within one of the files.

This problem is even more acute with encrypted files. Since a virus scanner has no way to decrypt a manually encrypted file, it will most likely miss any viruses that are present. You must first decrypt the file and then perform a virus scan to ensure that no viruses are present.

VIRUS SCANNER VARIATIONS

There are two basic types of virus scanners:

- ◆ On-demand
- ◆ Memory-resident

You must initialize *on-demand scanners* manually or through some automatic process. When you start an on-demand scanner, it typically searches an entire drive or system for viruses. This search includes RAM memory and storage devices such as a hard drive or a floppy disk.

Memory-resident virus scanners are programs that run in the background of a system. They are typically initialized at system startup and stay active at all times. Whenever a file is accessed, a memory-resident scanner intercepts the file call and verifies that no viruses are present before allowing the file to be loaded into memory.

Each of these methods has its trade-offs. On-demand scanners work after the fact. Unless you always initialize the scanner before accessing any file (an unlikely occurrence unless you are very meticulous or very bored), your system will contract a virus before it is detected. Although a memory-resident virus scanner is can identify a virus before it infects your system, it does so with a cost in performance. Every file scan degrades the system's file access speed, thus slowing the responsiveness of the system.

The manufacturers of memory-resident virus scanners are well aware that file access speed is important and recognize that many users would opt to disable the scanner rather than take a large performance hit. For this reason, many memory-resident scanners are not quite as thorough as their on-demand counterparts. Better performance can be achieved by only checking for the most likely virus signatures or by only scanning files that are the most likely to become infected (such as COM files).

TIP   A good security posture includes using both on-demand and memory-resident virus scanners.

PROBLEMS WITH LARGE ENVIRONMENTS

All virus-scanner vendors periodically release updated signature files to ensure that their products can detect as many known viruses as possible. Updating signature files can create a great deal of extra work for system administrators who are responsible for large networking environments. If you are running DOS, Windows, or Macintosh operating systems on the desktop, you will most likely have signature files on each of these systems that will need updating.

Many vendors have taken steps to rectify this problem. For example, Intel's LANDesk Virus Protect uses the concept of *virus domains* to group multiple servers and desktop machines. The network administrator can then update signature files, view alerts, and even control scanning parameters from a single console screen. This can dramatically reduce the amount of work required to administer virus protection in a large-scale environment.

A scalable virus-protection solution not only reduces overall costs, it helps to ensure that your environment remains well protected. As mentioned, virus-scanner vendors periodically release updated signature files. These signature files are of little use, however, if you don't install them on every system that requires them. A scalable solution provides a simple method for distributing these signature files to all systems that require them. A solid enterprise solution also includes some form of advanced alerting function so that the network administrator can be notified of all viruses detected on any system on the network.

Heuristic Scanners

Heuristic scanners perform a statistical analysis to determine the likelihood that a file contains program code that may indicate a virus. A heuristic scanner does not compare code with a signature file as a virus scanner does; it uses a grading system to determine the probability that the program code being analyzed is a virus. If the program code scores enough points, the heuristic scanner notifies the user that a virus has been detected. Most of today's virus scanners include heuristic scanning ability.

One of the biggest benefits of heuristic scanners is that they do not require updating. Since files are graded on a point system, no signature files are required for comparison. Thus, a heuristic scanner has a good probability of detecting a virus that no one else has ever seen. This can be extremely useful if you find that you are unable to update signature files regularly.

The biggest drawback to heuristic scanners is their tendency to report false positives. As mentioned, virus code is not all that different from regular program code. Distinguishing between the two can be extremely difficult. As system administrator, you may find yourself chasing your tail if you deploy a poor heuristic scanner that has a tendency toward reporting nonexistent viruses.

Application-Level Virus Scanners

Application-level virus scanners are a popular breed in virus protection. Instead of being responsible for securing a specific system from viruses, an application-level virus scanner is responsible for securing a specific service throughout an organization.

For example, e-mail makes a wonderful transport for propagating viruses through file attachments. Trend Micro manufactures a product called InterScan VirusWall, which can act as an SMTP (Simple Mail Transfer Protocol) relay with a twist. Instead of simply receiving inbound mail and forwarding it to the appropriate e-mail system, InterScan VirusWall can perform a full virus scan of all attachments before relaying them to an internal mail host.

Along with scanning SMTP traffic, InterScan VirusWall can scan FTP (File Transfer Protocol) and HTTP (Hypertext Transfer Protocol) traffic as well as raw files and many archive formats such as PKZIP. This helps to ensure that all files received from the Internet are free of viruses.

TIP Many vendors now make products that directly integrate with existing firewall products. For example, Cheyenne Software makes a virus-scanning plug-in for Check Point's FireWall-1 product. Using this product, you can manage virus scanning on the same system that is responsible for network security. Thus, the network administrator has a single point of management for both security and virus protection.

Deploying Virus Protection

Now that you have a good idea of how viruses work and what tools are available to prevent infection, let's take a look at some deployment methods to safeguard your network.

NOTE These suggestions should only be considered a guide; feel free to make modifications that better fit your specific needs.

The network diagram in Figure 10.1 shows a mixed environment that uses a number of different server operating systems. The desktop environment utilizes a mixture of operating systems, as well. Let's assume that you are consulting for the organization that owns this environment and you have been charged with protecting it from viruses, as well as Trojans and worms. You have also been asked to perform this task with a minimal impact on network performance. Take a moment to study the diagram and consider what recommendations you would make.

FIGURE 10.1

Sample network requiring virus protection

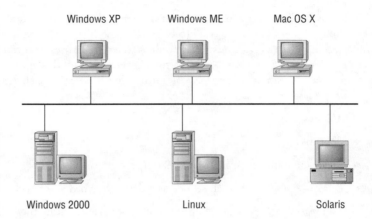

Protecting the Desktop Systems

Although the desktop environment uses a mixture of operating systems, the hardware platform is consistent (PC compatible). Thus, all desktop systems are susceptible to many of the same types of viruses. Try to standardize your desktop suggestions as much as possible, even though multiple operating systems are in use.

ENABLE BIOS BOOT SECTOR PROTECTION

One of the most cost-effective suggestions you can make is to enable boot sector protection through the systems' BIOS. This is a quick yet effective way to ensure that the boot sectors of all systems remain secure. You want to follow this up with some end-user education about what the boot sector warning means and how users should respond to it. Unless a user tries to upgrade their operating system, false-positive warnings should not be a problem.

ON-DEMAND SCANNING

Each desktop system should utilize an on-demand scanner configured to perform a full virus check of all local drives regularly. You can schedule this check to run nightly if desktop systems are typically left powered up at night. If nightly virus scans are not an option, you can run scans during some other period of inactivity (such as lunch time) or weekly as part of a server logon script.

The on-demand scanner must check all local files to ensure that a virus has not been planted through a dropper or sneaked in through some file with an obscure file extension. A proper on-demand scanner should also include heuristic scanning capability. You also need some way to report all scanning results to a central location so that a system administrator can review the data.

MEMORY-RESIDENT SCANNING

Each desktop should also launch a memory-resident scanner during system initialization to weed out viruses before they can be stored on the local file system or executed in memory. In the interest of performance, you might want to tweak which files are checked by the memory-resident scanner.

Since you will be performing a regular on-demand scan of each desktop system, you have a bit of leeway in how meticulous you need to be in verifying files with your memory-resident scanner. By only checking files that are most commonly infected by viruses, you can reduce the impact of the memory-resident scanner on system performance. Although this approach diminishes your security posture a bit, the gain in system performance might be worth the slightly higher risk.

Your memory-resident scanner should check the following:

◆ File reads only

◆ Worms

◆ Executable files such as COM and EXE files

◆ Macro-enabled documents, such as Microsoft Word and Excel

You want to check file reads, but not writes, because checking files that are written to disk is redundant. If a scanner failed to find a virus when the file was read into memory, it is extremely unlikely that the same scanner will detect the virus when it is written to disk. You also want to check for worms because many do not save any information to disk; thus, they may go undetected by an on-demand scanner. Finally, you want to configure your memory-resident scanner to check the files most likely to become infected. This includes executable files, as well as files that can save macro commands.

OPTIONS NOT CONSIDERED

We didn't mention setting file attributes or checksum verification because as you saw earlier, these methods are ineffectual against many strains of viruses. We didn't mention other types of process monitoring (besides the BIOS boot sector warning) for the same reason. The suggestions are designed to provide the greatest level of protection with the least amount of labor.

One additional option, however, is to use the file permissions on the client workstations in order to prevent the users from having Write access to any executable files. Although doing so decreases the chances of virus infection on these systems, it also breaks from the standard configuration used on the other desktop machines. It also means that individual users won't be able to update their own systems. That might be acceptable in your network. It depends on the particular systems, your support infrastructure, and, ultimately, your organizational security policy.

Also, this option does not address the macro viruses that are the most common forms of virus found in the wild. These viruses hide within document files. Users must have write access to their document storage folders to save their files. This option may cause more problems than it solves.

Protecting the Server Operating Systems

Since NT-based, Unix-based, and OS X servers provide shared resources, they require a slightly different method of protection than the desktop machines. Virus protection on these systems is far more critical, because they can be used as a transport for propagating viruses among the desktop machines.

ON-DEMAND SCANNING

As with the desktop systems, configure an on-demand virus scanner to perform a full scan of all files nightly. Most server-based virus-scanning products include a scheduler for just this purpose. If nightly backups are performed, set the on-demand scanner to scan the file system before performing the backup operation. This approach ensures that all archived files are virus-free.

MEMORY-RESIDENT SCANNING

Memory-resident software checks the server's memory and files stored on the local file system. Your server-based memory-resident scanner should check the following:

- Local memory for worms and Trojans

- Inbound executable files from the network

- Inbound macro-enabled documents from the network

As with the desktop machines, this minimal file checking is done in the interest of improving performance. On the off chance that a virus sneaks through, you would expect the nightly on-demand virus scan to catch it.

TIP *You can gain some additional benefits by using products from different vendors to secure each part of your network from viruses. For example, you can use a product from one vendor on the servers and another on the desktop machines. No two vendors' signature files are identical. By mixing and matching products, you can receive the maximum amount of virus protection.*

FILE PERMISSIONS

As mentioned earlier in this chapter, setting user-level file permissions ensures that executable files do not become infected. The benefits of this configuration depend greatly on how applications are stored on the network. If all applications are stored on the local workstation, there will be no executables on the server to protect by setting read-only user-level access. If, however, all applications are launched from one or both servers, you can decrease the likelihood of virus infection by setting the minimum level of required permissions.

OPTIONS NOT CONSIDERED

We have not suggested either process monitoring or checksum verification, because both methods are less effective than running virus-scanning software. Remember that the objective is to provide the greatest amount of protection while creating the least amount of administrative maintenance. The suggestions made achieve that goal.

Protecting the Unix-Based System

One important piece of information is missing: what exactly is the Unix system used for? You have not been told if it is a simple e-mail relay or a full-blown server accepting a full array of intranet services. The answer to this question could greatly affect your recommendation. For the purpose of this example, let's assume that this is an engineering system used to compile C code. Users connect to the system via Telnet and FTP.

TIP *Always be sure you have enough data to make an informed and logical decision!*

FILE INTEGRITY CHECKING

One of your biggest concerns with the Unix system should be the possibility that someone will attempt to load a Trojan on the system in order to capture authentication information. By replacing the Telnet server with one of their own creation, an attacker could record logon information from every user who authenticates with the system.

The easiest way to detect this type of activity is to perform a regular file integrity check. This should include a CRC checksum so that changes can be detected even if the current file has the same size and time stamp. Verify the Telnet and FTP servers, as well as any other process that accepts inbound connections. Run this check as an automated process and analyze the results on a different machine. By analyzing the results on a different machine, you are less likely to have the results altered by someone who has compromised the system.

PROCESS MONITORING

Another concern with the Unix machine is that someone can infiltrate the system with a worm. This attack would show up as a new process running on the system. As with the integrity check, automate this audit and analyze the results on a separate system. By knowing what should be running on the system, you can take action if a new process appears.

FILE PERMISSIONS

By default, only the root user can overwrite software that runs as a server on the system. An attacker would first need to crack the root account or perform a root-level exploit before they could replace any of the server software. Maintain this level of file access to reduce the chance of a system compromise. Don't grant regular user accounts write access to these files.

OPTIONS NOT CONSIDERED

What about virus-scanning software? Unix-compatible viruses are extremely rare. Given the described use of this particular system, it is extremely unlikely that a virus infection will occur. Your greater concern is with Trojans and worms.

Summary

In this chapter, we discussed the differences among viruses, Trojans, and worms and how each of them can affect an infected system. You saw what preventive measures are available and the effectiveness of each. You also looked at a mixed-network environment and considered how best to go about protecting it from infection.

In the next chapter, you will learn about backups and disaster recovery. These provide your last line of defense when catastrophic failures occur. From a security perspective, it is always best to plan for the worst.

Chapter 11

Disaster Prevention and Recovery

IN MARCH 2002, Gartner Research published a report stating that only 35 percent of small- to medium-sized businesses have a disaster recovery plan in place. Whether related to weather, fire, theft, network service disruption, hurricane, or human error, the remaining 65 percent of these companies have opened themselves to cost-consuming outages that affect not only their financial performance, but their credibility in the eyes of their customers.

Disaster prevention refers to the precautionary steps you take to ensure that any disruption of your organization's resources does not affect your day-to-day operations. Think of disaster prevention as insurance: you invest money in case you might need it—but you hope you never will.

Disaster recovery is all about contingency planning. Despite all the preparations that go into ensuring that the worst never happens, you need a backup plan that determines what you will do when disaster becomes reality. This plan is your last line of defense between recovery and complete failure.

In Chapter 2, we discussed risk analysis and the importance of identifying your critical resources. We also stressed placing a dollar value on resource unavailability in order to determine just how much downtime you can live with. In this chapter, we will discuss what options are available to you to keep those resources accessible.

Featured in this chapter:

◆ Disaster categories

◆ Server disasters

◆ Extreme disasters

Disaster Categories

Disaster solutions fall into two categories:

◆ Maintaining or restoring a service

◆ Protecting or restoring lost, corrupted, or deleted information

Each category has its place in guarding your assets, and no disaster solution is complete unless it contains elements from both categories.

For example, let's say you have two hard drives mirrored together installed in a server. *Mirroring* ensures that both disks always contain exactly the same information. When mirroring is used, a single hard drive failure will not bring down the entire server. The remaining hard drive can continue to provide file storage and give users access to previously saved information. Mirroring is considered a disaster recovery *service* solution because it helps to ensure that file services remain available.

Now let's assume that a user comes to you and claims that they need to retrieve a file that they deleted three months ago. Despite the passage of so much time, this information is now critical to performing their job, and the information cannot be re-created.

If mirroring is the only disaster recovery procedure you have in place on this file server, you are in deep trouble. Although mirroring ensures that files are saved to both hard drives in the mirrored pair, mirroring also ensures that deleted files are removed. Mirroring provides no way to recover this lost information, making it an ineffective information recovery solution.

TIP   When identifying a full disaster recovery solution, make sure you find methods to recover from service failures as well as to recover lost information. Both are critical to ensuring that you have a contingency plan in any disaster situation.

Network Disasters

As a result of the terrorist attacks on the World Trade Center (WTC) on September 11, 2001, companies are refocusing their attention on the wide variety of areas in which their organization may be vulnerable rather than focusing purely on server redundancy. In addition to server and service failure, it is important to plan and prepare for network disasters, which have the ability to shut down communications throughout an entire organization.

Consider the many companies in Manhattan that, though not physically affected by the attacks, found themselves without phone or Internet access for an extended period because their service providers held central offices at the WTC. Although they lost neither data nor power, they found themselves unable to reach customers, clients, or distributors because of an Internet outage completely beyond their control. Without a functioning network, your highly-available, fully redundant server becomes basically useless.

Media

Good disaster recovery procedures start with your network media. Although physical cables are still the predominant media for most LANs, wireless is rapidly growing as an option and must be considered as part of the overall disaster recovery. If you do choose cable, the cabling you select will go a long way toward specifying how resilient your network will be in case of failure. Whichever media you choose will carry all your network communications, so a failure at this level can be devastating.

TWISTED PAIR

Category 7 (CAT7) cabling is the current cabling standard for most network installations. For years the standard was Category 5. Because of this newer standard, UTP will most likely *not* be replaced with fiber-optic. Due to increasing bandwidth requirements, the wide installation base of CAT5 (and greater) cable guarantees that it will be included in future topology specifications for at least a few more years.

The problem arises from the fact that CAT7 does not guarantee that up to gigabit operation is possible; it only provides the ability to support these speeds. The CAT7 components must be properly assembled and tested to function properly.

It is entirely possible that improperly installed CAT7 cabling will allow you to hook up gigabit devices and have them communicate with each other. Problems typically do not occur until a heavy load is placed on the network. Of course, a heavy load typically means that you have many users relying on network services. Problems due to poor cabling can take the form of slow network performance, frequent packet retransmissions due to errors, or even disconnection of users from services.

Your best preventive medicine for avoiding twisted-pair cabling problems is to test and certify your cables before use. If this is not possible, or if you have been pressed into using below-grade cabling, consider segmenting these problem areas with one or more switches. A switch can trap packet errors and isolate transmissions into multiple collision domains. Although segmentation will not fix the errors, it will limit the scope of the effect that your cable problems have on the rest of your network.

FIBER-OPTIC CABLING

Since fiber-optic cable uses light for transmitting network information, it is immune to the effects of electromagnetic interference (EMI). EMI can also cause transmission errors, especially if the cabling is under heavy load. Fiber-optic is, therefore, an excellent choice for avoiding EMI failures, thus increasing the availability of services that the fiber-optic cable is connecting.

NOTE *For a detailed discussion of fiber-optic cable, see Chapter 4.*

EXCESSIVE CABLE LENGTHS

Every logical topology has specifications that identify the maximum cable lengths you can use. For example, 10Mb and 100Mb Ethernet both specify that twisted-pair cable runs cannot exceed 100 meters. These rules exist to ensure that a system at one end of the cable run can properly detect the transmissions of a system at the opposite end.

Exceeding these topology specifications for cable length can produce intermittent failures due to low signal strength and slow down communications along the entire segment due to an increase in collisions. Since these problems will not be consistent, they can be difficult to troubleshoot.

TIP   A good cable tester is the quickest way to tell if you have exceeded cable-length limitations for your logical topology.

WIRELESS TECHNOLOGIES

Wireless technologies have existed for some time, but slow transfer speeds and lack of open, common standards have limited their market penetration until recently. With the adoption of new technologies and standards (802.11b in particular), high-speed wireless LAN (WLAN) is now technically and financially feasible.

A WLAN is a transmission system that is designed to be location-independent, allowing network access using radio waves rather than a cable infrastructure. In corporate environments, WLANs are usually the final link between an existing wired network and a group of client computers.

However, there are still threats to a wireless infrastructure:

Interference   Although 802.11b is the preferred wireless LAN standard, other wireless standards still exist (HomeRF and Bluetooth). In the fall of 2000, the FCC (Federal Communications Commission) ruled that HomeRF could increase its range of frequencies to overlap with that of 802.11b. Although HomeRF uses frequency hopping that allows traffic to move from frequency to frequency in search of the best signal (and avoid other signals), 802.11b does not.

Installation and configuration   What seems like the advantage of a wireless network can actually be the source of most of its problems. Mobile users have to be handed off from one AP (Access Point) to another, just as a cell phone is handed off from one cell tower to another as the caller moves between cells. If there are not enough APs to cover an area, or if they are incorrectly configured, communication with the network can be lost.

Wireless technologies can be a positive part of any organization's disaster recovery plan—used as a backup in case of a wireless failure. Also, because WLANs are usually added gradually to an existing wire-based network, the wires themselves become the backup plan in case the WLAN fails.

Topology

The topology you choose can also have a dramatic effect on how resilient your network will be in case of failure. As you will see in the following sections, some topologies do a better job than others of recovering from the day-to-day problems that can happen on any network. Changing your topology may not be an option. If not, this section will at least point out some of the common problems you may encounter and give you an idea of possible contingency plans.

LAN Topology

There have been a number of changes in the past few years in LAN topologies. Although some old standards such as Token Ring have become almost extinct, others, such as wireless, are causing a revolution in networking flexibility (and providing a daunting security challenge in the process).

ETHERNET

Ethernet has become the topology of choice for most networking environments. When used with twisted-pair cabling, this topology can be extremely resistant to failure due to cabling problems on any single segment. You can isolate problems so that only a single system is affected. Of course, if this single system happens to be one of your servers, the break in connectivity can still affect multiple users.

The biggest flaw in Ethernet is that a single system can gobble up all the available bandwidth. Although this is an uncommon occurrence with today's network cards, older network interface cards (NICs) were prone to a problem known as *jabbering*. A jabbering network card was a NIC with a faulty transceiver that caused it to continually transmit traffic onto the network. Every other system on the network stopped transmitting and waited for the jabbering card to finish transmitting. Since the faulty card continued to jabber as long as it had power, network communications ground to a halt.

Because of the improvements in technology, jabbering network cards are now rare. The introduction of switching has also made jabbering NICs less of an issue. When a NIC jabbers, the packets it transmits are not legal Ethernet packets. A switch checking for errors rejects these packets and does not forward them on to the rest of the network. The problem system is thus isolated so that it does not affect the operation of other systems on the network.

FDDI

Fiber Distributed Data Interface (FDDI) is a ring topology that utilizes a second ring to rectify many of the problems found in Token Ring. Regular Token Ring users can access a token to indicate which computer (or node) is entitled to transmit at any given time. Whoever has the token, speaks. Everyone else must sit quietly and wait for their turn with the token. (Can you imagine if we could figure out a way to implement this with eight-year-olds?) Thus, data collisions are avoided, and all nodes are given an opportunity to transmit. With FDDI, a second ring remains dormant until an error condition is detected. When this occurs, the FDDI systems can work together to isolate the problem area. FDDI is considered a dying technology because no effort has been made to increase speeds beyond 100Mb. The technology is still worth considering, however, because of its fault-tolerant nature.

NOTE   *FDDI can be run in full duplex mode, which allows both rings to be active at all times. Enabling this feature, however, eliminates the use of the second ring for redundancy.*

In a FDDI ring environment, each station is connected to both rings to guard against cable or hardware failure. Let's assume that you have a cable failure between two of the routers shown in Figure 11.1. When this cable failure occurs, the system immediately downstream from the failure quickly realizes it is no longer receiving data. It then begins to send out a special maintenance packet called a *beacon*. A token station uses a beacon to let other systems around the ring know it has detected a problem. A beacon frame is a system's way of saying, "Hey, I think there is a problem between my upstream neighbor and me because I am no longer receiving data from my upstream neighbor." The station then initializes its connection on the secondary ring so that it can send and receive data on connector A.

FIGURE 11.1

Four routers con-
nected to a FDDI
ring

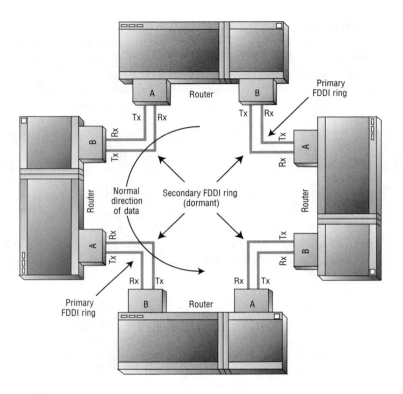

The beacon packet continues to be forwarded until it reaches the beaconing system's upstream neighbor. This upstream neighbor then initializes its connection to the secondary ring by sending and receiving on connector B. This in effect isolates the problem area and returns normal connectivity. When the beaconing station begins to receive its own beacons, it ceases transmission, and ring operation returns to normal. The final transmission path resembles the network shown in Figure 11.2. By using beacon frames, the systems on the network can determine the failure area and isolate it by activating the secondary ring.

If this had, in fact, been a hardware failure caused by a fault in the upstream neighbor and that system was unable to initialize the secondary ring, the faulty system's upstream neighbor would have detected this situation and stepped in to close the ring. This action isolates the problem hardware but allows the rest of the network to continue to function.

Each router continues to monitor the faulty links until connectivity appears to be restored. If the link passes an integrity test, the primary ring returns to full operation, and the secondary ring again goes dormant. This type of network fault tolerance can be deemed critical in environments in which connectivity must be maintained 24/7. This functionality is what still makes FDDI the most fault-tolerant networking topology available today for local area networks.

NOTE   *FDDI also supports a star topology that does not provide any redundancy. A FDDI network can consist of both star and ring connections.*

FIGURE 11.2

How FDDI stations recover from a cable failure

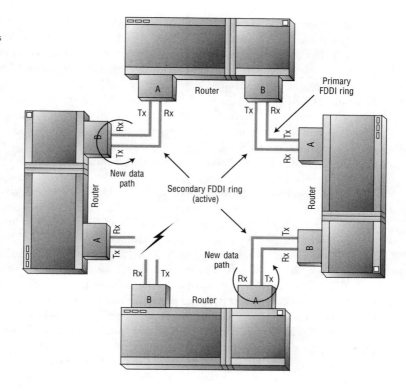

802.11B (WLAN)

The 802.11b standard defines two primary players:

Station   Usually a PC equipped with a wireless NIC.

Access Point (AP)   Acts as a bridge between a wired network and wireless computers. Consisting of a radio, a wired interface (Ethernet), and bridging software, the AP is the base that allows one or more stations to connect to the network.

The 802.11b standard also works in two modes:

Infrastructure   Also called a Basic Service Set (BSS), this mode is a wireless network that has at least one AP connected to a wired network and that has a group of one or more wireless stations. Two or more BSSs in a single subnetwork is an Extended Service Set (ESS). Infrastructure mode is the most common for corporate environments.

Ad hoc   Known as Independent BSS (IBSS) or peer-to-peer mode. Simply a group of wireless stations that communicate directly without the bridging services of an AP.

Like Ethernet (802.3), 802.11b forces the sender to listen to the medium before transmitting. In Ethernet, the full access protocol is known as Carrier Sense Multiple Access with Collision Detection (CSMA/CD). In a wireless network, however, collision detection is not possible, because a station cannot transmit and listen at the same time and therefore cannot "hear" a collision occurring.

To compensate, 802.11b uses a modification called Carrier Sense Multiple Access with Collision Avoidance (CSMA/CA). CSMA/CA works like this: the sender listens, and if no activity is detected, it waits an additional random amount of time and then transmits. If the packet is received intact, the receiver issues an acknowledgment to the sender, which completes the process. If an acknowledgment isn't received, a collision is assumed, and the packet is retransmitted. Unfortunately, CSMA/CA adds additional overhead, which means that an 802.11b network will be slower than an equivalent speed Ethernet network.

Another potential problem is known as the "hidden node," in which two stations on opposite sides of an AP can both "hear" activity from an AP, but not from each other. Fortunately 802.11b has an option called Request to Send/Clear to Send (RTS/CTS). This protocol dictates that a sender transmits an RTS first and then waits for a CTS from the AP. Since all stations can hear the AP, the CTS causes them to delay transmitting, allowing the sender to communicate without any chance of a collision. RTS/CTS causes overhead, however, which is another potential negative.

A WLAN with multiple APs avoids having a single point of failure. Reassociation with a new AP usually occurs because the station has physically moved away from its original AP, but can also occur if there is a change in radio characteristics or high network traffic—essentially load balancing.

Because newer cordless (noncellular) phones work in the same 2.4GHz frequency range, have increased power and range, and are increasingly common in business environments, contention is increasing contention between these phones and 802.11b networks. If you are having serious bandwidth issues, explore the possibility that a portable phone is causing problems.

WAN Topologies

There have been even more developments on the WAN front than with LAN topologies, especially with the increasing deployment (albeit not without some "birthing pains") of DSL and cable modems. As with any new technology, there are security implications to be dealt with.

LEASED LINE OR T1 CONNECTIONS

Private-circuit WAN topologies, such as leased lines or T1 connections, are good at ensuring privacy, but they also introduce a single point of failure. A leased line or a T1 circuit is the equivalent of a single, long cable run between two of your geographically separated sites. If any portion of this circuit is interrupted, there is no built-in redundancy to ensure that information can still be exchanged between these two sites.

If you will be using a private circuit, consider an analog or ISDN (Integrated Services Digital Network) redundancy option, discussed later in this section. This consideration is particularly important if you are following the latest trend of removing servers from field offices and consolidating them in a central location. Although this approach provides a single point of management, it also creates a single point of failure. If a field office that does not have a server loses its private circuit connection to the main office, that field office is without network resources. If the company has also moved to a thin-client architecture, this field office is down completely.

FRAME RELAY

Frame relay can also provide WAN connectivity, but it does so across a shared public network. This network is *packet switched*, meaning that if any segment within the frame relay cloud experiences a failure, traffic can be diverted across operational links. Although packet switching might cause a bit of traffic congestion, at least you still have connectivity.

It is not impossible, however, for the entire frame relay network to go down. This has happened recently to both MCI and AT&T. In both cases, all customers experienced downtime that varied from a few hours to a few days, depending on the client's location. Although outages are rare, these failures have shown that they are possible.

TIP   Although frame relay does provide better fault tolerance than private circuits, it is not immune to failure. If you have a WAN segment running over frame relay that absolutely must remain operational 24/7, consider building in some redundancy to the circuit.

ISDN

ISDN is a telephone company technology that provides digital service typically in increments of 64Kbps. ISDN has been available since the early 1980s, but it was broadly implemented only in the late '90s because of the limitations in analog modems and the rising popularity of the Internet. ISDN requires that the phone company install services within their phone switches to support digitally switched connections. Using two separate channels, consumers can access both voice and data communication over the same line. The second channel dynamically switches when the phone is in use to carry voice communications, but returns to data when the receiver is replaced, thus dynamically doubling the available bandwidth. ISDN was initially stalled by high costs, lack of standards, and low consumer acceptance. Although still in use, it has become less popular with the increase in home DSL availability and high-speed cable transfer. Because the circuits involved in an ISDN connection are dedicated, any interruption of a single circuit causes the entire connection to fail. Although still a viable option for organizations, most of today's companies find that emerging DSL technology is more flexible and cheaper.

DSL

Digital Subscriber Line (DSL) is similar to ISDN in that both use existing copper telephone lines and both require short distances to a central switching office (less than 18,000 feet). Because DSL is circuit oriented, each connection is independent of all others (similar to ISDN). Any single failure in the circuit causes the connection to fail. DSL, however, can provide a higher speed: up to 32Mbps downstream, and up to 1Mbps upstream. This speed is not fixed as in ISDN or a T1, which can cause problems for organizations that require dedicated throughput for multimedia purposes.

All DSL companies use existing phone cabling, but service and services vary greatly from one company to the next. In addition, many companies offer a range of guaranteed transfer rates to choose from based on your proximity to the central office and how much money you want to spend. Your best defense against poor service is to speak with other customers of the company or research any complaints that have been made against them in your area. Several websites (including `www.broadbandreports.com`) can assist you in selecting a service provider. Some business-grade DSL services, depending on how far the business is from the local phone companies POP (point of presence), can actually meet (and, in some instances, surpass) T1 speeds. And many business have chosen to replace their analog phone system with an all-in-one solution combining VoIP (Voice over IP) and Internet connectivity. But now *two* critical business systems rely on a single access point—a potential problem. Traditional dial-up as a backup strategy is effectively removed.

CABLE MODEMS

Cable modem service is the love child of a marriage between your cable television provider and an Internet Service Provider (ISP). Because in most instances the existing infrastructure is sufficient to offer high-speed access, cable modems have a much higher growth rate and market penetration than DSL and, in some cases, far exceed DSL speeds. Also, most cable providers tend to have increased local presence, which some claim improves service. Although cable modems might not be considered the first choice for business connectivity, remember that your disaster recovery plan should include any telecommuters. Some companies are looking at employee access from home as a business continuity operation, in case the physical business building becomes incapacitated.

A Yankee Group study showed that at the end of 2001, 60 percent of homes in the United States were cable ready, whereas only 45 percent were DSL ready. This study also predicted that cable modems would rule supreme over DSL for the next five years because of over-regulation of DSL. In March 2002, the FCC determined that cable modems fall under the same umbrella as DSL (you must have multiple providers per cable company) and will be regulated, so the future of cable modems is all but certain.

Single Points of Failure

As you may have surmised from the previous section, one of the best ways to eliminate disasters on a network is to identify all single points of failure and either build in redundancy or develop a contingency plan. Unknowingly creating a single point of failure is the most common mistake in network design.

For example, consider the configuration of the average network connection:

◆ A single firewall

◆ A single router

◆ A single CSU/DSU (channel service unit/data service unit)

◆ A single leased line or T1 connection

This configuration has three electronic devices, as well as a network circuit that is not under your control—all capable of interrupting Internet service. The electronic devices are not exactly components you can replace by running down to the local Radio Shack. You local exchange carrier controls the WAN circuit, so the response time you receive to problems may be directly affected by the business relationship you have with the local exchange carrier. (Translation: "The more money you spend on a monthly basis, the more likely you are to see a service tech by the end of the millennium.")

Although these issues may not be a big deal for some organizations, many rely on network connectivity, whether to another office or to the Internet, as part of their daily business practices. When Internet connectivity was first established, consistent access to Internet services might not have seemed important or might not have been considered a critical business function. Now that Internet access has become a critical business function, no one has gone back to evaluate the impact of the loss of this service.

Besides connectivity and equipment failures, you should also avoid single points of failure in other areas, including power, maintenance, and—believe it or not—employee knowledge. We call this the "beer truck" principle, because in principle, even the most vaunted, capable systems engineer can be run over, and unless the critical technical and business knowledge is retained or documented in some fashion, this employee's accident can cause a crisis just as severe as a hurricane or a power outage.

So you need to go back to your risk analysis and identify your single points of network failure. You also need to evaluate the effect that loss of service will have on your organization. If any point in your network can be considered critical, you need to build in redundancy.

CONSOLIDATED EQUIPMENT

In the early 1990s, chassis hubs became extremely popular because of their high port density and single point of management. It was not uncommon to connect 200 or more systems through a single hub. Of course, neither was it uncommon for 200 or more users to be unable to access network resources because a power supply or a single management board had failed. For this reason, many organizations have stuck with stackable hubs; although they require more rack space, the failure of a single unit does not bring down an entire network.

There has been a resurgence of interest in consolidated solutions with the release of Cisco's 5000 and 6000 series switches, as well as multiple product offerings from Cabletron. Like their chassis hub predecessors, these products claim lower administration costs due to a central point of management. Although there is validity in this claim, it does not speak to financial loss due to the catastrophic failure of a single device.

Stackable solutions provide you with more flexibility in recovering from a failure. For example, if you are using six stackable switches instead of a single consolidated unit and one of these switches fails, you will not experience a complete network outage. Although you still have a failed device to deal with, you at least have some breathing space. You can use the remaining five units to continue providing services to important users such as your boss (if the outage coincides with your review), the person who cuts the weekly payroll, and that administrative assistant who drops off brownies every holiday.

TAKING ADVANTAGE OF REDUNDANT LAN ROUTES

As you saw in Chapter 3, you can use dynamic routing to take advantage of multiple paths between network segments. Some routing protocols even take such metrics as network utilization into account when determining which path is the best route along which to forward your traffic.

Although static routes are your best bet when only a single path is available (such as a WAN link) or in areas where you are concerned that an attacker might corrupt the routing table (such as an Internet connection), for the majority of your internal network you should use a dynamic routing protocol such as OSPF (Open Shortest Path First). If there is only one connection point between each of your routed segments, consider purchasing another router for redundancy or adding more network cards to one of your servers. Using metrics such as hop count and cost, you can configure your network to route through the server only in case of emergency. This approach helps to ensure that the server does not experience additional load unless the primary router fails.

DIAL BACKUP FOR WAN CONNECTIONS

WAN connections are prime candidates for providing a single point of failure. Because of the recurrent costs of maintaining a WAN link, most organizations do not build any type of redundancy into their wide area network. This is a shame, because you have no real control over this portion of your network. You are at the mercy of your exchange carrier to feel your urgency and rectify the problem as soon as possible.

One potential solution is to configure your border routers to fail over to a backup circuit if the primary line fails. This backup can be an analog dial-up line along with a couple of modems, or you could go for increased bandwidth by utilizing an ISDN solution. In either case, you will have a lot less available bandwidth if the line that fails is a full T1, but you are better off being able to provide a minimal amount of bandwidth between your two locations than no bandwidth at all.

Configuring a router to perform dial backup is not difficult. The following example shows the commands required for a Cisco router to bring up an ISDN connection on bri 0 when the primary circuit on serial 0 fails to respond:

```
interface serial 0
 backup delay 10 120
 backup interface bri 0
 ip address 192.168.5.1 255.255.255.0
!
interface bri 0
 ip address 192.168.5.2 255.255.255.0
 dialer string 5551212
 dialer-group 1
 dialer in-band
 dialer string 5551212
 async dynamic routing
!
dialer-list 1 protocol ip permit
```

This configuration tells the router that if serial 0 fails to respond for 10 seconds, the bri 0 interface should be initiated as an alternate path. Likewise, if the serial 0 circuit returns to operation for a minimum of 120 seconds, the bri 0 line should be torn down. The dialer-list command identifies the type of traffic that can bring up the alternate circuit path. In this case, we have specified that any IP traffic can initiate the circuit.

Tip   If you are using ISDN as a backup solution, and you are using a primary rate ISDN (PRI) interface at your main office in order to accept basic rate ISDN (BRI) connects from multiple field offices, remember that the call will have to be initiated from the BRI side of the circuit.

Saving Configuration Files

All the network disaster solutions we've discussed until now have dealt with availability of service. As mentioned earlier in this chapter, no disaster recovery solution is complete unless you can restore lost information. In this case, we are not talking about your data that is traveling along the network.

Protocols do a good job of ensuring that this information does not become lost. The real concern is the configuration files that you use to program routers, switches, and even hubs along your network.

When a network device fails, chances are you will also lose the configuration that has been programmed into it. It is also possible that someone might inadvertently change the configuration to an unusable state. If either of these events occurs, it is a good thing to have a backup of your configuration file so that you can restore the original setup. A backup configuration file is also useful for historic purposes, when you want to see what changes have been made to your network and when.

The easiest way to save your configuration information is *terminal logging*. Most terminal emulation and Telnet programs have some method of recording all the information that passes by on the terminal screen. If your networking device has a single command that shows all configuration information, you can use terminal logging to archive this information for later retrieval.

Some devices, such as Cisco routers and switches, let you paste this information to your terminal screen in order to configure the device. For example, the `write term` command displays all configuration information to the terminal screen. You can then easily save this configuration information. If the device should fail later, simply open a terminal session with the new device and place it in configuration mode. Copy the original configuration of the original device to your Clipboard (using Notepad or WordPad), and paste it into the terminal screen connected to the new device. Save the configuration, and your replacement is ready for action.

The drawback to terminal logging is that it only works for configuration; you cannot save the operating system. Also, if your network device does not provide a single command for displaying all configuration information, the process of recording the full configuration can be tedious.

TFTP SERVER

Trivial File Transfer Protocol (TFTP) is similar to FTP, except that it uses UDP as a transport and does not use any type of authentication. When a client wants to retrieve a file from a TFTP server or save a file to a TFTP server, it simply needs to know the file's name and the IP address of the TFTP server. There are no command parameters that allow you to authenticate or even change to a new directory.

Given the lack of authentication, TFTP is not exactly something you want coming through your firewall. Most networking devices, however, support TFTP for saving or retrieving configuration information. A single TFTP server can archive configuration files for every device on your network. If a device on your network fails, simply plug it in, assign an IP address, and use TFTP to retrieve the required configuration file.

TIP *Most vendors use TFTP to configure devices with their latest operating system versions. This means that you can keep a known-to-be-stable operating system version on the TFTP server with the required configuration file. When a device needs to be replaced, simply use TFTP to load both the operating system and the configuration file from the TFTP server.*

By saving the configuration information from your network devices, you can be assured of recovering from a network disaster as quickly as possible. Few things in life are a greater letdown than having a network device fail and finally receiving the replacement, only to discover that you do not remember the configuration of the original device and that you will have to spend the next few hours playing trial and error.

Server Disasters

Now that you have seen how to make your network more fault tolerant, it is time to consider your servers. A wide range of options is available to make servers more disaster resistant. The only limiting factors are your budget and in some cases your operating system—not all solutions are available for every platform. Disaster prevention on a server is usually viewed as being the most costly, because typically we can justify the expenditure only on a single system.

Uninterruptible Power Supply (UPS)

Although all computers need a source of clean and steady power, power is even more important when the computer acts as a server, because multiple users rely on the system. A good power source is not just one that is free from blackout (power failure) or brownout (voltage sag) conditions; it should also protect your computer from power surges and spikes, electrical line noises, frequency variations, and harmonic distortions.

An Uninterruptible Power Supply (UPS) comes in a variety of flavors ranging from a basic $80 home computer system that offers little protection beyond the occasional power sag to a fully config-urable operating-system integrated device that saves any open files, notifies connected users several times prior to shut down, blares audible warnings when power levels have changed, and initiates e-mail notices to administrators for $3000 to $5000. The higher-end devices will do just about everything but call an electrician and order pizza for you while you wait for the electrician to arrive.

The reliability of these devices is as varied as the manufacturers who produce them. Network-computing.com performed a side-by-side cost and features comparison of many of the most popular UPS models used in homes and businesses today. Although reliability was not a central factor in the study, the MTBF (mean time between failures) value can be used as an initial benchmark in deter-mining what level of UPS redundancy is required simply to compensate for anticipated failure in the UPS itself. (The study is fascinating. You'll find it at `www.networkcomputing.com/ibg/Chart?guide_id=3504`.)

TRACKING DOWN POWER PROBLEMS

We were once called in by a client to troubleshoot a problem with some backup software on a NetWare server. The backup software appeared to be hanging the server and causing 100 percent CPU utilization. The prob-lem was not completely consistent: it happened during random stages of the backup process. What was odd, however, was that it only happened on Monday and Thursday nights between 7:30 P.M. and 8:00 P.M., even though the client ran the backup every night. The problem could not be reproduced during regular business hours. Installing all current patches had no effect.

We decided to work late one Thursday night to see if we could diagnose the problem. At 7:00 P.M., the cleanup crew came in and started emptying waste baskets and vacuuming the rugs. At approximately 7:40 P.M., a member of the cleaning crew plugged a vacuum into an outlet just outside the server room.

All ran fine until the vacuum was powered off. The resulting power spike immediately caused a 100 percent CPU race condition on the server. We asked the employee if the crew vacuumed this office space every night and was told that although the crew emptied wastebaskets every night, they only vacuumed on Mondays and Thursdays. Needless to say, the client had a UPS installed by Monday—and the problem was solved.

A UPS is designed to maintain power to your system only long enough to notify users before initiating a graceful shutdown of the system. It is not a solution for overcoming a long-term power outage.

As little as a 10 percent fluctuation in power can cause an error condition on a computer, even less if it is in the form of a steady stream of noise. Although brownouts or blackouts are easy to identify because they cause the system to reboot, spikes, surges, and noise can cause far more subtle problems, such as the application error just described. Electrical power is like network wiring: we do not think to check it until we have spent time chasing our tails replacing drivers and loading patches.

TIP   *Although a good UPS is an excellent idea for any computer system, it should be considered critical equipment for your servers. An intelligent UPS will include software that can shut down the server if power is unavailable for a specific amount of time. This ensures that your server does not come crashing down once the battery supply has run dry. In addition, any server performing file and data storage should be equipped with a UPS that is configured to notify all connected users prior to shut down, giving them the opportunity to save their files before being disconnected.*

RAID

RAID, or *redundant array* of *inexpensive disks*, not only provides fault tolerance against hard disk crashes; it can also improve system performance. RAID breaks up or copies the data you want to save across multiple hard disks. This approach prevents a system failure due to the crash of a single drive. It also improves performance, because multiple disks can work together to save large files simultaneously.

The process of breaking up data across multiple disks is referred to as *striping*. Depending on the level of RAID you are using, the system might also store parity information known as Error Correction Code (ECC). Some RAID systems are *hot swappable*, meaning you can replace drives while the computer is still in use, reducing downtime to zero.

You can implement RAID as either a hardware or a software solution. With hardware RAID, the RAID controller takes care of all RAID functionality, making the array appear as a single logical disk to the operating system. Software RAID is program code that is either part of the existing operating system or available as add-on software. Software RAID is usually slower than hardware RAID because it requires more CPU utilization. Regardless of the solution you use, RAID is classified into levels: RAID 0–RAID 5.

NOTE   *There are classifications for RAID 6–RAID 10, but these are simply variations on the original six specifications.*

RAID 0

RAID 0 is used strictly for performance gains and provides no fault tolerance. Instead of saving a file to a single disk, RAID 0 stripes the data across multiple hard drives. This approach improves performance by letting the drives share the storage load, but it also increases the chance of failure, because any one disk crash disables the entire array. Because of the lack of fault tolerance, RAID 0 is not widely used.

RAID 1

RAID 1 maintains a full copy of all file information on every disk and thus is sometimes referred to as *disk mirroring*. If a single disk fails, each of the remaining disks has a full copy of the entire file system. This approach prevents a system crash due to the failure of any one disk. It also means that disk storage is limited to the size of a single disk. In other words, if you have two 4GB drives mirrored together, you have only 4GB of available storage, not 8GB.

A RAID 1 disk array actually performs worse than a single disk solution because the disk controller must send a full copy of each file to every single drive. This approach limits the speed of the array to that of the slowest disk. Novell developed a term for a variation on disk mirroring called *disk duplexing*. Disk duplexing functions in the same way as disk mirroring, except that multiple controller cards are used. Using multiple controller cards helps to eliminate some of the performance degradation because each controller needs to communicate with only a single drive. Duplexing also helps to increase fault tolerance because the system can survive not only a drive failure, but a controller failure, as well.

RAID 2

RAID 2 is similar to RAID 5, except that data is stored to disk one byte at a time. Error correction is also used to prevent a single drive failure from disabling the array. The block mode data transfer used by other RAID specifications is far more efficient than the byte mode used by RAID 2. Thus, RAID 2 suffers from extremely poor performance, especially when dealing with multiple small files. Because of its poor performance, RAID 2 is not widely used.

RAID 3 AND RAID 4

RAID 3 and RAID 4 are identical specifications, except that RAID 3 involves the use of three disks and RAID 4 involves the use of four. These RAID specifications dedicate a single disk to error correction and stripe the data across the remaining disks. In other words, in a RAID 4 array, disks 1–3 contain striped data, and disk 4 is dedicated to error correction. In this way, the array can remain functional through the loss of a single drive.

The ECC is essentially a mathematical summation of the data stored on all the other hard drives. This ECC value is generated on a block-by-block basis. For example, consider the following math problem:

$$3 + 4 + 2 + 6 = 15$$

Think of all the values to the left of the equal sign as data that is stored to a specific block on each data disk in a RAID 4 array. Think of the total as the value stored to the same block on the parity drive. Now let's assume that disk 3 crashes and a file request is made of this group of blocks. The RAID array is presented with the following problem:

$$3 + 4 + ? + 6 = 15$$

As you can see, it is rather easy to derive the missing value. Although this requires a bit more processing, thus slowing down disk access a bit, the array can reproduce the missing data and return the file information. Although this example is greatly simplified, it essentially shows how RAID levels 3–5 recover from a disk failure.

You start to see an improvement in performance over using a single disk when you use RAID levels 3 and 4. You also take less of a storage hit in order to provide fault tolerance. Since data is stored on all the disks but one, the total storage capacity of a RAID 3 or RAID 4 array is the total storage of all the disks, minus the storage of one of them. In other words, if you have four 4GB drives in a RAID 4 configuration, you have 12GB of available storage.

RAID 5

RAID 5 is similar to RAID 3 and RAID 4, except that all disks are used for both data and ECC storage. This arrangement helps to improve speed over RAID 3 and RAID 4, which can suffer from bottlenecks on the parity drive. It also helps to improve capacity, because you can use more than five drives on a RAID 5 array. Like RAID 3 and 4, the total storage capacity is the combined storage of all the disks minus one. RAID 5 is by far the most popular RAID solution after disk mirroring.

RAID 0+1

Raid 0+1 is a combination that creates a mirrored pair of two stripe sets without parity. This configuration provides incredibly high I/O reads due to the multiple stripe sets and is often used in an external storage array (as in server clustering) or a storage area network. In an external storage array, several disks are housed in an external SCSI (Small Computer System Interface) drive cabinet (set of disks) and can be accessed by any server connected to the array. This approach boosts fault tolerance because a single server failure does not prevent other linked servers from accessing the information stored in the array. It also provides the same fault tolerance as Raid 0 (a mirror set) and can recover from a single disk failure. Bear in mind, this is not an appropriate solution if data loss creates a critical situation. If you house two stripe sets of 32 disks that are mirrored, you can recover from a single disk, but if a second disk fails before you repair the first, all information is lost.

A storage area network is an actual dedicated network, connected to your local area network, where data and information is stored. In addition to placing data in a centralized location, it isn't attached to a given server, so it doesn't use the server's resources. It also takes the resources used for backup off the production network and limits it to the SAN (System Area Network).

RAID 0 + 5

This is the same concept as RAID 0 + 1, but now we are mirroring two RAID 5 arrays, providing an incredibly level of fault tolerance while maintaining a high level of I/O performance.

Redundant Servers

Server redundancy takes the concept of RAID and applies it to the entire computer, which is sometimes referred to as *server fault tolerance*. Redundant servers provide one or more entire systems to be available in case the primary system crashes. It does not matter if the crash is due to a drive failure, a memory error, or even a motherboard failure. Once the primary server stops responding to requests, the redundant system steps in to take over.

As shown in Figure 11.3, redundant servers typically share two communication channels. One channel is their network connection, and the other is a high-speed link between the two systems. Depending on the implementation, you can create this link using proprietary communication cards or possibly 100Mb Ethernet cards. Updates are fed to the secondary via this high-speed link. Depending on the implementation, these updates might simply be disk information or might possibly include memory address information, as well.

NOTE *When memory address information is included, the secondary can step in for the primary with no interruption in service.*

FIGURE 11.3

A redundant server configuration

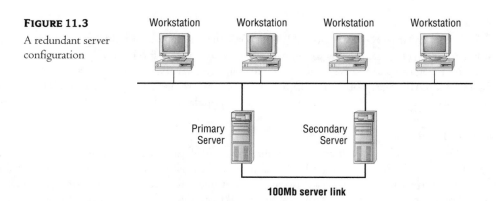

100Mb server link

Not all redundant server solutions include a high-speed link. For example, the VERITAS Storage Replicator, which is discussed at length at the end of this chapter, uses the server's network connection when exchanging information. Storage Replicator does not require a high-speed link between the two systems. The benefit of using the existing network is that the secondary server can be anywhere, even at a remote facility. Since the secondary server can be safely tucked away in another location that is miles away, the setup is far more fault resilient to facility-wide problems such as fire, lightning strikes, floods, or even cattle stampedes.

If you do not have a link between the two systems, memory information is not shared, and the secondary cannot step in immediately. A client request originally sent to the primary server has to time out and be reset before it can be serviced by the secondary server. This adds a delay of a minute or two before the secondary is fully utilized. Another drawback is increased network utilization. All information is shared over the network, not over an isolated link between the two systems.

You can implement server redundancy at the operating-system level or as an add-on product. Microsoft Cluster Service (MSCS) is a good example of support at the operating-system level for running redundant servers. Many third-party offerings from companies such as Legato and Veritas can add redundant server support. The option you choose depends on the features you want. Each product supports redundant servers in a slightly different fashion.

NOTE *Microsoft Cluster Service does not support true clustering at the time of this writing. It supports only redundant servers and a minimal amount of load sharing. Full clustering ability is expected to be included in a later release.*

Clustering

Many flavors of cluster implementations are available, each with its own advantages and disadvantages. Let's take a look at two of the most common types: active/passive and active/active

An *active/passive* cluster is similar to a redundant server. Each node in the cluster is attached to a shared storage space (external storage array or storage area network, usually). The active server handles all client requests, and the passive server sits in stand-by, ready to take over if the active server fails. In this setup, the passive server participates only during failover of the active server.

In *active/active* clustering, all systems take part in processing service requests. Since applications are loaded on each node, and each node has access to the shared storage space, the cluster acts as an intelligent unit in order to balance traffic load between the nodes. From a client's perspective, a cluster looks like a single, yet very fast server. If a server fails, all tasks that were running on the server are seamlessly moved to another server—at the most within seconds. Processing continues on another machine, but with an obvious degradation in performance. What makes clustering more attractive than server redundancy is that your secondary systems are actually providing processing time; they do not sit idle waiting for another system to fail. This approach ensures that you get the highest level of utilization from your hardware. Clustering is an excellent solution for boosting both fault tolerance and performance and is available for Linux, Unix, VMS, and Microsoft NT and 2000.

Data Backup

Keeping a duplicate copy of your data has always been the best way to protect against disaster, corruption, or loss. Traditionally, we relied on tape, but newer backup methods are starting to gain the attention of companies, including Internet-based backups that provide for off-site storage and a reduction of in-house maintenance of backup equipment and procedures. Many companies now offer real-time Internet backup solutions that guarantee complete recovery of data, regardless of the problem, within four hours.

TAPE BACKUP

The mainstay of most network administrators, *tape backups* are the method of choice for protecting or restoring lost, corrupted, or deleted information. All the server-based options we have discussed so far have focused on maintaining or restoring the server as a service. None can restore that proverbial marketing file that was deleted more than three months ago. Here is where tape backups come in: their strength is in safeguarding the information that is actually stored on the server.

NOTE *The ability to restore files becomes even more important if you are using Unix or any Windows-based system as a file server. Neither of these operating systems includes a utility for restoring deleted network files.*

Most backup software supports three methods for selecting which files are archived to tape:

- Full backup
- Incremental backup
- Differential backup

FULL BACKUPS

As the name implies, a *full backup* is a complete archive of every file on the server. A full backup is your best bet when recovering from a disaster: it contains a complete copy of your entire file system, consolidated to a single tape or set of tapes. The only problem with performing a full backup is that it takes longer to complete than any other backup. If you need to back up large amounts of information (say 10GB or more), it may not be feasible to perform a full backup every night.

INCREMENTAL BACKUPS

Incremental backups copy to tape only files that have been recently added or changed. This approach helps to expedite the backup process by archiving only files that have changed since the last backup. The typical procedure is to perform a full backup once a week and incremental backups nightly. If you need to rebuild your server, you first restore the full backup, and then you restore every incremental backup created since the full backup .

The one flaw in incremental backups is that they do not track deletions. You could potentially end up trying to restore more data than you have the capacity to store. For example, consider Table 11.1. Let's say you have a 12GB drive on which you are storing file information. At the beginning of the day on Monday, you have 10GB of files saved on this disk. In the course of the day, you add 1GB of file information. At the end of the day, you perform a full backup, which writes 11GB of data to tape.

TABLE 11.1: STORAGE PROBLEMS WITH INCREMENTAL BACKUPS

DAY	STORAGE USED	FILE ADDS	FILE DELETES	SAVED TO TAPE
Monday	10GB	1GB	0GB	11GB
Tuesday	11GB	1GB	3GB	1GB
Wednesday	9GB	2GB	0GB	2GB
Thursday	11GB	1GB	3GB	1GB

You start the day on Tuesday with 11GB out of the 12GB used for storage. In the course of the day, you add 1GB of files but delete 3GB to free up disk space. At the end of the day, you perform an incremental backup and save 1GB of new data to tape.

You start the day on Wednesday with 9GB out of 12GB used for storage. You add 2GB of files and perform an incremental backup, saving 2GB of data to disk. Thursday you save 1GB of data to disk but delete 3GB. You incrementally back up the 1GB of data to tape. At the end of the day on Thursday, you have 9GB out of 12GB used for storage.

Friday morning you walk in and find that someone has performed a bit of housekeeping, deleting all the files from your 12GB drive. You immediately fire up your backup software and restore the full backup performed on Monday. You then load the Tuesday incremental tape and restore that, as well. No sooner does the Tuesday tape finish the restore process than you get an "out of disk space" error from the server. Even though you still have two tapes with 3GB of data to restore, you have no free space left on your 12GB drive.

The capacity problem in this example is typical of incremental backups. For this reason, most system administrators perform differential backups instead of incremental.

DIFFERENTIAL BACKUPS

A *differential backup* differs from an incremental backup in that it backs up all files that have changed since a full backup was last performed. It does not back up files from the time of the last backup. For example, if you perform a full backup on Monday and then a differential backup every other night of the week, the differential backup performed on Thursday night will include all file changes from Tuesday through Thursday. This approach helps to reduce the chances of the capacity problem you saw in restoring incremental backups. Although it is still possible to end up with more data on tape than drive capacity, this problem is far less likely to occur.

Another benefit of performing differentials over incrementals is that you only need to restore two tapes after a server crash. This approach not only expedites the process but also reduces the chance of failure. For example, look again at Table 11.1. For an incremental backup, you need to restore four tapes to retrieve all your data. If you perform differentials, you have to restore only two. This approach reduces your chances of running across a bad tape.

TIP   Tape backups are fine for tape storage periods of a year or less. If you need to archive information for a longer period, consider using some form of optical media or storing your tapes in a climate-controlled environment.

INTERNET BACKUPS

An alternative or addition to tape backups can be Internet backups. Part of a larger outsourcing movement, Internet backups are typically included in a larger service package of outsourced, remote management. Products such as Connected's Connected TLM automatically and regularly copy encrypted data from an organization and store it off site in a secure facility.

The advantages of Internet backups include the following:

Low administrative overhead   Because local implementation and maintenance is usually limited to a small software package, Internet-based backups run seamlessly and without intervention or monitoring on behalf of the internal IT staff of an organization. You don't need to monitor tapes for quality or deterioration, and you don't need to take them off site or secure them.

Reduced risk   Because data is always stored off site, there is never a fear of an onsite disaster permanently destroying data. Because data is not being stored on tape, the risk of losing control of proprietary or confidential data through theft or negligence is more controlled. No one can simply walk off with a backup tape.

However, some significant disadvantages are associated with Internet backups:

Speed   Even with a T1, backups can take a significant amount of time. Although greater bandwidth is increasingly available, this bandwidth pales in comparison to the rate of growth of corporate data. For example, it takes 2–3 hours to back up a 450MB file over a T1 link.

Recoverability   The time it takes to restore data from an Internet backup is greater than that of a local backup, and not just because of the slower connection speed. Requesting the backup service, locating the data, and initiating the process adds extra overhead to an already slow transfer rate.

Despite the disadvantages, some organizations are adding Internet backups as part of their overall data recovery solution, using the benefit of offsite storage as an additional guarantee against data loss.

Application Service Providers

Application Service Providers (ASPs) solve the problem of server failure and data loss in a unique way. All data services are outsourced, with only the end-user client application running locally within an organization. All data and services are hosted through the Internet. The ASP is then responsible for ensuring the availability and redundancy not only of the data, but also of the entire application itself.

Although this solution is still emerging, it has become ideal for many smaller organizations that do not have the budget to maintain either an entire IT staff or hardware/software infrastructure. Larger organizations that use one or two primary line-of-business applications can also benefit from entering into a tight relationship with ASPs.

The drawbacks of using an ASP become obvious. If the Internet connection fails, no recourse is available to an organization to get access to their applications or their data. Billing or service disputes with the ASP can mean that data is held hostage, and business is halted until the dispute is resolved.

Also, service alternatives are restricted to a single company. Switching between ASPs can be difficult, and the portability of data can be impossible, leaving an organization without critical assets.

Server Recovery

Although tape backups are fine for protecting file information, they are not an efficient way to recover a server. Let's assume that you suffer a complete server failure and you need to rebuild the server on a new hardware platform. You need to take the following steps:

1. Install the server operating system.

2. Install any required drivers.

3. Install any required service packs.

4. Install any required hotfixes or security patches.

5. Install the backup software.

6. Install any required patches to the backup software.

7. Restore your last full backup tape.

8. Restore any incremental or differential tapes as required.

This process is obviously time-consuming and labor-intensive. It would be a minor miracle if you could place this server in operation in anything less than a full day, especially if the server stores a lot of data.

The alternative is to use a package specifically designed for server recovery. Typically, such packages create a small number of boot disks along with an image of the server. You can use the boot disks to start the system without an operating system. The server recovery software then accesses the previously created image and restores all the data to the server. Once the server reboots, it is back in operation.

Some vendors make server recovery products that integrate directly with a backup solution. For example, the ARCServe product line from Computer Associates includes both a backup program and a server recovery program. If you are using ARCServe to perform your nightly backups, it makes sense to also obtain a copy of the ARCServe disaster recovery option. The recovery option can read the ARCServe backup tapes, allowing the recovery program to automatically restore your server to the configuration it had during the last full backup. If you purchase a server recovery program from another vendor, you have to maintain the image file separately to ensure that it stays up-to-date.

The only drawback to a server recovery solution is that it saves the entire system as an image. Although this expedites both the backup and the restore process, you cannot access individual files. Even with a server recovery solution, you still need a regular backup solution to replace that occasional lost file.

One possible solution to the lengthy process of rebuilding a server is to *image* your server. Imaging is nothing more than taking a complete snapshot of your system partition (the hard drive or disk partition on which your system files are stored) and storing it as a single, compressed file in a different location. By taking frequent images, you can quickly restore (within minutes) an exact duplicate of your server (at the time the image was taken). Images work with working data, not just system files, but typically those images are larger and can take longer to restore.

The imagine process generally works in the same way, no matter which product is used. The source system (the one to be imaged) is booted from a special floppy or CD that loads a minimal operating system, enables networking, and launches the imaging client software. The imaging client either prompts you for image settings or contacts the image server directly to determine the nature of the imagine operation. Typically the imaging choices are the following:

- Which disk partition on the source system should be imaged
- The name that will be given to the image file stored on the server
- Which compression options should be applied to the image file

Once your system is imaged, it can be rebooted to continue normal operation. If your server was created with at least two distinct partitions—one for the operating system, the other(s) for working data—it is actually possible to re-image your system or data partitions separately from each other. The result is that you can restore system partitions separately from your data partitions, something that can save a lot of time when your are trying to recover a system as quickly as possible. One product that is well respected for its imaging capabilities is PowerQuest DriveImage.

Extreme Disasters

Okay, so you've identified each point of failure in your network and believe you've covered all your bases redundantly. You lock up the office, knowing that in case of power failure, your UPS system will kick in and keep you up and running as the automatic power generator switches on. You've implemented clustering, in case any server should fail. You've backed up your system regularly and stored copies of the data in an offsite location. You ensured several routes to and from your network, complete with back-up network/Internet connectivity, and now, you return home and snuggle into your warm bed, dreaming of the promotion that is certain to come your way.

Sadly, as your visions of sugar plums dance across happily redundant network wires, a ten-year-old boy playing with fireworks accidentally sets fire to your building, and it burns completely to the ground. Now what?

A good disaster recovery plan must include a contingency plan for complete destruction of your office. You can, of course, consider it the work of fate, pack your bags, and take a janitorial job at the local Dairy Queen. Or you can implement a well-conceived business continuity plan to keep your business running, even in the face of total disaster.

You've already completed a big portion of the recovery process by running your nightly backups and keeping offsite copies of the data. Although it is completely unfeasible to maintain backup computer equipment for each employee in the company, do you have a server to which you can restore the information? Is there a local organization, such as a training center or a computer reseller, that can provide space and equipment for an extended period of time? Is there another company office where employees can be relocated for the duration of your office reconstruction?

An insurance organization in Florida that relies heavily on Internet access to provide service to their customers has integrated a partnership with a local hotel chain that provides high-speed Internet access. In the event of a hurricane or a tropical storm, employees and their families will be relocated to a safe location and provided with food, shelter, and the ability to work. Although that may seem somewhat cold-hearted, the plan was initiated with the goal of meeting the needs of the company as well as the personal needs of its employees.

By now you should have a number of ideas about how to make your network more fault-resistant and how to plan for and recover from failures. It is not enough to simply plan a disaster solution; you must test and document your solution, as well. Testing is the only way to ensure that the recovery portion of your plan will actually work. Documenting the process is the only way to ensure that the correct procedure will be followed when disaster does occur.

THE IMPORTANCE OF DISASTER SIMULATION

We cannot overemphasize the importance of testing your disaster recovery solution. We once consulted for a company that wanted to implement a facility-wide disaster recovery solution. In other words, the company wanted to ensure that if the whole building went up in smoke, it could recover to a remote facility and be back in operation within 96 hours. It was expected that most of the data would be migrated to this other facility via backup tape, because the remote facility was also used for offsite tape storage.

Only when we simulated a disaster did we find one minor flaw. The DEC tape drive sitting on the main production server was incompatible with the tape drive on the replacement server. In fact, the tape drive on the production server was so old that we could not obtain a duplicate drive to read the tapes created by the production system. Had this been an actual failure, recovery would have taken a wee bit longer than 96 hours.

The solution was twofold:

◆ Replace the tape drive on the production server with an identical model to that of the replacement server.

◆ Document that any future tape-drive upgrades must be duplicated on both systems.

Nondestructive Testing

Nondestructive testing allows you to test your disaster prevention and recovery plans without affecting the normal workflow of your operation. This is the preferred method of testing: you do not want to cause a disaster while testing a potential solution. For example, 9:00 A.M. on a Monday morning is not the best time to initially test the hot-swappable capability in your server's drive array.

You can implement nondestructive testing in a number of ways. The most obvious is to use alternative hardware to simulate your disaster. For example, you can take another server that is identical to your production server and try to restore your backups to this alternative system.

Not everyone has the luxury of redundant components at their disposal to test their recovery plans. If you're not one of the lucky ones, try to plan your testing around plant shutdowns or extended holidays. Although the last thing anyone wants to do is to spend a long weekend simulating network outages, it is far preferable to experiencing an actual disaster. There is nothing worse than a server outage at 9:00 on a workday morning that has been caused by a part that must be special ordered. Simulating your disasters ahead of time helps to ensure that you will be capable of a full recovery when an actual disaster does occur.

Document Your Procedures

The only thing worse than spending a long weekend simulating network outages is spending a long weekend simulating network outages and writing documentation. As networking staff levels continue to drop, it is hard enough to keep up with the day-to-day firefighting, let alone simulate additional disasters and document your findings. We all like to think that we have minds like a steel trap and will remember every last detail when an actual disaster does occur.

The reality is that the stress of trying to restore a lost service or deleted information can make the best of us a little sloppy. It is far easier to document the process when you can take your time and think things through with a clear head. When you are under pressure, it is far too easy to try a shortcut to get things done more quickly—only to find that your shortcut has made matters worse. Documenting the process when you are not under the gun to restore service allows you to write a clear set of instructions.

VERITAS Storage Replicator

VSR (Veritas Storage Replicator) is designed to replicate data between Windows NT/2000 systems in a network, providing data redundancy in the case of the catastrophic failure of one or more systems. VSR uses the concept of a *source* server and a *target* server. A source server is simply a system on which the master copy of the data is stored. A target server stores the replicated changes made to the original file stored on the server. VSR is a complete management system that lets you define one or more source servers, one or more target servers, the files you want to replicate, and a replication schedule.

All replication happens under the heading of a *Job*. Even when a Job is activated, the source server is not considered protected until all files have been replicated to at least one target server—something that takes place in an initial synchronization (which is nothing more than a full copy of all data to be protected). Once this first step is finished, only changes to the source files are replicated, which saves bandwidth and time.

VSR is made up of several components:

RMS (Replication Management Server)   The RMS coordinates the replication process according to settings defined at the Console. As a result, it stores all the configuration data and starts and stops the replication process. The RMS also stores the logs, alerts, and histories for all Jobs. There is only one RMS per Replication Neighborhood (explained later in this section).

RSA (Replication Service Agent)   Required for a system that is either a source or a target for replication. You can install the software manually or have the Console "push" it out to the system across the network.

Console   The primary administrative utility of VSR, the Console is used to set replication servers (both source and target) as well as scheduling and other replication settings.

Status Applet   This small program displays replication status. This allows you to keep track of your system without displaying the entire Console

srTool   This is a command line tool that you can use instead of the GUI Console.

VSR uses the concept of a *Replication Neighborhood*. A Replication Neighborhood is simply one or more systems with an RMS, one or more RSAs, and a Console. None of the components have to be on the same machine, but an RSA is required for any machine that will be either a source or a target server.

VSR Planning

Before installing VSR, you need to consider the following items:

◆   What data needs to be replicated

◆   How often the data needs to be replicated

◆   How much bandwidth is available for replication (small data changes increase total bandwidth)

◆   How much space will be required on target servers

◆   What will the replication model entail (one-to-one, one-to-many, or a many-to-one)

◆   Which server will be the RMS

The decision that actually impacts the VSR installation is which replication model you implement. Each model has limitations and benefits.

ONE-TO-ONE

Also known as standard replication, this model is the simplest. You define a single source server, along with which volumes, directories, and files are to be replicated. You assign a single target server to the source server and define a replication frequency. This model is most often used when a small organization has just one or two critical data servers and wants to use both servers to back up each other's data.

MANY-TO-ONE

Also called the centralization model, this model entails multiple source servers pushing all their replicated data to a single target. This model is used when the data will be copied to an off-line medium (such as an optical disk or tape). This model is common when an organization has multiple servers that store critical data, but needs only a single machine to back up to tape.

ONE-TO-MANY

Using the concept of a published Job, this model allows multiple targets to receive the data from one server. This model is seen when common data sets need to be shared by multiple servers, for example, in a business that has multiple locations. In each location a server can host a common customer database. Each night the corporate server takes the changes that occurred that day to the master customer database and pushes them out to each location.

After you decide which model works for your environment, as well as which machines will be the source, target, and RMS servers, you are ready to install VSR.

Installing VSR

VSR requires that you install the RMS component first. After you do so, you can use the Console to push the RSA software over the network to the machines that will be source and target servers. To install VSR, follow these steps:

1. Insert the CD-ROM, and choose Setup.exe.

2. Enter you name and company information to display the RMS Retrieval screen:

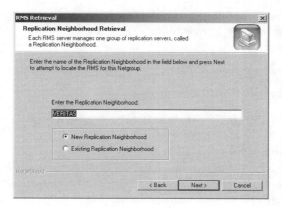

3. Select whether to create a new Replication Neighborhood or join an existing neighborhood. If you choose to create a new Replication Neighborhood, enter its name in the Enter the Replication Neighborhood box.

NOTE   Choosing the Existing Replication Neighborhood option forces the installation to search for a currently running RMS environment on your network. As a result, you might encounter a significant delay while your computer attempts to contact the RMS server for that neighborhood.

4. Click Next to open the Storage Replicator Setup screen:

5. If you are installing RMS on a system that will not be either a source or a target, you can choose to clear the Storage Replicator RSA check box. Otherwise, leave the default components selected. You can also change the destination folder for the software, as well as verify that you have sufficient disk space. Click Next.

6. In the next screen, specify whether you want to create a Program folder.

7. When prompted, enter a storage location for the VSR database.

8. Next you are prompted to supply a storage location for the VSR Journal files. We recommend storing the VSR Journal files on a separate disk or at least on a separate partition for fault tolerance.

9. You are then prompted to enter the VSR product serial number.

10. Confirm your installation settings.

11. Accept the license agreement, and you are prompted to restart your system.

Configuring VSR

After you restart the system, you can use the Console to configure your Replication Neighborhood, including adding and editing Jobs and servers, as well as installing RSA components on computers that will become source and/or target servers. Figure 11.4 shows the default view of the Console when you first start it.

You can also monitor the status of currently configured jobs and look through several online guides that present basic VSR concepts, as well as provide checklists and step-by-step instructions for configuring the various components.

FIGURE 11.4

The Storage Replicator Console

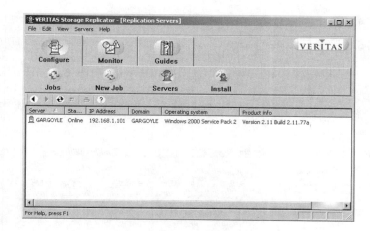

Before you configure anything, however, install at least one RSA on a system. Typically, if you are enabling only two servers in a one-to-one relationship, the server running RMS and the Console will be the target server, and the source server will host data of some type. To remotely install the RSA on your source server, follow these steps:

1. In the Storage Replicator Console, click the Configure tab.

2. Click the Install icon to start a wizard that walks you through installing RSA.

3. The wizard first prompts you for a username, password, and domain that will allow you to remotely connect and install the software on the source server, as shown in Figure 11.5. If you want to use the same account as the one you are currently using on the RMS server, leave these settings blank.

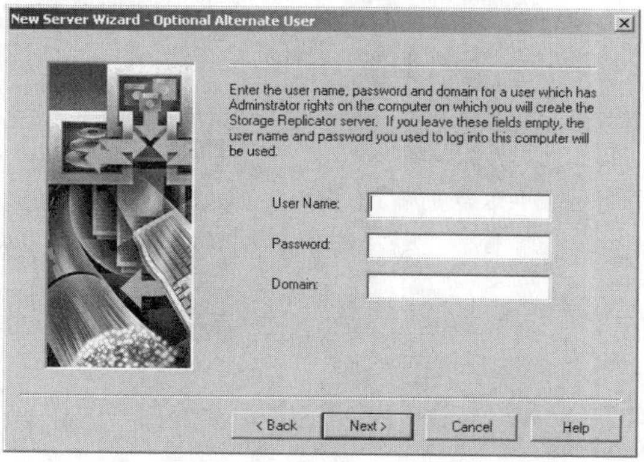

FIGURE 11.5

The Optional Alternate User screen

4. Click Next.

5. The next screen prompts you to select the destination computer. All available workgroups are displayed, along with all the known computers in those workgroups. When you select a computer in a workgroup, its icon turns green if you are authorized to access it, as shown in Figure 11.6. If not, the icon turns red. You can optionally choose to filter out all but those machines currently running RSA and those that are candidates for upgrading their RSA software to the latest version.

FIGURE 11.6

The Select the Destination Computer screen

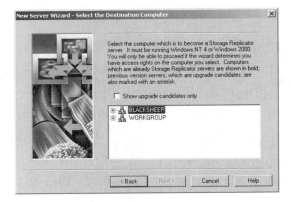

6. Click Next to open the Select the Destination Path screen:

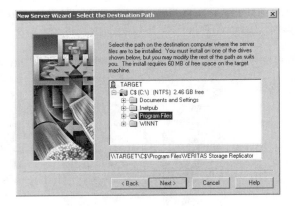

After you select the destination computer, you are prompted for the destination path where the RSA software will be installed, along with an indication of file system type and remaining free space, as shown in the previous graphic. The default location is the Program Files folder.

7. Click Next to open the Enter Serial Number screen:

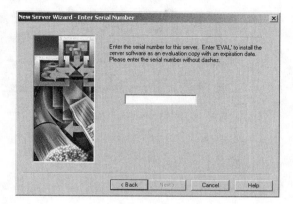

8. Enter the serial number for the source server, and click Next to open the Choose Whether Or Not To Reboot screen:

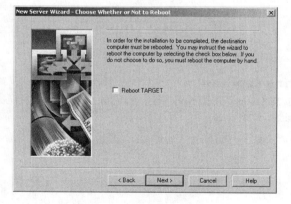

NOTE *You must reboot the system to activate the RSA software.*

9. Click the Reboot TARGET check box, and click Next to display a screen that shows your configuration choices.

10. When you are satisfied that the settings are correct, click the Finish button. The Console will finish installing the software and reboot the destination machine (if you selected that option in the wizard).

Once the destination system has been rebooted, both your RMS system and the new server will display in the Console on the Configure tab when you click the Servers icon, as shown in Figure 11.7—assuming you kept the defaults and installed the RMA on the RMS system during the initial setup. You are now ready to configure replication.

FIGURE 11.7

The Configure tab
in the Console

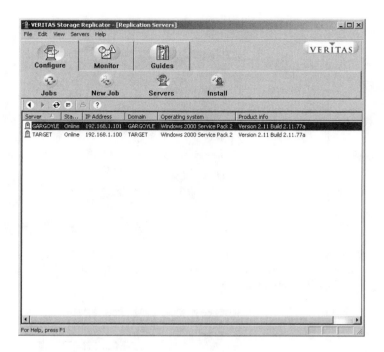

Configuring Replication

Once your RMS is installed, along with two (or more) RMAs, you are ready to configure a replication Job. Follow these steps:

1. In the Console, click the Configure tab, and then click the New Job icon to start the New Job Wizard:

2. In the Job Type screen, select a job type. We're choosing Standard in these steps. Click Next to open the Job Name screen:

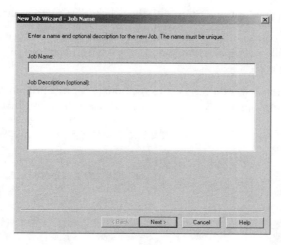

3. Enter the job name and a description, and then click Next to open the Replication Options screen:

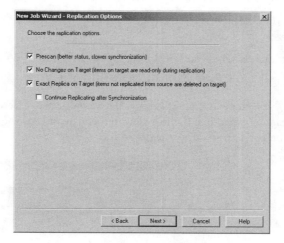

Notice that all but the last option are selected by default. The options are as follows:

Prescan This option enables progress bars and time estimates of replication jobs by calculating the amount of data to be replicated.

No Changes On Target This setting enables all replication changes to be made to a temporary file on the target, until the replication is successful. This ensures data integrity on the target server.

Exact Replica On Target This option deletes files on the target that are no longer on the source.

Continue Replicating After Synchronization   This option can be considered "just in time" replication. All changes are replicated to the target as they are made on the source.

4. Select a replication option, and then click Next to open the next screen of the wizard.

5. You are prompted to select the replication pairs—in other words, the source and target servers that will participate in this job. Click the Add Pair button to open the Add A Replication Pair dialog box.

6. Click the Select button next to the Source Server option to open the Replication Servers Select A Source Server dialog box, and select the server that will be your source:

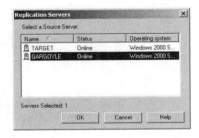

7. Click OK to return to the Add A Replication Pair dialog box.

8. Click the Select button next to the Target Server option to open the Replication Servers Select A Target Server dialog box.

9. Select a target server, and then click OK to return to the Add a Replication Pair dialog box.

10. Click OK to return to the Replication Pairs dialog box.

11. Click Next to open the Replication Rules dialog box. Select the areas of the file system to replicate by expanding the tree view in the main area of the dialog box, and then click the Add Rule button to open the Rule dialog box:

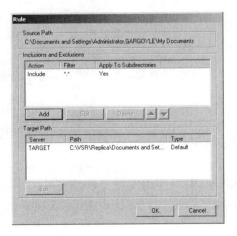

In this example, we selected the My Documents folder of the Administrator account by navigating the directory tree from the server level down to the C drive, through the Documents and Settings folder, and into the Administrator account.

12. To add an inclusion rule, click the Add button in the Inclusions And Exclusions section to open the Inclusion/Exclusion dialog box.

13. Accept the default settings that specify the rule will include all files and subdirectories under this directory, and click OK to return to the Rule dialog box.

14. Click OK to return to the Replication Rules dialog box, which now paints your My Documents folder with a blue circle.

15. Click Next to open the Replication Schedule dialog box:

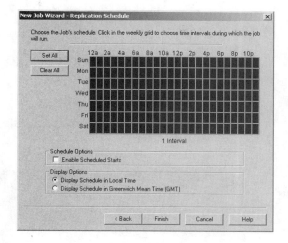

16. You can select the day and the intervals (in 1-hour increments) by dragging your mouse across the grid while holding down the left mouse button. In addition, you can specify replication start points by clicking the Entire Scheduled Starts check box, and you can specify whether the time is displayed in local or GMT by selecting the appropriate radio button. If you have servers in multiple time zones, consider displaying the time in GMT to avoid confusion for future administration and in your replication log files.

17. Click Finish.

RMS immediately begins synchronizing the data between your source server and your target server, as shown in Figure 11.8.

When the synchronization finishes, the Monitor tab in the Console changes to reflect that all is well and that both systems are now operational but idle, as shown in Figure 11.9.

FIGURE 11.8

A new job synchro-
nization in progress

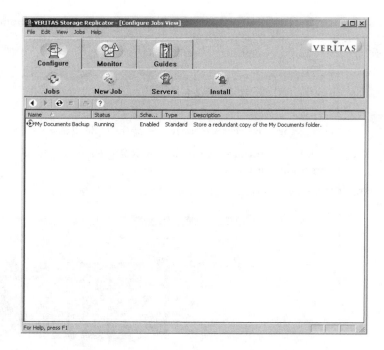

FIGURE 11.9

A normal status
window in the
Monitor tab

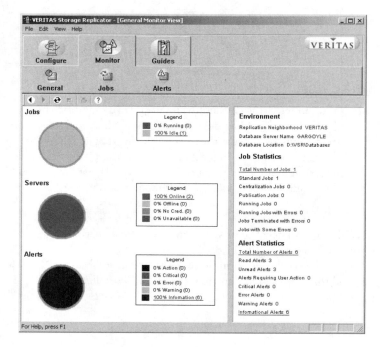

Compare the screen in Figure 11.9 with that in Figure 11.10, in which the source server has been disconnected from the network. Notice that the circle representing all the source and target servers (which, in our example, is only two) indicates that only 50 percent of the servers are active.

FIGURE 11.10

The status window reflecting a lost source server

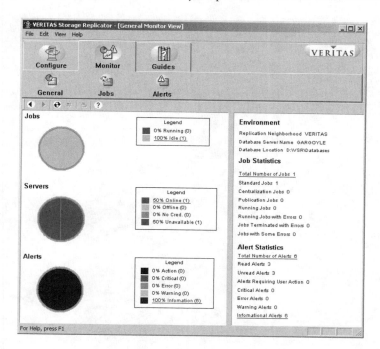

Although the source server can't be reached, the data is still available on the target and can be recovered to a new source server, or all clients can be reconfigured to point to the target server as their new source.

As a fundamental strategy for data duplication, VSR provides a quick and simple interface for implementing multiple redundant strategies that should fit most basic file server needs. As this example shows, the most difficult part of implementing a redundant file system is deciding which system to back up, which systems will hold the redundant data, and how your replication jobs should be scheduled. Keep in mind that network bandwidth will play a significant part in your replication plan, along with disk space, of course.

Summary

In this chapter, you saw what disaster prevention and disaster recovery options are available for protecting your network. We examined our network to eliminate any single point of failure, including network-based disasters, server-based disasters, and natural disasters. We also discussed the importance of testing and documenting your disaster recovery procedures. Finally, we took a look at a product designed to provide redundant-server fault tolerance in an NT/Windows 2000 server environment.

Chapter 12

The Wide World of Windows

MICROSOFT OPERATING SYSTEMS are ubiquitous, but in this chapter we'll only look at the NT-based family, from NT 4 through Windows 2000, and a little at the brand-new .NET line.

Featured in this chapter:

◆ NT overview and Active Directory

◆ The domain structure and user accounts

◆ File system, logging, and security patches

◆ Available IP services

◆ Packet filtering with Windows NT

◆ Securing DCOM

◆ Ports used by Windows services

◆ Additional Registry key changes

◆ Windows .NET

NT Overview

The core operating system of NT Server is 32-bit. Although this creates some backward compatibility problems with 16-bit Windows applications, it helps to ensure that the operating system kernel remains stable. NT is both multitasking and multithreaded, which helps prevent any single process from monopolizing all available CPU time.

NT Server uses the same Win32 application programming interface as NT Workstation, Windows 95, and Windows 98. This ensures a familiar programming environment that, in theory, allows a programmer to write a more stable application. For example, a programmer who is familiar with writing Windows desktop applications will find programming for NT Server similar because both use the Win32 interface. This technology is in contrast to the NetWare Loadable Module (NLM) technology used by a NetWare server. A programmer writing code for a NetWare server must be specifically aware of the NLM programming environment.

Because the server uses the same Win32 interface as a Windows workstations, most desktop applications are supported. This can be a real money saver for small environments that cannot afford to dedicate a system to server activities. Unlike NetWare, which requires you to dedicate a system as a server, NT Server can perform double duty as a user workstation. Server support for Win32 can also be a real time-saver for the system administrator. Most of the tools that you are used to running from a desktop machine will run from the server.

NOTE   *Unfortunately, NT is missing the remote control features of NetWare's Rconsole or Unix's Telnet. (A Telnet server is included with Windows 2000 Server.) Although tools are available from Microsoft's website and from its resource kits to manage some server functions remotely, you cannot directly add or remove protocols, launch applications, or access the NT Server Desktop from a remote workstation. Third-party software is required to provide this functionality.*

Out of the box, NT Server provides support for a maximum of four processors. With hardware support, you can increase this number to 32. The benefit of additional processors is that more CPU time can be made available to applications running on the server.

NT uses a database known as the *Registry* to save most of the system's configuration information. This information can concern user accounts, services, or even system device drivers. Related information is said to be stored under the same hive. For example, the hive `HKEY_USERS` stores information about user accounts. Fields within a hive that hold configuration values are known as *keys*.

The benefit of the Registry is that information is stored in a central location, simplifying the process of finding and changing information. Although you can change most of NT's settings through the graphical interface, you must manually change many settings in the Registry. The tool you use to view and change Registry information is known as `regedt32`.

WARNING   *Because the Registry contains a majority of the system's configuration information, be extremely careful when making changes. Never edit the Registry without first making a backup copy and creating an emergency recovery disk, and never make changes without first understanding the effects of the change.*

VIRTUAL MEMORY

NT Server supports memory isolation of all applications running on the system. It also supports the use of *virtual memory*. Virtual memory allows the server to utilize more memory space than is physically installed in the system. The benefit is that applications are free to use more memory to add features. The drawback is that virtual memory is stored to disk, which has a slower access time than physical memory by a factor of 100.

You take a performance hit once you start using a lot of virtual memory. It is true that you can follow Microsoft's minimum memory recommendations by installing 32MB of RAM in a server offering basic file, print, HTTP (Hypertext Transfer Protocol), WINS (Windows Internet Naming Service), and DHCP (Dynamic Host Configuration Protocol) services. You might even get the system to boot up and function. Performance on this system would be absolutely dismal, however. For a system with this or a similar configuration, plan to install at least 96MB–128MB of physical memory.

Active Directory

Although NT 4 provided a flat, nonextensible directory service, Active Directory (AD) provides a flexible, hierarchical, and expandable directory service. Active Directory is the directory service in Windows 2000. It's responsibility is to store information about each object within the network, enabling users to locate and manage printers, shared folders, files, and other objects throughout the organization. It facilitates a consistent way to name, describe, locate, access, manage, and secure information about distributed resources in an enterprise environment.

The information for each object is held in the AD database, which is the basis of the domain. Domains are named to correlate with DNS names, and when collected in a hierarchy, domain names make up a tree. Multiple trees can be collected into a hierarchical structure known as a forest. Multiple trees (with distinct naming structures) can belong to the same forest, as long as all trees share the schema, or database structure, of the forest as a whole. The AD database is automatically replicated to each domain controller within a domain. (For more information about domains, see the next section, "The Domain Structure.")

Because it is closely integrated with the operating system, AD is the central authority for network security. It works with the operating system to verify a user's identity and permissions, controlling logon and access to network resources regardless of the user's physical location. It also enforces the user's group policy settings, which is discussed in more detail later in this chapter.

There is only one AD database per forest. Tools are provided that enhance enterprise level administration. You'll find these tools on the Windows 2000 Server or Advanced Server CD-ROM, and you can install them on any computer running Windows 2000 (including Professional). To install the Active Directory Management tools and the Windows 2000 Administration Tools, follow these steps:

1. Open the I386 folder on the appropriate Windows 2000 Server CD-ROM. The latest version of the Windows 2000 Administration Tools is on the latest Windows 2000 Service Pack CD-ROM.

2. Double-click the `Adminpak.msi` file.

3. Click Next, and then click Finish.

NOTE *For more information, see Microsoft's Knowledge Base article Q308196 at* `http://support` `.microsoft.com/default.aspx?scid=kb;en-us;Q308196.`

The following are additional features of AD:

DNS integration All AD services use DNS (Domain Name System) to advertise, locate, and connect to all network services. As a result, DNS is a required service of AD and works to replace NetBIOS (Network Basic Input Output System) names for service naming and locating.

Extensible schema (or structure) Administrators or applications can add new classes of objects and new attributes of existing classes. You most often do this when adding the Exchange groupware server to an AD domain.

Object-based policies Also known as Group Policies, these settings determine user access to resources and how these resources can be used.

Scalability   AD uses one or more domains, each with one or more domain controllers. You can combine multiple domains into a domain tree, and you can combine multiple domain trees into a forest. A single domain network is still a single tree and single forest.

Multimaster replication   All domain controllers are created equal in the sense that a change to the directory can occur on any domain controller, which in turn updates all the other domain controllers. If one domain controller fails, the others can take over its load.

Centralized security   AD authorizes each user's access to the network. In addition, you can define access control not only on each object in the directory, but also on each property of each object.

Interoperability   LDAP (Lightweight Directory Access Protocol) allows AD to share object information with applications and other directory services.

Delegation of authority   The Delegation of Authority Wizard provides an easy interface that you can use to assign administrative permissions of varying degrees to your network. Instead of adding additional users to the Domain Admins group, you can assign someone the ability to perform only a specific task, or you can grant them full control over an entire Organizational Unit (discussed later in this chapter).

So how does Active Directory fit in with our goal of providing higher network security? Essentially, Active Directory centralizes all security controls and settings, as follows:

Password management   Users log in to the network with a single username and password and are provided an access token based on their assigned permissions. In addition, you can configure password complexity settings to ensure that secure, frequently changing passwords are being used.

Desktop functionality   Administrators can lock down the desktop configurations on their network and prevent access to things that might potentially endanger their system (such as software installations and Registry editing).

Internet protocols   Support for Internet protocols and authentication methods are built in to the operating system, providing secure standards without additional configuration or installation. These protocols include Kerberos authentication (the default among Windows 2000 machines), Secure Sockets Layer (SSL), Lightweight Directory Access Protocol (LDAP), and Public Key Infrastructure (PKI).

Object-level security   Every object held in AD contains an access control list (ACL) that can be configured to limit access based on your network's security model.

Although Microsoft has provided the necessary Microsoft Management Console (MMC) snap-in tools (small plug-in components that provide the ability to manage a specific element of Windows 2000 through a single utility) to secure your AD, it has also made available several additional general Windows security tools worth mentioning:

Windows Update   Microsoft's support website that contains critical and recommended software updates. It is especially good at catching Internet browser vulnerabilities and is recommended if your organization maintains an Internet presence. You can find Windows update at `http://windowsupdate.microsoft.com`.

Microsoft Baseline Security Analyzer   This tool, which replaced the Microsoft Personal Security Advisor, could be called a "supersized" version of HFNetChk. You can use it to analyze and identify security misconfigurations on any NT, 2000, or XP machine. In addition to checking for missing security patches and hotfixes, it also investigates the current password policies, scans servers running IIS (Internet Information Services) and SQL for common security misconfigurations, and checks the security zone settings in Microsoft Office, Outlook, and Internet Explorer. Find the BSA at `http://support.microsoft.com/default.aspx?scid=KB;EN-US;Q320454&`.

Microsoft Security Bulletin   This is a repository for the latest security news , patches, and hotfixes. You can also subscribe to the Microsoft Security Notification Service, which will send you an e-mail message as new security patches and dangers are announced. You can subscribe to the Microsoft Security Bulletin at `http://register.microsoft.com/regsys/pic.asp`.

Microsoft Network Security Hotfix Checker   This is a free, downloadable command-line tool from Microsoft that identifies security patches/hotfixes that are missing from your Windows NT, 2000, and XP computers (including patches for IIS, SQL Server, and Internet Explorer). (See the Microsoft Knowledge Base article Q305385 at `http://support.microsoft.com/default.aspx?scid=kb;en-us;Q305385` for more information.)

Qfecheck.exe   This is a free, downloadable command-line tool from Microsoft that tracks and verifies existing patch/hotfix installations (including XP systems) to ensure that they are properly applied/installed. You can use this tool to track patch installations across a network when you're concerned about consistency in your machines. See Microsoft Knowledge Base article Q282784 at `http://support.microsoft.com/default.aspx?scid=kb;en-us;Q282784`for more information.

Qchain   This is a free, downloadable utility from Microsoft that helps you apply multiple hotfixes simultaneously. Typically hotfixes require a system reboot after each installation. You can find Qchain at `http://support.microsoft.com/default.aspx?scid=KB;EN-US;Q296861&`.

Microsoft also distributes a CD containing white papers on security "best practices," service packs, and hotfixes. You can find this information at `http://www.microsoft.com/security/mstpp.asp`.

You can also use several third-party tools in conjunction with AD for ease of administration. The following list is in no way comprehensive, nor is it an endorsement of any particular product. It's just a sampling of what you can find out there. You will need to research each product and assess it against the needs of your network environment to determine which tool is right for you.

NetIQ Security Analyzer   This product gives you the opportunity to offload the constant researching and keep you up-to-date on the latest security threats and tests. It has a built-in auto sync process that keeps your server up-to-date with the most recent tests for security holes. You can fin the NetIQ Security Analyzer at `http://www.netiq.com/products/sa/default.asp`.

NetIQ Security Manager   This complementary product provides an advanced, central security console for real-time security event monitoring and automated response, host-based intrusion detection, event log consolidation, and security configuration management. You can fin the NetIQ Security Manager at `http://www.netiq.com/products/sm/default.asp`.

Sunbelt Software's Retina   This product is a vulnerability scanner (like a home security consultant who looks for points of entry *before* a burglar comes) that can fix/repair many of the vulnerabilities it finds. You can find Retina at `http://www.sunbelt-software.com/product.cfm?id=690`.

The Domain Structure

In a Windows 2000 environment, a domain consists of workstations, servers, individual users, groups, and other AD objects that are logically organized within a single security boundary. Each object within that boundary is subject to the domain level Group Policy, set by an administrator with the appropriate permissions, dictating a set of rules and policies that affect these objects. Policies can range from the length of a user's password to the forced installation of a virus protection software package on each computer.

Windows 2000 also incorporates the use of *Organizational Units*, or OUs, within a domain. Organizational Units allow administrators to further segregate objects within AD for the purpose of implementing different levels of Group Policy (for example, a forced Desktop configuration for a group of users) or for the purpose of delegating administrative authority.

By organizing users, computers, and other AD resources into logical groups (OUs), an administrator can delegate all or part of their administrative authority to another user or a group of users. For example, an administrator can grant the ability to perform simple, everyday tasks (such as making a name change on a user's account) for a particular OU to Ronnie, without giving her the power to do anything else. Or an administrator can give Keith full administrative authority over all objects in the OU without having to add him to the Domain Admins group (which would grant him power over other areas of the network that the administrator doesn't want him to access). Basically, OUs allow all objects in a network to be organized in a hierarchical structure, giving administrators far more flexibility in how objects are managed.

Storing Domain Information

Each domain controller in an AD environment contains a writable copy of the domain database. This multiple-master setup is a radical change from NT 4, which held all domain information in a flat file called the Security Accounts Manager (SAM). Replication between domain controllers occurs by default every five minutes and includes any changes to the domain partition.

Some domain controllers also act as Global Catalog Servers. The Global Catalog contains a listing of every object in the AD forest, allowing users to search for objects (such as e-mail addresses of their fellow employees or shared printers) across the enterprise. To maintain a manageable size, the global catalog only contains a small subset of the attributes associated with each object.

In other words, you might be able to search for the name, department, and e-mail address of anyone in the company, but additional attributes (such as to whom that employee reports, their home address, or their hire-date anniversary) are kept within the domain of that person's AD user object.

Each domain controller throughout the forest also holds a copy of the schema partition. The *schema partition* defines the rules for all objects and attributes created in the forest. For example, it dictates that a user object can have several attributes such as first name, last name, department, title, and so on, but does not contain an attribute (at least by default) named "credit card number."

Unlike Windows NT, a Windows 2000 server does not have to be installed as a domain controller. It can be promoted and demoted back to a member server at any time using the dcpromo.exe application located on your server operating system disk.

Domain Trusts

Trusts are also simplified in Windows 2000. Whereas in an NT environment, you had to create trusts between each domain in an enterprise network, all domains within an AD forest are automatically configured with two-way transitive trusts. Microsoft created an automatic two-way highway between all domains in a single forest. However, this does not imply that the security boundary between domains has been compromised. Although the highway still exists, no permissions pass between domains that are not specifically granted.

Let's say for the sake of argument that Austin has a high-end color printer in her domain that a group of vice-presidents in Hope's domain would like to use. Hope creates a global group that includes the appropriate users, and Austin adds that global group to her printer's access control list and grants the permission to print. The trust portion of this transaction exists in the power that Hope has over the members of that global group. Though she has no authority to change the permission on the printer, she can at any time change the membership of the global group should the organization restructure. Austin must trust that she will not abuse that privilege.

In an NT environment, you must manually create trusts to allow access between domains. You can configure trusts to be unidirectional (one domain trusts another) or bidirectional (each domains trusts the other equally). A unidirectional trust is referred to as a *one-way trust* and a bidirectional trust is referred to as a *two-way trust*.

User Accounts

In an AD network, user accounts are managed with the AD Users and Computers utility, which you can install on any workstation in the enterprise. You use this tool to add and remove users, assign groups, and create an appropriate OU structure for organization, administration, and delegation of objects within your domain. You manage all user access attributes through this interface except for file, directory, and share permissions. You set file system permissions through Windows Explorer.

In addition to domain accounts, non-domain controllers in a Windows 2000 network can also have local accounts. You create local accounts to assign permissions to non-domain users. You can grant someone access to your workstation and the applications or resources on it, but they won't have any access to network resources because they are not logged in to the domain.

You create local user accounts in Windows 2000 non-domain controllers using the Computer Management administrative snap-in.

Working with SIDs

A *Security Identifier*, or SID, is a unique identification number that is assigned to every user and group. The format of a SID is as follows:

```
S-Revision Level-Identifier Authority-Subauthority
```

The initial *S* identifies this number as a SID. For a given domain, all values are identical for every user and group, except for the subauthority. The subauthority provides a unique number to distinguish between users and groups. A number of subauthority numbers are referred to as *well-known SIDs* because the subauthority number is consistent in every NT domain. For example, the Administrator account always has a subauthority value of 500. An attacker can use this information to help target certain accounts for attack.

NOTE *The Microsoft Knowledge Base article Q163846 at* `http://support.microsoft.com/default` `.aspx?scid=kb;en-us;Q163846` *lists all well-known SID numbers, along with their associated accounts.*

Microsoft, as well as many security consultants, recommends that you rename the NT Administrator account. The logic is that if an attacker does not know the logon name being used by the administrator, the attacker will not be able to compromise this account. A set of utilities written by Evgenii Rudnyi, however, shows just how easy it can be to circumvent this attempt at security through obscurity.

Figure 12.1 shows Rudnyi's two utilities in use. The first, `user2sid`, allows you to input a user or group name and produce the SID for this account. As mentioned, the SID is identical for every account except for the subauthority key. By using the second utility, `sid2user`, we can substitute the well known SID number we want to look up (such as 500 for the Administrator account). As shown in Figure 12.1, the Administrator account has been renamed to `Admin_renamed`. Through this quick check, we now know which account to target.

FIGURE 12.1

The user2sid and sid2user utilities

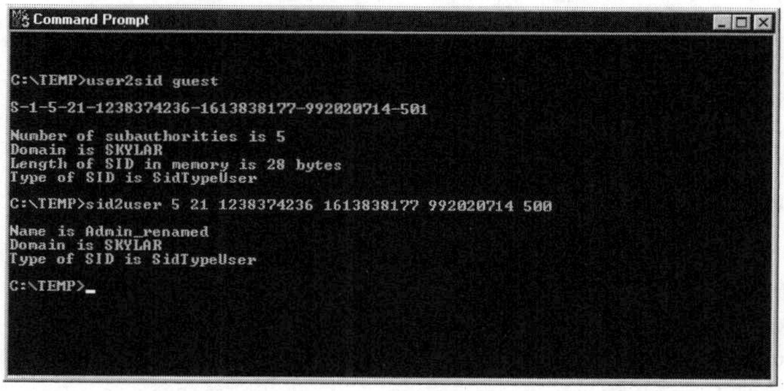

NOTE *You can download Rudnyi's SID utilities from* `http://www.ntbugtraq.com`.

NOTE *Renaming the Administrator account provides little help in protecting a system. A better tactic is to ensure that the Administrator account is using a strong password and that all failed logon attempts are logged.*

The Security Account Manager in Windows NT

The *Security Account Manager (SAM)* is the database that stores all user account information for an NT network. This information includes each user's logon name, SID, and an encrypted version of each user's password. The SAM is used by the Local Security Authority (LSA), which is responsible for managing system security. The LSA interfaces with the user and the SAM in order to identify what level of access should be granted.

The SAM is simply a part of the registry stored in a file that is located in the `\WinNT\system32\` `config` directory. Since the operating system always has this file open, users cannot access it. The SAM file can be located in a number of other places, however, and you need to monitor these locations carefully:

`\WinNT\repair`

This directory contains a backup version of the SAM file stored in compressed format. At a minimum, it contains entries for the Administrator and Guest accounts.

Emergency repair disks   When you create an emergency repair disk, a copy of the SAM is saved to the floppy.

Backup tape   An NT-aware backup program can save the SAM file.

If an attacker can get access to the SAM file from one of these three places, they may be able to compromise the system.

NOTE   *In Chapter 14, we will look at how a brute force attack can be launched against the SAM file to recover account passwords.*

Configuring Group Policies for Windows 2000

Group Policy allows you to stipulate users' environments only once and to rely on the operating system to enforce them thereafter. Group Policy objects are not profiles. A profile is a user environment setting that a user can change, such as Desktop settings, Registry settings in the NTUser.dat files, the Profiles folder, the My Documents folder, or the Favorites folder. You, as the administrator, manage and maintain Group Policy by using an MMC-hosted administrative tool used to set policy on groups of users and computers.

Group Policy is represented by one or more Group Policy objects, which are discrete, named collections of policy settings. These objects are stored in AD and take effect when they are linked to other AD objects such as sites, domains, and Organizational Units.

NOTE   *The Microsoft Management Console is a program that acts as an administrative template. Actual functionality is provided through a series of plug-ins, while the MMC provides a consistent "look and feel."*

By default, Group Policy is inherited from site, to domain, and finally to the Organizational Unit level. The order and level in which you apply Group Policy objects (by linking them to their targets) determines the Group Policy settings that a user or computer actually receives. Furthermore, you can block policy at the AD site, domain, or Organizational Unit level; or you can enforce policy on a per Group Policy object basis. You do so by linking the Group Policy object to its target and then setting the link to No Override.

By default, Group Policy affects all computers and users in the site, domain, or Organizational Unit, and does not affect any other objects in that site, domain, or Organizational Unit. In particular, Group Policy does not affect security groups.

Instead, you use security groups to filter Group Policy, that is, to alter its scope. You do so by adjusting the Apply Group Policy and the Read permissions on the Group Policy object for the relevant security groups, as explained later in this chapter.

Windows 2000 Group Policy settings have the following characteristics:

◆   They can be associated with sites, domains, and Organizational Units.

◆   They affect all users and computers in the site, domain, or Organizational Unit.

◆   They can be further controlled by user or computer membership in security groups.

◆   They are secure. Only an administrator can change the settings.

◆   They are removed and rewritten whenever policy changes.

◆   They can be used for finely tuned desktop control and to enhance the user's computing environment.

NOTE   *Windows NT 4 System Policy settings in the Registry sometimes persist past their useful life because these settings remain in effect until they are explicitly changed. Windows 2000 Group Policy settings do not persist past their useful life because Windows writes them to the following secure Registry locations, and removes them when a Group Policy object no longer applies:* HKEY_LOCAL_MACHINE\Software\Policies *and* HKEY_LOCAL_MACHINE\Software\ Microsoft\Windows\CurrentVersion\Policies.

SYSTEM POLICY SETTINGS IN WINDOWS NT

You specify the System Policy settings in Windows NT using the System Policy Editor (Poledit.exe). System Policy settings have the following characteristics:

◆   They are applied to sites, domains, and Organizational Units.

◆   They can be further controlled by user membership in security groups.

◆   They are not secure. A user can change them with the Registry Editor (Regedit.exe).

◆   They persist in users' profiles, sometimes beyond their useful lives. After you set a Registry setting using Windows NT 4 System Policy, the setting persists until the specified policy setting is reversed or the user edits the Registry.

◆   They are limited to administratively mandated desktop behavior based on Registry settings.

Windows NT 4 Registry settings can be problematic when a user's security group membership changes. You might need to manually update or remove the Registry settings.

The root node of the Group Policy snap-in displays as the name of the Group Policy object and the domain in which it is stored, in the following format:

```
<Group Policy object name> [<server name>] Policy
```

For example:

```
Default Domain Policy [MSMSRV01.Reskit.com] Policy
```

The next level of the namespace has two nodes: Computer Configuration and User Configuration. These are the parent folders that you use to configure specific desktop environments and to enforce Group Policy on groups of computers and users, respectively, on the network.

COMPUTER CONFIGURATION

Computer configuration includes all computer-related policy settings that specify operating system behavior, desktop behavior, security settings, computer startup and shutdown scripts, computer-assigned application options, and application settings. Computer-related Group Policy is applied when the operating system initializes and during the periodic refresh cycle (explained later in this chapter). In general, computer policy takes precedence over conflicting user policy. Figure 12.2 shows the Group Policy snap-in console Computer Configuration.

FIGURE 12.2

The Group Policy snap-in console showing Computer Configuration options

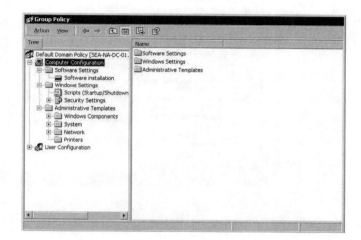

USER CONFIGURATION

The User Configuration category (or node) includes all policies that can be applied to a given user, as shown in Figure 12.3. These policies cover areas (or subnodes) of diverse topics, including how the Desktop works, the function of the operating system, how applications are provided to the user, and even folder redirection. User policies are applied when a user logs on and are also periodically "refreshed"—updated from an AD server.

Some computers require specific and strict configurations regardless of the user that is working on the system. Augmenting or even replacing User Configuration settings with Computer Configuration settings allows for a more secure Desktop environment in which the computer in question is used in a highly public area (such as a school or a kiosk). Microsoft refers to this process as policy "loopback."

The following are the main sub (or child) nodes under each major (or parent) node:

Software Settings   Basically a placeholder for third-party software vendors to include their own extensions. This allows Group Policy to be a central point of control no matter who created the software that is included on the system.

Windows Settings   Operating system extensions that are defined by Microsoft.

Administrative Templates   Collections of Registry-based settings that can be stored separately in files ending in the .adm extension and that can be exported and imported with the Group

Policy snap-in. By right-clicking the Administrative Templates node, you can further select the Add/Remove Templates option. This powerful feature allows administrators in different organizations to share customized Registry settings.

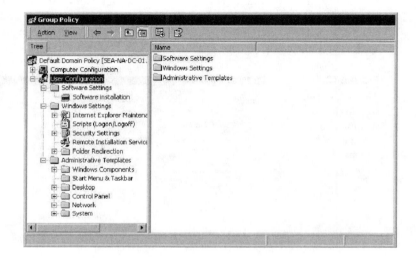

FIGURE 12.3

The Group Policy snap-in console showing User Configuration options

GROUP POLICY EXTENSIONS

Although both User and Computer parent nodes share common extensions and child nodes, the nodes are context-sensitive. In other words, they present different options for each parent node. The following are the default Windows 2000 extensions.

Administrative Templates   As mentioned, these settings (more than 450 by default) control the workings of the Desktop, applications, and the operating system itself. You can import additional settings from the `.adm` files. Although these files can include any Registry setting, , additional keys should be located only in the `HKEY_LOCAL_MACHINE\Software\Policies` or `HKEY_LOCAL_MACHINE\Software\Microsoft\Windows\CurrentVersion\Policies` tree of the Registry in order to take advantage of automatic Registry deletion.

Security Settings   You can define general security settings for the local computer, the domain in which a computer resides, or the entire network.

Software Installation   The backbone of software management in Windows 2000, this child node is used to assign or publish applications to users or to assign software to computers.

Scripts   You use scripts to automate tasks that are to be performed when a computer starts or shuts down or when users log on or log off. Supported scripting languages include VBScript, JavaScript, Perl, and `.bat/.cmd` DOS files.

Remote Installation Services (RIS)   You use RIS to control which options are presented to a user who is installing a system through RIS. RIS allows a computer with a PXE-enabled NIC (network interface card) or network boot floppy to boot a minimal menu-based operating system. (PXE stands for Pre-Boot Execution Environment.) From the menu, the user can select from among various operating system configurations that are then installed on the client system.

Internet Explorer Maintenance   Used for the centralized configuration of Internet Explorer, this child node allows administrators to specify the settings for Internet Explorer throughout the enterprise. Usually you specify updates, proxy settings, and security levels through this policy area.

Folder Redirection   This extension allows Windows 2000 special folders (My Documents, Application Data, Desktop, and Start Menu) to be redirected to another location on the network. Although this solution can dramatically increase logon time and network traffic, it is nice for users who are highly mobile within your organization.

ADMINISTRATIVE TEMPLATES

So what types of Administrative Templates come with Windows 2000? In reality, most of the options that were part of NT 4 system policies are included, along with some additions. Figure 12.4 illustrates a few of these settings.

FIGURE 12.4

The Administrative
Template settings

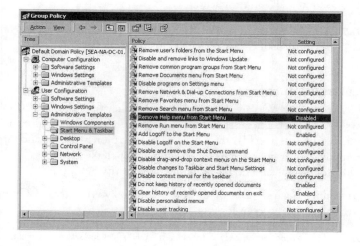

NOTE   *Similar to NT 4* `.adm` *files, Windows 2000* `.adm` *files have new features, such as Explain text. The Windows 2000 Resource Kit CD-ROM includes a file called* `GP.chm` *that covers the details about which policy settings are part of Windows 2000 Server.*

.ADM FILES

Although they contain only text, `.adm` files use parent and child categories to define not only what Registry settings can be modified as part of the policy, but also how these settings are displayed in the Group Policy snap-in. Entries in the file also indicate any value or range restrictions, possible default values, Registry key locations, and optional settings. The three .adm files that make up the default grouping of more than 450 settings are System.adm (the majority of the settings), Inetres.adm (for Internet Explorer), and Conf.adm (for Microsoft NetMeeting; not loaded by default).

NOTE   See the Explain tab of each Group Policy setting's Properties dialog box for more details on the policy settings within the .adm file.

REGISTRY SETTING PERSISTENCE

NT 4 Registry settings had to be explicitly overwritten to be changed. Under Windows 2000, though, settings are removed and possibly rewritten when a policy changes, which means that when a policy no longer applies to a Windows 2000 machine, the previously applied policy Registry settings are removed. This allows for a much cleaner and consistent security environment.

OTHER REGISTRY-BASED EXTENSIONS

RIS and Disk Quotas rely on settings stored in the Registry. Although RIS has a child node in the Group Policy snap-in, there is no client-side .dll, which is normal because RIS is usually used in an environment where a client machine has no native operating system and is using RIS to obtain one. Disk Quotas, on the other hand, does not have a node in the Group Policy snap-in, but does have a .dll (Dskquota.dll) on the client.

NOTE   RIS policies are stored in the Sysvol folder at the following location: Policies\{<GUID of GPO>}\User\Microsoft\RemoteInstall\oscfilter.ini.

SECURITY SETTINGS

Multiple security areas are defined in Group Policy for Windows 2000 Professional and Windows 2000 Server. These settings work with other security components such as the permissions applied to objects and files through Windows Explorer or User and Group assignments through the Computer Management or AD Users and Computers snap-ins.

The following child nodes are under the Security Settings:

Account Policies   One of the more commonly used areas of Group Policy, these settings control password, account lockout, and Kerberos policies.

NOTE   These settings are set only at the domain level. If they are set at the Organizational Unit level, they are ignored.

Local Policies   Another critical area from a security perspective, the settings located under this node establish audit policies that track successful resource usage or unsuccessful attempts at resource usage. Additionally, the policy that specifies which users or groups of users can access a specific computer are placed here, along with general access security settings (such as anonymous access to shared resources).

Event Log   These policies control how event logs (Application, Security, and System) are allowed to grow and are retained. A common technique for attackers is to flood the Security log with innocuous events in order to cover their pernicious activities.

Restricted Groups   This setting is used to make sure that only specific user or group accounts are allowed to be members of selected sensitive groups such as the Enterprise Administrators group. If additional users or groups are added to a restricted group, they are removed the next time the policy is applied (either through period refresh intervals or computer boot/user login). This is a nice feature to enable for high-risk groups that might be the target of an attack in which the cracker attempts to add a normal, but compromised, user account to a more powerful group. Defining the membership of your most sensitive groups means that an attacker has to work harder to maintain a higher level of access to your system. This work usually translates into activity that can be noted through an active policy of reviewing event logs for unallowed or unusual object access.

System Services   Service policies define the startup mode (Automatic, Manual, or Disabled) of system services, along with which accounts are allowed to start or stop a given service. Because good security focuses on disabling unused services, especially those that have had exploitable weaknesses in the past (such as the Internet Printing Protocol or the Task Scheduler), it can be a good idea to restrict activation of these potentially vulnerable services to those accounts that have administrative privileges.

Registry   This node can be a bit misleading. The purpose is not to specify which Registry settings are applied to the Registry of the destination machine, but rather to define the security settings (access control, auditing, and ownership) of the keys that already exist. This becomes an issue if third-party software makes unsecured Registry entries that could later be used by an attacker to bypass system security.

File System   Although you can set security settings through Windows Explorer, this method isn't efficient for applying consistent settings across multiple machines. This node allows settings to be applied to common file objects.

SECURITY TEMPLATES

Microsoft provides some default security templates that allow for incremental changes to system security. By using the Security Templates snap-in, you can customize these templates (stored in `%systemroot%\Security\Templates` by default) or create your own. Once modified or reviewed, the settings stored in these templates can be imported in the Security Settings node in the Group Policy snap-in. These settings are incremental on purpose; they allow you to make small, related changes so that you can verify that essential functionality remains after the settings have been applied. There is nothing more frustrating than trying to determine which specific security setting (among hundreds) is responsible for "breaking" your system!

WARNING   *Incremental security templates won't function correctly on Windows NT 4 machines that have been upgraded to Windows 2000.*

TEMPLATE CATEGORIES

The preconfigured incremental templates are categorized as Compatible, Secure, or High Secure.

Basic

Because of the increased security settings on Windows 2000 Registry keys, regular user accounts won't be able to run some older applications. Although you can make all local users members of the

Power Users group, that isn't considered an ideal solution from a security standpoint. The Compatible template (`Compatws.inf`) makes specific Registry key security changes so that regular users can in fact run older applications (on servers as well as workstations). However, remember that this is still considered the "lesser of two evils" approach; the system cannot be considered really secure.

Secure

Two templates (`Securews.inf` for Windows 2000 Professional and any non-domain controller Windows 2000 Server; `Securedc.inf` for domain controllers) include more restrictive settings for the Account Policy and Auditing nodes, as well as other Registry keys. In addition, both templates remove any and all members of the Power Users group.

High Secure

Like the Secure templates, two files (`Hisecws.inf` and `Hisecdc.inf`) are used to increase the security for Windows 2000 Professional, Server, and domain controllers. Areas that are affected include network traffic (forced to be encrypted and digitally signed by both parties in a session), the Power Users group (restricted to the same Registry/file system access level as regular users), and Terminal Services (TS users are restricted in the same fashion as the Power Users group and regular users).

MISCELLANEOUS

This template provides three files (`ocfiless.inf`, `ocfilesw.inf`, and `setup security.inf`) used to apply security settings that are specific to optional components such as Terminal Services and certificate services.

DEFAULT SETTINGS TEMPLATES

So what happens if you really make a mess of things? Or you upgraded a Windows NT 4 machine to Windows 2000, and you want to make sure security is consistent with your native Windows 2000 machines? Fortunately, Microsoft has provided some templates to take you back to a baseline security configuration:

`Basicwk.inf`　This template sets all security settings back to the default for Windows 2000 Professional, with the exception of User Rights and Group Membership.

`Basicsv.inf`　This template is just like `Basicwk.inf`, except for Windows 2000 Server (stand-alone or member server).

`Basicdc.inf`　This template is for domain controllers and has the same exceptions as the previous two templates.

SOFTWARE INSTALLATION

Software installation might seem an unusual system security topic, but in reality a well-formed security policy should define who is allowed to use specific applications—not just because of potential security holes, but to ensure that an organization is in compliance with licensing requirements. Additionally, centrally managing software allows for more consistent software updates and patches—something that directly applies to organization security in light of how many viruses have used weaknesses in Microsoft Outlook, Outlook Express, and Internet Explorer to shut down entire networks.

Applications can be either assigned or published. When applications are assigned, all users subject to the policy automatically have the application installed the next time they log on to a computer that doesn't already have the software installed, when they select the icon representing the application from the Start menu, or when they attempt to open a file that has an extension associated with the application.

Published applications are merely located in the Add/Remove Programs applet in Control Panel. Users can either select to install the application from this applet, or (as in application assignment) users can open a file with an extension that is mapped to the specific application.

SCRIPTS

Windows 2000 includes a script interpreter known as WSH (Windows Scripting Host). WSH is powerful and supports scripts written in various languages, something that has already been exploited by several viruses. As originally designed, WSH could be controlled by Group Policy to allow for "legacy" logon scripts, as well as newer Group Policy logon and logoff scripts, and, finally, system startup and shutdown scripts.

However, as a result of successful hostile code attacks that take advantage of WSH, many organizations have chosen to disable WSH on all client systems. If scripting will play a part in your organization, consider upgrading to version 5.6 of WSH. This new version (initially designed for Windows XP) has several new features that make sure that only authorized scripts run on client machines, including the ability to require scripts to authenticate themselves before they are run.

WSH 5.6 considers a script authentic when that script is accompanied by a digital certificate issued by a trusted authority. Of course, most organizations have their own certificate authority to maintain authentication control within their network. Because a script is signed with this certificate, any unauthorized modifications to the script itself are automatically determined by WSH, which then stops execution and displays an error message.

FOLDER REDIRECTION

Folder redirection is a nice solution when client systems are unstable or when an end user moves around a lot. Although there are many advantages from a general administrative perspective, security can also be enhanced by ensuring that critical data is stored in one central place, which means that security settings can also be centralized. Although hostile code running on a desktop could still get access through the redirected folder to the data, this access is limited to the current session. Once a user logs out, the folder redirection is stopped.

Configuring User Manager Policies for Windows NT

NT provides a number of settings that allow you to define a user access policy. You set account properties and user access rights through the User Manager for Domains utility. You enforce Desktop customization through User Manager, but you create policies through the System Policy Editor.

ACCOUNT POLICIES

To set account policies, open User Manager for Domains and choose Policies ➢ Account to open the Account Policy dialog box, which is shown in Figure 12.5. You can customize all settings that deal with system authentication in this dialog box. These settings are global, meaning that they affect all system users. A brief explanation of each option follows.

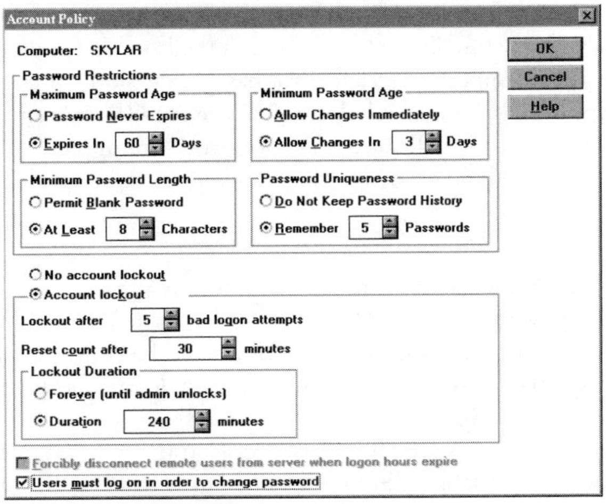

FIGURE 12.5

The Account Policy dialog box

Maximum Password Age

This setting determines the amount of time before a user is forced to change their password. Too long a period can be considered a security risk, and too brief a period of time might tempt a user to write down their password. Typically, a maximum password age of 30–90 days is considered acceptable.

Minimum Password Age

This setting determines the amount of time that must pass before a user is allowed to change their password. When prompted to change their passwords, some users like to make repetitive password changes in order to cycle past the Password Uniqueness value. This allows the user to exceed the history setting and reset their password to the current value. By setting a minimum password age, you can prevent users from reusing the same password. A value of three to seven days is usually sufficient to deter this user activity.

Minimum Password Length

This setting determines the smallest acceptable password. Due to vulnerabilities in the LanMan password hash that we will discuss in Chapter 14, it is suggested that you use a minimum of eight characters for passwords.

Password Uniqueness

This setting allows you to configure how many previous passwords the system remembers for each user. This setting prevents a user from reusing an old password for the number of password changes recorded in this setting. Typically, you want to combine this setting with the Maximum Password Age value so that users will not use the same password more than once a year.

Account Lockout

The Account Lockout setting defines how many logon attempts a user is allowed to try with an incorrect password before the account becomes administratively locked. This setting is used to prevent attackers from attempting to guess the password for a valid user account. Usually five or six attempts is a good balance between not giving an attacker too many tries at an account and giving the user a few attempts at getting their password right.

Reset Count After

This setting defines the period of time in which a number of bad logons are considered part of the same logon attempt. For example, if the Account Lockout setting is set to five attempts and the Reset Count After setting is set to 30 minutes, the system will lock the account only if five failed logon attempts occur in a 30-minute period. After 30 minutes, the counter is reset, and the next failed logon is counted as attempt number one. Depending on your environment, you might want to set this value as low as 30 minutes or as high as one day.

Lockout Duration

If an account does become locked due to an excessive number of logon attempts, the Lockout Duration setting defines how long the account remains locked. For high-security networks, set this value to Forever. When you do so, the account is locked until the system administrator resets it. The administrator can then investigate whether the lockout is due to an intruder or to a user who cannot remember their password.

In many environments, a lockout setting that enables the account after a specific period of time is sufficient. This setting is useful when a user locks their account and the administrator is not available to clear the lockout. It is also useful for preventing DoS (denial of service) attacks. An attacker could purposely attempt multiple logons with a bad password in order to lock out the legitimate user. By setting a duration, the account can clear itself without administrator intervention.

Forcibly Disconnect Remote Users from Server When Logon Hours Expire

When time restrictions are used, this setting disconnects all users who do not log off when the time restriction expires. This setting is useful to ensure that users do not remain logged on after business hours, thus giving an attacker an active account to work with.

TIP   This setting is also useful to ensure that all document files are closed so that a proper backup can be performed.

Users Must Log On in Order to Change Password

In a Windows environment, users can change their passwords locally and then later update the server with these password changes. This setting means that the user can only change their password during an authenticated session with the domain. This setting ensures that an attacker cannot use a local vulnerability in order to modify a password throughout an NT domain.

INCREASING PASSWORD SECURITY WITH *PASSFILT.DLL* AND *PASSPROP.EXE*

Within Service Pack 2 and later, Microsoft included the `passfilt.dll` file. This file allows you to increase you password security by challenging a user's password to meet more stringent criteria. The `passfilt.dll` file performs the following checks:

- ◆ Passwords must be six characters or more.
- ◆ Passwords must contain a mixture of uppercase, lowercase, numeric, and special characters (at least three of the four categories are required).
- ◆ Passwords cannot be a variation of your logon name or full username.

You can use Account Policies to require a longer password, but you cannot specify a shorter one. The domain administrator is able to override these settings on a user-by-user basis. This is done by managing the specific user with User Manager and setting a specific password in the password field. This password is not subjected to `passfilt.dll`.

To implement `passfilt.dll`, edit the Registry key

```
HKEY_LOCAL_MACHINE\System\CurrentControlSet\Control\LSA\Notification Packages
```

and add the character string **PASSFILT**. Do not delete the existing key value.

The NT 4 Resource Kit includes another utility that you can use to further increase password security. `Passprop.exe` can be used to restore simple passwords, force passwords to include complex elements (upper- and lowercase letters, symbols, and numbers) and allows the Administrator account to be locked out (except in an interactive session at a Domain Controller).

USER RIGHTS

To set user rights, open User Manager, and choose Policies ➤ User Rights to open the User Rights Policy dialog box, which is shown in Figure 12.6. User rights allow users or groups to perform specific actions on the server. Select the right from the Right drop-down menu; the Grant To box identifies which users and groups have been granted this right. Checking Show Advanced User Rights displays additional options in the Right drop-down menu. Some of the more important rights are described in the following sections.

Access This Computer from Network

This right defines which domain users can remotely authenticate with each of the servers within the domain. This right applies to all domain servers—not just this specific server, as the name implies.

FIGURE 12.6

The User Rights Policy dialog box

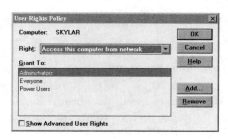

TIP *Instead of renaming the Administrator account, create a new account that is an administrator equivalent, and use this account to manage the domain. This allows you to remove the Access This Computer from Network right from the Administrator account. The administrator will still be able to log on from the console, just not over the network. If you also log failed logon attempts, you can see when someone is trying to break in to your domain as Administrator.*

Back Up Files and Directories

This right supersedes all file permission settings and allows the users with this right to have read access to the entire file system.

WARNING *Back Up Files and Directories is a dangerous right, because it gives the user access to the entire system without being flagged as an administrator equivalent. This right allows a user to copy the SAM in order to run it through a password cracker.*

Bypass Traverse Checking

An advanced user right, Bypass Traverse Checking allows a user to navigate the file system regardless of the permission levels that have been set. File permissions are still enforced; however, the user is free to wander through the directory structure.

Log On Locally

When you manage a domain, this right defines who is allowed to log on from the PDC (Primary Domain Controller) or BDC (Backup Domain Controller) console. You might want to limit console access to only administrator-level accounts. Doing so can help deter (but not completely prevent) physical attacks against the server. As with the Access This Computer from Network right, you can use failed logon attempts to track whether any of your users have sneaked into the server room and attempted to access the server directly.

Manage Auditing and Security Logs

If file and object auditing has been enabled, this right defines which users are allowed to review security logs and specify which files and objects will be audited.

WARNING *Be careful to whom you grant this right. An attacker can use this right to cover their tracks once they penetrate a system.*

Policies and Profiles

Policies allow you to control the functionality of the user's workstation environment. This can include everything from hiding Control Panel to disabling the ability to run programs that are not part of the Desktop. You can set policies globally for a domain, or you can apply them to specific users or groups.

Profiles allow you to customize the look and feel of a user's Desktop. You do this by authenticating to the domain using a special account and laying out the Desktop environment in exactly the way you want it to appear to your end users. This can include special program groups or even a choice of color schemes and screen savers. You can implement profiles in a number of ways:

Mandatory profile   Absolute enforcement of the Desktop environment. Mandatory profiles are loaded from the server and do not allow any customization. If the user changes their Desktop environment, it is reset at their next logon.

Local profile   A customizable profile that is stored on the local machine. If the user authenticates from a different workstation, their Desktop environment may appear different.

Network profile   Also referred to as a *roaming profile*. Network profiles allow the user to display their Desktop settings from any network workstation. Network profiles can be mandatory or customizable.

Policies are useful for deploying a security policy. For example, if your policy states that users are not allowed to load software programs onto the system, policies can remove the tools required to run the Setup program of a new software package. Profiles are a type of management tool in that you can use them to implement a standard Desktop.

USING POLICIES

You create policies using the System Policy Editor (shown in Figure 12.7), which is located in the Administrative Tools program group. From the NT server, you can create only policies that will be applied to other NT systems. If you want to create policies for Windows 95/98 systems, you must copy the `Poledit.exe` file from the `WinNT` directory to a Windows 95/98 machine. You must then run the Policy Editor from the Windows 95/98 system.

NOTE   *You must run the Policy Editor on the operating system for which you want to create a policy.*

FIGURE 12.7

The System
Policy Editor

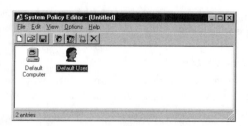

You use the Policy Editor to control the functionality of the user's workstation environment. You can do so by system, by user, or by groups of users. The default settings for the Policy Editor allow you to create a policy that will be defined for all systems and all users. If you want to create a more granular environment, you can use the Edit menu to define additional systems, groups, or users.

The policy in Figure 12.8 is made up of four groups:

- ◆ Domain Guests
- ◆ Domain Admins
- ◆ Domain Users
- ◆ Power Users

FIGURE 12.8

A sample policy

FIGURE 12.8

A sample policy

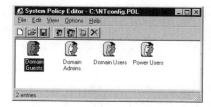

Using these groups you can customize the Desktop based on the level of access granted to each group member. For example, Domain Guests might have their Desktop environment stripped clean, while Domain Admins enjoy access to all Desktop functions. The Domain Users and Power Users groups might be permitted a level of Desktop functionality that falls in between Domain Guests and Domain Admins. Thus, you can define multiple levels of Desktop access.

MACHINE POLICIES

To configure machine policies, double-click the machine object you want to manage to open the Default Computer Properties dialog box, which is shown in Figure 12.9. By navigating the structure, you can enable policy settings that will be enforced either on all machines (if the default policy is modified) or on specific machines (if you choose Edit ➢ Add Computer). The following are some of the more useful machine policy settings you can configure.

FIGURE 12.9

The Computer Properties dialog box for the default computer policy

Enable SNMP updates   This setting allows the system to transmit SNMP (Simple Network Management Protocol) updates to an SNMP management console.

Run   This setting determines which programs run during system startup.

Sharing   This setting determines whether administrative shares should be created.

Custom shared folders This setting determines whether shared program groups can be created on the system.

Logon banner This setting defines a logon banner. A banner is a useful way to display corporate policies regarding system access.

Shutdown from Authentication box This setting determines whether the shutdown option is available from the logon authentication screen. This setting allows a user to shut down the system without first authenticating with the system. By default, this option is disabled. Selecting this box enables the shutdown option.

Do not display last logon name Selecting this option causes the last logon name not to be filled in. By default, Windows remembers the last user who performed a system logon and fills in the logon name field of the authentication window.

USER AND GROUP POLICIES

To configure user or group policies, double-click the object name that you want to manage to open the Default User Properties dialog box shown in Figure 12.10. The following are some useful policy settings.

Remove Run command Prevents a user from choosing Start ➢ Run from the Taskbar

Remove folders from Settings Prevents a user from choosing Start ➢ Settings in order to modify the system configuration

Remove Find command Prevents a user from choosing Start ➢ Find, which prevents the user from searching the local drives

FIGURE 12.10

The Properties dialog box for the default user policy

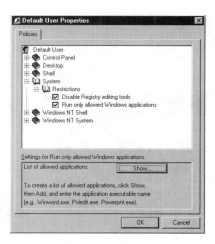

Hide drives in My Computer   Prevents a user from browsing local or mapped drives using the My Computer icon

Hide Network Neighborhood   Prevents a user from browsing the network

Disable Registry editing tools   Prevents a user from modifying the Registry keys

Run only allowed Windows applications: Allows the administrator to define which applications can be run by the user

ENABLING POLICIES

After you create your policy, enable it by saving the policy to the `NETLOGON` share. The `NETLOGON` share is in the `\WinNT\System32\Repl\Import\Scripts` directory. You must copy the policy to the `NTLOGON` share of every PDC and BDC.

To apply a policy to all NT systems, save the policy under the name `Ntconfig.pol`. If you created a policy that will be applied to Windows 95/98 users, save the policy using the name `Config.pol` and copy this file to the `NETLOGON` share as well. When a Windows system authenticates with a domain, it looks for these specific files to see if a policy has been enforced. Windows NT systems specifically look for the file `Ntconfig.pol`; Windows 95/98 systems are configured to look for the file `Config.pol`.

The File System

NT Server supports two file systems: FAT (file allocation table) and NTFS (New Technology File System). Although both support long filenames, FAT is optimized for drives up to 500MB, and NTFS is designed for drives of 500MB and larger. NTFS is the preferred file system for storing applications and user files because it supports file and directory-level permissions; FAT does not.

NOTE   Recovering deleted files is supported only under the FAT file system. NT provides no tools for recovering files that are remotely deleted from an NTFS drive.

You can associate two types of permissions with files and directories: *share permissions* and *file permissions*. Share permissions are enforced when users remotely attach to a shared file system. When a user attempts to access files through a share, the share permissions are checked to see if the user is allowed access.

File permissions are access rights that are assigned directly to the files and directories. Unlike share permissions, file permissions are enforced regardless of the method used to access the file system. Although a user is not subjected to share permissions if they access the file system locally, they are still challenged by the file-level permissions.

NOTE   This distinction between types of permissions is important when you start setting permissions for services such as your web server. Access permissions for a web server are regulated only by file-level permissions. Share permissions have no effect. That said, the web server—such as IIS—also has its own set of permissions that are also checked. You can, for example, configure NTFS permissions to be read and write, but define web-access as read-only, in which case users accessing the file would have only (surprise) read access.

When accessing a share over the network, permissions are *cumulative*. This means that a user is subjected to the strictest level of access. For example, if a remote user has Full Control access set as a file permission but only has Read access to a share, that user will only be allowed Read access.

Share Permissions

You set share permissions through Windows Explorer. Follow these steps:

1. Right-click the directory name on which you want to set share permissions and choose Sharing from the shortcut menu to open the Shared Documents Properties dialog box:

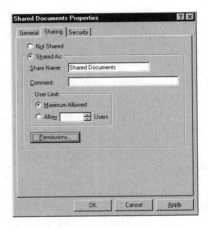

NOTE   *Notice the Security tab. You use the options on this tab to set file-level permissions, which we'll discuss in the next section.*

2. Click the Permissions button to open the Access Through Share Permissions dialog box:

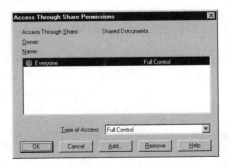

The default is to give Everyone Full Control access to the share.

TIP *NT file sharing always grants full access to everyone. Make a habit of reviewing the share permission level and reducing the level of access whenever possible.*

To set access levels you associate groups or specific users with certain share permissions. Doing so defines the level of access each user or group has when attempting to access this specific share. You can assign only four share permissions:

No Access No access to the share is permitted.

Read The user or group can navigate the directory structure, view files, and execute programs.

Change The user or group has Read permission and can add or delete files and directories. Permission is also granted to change existing files.

Full Control The user or group has Change permission and can also set file permissions and take ownership of files and directories.

A more appropriate set of share permission than the default setting is shown in Figure 12.11. In this configuration, Everyone has No Access rights by default. A user who is part of the Domain Users group is allowed Change-level access. Finally, Domain Admins are allowed Full Control of the share. With Full Control right, the Domain Admins can perform any required administrative functions.

FIGURE 12.11

Some suggested share permissions

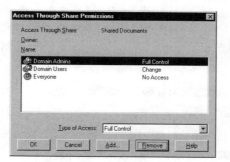

TIP *When modifying share permissions, always add permissions for the domain admins first. It is possible to configure a share so that the domain administrators have no access rights!*

After you configure your share permissions, click OK to save your changes. Make a habit of checking these permission levels twice before leaving this screen. Share permissions take effect immediately and affect any future users who try to access the share.

File Security

You can also set file permissions by right-clicking a directory name in Windows Explorer and choosing Properties from the shortcut menu to open the Shared Documents Properties dialog box. Click the Security tab, which is shown in Figure 12.12. This dialog box has three buttons, which allow you to work with file permissions, auditing, or file ownership.

FIGURE 12.12

The Security tab of the Shared Documents Properties dialog box

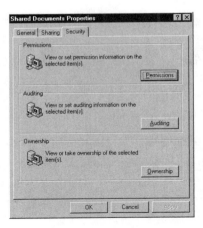

THE PERMISSIONS BUTTON

To modify file and directory permissions, click the Permissions button on the Security tab to open the Directory Permissions dialog box, which is shown in Figure 12.13. To alter a permission, select the user or group for which permission will be altered, and then click either the Allow or Deny check box corresponding to the desired permission. As you can see, working with file and directory permissions is similar to working with share permissions. The only difference is that you have a few more options.

FIGURE 12.13

The Directory Permissions dialog box

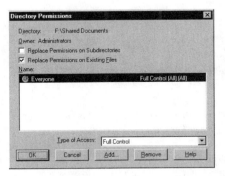

Two check boxes are at the top of the dialog box. Since you are working with a directory instead of a share, the system realizes that you might want to apply your security changes to all objects within the directory. If only the Replace Permissions on Existing Files check box is checked, the permissions are applied to files within this directory only. Checking the Replace Permissions on Subdirectories check box allows this permission change to be recursively applied to all files and directories located below the current location. If neither box is checked, the permissions are applied to the directory only, and no other directories or files are updated.

Like share permissions, file or directory permissions are set by associating a user or group with a specific level of access. When working with directory permissions, you have seven permission levels available. Thus, you have a bit more granularity when setting access permissions. The permission settings are as follows:

No Access   No access to the directory is permitted.

List   The user or group can navigate the directory structure and see listed files. This setting does not provide the user or group any file access beyond seeing the file's name.

Read   The user or group has List permission, can view files, and can execute programs.

Add   The user or group has List permission and can add files and directories. The user or group cannot view or execute files.

Add & Read   This setting combines the permissions of Read and Add so that files can be viewed and added but not deleted or changed.

Change   The user or group has Add and Read permissions and can delete files and directories. The user or group can also change existing files.

Full Control   The user or group has Change permission and can set file permissions and take ownership of files and directories.

Special Access   This setting allows you to specify the exact right assigned to files or directories. Options are Read, Write, Execute, Delete, Change Permissions, and Take Ownership. This setting is useful for those unique cases when the generic groups will not suffice. For example, setting the Execute permission for a file allows a user to run the program without having access to view the directory.

As with share permissions, decide on the minimum level of access required by each user or group and set permissions accordingly. Keep in mind that membership in a group can both allow and deny access not explicitly assigned to a user account. In other words, if a user does not have explicit permissions to a resource, but is a member of a group that does, that user can still gain access to the resource through the permissions assigned to the group. Likewise, if a user belongs to a group that has been *explicitly* denied access to a resource, the user will not be able to use that resource, even if they have explicitly been granted permission through their user account!

THE AUDITING BUTTON

Auditing allows you to monitor who is accessing each of the files on your server. Clicking the Auditing button in the Shared Documents Properties dialog opens the Directory Auditing dialog box, which is shown in Figure 12.14. From this dialog box, you can select specific users and groups and define the activity you want to record. For example, in Figure 12.14 we are auditing the directory for ownership and permission changes.

To use this feature, open User Manager and choose Policies ➢ Audit to open the Audit Policies Properties dialog box. You must enable Auditing, and select the File And Object Access option. All audit entries are reported to the Security log in Event Viewer.

NOTE   *Auditing is discussed in greater detail in the "Logging" section of this chapter.*

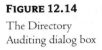

FIGURE 12.14

The Directory
Auditing dialog box

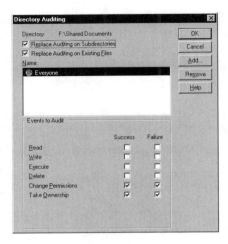

THE OWNERSHIP BUTTON

Clicking the Ownership button in the Shared Documents Properties dialog box opens a window in which you can confirm the action of taking ownership of a file or directory structure. Domain administrators are always allowed to take ownership (provided they have full control of the file or directory). If Full Control is enabled for domain users, they can designate other domain users who can take ownership of files or directories they own.

Logging

All NT events are reported through Event Viewer. You access Event Viewer through the Administrative Tools program group. By default, only system and application messages are logged. You can, however, enable auditing, which provides feedback on a number of security-related events and provides a greater level of detail about what is taking place on the system.

Configuring Event Viewer

You might want to change a few settings in Event Viewer. To do so, open Event Viewer, and choose Log ➢ Log Settings to open the Event Log Settings dialog box, which is shown in Figure 12.15. Click the Change Settings For drop-down menu to configure the System, Application, and Security logs separately. You can also set the maximum size of the log as well as specify what Event Viewer should do if the log grows too large.

TIP Given the price of disk space, the default log size setting of 512KB is far too small. Event Viewer keeps track of important events. You want to make sure that you provide enough space to record them. Increase the log size of all three logs to 4098KB. This will use a maximum of 12MB of disk space for log entries—a small price to pay for keeping tabs on your system's health.

FIGURE 12.15

The Event Log Settings dialog box

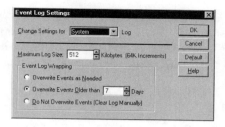

The default setting for Event Log Wrapping is also a problem. What happens if you find out that your system was compromised at some time during the last 60 days? If you are overwriting events after seven days, you have no real history to go through in order to track what has happened. Change this setting to Do Not Overwrite Events for all three logs. This setting produces a console error message if the log file becomes full, but it is better than losing your log history.

Reviewing the Event Viewer Logs

Review your logs regularly. Your logs are your best tools for determining whether someone has infiltrated your system. The logs show you what has gone on with your system when you were not there to watch it. Depending on your setup, you can choose from a number of manual and automated methods for reviewing log entries.

MANUAL LOG REVIEW

One of the simplest ways to review your logs is to log on to each system from the console and review the log entries. If you have only one or two servers, this may be sufficient. To archive logs, choose Log ➢ Save As in Event Viewer and save each log to file. You might want to save the logs as a `.txt` files so that you can import them into another program, such as Excel or Access, for further review. If you will be transporting the files via floppy disk, consider compressing them first. You can easily fit 12MB worth of logs onto a floppy in `PKZIP` format.

If you are managing 10 or more NT systems, it may not be practical to walk around to every system. In this case, choose Log ➢ Select Computer in Event Viewer to open the Select Computer dialog box, which is shown in Figure 12.16. From this dialog box, you can select any Windows NT system and remotely view the Event Viewer log. In this way, you can monitor all your logs from a central location. You can even save the logs locally, making log archiving a single-step process.

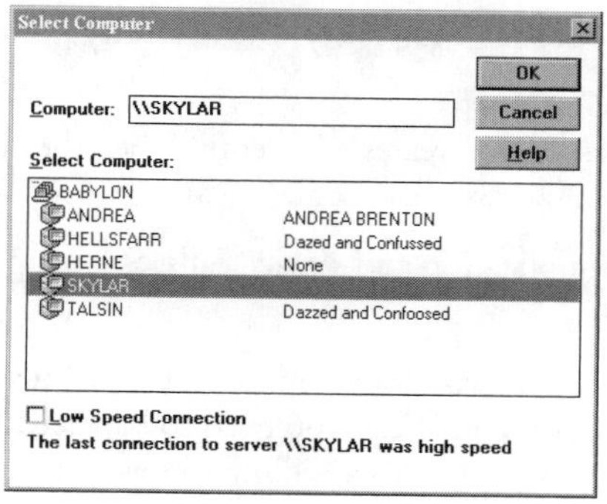

FIGURE 12.16

The Select Computer dialog box

TIP *If your desktop system is Windows 95/98, you can still view Event Viewer log entries remotely. You simply need to acquire the NT Administration Tools for Windows 95/98. A self-extracting executable named* nexus.exe *includes Event Viewer, User Manager, and Server Manager for Windows 95/98. You can use all these tools to manage an NT domain from a Windows 95/98 system. You can find the* nexus.exe *archive on the Microsoft website.*

AUTOMATED LOG REVIEW

If you have hundreds or thousands of NT systems to monitor, manually reviewing all the Event Viewer logs is out of the question. You need to automate the process. Doing so allows you to search the Event Viewer logs to see if anything interesting has happened on the system. By first exporting the log files to a database, you flag the log where an interesting event has been found so that the system administrator knows that the log is in need of further review. Automating the log review process can drastically reduce the amount of human work required to locate critical events.

The safest way to automate the review process is to transmit the log entries to a remote system. Although this places log information out on the wire, it also prevents attackers from being able to modify log entries on the compromised system in order to cover their tracks EventReporter is a commercial program that allows a Windows-based system to forward log entries to any Unix-based system running syslogd. Centralized logging does more than simply easing and simplifying an administrative burden; it also provides another layer of defense for your intrusion detection strategy. When you export event logs, crackers face a greater challenge in covering or erasing the evidence of their activity.

Auditing System Events

To enable auditing, open User Manager and choose Policies ➤ Audit. to open the Audit Policy dialog box, which is shown in Figure 12.17. For each of the listed events, you can select whether you want to log event successes, failures, or both. A description of each event follows:

Logon and Logoff   Creates a log entry as users log on and log off the system.

File and Object Access   Creates a log entry when files or objects flagged as audited are accessed.

Use of User Rights   Creates a log entry whenever user rights are verified. Selecting this event can create very large log files.

User and Group Management   Creates a log entry when user and group entries are added, deleted, or modified.

Security Policy Changes   Creates a log entry when security policies, such as group rights or audited events, are modified.

Restart, Shutdown, and System   Creates a log entry when the system is restarted or shut down or when the Security log settings are changed.

Process Tracking   Tracks application and service calls. Selecting this event can create very large log files.

You must now select which events you want to monitor. The knee-jerk reaction is to monitor everything; however, this may not be practical. You need to balance the amount of detail collected with the amount of time and resources you are willing to invest in reviewing the logs. If the logs will be reviewed automatically, this may not be a problem. If you will be reviewing the logs manually, having Event Viewer generate 20MB worth of daily log entries will not help you track what is going on with your system.

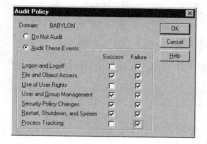

The key is to track only the events that you deem critical to your environment's security policy. For example, you might not want to sift through all the successful logon events. Auditing this information might only help to create additional log entries for you to filter through. You should, however, be interested in logon failures, because one of these events might be an attacker's first attempt at gaining system access.

TIP   The bottom line is to keep your log size manageable. It does absolutely no good to collect all this information if you are not going to review it to check for problems.

Security Patches

No doubt you've heard stories about the recent vulnerabilities discovered in the Windows NT and 2000 operating systems, as well as IIS, SQL, and so on. It is not uncommon to see two or three major security flaws exposed monthly. For this reason, apply all security-related patches once they are known to be stable. Stability is usually determined within a few weeks. During this testing period, you might want to consider testing the security patch on a nonproduction server. Microsoft has needed to recall security patches in the past due to the problems they created.

WARNING   Do not apply a new security patch to a production server until you know it will not cause a problem.

Although the latest Service Pack is SP 2, Microsoft has released an updated security package known as the Windows 2000 Security Rollup Package. This collection of fixes provides a cumulative rollup of security updates that have been released since Service Pack 2. All these software packages are available for free from Microsoft's website and may contain several hundred small fixes (as well as a few large ones) that affect various hardware setups and configurations. Service Packs are cumulative, meaning you need install only the latest version to gain all repairs; rollups usually require that you apply the latest Service Pack first. Service Pack 2, for example, fixed problems with system services, errors that arose due to interaction with other services (such as IIS), and a few new difficulties that arose as a result of companies installing Service Pack 1! You can see a complete listing of the fixes for each Service Pack at www.microsoft.com.

For NT machines, the most recent Service Pack is version 6a, though there have been several security patches released that target specific loopholes and may or may not be necessary for your machines.

SP6a is significant because it finally allowed NT 4 to be C2 certified. C2 certification is established through the National Computer Security Association (NCSA), a branch of the National Security Agency (NSA). C2 certification requires the following security features:

Mandatory user identification and authentication   The ability of the system to identify authorized users and allow only them to access system resources.

Discretionary access control   Users can protect information as they see fit.

Auditing and accountability   Tracking and logging all user resource access.

Object reuse   The capability of the operating system to block user access to previously utilized resources.

The NCSA does the following to certify an operating system as C2:

◆ Examines source code

◆ Examines detailed design documentation

◆ Retests to ensure that any errors identified during the evaluation have been corrected

TIP   *If you will be running Internet Information Server (IIS), you'll want to install a number of other security patches as well. See the Microsoft website for the latest list of available security patches.*

Available IP Services

This section discusses the IP services that ship with NT Server. To add a service, follow these steps:

1. Right-click Network Neighborhood, and choose Properties from the shortcut menu to open the Network Properties dialog box.

2. Click the Services tab

3. Click the Add Service button to open the Select Network Service dialog box:

4. Select the service, and then click OK to add the service.

5. Close the Network Properties dialog box, and then reboot the system as needed.

Computer Browser

When you use NetBIOS over IP, the computer browser creates and maintains a list of system names on the network. It also provides this list to applications running on the system, such as Network Neighborhood.

DHCP Relay Agent

When a DHCP client and server exist on two separate network segments, the *DHCP Relay Agent* acts as a proxy between the two systems. The DHCP Relay Agent ensures that the client's DHCP requests are passed along to the segment where the DHCP server resides. In turn, it also ensures that the replies sent by the server make it back to the client. The benefit of the DHCP Relay Agent is that it removes the necessity of a separate DHCP server on each logical network. The relay agent can be located on the same network segment as the client or at the border between the client's and the DHCP server's network segments (acting as a router).

The DHCP Relay Agent requires that IP be installed. It also requires the IP address of at least one DHCP server.

Microsoft DHCP Server

The DHCP Server allows the NT Server to automatically provide IP address information to network clients. When a client sends out a DHCP request, it can receive all information required to communicate on an IP network, including an IP address, a subnet mask, a domain name, and DNS Server.

The DHCP Server requires that IP be installed. When you install the DHCP Server, it automatically adds a menu option for DHCP Manager to the Administrative Tools menu.

Microsoft DNS Server

The Microsoft DNS Server allows NT Server to respond to clients and other DNS servers with IP domain name information. When you configure DNS Server to use WINS resolution, host name information is provided by WINS, based on NetBIOS system names.

A DNS server normally requires that host name information be manually maintained in a set of text files. If a machine changes its IP address, you must update the DNS tables to reflect this change. If DHCP provides IP address information, DNS has no way of knowing which host names will be assigned to which IP address.

By using WINS resolution, the DNS server can query the WINS server for host information. The DNS server passes the query along to WINS, which uses its NetBIOS table to match an IP address to a host name. The WINS server then returns this information to the DNS server. To a client querying a DNS server, the transaction is transparent. As far as the client is concerned, the DNS server is solely responsible for responding to the request. The two services do not need to be configured on the same NT Server.

The DNS server requires that IP be installed. When you install DNS Server , it automatically adds a menu option for DNS Manager to the Administrative Tools menu.

Microsoft Internet Information Server (IIS)

The Microsoft Internet Information Server adds web, FTP, and Gopher functionality to NT Server. (Version 5, which comes with Windows 2000, removes Gopher capability, but adds a limited SMTP service.) After you install IIS, clients can access HTML pages, transfer files via FTP, and perform Gopher searches for files. Installing Service Pack 3 upgrades IIS to version 3. At the time of this writing, IIS 4 is the latest release for NT, and version 5 is the latest release for Windows 2000.

By default, the IIS installation creates the directory `InetPub` and places four directories inside it. The first three are the root directories for each of the three servers. Place all files and directories for each of the three services under their respective root directory.

The fourth directory is for scripts. Web applications developed with CGI (Common Gateway Interface), WINCGI, Visual Basic, or Perl can be stored in this directory. It also contains some sample scripts and a few development tools.

NOTE   A number of vulnerabilities have been found with IIS—probably more than with the NT operating system itself. Be sure you install all available and stable security hotfixes. Also review the IIS directory structure and set appropriate permission levels according to the various guidelines on the Microsoft website for securing IIS.

IIS requires that IP be installed. During IIS installation, a menu folder called `Microsoft Internet Server` is created for the management tools required for these services.

Microsoft TCP/IP Printing

Microsoft TCP/IP Printing allows NT Server to support Unix printing, referred to as *line printer daemon* (lpd). TCP/IP Printing allows NT Server to print to a print server that supports lpd or to a Unix system that has a directly connected printer.

TCP/IP Printing also allows NT Server to act as a printing gateway for Microsoft clients. NT Server connects to lpd via IP and can advertise this printer as a shared resource on NetBEUI (NetBIOS Enhanced User Interface). Microsoft clients using only NetBEUI can send print jobs to this advertised share. NT Server then forwards these jobs to the lpd printer.

Microsoft TCP/IP Printing requires that IP be installed. During installation, it adds a new printer port type called `LPR` (Line Printer Remote), as shown in Figure 12.18. `LPR` provides remote access to lpd printers.

FIGURE 12.18

Installing TCP/IP Printing adds a printer port called the **LPR** port, through which NT Server can access Unix printers.

Network Monitor Agent and Tools

The Network Monitor Agent allows NT Server to be remotely accessed and monitored by systems running the NT Server Network Monitoring Tools.

The Network Monitor tool installs a network analyzer similar to Novell's LANAlyzer or Network General's Sniffer, except that it can capture only broadcast frames or traffic traveling to and from NT server. The Network Monitor tool allows the server to capture and decode network frames for the purpose of analysis. Figure 12.19 shows a typical packet capture with Network Monitor. The tool displays the source and destination address of each system, as well as the protocol in use. A more fully developed version of Network Monitor (supplied with Microsoft's Systems Management Server) can capture *all* traffic on a subnet.

FIGURE 12.19

Network Monitor can capture network traffic so that it can be decoded and analyzed.

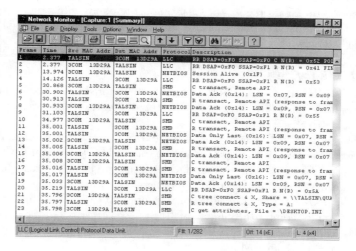

WARNING *Network Monitor is a great tool for monitoring traffic headed to and from the server. It can also be a major security problem if an attacker is able to access Network Monitor data through a remote agent. Network Monitor can be a useful troubleshooting tool, but you should not leave it active unless you are using it.*

RIP

The RIP service allows NT Server to use and propagate routing information broadcasts for IP. RIP is the only dynamic routing protocol supported for IP by the base NT installation. You can, however, download a copy of RRAS (Routing and Remote Access Service) from the Microsoft website, which adds support for the OSPF (Open Shortest Path First) routing protocol.

RPC Configuration

The RPC Configuration service enables NT Server support for Remote Procedure Call (RPC). RPC allows an application running on the local system to request services from another application that is running on a remote system. In order for the application to function correctly, both systems must support RPC. RPC provides similar functionality to a normal function call, except that RPC supports the calling of a subroutine located on a remote system.

Simple TCP/IP Services

Simple TCP/IP Services installs support for some little-used IP applications such as Echo, Chargen, and Quote of the Day.

WARNING   *Unless you really need these services, don't install Simple TCP/IP . The Echo and Chargen ports can be used to launch a DoS attack against the server or even an entire network segment.*

When the Chargen port is transmitted a character, it responds by returning a full set of alphanumeric characters. The Echo port is designed to reflect all the traffic that has been transmitted to it. A DoS exploit spoofs a packet in order to get two systems communicating between these two ports or even to get a single server speaking to itself. The result is that for every character the Echo port reflects to the Chargen port, the Chargen port responds with a full set of alphanumeric characters. The result is that network utilization can reach 100 percent, preventing legitimate traffic from reaching its destination.

SNMP Service

The SNMP Service allows NT Server to be monitored by an SNMP management station. It also allows Performance Monitor on NT Server to monitor IP statistics and statistics for IP applications (DNS, WINS, and so on).

When the SNMP service is installed, NT Server can send configuration and performance information to an SNMP management station such as Hewlett-Packard's Open View. This allows the status of NT Server, as well as other SNMP devices, to be monitored from a central location. Monitoring can be over IP or IPX (Internetwork Packet Exchange).

The SNMP Service also adds functionality to the NT Performance Monitor. For example, it allows you to monitor the number of IP packets with errors or the number of WINS queries the server has received. Both SNMP and the applicable service must be installed for these features to be added to Performance Monitor.

Windows Internet Naming Service (WINS)

A WINS server allows NetBIOS systems to communicate across a router using IP encapsulation of NetBIOS. The WINS server acts as a NetBIOS Name Server (NBNS) for p-node and h-node systems located on NT Server's local subnet. WINS stores the system's NetBIOS name, as well as its IP address.

Each WINS server on the network periodically updates the other WINS servers with a copy of its table. The result is a dynamic list, mapping NetBIOS names to IP addresses for every system on the network. A copy of the list is then stored on each WINS server.

When a p-node system needs the address of another NetBIOS system, it sends a discovery packet to its local WINS server. If the system in question happens to be located on a remote subnet, the WINS server returns the remote system's IP address. This allows the remote system to be discovered without propagating broadcast frames throughout the network. When h-nodes are used, the functionality is identical to that of the p-node, except that an h-node can fall back to broadcast discovery if the WINS server does not have an entry for a specific host.

WINS requires that IP be installed. During WINS installation, a menu option for WINS Manager is added to the Administrative Tools menu.

Packet Filtering with Windows NT

Windows NT supports static packet filtering of IP traffic. Although the capabilities of this filtering are somewhat rudimentary, they can provide some additional security. Because NT uses static packet filters, it cannot maintain state. This means that NT's filters are unable to distinguish between legitimate acknowledgment traffic and possible attacks.

NOTE   *See Chapter 5 for an in-depth discussion of static packet filtering versus dynamic packet filtering.*

Windows NT does not allow you to specify the direction of traffic when applying your packet filters. All filtering is done on inbound SYN=1 traffic only. This means that if someone is able to compromise your system, NT's packet filters will be unable to prevent the attacker from relaying information off the system. Finally, NT does not allow you to filter on IP address. Any access control policy you create is applied to all systems equally. In other words, you cannot create an access control policy that allows access only from a specific subnet.

Enabling Packet Filtering

To enable packet filtering, follow these steps:

1. Right-click Network Neighborhood, and choose Properties from the shortcut menu to open the Network Properties dialog box.

2. Click the Protocols tab, and then double-click TCP/IP Protocol to open the Microsoft TCP/IP Properties dialog box.

3. Click the IP Address tab.

4. Click the Advanced button to open the Advanced IP Addressing dialog box:

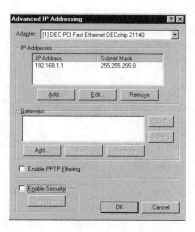

5. Click the Enable Security check box, and then click the Configure button to open the TCP/IP Security dialog box, which is shown in Figure 12.20.

FIGURE 12.20

The TCP/IP Security dialog box

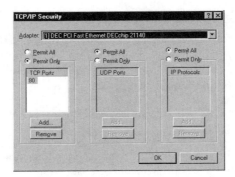

Configuring Packet Filtering

Click the Adapter drop-down list to scroll through all the network adapter cards installed in the system. You can assign a different access control policy to each one. This is useful if you have a multi-homed server that connects to two different subnets and you want to provide different services to each. For example, you can leave all services enabled on one network card while limiting hosts on the other subnet to accessing only HTTP (TCP port 80).

You use the TCP/IP Security dialog box to specify which services can be accessed through the selected network card. For example, in Figure 12.20 we specified that all users located off the DEC PCI network card be allowed access only to services on TCP port 80. This access rule applies to the subnet directly connected to the DEC PCI card, as well as to any other subnets that might be sitting behind this one on the other side of another router.

To understand the effects of the packet filter setting, take a look at Figure 12.21. This figure is the result of an IP port scan performed on NT Server. Notice that the scan has detected a number of open ports on this server.

FIGURE 12.21

A port scan performed against an unprotected NT Server

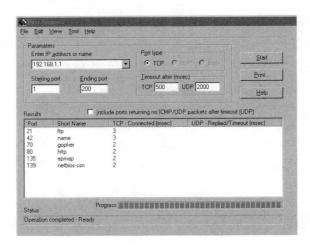

Figure 12.22 shows a port scan of the same NT Server after it has been configured with the access control policy shown in Figure 12.21. Notice that the only port still responding to service requests is port 80 (HTTP). If this were a multihomed system, we could continue to offer all services off another network card, while hosts connecting through this network would have access only to web services.

FIGURE 12.22

A port scan performed against an NT Server using packet filtering

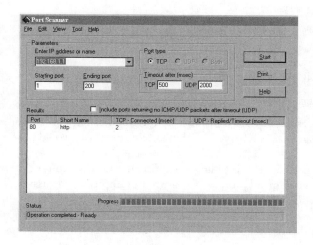

In the TCP/IP Security dialog box, you have three options for controlling IP traffic. You use the TCP Ports box to specify which inbound ports are active on the system. Choose Permit All, to allow all TCP traffic, or choose Permit Only to specify inbound access to only certain ports. To add a new port, simply click the Add button, which opens the Add Port dialog box and type the number of the port you want to leave open in the Protocol field. These filter settings will affect only TCP packets with the flag setting SYN=1. If traffic is received for a specific port but the SYN flag is not set, the packet filters will not block the traffic.

NOTE *Remember that NT's packet filters filter only in an inbound direction. You are not required to open upper port numbers in order to allow acknowledgments back to the requesting host.*

Along with filtering TCP traffic, NT's packet filters allow you to filter on UDP (User Datagram Protocol). Remember that NT's packet filters are static, not dynamic. Consequently, NT may not be as effective at filtering UDP traffic as a real firewall. With TCP traffic, NT can make filtering decisions based on the value of the SYN flag. Since UDP does not use flags, this is not an option. Finally, you can use the TCP/IP Security dialog box to filter traffic based on transport. In the IP Protocols box, click the Add button to open the Add Transports dialog box and specify only certain transports by name.

After you configure your packet filter settings, click the OK button on each of the four open dialog boxes. You will need to reboot the system for your filters to take effect.

A Final Word on Ports

NT does not report conflicts caused by two or more applications acting on a specific port. Any ports that are blocked by packet filters will not produce an error message in Event Viewer. You need to inspect your system carefully to identify running services.

For example, review the port scan that's shown in Figure 12.22. The server appears to be running the following services:

◆ WINS (port 42)

◆ RPC (port 135)

◆ NetBIOS over IP (port 139)

◆ Internet Information Server (IIS)

IIS includes port 21 for FTP, port 70 for Gopher, and port 80 for HTTP. In other words, this looks like a normal NT Server. Nothing in this port scan would raise a network administrator's suspicions.

The fact is, this server is hiding a surprise. If you telnet to port 70 of this system, you are presented with a command prompt. You are not prompted for a password, and you can gain immediate access to the file system. Obviously, this is not the type of response you would expect from a Gopher server.

How did this happen? The NT Server in question is running a copy of L0pht's Netcat for NT. Netcat is an all-purpose utility that can act as a client as well as a server. It can also bind itself over another service listening on the same port number. Thus, Netcat can accept and process inbound service requests before the Gopher service is able to detect the traffic. The network administrator must actually attempt a connection with every active port in order to ensure that the correct service is listening.

Since NT does not report conflicts between multiple applications that attempt to bind to the same listening port, Netcat produces no telltale error messages. In fact, it is even possible to launch Netcat so that it listens for inbound service requests on a port that is supposed to be blocked by your packet filter policy. In other words, it is possible for applications to accept inbound connection requests before the request is subjected to the filters. Again, this type of activity generates no error log messages.

TIP *The moral of this story is that even if you think you have locked a system down tight, it is always a good idea to review the system regularly. This review should include a check of which processes are running in memory, as well as what type of response you receive when connecting to each of the active ports.*

Securing DCOM

The *Distributed Component Object Model* (DCOM) is an object-oriented approach to making Remote Procedure Calls (RPCs). Thus, DCOM is sometimes referred to as Object RPC. DCOM is designed to replace Microsoft's original specification Object Linking and Embedding (OLE) remote automation. The benefit of DCOM over OLE is that DCOM is designed to support multiple flavors of operating systems.

A DCOM client initially connects to the DCOM server using a fixed port number of UDP 135 (NT RPC). The DCOM server then dynamically assigns the ports it will use. This makes DCOM applications such as NetMeeting and Exchange extremely difficult to support if client traffic must pass through a firewall. Unlike most applications, which require that you open only a single port (such as SMTP which uses TCP port 25), DCOM requires that all ports above 1023 be left open. Depending on which Windows platforms you are using, you might need to open ports for TCP, UDP, or both. Obviously, this makes supporting any DCOM application across a firewall a severe security threat.

Selecting the DCOM Transport

An excellent white paper written by Michael Nelson is located at www.microsoft.com/com/wpaper/ dcomfw.asp. This article discusses how to limit the range of ports used by DCOM applications. In short, the article mentions that all Windows operating systems default to TCP as the DCOM transport, except for Windows NT version 4.

TIP *One of the best ways to begin limiting the number of ports used by DCOM is to ensure that all your systems are using the same transport.*

To configure your NT 4 systems to use TCP as their default DCOM transport, follow these steps:

1. At a command prompt, type **regedt32** to start the Registry Editor.

2. Locate the following key, as shown in Figure 12.23.

    HKEY_LOCAL_MACHINE\Software\Microsoft\Rpc

FIGURE 12.23

Using Registry Editor to change the DCOM default protocol

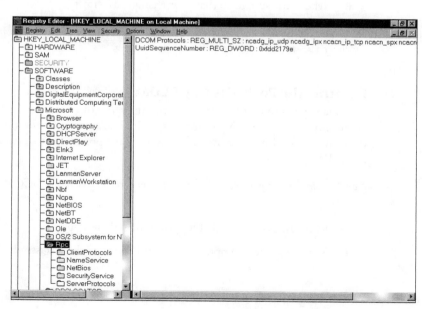

The left pane shows the hive objects we needed to navigate in order to find this specific key. The right pane shows the actual key value. This key defines the protocol search order to be used by DCOM. Notice that the first protocol that DCOM is set to use is UDP/IP which is defined by the `ncadg_ip_udp` key value.

3. Double-click the values in the right pane to open the Multi-String Editor:

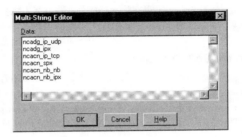

From top to bottom, each line defines the protocol search order for DCOM to use. For example, if DCOM attempts to connect to a remote system using UDP/IP and that connection fails, the Multi-String Editor specifies that DCOM then attempt a connection using IPX.

4. To change the default search order so that the TCP/IP connections are attempted first, use Cut and Paste to move `ncacn_ip_tcp` from third in the list to first.

5. Click OK, and then exit the Registry Editor.

6. Reboot the system so that your change take effect.

TIP *Since the Multi-String Editor does not have an Edit menu option, press Ctrl+X to cut the highlighted text string, and then press Ctrl+V to paste it.*

Limiting the Ports Used by DCOM

Nelson's paper also describes how to limit the range of ports used by DCOM, forcing DCOM applications to use only the ports you specify. This approach eases the burden of supporting DCOM through a packet filter or a firewall by limiting the ports used to a select few, rather than all, ports above 1023.

NOTE *Limiting the ports does not limit which applications try to use DCOM; it simply limits the ports used by DCOM itself.*

To define the ports used by DCOM, follow these steps:

1. At a command prompt, type **regedt32** to start the Registry Editor.

2. Locate and highlight the following key:

   `HKEY_LOCAL_MACHINE\Software\Microsoft\Rpc`

3. Choose Edit ➢ Add Key to open the Add Key dialog box.

4. In the Key Name field, type **Internet** and click OK. A key value named Internet appears below Rpc.

5. Select the Internet object.

Table 12.1 shows the values that you need to add to this key. To add a value, follow these steps:

1. Choose Edit ➢ Add Value to open the Add Value dialog box.

2. Enter the value name and data type.

3. Click OK to open the String Editor.

4. Enter the string value shown in Table 12.1.

5. Click OK to return to the Registry Editor main window.

TABLE 12.1: REQUIRED KEY CHANGES TO MAKE DCOM USE FIXED PORT NUMBERS

VALUE NAME	DATA TYPE	STRING VALUE
Ports	REG_MULTI_SZ	57100-57120,57131
PortsInternetAvailable	REG_SZ	Y
UseInternetPorts	REG_SZ	Y

The Ports string value defines which ports DCOM can use. Each line can specify a specific port number or a range. For example, in Table 12.1, ports 57100–57120 are defined as ports that DCOM can use. An additional port, 57131, is also defined. If you will support DCOM through a firewall, the string values you associate with the Ports key are the inbound port numbers you will need to open from the Internet to your server.

NOTE *When assigning DCOM ports, it is a good idea to never statically assign the ports 1–49151. These ports may be in use by another service or may be dynamically assigned by the system before the DCOM application is activated. When statically assigning ports, use only private port numbers that range from 49152 through 65535. For more information, see* `www.iana.org/assignments/port-numbers`*.*

DCOM and NAT

One caveat about DCOM is that raw IP address information is passed between systems. Thus, Network Address Translation (NAT) cannot be used. NAT is typically used to translate private IP address space into legal IP address space for the purpose of communicating on the Internet. If the DCOM server is sitting behind a device performing NAT, DCOM will not work. The client attempts to reach the system using the IP address information embedded in the data stream. If you need to support DCOM applications over the Internet, you cannot use NAT to translate IP address information.

TIP   You can use DCOM applications across the Internet using private address space if the data stream will travel along a VPN (virtual private network) tunnel. A tunnel supports the use of private address space without performing NAT. See Chapter 9

Ports Used by Windows Services

NT uses a number of ports and services that are unique to the operating system. Although the port numbers used by services such as SMTP, FTP, and HTTP are documented in Request For Comment (RFC) 1700, many of the ports used for Windows-specific services, such as WINS or remote event viewing, are not as well documented. For this reason, supporting Microsoft services across subnets where firewalls or packet filters are being used can be extremely difficult.

Table 12.2 lists a number of popular Windows services along with the transport and port numbers they use.

TABLE 12.2: TRANSPORT AND PORT NUMBERS FOR POPULAR WINDOWS SERVICES

NAME	TRANSPORT/PORT NUMBER
b-node browsing	UDP/137, UDP/138
p-node WINS registration	TCP/139
p-node WINS query	TCP/139
WINS replication	TCP/42
Logon	UDP/137, UDP/138, TCP/139
File share access	TCP/139
Printer share access	TCP/139
Event Viewer	TCP/139
Server Manager	TCP/139
User Manager	TCP/139
Performance Monitor	TCP/139
Registry Editor	TCP/139

NOTE   Keep in mind that in some cases you may need to open more than just the port number listed in Table 12.2. For example, Event Viewer needs to know the IP address used by the remote NT system. If you are not using a local LMHOSTS file, you may need to enable the ports used by WINS, as well.

Table 12.3 lists a number of Windows applications that rely on DCOM. The service uses one or more fixed ports, as well as random ports above 1023, unless you have made the Registry changes documented in the previous section. Also, RPC 135 defaults to UDP (as shown in Table 12.3) unless you have modified the Registry to use TCP.

TABLE 12.3: WINDOWS APPLICATIONS THAT USE DCOM

NAME	TRANSPORT/PORT NUMBER
Domain Trusts	UDP/135, UDP/137, UDP/138, TCP/139
DHCP Manager	UDP/135
WINS Manager	UDP/135
Message Queue	UDP/135, TCP&UDP/1801, TCP/2101, TCP/2103, TCP/2105
Exchange Client	UDP/135
Exchange Replication	UDP/135

NOTE   You must make a number of additional Registry key changes to an Exchange server in order to support client communications through a firewall. For more information, see Microsoft's Knowledge Base article Q148732 at `http://support.microsoft.com/default.aspx?scid=kb;EN-US;q148732` *and Q155831 at* `http://support.microsoft.com/default.aspx?scid=kb;en-us;Q155831`.

Additional Registry Key Changes

A review of Microsoft's website reveals a number of other Registry keys that you might want to modify to enhance security. Change key entries using the `regedt32` utility. The predecessor to this utility, `regedit`, does not have some of the advanced functionality of `regedt32`, such as support for multipart keys.

TIP   As mentioned earlier in this chapter, be sure you have an emergency recovery disk and back up the Registry before attempting to edit the Registry.

Producing a Logon Banner

By modifying certain Registry keys, you can change the Windows NT logon process so that pressing Ctrl+Alt+Del produces a logon banner. This banner is a dialog box in which you can display a legal notice or system usage policy. Before users can authenticate to the system, they must click OK or press Enter to display the actual logon screen.

To add a logon banner, follow these steps:

1. At a command prompt, type **regedt32** to open the Registry Editor.

2. Locate the following key:

    ```
    HKEY_LOCAL_MACHINE\Software\Microsoft\Windows NT\
        Current Version\Winlogon
    ```

3. Within this key you will find two key values, LegalNoticeCaption and LegalNoticeText. Click either value to modify the value.

NOTE *The* LegalNoticeCaption *value is the text that appears in the title area of the dialog box. The* LegalNoticeText *value is the actual text that appears within the dialog box itself.*

4. Exit the Registry Editor, and reboot the system so that your changes take effect.

Hiding the Last Logon Name

As a convenience, Windows NT retains the logon name of the last user to log on to the system locally. The system fills in the logon name field the next time someone attempts to authenticate to the system by pressing Ctrl+Alt+Del. For a high-security environment, this may not be acceptable because it can provide anyone passing by the system with a valid logon name.

To prevent Windows NT from presenting the name of the last user to log on to the system, follow these steps:

1. Open the Registry Editor and locate the following key:

    ```
    HKEY_LOCAL_MACHINE\Software\Microsoft\Windows NT\
        Current Version\Winlogon
    ```

2. Highlight the Winlogon key, and choose Edit ➢ Add Value to open the Add Value dialog box.

3. Add a value name of **DontDisplayLastUserName** with a data type of REG_SZ.

4. Click OK to open the String Editor, and enter a string value of **1**.

5. Click OK, and then close the Registry Editor.

6. Reboot the system so that your changes take effect.

Securing the Registry on Windows NT Workstation

You can edit the Registry on a Windows NT system across the network, as well as from the local machine. On a Windows NT Server, remote Registry access is restricted to administrator-level accounts. On Windows NT Workstation, however, no such restriction exists.

To restrict Registry access to administrators on NT Workstation, follow these steps:

1. Open the Registry Editor, and locate the following key:

    ```
    HKEY_LOCAL_MACHINE\SYSTEM\CurrentcontrolSet\
        Control\SecurePipeServers
    ```

2. To create a winreg key beneath this object, select SecurePipeServers, and choose Edit ➢ Add Key to open the Add Key dialog box.

3. In the Key Name field, type **winreg** and click OK. A key value named `winreg` appears below Rpc.

4. Reboot the workstation so that the changes take effect.

Securing Access to Event Viewer

By default, Windows NT allows guests and null users access to entries in the Event Viewer System and Application logs. An attacker can use this information to identify vulnerabilities on the system. The Security log is exempt from this setting because access is controlled by the Manage Audit Log settings in User Manager. To ensure that the System and Application logs are accessed only by administrator-level accounts, follow these steps:

1. Open the Registry Editor and locate the following keys:

```
HKEY_LOCAL_MACHINE\System\CurrentControlSet\Services\
    EventLog\Application
HKEY_LOCAL_MACHINE\System\CurrentControlSet\
    Services\EventLog\System
```

2. Select the `Application` key.

3. Choose Edit ➢ Add Value to open the Add Value dialog box.

4. Enter a value name of **RestrictGuestAccess** and a data type of `REG_DWORD`.

5. Click OK to open the String Editor, and enter a string value of **1**.

6. Click OK.

7. Select the `System` key, and repeat steps 3 through 6.

8. Close the Registry Editor, and then reboot the system so that the changes take effect.

Cleaning the Page File

The *page file* is the area of the hard disk used by Windows NT as virtual memory. As part of memory management, Windows NT moves inactive information from physical memory to the page file so that more physical memory is available for active programs. When the Windows NT system is shut down, there is no guarantee that this information will be completely removed. Thus an attacker who can boot the system to another operating system might be able to read information stored in this file.

To ensure that the contents of the page file are purged during shutdown, follow these steps:

1. Open the Registry Editor, and locate the following key:

```
HKEY_LOCAL_MACHINE\SYSTEM\CurrentControlSet\Control\Session Manager\
    Memory Management
```

2. Select the `Memory Management` key, and choose Edit ➢ Add Value to open the Add Value dialog box.

3. Enter a value name of **ClearPageFileAtShutdown** and a data type of `REG_DWORD`.

4. Click OK to open the String Editor, and enter a string value of **1**.

5. Click OK, and close the Registry Editor.

6. Reboot the system twice to wipe the page file.

Windows 2000

Windows 2000 includes many security features:

◆ Active Directory, which is designed to replace the flat security structure of the current domain architecture (discussed earlier in this chapter)

◆ Encrypting File System

◆ Kerberos version 5

◆ Public key certificate services

◆ IPSEC support

◆ Support for smart cards

File System Permissions

The Windows 2000 NTFS permissions build on those established with NT, but with some differences. The following permissions are available for folders and files:

List Folder Contents   The user or group can navigate the directory structure and see listed files. This setting does not provide the user or group any file access beyond seeing the file's name.

Read & Execute   The user can view files and execute programs.

Read   The user can view files but not delete or change them.

Write   The user or group can create files and folders and write or append data to files.

Modify   The user or group can delete files and directories and change the existing content of files.

Full Control   The user or group has Change permission and can set file permissions and take ownership of files and directories.

Encrypting File System

In Windows 2000, you can encrypt data that is stored on NTFS volumes using the built in Encrypting File System (EFS), which keeps data safe from everyone except the encrypting user and a designated recovery agent. Choosing to encrypt files (or folders) is simply a matter of setting an attribute in the file object's Properties dialog box.

Because EFS activities are invisible to users, administrators need to make sure that all encryption is done within the context of an overall security policy, especially the file and e-mail retention policy!

So, why is EFS so valuable? Let us give you a real-life example. Because we travel extensively, we routinely end up sitting next to someone who is using a laptop for business. On one such flight, we sat next to an individual who was using one of Sony's new Vaio laptops—the very tiny model. Initially we were quite disturbed at the cavalier way in which this person was entering what was obviously proprietary and sensitive company information (regarding medical technology that had not yet been patented!) without concern for who might be looking over his shoulder. Then we questioned him and learned that he had no password on his system, had taken no steps to back up his data, and had actually had a previous laptop stolen! Although not a complete solution, EFS is certainly a candidate for this type of knowledge worker. By encrypting sensitive information on systems that are at a high risk for unauthorized physical access (such as theft), organizations can implement another layer in their defense plan. Because EFS uses a unique file encryption key for each file, attackers have to do a significant amount of work to crack multiple files—making the cost (and time) to do so prohibitive.

You can choose to encrypt a single file, a folder only (although any new files placed in the folder will be encrypted), or a folder and all its contents. To enable encryption, follow these steps:

1. Open Windows Explorer.

2. Right-click the file or folder you want to encrypt, and choose Properties from the shortcut menu to open the Properties dialog box for the file or folder.

3. Click the General tab.

4. Click the Advanced button to open the Advanced Attributes dialog box:

5. Click the Encrypt Contents to Secure Data check box, and then click OK.

NOTE   Files that are compressed, that are marked with the System attribute, or that are in the system root folder (usually **WINNT***) cannot be compressed.*

Here are some recommendations about how to best use EFS:

◆ Make it policy to encrypt the My Documents folder for each user. If you allow users to enable encryption themselves, show them how to enable folder-level encryption, which is more consistent and less likely to lead to unexpected encryption behavior.

◆ Treat the private keys that are associated with the recovery agent (remember that each file is encrypted with the user's key and the recovery agent's key) as sensitive. Store a copy on a floppy in secure, logged, and authenticated manner. If new recovery agents are designated or if old accounts terminated, make sure that an archive exists of *all* recovery agent private keys. If you do so, you can recover files encrypted with an old or a deleted recovery agent account.

◆ Encrypt temporary files and print spools if they are used to process sensitive information.

To disable EFS, follow the steps given earlier for enabling it, except clear the Encrypt Contents to Secure Data check box in step 5.

If you decide that EFS is not appropriate for a given domain, you can deactivate on a domain-wide basis. Follow these steps:

1. Open the Active Directory Users and Computers snap-in

2. Right-click the domain and choose Properties from the shortcut menu to open the Properties dialog box for the domain.

3. Click the Group Policy tab, and then select Default Domain Policy, and click the Edit button.

4. Locate the Encrypted Data Recovery Agents node (under `Computer Configuration\Windows Settings\Security Settings\Public Key Policies`) and delete any certificates that appear in the right pane.

5. Right-click the Encrypted Data Recovery Agents node and choose Delete Policy from the shortcut menu. Choose Yes when prompted.

6. Right-click the Encrypted Data Recovery Agents node and choose Initialize Empty Policy from the shortcut menu.

7. Click OK to close the dialog box.

After you make this change, users receive an error message if they attempt to enable encryption for any file or folder.

Kerberos Version 5

Before Windows 2000, Microsoft relied on the NTLM (NT LanManager) protocol for user authentication. Starting with Windows 2000, Microsoft integrated an open, industry-standard protocol developed by MIT called Kerberos. Now in it's fifth version, Kerberos is a mature and robust protocol that provides many advantages over NTLM, including the following:

More efficient authentication to servers   With NTLM, an application server must connect to a domain controller in order to authenticate each client. With Kerberos, the server authenticates the client by examining credentials presented by the client. Credentials can be reused throughout the entire session.

Mutual authentication   NTLM allows servers to verify the identities of their clients. It does not allow clients to verify a server's identity or one server to verify the identity of another. Kerberos assumes nothing. Parties at both ends of a connection can know that the party on the other is who it claims to be.

Delegated authentication   Windows services impersonate clients when accessing resources on their behalf. Some distributed applications are designed so that a front-end service must impersonate clients. The Kerberos protocol has a proxy mechanism that allows a service to impersonate its client when connecting to their services. No equivalent is available with NTLM.

Simplified trust management   One of the benefits of Kerberos is that trust between the security authorities for Windows 2000 domains is two-way and transitive (by default). Credentials issued by the security authority for any domain are accepted everywhere in the tree.

Interoperability   Microsoft follows the Kerberos standards as specified by the Internet Engineering Task Force (IETF), which allows Windows 2000 to play nice with other networks using Kerberos for authentication.

So, how does it work? Well, Kerberos defines all participants in network activity as *entities*. These entities, whether they are users or services (such as web or file servers), have a private (secret) key. This key is known only to the user (of course) and the central authentication server that is in charge of a particular Kerberos domain. For an entity to get access to the services provided by another entity, the entity (or client) has to get a *ticket* from the authentication server.

Now, the ticket is made up of several things, including data that is encrypted with the key belonging to the requested service. The client, after receiving the ticket from the authentication server, presents it to the application server, which then determines if the ticket is authentic. Because the client doesn't actually know the server's key, it can't forge or tamper with a ticket (without being detected).

But another step occurs before this procedure, and it is linked to the logon of a user. When a user is authenticated, the client system gets a TGT (Ticket-Granting Ticket) from the authentication server. The authentication server (also called a TGS [Ticket-Granting Server]) uses this TGT to determine if a user should be *allowed* to get a ticket that grants the user access to the requested service.

The benefit of this system is that each entity involved in a network transaction is authenticated automatically; the end user has to be authenticated to the network as a whole only once.

This is the point at which most explanations of Kerberos stop. But to really understand and work with Kerberos, it's necessary to delve a bit deeper into the technical details of what is happening "under the hood". So, let's start with the request that is created when a user logs on. The request packet has a format shown in Table 12.4

TABLE 12.4: THE KERBEROS REQUEST FORMAT

FIELD	CONTENTS	LENGTH
1	Protocol Version Number	1 byte
2	Message Type Identifier	1 byte
3	Username	string
4	Requested Ticket Instance	string
5	Kerberos Realm	string
6	Timestamp	4 bytes
7	Requested Ticket Lifetime	1 byte
8	Requested Service	string
9	Requested Service Instance	string

We know what you're thinking: a cracker could easily intercept this packet and reproduce it at a later time, attempting to impersonate a legitimate user. This isn't really a problem, because the authentication server doesn't attempt to validate this packet. Rather, it returns an encrypted packet in the format shown in Table 12.5.

TABLE 12.5: THE TGT RESPONSE PACKET

FIELD	CONTENTS	LENGTH
1	Session Key	8 bytes
2	Service Name	string
3	Instance	string
4	Realm (Domain)	string
5	Ticket Lifetime	1 byte
6	Version Number	1 byte
7	Length of Encrypted Ticket Block	1 byte
8	Encrypted Ticket Block	varies
9	Timestamp	4 bytes

This is where Kerberos gets clever. The TGT return packet (in its entirety) is encrypted with a key created from the user's password (using DES [Data Encryption Standard]). The only way to unencrypt the packet is with the same password, and the system counts on the fact that an attacker doesn't have that password and as result can't decrypt the message to get at the TGT.

But the cleverness of Kerberos has limits. See, if you're a smart attacker, you simply copy the encrypted TGT returned by the authentication server and then use a hacked Kerberos client to initate a dictionary attack against the packet, using millions of possible combinations in an attempt to match the real user password. K-DUMP is a program that can grab encrypted TGT response packets off the network and store them in a file for later hacking attempts.

As you can imagine, this weakness of Kerberos could leave your network particulary vulnerable. Fortunately, Microsoft extended Kerberos in ways that reduce the risk of brute-force dictionary attacks succeding in creating forged Kerberos tickets.

To understand Microsoft's additions, we need to cover the various subprotocols at work with Kerberos: Authentication Service (AS) Exchange, TGS (Ticket-Granting Service) Exchange, and CS (Client-Server) Exchange. These protocols work together to provide the overall functionality of Kerberos.

AUTHENTICATION SERVICE EXCHANGE

This protocol works from the beginning of the Kerberos process, as mentioned earlier. The user logs on to the network by providing a username and a password. (Or, in the case of biometric or smart card authentication, the authorizing mechanism retrieves the user's password from Active Directory once the user is authenticated through that mechanism.) The Kerberos client uses the password to create an encryption key.

The Kerberos client then sends the authentication server (Microsoft calls this the KDC [Key Distribution Center]) a Kerberos Authentication Service Request. This packet has information that identifies the user and the TGS being requested, it has a timestamp, and it has pre-authentication information that proves that the user knows the correct password. (This is a simple message that has been encrypted with the user's logon password.)

The KDC receives the request and then verifies the password and timestamp. The password and timestamp are essential. If a request is received and the timestamp is "old,", an attacker might have captured a request packet, cracked the password (using a brute force method), and reissued the request—something that should take longer than the allowed grace period for incoming requests.

If the KDC has authenticated the user, credentials are created that the client can use to request a ticket from the ticket-granting service. These credentials consist of a logon session key that has been encrypted with the user's key. An additional copy of the logon session key is placed, along with the user's authorization data, in a TGT, which is then encrypted with the KDC's key.

The client recieves a copy of the credentials through the Kerberos Authentication Service Reply, decrypts the logon session key using the user's password, and stores the new key in its ticket cache, along with the TGT.

TICKET-GRANTING SERVICE EXCHANGE

Once a client has a TGT, it sends a Kerberos Ticket-Granting Service Request to get the credentials necessary to use a particular service. This request contains the identify of the service, a message encrypted with user's logon session key (used to authenticate the request as coming from that user), and the TGT.

The KDC decrypts the TGT with its key (it was the one that signed it, remember?) and pulls out the user's logon session key, which it then uses to decrypt the user authentication message. Finally, it creates a session key for use between the user and the server that actually provides the requested service. The KDC creates two copies of the service session key: one is encrypted with the user's logon session key, and the other is embedded in a ticket along with the user's authorization data. This second copy is then encrypted with the destination server's key.

When the KDC is finished with all this work, it returns the service credentials to the cliet with a Kerberos Ticket-Granting Service Reply. When the client receives the reply, it unencrypts the service session key and stores it in its cache, along with the ticket to the server.

CLIENT-SERVER EXCHANGE

Finally, the client is ready to request the application that it needed in the first place. It sends the application server a Kerberos Application Request message that contains data encrypted with the key sent by the KDC, the session's ticket, and an indicator from the client that specifies whether the client would like the application server to authenticate itself to the client!

The application server decrypts the ticket and pulls out the user's authentication information and the session key, which it then promptly uses to decrypt the user's encrypted message. Because the encrypted user message has a timestamp, the application server can evaluate whether the request falls within an acceptable time period.

If the request doesn't violate acceptable time parameters, the server checks to see if it needs to authenticate itself to the client. If so, it encrypts the same timestamp it received from the client and returns it to the client. Once the client has positively authenticated the server, the service request continues as normal.

Public Key Certificate Services

Before Windows 2000, encryption was implemented in a fragmented and isolated fashion. With the growth of the Internet and distributed, interoperating networking systems, authenticating the participants of a data session and then encrypting the subsequent session have become minimum standards of data processing.

Public-key cryptography provides three capabilities that are critical for today's networks:

Privacy   Encrypting all network communication, including e-mail, voice, and instant messaging

Authentication   Verifying the identity of all participants in a session for the full duration of the session

Nonrepudiation   Creating a binding record of all transactions performed by all parties during a session

Traditional cryptography relies on secret keys, wherein two parties share a single secret key that is used to both encrypt and decrypt data. Loss or compromise of the secret key makes the data it encrypts vulnerable. Public-key systems, on the other hand, use two keys: a public key that is shared, and a private key that is closely held. These keys are complementary in the sense that if you encrypt something with the public key, it can only be decrypted with the corresponding private key, and vice versa.

For example, if Bob wants to send Alice some private data, he uses her public key to encrypt it and then sends it to her. Upon receiving the encrypted data, Alice uses her private key to decrypt it. The important concept here is that Alice can freely distribute her public key in order to allow anyone in the world to encrypt data that only she can decrypt. If Bob and Chuck both have copies of her public key, and Chuck intercepts an encrypted message from Bob to Alice, he will not be able to decrypt it; only Alice's private key can do that, and she is the only person who holds it.

This example takes care of privacy, but what about authentication and nonrepudiation? For this we turn to the concept of *signing*. Signing also uses encryption, but the goal is to prove the origin of the data. If Alice wants the world to know that she is the author of a message, she encrypts it using her private key and posts the message publicly. The only way this message can be decrypted is to use Alice's freely available public key, thus verifying the source of the message as Alice.

Used together, encryption and signing provide for privacy, authentication, and nonrepudiation. The framework that provides these services is known as Public Key Infrastructure (PKI). PKI is the operating system and services that make it easy to implement and manage public keys and provides features that include the following:

Key Management   PKI makes it easy to issue, review, and revoke keys, as well as manage the trust level attached to keys.

Publish Keys   PKI offers an easy format for users to locate, retrieve, and validate public keys.

Use Keys   PKI provides integration with third-party applications to easily select which combination of services to perform (encryption and signing).

Although public keys are the objects that PKI uses (private keys are always stored privately), they are usually packaged as digital certificates. The certificate contains the public key and a set of identifying details such as the keyholder's name. The binding between attributes and the public key is present because the certificate is digitally signed by the entity that issued it; the issuer's signature on the certificate vouches for its authenticity and correctness.

The problem is, of course, in determining the validity of the entity that issues a certificate in the first place. The answer lies in the concept of a certificate hierarchy. In a hierarchy, each issuer (known as a certificate authority [CA]) signs each certificate that it issues (with its private key). The public half of the CA's keypair is itself packaged in a certificate—one that was issued by a higher-level CA. This pattern can continue through many levels, but eventually there must be a top-level CA. This CA, known as the root certificate authority, signs its own certificate. Obviously, an end user has to trust that the root certificate is who it says it is.

Well-known commercial CA's such as Thawte and Verisign issue certificates to millions of users. Windows 2000 includes its own PKI that can be used to issue certificates, but also provides services to manage and use them. The following are the primary components of Windows 2000 PKI:

Certificate services   The central PKI service that allows organizations to act as their own CA's and to issue and manage digital certificates.

Active Directory   As a directory service, AD serves as the publication service for PKI.

PKI-enabled applications   Internet Explorer, Microsoft Money, Internet Information Server, Outlook, and Outlook Express as well as many other third-party applications can use Windows 2000 PKI.

Exchange Key Management Service (KMS):   A component of Microsoft Exchange that archives and retrieves keys used to encrypt and sign e-mail messages.

Microsoft has made an effort to follow open PKI standards. Table 12.6 lists and describes some of these are standards.

TABLE 12.6: PKI STANDARDS SUPPORTED BY WINDOWS 2000

STANDARD	DESCRIPTION
X.509	Format and content of digital certificates
CRL ver. 2	Format and content of certificate revocation lists
PKCS family	Format and behavior for public-key exchange and distribution
SSL ver. 3	Encryption for web sessions
SGC	Provides SSL-like security without export complications
IPsec	Encryption for network sessions using IP
PKINIT	Emerging standard for using public keys to log on to networks that use Kerberos
PC/SC	Smart card standard

IPsec

NT 4 did not provide robust and routine network data encryption, a critical weakness in today's environment of mixed networks and global information exchange. Windows 2000 includes IP Security (IPsec) protocol, which ensures that data traffic is safe on two basic levels:

Modification   Data is protected en route.

Interception   Data cannot be viewed or copied en route

IPsec is an open standard designed by the IETF for IP, and it supports network-level authentication, data integrity, and encryption. Because IPsec in Windows 2000 is deployed below the transport level of the OSI (Open Standards Interconnect) Reference Model, application-specific configuration is no longer necessary. This also dramatically simplifies VPNs. Additional IPsec services provided by Windows 2000 include the following:

Data integrity   IP authentication headers ensure data integrity during communications.

Dynamic rekeying   Regenerating keys at variable intervals during a session dramatically improves protection against attacks.

Centralized management   Windows 2000 administrators can set security policies and filters to define granular security based on user, workgroup, or other criteria.

Flexibility   IPsec policies can be applied to a single workstation, to a user, to a group, or to enterprise-wide data communications.

IPsec provides for privacy, authentication, and nonrepudiation by using an Authentication Header (AH) and Encapsulating Security Payload (ESP). The AH provides source authentication and integrity. The ESP provides confidentiality (along with authentication and integrity). With IPsec, only the sender and the recipient know the security key. If the authentication data is valid, the receiver knows that the data comes from the purported sender and has not been altered in transit.

Microsoft has included the following industry-standard technologies in their implementation of IPsec:

Diffie-Hellman   The preferred method for sharing keys, Diffie-Hellman starts with the two participants exchanging public information. Each entity then combines the other's public information along with its own secret information to generate a shared-secret value.

Keyed Hashing for Message Authentication code (KHMAC)   Used to verify data integrity, HMAC produces a digital signature for each packet. If the contents of the packet change, the resulting discrepancy is calculated from the encrypted digital signature, and the packet is discarded.

Data Encryption Standard (DES)   Used to enforce confidentiality, DES uses a secret key algorithm known as cipher block chaining (CBC) to generate a random number that is used with the secret key to encrypt data.

Other security protocols that support IPsec in Windows 2000 are the following:

Internet Security Association and Key Management Protocol (ISAKMP):   This protocol defines a common framework to support the establishment of security associations (SAs). An SA is a set of parameters that defines the mechanisms (such as keys) for secure communication between two computers.

Oakley Key Determination   Oakley uses Perfect Forward Secrecy (PFS) to make sure that only data directly encrypted by a key can be compromised if they key encryption is broken. It never reuses a key to compute additional keys and never uses the original key-generation material to compute another key.

Because IPsec has been integrated into Windows 2000, it can take advantage of Windows 2000 PKI services, including AD, Group Policies, and Certificate Services. Windows 2000 thus allows centralized management of all security services, a powerful security advantage.

Smart Cards

NT 4 user authentication methods were limited to passwords, unless third-party products were installed. Passwords present numerous problems, including management overhead and personnel issues (users setting weak or easily guessed passwords or users' frustration with high password turnover). The security industry as a whole has turned to more secure and easily managed ways to verify identity. One of the most popular methods is the smart card, which strikes a balance between cost and functionality.

A smart card is a credit-card–sized device that uses an integrated circuit to store information including certificates, private keys, and any other personal data. To gain access to a computer system with a smart card, you use a smart card reader. Typically, you swipe (or insert) your smart card through a smart card reader. You are then prompted to enter some additional unique and private information such as a PIN (Personal Identification Number), similar to the concept of an ATM card. Smart cards, however, store their information not in an unencrypted magnetic strip, but in an encrypted format on the integrated circuit.

Smart cards are attractive from a security perspective because they enhance software-only solutions such as client authentication, logon, and secure e-mail. Smart cards really exist at the center of several technologies of PKI because they do the following:

◆   Provide tamper-resistant storage for protecting private keys along with personal information

◆   Isolate sensitive security operations (such as authentication, digital signatures, and key exchanges) from other parts of the system that do not have a need to know

◆   Provide portability to credentials and private information between computers at any geographical location (work, home, on the road, and so on)

Traditionally smart cards have had limited success because of nonstandardization. The International Organization for Standardization (ISO) developed ISO 7816 in an attempt to centralize smart card development. In 1996, Europay, MasterCard, and VISA (EMV) defined a specification that adopted ISO 7816 standards and added other standards to support the financial services industry. The European telecommunications industry split the standards process by creating their own variant of ISO 7816 for their Global System for Mobile Communications (GSM) specification to enable identification and authentication of mobile phone users.

None of these specifications met the needs of the computer industry, so in 1997 the PC/SC (Personal Computer/Smart Card) Workgroup (formed by several industry leaders including Microsoft) released the PC/SC specifications. Also based on ISO 7816, these standards include issues relating directly to information systems. Microsoft implemented the standards using the following technology:

CryptoAPI   This component allows for any Smart Card Service Provider (SCSP) to take advantage of cryptographic features integrated into Windows 2000 without having to know cryptography.

SCard COM   A noncryptographic interface, SCard COM allows applications to gain access to generic smart card services.

Because of their integration with Windows 2000 services, smart cards can be used as the primary contributor to the PKI of an organization, at the same time providing a high degree of management and risk-avoidance.

Windows .NET

Although still in beta, the Windows .NET Server line promises to improve on the many significant improvements Microsoft made with Windows 2000 Server. Don't get confused. There is a difference between .NET servers and .NET in general, with the latter really referring to a software platform and the various pieces (.NET servers, Passport, and XML) that support it. As for the server operating system, Microsoft plans to release four versions:

Windows .NET Web Server   This new product has been streamlined to focus on web hosting and e-commerce applications. From a security perspective, this is a proper approach that comes from a philosophy of enabling only the minimum functionality required to perform a task.

Windows .NET Standard Server   This is the basic .NET server that will support a maximum of two processors.

Windows .NET Enterprise Server   Supporting a maximum of eight processors (including the new 64-bit Itanium), this server is for large database-clusters and web services.

Windows .NET Datacenter Server   Capable of supporting 32 processors, this server is Microsoft's most powerful server and is to be used for data-center and mission-critical applications.

You should be familiar with several new technologies that are integrated into Windows .NET:

XML   The foundation for Microsoft's vision for future applications, XML (Extensible Markup Language) is being hailed as the next great protocol for allowing applications and services to interconnect and exchange data. One of the more interesting security-related developments with XML is the proposed XMLDSIG (XML Digital Signature) specification, which promises to allow programs to natively sign and encrypt XML messages—something that is critical for asynchronous data transmissions (such as an e-mail document).

.NET Passport   Although heavily criticized because of privacy concerns, Passport is nonetheless a significant advance in the integration of user data and authentication. By integrating Passport into Active Directory, Microsoft has made personal data that much more portable, while retaining the ability to integrate within a corporate structure.

.NET Assemblies   Part of the new software development paradigm that .NET embodies, Assemblies are collections of application code that contain not only the compiled code itself, but versioning and metadata as part of a *Manifest*. The Manifest indicates the list of files that make up the Assembly, along with data about each of the files, and is normally stored encrypted—a technique that alerts the system if any of the files is corrupted or infected with a virus.

Common Language Runtime (CLR)   The CLR is the new environment in which applications run. The primary security impact from the CLR is that it enforces a policy that places restrictions on running code, including prohibiting the conditions that lead to buffer overflow attacks and unapproved system access. This concept is similar to the Java "Sandbox," which prohibited web-based Java applets from writing data to any place other than the screen.

The .NET Security Policy

One of the more innovative features of .NET is the integration of code access restrictions into system policies. As is the case with any new security feature, there are benefits from increased control, as well as greater risks from the inherent complexity and possible misconfiguration.

The .NET Security Policy is simply a collection of rules, which you can adjust, that determines which network resources are made available to running code—which ultimately translates into restricting the applications that can run in your environment, period! For example, if you are bedeviled by employees wasting precious company bandwidth as they listened to Internet-based MP3 radio, you can simply set an enterprise security-level policy that prevents the program from running.

Although the policy can apply in a general way to any software, it is really designed to take advantage of the security and code identification controls built into the Assemblies that make up the new CLR. These controls take the form of security objects, and application developers can use them to provide you—the security administrator—with policy hooks that can be used to tightly control how applications run on your network.

There are four policy levels (in descending order of magnitude):

Enterprise   Policies that can be applied to any domain in your Active Directory forest

Machine   A policy that is applied to a specific machine

User   A policy that is applied to a specific user

Application Domain   A policy that is defined by whatever machine is running a given instance of a program, and as a result cannot be administered

An administrator can tighten the policy at a lower level, but never loosen it, with the default policy residing at the machine level. The default settings are that the Enterprise and User levels are unrestricted, and anything else is configured at the Machine level (which has several restrictions in its default setting).

You manage policies by first grouping applications together and then mapping those code groups to sets of permissions. You determine group membership based on several possible code attributes, including the installation directory, the digital signature, the website of origin, and even the hash.

Default security settings include the following characteristics:

◆ Code originating from outside the machine (Internet/intranet) can't read or write to the Registry or local drives.

◆ Internet/intranet code can communicate with the website from where it was downloaded.

◆ Intranet code has complete access to user interface resources, but Internet-based code has access only to subwindows and the Clipboard.

Policy Tools

A proliferation of tools are available to enforce security policies. Because Microsoft has invested so much of their security reputation (and their business) on .NET deployment, these tools will be central to their security efforts.

FRAMEWORK CONFIGURATION

The .NET Framework Configuration tool (Mmscorcfg.msc) provides several wizards that you can use to modify security policy, including allowing certain applications to be trusted, adjusting the security settings for various zones (My Computer, Intranet, Internet, Trusted Sites, Untrusted Sites), and support for creating a .msi (Windows Installer package) that can be used to deploy a security policy using Group Policy.

PERMISSIONS VIEW

You use the Permission View tool (Permview.exe) to view the minimum permissions needed to run a program, optional permissions, and permissions refused by a program. This is useful if you're trying to track down why an application isn't running or has inconsistent or inappropriate access to resources—or simply not enough freedom on the system to do what it needs to.

CODE ACCESS SECURITY POLICY

You use the Code Access Security Policy tool (Caspol.exe) to create code groups (from unique identifiers such as the name, hash, public key, or some other custom attribute), permission sets, and mappings between groups and sets.

Policy Recommendations

So what kind of approach should we use with this new powerful security infrastructure? Well, for starters, we can use our organizational policies to help determine who should get access to what. Starting at the Enterprise level, we can apply an attribute known as LevelFinal to any code group in which the Enterprise-level administrators (in a multidomain, decentralized administration model) do not want lower-level administrators giving greater access to those applications that make up that code group.

The Machine Policy level is where most of the security policy settings (the defaults, that is) are located, and usually changes are only made here when the machine is not on a network, is not a domain controller, or serves a specialized function (such as a kiosk).

The lowest level that we can administer is that of the User Policy. Keep in mind that users themselves can change their policy—something that can be a problem if a user becomes more paranoid than the network security team—and lock down their system as a result, eliminating the functionality of critical programs.

Summary

In this chapter, we discussed how to go about securing a Windows server environment. You saw how to manage user accounts, as well as how to set file permissions. We also discussed the importance of installing security patches. Finally, we looked at the new technologies included with Windows .NET that improve upon the existing Windows 2000 features that provide a very powerful, centrally managed infrastructure for network security, including increased protection from hostile code.

In the next chapter, we will discuss how to secure a Unix system. Since many environments still use Unix for mission-critical applications, the operating system is a strategic component of many networking environments.

Chapter 13

Unix-Based Systems

To SECURE A SYSTEM running Unix, you must have a firm handle on how the operating system works. Although most Unix systems come with some type of GUI (Graphical User Interface), these systems usually won't walk you through the process, nor are there extensive Help buttons to click that will describe a particular setting and when it should be used. Unix systems are predominantly managed from the command line, although some utilities have been ported to the X Window System. Securing a Unix system, therefore, is extremely difficult for those not versed in the operating system.

The reward to learning Unix is the ability to manage a system that still controls a majority of the world's critical data. Although Unix has lost market share in the small markets, it is still the major player in supporting mission-critical applications. It can also become an extremely secure application server.

Featured in this chapter:

◆ The history of Unix

◆ The Unix file system

◆ Account administration

◆ Optimizing the Unix kernel

◆ IP service administration

◆ Unix checklist overview

Unix History

Developed in 1969 at Bell Labs, Unix is by far the oldest distributed NOS (network operating system) in use today. Its creation is credited to Ken Thompson, who was working at that time for Bell Labs on the Multiplex Information Computing System (MULTICS) for a General Electric mainframe. Bell Labs eventually dropped the project, and with it went an important piece of software: a game called Space Travel.

It is rumored that Thompson set out to create a new operating system to which the game could be ported. MULTICS assembly code was rewritten for an available DEC PDP-7, and the new operating system was named UNICS.

Bell Labs eventually took interest in UNICS, as additional functionality beyond the game Space Travel was added, which gave the operating system some commercial appeal. By 1972, it was named Unix and had an installed base of 10 computers. In 1973, Thompson and Dennis Ritchie rewrote the kernel in C, making the operating system much more portable.

In 1974, IP was developed and integrated into the Unix operating system. No longer were multiple terminals required to access a single Unix system. A shared media called Ethernet could be used to access the system. Unix had become a true NOS.

In the mid-'70s Bell Labs started releasing Unix to universities. Since Ma Bell was still regulated at the time, it was not allowed to profit from Unix's sales. For this reason, only a minimal fee was charged for the Unix source code, which helped to make it widely available.

Once Unix hit the universities, its development expanded from the injection of fresh blood. Students began improving the code and adding features. So dramatic were these changes at the University of California at Berkeley that the university began distributing its own flavor of Unix: the Berkeley Software Distribution (BSD). The Unix version that continued to be developed by Bell Labs is known as System V (pronounced "five").

Because Unix could meet so many needs (and could run on so many platforms), many versions proliferated in the early 1980s. AT&T contributed to this diversity because of its licensing policy at the time; it retained the Unix name, allowing any other distributor to name their own version of Unix—with results such as Solaris (Sun) and HP-UX (Hewlett-Packard). Even Microsoft released a version of Unix called XENIX.

Finally, in 1987, AT&T along with Sun Microsystems and Microsoft agreed to combine the major versions of Unix into a single distribution. Called System V Release 4 (abbreviated to SVR4), this version combined the best features of XENIX, BSD, and System V Release 3—and as a result became a de facto standard well into the 1990s. In 1993, six other vendors created a standard called COSE (Common Open Software Environment), including Hewlett-Packard, SCO (The Santa Cruz Operation), SunSoft, Univel, and Unix System Laboratories. That same year, AT&T sold Unix to Novell, which in turn sold it to SCO in 1995. Despite the repeated (and occasional) efforts to standardize Unix, it is still a fragmented, but respected operating system.

The beginning of the 1990s saw another trend—noncommercial clones of the Unix operating system, most notably FreeBSD and Linux.

FreeBSD

FreeBSD was born from a tumultuous legal battle involving Novell and U.C. Berkeley in the early 1990s. Originally developed as a patch for an existing i386 version of BSD, then re-created from the bits of the 4.4BSD-Lite2 version of Unix remaining after the settlement of the lawsuit between Novell and U.C. Berkeley, FreeBSD has used a controlled development model to create an exceptionally stable (and secure) but free operating system.

So how does FreeBSD differ from Linux, in that they both employ an open model when it concerns their source code and price? For starters, FreeBSD is not dependent on any one person—unlike Linux, which is ultimately controlled by Linus Torvalds. And because FreeBSD inherited so much technology from an earlier, mature version of Unix (BSD), its networking traditionally has been much more robust and has performed better than Linux (although that is rapidly changing). A third reason is that Linux takes after the other main family of Unix, SVR4, in terms of file system layout, boot process, and executable standard. And finally, there is the issue of licensing; although Linux depends on the GNU CopyLeft license (which severely limits the commercial advantages to investing in Linux development), FreeBSD has its own license that permits much more commercial investment.

In the end, the decision to run FreeBSD over Linux (or even a mainstream version of Unix) comes down to many personal preferences. One negative is that FreeBSD does not support the same extensive range of hardware (such as obscure video cards) that Linux does. However, FreeBSD is dramatically easier to update and maintain "in sync" with the latest releases. Some organizations (such as Yahoo!) have decided to overcome the quandary by installing both, taking advantage of the numerous similarities as opposed to the few differences.

Linux

There is a myth (and it is only a myth) that Linux was created to compete against Microsoft. The truth, however, is much more humble, and, to make a play on an old saying—dissatisfaction is the mother of invention.

In 1991, Linus Torvalds, a student at the University of Helsinki in Finland, was frustrated with his choice of operating systems that would run on the Intel 386 processor. Not inclined to DOS, and unable to afford the more expensive Unix versions, he decided to create his own Unix clone based on a limited PC clone called Minix. Linus then made two decisions that set the stage for the entire culture of open development that has grown with the operating system itself: he released (and publicized) the source code on the Internet, and he asked for volunteers to help him further develop the operating system.

Linux had two assets that immediately gave his new operating system life: an FTP site at the University of Helsinki (where anyone could download the latest and previous versions), and a variety of experienced volunteers who added device drivers, compilers, and code libraries. These elements formed a cohesive whole that allowed anyone to download a relatively complete operating system (albeit, initially, one without a full feature set).

Over time, the open source efforts have given Linux a full range of capabilities that are required for the success of any NOS—multitasking, memory management, and especially networking. The open approach to software (with critical changes to the kernel still controlled by Torvalds) has created some hesitation in the business community (although it wholly embraces the fact that Linux is technically free of purchasing or licensing costs), simply because no single organization ensures the commercial orientation or timeline of traditional operating systems.

However, despite the reservations that Linux might suffer the same "fragmentation" suffered by Unix, there has been a dramatic growth in the past few years of corporations adopting Linux in core business applications, not just for peripheral network services such as DNS (domain name service), DHCP (Dynamic Host Configuration Protocol), and HTTP (Hypertext Transfer Protocol). Combined with the broad hardware and platform support, Linux has gained significant commercial support. This includes a 1.15 billion dollar investment into Linux by IBM (which, along with Compaq and Dell, offers Linux preinstalled on their flagship server products) and major application vendors (including Oracle and Informix) choosing Linux as their platform of choice.

The Unix File System

Most Unix operating systems are POSIX-compliant file systems that accept filenames up to 254 characters. Names are case sensitive, so `Myfile.txt` and `myfile.txt` are considered two different files. *POSIX* (Portable Operating System Interface) is a high-performance file system that helps to reduce the amount of file fragmentation.

Unix uses *mount points* instead of drive letters when disks are added. A mount point is simply a point in the directory structure when the storage of the new disk has been added. This approach provides a cleaner feel to the file structure and helps to consolidate information.

For example, you are setting up a Unix machine and you have two physical hard drives that you want to use. You want to dedicate the first drive to the operating system and use the second drive for your users' home directories.

Instead of installing the operating system on drive C and putting the users' home directories on drive D, you simply assign the second drive for storage of all files under the `/home` directory. This stores all files on the primary drive, except for those under the home directory.

A few benefits are associated with this approach. First, it allows the addition of extra drives to be transparent. If you are looking for a file and have no idea where it is, you can simply go to the root and perform a single search. You are not required to repeat the search for each additional drive, because they have been woven into the fabric of the directory structure.

Using mount points also helps to reduce system-wide failures due to a crashed drive. For example, if your second disk fails, you lose only the users' home directories, not the entire system. This arrangement is in contrast to NetWare, which requires you to span the entire volume structure over both disks. If one of those drives fails, none of the files on the volume can be accessed.

Understanding UID and GID

Unix uses two numbers as part of associating file permissions with their correct user and group. The *User ID* (UID) is a unique number assigned to each logon name on a system. The *Group ID* (GID) uniquely identifies each group. When a file is saved to the system, the user's UID and GID are saved along with it. This allows the Unix system to enforce access restrictions to the file. For example, if your UID is 501, this information is recorded with every file you write to the system so that you can be properly identified as the file's owner.

Two files are used to store the UID and GID information:

passwd   Identifies the UID for each user and the GID of the user's primary group

group   Identifies the GID for each group and lists secondary groups for each user

We'll discuss the `passwd` (password) file and the `group` file in greater detail later in this chapter. For now, just be aware that every user is associated with a unique UID and that every group is associated with a unique GID.

File Permissions

If Unix has one major security weakness, it is its file permission settings. Permissions are set by three distinctive classes—owner, group, and everyone. You can set specific permissions for when you access a file, for when anyone in your group accesses a file, or for when anyone else on the system accesses the file. Permission settings are limited to read, write, and execute. Unix does not support some of the more granular permission settings such as change, modify, and delete.

For example, you have a file called `serverpasswords.txt` in your home directory (a bad idea, we know, but this is only an example). You are part of a group called `admin`. You can set permissions on this file so that you can read and write to it, members of the `admin` group have read-only access, and everyone else on the system has no access.

There are a few problems with this setup. First, even though "everyone else" has no access, they will still see that the file exists unless you remove all read permissions for the entire directory. Seeing a file may prompt others to take further steps and try to access the file, now that they know it is there. Although removing all access to a directory might be acceptable in some cases, it may not be possible to do this in every situation, such as when you're working with shared file areas.

Another problem is that permissions are too general. You cannot say, "Give read and write access for this file to Sean and Deb from the `admin` group, but give all other members read-only access." Unix was spawned in a much simpler time, when complicated file access was not required. In fact, for many years the focus was on making system access easier, not more difficult.

NOTE *The administrator account called* root *always has full access to all system files. You cannot remove this attribute.*

VIEWING FILE PERMISSIONS

You can display a listing of directory files by using the `ls` (list) command. When combined with the `-l` (long) switch, file permission information is displayed. It is also useful to include the `-a` (all) switch, which will show hidden files, as well. A sample output from the `ls` command is as follows:

```
[granite:~]$ ls -al
drwx------      3 cbrenton   user      512 Aug 25 18:15 .
drwxr-xr-x   5400 root       wheel   95744 Aug 28 17:01 ..
-rw-r--r--      1 cbrenton   user        0 Oct 31  2002 .addressbook
-rw-r--r--      1 cbrenton   user     1088 May  6  2002 .cshrc
-rw-r--r--      1 cbrenton   user      258 May  6  2002 .login
-rw-r--r--      1 cbrenton   user      176 May  6  2002 .mailrc
-rw-------      1 cbrenton   user     7881 Aug 25 18:15 .pine-debug1
-rw-------      1 cbrenton   user     8410 Aug 25 16:30 .pine-debug2
-rw-------      1 cbrenton   user     7942 Aug 25 15:08 .pine-debug3
-rw-------      1 cbrenton   user     8605 Aug 25 14:49 .pine-debug4
-rw-r--r--      1 cbrenton   user    11796 Aug 25 18:15 .pinerc
-rw-r--r--      1 cbrenton   user     1824 May  6  2002 .profile
-rw-r--r--      1 cbrenton   user       52 May  6  2002 .profile.locale
-rw-r--r--      1 cbrenton   user      749 May  6  2002 .shellrc
-rw-------      1 cbrenton   user     2035 Jul 13 14:33 dead.letter
drwx------      2 cbrenton   user      512 Aug 25 16:29 mail
```

The first column holds permission information. This output is a string of 10 characters that describes the type of entry, as well as the permissions assigned to the entry. Any entry beginning with a dash (-) is identified as a regular file. Table 13.1 contains a list of valid first characters and the type of entry each describes.

TABLE 13.1: UNIX FILE TYPES

FIRST CHARACTER ENTRY	DESCRIPTION
–	File
d	Directory entry
l	Symbolic link to a file in a remote directory
b	Block device (used for accessing peripherals such as tape drives)
c	Character device (used for accessing peripherals such as terminals)

The remaining nine characters are classified in three groups of three characters each. The first group of three describes the permissions assigned to the file's owner. In the sample directory listing, all the files are owned by the user cbrenton. The second group of three characters describes the permissions assigned to the file owner's group. In the sample directory listing, cbrenton is a part of the group user; therefore the second group of permissions is applied to that group. Finally, the third group of three characters describes the permissions granted to everyone else with a valid logon account to the system. Table 13.2 describes the possible permissions.

TABLE 13.2: UNIX PERMISSION SETTINGS

CHARACTER ENTRY	DESCRIPTION
r	Entry can be viewed or accessed in read-only mode.
w	Entry can be modified or deleted. If assigned to a directory, new files can be created, as well.
x	If the entry is a file, it can be executed. If the entry is a directory, it can be searched.

For example, the file .login in the sample output is interpreted as follows:

◆ This is a regular file (- is the first character).

◆ The owner of the file can read it (r is the second character).

◆ The owner of the file can write to it (w is the third character).

◆ The owner of the file cannot execute it (x is not the fourth character).

◆ The owner's group can read it (r is the fifth character).

◆ The owner's group cannot write to it (w is not the sixth character).

◆ The owner's group cannot execute it (x is not the seventh character).

◆ Everyone else can read it (r is the eighth character).

◆ Everyone else cannot write to it (w is not the ninth character).

◆ Everyone else cannot execute it (x is not the tenth character).

For a final example, review the last entry, which is for the directory named `mail`. The owner (`cbrenton`) has permission to read, write, and even search this directory. Everyone else on the system (including the group `user`) has no permissions to this directory. Anyone else who tries to access this directory will receive a "permission denied" error message.

CHANGING FILE PERMISSIONS

You can use the `chmod` utility to change the permissions assigned to a file or directory. Although you can use a number of variations on the switches, most users find the numeric system easiest to work with. The numeric system assigns an integer value to the read, write, and execute permissions. The assigned values are as follows:

- ◆ `r` (read): 4
- ◆ `w` (write): 2
- ◆ `x` (execute): 1
- ◆ No permissions: 0

By combining the numeric values, you can assign a specific level of access. For example, a numeric value of 6 indicates that the read and write permissions should be assigned, but not the execute permission. A numeric value of 5 assigns read and execute, but not write.

When working with `chmod`, you set permissions using a three-digit number. The first digit assigns the permission level for the owner. The second digit assigns the permission level for the group. Finally, the third digit assigns the permission level for all other users on the system. For example, executing the command

```
chmod 640 resume.txt
```

assigns the following:

- ◆ Read and write access for the owner of `resume.txt` (6)
- ◆ Read-only access for the owner's group (4)
- ◆ No access for all other system users (0)

As with any multiuser operating system, restrict access permissions as much as possible, while still allowing users to perform their jobs. Most Unix operating systems default to a loose level of permissions, so review the file system and tighten restrictions before allowing users access. Unfortunately, users do require at least read access to many of the system files. This can be a problem because it allows them to snoop around the system—and perhaps find a vulnerability that will provide a higher level of access.

CHANGING FILE OWNERSHIP AND GROUPS

Two other utilities for maintaining access control are `chown` and `chgrp`. You use the `chown` command to change the ownership of a file. This command is helpful if you need to move or create files and directories. The syntax of the command is as follows:

```
chown <switches> <new owner><file or directory name>
```

The most useful switch is -R, which allows you to change ownership through a directory structure recursively. For example, the command

```
chown -R lynn *
```

gives Lynn ownership of all files in the current directory as well as any subdirectories below the current location. Lynn can't take ownership of these files by running the chown command herself; the root user must run the command for her.

NOTE *Remember: Unix is case sensitive, so the* R *must be capitalized.*

You use the chgrp command to change the group associated with a file. This command is useful if you want to associate a file with a different group than your primary group. For example, the passwd file defines your primary group as users. You are also a member of the group admin. When you create a file, the file is automatically associated with the group users. If you want instead to associate this file with the admin group, you need to run the following command:

```
chgrp admin file_name
```

This command changes the group association of the file to the admin group. Any group permissions that have been set are now associated with admin, not users. As with the chown command, you can use the -R switch to recursively change the group association of every file in an entire directory structure.

Account Administration

Unix systems can be self-sufficient when it comes to administering users and groups. If you have multiple Unix systems, you can administer account information administered separately on each. You can also centrally manage many Unix flavors through Network Information Services Plus (NIS+), an updated version of NIS (formerly known as Yellow Pages).

NIS+ is a hierarchical database system designed to share user and group information across multiple systems. A collection of systems sharing NIS information is called a *domain*. To give a user access to the domain, an administrator simply needs to add that user's account to the master NIS server. If the user attempts to access a system within the domain, that system contacts the master to validate the user's logon. This allows the user to gain access to the system, even though no local account is defined.

The Password File

All user authentication requests are verified against the password file named passwd. Here is a sample passwd file:

```
[cbrenton@thor /etc]$ cat passwd
root:Y2YeCL6KFw10E:0:0:root:/root:/bin/bash
bin:*:1:1:bin:/bin:
daemon:*:2:2:daemon:/sbin:
adm:*:3:4:adm:/var/adm:
lp:*:4:7:lp:/var/spool/lpd:
```

```
sync:*:5:0:sync:/sbin:/bin/sync
shutdown:*:6:0:shutdown:/sbin:/sbin/shutdown
halt:*:7:0:halt:/sbin:/sbin/halt
mail:*:8:12:mail:/var/spool/mail:
news:*:9:13:news:/var/spool/news:
ftp:*:14:50:FTP User:/home/ftp:
nobody:*:99:99:Nobody:/:
cbrenton:7aQNEpErvB/v.:500:100:Chris Brenton:/home/cbrenton:/bin/bash
deb:gH/BbcG8yxnDE:501:101:Deb Tuttle:/home/deb:/bin/bash
dtuttle:zVKShMTFQU4dc:502:102:Deb Tuttle(2):/home/dtuttle:/bin/csh
toby:PpSifL4sf5lMc:503:103:Toby Miller:/home/toby:/bin/bash
```

Each row indicates authentication information for a single user. Entry fields are separated by a colon (:). From left to right, the fields are identified as follows:

◆ The logon name

◆ The encrypted password

◆ The User ID

◆ The primary GID

◆ The description for this logon name (usually the user's full name)

◆ The location of the user's home directory

◆ The shell or command line interpreter for this user

The root user always has a UID and a GID of 0. Processes such as FTP (File Transfer Protocol) are also assigned a unique UID and GID so that these processes do not have to run on the system as root. This approach limits the amount of damage an attacker can cause by compromising one of these services.

Any password field that has a value of an asterisk (*) is a *locked account*. You cannot authenticate to the system using a locked account. Locked accounts are useful for disabling user access or for securing processes that will be running on the machine. If you feel that an account, albeit locked, is unnecessary, you can remove it by using the system administration utilities for your flavor of Unix, or you can simply delete the user account entry in /etc/passwd.

TIP   Any account that has a blank or invalid shell entry cannot telnet to the system or log on from the console. This is useful if you want to offer services such as POP (point of presence) and IMAP (Internet Message Access Protocol) but do not want to allow people to gain shell access to the system via Telnet.

THE PASSWORD FIELD

As you can see from the sample output of our passwd file, the ciphertext of each encrypted password is clearly visible. Visibility is required because users need read access to the passwd file in order to authenticate with the system. This can also be a major security problem: any user with legitimate access to the system can copy the passwd file to another machine and attempt to crack user passwords using a brute force attack.

Unix uses a strong encryption algorithm when encrypting user passwords. Unix uses a twist on 56-bit DES (Data Encryption Standard), in which the plain text is all zeros and the encryption key is the user's password. The resulting ciphertext is then encrypted again, using the user's password as the key. This process is repeated a total of 25 times.

To make the final ciphertext even more difficult to crack, a second key is introduced known as a *grain of salt*. This salt is based on the time of day and is a value between 0 and 4095. This process ensures that if two users have identical passwords, the resulting ciphertexts will not be identical. For example, look again at the output of the passwd file. One user, Deb Tuttle, has two accounts. Even though both accounts use the exact same password, you would never be able to tell from the resulting ciphertext.

The salt value used to encrypt the password is the first two characters of the ciphertext. When the password for deb was created, the salt used was gH, and the salt used for the dtuttle password was zV. When a user authenticates with the system, the salt is extracted from the ciphertext and used to encrypt the password entered by the user. If the two ciphertext values match, the user is validated and permitted access to the system.

CRACKING UNIX PASSWORDS

Unix is said to use *one-way encryption* when creating ciphertext for the passwd file. It is not practical to try to directly crack a file that has been encrypted 25 times. Also, it is not the data an attacker is trying to read; this is a known value of all zeros. An attacker is trying to find the actual password value, which is also the key. Of course, to decrypt the ciphertext, you need the key, but if you have the key, you already have the user's password.

So how does one go about cracking Unix passwords? By applying the same process that the system does to authenticate a user. When Woolly Attacker tries to crack a password, he pulls the salt from the ciphertext entry within the passwd file. He then systematically encrypts a number of words, trying to produce a matching ciphertext string. When a match is found, Woolly knows he has the correct password.

NOTE *The file that contains the list of words used for cracking purposes is known as a dictionary file.*

An attacker cannot reverse-engineer the ciphertext, but they can attempt to guess the correct value using a brute force attack. Thus, it is important not to use common words or variations on server names and user names for passwords. These terms are typically the first words an attacker tries.

SHADOW PASSWORDS

One way to resolve the problem of users' viewing the encrypted passwords within the passwd file is to locate the ciphertext somewhere else. The *shadow password* suite serves this purpose: it allows you to locate the ciphertext within a file that is accessible only to the root user. This prevents all users on the system from having access to this information.

When shadow passwords are used, the password field within the passwd file contains only the character x. This character tells the system that it needs to look in the file named shadow for the password ciphertext. The format of the shadow file is identical to the passwd file in that all fields are separated by a colon (:). At a minimum, each line of the shadow file contains the user's logon name and password. You can optionally include password aging information, such as the minimum and maximum allowable time before forcing a user to change their password.

WARNING *If you decide to use shadow passwords, be sure that any other authentication system you are using is compatible with the shadow format. For example, many older versions of NIS (but not NIS+) expect the password information to be stored within the* passwd *file. If you install the shadow password suite on one of these systems, NIS will break—and it is possible that you will no longer be able to gain access to the system.*

The Group File

As mentioned earlier, the group file identifies the GID associated with each group, as well as the group's members. Most Unix versions allow users to be a member of more than one group. A sample group file is shown here:

```
disk::6:root
lp::7:daemon,lp
mem::8:
kmem::9:
wheel::10:cbrenton
mail::12:mail
news::13:news
ftp::50:
nobody::99:
users::100:cbrenton,deb,dtuttle,toby
cbrenton::500:cbrenton
deb::501:deb
dtuttle::502:dtuttle
toby::503:toby
```

Notice that the users cbrenton, deb, dtuttle, and toby are all members of a unique group that shares their logon name, as well as members of the group users. If you refer to the passwd file, you will see that the primary group for each of these users is the group that matches their logon name. This security feature helps prevent users from unintentionally providing more access to a file than was intended.

When a user creates a file, the system provides read and write access for the file's owner as well as the owner's group. For example, if you create a file called resume.txt, everyone in your primary group has write access to this file. This set of permissions is rather loose to be assigned by default; the user might forget or might not know enough to go back and use the chmod command.

To resolve this file permission problem, every user is assigned to a unique group. By default, all other users are viewed as "everyone else" and provided only a minimum level of file access (usually read-only). If, however, you want to allow other users to have a higher level of access to the file, you can use the chgrp command. You have to think about what you're doing before you can grant further access to the file.

For example, the user cbrenton creates a file named smtp.txt. A list of the file would produce the following:

```
[cbrenton@thor cbrenton]$ ls -al smtp.txt
-rw-rw-r--   1 cbrenton cbrenton      499 Feb  5  1997 smtp.txt
```

Since the user cbrenton is in a unique group named cbrenton, all other users on the system have read-only access to the file. If cbrenton wants to allow deb, dtuttle, and toby write access, he can use the chgrp command to associate this file with the group users. The syntax of the command is as follows:

```
chgrp users smtp.txt
```

After running this command, a new listing of the file smtp.txt appears as follows:

```
[cbrenton@thor cbrenton]$ ls -al smtp.txt
-rw-rw-r--   1 cbrenton users           499 Feb  5  2002 smtp.txt
```

Now all members of the group users (deb, dtuttle, and toby) have read and write access to the file smtp.txt. Any user on the system who is not part of the group users still has just read-only access to the file.

On a Unix system, users are allowed to assume the identity of another user using the su command. If no logon name is specified with the su command, su defaults to the root account and prompts you for the root user password. Here is an example of using the su command:

```
[cbrenton@thor cbrenton]$ whoami
cbrenton
[cbrenton@thor cbrenton]$ su
Password:
[root@thor cbrenton]# whoami
root
[root@thor cbrenton]# who am i
thor.foobar.com!cbrenton ttyp0    Aug 30 23:34 (192.168.1.25)
[root@thor cbrenton]#
```

First, verify your current logon name. As you can see from the output of the whoami command, the system identifies you as cbrenton. You then type **su** with no switches, and the system prompts you for the root user's password. Once you enter the password, a repeat of the whoami command identifies you as now being the root user. Notice that if you use the who am i command, the system still knows your true identity.

This is extremely useful for tracking who has assumed administrator privileges. If you check the final entry in the /var/log/messages file, you find the following entry:

```
Aug 30 23:34:56 thor su: cbrenton on /dev/ttyp0
```

This tells you who assumed root-level privileges and at what time the event occurred. If you are worried that a user improperly assuming root might attempt to delete this entry in order to cover their tracks, you can use syslog to export all log entries to a remote system.

One way to reduce the number of people capable of assuming root-level privileges is through the use of the wheel group entry within the group file. Only members of the wheel group are allowed to assume root-level privileges. If you review the group file in this section, you will see that only the user cbrenton is allowed to su to root. Even if the user deb knows the root-level password, she cannot assume root from her account. She must either log on to the system directly as the root user or by first breaking into the account cbrenton. This makes it far more difficult to compromise the root-level account.

PAM (Pluggable Authentication Module)

PAM is a system of shared libraries that allow PAM-compatible applications to authenticate users through the administrator-configured (and extended) PAM system. Although PAM was implemented originally on Sun Solaris, a free clone has been created that is widely integrated on Linux and BSD-based systems (even Apple has incorporated it into their BSD-based operating system X as well). PAM is a significant, although technically challenging, addition to Unix-based authentication.

PAM's significance comes from the ability given to an administrator to change the authentication mechanism (say, implementing a biometric-based scheme instead of one using simple passwords) of an application, without needing to recode and recompile the application. PAM is implemented as a collection of functions that can be used by an application to authenticate a user.

You configure PAM through a system file (`/etc/pam.conf`) or a collection of files (stored in `/etc/pam.d/`). The actual PAM modules (implemented as object files that are dynamically loaded and unloaded as needed) are stored in `/usr/lib/security`.

PAM MANAGEMENT

PAM provides for four distinct management services:

Authentication   This service not only authenticates the user (through passwords, biometric devices, and so on), but also grants additional credentials to the user (such as group membership).

Account   All other nonauthentication account restrictions are enforced with this service. Examples include restricting access based on time of day, type of access (prohibiting remote root logins), or even system load.

Session   This service performs any additional work related to setting up a session for user, including logging, mounting resources, or creating remote sessions for data synchronization.

Password   Each user gets an authentication token. This service is in charge of updating this token for each authenticated user.

How a particular application uses these services depends on the contents of the PAM configuration files; the application itself is ignorant of how authentication happens. In other words, an application calls the PAM library, which uses the configuration files to choose which management services (and in what order and priority) will be used to authenticate the user requesting the application. Once the process is complete, the PAM library returns either a confirmation or a denial to the application requesting the service.

Before we look at an example of the configuration file, we need to point out that an application can take advantage of multiple modules of the same type (modules in this configuration are said to be stacked). Although each module is processed for success or failure in order, only a final (and summary) success or failure is passed back to the application.

PAM CONFIGURATION

The PAM configuration file (`/etc/pam.conf`) consists of entries with the following original format:

```
service name      module-type      control-flag      module-path      arguments
```

The service name entry corresponds to the name of the application, module-type represents the management service, and control-flag is one of four options:

required   The user must successfully meet the criteria established by this module in order to gain access to the application; however, processing of the rest of the stacked modules continues.

requisite   Functionally, this option is the same as the required keyword, except that processing of the stacked modules stops and a failure is returned immediately to the application.

sufficient   As long as no required module (of the same type) has not failed, successful processing of a module with this control flag returns a success to the application. (No other required modules are processed.)

optional   This option is useful only when the summary outcome of previous module processing is not definite.

The module-path keyword indicates the path name of the module file itself, and arguments represent a list of tokens that can be passed to the token when it is activated.

Changes in more recent PAM versions (similar to xinetd) allow for a directory containing files whose names and configurations correspond to the application they support. In this case, the entries are the same, except that service name is no longer included (or necessary, since it is specified in the filename).

Here's an example of a PAM application configuration file for the Telnet service:

```
auth       required   /lib/security/pam_securetty.so
auth       required   /lib/security/pam_unix.so shadow
auth       required   /lib/security/pam_nologin.so
account    required   /lib/security/pam_unix.so
password   required   /lib/security/pam_cracklib.so retry=3
session    required   /lib/security/pam_unix.so
```

The first line checks to see if the user is allowed to log in remotely by scanning the /etc/securetty file (if it exists) for an entry. The second line forces Telnet to prompt the user for a password and then checks that password against the shadow file (hence, the shadow argument). The third line checks to see if the /etc/nologin file exists and is actually the final authentication step. But once passed, it doesn't mean that the user is home free. The user still has to go through *all* modules to have their connection accepted. (If the /etc/nologin file does exist and the user is not root, their attempt fails.)

The fourth line checks any account verification, including account expiration and password updates. If the password has expired, the fifth line is called, prompting for a new password and verifying that it meets complexity requirements within three trys. The last line indicates which PAM module will manage the session as a whole. By default, pam_unix.so records the username and application in /var/log/messages at the beginning and end of each session.

NOTE   *PAM configuration can be extensive and is highly customizable. Each PAM installation comes with a system administrator guide and manuals for module and application developers.*

Limit Root Logon to the Local Console

As mentioned, if Deb knows the root-level password, she can circumvent the wheel group security by logging on to the system directly as root. This is a bad thing, because we now lose the ability to log these sessions. Clearly, it would be beneficial to limit the types of connections that the root user can make with the system.

For example, you can limit the root account so that logon is only permitted from the local console. Someone must then gain physical access to the machine in order to directly log on as the root user. Any users connecting to the system remotely (with a program such as Telnet) are forced to first log on as themselves and then su to root. This approach allows you to enforce the wheel group restrictions for all remote users.

Most flavors of Unix allow you to limit root's ability to access the system. Typically, you do so by creating entries in the /etc/securetty file. The following is a sample securetty file:

```
[root@thor /etc]# cat securetty
tty1
tty2
tty3
tty4
```

The entries within the securetty file identify which interfaces root is allowed to use when accessing the system. Direct terminal sessions with the system are identified as tty. This file specifies that root can only gain system access from the first four local consoles. All other connection attempts are rejected. If Deb tries to telnet to the system as root, the logon will be rejected even if she knows the correct password. The following is an example of such a session:

```
Trying 192.168.1.200 (thor) ...
Connected to thor.foobar.com
login: root
Password:
Login incorrect
login: root
Password:
Login incorrect
login:
```

As you can see, there is no visible indication that root is not allowed to access the system via Telnet. As far as an attacker is concerned, the root password could have been changed. This helps to keep Woolly Attacker from trying to come at the system from a different console.

Optimizing the Unix Kernel

Removing kernel support for any unneeded services is a great way to further lock down your system. Not only does this help to optimize system performance, it can improve security. For example, if you will be using your Unix system as a router or a firewall, you might want to disable support for source-routed packets. Doing so prevents an attacker from using source routing for spoofing or to circumvent the routing table.

Configuring a Unix kernel varies slightly with each implementation. Which options you can configure when rebuilding the kernel depend on which options are included by the manufacturer. For the purpose of demonstration, we'll work with Red Hat's version of Linux. Red Hat supports a number of graphical utilities that can be used when rebuilding a Unix kernel, something that is not available with every platform.

NOTE *Linux supports the largest number by far of configurable options. If you are rebuilding the kernel on another Unix flavor, chances are you will see fewer configurable settings.*

Running *make*

The stock Linux kernel is designed to support the lowest common denominators. Although this design allows it to run on the widest range of systems, it is probably not optimized for your specific configuration.

TIP *Most distributions install a kernel that is configured to support a 386 processor. Recompiling the kernel to match your unique hardware requirements can greatly optimize your system's performance.*

You can use several commands to reconfigure the kernel on a Red Hat Linux system:

◆ `make clean`

◆ `make config`, `make menuconfig`, or `make xconfig`

◆ `make dep`

◆ `make zImage` or `make bzImage`

◆ `make modules`

◆ `make modules_install`

◆ `make zlilo` or `make bzlilo`

You need use only one of the three commands listed in the second bullet. The differences are explained in the following section. The `make clean` command removes any "leftovers" from previous compile attempts with the same source. If this is your first attempt with brand-new source code, it isn't necessary Execute all commands from the directory where your Linux kernel source files have been placed on your system.

CONFIGURING THE KERNEL

Always back up your kernel before you start. That way, if something embarrassing happens, you can always fall back on your original configuration. The kernel file is `/vmlinuz`. Simply copy—do not move!—the file to `/vmlinuz.old`. There are three command choices when it comes to selecting the configuration parameters of the kernel:

◆ `make config`

◆ `make menuconfig`

◆ `make xconfig`

The make config command is the oldest and the most familiar command to administrators who are old salts with Linux. The make config interface is completely command-line driven. Although not pretty, the make config interface provides default settings that should be fine if left alone. If you don't understand a prompt, don't change it. You can access online Help by typing a question mark in the prompt answer field. The biggest drawback is that you pretty much have to walk through each and every prompt. With the menu utilities, you can jump in and just change what you need to. Figure 13.1 shows the typical output when a make config is performed.

Typing **make menuconfig** enables the ASCII character interface shown in Figure 13.2. Using the arrow keys, you can navigate between menu options. Selecting y for a highlighted option enables support; pressing n disables support. Some menu items allow you to select m for *modular support*. This allows the driver to load or unload as required while the system is running. Pressing h displays a brief Help menu.

FIGURE 13.1

The output of a make config

```
[root@toby linux]# make config
rm -f include/asm
( cd include ; ln -sf asm-i386 asm)
/bin/sh scripts/Configure arch/i386/config.in
#
# Using defaults found in arch/i386/defconfig
#
*
* Code maturity level options
*
Prompt for development and/or incomplete code/drivers (CONFIG_EXPERIMENTAL) [N/y/?]
*
* Loadable module support
*
Enable loadable module support (CONFIG_MODULES) [Y/n/?]
Set version information on all symbols for modules (CONFIG_MODVERSIONS) [Y/n/?]
Kernel daemon support (e.g. autoload of modules) (CONFIG_KERNELD) [Y/n/?]
*
* General setup
*
Kernel math emulation (CONFIG_MATH_EMULATION) [Y/n/?]
Networking support (CONFIG_NET) [Y/n/?]
```

FIGURE 13.2

The menu-based kernel configuration screen

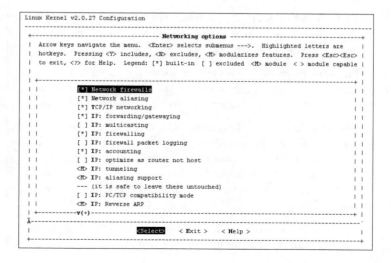

The make xconfig command is intended to be run from a shell within the X Window System. It is similar to menuconfig, but it's a lot prettier. It is also a bit easier to navigate. Figure 13.3 shows the network section of the xconfig utility.

FIGURE 13.3

The X Window System kernel configuration screen

CONFIGURATION OPTIONS

Regardless of the method you choose, you need to select the features you want to enable or disable. Brief descriptions of features related to networking are listed here.

TIP   For a more complete list, see the online Help and How-To files.

Networking Support?   This feature enables networking. If you don't answer yes to this prompt, you won't receive any of the other networking prompts. The default is yes.

Limit Memory to Low 16MB?   This feature is provided for older systems that have trouble addressing memory above 16MB. Most systems do not need this support. The default is no.

PCI BIOS Support?   This feature provides support for systems that have one or more PCI (Peripheral Component Interconnect) bus slots. Most newer systems support PCI. The default is yes.

Network Firewall?   This feature allows the Linux system to act as a firewall. This option enables firewalling in general, although firewalling for IP is the only protocol supported at this time. If you want to do IP masquerading, you must enable this option. The default is yes.

Network Aliasing?   This feature allows multiple network addresses to be assigned to the same interface. Currently, the only supported protocol is IP. This feature is useful if you need to route two logical networks on the same physical segment. Enable this option if you plan to use the Apache web server in a multihomed capacity. Apache can use the different IP addresses assigned to the interface to direct HTTP requests to different websites running on the machine. The default is yes.

TCP/IP Networking?   This feature enables or disables IP networking. If you want to use IP to communicate, enable this option. The default is yes.

IP: Forwarding/Gateway? This feature allows the Linux system to forward IP traffic from one interface to another acting as a router. This configuration can be LAN to LAN or LAN to WAN. If the Linux box will be providing firewall services, disable this option. If you will be using IP masquerading (even if the system will be a firewall as well), enable this option. The default is yes.

IP: Multicasting? If you will be using IP multicasting or transmitting routing updates using OSPF (Open Shortest Path First), enable this option. The default is no.

IP: Firewalling? This option enables firewall support for IP. You must enable this option if you want to do IP masquerading or traffic accounting or if you want to use the transparent proxy. The default answer is yes.

IP: Firewall Packet Logging? When the system is used as a firewall, this option creates a file that logs all passing traffic. It also records what the firewall did with each packet (accept, deny). Logging is a good way to keep an eye on who might be knocking at the front door. We usually enable this option. That way, if you do not need the information, you can simply clean it out from time to time. The default is no.

IP: Accounting? When the system acts as a firewall or a gateway, this option logs all passing traffic. If Linux will be routing on the internal network, you might want to disable this option because the log can get quite large. If Linux will be routing to or firewalling a WAN connection, you might want to enable this option if you want to keep track of WAN utilization. The default is yes.

IP: Optimize as Router Not Host? If the Linux box will be acting strictly as a router, a firewall, or a proxy, enable this option. If the system will be hosting an HTTP, an FTP, a DNS, or any other type of service, disable this option. The default is no.

IP: Tunneling? This feature enables support for IP encapsulation of IP packets, which is useful for amateur radio or mobile IP. The default is modular support, which means you can load it while the system is active if you need it.

IP: Aliasing Support? This option allows you to assign two or more IP addresses to the same interface. Network Aliasing must also be enabled. The default is modular support.

IP: PC/TCP Compatibility Mode? PC/TCP is a DOS-based IP stack. There are some compatibility issues: older versions do not quite follow the same set of communication rules as everyone else. If you have trouble connecting to a Linux system from a host running PC/TCP, enable this option. Otherwise, disable this option. The default is no.

IP: Reverse ARP? This option is typically used by diskless workstations to find their IP addresses. Enabling this option allows the Linux system to reply to these requests. If you plan to run bootp services, you might want to enable this option in case you need it (either now or later). If the Linux system will not be providing bootp or DHCP services, you can disable this option. The default is modular support.

IP: Disable Path MTU Discovery? Maximum transmission unit (MTU) allows a system to discover the largest packet size it can use when communicating with a remote machine. When

MTU is disabled, the system assumes it must always use the smallest packet size for a given transmission. Because this option can greatly affect communication speed, use MTU unless you run into a compatibility problem. The default is no, which enables MTU discovery.

IP: Drop Source Routed Frames?   Source routing allows a transmitting station to specify the network path along which replies should be sent. This forces the system replying to the request to transmit along the specified path instead of the path defined by the local routing table.

NOTE   *There is a type of attack in which a potential attacker can use source-routed frames to pretend to be communicating from a host inside your network when the attacker is actually located on the Internet. Source routing is used to direct the frame back to the Internet, instead of toward the network where the host claims to be. When source routing is used for this purpose, it is called IP spoofing.*

Some network topologies, such as Token Ring and FDDI, use source routing as part of their regular communications. If the Linux box is connected to one of these token-based topologies, enable source routing. If you are not using these topologies to communicate, disable this option to increase security. The default is yes, which will drop all source-routed frames.

IP: Allow Large Windows?   This option increases the transmission buffer pool to allow a greater number of frames to be in transit without a reply. This feature is useful when the Linux box is directly connected to a high-speed WAN link (multiple T1s or faster) that connects two sites separated by an extremely large distance (for example, a coast-to-coast connection). The additional buffer space does require additional memory, so enable this option only on systems that meet this criterion and have at least 16MB of physical memory. The default is yes.

The IPX Protocol?   This option enables support for the IPX (Internetwork Packet Exchange) protocol. You must answer yes to this prompt in order to configure any IPX services. The default is modular support.

Full Internal IPX Network?   NetWare servers use an internal IPX network to communicate between the core operating system and different subsystems. This option takes this concept one step further by making the internal IPX network a regular network capable of supporting virtual hosts. This option is more for development than anything else right now, as it allows a single Linux system to appear to be multiple NetWare servers. Unless you are doing development work, disable this option. The default is no.

AppleTalk DDP?   This option enables support for the AppleTalk protocol. When used with the netatalk package (Linux support for AppleTalk), the Linux system can provide file and printer services to Mac clients. The default is modular support.

Amateur Radio AX.25 Level 2?   This option is used to support amateur radio communications. These communications can be either point to point or through IP encapsulation of IP. The default is no.

Kernel/User Network Link Driver?   This option enables communications between the kernel and user processes designed to support it. As of this writing, the driver is still experimental and is not required on a production server. The default is no.

Network Device Support?   This option enables driver-level support for network communications. You must answer yes to this prompt to enable support for network cards and WAN communications. The default is yes.

Dummy Net Driver Support?   This option enables the use of a loopback address. Most IP systems understand that transmitting to the IP address 127.0.0.1 directs the traffic flow back at the system itself. This option should be enabled because some applications do use the loopback address. The default is modular support.

EQL (Serial Line Load Balancing) Support?   This option allows Linux to balance the network load over two dial-up links. For example, you might be able to call your ISP on two separate lines, doubling your available bandwidth. The default is modular support.

PLIP (Parallel Port) Support?   This option enables support for communication between two systems using a null printer cable. Both systems must use bidirectional parallel ports for communications to be successful. This arrangement is similar to connecting two systems via the serial ports with a null modem cable, except it supports faster communications. The default is modular support.

PPP (Point-to-Point) Support?   This option allows the Linux system to create or accept PPP WAN connections. Enable this option if you plan to use your Linux system to create dial-up connections. The default is modular support.

SLIP (Serial Line) Support?   SLIP (Serial Line Internet Protocol) is the predecessor to PPP. It provides IP connectivity between two systems. Its most popular use is for transferring e-mail. Because of the additional features provided by PPP, SLIP is seldom used. The default is to provide modular support.

Radio Network Interfaces?   This option allows the Linux system to support spread-spectrum communications. Spread spectrum is most commonly used for wireless LAN communications. You must answer yes to this prompt in order to receive prompts to configure the radio interface. The default is no.

Ethernet (10 or 100Mbit)?   This option allows the Linux system to communicate using Ethernet network cards. You must answer yes to this prompt to select an Ethernet driver later. The default answer is yes.

3COM Cards?   This option allows you to select from a list of supported 3COM network cards. If you answer no, you will not be prompted with any 3COM card options. If you select yes, you will receive further prompts, allowing you to selectively enable support for each 3COM card that is supported by Linux.

Upon startup, Linux attempts to find and auto-detect the setting used on each network card. When you reboot the system, watch the configuration parameters it selects for the card. If these are correct, you're all set. If they are wrong, you will need to change either the card settings or the configuration parameters. You set the card using the configuration utility that ships with it. You can change the startup settings through the Red Hat Control Panel's Kernel Daemon Configuration option. The default for this prompt is yes.

AMD LANCE and PCnet (AT1500 and NE2100)? This option is similar to the 3COM prompt, except that this option enables support for AMD and PCnet network cards. The default is yes.

Western Digital/SMC Cards? This option is similar to the 3COM prompt, except that this option enables support for Western Digital and SMC network cards. The default is yes.

Other ISA Cards? This option is similar to the 3COM prompt, except that this option enables support for some of the more obscure network cards, such as Cabletron's E21 series or HP's 100VG PCLAN. If you select yes, you will receive further prompts, allowing you to selectively enable support for a variety of network cards that are supported by Linux. The default is yes.

NE2000/NE1000 Support? This option deals with the generic Ethernet network card support. If your card has not been specifically listed in any of the previous prompts, enable this option. The default is modular support. Most Ethernet network cards are NE2000 compatible, so this prompt is a bit of a catchall.

EISA, VLB, PCI and on Board Controllers? A number of network cards are built directly into the motherboard. If you select yes, you will receive further prompts, allowing you to selectively enable support for a variety of built-in network cards that are supported by Linux. The default answer is yes.

Pocket and Portable Adapters? Linux also supports parallel port network adapters. If you select yes, you will receive further prompts, allowing you to selectively enable support for a variety of parallel port network adapters supported by Linux. The default answer is yes.

Token Ring Driver Support? Linux supports a collection of Token Ring network adapters. If you select yes, you will receive further prompts, allowing you to selectively enable support for a variety of Token Ring network adapters supported by Linux. The default answer is yes.

FDDI Driver Support? Linux supports a few FDDI (Fiber Distributed Data Interface) network adapters. If you select yes, you will receive further prompts, allowing you to selectively enable support for different FDDI network cards supported by Linux. The default answer is no.

ARCnet Support? ARCnet is an old token-based network topology that is seldom used today. If you select yes, you will receive further prompts, allowing you to selectively enable support for different ARCnet network cards supported by Linux. The default support is modular.

ISDN Support? This option enables support for ISDN (Integrated Services Digital Network) WAN cards. If you plan to use ISDN, also enable the PPP support listed previously. The default support is modular.

Support Synchronous PPP? This option provides support for synchronous communications over an ISDN line. Some ISDN hardware requires this to be enabled and will negotiate its use during connection. If you plan to use ISDN, enable this option in case you need it. The default is yes.

Use VJ-Compression with Synchronous PPP? This option enables header compression when synchronous PPP is used. The default is yes.

Support Generic MP (RFC 1717)? When synchronous PPP is used, this option allows communications to take place over multiple ISDN lines. Since this is a new specification and not yet widely supported, the default answer is no.

Support Audio via ISDN? When supported by the ISDN card, this option allows the Linux system to accept incoming voice calls and act as an answering machine. The default answer is no.

NFS Filesystem Support? This option enables support for mounting and exporting file systems using NFS (Network File System). NFS is most frequently used when sharing files between Unix systems; however, it is supported by other platforms, as well. The default answer is yes.

SMB Filesystem Support? This option enables support for NetBIOS/NetBEUI shares. It is most frequently used between Microsoft Windows systems for sharing files and printers. The default answer is yes.

SMB Win95 Bug Workaround? This option fixes some connectivity problems when the Linux system attempts to retrieve directory information from a Windows 95 system that is sharing files. The default is no. If you use file sharing for Windows 95, enable the SMB Win95 Bug Workaround.

NCP Filesystem Support? This option allows the Linux system to connect to NetWare servers. Once connected, the Linux system can mount file systems located on the NetWare server. The default support is modular.

DEPENDENCIES CHECK

When you finish the configuration, it is time to run make dep. This command performs a dependencies check to ensure that all required files are present before compiling the kernel. Depending on your system speed, this command could take between 1 and 15 minutes to run. Although it is not quite as thrilling as watching grass grow, keep an eye on the dependencies check to make sure there are no errors.

TIP   Errors are usually in the form of missing files. If you note what is missing, you can go back and see where you lost it.

CLEANING UP THE WORK SPACE

Next you can run a make clean to ensure that any object files are removed. Running this command is typically not required with the latest revision kernels, but it does not hurt to run it just in case. This command usually takes less than one minute to execute.

COMPILING THE KERNEL

Until now we have not changed the active system. All our changes have been to configuration files. The next command, make zImage, creates a kernel with the configuration parameters you selected and replaces the kernel you are currently using. If you receive an error message that the kernel is too large (which is common with kernel versions later than 2.2.*x*), try make bzImage, which creates a compressed image of the kernel.

NOTE   Be sure you type a capital I in zImage or bzImage. Remember, Unix commands are case sensitive.

How long this command will take to run depends on your processor speed and the amount of physical memory that is installed in the system. A 400MHz Pentium with 128MB of RAM should create a new kernel within 10 to 20 minutes.

CONFIGURING THE BOOT MANAGER

The last step is to tell Linux's boot manager LILO that it needs to set pointers for a new image. You do so with the command `make zlilo` or `make bzlilo` or by copying the kernel image to the `/boot` directory, editing `/etc/lilo.conf` by hand, adding an entry for the new kernel, and rerunning the `lilo` command.

You can now reboot the system and boot off the new kernel. You should not notice any new errors during system startup. If you do, or if the system refuses to boot altogether, you can use the emergency recovery disk to boot the system and restore the backup kernel we discussed in the "Configuring the Kernel" section of this chapter. When you restart the system, you can figure out what went wrong.

Changing the Network Driver Settings

You might need to change the network driver settings if auto-probe fails to configure them properly. You can do so through the Red Hat Control Panel using the Kernel Daemon Configuration option. Figure 13.4 shows the Kernel Configurator window, in which you can add, remove, or change the settings of device drivers.

FIGURE 13.4

The Kernel Configurator

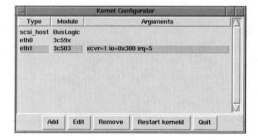

Highlighting a specific driver and clicking Edit opens the Set Module Options dialog box, shown in Figure 13.5. You can use the options in this dialog box to change the configuration parameters that Linux uses to initialize your network card. Once the changes are complete, you can restart the kernel to have these changes take effect.

FIGURE 13.5

You use the Set Module Options dialog box to change the startup parameters for a specific driver.

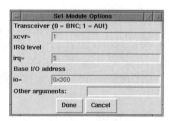

You should now have an optimized kernel, which includes support only for the options you want to use. Optimizing the kernel prevents an attacker from accessing any of these services, because support has been removed from the kernel itself. To add support back in, an attacker would have to rebuild the system kernel. Most likely, such an event would not go unnoticed.

TIP   *Once the kernel has been optimized, remove any unneeded IP services from the machine, as well.*

IP Service Administration

Unix has evolved into a system that can support many IP services. This characteristic is excellent from a functionality perspective, but not so good for security. Service-rich systems are easier to exploit because the chances of finding a vulnerability are greater. For example, someone wanting to attack your Unix system might find that you have done a good job of locking down HTTP, FTP, and SMTP services but that you have missed a Finger exploit.

In the next few sections, we'll look at the IP services available on most flavors of Unix and discuss how you can disable the services you do not need.

IP Services

A large number of IP services are available for Unix. The specific flavor of Unix that you are using determines which services are enabled by default. Under each service description, we note which services are commonly enabled. You will need to check your specific configuration, however, to see which services you are running and which ones you are not.

BOOTP SERVER

The Unix bootp server provides bootp and DHCP services to network clients. DHCP and bootp clients can be serviced independently or in a mixed environment. The bootp service allows a client to dynamically obtain its IP address and subnet mask. DHCP supports these configuration settings and many others, such as default route, domain name, and so on. Most flavors of Unix do not ship with a bootp server running.

DNS SERVER

The domain name server of choice for the Unix platform is the Berkeley Internet Name Domain (BIND) server. BIND is the original, and still the most popular, utility used to exchange domain name information on the Internet. You can configure a BIND server to provide primary, secondary, or caching-only domain name services.

Most Unix operating systems ship with a local DNS server running. BIND is configured to act as a caching name server by default, unless you specifically configure the system to act as a primary or secondary. As a cache-only name server, BIND can still respond to queries on TCP and UDP (User Datagram Protocol) ports 53. BIND runs as its own separate process called named.

BIND is infamous for the way in which crackers have exploited it over the years in order to gain access to Unix systems. Verify that you have the latest version of BIND, and check with CERT (www.cert.org) for the latest security information regarding this critical network service.

FTP SERVER

Unix provides FTP services, including the ability to service anonymous FTP requests. When someone uses FTP to connect to the system and they use a valid logon name and password, they are dropped into their home directory and have their normal level of access to the file system. If, however, someone authenticates using the logon name **anonymous**, they are dropped into a subdirectory (typically /home/ftp) and are not allowed to navigate the system beyond this point. As far as anonymous FTP users are concerned, /home/ftp is the root-level directory.

NOTE *Subdirectories set up under* /home/ftp *can allow anonymous users to receive read-only or read-write access to files. Such access is called* anonymous FTP access, *and it prevents people from gaining access to the complete file system without proper authentication.*

FTP runs as a process under inetd. Although most versions of Unix ship with the FTP server enabled, not all support anonymous FTP access. The most popular version of FTP, wu-ftp, is also notorious for weaknesses that have allowed crackers to penetrate systems. Be sure you have the latest secure version, and verify with CERT that there are no known issues with the version you are running.

HTTP SERVER

Many Unix systems ship with a web server called Apache (the most popular Web server to date). Apache predominates among Unix-based web servers because it supports advanced features such as Java scripting and *multihoming*. Multihoming is the ability to host multiple domain names on the same web server. Apache looks at the destination web server address and directs the query to the appropriate directory structure for that domain.

HTTP can be a particularly nasty process to leave running because vulnerabilities have been found with some of the older, stock CGI (Common Gateway Interface) scripts and in the Apache daemon itself. If you are actively maintaining your server, you have probably updated many of these scripts already. The situation you should avoid is an HTTP process that has been loaded on the system and forgotten about. Web services run as their own separate process called httpd.

IMAP AND POP3 SERVERS

Unix supports remote e-mail retrieval using both POP3 and IMAP. POP3 is the older standard and is supported by most remote e-mail clients. IMAP has more features than POP3, but IMAP is just starting to become popular. IMAP has some known vulnerabilities, so be sure that you are running the most current version.

Most Unix flavors ship with both POP3 and IMAP services active. Both run as a process under inetd.

NOTE *For more information on POP3 and IMAP, see Chapter 3.*

LOGIN AND *EXEC*

These two daemons—login and exec—are referred to as the *trusted hosts* daemons because they allow remote users to access the system without requiring password authentication. The commands that use these daemons are `rcp` (copy a file to a remote system), `rlogin` (log on to a remote system), and `rsh` (execute a command on a remote system). Collectively, these are known as the *R commands*.

Trust is based on security equivalency. When one system trusts another, it believes that all users will be properly authenticated and that an attack will never originate from the trusted system. Unfortunately, this trust can create a domino effect. All an attacker needs to do is compromise one Unix machine and then use the trusted host equivalency to compromise additional systems.

Trusted hosts are determined by the contents of the `/etc/hosts.equiv` file. This file contains a list of trusted systems, as you can see in the following example:

```
loki.foobar.com
skylar.foobar.com
pheonix.foobar.com
```

If this `host.equiv` file is located on the system named `thor.foobar.com`, Thor will accept `login` and `exec` service requests from each of these systems without requiring password authentication. If any other system attempts to gain access, the connection request is rejected.

WARNING *It is far too easy to exploit the minor level of security provided by the R commands. An attacker can launch a spoof attack or possibly corrupt DNS in order to exploit the lack of password security. Both `login` and `exec` run as daemons under `inetd`. It is highly recommended that you disable these services. Using `ssh` (secure shell) will provide the same functionality but with authenticated and encrypted communications.*

E-MAIL SERVER

Most flavors of Unix include Sendmail for processing SMTP traffic. Although a few other SMTP programs are available for Unix, Sendmail is by far the most popular.. Older versions of Sendmail (especially versions prior to 8) have many known exploits. If you are running an older version, you should seriously consider updating.

WARNING *Unfortunately, many Unix vendors do not stay up-to-date on Sendmail releases, so it is entirely possible that you will install a new operating system version, only to find that Sendmail is one or two years old.*

Most versions of Unix ship with Sendmail installed and running. Sendmail runs as its own separate process. The name of the daemon is `sendmail`.

NEWS SERVER

The most popular Unix news server is the InterNetNews daemon (INND). When a Unix news server is provided with an appropriate feed, remote users can connect to the server to read and post news articles. If no feed is available, the server can be used for intranet discussion groups.

News is not included with most Unix packages, primarily because of the number of resources the typical news server uses. Besides gobs of disk space (8GB to store a few weeks' worth of articles is not uncommon), an active news server will bring a low-grade processor to its knees.

TIP *If you decide to run news, it is a good idea to dedicate a system to the task.*

NFS SERVER

Unix can use NFS to export portions of the server's file system to NFS clients or to act as an NFS client itself and mount remote file systems. Functionality is similar to NetWare (in which you map a drive letter to a section of the remote file system) or to NT server (in which you map to a share). The difference is that the remote NFS file system can be mounted to any point in a Unix client's file system.

Most flavors of Unix that ship with NFS support NFS version 1. The original version of NFS was rather insecure, mostly because it used UDP as a transport. NFS version 2 supports TCP, which helps to make the protocol easier to control with static packet filtering. Many Unix operating systems ship with the NFS server active. Unless you specifically configure it otherwise, no file systems are exported by default.

Using NFS is still considered a risky venture because packet filtering is easily exploited and overcome by any skilled cracker. Consider using NFS only if necessary, and then only behind firewalls.

SAMBA

SAMBA is a suite of tools that allow a Unix machine to act as a session message block (SMB) client or server. This is the same protocol used by Windows systems, which means that a Unix system running SAMBA can participate in a Windows workgroup or NT 4 domain, -even acting as a Primary or Backup Domain Controller. (Work is underway to allow SAMBA systems to work with Active Directory.) This arrangement allows the Unix machine to share files or printers with Windows systems.

Most Unix flavors do not ship with SAMBA installed. The exception is Linux. SAMBA is available for free, however, and supports many flavors of Unix. SAMBA runs its own set of daemons (smbd and nmbd), which are not controlled by inetd. .

TALK

Unix supports Talk, which is similar to Internet Relay Chat (IRC). Talk does not require a dedicated server, because a session is created directly between two Unix machines. You establish a connection by typing **talk user@host.domain.**

The recipient of a Talk request accepts or rejects the connection. Once a connection is established, the screen is split so that users can type messages simultaneously. Most flavors of Unix ship with Talk installed and activated. Talk is run as a process under inetd.

Because today's security philosophy is minimalist, activate Talk only if it is absolutely necessary. Using Talk-like clients (thus avoiding the activation of daemons) can achieve the same communication capability. Some examples include IRC, ICQ, and America Online's Instant Messenger (AIM).

TIME SERVER

Unix can use Network Time Protocol (NTP) to both send and receive time synchronization updates. Typically, one system on the network is set up as a *time reference server*. This server syncs its time with one of the many available time servers on the Internet. Other systems on the network then check with the reference time server to ensure that their system time remains accurate.

Most flavors of Unix ship with NTP installed and active. NTP is run as a process under inetd. NTP 3, the most current version, can use certificates to verify the identity of reference servers on the network, thereby eliminating unknown servers from posing as reference servers.

TELNET SERVER

Unix can accept Telnet requests to provide remote console access to the server. Clients connecting to the system through Telnet have the same abilities they would have if they were sitting in front of the server console.

NOTE *Telnet is a powerful feature, so take additional steps to limit who has Telnet access to your Unix machines.*

Telnet is supported by all current versions of Unix. By default, the Telnet server is active. Telnet runs as a process under `inetd`.

Additional steps taken to secure Telnet include limiting the administrative functions that can be performed in a Telnet session (including logging in as root) or replacing Telnet with `ssh` (secure shell), which provides the same functionality but encrypts the communication. (In Telnet, the username and password are sent over the network media in clear text.)

inetd and *xinetd*

The `inetd` service is the super server that is responsible for monitoring service ports on a Unix system. (Starting in Red Hat Linux 7, `inetd` has been replaced with `xinetd`, an improved version that provides better security and management.) The `inetd` service is also responsible for launching the appropriate daemon when a service request is received. The `inetd` service uses two files to determine how to handle service requests:

services   Identifies the service associated with each port

inetd.conf   Identifies the daemon associated with each service

THE SERVICES FILE

The services file was discussed at length in Chapter 3, so we'll only briefly mention it here. The services file contains a single line entry, which identifies each port that `inetd` is expected to monitor. For example, the line entry for Telnet appears as follows:

```
telnet          23/tcp              #Provide remote terminal access
```

This line tells `inetd` that any request using TCP as a transport that is received on port 23 is attempting to access the service Telnet. Once `inetd` discovers that a remote user is trying to access Telnet, `inetd` references the `inetd.conf` file to determine how to handle the request.

INETD.CONF

The `inetd.conf` file tells `inetd` which daemon to launch for a given service request. Here is an example of an `inetd.conf` file:

```
# These are standard services.
#
ftp     stream  tcp     nowait  root    /usr/sbin/tcpd  in.ftpd -l -a
telnet  stream  tcp     nowait  root    /usr/sbin/tcpd  in.telnetd
gopher  stream  tcp     nowait  root    /usr/sbin/tcpd  gn
#smtp   stream  tcp     nowait  root    /usr/bin/smtpd  smtpd
#nntp   stream  tcp     nowait  root    /usr/sbin/tcpd  in.nntpd
#
```

```
# Shell, login, exec and talk are BSD protocols.
#
shell   stream  tcp     nowait  root    /usr/sbin/tcpd  in.rshd
login   stream  tcp     nowait  root    /usr/sbin/tcpd  in.rlogind
#exec   stream  tcp     nowait  root    /usr/sbin/tcpd  in.rexecd
talk    dgram   udp     wait    root    /usr/sbin/tcpd  in.talkd
ntalk   dgram   udp     wait    root    /usr/sbin/tcpd  in.ntalkd
#dtalk  stream  tcp     waut    nobody  /usr/sbin/tcpd  in.dtalkd
#
# Pop and imap mail services et al
#
pop-2   stream  tcp     nowait  root    /usr/sbin/tcpd  ipop2d
pop-3   stream  tcp     nowait  root    /usr/sbin/tcpd  ipop3d
imap    stream  tcp     nowait  root    /usr/sbin/tcpd  imapd
#
# Tftp service is provided primarily for booting.  Most sites
# run this only on machines acting as "boot servers." Do not uncomment
# this unless you *need* it.
#
#tftp   dgram   udp     wait    root    /usr/sbin/tcpd  in.tftpd
#bootps dgram   udp     wait    root    /usr/sbin/tcpd  bootpd
#
# Finger, systat and netstat give out user information which may be
# valuable to potential "system crackers."  Many sites choose to disable
# some or all of these services to improve security.
#
# cfinger is for GNU finger, which is currently not in use in RHS Linux
#
finger  stream  tcp     nowait  root    /usr/sbin/tcpd  in.fingerd
#cfinger stream tcp     nowait  root    /usr/sbin/tcpd  in.cfingerd
#systat stream  tcp     nowait  guest   /usr/sbin/tcpd  /bin/ps -auwwx
#netstat stream tcp     nowait  guest   /usr/sbin/tcpd  /bin/netstat -f inet
#
# Time service is used for clock synchronization.
#
time    stream  tcp     nowait  nobody  /usr/sbin/tcpd  in.timed
time    dgram   udp     wait    nobody  /usr/sbin/tcpd  in.timed
#
# Authentication
#
auth    stream  tcp     nowait  nobody  /usr/sbin/in.identd in.identd -l -e -o
#
# End of inetd.conf
```

From left to right, each line entry includes the following:

◆ The service, as identified in the services file

◆ The socket type

◆ The transport

◆ The flags to use at initialization

◆ The user account that provides privileges for this daemon

◆ The name of the daemon, including any required switches

Once `inetd` checks the services file and identifies a service request as looking for Telnet, `inetd` accesses the `inetd.conf` file and references the following line:

```
telnet  stream  tcp    nowait  root    /usr/sbin/tcpd  in.telnetd
```

This line tells `inetd` to go to the `/usr/sbin` directory and run the `tcpd` daemon using `in.telnetd` as a switch while using root-level privileges.

WARNING   Be careful with any service that runs under root-level privileges, because such services are prime targets for attack. An attacker who can compromise a root-level service might be able to steal information or install a back door to provide future access. Thus, many services run as guest *or* nobody. *Compromising the service can then provide little access.*

DISABLING SERVICES CALLED BY *INETD*

One of the best ways to secure a Unix system is to shut down all unneeded services. The more services running on the system, the easier it is for an attacker to find an exploit that will allow access to the system.

TIP   Disabling unneeded services is also an easy way to boost system performance. The fewer processes you have enabled, the more resources you will have available for the services you need to run.

To disable services running under `inetd`, simply add a pound sign (#) to the beginning of the entry within the `inetd.conf` file. For example, to disable Telnet access to the system, simply change the entry to the following:

```
#telnet  stream  tcp    nowait  root    /usr/sbin/tcpd  in.telnetd
```

After you comment out all the services you do not want to run, you simply need to restart the `inetd` process. Do this by identifying the process ID being used by the service and sending that process ID a restart request. To find the process ID for `inetd`, type the following:

```
[root@thor /etc]# ps -ax|grep inetd
  151  ?  SW   0:00 (inetd)
 7177  p0 S    0:00 grep inetd
[root@thor /etc]# kill -HUP 151
[root@thor /etc]#
```

The `ps -ax` portion of the first command lists all running processes. Instead of letting this output scroll past the top of the screen, we have piped (|) it to the `grep` command. We are telling `grep` to filter through the output produced by `ps -ax` and show us only the entries that include the keyword `inetd`. The first entry (process ID `151`) is the actual `inetd` process running on the Unix system. The second listing (process ID `7177`) is our `grep` command performing its search.

Now that you know the process ID being used by `inetd`, you can signal to the process that you want it to restart. You do so with the `kill -HUP 151` command.

NOTE   *Remember that case is important. You must type the command exactly.*

After you restart `inetd`, it should ignore service requests that you have commented out. You can test this by using Telnet and pointing it to the service port in question. For example,

```
telnet thor 110
```

creates a connection with the POP3 service port (110). If you have commented out the POP3 service, you should immediately receive a Connection Refused error message.

XINETD

The `xinetd` service is the next generation of `inetd` that provides a new framework for configuring services. Instead of listing all services within an `xinetd.conf` file (which does exist for global options), individual components have their own file located within the `/etc/xinetd.d/` directory. By default (starting with RedHat 7.2), all services are deactivated. To activate them, simply replace the `disabled = yes` line in the file with `disabled = no`, and restart the `xinetd` daemon.

Working with Other Services

Not all services are called by `inetd`. BIND, Sendmail, and SAMBA, for example, each commonly runs as its own process. HTTP is another service that is commonly run as its own process and is not called by `inetd`. This is done for performance reasons: the service can respond to requests faster if it does not have to wait for `inetd` to wake it up. On an extremely busy system, this can provide a noticeable improvement in performance.

DISABLING STAND-ALONE SERVICES

To disable a stand-alone service, you need to disable the initialization of that service during system startup. Many services look for key files before they initialize. If they don't find this key file, the service is not started. This approach prevents errors. For example, BIND looks for the file `/etc/named.boot` during startup. Sendmail checks for a file named `sendmail.cf` before it will initialize. If these files are not found, the process fails to start.

One way to disable a process from starting is to delete or rename the process's key file. For example, the command

```
mv named.boot named.boot.old
```

renames the `named.boot` file to `.boot.old`. This renaming prevents BIND from being able to locate its key file, thus causing initialization to fail.

You can also disable a stand-alone service by renaming its initialization script or by commenting it out. For example, in the Linux world, all process initialization scripts are stored under `/etc/rc.d/init.d`. These initialization files bear the names of the processes that they start. For example, the Sendmail initialization script is named `sendmail.init`. By renaming this file to `sendmail.init.old`, you can prevent Sendmail from being called during system initialization.

After you change your initialization files so that all unnecessary daemons will not start, you can restart the system or simply kill the current process. To kill a running process, use the `ps` and `grep` commands, as we did in the `inetd` example. You then issue the `kill` command without any switches. The output of these commands is similar to this:

```
[root@thor /root]# ps -ax|grep sendmail
  187  ?   S    0:00 (sendmail)
  258  p0  S    0:00 grep sendmail
[root@thor /root]# kill 187
[root@thor /root]# ps -ax|grep sendmail
  263  p0  S    0:00 grep sendmail
[root@thor /root]#
```

After you reduce the number of services running on your Unix system, you can use *TCP Wrapper* to limit who can access these services.

TCP Wrapper

TCP Wrapper allows you to specify which hosts are allowed to access each service managed by `inetd`. Most of today's versions of Unix ship with TCP Wrapper installed.

NOTE *Despite its name, TCP Wrapper can be used with services that require either TCP or UDP as a transport.*

TCP Wrapper is activated by having `inetd` call the TCP Wrapper daemon instead of the actual service daemon. In our Telnet example:

```
telnet  stream  tcp     nowait  root    /usr/sbin/tcpd  in.telnetd
```

`inetd` is actually calling the TCP Wrapper daemon (`tcpd`), not the Telnet daemon (`in.telnetd`). Once `tcpd` is called, the service request is compared with a set of access rules. If the connection is acceptable, it is allowed to pass through to the `in.telnetd` daemon. If the connection request fails access control, the connection is rejected.

Access control is managed using two files:

hosts.allow Defines which systems are permitted access to each service

hosts.deny Defines which service requests are rejected

When verifying access from a remote system, `tcpd` first checks the `hosts.allow` file. If no matching entry is found, `tcpd` then checks the `hosts.deny` file. If no matching entry is found in either file, access is allowed. The syntax of both files is as follows:

```
<comma separated list of services>:<comma separated list of hosts>
```

Valid services are only those managed by `inetd`. Valid hosts can be listed by host name, domain, or IP address. For example, consider the following output:

```
[root@thor /etc]# cat hosts.allow
pop-3, imap: ALL
ftp: .foobar.com
telnet: 192.168.1
finger: 192.168.1.25
```

```
[root@thor /etc]# cat hosts.deny
ANY: ANY
```

The `hosts.allow` file states that all hosts with connectivity to the system are permitted to access POP3 and IMAP services. FTP, however, is limited to hosts within the `foobar.com domain`. We have also limited Telnet access to source IP addresses on the `192.168.1.0` network. Finally, only the host at IP address `192.168.1.25` is allowed to finger the system.

The `hosts.deny` entry allows us to define the security stance "that which is not expressly permitted is denied." If a service request is received and a match is not found in the `hosts.allow` file, this catchall rule specifies that we do not want to allow the remote system access to our Unix server.

TCP Wrapper is an excellent way to fine-tune access to your system. Even if all your Unix systems are sitting behind a firewall, it can't hurt to take preventive measures and lock them down even further. Doing so helps to ensure that anyone who manages to sneak past the firewall is still denied access to your Unix system.

Unix Checklist Overview

Many excellent security checklists exist for the various Unix-based systems. This section provides a simple conceptual overview along with specific general steps that you can take to secure an out-of-the-box installation. The current trend is for more and more vendors to release systems preconfigured to be more secure.

Preinstallation

The most important instruction concerning operating system security has to do with network connectivity. In a word, don't. Be sure that a system has as many security controls set as possible (including patches) before connecting it to any type of network that might be possibly compromised. Although implementation is difficult in reality, you can have a dedicated "patch" machine that, along with a switch, can be connected to a newly installed system in order to configure, update, and validate the new system's security.

TIP   By subscribing to vendor or security-related mailing lists for your operating system, your vulnerability to late-breaking exploits and security holes can be minimized.

System Configuration

As you install your operating system, keep in mind the basic principle of system security :enable only what you will use. This approach not only conserves critical resources, but it helps you avoid unnecessary complexity. To paraphrase Einstein, systems should be kept as simple as possible—but no simpler. Once your essential operating system install is finished, you need to bring it up to date by applying the latest patches.

PATCHES

Patches are critical to system security. Even if no patches exists for the operating system itself, the services and applications that run *on* the operating system most certainly do, and these are the most vulnerable, most often exploited, and most often updated components on a computer.

In addition to general and security-specific patches, many vendors (and third parties) have produced "hardening" scripts that you can use to lock down all the various components of any Unix-based system. Well-written scripts can use basic "find and replace" text functionality to replace general values with your specific information (typically network parameters). Another variant of the "hardening" script is a testing script that is used to probe the now-locked-down system to test if the script really worked as advertised.

GENERAL CONFIGURATION

Make the following changes to any Unix-based system:

◆ Deactivate any applications that run underneath `inetd/xinetd`.

◆ Configure `inetd/xinetd` to use the `tcp_wrappers` function to provide additional protection. (See your system's documentation for specific instructions.)

◆ Remove or empty the `/etc/hosts.equiv` file (used by the R programs to grant access to remote systems based on IP address only).

◆ Edit `/etc/hosts.allow` by adding the following line *after* any lines allowing specific system access:

`ALL:ALL:deny`

◆ Edit `/etc/hosts.deny` by adding the following line as the first (uncommented) line in the file:

`ALL:ALL`

◆ Verify that all unnecessary daemons, services, and applications have been removed from the system or at least removed from activation through any startup scripts (variously stored in `/etc/`, `/etc/rc.d/`, and `/etc/init.d`)

◆ Verify that no unnecessary or unused user or group accounts exist and that system accounts (`bin`, `nobody`, and so on) are not allowed interactive (through the console or remotely) logon.

◆ Review the terminal security file (usually `/etc/securetty` or `/etc/ttys`) to ensure that remote access to any privileged account (especially root) is not allowed.

◆ If your system is using PAM (Pluggable Authentication Module), take a look through the configuration files (`/etc/pam.conf` and the various files stored in `/etc/pam.d/`) to make sure you understand the default settings, and change them if necessary.

◆ Verify that `syslogd` (the system logging daemon) will not accept any incoming connections.

NETWORKING

The following steps are considered critical for systems that provide services to the Internet (or any unsecured network) or are otherwise in a position to be vulnerable to attack:

◆ Implement any built-in firewall capabilities of your operating system. Linux has `iptables` (kernel version 2.4.x) and `ipchains` (kernel version 2.2.x), BSD has `ipfw`, and Sun Solaris has SunScreen on Solaris 8 (Solaris 9 has not been released for the Intel platform). Firewall settings should focus on packet filtering, DoS attacks, and logging.

◆ Carefully consider remote administration. At a minimum, use the latest patched version of SSH (Secure Shell). Remove backward compatibility with previous SSH protocols (especially protocol 1).

MONITORING

Keeping track of system access (both successful and unsuccessful) is critical for security. Most experts agree that putting resources into monitoring and logging is more valuable in the long run that blowing the bank on the latest firewall software. In particular, consider the following:

◆ Install and integrate a host-based IDS (intrusion detection system) on your Unix system. If you have network-wide IDS, be sure that your system is integrated to the degree required by your security plan.

◆ An excellent addition to network-activity IDS is a system integrity scanner. The most popular example of file system integrity checking is Tripwire, but many other systems exist.

MAINTENANCE

Throughout the life of the system, plan for and implement the following:

◆ Regularly review intrusion detection and system access logs.

◆ Make regular backups of the entire system, focusing not just on data but system configuration. Consider the use of a disk imager (such as Ghost) to maintain a complete system copy that is useful for rapid backups of compromised systems.

◆ Maintain effective and current security configurations, to include a history of previous changes.

Summary

In this chapter you saw how to go about locking down your Unix (or Unix-based system, such as Linux and FreeBSD) system. We discussed file permissions and how they can be tuned to restrict access to sensitive files. We also looked at how the Unix system deals with authentication and why it is so important to lock down the root user account. Finally, we looked at IP services and how you can limit which hosts have access to them.

The next chapter will look at some common exploits, describing how each vulnerability is exploited and what you can do to protect your network.

Chapter 14

The Anatomy of an Attack

IN THIS CHAPTER, WE will look at some of the common tricks and tools that an attacker can use to compromise your assets. This material is not intended to be a how-to on attacking a network (so please don't use it on live networks or on networks for which you do not have explicit written permission to use these techniques). Rather, it is intended to show you, the network administrator, how an attacker is likely to go about finding the points of vulnerability within your network. Here, we will focus on how you can identify the signs of an attack and what you can do to prevent it.

The initial discussions will assume that the attacker is someone outside your network perimeter who is trying to break in. We'll show you the steps an attacker must take when working with limited information. A regular user on your network, who already has an insider's view, would be able to skip many of these steps. Because an overwhelming majority of network attacks originate from inside the network, the precautionary steps you take to secure your network resources cannot concentrate solely on the network perimeter.

Featured in this chapter:

◆ Collecting information

◆ Probing the network

◆ Launching an attack

Collecting Information

Woolly Attacker has seen one of your TV ads and decided that your political views do not match his own. He decides his best recourse is to attack your network. The question is, where to begin? At this point, Woolly does not even know your domain name. In order to attack your network, he has to do some investigative work.

NOTE   *The attack techniques described here assume a cracker is attempting to penetrate a specific network. In reality, most hackers indiscriminately attack any systems that exhibit specific vulnerabilities. With the advent of fast, automated tools (used by "script kiddies," individuals without sophisticated technical knowledge beyond what is needed to employ these tools), crackers can scan entire IP subnets for the many vulnerabilities discovered throughout the years. Your system could be attacked simply because you are unlucky enough to have an (unsecured) server located on a subnet chosen at random by an attacker.*

The *whois* Command

The first thing Woolly can try is a whois query at the InterNIC. The InterNIC maintains a publicly accessible database of all registered domain names. You can search this database using the whois utility. By querying for the name of the organization, Woolly can find out if it has a registered domain name. For example, searching for an organization named CameronHunt.com would produce something that looks like the following:

```
[granite:~]$ whois CameronHunt.com
Registrant:
Cameron Hunt (CAMERONHUNT-DOM)
      392 E. 12300 So. Ste A.
      Draper, UT 84020
      US

      Domain Name: CAMERONHUNT.COM
      Administrative Contact, Technical Contact, Billing Contact:
         Hunt, Cameron (CHL150)  cam@cameronhunt.com
         10312 Bay Club Ct.
         Tampa, FL 33607
         (813) 207-0363

      Record last updated on 05-Apr-2002.
      Record expires on 19-Jan-2004.
      Record created on 19-Jan-2002.
      Database last updated on 12-Feb-2002 16:21:38 EST.

      Domain servers in listed order:

      DNS.CAMERONHUNT.COM        64.36.56.58
      DNS.COPPERKNOB.COM         64.36.56.59
```

By running this simple command, we now have some interesting information to work with. So far we know the following:

◆ The organization's domain name

◆ The organization's location

◆ The organization's administrative contact

◆ The phone number and fax number for the administrator

◆ A valid subnet address within the organization (64.36.56.0)

DOMAIN NAME

The organization's domain name is important because the attacker can use it to collect further information. Any host or users associated with this organization will also be associated with this domain name. Thus, Woolly has a keyword to use when forming future queries. In the next section, we will use the domain name discovered here to produce some additional information.

PHYSICAL LOCATION

Woolly also knows where this organization is located. If he is truly intent on damaging this network or stealing information, he might now attempt to apply for a temporary job or, even better, offer his consulting services. Once he's inside the organization, he might be granted a certain level of access to network resources in order to continue his investigation or possibly to install backdoor access into the network. Although this would require some legwork, the easiest way to breach a network perimeter is to be invited inside it.

The address also tells Woolly where to go if he wants to do a bit of dumpster diving—rummaging through a dumpster in an effort to find private company information. This information can be valid account names, passwords, or even financial data. Although many companies shred sensitive information, this practice tends to be commonplace only in the financial or HR departments. Many IT shops still dump sensitive information in the trash. Also consider the many types of sticky notes that are ubiquitous in offices everywhere. Many times users write down their password "temporarily" until they have used it enough times to memorize it. Over the years, this process has been simplified because many organizations separate their paper trash from the rest for recycling. This makes finding useful information far easier and a lot cleaner.

ADMINISTRATIVE CONTACT

The administrative contact is typically an individual who is responsible for maintaining the organization's network. In some cases, a technical contact, who is subordinate to the administrative contact, will be listed as well. This information can be extremely useful if Woolly wants to attempt a social engineering attack. For example, he could now call an end user and state, "Hi, I'm Sean, who has just been hired on the help desk. Tom Smith asked me to call you because there is a problem with your account on one of the servers. What's your password?" This attack tends to be less successful in large organizations that have formal security policies and training, but you would be surprised to learn the number of mid-sized or smaller organizations that don't even have a password rotation policy in place, much less an education program. If Woolly gets lucky, he will end up with a valid logon name and password, which will provide at least minimal access to network resources. This minimal access is all that is required to get a foothold and go after full administrator access.

E-mail is another tool that crackers can use to abuse the concept of an administrative contact. It's quite simple for a cracker to send a spoofed e-mail message that contains hostile code (ideally a Trojan) to the administrative contact. If the e-mail is activated by the administrative contact (or through an unpatched vulnerability), the cracker might succeed in gaining backdoor access to a system (and an account!) used to perform administrative functions.

PHONE NUMBERS

Phone numbers may seem like strange pieces of information to go after, but they can actually be quite useful. Most organizations use a phone service called *Direct Inward Dial* (DID). DID allows someone to call a seven-digit phone number and directly reach the desk of an employee without going through an operator. The numbers are usually issued in blocks. For example, 555-0500 through 555-0699 might be a block of DID numbers assigned to a specific organization. DID makes it easy for an attacker to discover every phone number your organization uses.

> ### WHAT A WAR DIALER CAN FIND
>
> It is not uncommon for organizations to overlook security on their dial-in devices. For example, in the spring of 1998, Peter Shipley (who designed a well-known vulnerability analysis tool known as SATAN) used a war dialer to systematically call phone numbers within the San Francisco Bay area. He found multiple systems that granted full access without any type of authentication, including:
>
> ◆ A firewall that protected a financial services organization
>
> ◆ A hospital system that allowed patient records to be viewed or modified
>
> ◆ A fire department system allowing fire engines to be dispatched
>
> Although these are extreme examples, it is not uncommon for organizations to allow their users to have modems on their desktops. This, in effect, puts the employee in charge of security for that modem line, something many employees may not be qualified to handle.

So Woolly might try calling phone numbers that are just a few numbers off from the listed contact. Doing so might allow him to reach other employees on whom to attempt the previously described social engineering attack. Woolly might also set up a *war dialer* in order to test consecutive phone numbers. A war dialer is simply a piece of software that dials a series of phone numbers and then identifies which phone numbers were answered by a computer. Woolly can review the lists and attempt to infiltrate any phone number that was answered by a computer. If his social engineering attack was successful, he even has a valid account to try.

VALID SUBNET

One of the last pieces of information produced by the whois command is an IP address entry for DNS.CAMERONHUNT.com. Since this host is part of our target domain, we can assume that the subnet it sits on is also part of this same domain. Woolly does not know whether the host is inside or outside the firewall, but he now knows one valid subnet to use once he decides to launch his attack.

The *nslookup* Command

Now that the whois command has given Woolly a starting reference point, he can use the nslookup command to collect even more information. The nslookup command allows you to query DNS servers to collect host and IP address information. If Woolly wants to attack the network, he must find out which hosts are available as targets. The nslookup utility does an excellent job of supplying this information.

When Woolly launches the nslookup utility, he is informed of the current DNS (domain name server) that nslookup will use, as shown in the following output:

```
[granite:~]$ nslookup
Default Server:  granite.sover.net
Address:  209.198.87.33
>
```

This output tells us that `nslookup` will use the server `granite.sover.net` when making DNS queries. Since Woolly wants to find out information about `CAMERONHUNT.com`, he can change the default DNS server to one of the two systems listed in the `whois` output, as shown in the following output:

```
> server DNS.CAMERONHUNT.COM
Default Server:  DNS.CAMERONHUNT.COM
Address:  64.36.56.58

>
```

The `nslookup` utility is now pointed at `DNS`, one of CameronHunt's DNS servers. All queries will now be directed to this system instead of to `granite`. The first thing that Woolly will want to try is to perform a *zone transfer*. A zone transfer allows Woolly to collect all host and IP address information with a single command, as shown in the following output:

```
> ls -d CAMERONHUNT.COM > hosts.1st
[DNS.CAMERONHUNT.COM]
Received 20 answers (0 records).
> exit
```

The first command attempts to get the DNS server to list all valid host information for the `CAMERONHUNT.com` domain and output this to a file called `hosts.1st`. Since Wooly received 20 answers to his query, he knows that the command was successful, and he now has a valid list of all hosts registered with the DNS. Of course, newer DNS systems (such as Windows 2000 DNS, which stores its zone files within Active Directory) will refuse such a request unless the transfer is initially authenticated. But many administrators (as evaluated by security experts and demonstrated by the many number of DNS hacks—even at Microsoft) do not activate this simple security procedure. At this point, Woolly exits the `nslookup` utility because he was able to gather quickly all the information he required.

TIP   *You can limit who can perform zone transfers from your name servers by using the* `xfers` *command (if your DNS system supports the* `named.boot` *file). Place this command in the* `named.boot` *file preceding a list of IP addresses that are the only systems allowed to perform zone transfers with the name server.*

Had Woolly received a "Can't list domain" error message, he would have learned that zone transfers from this name server were limited to only specific hosts. Woolly would now be forced to systematically try some common names such as `mail`, `ftp`, `www`, and so on to discover additional subnets within the CameronHunt network. There is no guarantee that Woolly would have been able to identify every valid name using this method, because this process would become a guessing game. The zone transfer was successful, however, as shown by the contents of the `hosts.1st` file:

```
[DNS.CAMERONHUNT.COM]
$ORIGIN CAMERONHUNT.COM.
@                      1H IN SOA     DNS postmaster (
                                     5              ; serial
                                     1H             ; refresh
                                     10M            ; retry
                                     1D             ; expiry
```

```
                                    1H )                   ; minimum
                        1H IN NS    dns
                        1H IN NS    206.79.230.10
                        1H IN MX    5 mail
    cam                 1H IN CNAME mail
    ftp                 1H IN CNAME web
    web                 1H IN A     64.36.56.58
    honeypot            1H IN A     64.36.55.57
    www                 1H IN A     web
```

This file has produced some useful information. Woolly may have two valid IP subnets at which he can direct his attacks instead of just one (64.36.56.0 and 64.36.55.0). The 206.79.230.0 subnet is not a target because the whois information lists this host as being part of another domain (exodus.net).

Woolly also knows that mail is the mail system for the domain because of the MX record entry. In addition, he knows that mail is the only mail system, so if he can disable this one host, he can interrupt mail services for the entire domain. Finally, this file shows that the web server is also acting as the FTP server. It may be possible for Woolly to use the FTP service to compromise the web server and corrupt web pages. This would allow him to penetrate potentially sensitive information.

Search Engines

Using search engines can be an excellent way to collect additional information about an organization's internal network. If you have not done so already, try searching for hits on your organization's domain name. You will be amazed at the amount of information that accrues once an organization has been online for a while. This information can include mail messages, newsgroup posts, and pages from internal web servers (if they are visible from the Internet).

For example, look closely at Figure 14.1. The domain ssc.com has a mail relay named mail.ssc.com that is responsible for sending and receiving all e-mail. As far as the outside world is concerned, mail is ssc.com's only mail system. If you look closely at this mail header, however, you will see another mail system hiding behind mail named palace.ssc.com.

FIGURE 14.1

A search engine hit that displays an e-mail header

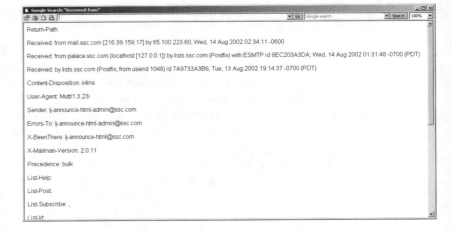

This mail header reveals some information that could be used to attack the internal network, including the following:

♦ The newsgroup server `lists.ssc.com` is a Unix-based machine running Postfix with a userid of 1048.

♦ The mail relay `palace` is on IP `127.0.0.1`, which means that it operates on the same physical machine as `lists.ssc.com` and is therefore also Unix-based.

We now have not only the IP address of the mail server, but we also know that the relay and newsgroup server that created this message share the same Unix-based system. Not bad for a single search engine hit.

TIP   The way to avoid this problem is to have the mail relay strip all previous outbound mail header information. This will make it appear as though all mail originates from the relay itself, thus preventing any information about your internal network from leaking out.

Probing the Network

Now that Woolly has collected some general information about the target, it is time for him to begin probing and prodding to see what other systems or services might be available on the network. Woolly would do this even if he has already found his way inside the firewall through some other means, such as a contract job or dial-in access. Probing gives an attacker a road map of the network, as well as a list of available services.

The *traceroute* Command

You can use the `traceroute` command to trace the network path from one host to another. This is useful when you want to document the network segments between two hosts. An example of the output created by `traceroute` is shown in Figure 14.2.

NOTE   In the Windows world, the command name is truncated to `tracert` to accommodate an eight-character filename.

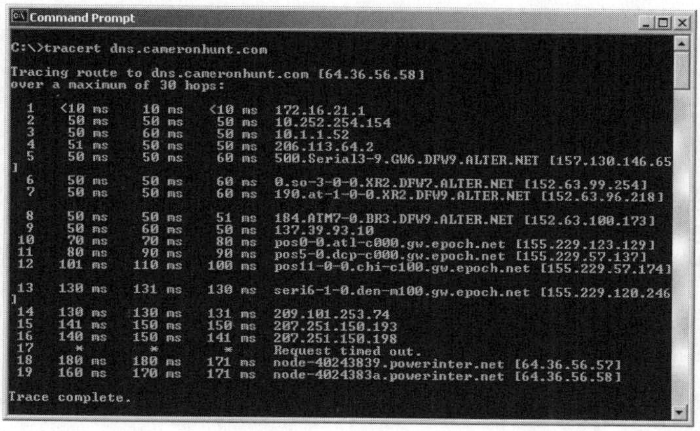

FIGURE 14.2

Output from the
`traceroute`
command

```
C:\>tracert dns.cameronhunt.com

Tracing route to dns.cameronhunt.com [64.36.56.58]
over a maximum of 30 hops:

  1    <10 ms     10 ms    <10 ms   172.16.21.1
  2     50 ms     50 ms     50 ms   10.252.254.154
  3     50 ms     60 ms     50 ms   10.1.1.52
  4     51 ms     50 ms     50 ms   206.113.64.2
  5     50 ms     50 ms     60 ms   500.Serial3-9.GW6.DFW9.ALTER.NET [157.130.146.65]
  6     50 ms     50 ms     60 ms   0.so-3-0-0.XR2.DFW7.ALTER.NET [152.63.99.254]
  7     50 ms     50 ms     60 ms   190.at-1-0-0.XR2.DFW9.ALTER.NET [152.63.96.218]
  8     50 ms     50 ms     51 ms   184.ATM7-0.BR3.DFW9.ALTER.NET [152.63.100.173]
  9     50 ms     60 ms     50 ms   137.39.93.10
 10     70 ms     70 ms     80 ms   pos0-0.atl-c000.gw.epoch.net [155.229.123.129]
 11     80 ms     90 ms     90 ms   pos5-0.dcp-c000.gw.epoch.net [155.229.57.137]
 12    101 ms    110 ms    100 ms   pos11-0-0.chi-c100.gw.epoch.net [155.229.57.174]
 13    130 ms    131 ms    130 ms   seri6-1-0.den-m100.gw.epoch.net [155.229.120.246]
 14    130 ms    130 ms    131 ms   209.101.253.74
 15    141 ms    150 ms    150 ms   207.251.150.193
 16    140 ms    150 ms    141 ms   207.251.150.198
 17      *         *         *      Request timed out.
 18    180 ms    180 ms    171 ms   node-40243839.powerinter.net [64.36.56.57]
 19    160 ms    170 ms    171 ms   node-4024383a.powerinter.net [64.36.56.58]

Trace complete.
```

The output in Figure 14.2 shows us the host name and IP address of each router that must be crossed between the source and destination systems. The three preceding columns identify the amount of time it takes to cross the previous network segment.

Just before reaching DNS, we crossed a few network segments on powerinternet.net. Notice also that several hops timed out and failed to respond to a traceroute query. This could be because of a slow link speed or possibly because the device is filtering out these requests.

Returning to our nslookup information, Woolly still needs to verify whether the honeypot address is within the CameronHunt.com domain or whether the website is hosted at an alternate location. To find out, he can rerun the traceroute command, only this time using honeypot.CameronHunt.com as a target system. The output of this test is shown in Figure 14.3. As you can see, the trace terminates on an unknown network. This verifies that honeypot is a host that doesn't exist and that Woolly has only the 64.36.56.0 subnet to use when targeting attacks.

FIGURE 14.3

Woolly verifies that honeypot isn't a valid host.

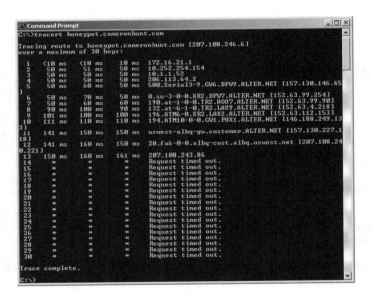

NOTE *If Woolly had taken a contract job with CameronHunt.com or found his way into the network by some other means, the* traceroute *command would be able to produce even more information; it would document each of the internal IP subnets, as well as which routers connect them. By choosing a few selective hosts, Woolly would be able to generate a full network diagram.*

One final probing technique that relies on traceroute-like techniques is known as *firewalking*, which uses various ICMP packet types to determine whether a packet can identify open or "pass-through" ports on a firewall/router. Sophisticated versions of this attack can also find routers behind any packet-filtering device (and determine their Access Control List settings) and possibly even map the entire contents of a private network. The best protection against firewalking is to disallow *outbound* ICMP messages at your firewall.

Host and Service Scanning

Host and service scanning allows you to document which systems are active on the network and which ports are open on each system. This is the next phase in identifying which systems might be vulnerable to attack. Woolly would follow these steps:

1. Find every system on the network.

2. Find every service running on each system.

3. Find out which service is vulnerable to which exploits.

You can perform these steps individually, or you can locate a tool that performs all of them at once. For the sake of completeness, we will look at each of these steps one at a time.

PING SCANNING

A Ping scanner simply sends an ICMP (Internet Control Message Protocol) request to each sequential IP address on a subnet and waits for a reply. If a reply is received, the scanner assumes that there is an active host at this address. The scanner then creates a log entry of the systems that respond and possibly attempts to resolve the IP address to a host name. You can use a simple batch or script file to create a homespun Ping scanner. You can also find a number of graphical utilities such as WildPackets' (formerly AG Group) iNetTools, shown in Figure 14.4.

TIP   An additional feature of the iNetTools utility is that if the tool cannot resolve the IP address to a DNS host name, it will attempt to look up the system's NetBIOS name instead. This is helpful if you are scanning a network with many Windows desktop systems that may not have entries on the DNS server.

FIGURE 14.4

The Ping scanner included in the iNetTools utility

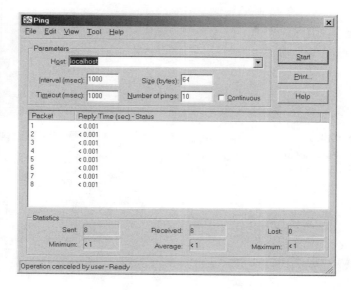

PORT SCANNING

A port scanner allows you to sequentially probe a number of ports on a target system to see if a service is listening. Think of a burglar walking through an apartment building and jiggling all the doorknobs to see if one is unlocked, and you will get the idea. A port scanner simply identifies which well-known services are listening and waits for connection requests.

Figure 14.5 shows the results of a scan against the system `64.36.56.59` using iNetTools. As you can see, iNetTools has identified a number of open ports on this system. Notice that the information about which ports are open reveals the functionality of a system, which in this case is acting as an FTP, mail, DNS, and web server.

Figure 14.6 shows how a port scanner works. If you look at packet 35, the port scanner initiates a TCP three-packet handshake with a machine named Thor. The port scanner transmits a packet with a flag setting of SYN=1 with a destination port of 23 (telnet). In packet 36, Thor replies by transmitting a response of SYN=1, ACK=1. Because of this response by Thor, the port scanner knows that a service is listening at the telnet port. In packet 37, the scanner completes the three-packet handshake by transmitting ACK=1. The scanner then immediately ends the session in packet 38 by transmitting ACK=1, FIN=1. In packet 39, Thor acknowledges this request by transmitting ACK=1.

FIGURE 14.5
A port scan of a system

FIGURE 14.6
An analyzer trace of a TCP port scan

No.	Source	Destination	Layer	Summary	Error	Size	Interpacket Time	Absolute Time	Relative Time
35	Scanner	Thor	tcp	Port:1546 ---> TELNET SYN		64	68 ms	11:31:02 PM	2 s
36	Thor	Scanner	tcp	Port:TELNET ---> 1546 ACK SYN		64	1 ms	11:31:02 PM	2 s
37	Scanner	Thor	tcp	Port:1546 ---> TELNET ACK		64	367 µs	11:31:02 PM	2 s
38	Scanner	Thor	tcp	Port:1546 ---> TELNET ACK FIN		64	710 µs	11:31:02 PM	2 s
39	Thor	Scanner	tcp	Port:TELNET ---> 1546 ACK		64	681 µs	11:31:02 PM	2 s
40	Scanner	Thor	tcp	Port:1547 ---> 24 SYN		64	9 ms	11:31:02 PM	2 s
41	Thor	Scanner	tcp	Port:24 ---> 1547 ACK RESET		64	642 µs	11:31:02 PM	2 s
42	Scanner	Thor	tcp	Port:1545 ---> 22 SYN		64	450 ms	11:31:02 PM	3 s
43	Scanner	Thor	tcp	Port:1543 ---> FTP-DATA SYN		64	136 µs	11:31:02 PM	3 s
44	Scanner	Thor	tcp	Port:1547 ---> 24 SYN		64	69 µs	11:31:02 PM	3 s
45	Thor	Scanner	tcp	Port:22 ---> 1545 ACK RESET		64	687 µs	11:31:02 PM	3 s
46	Thor	Scanner	tcp	Port:FTP-DATA ---> 1543 ACK RESET		64	405 µs	11:31:02 PM	3 s
47	Thor	Scanner	tcp	Port:24 ---> 1547 ACK RESET		64	412 µs	11:31:02 PM	3 s
48	Scanner	Thor	tcp	Port:1548 ---> SMTP SYN		64	68 ms	11:31:02 PM	3 s
49	Thor	Scanner	tcp	Port:SMTP ---> 1548 ACK SYN		64	1 ms	11:31:02 PM	3 s
50	Scanner	Thor	tcp	Port:1548 ---> SMTP ACK		64	356 µs	11:31:02 PM	3 s
51	Scanner	Thor	tcp	Port:1548 ---> SMTP ACK FIN		64	715 µs	11:31:02 PM	3 s
52	Thor	Scanner	tcp	Port:SMTP ---> 1548 ACK		64	691 µs	11:31:02 PM	3 s
53	Scanner	Thor	tcp	Port:1549 ---> 26 SYN		64	9 ms	11:31:02 PM	3 s
54	Thor	Scanner	tcp	Port:26 ---> 1549 ACK RESET		64	653 µs	11:31:02 PM	3 s
55	Scanner	Thor	tcp	Port:1545 ---> 22 SYN		64	450 ms	11:31:03 PM	3 s
56	Scanner	Thor	tcp	Port:1549 ---> 26 SYN		64	165 µs	11:31:03 PM	3 s
57	Scanner	Thor	tcp	Port:1547 ---> 24 SYN		64	24 µs	11:31:03 PM	3 s
58	Thor	Scanner	tcp	Port:22 ---> 1545 ACK RESET		64	761 µs	11:31:03 PM	3 s
59	Thor	Scanner	tcp	Port:26 ---> 1549 ACK RESET		64	413 µs	11:31:03 PM	3 s
60	Thor	Scanner	tcp	Port:24 ---> 1547 ACK RESET		64	389 µs	11:31:03 PM	3 s

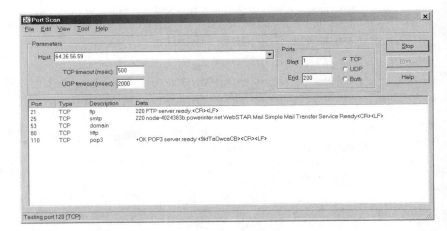

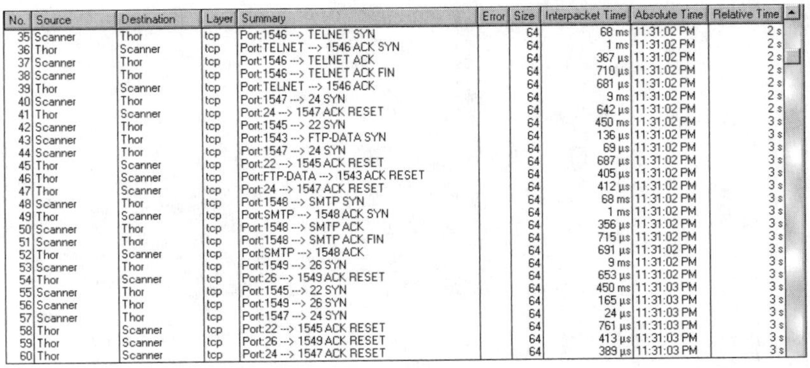

The scanner knew that Thor was listening on port 23 because it was able to complete a full TCP three-packet handshake with the system. To find out what happens when a service is not active, look at packets 55, 56, and 57. In these three transmissions, the scanner is probing Thor at ports 22, 26, and 24 to see if a service is listening. In packets 58, 59, and 60, Thor replies by transmitting ACK=1, RST=1. This is a target system's way of letting the source know that no service is available on that port. By sorting through the responses, a port scanner can accurately log which ports have active services.

Port scanning has a couple of shortcomings. The first is that the connection attempt will most certainly be logged by the target system. This provides the system administrator on the target system with a record that a port scan has taken place. The second is that port scanning can easily be filtered out by any packet filter or firewall because the port scanner relies on the initial connection packet with SYN=1.

TCP HALF SCANNING

TCP half scanning was developed to get past the logging issue. A TCP half scan does not try to establish a full TCP connection. The half scanner transmits only the initial SYN=1 packet. If the target system responds with a SYN=1, ACK=1, the half scanner knows that the port is listening and immediately transmits an RST=1 to tear down the connection. Since a full connection is never actually established, most (but not all) systems would not log this scan. Since a TCP half scan still relies on the initial SYN=1 packet, it can be blocked by a packet filter or firewall, just like a full scanner.

FIN SCANNING

A FIN scanner does not transmit a SYN=1 packet in an attempt to establish a connection. Rather, a FIN scanner transmits a packet with ACK=1, FIN=1. If you look back at packet 38 in Figure 14.6, you will remember that these are the flags we used to tear down our TCP connection. In effect, the FIN scanner is telling the target system that it wants to tear down a connection, even though no connection exists.

NOTE *How the target system responds is actually kind of interesting (to a bit weenie, anyway). If the target port does not have a service listening, the system responds with the standard ACK=1, RST=1. If a service is listening, however, the target system simply ignores the request because there is no connection for the target system to tear down. By sorting through which ports elicit a response and which do not, a FIN scanner can determine which ports are active on the target system.*

What makes this type of scanner even more lethal is that neither a static packet filter nor many firewalls block this type of scan. Thus, an attacker can identify systems even if they are on the other side of a firewall.

FIN scanning does not work on every type of system. For example, a Microsoft TCP stack responds with an ACK=1, RST=1 even if the port is active. Although Microsoft's TCP stack does not comply with RFC 973, you cannot use a FIN scanner against a Windows systems to identify active ports because it will appear that none of the system's ports has active services. The ACK=1, RST=1 still informs the attacker that a system is present, however, and that it is some form of Microsoft operating system.

Passive Monitoring

To collect more information about your network, an attacker might attempt to monitor traffic. They can do so by directly installing an analyzer onto your network or, more subversively, by identifying internal systems. You have seen what an attacker can learn by installing a network analyzer on your network to monitor traffic flow. In this section, we will look at one of the more subtle methods an attacker can use to collect information about your internal systems.

For example, take a look at the packet capture in Figure 14.7. This is a standard HTTP data request that a client sends to a web server. If Woolly Attacker can get some of your internal users to connect to his website (perhaps through an enticing e-mail), he has the possibility of collecting a wealth of information. Starting at about halfway through the packet capture, our web client is telling the remote web server several things:

FIGURE 14.7

An HTTP data request

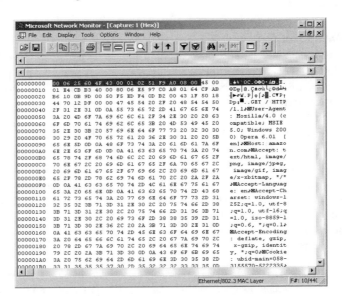

- ◆ The preferred language is English.

- ◆ The acceptable encoding types (including gzip).

- ◆ The cookie id placed (and retrieved) by Amazon.

- ◆ The operating system is Windows 2000.

- ◆ The browser is Opera 6.01 (but compatible with Internet Explorer 5).

The last two pieces of information are the most interesting. Woolly now knows that if he wants to attack this system, he needs to focus on exploits that apply to a system running Windows 2000 and Opera 6.02. As you will see later in this chapter, many of these vulnerabilities can be exploited simply by having a user download a web page.

One of the reasons for the popularity of proxy firewalls is that most of them filter out information regarding operating system and browser type. This puts an attacker in a hit-or-miss position: the exploit may or may not work on the target system.

NOTE   *The less information you unknowingly hand out about your network, the more difficult it will be for an attacker to compromise your resources.*

Checking for Vulnerabilities

Now that Woolly has an inventory of all systems on the network and he knows what services are running on each, he can turn his attention to finding out which vulnerabilities can be exploited. He can do so in a hit-or-miss fashion by simply launching the exploit to see what happens. A dangerous attacker, however, will take the time required to know that an exploit will work before trying it. This helps to ensure that the attacker does not set off some kind of alarm while bumping around in the dark. An attacker can check for vulnerabilities manually or automatically through some form of software product.

MANUAL VULNERABILITY CHECKS

Manual vulnerability checks are performed by using a tool, such as Telnet, to connect to a remote service and see what is listening. Most services do a good job of identifying themselves when a remote host connects to them. Although this is for troubleshooting purposes, it can provide an attacker with more information than you intended to give out.

For example, take a look at Figure 14.8. We have opened a Telnet session to the SMTP (Simple Mail Transfer Protocol) port on `mailsys.foobar.org`. To do so, we typed the following command at a command prompt:

```
telnet mailsys.foobar.org 25
```

FIGURE 14.8

Using Telnet to connect to a remote mail server

The trailing 25 tells Telnet not to connect to the default Telnet port of 23 but to port 25, which is the well known port for SMTP. As you can see, this mail server is more than happy to let us know that it is running Lotus Domino and that the software version is 5.0.8. An attacker looking to disable this system now knows to search for vulnerabilities that pertain to Lotus 5.0.8. Table 14.1 shows a number of commands you can use when connecting to a service port via Telnet.

TABLE 14.1: SERVICE PORT COMMANDS WHEN USING TELNET

SERVICE	PORT	COMMANDS		COMMENTS
FTP	21	`user, pass, stat, quit`		This provides a command session only. You cannot transfer a file.
SMTP	25	`helo, mail from:, rcpt to:, data, quit`		E-mail can be forged using these commands.
HTTP	80	`get`		You will receive a page error, but you will at least know the service is active.
POP3	110	`user, pass, stat, list, retr, quit`		Mail can be viewed by connecting to the POP3 port.
IMAP4	143	`login, capability, examine, expunge, logout`		All commands must be preceded by a unique line identifier.

Clearly, manual vulnerability-checking takes some work. Manually intervening to verify the target service is time-consuming. Manual vulnerability-checking also requires that attackers have at least half a clue about what they are doing. Knowing which service is running on the target system is of little help to an attacker who cannot figure out how to exploit this information.

AUTOMATED VULNERABILITY SCANNERS

An *automated vulnerability scanner* is simply a software program that automatically performs all the probing and scanning steps that an attacker would normally do manually. These scanners can be directed at a single system or at entire IP subnets. The scanner first identifies potential targets. It then performs a port scan and probes all active ports for known vulnerabilities. These vulnerabilities are then reported to the user. Depending on the program, the vulnerability scanner might even include tools to actually exploit the vulnerabilities that it finds.

For example, Figure 14.9 shows the Security Analyzer from WebTrends. By defining an IP subnet range, this scanner finds all active systems on that subnet. It then performs a port scan and reports any vulnerabilities. The program even includes an Ethernet sniffer so that traffic along the local subnet can be monitored. As you can see, Security Analyzer has identified some potential vulnerabilities on ports 21 and 25 of the system at IP address `192.168.1.200`.

Vulnerability scanners are not some mystical piece of software that can magically infiltrate a system and identify problems. They simply take the manual process of identifying potential vulnerabilities and automate it. In fact, an experienced attacker performing a manual vulnerability check is far more likely to find potential problems because they are in a better position to adapt to the characteristics of each specific system. A vulnerability scanner is no better at performing a security audit than whoever programmed it.

FIGURE 14.9

FIGURE 14.9

The Security
Analyzer from
WebTrends

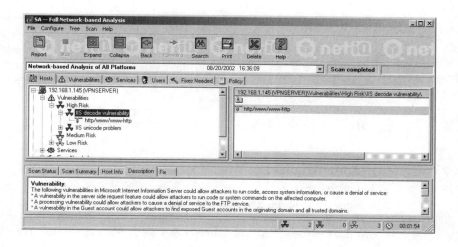

WARNING *Beware of security experts who make their living by strictly running automated vulnerability software. Most will provide the canned reports created by the software package and little extra value. We've run into more than one so-called expert who did not even understand the output of the reports they were producing. Ask for references before contracting with anyone to perform a security audit.*

It is impossible for a remote vulnerability scanner to identify all exploits without actually launching them against the remote system. For example, you cannot tell whether a remote system is susceptible to a teardrop attack without actually launching the attack to see if the system survives. Don't assume that a system has a clean bill of health just because a remote vulnerability scanner does not identify any specific problems.

It is possible for a vulnerability scanner to identify exploits without having to launch them when the software is running on the system that you want to check or when it has full access to the file system. A software program running locally has the benefit of being able to check application and driver dates and compare these with a list of known fixes. For example, a vulnerability scanner running on a Windows 2000 server that you want to check can verify that the IIS server is vulnerable to an IIS decode attack, which would allow an attacker to run system commands on the server.

Vulnerability scanners are simply a tool; they are not a magic bullet for finding all known security problems. Although vulnerability scanners are fine for providing some initial direction about which system is in the most need of attention, don't consider them a final authority on which systems are secure and which are not. No tool can replace an experienced administrator who stays informed of security issues and has an intimate understanding of the systems they manage.

Launching the Attack

Once Woolly Attacker knows your weak spots, he is ready to launch an attack. The type of attack he launches will depend greatly on his final objectives. Is he after one specific resource, or does he want to go after all systems on the network? Does he want to penetrate a system or will a denial of service suffice? The answers to these questions will decide his next course of action.

In this section, we will look at a number of exploits. The intent is not to give a listing of all known exploits—any such list would be out of date before this book even went to print. Rather, the goal is to show you a selective sampling of the exploits found in the wild so that you can better understand what can and cannot be done when attacking a target system or network. The idea is to make you aware of the types of attacks that can be launched so that you will be better able to determine whether a particular resource is safe.

NOTE   Some exploits that were briefly described earlier in this book have been included here for completeness.

Hidden Accounts

Although not an exploit *per se*, hidden user accounts can completely circumvent a security policy. For example, let's say you have a border router that is protecting your network by providing packet filtering. Imagine the security breach of having that device contain a hidden, administrator-level account that has a password that cannot be changed. Far-fetched, you say? Try telling that to 3COM.

In the spring of 1998, it came to light that 3COM was configuring layer-2 and -3 switches within its CoreBuilder and SuperStack II product line with hidden administrator accounts. The authentication pair used for most of these devices was a logon name of `debug` with a password of `synnet`. This administrator-level account could not be changed or deleted and was not visible from the management software. This meant that you could take all the right steps to secure your network hardware—only to have an attacker come in through the back door.

This problem used to be quite common, but seems to have decreased in frequency somewhat in the past few years. Nonetheless, from time to time you still hear reports about one vendor or another who has a default account embedded in the firmware or executable software. These vendors reason that, by including a hidden administrator account, a technical-support person can help a user who has forgotten the administrator password on the visible account. Many vendors, such as Cisco, have taken a more secure approach to handling such problems. For example, if you forget the password to your Cisco router, you can still recover it, but you need physical access to the device, and you must take it offline during the recovery process. This method of password recovery is far more secure.

TIP   Unless a vendor has made a statement to the contrary, it is impossible to know which network devices have hidden administrator accounts. This means that you should not rely solely on password authentication; rather, you should take additional measures to secure these devices. For example, you might want to consider disabling remote management of the device altogether or limiting management access to only certain IP addresses.

MITM (Man in the Middle)

In the classic man-in-the-middle exploit, an attacker sits between the client and the server with a packet analyzer. This is the variation that most people think of when they hear the term *man in the middle*. There are, in fact, many other forms of man-in-the-middle attacks that exploit the fact that most network communications do not use a strong form of authentication. Unless both ends of the session frequently verify whom they are talking to, they may very well be communicating with an attacker, not the intended system.

   Stepping in on a conversation is typically referred to as *session hijacking*. An attacker waits for two systems to begin a legitimate communication session and then injects commands into this data stream, pretending to be one of the communicating systems. Although there have been many MITM programs over the years, the current leader of the pack is the `dsniff` collection. The `dsniff` package was created to perform network auditing as well as penetration testing, and it does both quite well. Table 16.2 lists and describes a few of the various tools.

NOTE   *It is becoming increasingly common for security administrators to use the latest cracker tools to attempt penetration of their own network. This has actually led to a gray area in which security researchers create and release tools used to test network security. Once in the wild, however, these tools are often used by crackers in actual penetrations.*

TABLE 16.2: SAMPLE `dsniff` TOOLS

TOOL	DESCRIPTION
`sshmitm`	Stores and relays information as sent by `dnsspoof`. Can hijack interactive SSH (Secure Shell) sessions and can grab access passwords.
`webmitm`	Relays and stores HTTP/HTTPS (SSL) traffic as sent by `dnsspoof`. Used to capture form submissions (such as credit card numbers) and webmail logons (such as Hotmail)
`dsniff`	Grabs clear text passwords from more than 30 protocols. Reassembles TCP/IP session data and parses HTTP query and form encoding.
`arpspoof`	Used to hijack the ARP process.
`dnsspoof`	Used to hijack DNS information.
`filesnarf`	Captures file transfers.
`mailsnarf`	Captures mail transfers.
`msgsnarf`	Captures instant message traffic.
`urlsnarf`	Captures URLs.
`webspy`	Reassembles web pages.
`tcpkill`, `tcpnice`	Used to kill or create forged TCP information.

   Let's put these tools together. Assuming that Wooly Attacker has a physical connection on the same network as the host or client computer to be intercepted, the approach is straightforward. Old W.A. starts with `arpspoof`, which begins to tell all the computers on the network that W.A.'s computer is the new router out of the network. Now, if W.A. remembers to enable routing on his computer (`dnsiff` is a Unix-based suite of utilities), no one will realize that *all* their traffic out of the network is now passing through the clutches of an attacker.

   Now the real fun begins. By using `dnsspoof`, W.A. can *impersonate* any other computer on the Internet, especially web and SSH servers. Once a client attempts to create an SSL session to a web server (say, to buy flowers, to buy a book, or to enter a webmail site such as Hotmail), W.A. uses the web-mitm tool to send a bogus certificate to the client machine. This is where user education comes into play, because the web browser will (by default) display a warning to the user that the certificate presented by the "webserver" (really our W.A.) does not match the DNS name or has not been signed by a recognized authority (such as VeriSign). If the user accepts the certificate anyway, they have now created a completely secure, encrypted session with—that's right—Wooly Attacker! Of course, W.A. creates an actual encrypted session with the real web server involved. As a result, when the client enters sensitive information, webmitm (and the other snarf utilities) can extract all the juicy parts such as credit card numbers and passwords.

The scary part is that this type of attack can work with SSH sessions that rely on the older (and *much* less secure) version 1 of the SSH protocol. Even worse, if the user has never created a session to this particular SSH server before, the SSH client will *not realize* that the session has an eavesdropper. If the client has connected with this server before, they will be presented with a warning message that the public key presented by the server in order to encrypt the session has been changed. An administrator who ignores (or is ignorant of the meaning of) this message has just lost the secrecy that is the reason for using SSH.

Buffer Overflows

When a programmer writes an application, they must create memory pools, referred to as *buffers*, to accept input from users or other applications. For example, a login application must allocate memory space to allow the user to input a logon name and password. To allocate enough memory space for this information, the programmer must make an assumption about how much data will be received for each variable. For example, the programmer might decide that users will not need to enter a logon name larger than 16 characters and that passwords will never be larger than 10 characters. A *buffer overflow* is created when more data is received by a process than the programmer ever expected the process to see and when no contingency exists for when the process has to deal with an excessive amount of data.

BUFFER OVERFLOW DETAILS

Buffer overflows have become the most popular way to cause a denial of service or to attempt to execute commands on a remote system. Many exploits rely on sending a process too much information in order to attack the target system. The following are some of the more popular buffer overflow attacks over the last few years:

♦ Sending oversized ICMP request packets (ping of death)

♦ CodeRed, which exploited a buffer overflow in IIS 4 and 5

♦ Sending e-mail messages that have 256-character filename attachments to Netscape and Microsoft mail clients

♦ Sending an SMB (Server Message Block) logon request to an NT server with the data size incorrectly identified

♦ Sending a Pine user an e-mail with a From address in excess of 256 characters

♦ Connecting to WinGate's POP3 port and entering a username with 256 characters

As you can see, buffer overflow problems exist over a wide range of applications and affect every operating system. The only way to know for sure if an application is susceptible to buffer overflows is to review the source code.

NOTE *You may be able to find a buffer overflow problem through trial and error, but failing to produce a buffer overflow does not mean that the software is secure. You simply might not have tried enough characters. The only surefire method of verifying that a program is not susceptible to buffer overflows is to review the original source code.*

SYN Attack

A *SYN attack* exploits the use of a small buffer space during the TCP three-packet handshake in order to prevent a server from accepting inbound TCP connections. When the server receives the first SYN=1 packet, it stores this connection request in a small "in-process" queue. Since sessions tend to be established rather quickly, this queue is small and can store only a small number of connection requests. This approach was taken to optimize memory, in the belief that the session would be moved to the larger queue rather quickly, thus making room for more connection requests.

A SYN attack floods this smaller queue with connection requests. When the destination system issues a reply, the attacking system does not respond. This leaves the connection request in the smaller queue until the timer expires and the entry is purged. By filling up this queue with bogus connection requests, the attacking system can prevent the system from accepting legitimate connection requests. Thus, a SYN attack is considered a denial of service.

Since the use of two memory spaces is a standard TCP function, there is no way to actually fix this problem. You have two options:

◆ Increase the size of the in-process queue

◆ Decrease the amount of time before stale entries are purged from the in-process queue

Increasing the queue size provides additional space so that additional connection requests can be queued, but you would need an extremely large buffer to ensure that systems connected to a 100MB or 1GB network would not be vulnerable to a SYN attack. For systems connected to slower network connections, this use of memory is a complete waste. As for decreasing the time before connection requests are purged, a timer value that is set too low prevents busy systems or systems connected by a slow network link from being refused a connection.

Tuning a system so that it cannot fall prey to a SYN attack becomes a balancing act. You want to increase the in-process queue in order to handle a reasonable number of concurrent connection requests without making the buffer so large that you are wasting memory. You also want a purge time that is low enough to remove stale entries but not so low that you start preventing legitimate systems from establishing a connection. Unfortunately, most operating systems do not allow you to tune these values. You must rely on the operating system vendor to select appropriate settings.

Teardrop Attacks

To understand how a *teardrop attack* is used against a system, you must first understand the purpose of the fragmentation offset field and the length field within the IP header. The fragmentation offset field is typically used by routers. If a router receives a packet that is too large for the next segment, the router needs to fragment the data before passing it along. The fragmentation offset field is used along with the length field so that the receiving system can reassemble the datagram in the correct order. When a fragmentation offset value of 0 is received, the receiving system assumes either that this is the first packet of fragmented information or that fragmentation has not been used.

If fragmentation has occurred, the receiving system uses the offset to determine where the data within each packet should be placed when rebuilding the datagram. For an analogy, think of a child's set of numbered building blocks. As long as the child follows the numbering plan and puts the blocks together in the right order, they can build a house, a car, or even a plane. In fact, they do not even need to know what they are trying to build. They simply have to assemble the blocks in the specified order.

The IP fragmentation offset works in much the same manner. The offset tells the receiving system how far from the front of the datagram the included payload should be placed. If all goes well, this schema allows the datagram to be reassembled in the correct order. The length field is used as a verification check to ensure that there is no overlap and that data has not been corrupted in transit. For example, if you place fragments 1 and 3 within the datagram and then try to place fragment 2, but you find that fragment 2 is too large and will overwrite some of fragment 3, you know you have a problem.

At this point, the system tries to realign the datagrams to see if it can make them fit. If it cannot, the receiving system sends out a request that the data be resent. Most IP stacks can deal with overlaps or payloads that are too large for their segment.

LAUNCHING A TEARDROP ATTACK

A teardrop attack starts by sending a normal packet of data with a normal-size payload and a fragmentation offset of zero. From the initial packet of data, a teardrop attack is indistinguishable from a normal data transfer. Subsequent packets, however, have modified fragmentation offset and length fields. This ensuing traffic is responsible for crashing the target system.

When the second packet of data is received, the fragmentation offset is consulted to see where within the datagram this information should be placed. In a teardrop attack, the offset on the second packet claims that this information should be placed somewhere within the first fragment. When the payload field is checked, the receiving system finds that this data is not even large enough to extend past the end of the first fragment. In other words, this second fragment does not overlap the first fragment; it is actually fully contained inside it. Since this was not an error condition that anyone expected, there is no routine to handle it, and this information causes a buffer overflow—crashing the receiving system. For some operating systems, only one malformed packet is required. Others will not crash unless multiple malformed packets are received.

Smurf

Named after the original program that launched this attack, *Smurf* uses a combination of IP spoofing and ICMP replies to saturate a host with traffic, causing a denial of service. The attack goes like this: Woolly Attacker sends a spoofed Ping packet (echo request) to the broadcast address of a network with a large number of hosts and a high-bandwidth Internet connection. This network is known as the bounce site. The spoofed Ping packet has a source address of the system Woolly wants to attack.

The premise of the attack is that when a router receives a packet sent to an IP broadcast address (such as `206.121.73.255`), it recognizes this as a network broadcast and maps the address to an Ethernet broadcast address of `FF:FF:FF:FF:FF:FF`. So when our router receives this packet from the Internet, it broadcasts it to all hosts on the local segment.

You can guess what happens next. All the hosts on that segment respond with an echo-reply to the spoofed IP address. If this is a large Ethernet segment, 500 or more hosts might respond to each echo request they receive.

Since most systems try to handle ICMP traffic as quickly as possible, the target system, whose address Woolly Attacker spoofed, quickly becomes saturated with echo replies. This can easily prevent the system from being able to handle any other traffic, thus causing a denial of service.

This not only affects the target system, but the organization's Internet link, as well. If the bounce site has a T3 link (45Mbps), but the target system's organization is hooked up to a leased line (56Kbps), all communication to and from the organization grinds to a halt.

So how can you prevent this type of attack? You can take steps at the source site, bounce site, and target site to help limit the effects of a Smurf attack.

BLOCKING SMURF AT THE SOURCE

Smurf relies on the attacker's ability to transmit an echo request with a spoofed source address. You can stop this attack at its source by using router access lists, which ensure that all traffic originating from your network does in fact have a proper source address. This prevents the spoofed packet from ever making it to the bounce site.

BLOCKING SMURF AT THE BOUNCE SITE

To block Smurf at the bounce site, you have two options. The first is to simply block all inbound echo requests. Doing so prevents these packets from ever reaching your network.

If blocking all inbound echo requests is not an option, you need to prevent your routers from mapping traffic destined for the network broadcast address to the LAN broadcast address. By preventing this mapping, your systems will no longer receive these echo requests.

To prevent a Cisco router from mapping network broadcasts to LAN broadcasts, enter configuration mode for the LAN interface and then enter the following command:

```
no ip directed-broadcast
```

NOTE *You must enter this command on every LAN interface on every router. This command will not be effective if you enter it only on your perimeter router.*

BLOCKING SMURF AT THE TARGET SITE

Unless your ISP is willing to help you, there is little you can do to prevent the effects of Smurf on your WAN link. Although you can block this traffic at the network perimeter, this is too late to prevent the attack from eating up all your WAN bandwidth.

You can, however, minimize the effects of Smurf by at least blocking it at the perimeter. By using dynamic packet filtering or some form of firewall that can maintain state, you can prevent these packets from entering your network. Since your state table is aware that the attack session did not originate on the local network (it does not have a table entry showing the original echo request), this attack is handled like any other spoof attack and promptly dropped.

Brute Force Attacks

A *brute force attack* is simply an attempt to try all possible values when attempting to authenticate with a system or crack the crypto key used to create ciphertext. For example, an attacker might attempt to log on to your server as administrator using a list of dictionary words as possible passwords. No finesse is involved; the attacker simply going tries every potential word or phase to come up with a possible password.

One of the most popular ways to perform a brute force attack is with a *password cracker,* and no program displays how effective these programs can be like Security Software Technologies' L0pht-Crack (developed by L0pht, which later became @stake). L0phtCrack uses both a dictionary file and a brute force guessing attack to discover user passwords. Figure 14.10 shows L0phtCrack attempting to crack a number of user passwords. This particular session has just been started. Notice that several passwords have already been cracked.

FIGURE 14.10

L0pht's L0phtCrack utility

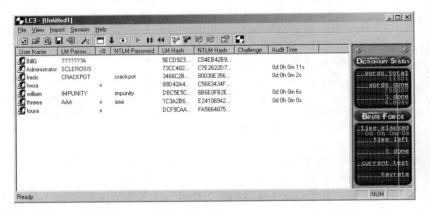

Encrypted Windows 2000 passwords are saved in the \WinNT\system32\config folder in a file named SAM. L0phtCrack provides three ways to access this information:

◆ By directly importing them into L0phtCrack if the software is running on the Windows 2000 server

◆ By reading a backup version of the SAM file saved to tape, an emergency recovery disk, or the \WinNT\repair directory

◆ By sniffing them off the network using the included readsmb.exe utility

Once the authentication information is collected, it is imported into the L0phtCrack utility. Unlike some password crackers that attempt to crack the entire ciphertext, L0phtCrack takes a few shortcuts to reduce the time required to crack passwords. For example, in Figure 14.10, the <8 column indicates accounts with a password of fewer than eight characters. This is determined by looking at the ciphertext in the LanMan hash. Any password that contains fewer than eight characters always has the string AAD3B435B51404EE appended to the end for padding. This allows L0phtCrack to quickly determine that the password string contains fewer than eight characters.

The passwords are first checked against a dictionary file that contains thousands of words. If you want to add word, you can edit this dictionary file with any text editor. Dictionary checking is extremely fast—checking the accounts shown in Figure 14.10 took less than 10 seconds. Any passwords that are not cracked by the dictionary search are then subjected to a brute force attack, which can test both alphanumeric and special characters. The amount of time it takes to brute force the password depends on the number of characters in the password. For example, the account Administrator in Figure 14.10 has a 9-character password. Had this password been seven characters or fewer, the search time would have been reduced by roughly one-third.

As system administrator, you simply cannot control the use of password crackers; password crackers are available for every platform. Although you might be able to prevent an attacker from running a password cracker directly on your server, they can always run the cracking software on some other machine. Your only true defense is to protect any files that include password information, as well as prevent sniffing on your network through the use of routers and switches.

Physical Access Attacks

With all the attention given to network-based attacks, many people forget that the most straightforward way to compromise a network is by gaining physical access to one or more network systems. Systems that are kept in secluded or locked areas are the most vulnerable, because this provides the attacker with the necessary privacy to compromise a system. As we have emphasized, an overwhelming majority of attacks originate from within an organization. This provides an attacker with a certain level of legitimate access to network resources. With physical access to a system, it is not difficult to increase access to that of an administrator.

For example, let's assume that you have a Windows 2000 Professional environment for all your client systems. Profiles are mandatory, and users are provided with minimal access to both the local system and network resources. All service packs have been installed, as have all security hotfixes. Every Professional workstation has full auditing enabled so that every event is recorded and sent to a remote process that looks for suspicious activity and archives the logs for future review.

This certainly sounds like a secure client environment, doesn't it? If Woolly Attacker has private physical access to the machine, he can easily do the following:

♦ Pop the cover on the computer and disconnect the battery in order to clear the CMOS (Complementary Metal Oxide Semiconductor) password

♦ Boot the system from a floppy to gain access to the local file system

♦ Copy the SAM file so that password information can be run through a password cracker

♦ Remove the local administrator password so that they have full access to the local operating system

♦ Reboot the system with the NIC disconnected so that they can log on locally as administrator without tripping any alarms

♦ Change the logging level so that suspicious activity is not reported

♦ Install sniffing software so that other network communications can be monitored

♦ Use the compromised passwords to attack other network systems

In short, a savvy attacker can completely circumvent the security of this environment in less than half an hour. The greatest delays are in waiting for the system to boot or shut down. If you are managing security for a large environment, don't plan on being able to fully secure any of your client systems. As you can see from this scenario, they are far too easy to compromise.

NOTE   *The exception is a thin client environment such as WinFrame or MetaFrame. In this environment, local workstations are little more than terminals; all security is managed on the server itself.*

Summary

In this chapter we discussed some of the ways an attacker might go about attacking your network. We started by looking at how an attacker can collect information about your network with little more than your organization's name. We then discussed how an attacker could go about collecting even more information about your specific network environment in order to determine which vulnerabilities might be exploitable. Finally, we looked at some of the assault methods available to an attacker who wants to compromise your resources.

In the next chapter, we will discuss how to stay ahead of these attacks. We will look at how to stay informed of the exploits that have been found—and how to find your vulnerabilities before an attacker does.

Chapter 15

Security Resources

THANKS TO THE COMPLEXITIES of today's software, it is safe to say that security vulnerabilities will be with us for many years to come. Although public discussion of those vulnerabilities goes a long way toward ensuring that current software is purged of exploitable code that can be exploited, there is no guarantee that future releases will be free from the same problems. For example, buffer overflows have plagued programmers since the early '70s and are still very much a problem today.

To maintain a secure environment, you need to stay abreast of these exploits as they are discovered. Gone are the days when you could wait for a product upgrade or a service pack in order to fix a security problem. For example, Microsoft releases security-related hotfixes frequently. Clearly, you would not want to leave security holes simply because you were waiting for a patch from a vendor.

Featured in this chapter:

◆ Information from the vendor

◆ Third-party channels

Information from the Vendor

Vendor channels are your best bet for finding the latest security patches. Although most vendors also issue security advisories, you can usually find out about specific exploits much sooner through third-party sources. You are also far more likely to get an accurate description of the exploit that is free from marketing spin. For example, a Microsoft press release regarding Back Orifice (a famous Trojan horse) stated:

> "Back Orifice" does not expose or exploit any security issue in Windows, Windows NT, or the Microsoft BackOffice suite of products. As far as demonstrating an inherent security vulnerability in the Windows platform, this is simply not true.

Obviously, this was a great public relations spin, but it was not helpful to the system administrator who was trying to determine how much of a threat this vulnerability posed to their local networking environment. Although the vendor may be willing to tell you that the vulnerability exists, you might have to look elsewhere for the full scoop.

3COM

This company makes a variety of networking products, including network cards, switches, and routers. It also has a popular handheld computer line called the Palm. The 3COM company made a name for itself by supplying reasonably priced products that provide above-average performance. You can find the 3COM website at www.3com.com.

TECHNICAL INFORMATION

The 3COM website contains a wealth of technical papers and briefs. Although the inventory is not quite as extensive as the one maintained by Cisco, the 3COM site includes papers on topics ranging from ATM to network management to security. Some of these papers are product specific; for example, one of the security papers deals with using a 3COM SuperStack 3 switch to block streaming media on a network. Many papers, however, simply deal with a specific technology. You can find these papers at www.3com.com/corpinfo/en_US/technology/index.jsp.

You can also find a decent amount of product support on 3COM's website, including a knowledge base, and tips and release notes for each of its products. Product documentation is also available online.

You can find technical support for 3COM products at www.3com.com/products/en_US/supportindex.jsp.

This company has made improvements in the past few years in issuing security advisories for their products. This is in sharp contrast to previous years, when you had to pay to get access to the 3COM knowledge base. Unfortunately, 3COM does not have a mailing list dedicated to security issues, something other vendors have implemented to improve timely notification of product vulnerabilities.

PATCHES AND UPDATES

Patches and updates are available free to all 3COM customers. You do not need a service contract to receive patch updates, nor are you not required to purchase a service contract simply to fix known bugs. There is also some helpful third-party software on 3COM's support site, such as a Windows-based TFTP (Trivial File Transfer Protocol) server. A TFTP server is required if you want to update the firmware on a 3COM router or switch. All 3COM downloads are available through the main technical support website (listed earlier).

Cisco

Cisco specializes in infrastructure hardware. It has a diverse product line that includes switches, routers, firewalls, and even intrusion detection systems. Since most of the Internet runs on Cisco hardware, Cisco is obviously a major player in the network connectivity field. You can find the Cisco website at www.cisco.com.

TECHNICAL INFORMATION

Cisco provides one of the best sites on the Internet if you are looking for network-related advice. Along with product-specific documentation, there is a wealth of technology information. Looking to implement BGP (Border Gateway Protocol) or OSPF (Open Shortest Path First) in your environment? The Cisco site contains a number of white papers and tutorials that explain these and most other Internet technologies and how to implement them.

The Cisco website has a large number of security-related documents geared toward helping the network administrator lock down their environment. You can literally perform a search on just about any vulnerability (such as teardrop, Smurf, and so on) to receive information that describes the exploit and what you can do to protect your internal systems. To make life even easier, all documents can be retrieved directly from the search engine on the main page.

Cisco does an excellent job of publicizing vulnerabilities once they are discovered and resolved. Cisco announces patches through CERT (Computer Emergency Response Team), as well as through its own distribution channels. As a major Internet player, Cisco has set the standard for commercial vendors in acknowledging vulnerabilities when they are found and issuing patches in a timely manner.

PATCHES AND UPDATES

If Cisco falls short in any area, it would have to be in making new patches publicly available. Cisco does not issue hotfixes to patch its routers or switches. Rather, the company releases a new revision of the device's operating system. Because these updates can also include product enhancements, Cisco does not make them available via publicly accessible areas such as its web or FTP sites. You need a Cisco support contract to receive these updates.

To its credit, Cisco provides free updates when a major security hole is found. For example, when it was found that the Cisco 700 series routers were vulnerable to a buffer overflow attack if a user entered an extremely long password string, Cisco made updates freely available to all Cisco 700 series customers, regardless of whether the customer had a support contract.

Linux

Although the core Linux operating system is not considered a commercial product, it is actively produced and supported by a large number of volunteers, as well as by the organizations that distribute it. Linux has established itself as a robust operating system that can handle mission-critical operations. It can act as an application server, a router, or even a firewall. Most Linux-related information is linked to the main website at `www.linux.org`.

TECHNICAL INFORMATION

The Linux website is host to a plethora of documents created by the Linux Documentation Project (LDP). There are FAQs, HOWTOs, and mini-HOWTOs on literally every function and service supported by Linux. No matter what you are trying to do with your Linux operating system, chances are there is documentation to walk you through the process. These documents even include many installation caveats. You'll find links to documentation at `www.linux.org/docs/index.html`.

This page even includes links to many Linux-related mailing lists and newsgroups. Mailing lists provide an excellent way to get real-time help when a Linux problem has you completely stumped. If phone support is more to your liking, you'll be pleased to know that a number of vendors provide this service for a fee. You can find a list at `www.linux.org/vendors/index.html`.

The Linux development team actively propagates information about and issues patches for security-related vulnerabilities as these are discovered. This information is circulated through CERT and through a number of Linux discussion channels.

PATCHES AND UPDATES

Because Linux is a noncommercial operating system, you can obtain it free of charge. Security-related patches and fixes are also free. You can download Linux source code from a number of locations. Some of the more popular include the following:

- `ftp://ftp.kernel.org`
- `ftp://sunsite.unc.edu`
- `ftp://ftp.caldera.com/pub/`
- `ftp://ftp.redhat.com/redhat`

Microsoft

Microsoft has come under heavy fire over the last few years for the large number of security vulnerabilities found in its software products. Although Microsoft was initially somewhat unresponsive when security exploits were identified, the company has picked up the pace recently. It is not uncommon for Microsoft to release a security patch within hours of the vulnerability's being reported. You will find the Microsoft website at `www.microsoft.com`.

TECHNICAL INFORMATION

Microsoft provides extensive technical information, a change from previous years when most of the highly detailed white papers were available only through an expensive subscription. To best access the resources (and interface), use Internet Explorer to visit the site. Other browsers work for most areas, but lack many of the nice navigational capabilities provided by the site.

You can find extensive security resources, including patches, white papers, and tutorials at `www.microsoft.com/security/`.

PATCHES AND UPDATES

Microsoft makes all security fixes freely available via its website. It also makes updates known through the Critical Update Notification program. This utility runs in the background on Windows systems and periodically connects to Microsoft's network to determine if there are any recently released patches. The user is notified and given the opportunity to download any fixes as soon as they are released. You can retrieve these patches from `ftp://ftp.microsoft.com`.

Novell

Novell makes a wide range of networking products that are focused on its NetWare operating system, and Novell has a good track record with regard to security. You'll find Novell's website at `www.novell.com`.

TECHNICAL INFORMATION

The Novell website contains a number of white papers; however, all are specific to Novell product offerings. Little general information is available about a specific technology. The Novell documentation site, at `www.novell.com/documentation`, contains online manuals for product offerings.

Novell also maintains a knowledge base that you can search to find resolutions to known problems. The knowledge base is extensive and documents support calls handled by Novell's technical support staff. Here you can find answers to just about any Novell-related issue. The problem is that the search engine does not do a good job of helping you locate documents. For example, entering the phrase **security AND alert** displays product information on WordPerfect, NetWare Connect, and NetView as the closest matches. These documents are not exactly what you might be looking for if you are searching for recent vulnerabilities. You can find the Novell support site at `http://support.novell.com`.

NOTE   *Novell does not participate in CERT advisories and does not dedicate space on its website to announcing security-related problems. You might be able to find security issues in the knowledge base, but you must already know what you are looking for in order to find it. Thus, you must rely completely on third-party channels for vulnerability information regarding NetWare products.*

PATCHES AND UPDATES

Novell makes all patch updates freely available through its support website. You can use a file find utility to see if a patch update is available for a specific file. You can also view Novell's suggested minimum patches and download them from the same page. Finally, you can view all recent patches from a single page and quickly find the latest updates.

Sun Microsystems

Sun manufactures one of the most popular lines of Unix operating systems. These boxes have found homes as engineering workstations and high-end application servers. Sun is known for pushing the performance envelope with its UltraSPARC product line, which is already using 64-bit processors running at speeds of 900MHz.

Sun has made a tremendous improvement to its support infrastructure, and most patches and support information can be found (for free) on their website, `www.sun.com`. This is in sharp contrast to several years ago when even patches had to be purchased.

NOTE   *Sun also actively participates in CERT advisories and has posted a number of vendor bulletins.*

Sun also maintains a section of its website for updating clients on security-related information. You can access this page through `http://sunsolve.sun.com/pub-cgi/show.pl?target=security/sec`.

Third-Party Channels

You can access a number of third-party resources to stay informed about the latest security-related exploits. Typically, these resources are established by helpful netizens or organizations that specialize in network security. All the resources listed here are free, meaning that no entry fee is required to access security-related information. Some resources do post advertisements, however, to defray the cost of maintaining the resource.

Third-party security resources include vulnerability databases, websites, mailing lists, and newsgroups. Each has its own drawbacks and benefits.

Vulnerability database   Provides search capability for finding exploits but no feedback if you have additional questions

Website   Might have direct links to patch information, as well as a more detailed description, but you will have a harder time finding a specific exploit

Mailing list   Provides immediate notification of exploits as they are found, but some lists can bury your mailbox with 50+ messages a day

Newsgroup   Offers more detailed discussions regarding specific exploits, but you might have to sift through lots of messages to find the information you want

TIP   Generally, it is best to subscribe to only one or two mailing lists in order to be informed of exploits as they are found. You can then use the vulnerability databases and websites when you want to research a specific issue.

Vulnerability Databases

Vulnerability databases let you search for an exploit based on specific criteria. For example, you might be able to search for exploits that affect a specific operating system (Windows NT, 2000, XP; Linux; Unix; and so on) or product (Apache, SendMail, MS SQL, and so on) that meet a specific attack signature (denial of service, cracking, and so on), or even exploits that have been discovered over a specific range of dates.

ISS's X-Force Database

You can search Internet Security System's X-Force database by platform or by keyword. You can choose from seven flavors of Unix, as well as all Windows operating systems, which are grouped into a single category. The database lists only operating system exploits; there are no entries for networking hardware such as 3COM or Cisco devices. You can display a month's worth of exploits or all entries for a specific platform. You can also select to display hits with a short summary or the entire search result on one page (as opposed to only showing a particular number per page).

A unique feature of the X-Force database is that each entry is assigned a level of risk. If your query produces multiple entries, you can quickly scan the list to find the worst of the bunch. The database entries are sufficiently descriptive, although not always 100 percent accurate.

You can find the X-Force database at `http://xforce.iss.net`.

PACKET STORM

Packet Storm is one of the most comprehensive search and reporting engines on all aspects of information security. It covers not only the weaknesses of a system but also provides a news service covering the latest happenings in the information security realm.

Packet Storm provides a unique feature called Storm Watch, which reports on the topics searched most often in their database. Table 15.1 lists the top 20 searches (at the time of writing). You can find Packet Storm at `http://packetstorm.decepticons.org/`.

TABLE 17.1: TOP 20 REQUESTED AREAS OF SECURITY INTEREST

QUERY	DATE
"cracker"	Fri Aug 2 21:41:13 CDT 2002
maya	Fri Aug 2 21:41:07 CDT 2002
VP-ASP shop cart	Fri Aug 2 21:40:58 CDT 2002
free authentication	Fri Aug 2 21:40:45 CDT 2002
iis 5	Fri Aug 2 21:40:39 CDT 2002
3d max	Fri Aug 2 21:40:37 CDT 2002
retina	Fri Aug 2 21:40:36 CDT 2002
cm-ssh	Fri Aug 2 21:40:31 CDT 2002
xscan	Fri Aug 2 21:40:29 CDT 2002
exploit	Fri Aug 2 21:40:02 CDT 2002
sub7	Fri Aug 2 21:39:42 CDT 2002
lpd exploit	Fri Aug 2 21:39:35 CDT 2002
identd	Fri Aug 2 21:39:33 CDT 2002
bullworm	Fri Aug 2 21:39:30 CDT 2002
"openssh"	Fri Aug 2 21:38:10 CDT 2002
serv-u	Fri Aug 2 21:37:59 CDT 2002
browser authentication	Fri Aug 2 21:37:55 CDT 2002
frontpage 5	Fri Aug 2 21:37:35 CDT 2002
encrypt	Fri Aug 2 21:37:29 CDT 2002
Palante	Fri Aug 2 21:35:01 CDT 2002

SECURITYFOCUS

SecurityFocus is a company that provides security consulting and services. Although their website provides an amazing amount of information, the real gem is their vulnerability database. Unfortunately, this database is available in a license-only arrangement so that other vendors can integrate it into their products.

You'll find a wealth of information at the SecurityFocusOnline website, `http://online.securi-tyfocus.com/`, and you can search all the major security newsgroups and mailing lists. The site also includes a news area, security articles, and a list of the most recent incidents, vulnerabilities, and advisories.

Websites

Third-party websites can contain a wealth of information about all forms of security-related issues. Some sites give you pointers on securing your environment, and other sites provide the tools an attacker would use against your network. In this section, we'll discuss a few of our favorite third-party security websites.

ANTIONLINE

AntiOnline is one of those sites with a little bit of everything. The main page lists current news events that pertain to network security. A "Quick Tips" section provides some excellent hints on dealing with some of the day-to-day security issues a network administrator faces, such as tracking spoofed addresses or dealing with spam. Another link brings you to an online library that contains papers on a wide range of security topics. A file archive contains a large number of security tools, both positive and negative in functionality. You can access AntiOnline at `www.antionline.com/`.

THE CERT HOME PAGE

CERT maintains a site responsible for collecting Internet-based exploits and works with vendors to resolve vulnerabilities. CERT also issues public bulletins on known vulnerabilities.

NOTE   *Although CERT primarily focuses on Unix vulnerabilities, it does issue Windows bulletins, as well.*

The site also contains helpful pointers for securing your environment. You can find CERT at `www.cert.org/`.

SANS

The SANS (System Administration, Network, and Security) site holds an amazing quantity of white papers and tutorials on security topics, as well as a world-class collection of alerts and notifications. Not to be outdone by CERT, they also host the top 20 exploits as reported by the FBI. You can find SANS at `www.sans.org`.

L0PHT AND @STAKE

L0pht started out as a group of hackers working out of the Boston area who specialized in system security and cryptography. Their site was a wealth of security-related information, including advisories and tools. Some of the best-known vulnerabilities were discovered in L0pht's test lab. Thus, most of L0pht's advisories are based on firsthand information.

In January 2000, L0pht joined a newly formed company called @stake (created by former executives of Compaq, Forrester Research, and Cambridge Technology Partners). Because the former members of L0pht now run the research lab at @stake, the website continues to be one of the best sources of security advisories.

You'll find the entire research lab at `www.atstake.com/research/index.html`.

THE NATIONAL SECURITY INSTITUTE

The National Security Institute (NSI) home page goes beyond the network and publishes security-related information on a variety of topics. Along with computer security, the site covers personal security, terrorism, security legislation, and even travel advisories. The information on the site is extremely diverse. You can even read papers on the psychological effects of implementing an information security policy. This site is an excellent resource if you are looking to expand your knowledge of the security field. You'll find the NSI home page at `http://nsi.org/`.

PHRACK MAGAZINE HOME PAGE

Phrack magazine is one of the longest-running electronic periodicals dealing with system vulnerabilities. A number of exploits have been made known to the public through the pages of *Phrack*. Although most articles are written from the perspective of how to perform an exploit, the articles do an excellent job of describing all the gory details of why an exploit is effective. This is just the information you need to ensure that you do not fall prey to attack. Phrack is not published on any set schedule. The most recent issue, #59, was released in the summer of 2002. You can find *Phrack* at `www.phrack.org/`.

Mailing Lists

Mailing lists are an extremely useful tool for staying informed about security vulnerabilities. They provide immediate notification when vulnerabilities are released to the public. They also supply a forum where the fine points of a particular exploit can be discussed in detail. A mailing list can provide far more information regarding a specific exploit than a vulnerability database, because most mailing lists are interactive. If the list is an open forum, you are free to ask questions.

NOTE *To join a mailing list, you must send an e-mail message to the mailing list server. This message must include some form of keyword or words in the body of the message (not the subject line) such as* `subscribe`. *To be removed from a list, you typically repeat the process using the word* `unsubscribe`.

BUGTRAQ

The mother of all vulnerability discussion lists, Bugtraq is a moderated mailing list for the discussion of exploits. Many vulnerabilities are announced publicly for the first time on this list. The mailing list focuses on which exploits have been found, as well as on what can be done to fix them. This is the one list you can subscribe to that will guarantee that you hear about any exploits that are discovered. Although traffic volume is a bit high, the information collected through this list is well worth the price of pressing your Delete key a few extra times a day.

Security Focus hosts the Bugtraq archive and the subscription form at `http://online.security-focus.com/cgi-bin/sfonline/subscribe.pl`.

INFOSEC NEWS

The InfoSec News mailing list disseminates security-related news articles. These include excerpts from newspapers, magazines, and online references. The mailing list is closed, meaning that only the moderator is allowed to post. You can, however, contribute by sending the moderator security-related news articles. The list does not discuss vulnerabilities as much as what is going on in the security field. For details on how to join the list, go to `www.c4i.org/isn.html`.

ISS'S X-FORCE IDS DISCUSSION LIST

ISS hosts a number of discussion lists under the X-Force branch of its website; one of the more popular is the intrusion detection system mailing list. This list is not moderated and focuses on topics related to intrusion detection systems. The list is an open discussion forum, meaning that anyone is free to post questions or comments. To join the list, point your browser to http://www.iss.net/security_center/maillists/.

THE NTBUGTRAQ MAILING LIST

The NTBugtraq mailing list focuses solely on Microsoft Windows exploits and vulnerabilities. Despite the list's name, it discusses all Microsoft operating systems and applications. The list is heavily moderated, keeping postings to an absolute minimum. In fact, most of the postings originate from the list moderator or from the Microsoft programming staff. If you are interested primarily in Windows, this might be a good list to join.

NOTE　*Windows-related vulnerabilities that originate on the Bugtraq mailing list eventually find their way to this list, as well.*

For more NTBugtraq information and to join the list, go to www.ntbugtraq.com.

Newsgroups

A number of newsgroups deal with security-related topics. Newsgroups are useful in that you do not have to worry about filling up your Inbox. Messages are posted to newsgroup servers, which you can review at your leisure. The only problem with newsgroups is that they tend to have a high signal-to-noise ratio because they are not moderated.

NOTE　*A high signal-to-noise ratio means that you might have to filter through a lot of postings to find the information that interests you.*

Here are some newsgroups that might be of interest:

◆ comp.os.ms-windows.nt.admin.security

◆ comp.os.netware.security

◆ comp.security

◆ comp.security.firewalls

◆ comp.security.ssh

◆ comp.security.unix

◆ comp.security.misc

◆ microsoft.public.access.security

You can also use Google to search newsgroups for a particular reference. Go to www.google.com, select Groups, and then enter your search criteria. You can even limit your search to a particular newsgroup.

Summary

In this chapter we discussed how you can stay better informed about exploits as they are found. We discussed which vendor and third-party resources are available for investigating vulnerabilities and where to find patches. We also discussed which mailing lists and newsgroups are available if you need to find out more information.

Appendix A

Operating System Security Checklists

THE FOLLOWING CHECKLISTS can be a great help in securing newly installed systems. Although this list is more a collection of the general security concepts, and not a step-by-step detailed outline, it is still quite useful in your planning process. Also, this list is not guaranteed to be unchanging or complete for all uses (remember that new vulnerabilities are constantly discovered), these checklists still help protect you from the most common vulnerabilities.

Windows 2000 Server Security Checklist

Before you begin this checklist, be sure that you have a complete system backup. Also, read through the entire checklist before taking any specific actions. If your Windows 2000 Server will perform special functions (such as hosting an Exchange service), be sure that the changes don't break functionality. Refer to Microsoft's online Knowledge Base (http://support.microsoft.com) for more information concerning additional security settings:

Physical Security   Physical security is more than just locking a server in a room. It includes providing adequate protection against climate effects (including static electricity and heat) and logging users who gain access to physical resources—IS professionals can commit crimes as well as outsiders.

Disable/Rename the Guest Account   Verify that the Guest account default has been renamed. Also, consider assigning an extensive, complicated password to the account.

Eliminate Unneeded Accounts   Unused accounts are prime targets for crackers, because they know that those accounts are not usually monitored for vulnerability, let alone the normal procedure of account lockout that indicates cracking attempts.

Create Additional Administrator Accounts   Having an additional administrative account is a valuable protection against compromise of an account. Also, be sure that your administrators use a nonprivileged account for daily activities.

Rename the Administrator Account   This won't stop a determined attacker, but it might slow them down. It might also filter out the "weekend" attacker that is just browsing around. Also, consider creating a dummy account (remember to include the account description that is created for the real Administrator account during installation) to throw off attackers.

Replace File System Permissions   Change the permissions for the Everyone group to Authenticated Users on all file shares and printers.

Enforce Password Security   By using complex passwords (of 12 characters or more that combine numbers, symbols, and upper- and lowercase letters) and forcing frequent changes, you can limit the number of simple password-guessing attempts as well as delay brute force attacks, giving you valuable time to respond.

Enable Password-Protected Screensavers   By setting a screensaver that blanks the monitor within 15 minutes of inactivity, you can avoid not only access violations, but "identity theft," whereby one user performs forbidden activities under the guise of an innocent party.

Restrict File Systems to NTFS   File systems other than NTFS (New Technology File System) don't provide DACL (discretionary access control list) capabilities, nor do non-NTFS systems allow for encryption.

Apply Appropriate Security Templates   Microsoft has made several levels of security templates available. The NSA (National Security Agency) has also released their own version of (slightly) stronger templates. Remember that applying the highest level of security template requires that *all* systems have the same level of security to be able to communicate.

Disable Unnecessary Services   In particular, Terminal Services, RRAS (Routing and Remote Access Service), and IIS (Internet Information Services) are vulnerable to exploitation. The following are the minimum services necessary for functionality:

◆ Computer Browser

◆ Microsoft DNS Server

◆ Netlogon

◆ NTLM SSP (NT LanManager Silicon Switch Processor)

◆ RPC (remote procedure call) Locator

◆ RPC Service

◆ TCP/IP (Transmission Control Protocol/Internet Protocol) NetBIOS Helper

◆ Spooler

◆ Server

◆ WINS (Windows Internet Naming Service)

◆ Workstation

◆ Event Log

Install a System Firewall   Shutting down unused ports is an excellent way to provide multiple layers of defense. By using ZoneAlarm or any other software-based firewall, you can achieve a higher level of security.

Auditing and Logs   Auditing system events is key to intrusion detection. If possible, audit all logs to detect intrusions and also as a forensic record. Set permissions and options so that only administrators can review security logs and so that the system is forcibly shut down if the logs fills to capacity.

Logon Settings   Set system policies so that the last username to be logged in is not displayed and a warning banner is displayed. Prevent the system from being shut down unless someone has logged on. And set a screen saver (preferably one that blanks the screen) that requires a password and is activated no more than 15 minutes after the system is inactive.

Deactivate DirectDraw   This graphic technology allows direct access to video hardware memory by applications, but is not needed in a business environment and could allow certain information to be vulnerable to exposure.

Activate EFS   Apply the Encrypting File System to all folders (including the Temp folder) that store documents, especially on any portable systems that are at risk for physical theft.

Disable Removable Media autorun   By default, Windows 2000 runs the autorun.exe file on any CD-ROM as soon as it is inserted into the system. Disabling this feature helps protect against hostile code.

Remove OS/2 and POSIX Subsystems   Delete all keys relating to POSIX and OS/2 support, along with the OS2 directory under System32.

Implement IPsec   IPsec, while extracting a heavy processor and bandwidth load, still provides unparalleled data protection for network traffic. The 3DES (Triple Data Encryption Standard) cards can offload the encryption from the operating system, and switched high-speed networks are making it more practical to encrypt LAN traffic, especially in segments devoted to the network backbone or network servers.

Apply Latest Service Packs   Ensure that the latest Service Packs and hotfixes have been applied to the system and are re-applied after any additional software installations.

Linux Security Checklist

Securing Linux can be more complicated than securing Windows 2000 machines, simply because there are more varieties of Linux distributions. Adding to the difficulty is that the most insecure parts of a system are the additional programs and services offered, not necessarily the code itself. This checklist assumes that you are using the Red Hat Linux distribution.

Upgrade the Kernel   New installations of Linux will most likely use the 2.4.18 kernel or newer. At the time of this writing, it is the most stable. Any kernels earlier than 2.4.13 have a serious vulnerability in how they handle symbolic links and should not be used.

Patch the System   Always download newer versions of software. One of the most valid criticisms of open-source software comes from its success; so many people are using the programs and looking at the code that problems are constantly found and fixed. The flipside, however, is that you have to do a lot of work to keep the system up-to-date.

Remove User Accounts   Remove unnecessary user accounts and groups installed by default at system install. Most installs create some user accounts and groups by default. Usually these are never used and retain their default passwords, making them easy prey for crackers. Disable or remove these.

Change the Telnet Banner   The system banner displayed when a remote user telnet's to a server can reveal a lot of useful information to crackers. If you allow telnet connections, change the Telnet banner.

Increase the Logging Level   This steps is closely allied to tuning SYSLOGD: improve the default logging level of the system. In particular, configure the system to record *all* logging activity.

Disable Ctrl+Alt+Delete   By default, most Linux distributions include the ability to shut the system down from the console by entering the famous "three-fingered salute." Disabling this feature provides an additional layer of defense (beyond simple physical security) for your system.

Disable Interactive init   The init process is the parent process of Linux and can be told to change the run level of a currently operating system. Changing the run level could leave the system in single-user mode (a type of DoS [denial of service] attack), or, conversely, enable services that are not secured.

Install vlock   This utility is the equivalent of a password-protected screensaver, and yet it works on a terminal. The purpose is to provide a way for an administrator to temporarily lock a session without having to log off.

Turn Off Network Services   "Disable, disable, disable"—that should be the repeated chant of every security professional who wants to secure a newly installed system. Deactivating unneeded services means not only that you reduce the number of entry points a cracker has to your system, but you also reduce your administrative burden when it comes to system updates.

Tune SYSLOGD   The SYSLOG daemon is the main logging tool for Linux and is your primary indicator for intrusion activity. The appropriate sensitivity to events, however, will be unique to your situation. Consider exporting all logging to an external system. Doing so makes it difficult for an attacker to cover their tracks once they have compromised a system.

Delete the History File   Place a command in a logoff script of all user accounts to empty the history file every time that user logs off. This serves primarily to cover any passwords or sensitive information that user might have accidentally entered on the command line.

Enable Netfilter   Also called IPTABLES, Netfilter provides kernel-level packet, stateful, and NAT ((Network Address Translation; called IP Masquerade) filtering services. Even if your Linux system sits behind a firewall, you can still specify that all traffic follow your local network rules. Consider Netfilter a type of system firewall, like ZoneAlarm.

Use CHROOT   The CHROOT feature restricts a given service to an isolated area. This is similar in concept to FTP (File Transfer Protocol), in which a user "sees" a filesystem root that is actually only a small area located in the FTP server's area.

Install Tripwire   Tripwire is a file-system IDS (intrusion detection system) and one of the greatest security tools since the firewall. Using Tripwire with SYSLOGD and Snort (see next) provides a full-featured and robust host IDS.

Install Snort   Snort is an IDS used to identify network attacks and is typically placed on (or near) the firewall in the network scheme. There is no reason, however, that you can't install Snort on all your internal Linux systems as well, as an additional level of security.

Keep in mind that you will need to take additional security steps for the specific applications and services you activate on your Linux system. Also, remember that this is *very* fast moving code, so vulnerabilities will be found where you least expect them.

Appendix B

Sample Network Usage Policy

ALTHOUGH THIS APPENDIX is included to provide you with a sample network usage policy, ideally usage policies are process-driven and usually go through several steps that are part of a never-ending cycle as business needs and technology change.

NOTE *The following link is an example of a real-world usage policy:* `http://www.security.gatech.edu/policy/usage/policy.html`.

Principles Behind an Effective Network Usage Policy

Two principles are traditionally used to justify network usage policies: total cost of ownership (TCO) and risk mitigation.

Total Cost of Ownership

TCO includes measuring employee productivity versus resource utilization.

Employee Productivity   Networks exist to ease the transfer of information, thereby making workers more productive. Ideally this productivity can be measured, which allows management to tie appropriate network usage to productivity goals.

Resource Utilization   The utilization of resources within a company must be suitably justified. Network activities that do not contribute to the bottom line simply cannot be justified from a cost perspective. Usage policies help define which activities are a justifiable use of resources; all other activities are automatically prohibited.

Risk Mitigation

Policies reduce the threat of information activity by defining those network activities that unjustifiably compromise company liability, threaten sensitive information, or open the organization to negative publicity:

Liability   Traditionally considered the domain of discrimination or sexual harassment, liability issues have expanded to include any communication that would result in the company being held liable.

Sensitive Information   Any information that would provide an advantage to a competitor; sensitive information is often the subject of intense scrutiny from rivals.

Negative Publicity   Any communication or use of resources that would lead to a negative image of an organization, negative publicity often has a direct impact on the revenue flow of an organization due to lost sales and stock revenue.

The Developmental Process

The process of fine-tuning the network usage policy for a specific organization goes through many phases:

Discovery   This first step is ideally performed with input from all levels of an organization that use the network. This not only provides a comprehensive policy, but eases employee support and education efforts. Here are some typical questions that you need to answer:

- Which company roles (or individuals) need access?

- Which specific network services do they need?

- What are the current methods of access (including time and location)?

- Which core business applications are Internet-integrated?

- What constitutes sensitive data?

- What are the measurable productivity goals, and how do network resources achieve those goals?

- What risks to network (and information) resources exist (for example, corporate espionage, liability, and negative publicity)?

- What are the legal issues surrounding employee monitoring vs. privacy?

Definition   The second step synthesizes the collected information from the first step to create the policy. Topics include the following:

- Definitions of acceptable use as they fit into overall company vision/mission, core business process/applications, and individual/collective roles

- Definitions and examples of sensitive data, processes, and resources

- Risks to data, including corporate espionage, liability, and negative publicity

- Declaration of intent to monitor employee communication along with definition and examples of appropriate private communication and employee consent procedures

- Consequences of policy violation, including penalty and appeal process

- Procedures for complaint and/or modification of the policy

- Methods for disseminating the policy

- Update frequency of the policy, whether it is time drive, event driven, or both

Implement   The third step is to implement the policy. Implementation fundamentally consists of two steps:

1. Disseminate the policy and educate the employees

2. Enforce the policy

Review   The final step is to review the effectiveness of the policy against the two principles underlying the policy, namely (and in review) total cost of ownership and risk mitigation. If the policy is not effective in satisfying these principles, the process is run again.

This sample policy that follows has been developed for Fubar Corporation. Fubar makes a wide range of desktop applications including FuMeeting, which is its premier meeting scheduler, and FuHR, which is an employee database system. A main office is in New York, and a small sales office is in San Diego. The sales office is connected to the main office via a 128KB frame relay. The corporate office also has a T1 connection to the Internet.

More than 200 employees work out of the corporate office; about half of them are programmers. Fubar has a contemporary telecommuting policy and allows each programmer to work from home one day a week. In addition, Fubar's sales personnel spend a lot of time on the road doing presentations and making sales calls. Because so many employees spend time working away from the office, Fubar has deployed two remote-access solutions. Remote access is provided via a dial-in modem pool, as well as over the Internet using special VPN (virtual private network) software.

The sensitivity of the information entering the network via remote connections is considered moderate. Since the programmers are working on the latest code, Fubar could lose its business edge if this information were to fall into the hands of a competitor. Additionally, the sales information is considered sensitive because this data could give a competitor clues about new product releases.

Scope

The scope of this document is to define the company policies on proper network usage. The corporate network is a substantial investment toward profitability. It exists to improve employee productivity and to increase workflow efficiency. The components of the network are as follows:

◆ All cabling used for carrying voice and electronic information

◆ All devices used for controlling the flow of said voice and electronic information

◆ All computer components including (but not limited to) monitors, cases, storage devices, modems, network cards, memory chips, keyboards, mice, network cards, and cables

◆ All computer software

◆ All output devices including printers and fax machines

Disciplinary action for failure to comply with any of the policy guidelines described in this document will be rendered on a per-incident basis. The company reserves the right to seek legal action when local, state, or federal laws have been broken or when financial loss has been incurred.

Network Management

All network maintenance, including configuration changes to desktop systems, are to be made solely by the operations staff. Employees or contractors who are not members of the operations staff are not allowed to make system modifications, even to the workstations issued to them by the company. Any of the following activities is considered a modification to the system:

♦ Patching a system's network drop to a new location

♦ Using a system's floppy drive to boot an alternative operating system

♦ Removing a system's case or cover

♦ Installing any software package, including software downloaded from the Internet

Hardware management is restricted to ensure that warranties are not inadvertently voided and that security precautions are not circumvented. Software installation is restricted in order to ensure that the company remains in compliance with software licensing laws. This restriction also ensures that proper support for the software can be provided by the internal operations staff and that software incompatibilities are avoided.

Password Requirements

Each employee will be issued a unique logon name in order to gain access to network resources. Every logon name will also have an associated password. The password provides verification that only the authorized user can access network resources using this unique logon name. It is the responsibility of every employee to ensure that their password remains secret. Passwords are to be used under the following guidelines:

♦ Passwords are to be a minimum of eight characters. Two of the characters must be special symbols (for example, !, $, ^, and &), and two must be numbers.

♦ Passwords cannot consist of common words or variations on the employee's name, logon name, server name, or company name.

♦ The employee must change their password every 60 days. If the employee does not do so, their account will be disabled. To reactivate a disabled account, the employee's direct supervisor must contact the network operations staff.

♦ During authentication, the employee will have three attempts at entering their password correctly. If all three attempts fail, the account will be disabled. To reactivate the account, the employee's direct supervisor must contact the network operations staff.

♦ Every company computer is required to use a screen saver that activates after 15 minutes of inactivity. Once the screen saver becomes active, it should require that the user again authenticate with the system before gaining access.

- For accessing the network remotely, either through the dial-in modem pool or through an Internet-based VPN, the employee will be issued a security token that produces a new password every 60 seconds. The password generated by the security token is to be used when the employee is accessing the network remotely.

- Passwords are to be kept private. The employee is expected to not write down their password or share it with other individuals. The exception is that an employee will surrender their password if requested to do so in the presence of their direct supervisor and a member of human resources.

- When accessing resources outside the corporate network, the employee is required to use a different password from the one used for internal systems. This is to ensure that critical password strings are not transmitted over public networks. Any questions about which systems are internal to the corporate network should be directed to the employee's direct supervisor or to a member of the network operations staff.

- The company reserves the right to hold the employee liable for damages caused by the employee's failure to protect the confidentially of their password in accordance with these guidelines.

A strong password policy ensures that all network resources remain secure.

Virus Prevention Policy

All computer resources are to be protected by antivirus software. It is the responsibility of the employee to ensure that the virus software running on their system is not disabled or circumvented. If the employee receives any type of warning from the antivirus software running on the system, they are to immediately cease using the system and contact a member of the network operations staff or their direct supervisor.

It is the responsibility of the network operations staff to keep all antivirus software up to date. This will be performed through an automated process while the employee is connected to network resources. Employees who suspect that their antivirus software has not been updated in the last 60 days should contact a member of the network operations staff.

Workstation Backup Policy

The network operations staff will back up documents stored on each employee's workstation weekly. Every employee is assigned a day of the week during which they must leave their system powered up at the end of the day. The employee is to log off of the system, but the system must remain powered up. It is the responsibility of the employee to ensure that their system remains powered up on the correct day. Employees should contact their direct supervisor to find out which day they have been assigned.

When an employee's workstation is backed up, only documents within the `C:\My Documents` folder will be saved. Documents stored in any other folder will be ignored. The employee bears responsibility for ensuring that they save all documents to this folder. All company-issued applications are designed to save file information in this folder by default.

Remote Network Access

The company provides both a dial-in modem pool and Internet-based VPN access in order to remotely connect to network resources. These are the only sanctioned methods of remote network access. Connecting a modem and a phone line to any part of the network (including desktop systems) is strictly prohibited and can be considered grounds for immediate dismissal.

Remote network access is provided on an as-needed basis. Any employee who requires remote access to network resources must have their direct supervisor submit a request form to the network operations department. The employee will then be issued the following:

- A security token for accessing network resources
- A list of modem pool phone numbers
- Required software for creating an encrypted VPN session over the Internet
- Directions for installing the VPN software
- Directions for accessing the network remotely

The company bears no responsibility for supporting the system that the employee plans to use for remote access. The employee agrees that by accepting the software, they are responsible for any and all upgrades required to support remote access. This includes (but is not limited to) the following:

- A phone line
- A modem
- A faster processor
- Additional disk drive space

In addition, support for remote access will be provided by the network operations staff only for the internal network up to and including the network perimeter. The employee is responsible for providing their own support for connectivity problems outside this scope.

The employee agrees to keep all information regarding remote network access confidential. The employee will not disclose password information or make copies of the VPN software, even for other employees. Propagating remote access details is considered a security breach and grounds for immediate dismissal.

General Internet Access Policy

Company network resources, including those used to gain access to Internet-based sites, are only to be used for the express purpose of performing work-related duties. This policy is to ensure the effective use of networking resources and shall apply equally to all employees. Direct supervisors can approve the use of network resources beyond the scope of this limited access policy when said use meets the following conditions:

- The intended use of network resources is incidental.
- The intended use of network resources does not interfere with the employee's regular duties.

- The intended use of network resources serves a legitimate company interest.

- The intended use of network resources is for educational purposes and within the scope of the employee's job function.

- The intended use of network resources does not break any local, state, or federal laws.

- The intended use of network resources will not overburden the network.

Internet Website Access Policy

When accessing an Internet-based website, employees are to use a web browser that meets the corporate standard. This standard requires the use of Internet Explorer 6 with the following configuration:

- There are no additional plug-ins.

- Java, JavaScript, and ActiveX are disabled.

These settings are to ensure that the employee does not inadvertently load a malicious application while browsing Internet websites. Failure to comply with these security settings can result in the loss of Internet access privileges. Web browser software should only be installed by network operations personnel. To maintain proper software licensing, employees are prohibited from retrieving browser software or upgrades from any other source. Any employee who is unsure whether their browser meets these company standards should contact network operations.

Internet Mail and Newsgroup Access Policy

Inbound and outbound Internet mail messages are limited to a maximum size of 8MB. Any employee who needs to transfer a file that exceeds this requirement should contact the network operations group for access to the corporate FTP server. This limitation is enforced to ensure that one oversized e-mail message does not affect the flow of all corporate messages.

All messages transmitted to Internet-based mailing lists or newsgroups should include a company disclaimer as part of each message. The required disclaimer is "The opinions expressed in this message do not reflect the views of my employer." The company reserves the right to monitor these transmissions and discard any messages that do not include this disclaimer.

Personal Internet-Based Accounts

Company network resources may not be used to access personal Internet-based accounts. These include (but are not limited to) the following:

- Personal e-mail accounts

- Personal shell accounts

- Personal accounts with a service provider such as AOL or CompuServe

Personal accounts on online services should not be accessed from company systems. This does not include company-based accounts or subscriptions that might exist on Internet-based systems. Access to corporate accounts is considered acceptable, provided that access falls within an employee's job duties.

Privacy and Logging

It is the position of the company that all corporate network resources are owned solely by the company itself. This includes (but is not limited to) e-mail messages, stored files, and network transmissions. The company reserves the right to monitor and/or log all network-based activity. The employee is responsible for surrendering all passwords, files, and/or other required resources if requested to do so in the presence of their direct supervisor and a member of human resources.

Security Incidents

All suspected security incidents (regardless of whether they involve computer-related violations) should be reported to an employee's immediate supervisor and to the organization's security department. Security is the responsibility of all employees, and each employee has the right to stop any suspected security violations.

Additional Information

All queries regarding information within this document, as well as issues that have not been specifically covered, should be directed to the employee's immediate supervisor. The immediate supervisor is responsible for relaying all queries to network operations or human resources, whichever is more appropriate.

Index

Note to the Reader: Throughout this index **boldfaced** page numbers indicate primary discussions of a topic. *Italicized* page numbers indicate illustrations.

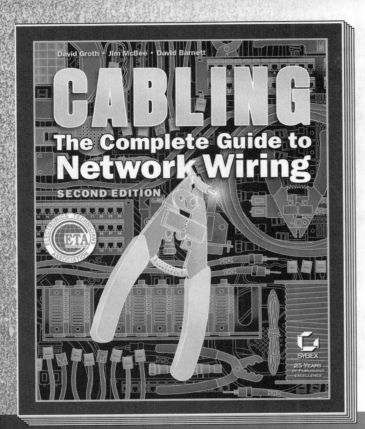

CABLING:
The Complete Guide to Network Wiring

*Cabling: The Complete Guide
to Network Wiring*
David Groth, Jim McBee, and David Ba
ISBN 0-7821-2958-7
808pp • $49.99

The most comprehensive guide to network cabling available!

- Coverage spans cabling system design and installation, electrical and security issues, cabling components, and documenting and troubleshooting your system.

- Provides all the information you need to know to work safely and effectively with cables in the workplace.

- Includes a full-color section for quick identification of connectors and cables, as well as vendor information and recommendations.

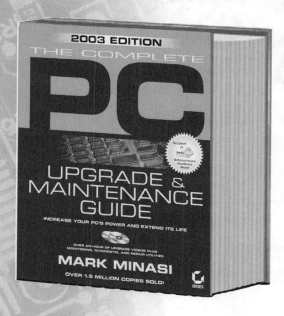

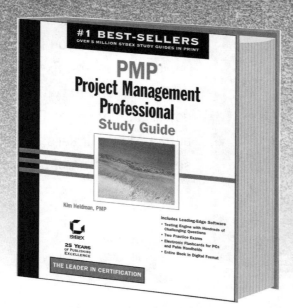

Mastering™ Cisco® Routers

2nd Edition

FROM SYBEX™

Mastering™ Cisco® Routers
Chris Brenton
ISBN 0-7821-4107-2
708pp • $49.99

Designed for administrators and students who need to get up to speed quickly with Cisco routers

- Learn how to administer, configure, and manage Cisco routers

- Install, configure, and manage the Cisco Internetworking Operating System

- Implement secure and reliable virtual private networking

SYBEX®

www.sybex.com

TELL US WHAT YOU THINK!

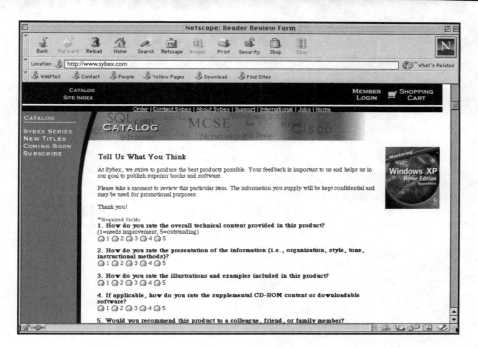

Your feedback is critical to our efforts to provide you with the best books and software on the market. Tell us what you think about the products you've purchased. It's simple:

1. Go to the Sybex website.
2. Find your book by typing the ISBN number or title into the Search field.
3. Click on the book title when it appears.
4. Click **Submit a Review.**
5. Fill out the questionnaire and comments.
6. Click **Submit.**

With your feedback, we can continue to publish the highest quality computer books and software products that today's busy IT professionals deserve.

www.sybex.com

SYBEX Inc. • 1151 Marina Village Parkway, Alameda, CA 94501 • 510-523-8233